AMERICAN CONTRADICTION

AMERICAN CONTRADICTION

Revolution and Revenge
from the 1950s to Now

PAUL STARR

Yale
UNIVERSITY PRESS
New Haven and London

Published with assistance from the foundation established
in memory of Amasa Stone Mather of the Class of 1907,
Yale College.

Copyright © 2025 by Paul Starr.
All rights reserved.

This book may not be reproduced, in whole or in part,
including illustrations, in any form (beyond that copying
permitted by Sections 107 and 108 of the U.S. Copyright Law
and except by reviewers for the public press), without written
permission from the publishers.

Yale University Press books may be purchased in quantity
for educational, business, or promotional use. For information,
please e-mail sales.press@yale.edu (U.S. office) or
sales@yaleup.co.uk (U.K. office).

Set in Janson by Westchester Publishing Services
Printed in the United States of America.
Library of Congress Control Number: 2025936905
ISBN 978-0-300-28243-6 (hardcover)

A catalogue record for this book is available
from the British Library.

Authorized Representative in the EU: Easy Access System
Europe, Mustamäe tee 50, 10621 Tallinn, Estonia,
gpsr.requests@easproject.com

10 9 8 7 6 5 4 3 2 1

To Ann

Contents

Preface xi

Introduction: A New People, an Old Nation: America in the Twenty-First Century 1
   Origins of the Upheaval 4
   Why the Full Backlash Took So Long 8
   Marchers and Sleepwalkers 12
   The Progressive Project and American Identity 16

PART I AMERICAN REVOLUTIONS OF THE TWENTIETH CENTURY

1. Midcentury Normal 23
   Consensus as a Contested Political Project 25
   "The Area of American Agreement" 32
   Consensus as Intellectual Framework 45

2. Black Americans, Model Minority 49
   Black Prototypes 53
   The New Model Movement 61
   Black Power as a Political and Cultural Prototype 69
   The New Family of Minorities 74
   Individual versus Group Striving 79

3. How Sex Got Serious   84
   Feminism as Equal Rights   87
   Feminism as Women's Liberation   97
   Gay Rights and the Turn toward Sexual Pluralism   102
   The New Centrality of Gender Politics   111

4. Half a Counterrevolution   117
   The Conservative Project and Political Realignment   119
   The Conservative Take-Off (1): Religion   130
   The Conservative Take-Off (2): Business and the Counter-Establishment   135
   The Democrats' Squandered Opportunity   142
   The Half-Truth of the Reagan Revolution   144

PART II SLEEPWALKING INTO REVENGE

5. Americans as Enemies: The 1990s as Historical Pivot   157
   From Cold War to Culture War   160
   The 1990s as the Beginning of a New Era   171
   The Limits of Democratic Victories   178

6. Sleepwalking (1): Immigration   183
   A Quiet Explosion   186
   The Return of Nativism   190
   The New Immigrants versus the Old   196

7. Sleepwalking (2): Race   201
   A Majority of Minorities?   203
   The Return of "People of Color"   212
   Diversity as an Ideal and Legal Standard   217
   Obama and the Racial Loop   221
   America, the Boiling Pot   228

8. How America Stopped Working
for Working-Class Americans   232
    Post-Industrial Capitalism: Two Elites, One Loser   234
    The Growing Divide among the 99 Percent   241
    Labor's Decline and the Struggle for Labor's Revival   244

9. Trumpism as Total Revenge   254
    The Interplay of Elite and Base in the Republican Party   258
    A Truly Hostile Takeover   265
    The Pandemic Stress Test   278
    Trump and the American Contradiction   285

10. A New, Old America:
Counterrevolution through the Courts   291
    Gay Rights and the Waning of the Liberal Rights Revolution   295
    Rights Subtraction, the Quiet Counterrevolution   302
    The Right's Rights   308
    History and Traditionalism   312
    Law versus Culture   318
    The Partisan Court   322

11. The American Contradiction, 2024   332
    The Third Trump Election   336
    The 2024 Fault Lines   339
    The Democrats Try to Occupy a New Center   348
    Trump's Restoration   354

Notes   361
Acknowledgments   419
Index   421

Preface

> I will not gloss over the appalling dangers of universal suffrage in the United States. In fact, it is to admit and face those dangers I am writing. To him or her within whose thought rages the battle, advancing, retreating, between Democracy's convictions, aspirations, and the People's crudeness, vice, caprices, I mainly write this book.
>
> —WALT WHITMAN, *Democratic Vistas*, 1871[1]

HOW DID THE COUNTRY that twice elected Barack Obama then go on to elect Donald Trump? That's the question that preoccupied me while writing *American Contradiction*. Since Trump's re-election in 2024, it is no longer plausible to dismiss his victory in 2016 as an aberration, but neither is it accurate to say that Trump and Trumpism sum up the whole truth about America.

The whole truth about America has never been found in one consistent set of principles, prejudices, or interests. The United States was born in the contradiction between freedom and slavery, and that contradiction has had its lineal descendants down to the present. It takes the form today of a contradiction between a changing people and a resisting nation, a nation with entrenched institutions that have empowered those who fear the changes and look to restore an old America of their imagining. The divisions over race, immigration, gender, and religion have all become part of this great conflict at a time when economic inequalities have risen and many Americans feel dispossessed of their country. The successive choices of Obama and Trump reflect the uncertain path of a fifty-fifty country careening from one side of the American divide to the other.

During the Cold War, historians identified the long-neglected words of a colonial sermon as the beginning of American consciousness, a kind of mission statement for the nation. "We shall be as a city upon a hill; the eyes of all people are upon us," John Winthrop, the governor of the Massachusetts Bay Colony, wrote in 1630 in a lay sermon said to have been given to passengers aboard one of the thirty ships the Puritans sent that year to the New World. Winthrop was using the image of "a city on a hill," which he drew from Jesus's Sermon on the Mount, as both an admonition to observe godly conduct and an assurance of a divinely inspired mission. But in the twentieth century, Winthrop's city took on a one-sided, self-congratulatory meaning. The United States became, at least as America's leaders imagined it, a beacon of freedom to the world.[2]

Another image, however, may better fit the United States. Ever since its birth, the American republic has been like a city built on a geological fault, shaken often by tremors and periodically by earthquakes. The tremors have gotten stronger in recent decades. The question that troubles Americans now is whether the earthquake they are experiencing will reduce their republic to rubble. Since the forces shaking the American city lie not beneath the earth's surface but deep within society, they require a social and historical explanation. In light of the successive elections of Obama and Trump, they also require a fresh explanation—a rewriting of the American story. That is what I hope the following pages can help provide.

November 8, 2024

Introduction
A New People, an Old Nation:
America in the Twenty-First Century

AMERICANS ARE BOTH a people and a nation, two things that may seem the same. But since the middle of the last century, the people have evolved far more than the nation. The changes in the American people have come from new understandings of identity and rights, infusions of new immigrants, and younger generations, especially of women, prepared to live in a different world from that of their parents. As a nation, though, the United States is still moored to an old version of itself. It has an eighteenth-century constitution that, among those of all major democracies, is the hardest to amend, with a Senate and Electoral College that underrepresent urbanized populations. The Supreme Court holds the power to interpret that nearly unamendable constitution, a power that it used in the mid-twentieth century to advance a revolution in rights, race, and gender. But today, in the name of "history and tradition" and the original meaning of the Constitution, the Court insists on a return of the law to a time before women, Black people, and other minorities had a say.

For all their flaws, the nation's institutions and symbols have historically proved adaptable. They haven't served all Americans equally well, but they have enabled the country to grow, prosper, and come closer to fulfilling the Constitution's promise of "a more perfect union." Whether the nation can do that again in the twenty-first century is no sure thing. Its institutions may now be too skewed in favor of an older America that cannot accept the new America its people are becoming.

Some Americans welcome that new America, but others are afraid of it. Movements for progressive change have opened new life possibilities for millions who would not otherwise enjoy the freedom and personal relationships, families, and careers they have now. But economic inequalities are greater than they used to be, and many people who once had a secure footing in industrial America have lost it in a post-industrial economy that has devalued their skills. They identify the old America with a normal and a good life and see the forces changing the American people as a dire threat. For them, the promise of a return to America as it once was, or as they imagine it, is a source of hope.

It was a movement to fulfill the promise of the Constitution, the Black freedom struggle of the mid-twentieth century, that sparked the recent changes in the American people, not only because of the struggle's direct impact but because of what it indirectly set in motion: other movements for rights and recognition, the reactions against those demands, changes in immigration laws, and far-reaching shifts in sexuality and culture, as well as law and politics. The themes weren't entirely new; they were old American themes remixed in a new tempo and with new words. The young especially wanted to break down barriers. When feet started moving in demonstrations and on dance floors, no one could have known, as the heat rose, where the marching and the music would lead.

Imagine, if you will, a scene that has unfolded in my mind like a science-fiction movie or an episode of the TV show *The Twilight Zone* that I watched as a teenager. The time is near the end of the summer of 1963, and I am a junior counselor at an integrated, progressive summer camp in the Hudson Valley for "underprivileged" kids from New York City, mostly Black and Puerto Rican. Pete Seeger has come from his home nearby to sing with them, finishing up with the old Black classic "This Little Light of Mine." In the evening, my peers and I find ourselves watching what we think is a television documentary about the civil rights movement. It begins with familiar scenes: sit-ins, freedom rides, the speech that Martin Luther King Jr. has just given at the March on Washington. But then it goes on to show events that have not yet happened: Congress passing the Civil Rights Act in 1964, the Voting Rights Act in 1965, and immigration reforms the same year that end the racist national-origins quotas. My friends are looking quizzically at each other but cheering. The mysterious documentary continues with the rise of Black Power and the women's and gay liberation movements, strange ideas even to young progressives in the early 1960s. While a few of my friends are thrilled, others are watching uncomfortably, occasionally rolling their eyes at the absurdity of it all. The documentary continues with scenes of racial backlash ("That figures," someone says), antiwar protest, a terrible plague we have never heard of, and ministers warning of doom; a flash of a familiar face, the actor Ronald Reagan ("President? You must be kidding"); a description of how, during all this time, labor unions are in decline and economic inequality is growing; and a rash of incomprehensible terms (multiculturalism, LGBTQ+, transgender, cisgender). Finally, someone says this is all ridiculous and could never happen and switches the TV to something with a more familiar and reassuring plot, a movie about aliens invading from outer space.

Since the mid-twentieth century, the struggle for freedom and equality has taken more imaginative leaps than a scriptwriter would ever dare. Like a Hollywood action hero only more fantastic, the movements for progressive change have jumped from one impossible challenge to the next: the impossible challenge of taking down racism, the impossible challenge of ending poverty, the impossible challenge of achieving equality between men and women, the impossible challenge of gaining acceptance for alternative forms of sexuality and gender identity.

The resulting conflicts have not stopped there. Based in the Black church, the civil rights movement certainly did not set out to take on religion. But the pursuit of both gender and racial equality has nonetheless brought about a religious realignment, as faith communities have divided on liberal versus conservative lines, and the more religiously observant, at least among whites, have become aligned with conservatism. Progressives also did not set out to bring in new waves of people from Latin America, Africa, and Asia, but the arrival of those immigrants has added another dimension to the conflict, reviving an old and recurrent pattern of nativist opposition to immigration.

In short, what began as the civil rights movement has become a fight to transform almost every hierarchical relation in the society: white over Black, men over women, straight over queer, the traditionally religious over the irreligious and more secular, native-born over immigrant—all this in a nation whose institutions are notoriously hard to change. Wisely or foolishly, the progressive project has challenged virtually the whole system of social precedence: who stands higher, who comes first, whose values and interests are identified with the whole of America. Its aims for freedom and equality have been more comprehensive than the aims of any similar struggle in the past—except in one respect. While other movements have risen, the labor movement has receded and the distance between rich and poor has widened. The progressive project has tried to achieve greater social equality amid increasing economic inequality—and that challenge may be genuinely impossible.

Origins of the Upheaval

One common explanation for the contemporary American upheaval points to technology and the economy. A second is all about race, or what might be called racial reductionism. Alone, neither is sufficient, but together they help explain how the upheaval began.

The economic and technological changes that since the mid-twentieth century have swept through all the high-income countries and affected the entire world are the source of much of the novelty in American life. Americans are not alone in using devices that didn't exist to do jobs that didn't exist in industries that didn't exist. The transformation of the media has been so dramatic that it may seem as though changes in politics have been entirely a technological byproduct. These have been years when new technologies have drastically altered commerce as well as communication; when the economies of high-income countries have undergone a massive shift from manufacturing to services and information; when global trade has increased; and when higher education has expanded, and educational systems have become critical in determining opportunity. For a while, particularly during the 1990s, these developments were unambivalently celebrated. "Disruption" became a word of the highest praise, at least among an elite who profited from the upside of "creative destruction." Some social scientists claimed the people of the advanced societies had moved on from material to "post-material" concerns.

But material concerns had hardly gone away. Even the movements concerned with rights and identity were also concerned with material well-being. And while the transformative developments in the techno-economy yielded wealthier societies overall, they undermined the material circumstances and communities of people who were on the receiving end of disruption's wrecking ball. The changes sharpened the divide between Americans with college degrees and those without, and were nothing short of a catastrophe for the old industrial working class. How they responded to being treated as expendable is a crucial part of our story. The struggles over freedom and equality in American society need to be understood in this changing context of economic and class relations, though they cannot be fully explained by it.

The other partial but inadequate explanation for America's upheaval focuses wholly on race and proposes that the opposition to the progressive project arises from racism alone, and especially from a reaction to the prospect of a multiracial democracy. Race has always been central to America's political conflicts, but it sells the progressive project short to say it has been only about racial equality. Liberals and progressives may find racial reductionism attractive because it suggests that a morally illegitimate racial animus—"racial resentment," as many political scientists call it— wholly explains the opposition they face.

But the ambitions of the progressive project have gone much further, and it should not be surprising that the opposition has a broader basis with its own moral sense. What racial reductionism particularly neglects is the masculine revolt against cultural change and the sense among conservatives that they are upholding a natural order with men on top and the right-side up. The exclusive focus on race also neglects the ongoing working-class catastrophe and the failure of many Americans with progressive sympathies to give labor's interests high enough priority. The movement for racial justice ignited more encompassing efforts to transform American society— indeed, it shaped the moral framework of those efforts and the resistance by people who felt diminished by them.

Alongside the forces that have disrupted the status quo have been highly entrenched institutions, the tenacious understructure of the American nation. Even as radical changes have unfolded in the techno-economy and in Americans' identities and social relations, the national institutions of the United States have been little altered. Americans like to think of their country as young, "the country of tomorrow" as Emerson called it. It was, once, but its political institutions are no longer young or a model for other democracies. The Constitution retains outdated undemocratic features, like an unrepresentative upper house of the national legislature, which other democracies have done away with. The requirements for constitutional amendments are so rigid that for more than a century, no major change in American society has come via a constitutional amendment. Major reforms have generally required the blessing of the justices of the Supreme Court or ingenious workarounds. Other peculiarities of a constitutional system handed down from the late eighteenth century, such as the role of the Electoral College in the choice of the president, remain untouched. Like the nation's political institutions, its system of free-market capitalism seems so deeply entrenched as to be protected from change, although it is itself a potent source of change.

For some time now, these institutional realities have systematically skewed American politics to the right. While welcoming economic and technological innovation, the United States has strong conservative reflexes, or what some describe as a deep institutional status quo bias. That bias can be broken, but it is a rare event when it happens.

Full and equal citizenship for all has nonetheless been, throughout the nation's history, a recurrent source of conflict and acute pressure on its constitutional system and political economy. This book begins with the seemingly broad political and cultural consensus of the 1950s and the singular role of the Black freedom struggle as the initiator of a family of movements for equal rights and respect. The Black movement established models of protest, legal principles, and cultural ideals that other historically subordinated groups came to see as relevant to their own situation. In this sense, Black people became a true model minority, a model of a collective and disruptive kind. Those insurgent movements led to counter-movements; to new points of confrontation over everyday practices, cultural symbols, and the role of government; to new party alignments and partisan identities—in short, to a radical reconfiguration of American politics, culture, and social structure.

The Black struggle was a rebuke to America's claims about itself, a reminder of the nation's original sin of racial slavery and the conflict between America's founding promise and its long history of white supremacy: How could a nation pledged to uphold the inalienable rights to life, liberty, and the pursuit of happiness deny those rights so flagrantly to enslaved people?

The gentle but inexact term for this stark conflict is a paradox, but contradiction is more apt. The elements in a paradox are opposed only superficially; once we grasp the paradox, we see that the elements fit together and make sense. In a contradiction, the elements negate each other, and there can be no genuine resolution except through change. Unlike a paradox, a dilemma, or mere hypocrisy, a social contradiction is a source of conflict at a deep level, over first principles, as slavery was. Some may shy away from the word "contradiction" because of its association with discredited Hegelian and Marxist conceptions of historical necessity. But "contradiction" is a fine word, independent of those philosophical traditions, and it is an honest and true word for the historical situation of Black people in the United States. The legacies of the founding contradiction between racial slavery and freedom have never been wholly overcome, and it was the struggle against those legacies that set off the latest phase of that contradiction in American history.

The resolution of a social contradiction does not depend solely on the facts but on their manifestation and the ability of those who see the contradiction to do anything about it. Often contradictions are latent; at least publicly, no one admits to seeing them. Just as individuals live with contradictions, so do societies. Human inventiveness takes many forms, none more consistently impressive than the capacity for devising evasions. Plausible deniability, or even sheer willful denial in the face of stark contradictions, is an ability many political leaders cannot do without.

A latent social contradiction may surface in several ways: through new conditions like demographic shifts, a crisis like a war, or social movements that dramatize the contradiction and use it as leverage for change. All three had a role in the manifestation of the American contradiction in the mid-twentieth century. The Great Migration brought Black people from the rural South not only into cities but into the center of American politics. The nation sent them into battle in World War II but never gave them just recognition; then the Cold War turned an international spotlight on racial injustice in the United States. And the Black civil rights leadership used the contradiction between that injustice and American ideals to break through the entrenched opposition to equal rights.

What especially distinguished the Black struggle in the second half of the twentieth century was how its influence traveled. Not only did other groups come to see their own problems through the lens of a Black analogy; the civil rights laws and judicial decisions adopted in response to Black protest provided the legal grounds for other groups' claims. The Black analogy was central to the ideas and strategies of the new feminist and gay rights movements that brought about a revolution in gender relations, roles, and identities. The demands for equality escalated into a broader struggle to overcome the old, taken-for-granted hierarchies of American life. These were the American revolutions of the twentieth century.

The analogy with the Black condition was also crucial for the movements that arose among the new immigrants after the 1965 immigration reforms. None of the other earlier ethnic and racial minorities—not the Irish, Italian, Jewish, and other European immigrants in the nineteenth and early twentieth centuries; not the Chinese or Japanese who came to the West Coast; not even the Mexicans or indigenous tribes incorporated into the nation—had affiliated with Black Americans in a joint movement or regarded themselves as sharing a common identity (though Jews came closest as allies in legal reform efforts). But after the adoption of civil rights protections and other new legal and statistical practices in the 1960s and 1970s, the growing Latin American and Asian American populations, along with Native Americans, came to be grouped together with Black people, eventually under the term "people of color." Women, LGBTQ+ people, and people with disabilities were included in a still-broader grouping of the historically marginalized, eligible for protection against discrimination and abuse.

Why the Full Backlash Took So Long

The popular and legal understanding of identities and rights growing out of the Black struggle created a new configuration of potential progressive political allies, but they were only one side of the change—the challenge to traditional hierarchies and norms. The other side, the defensive response, consisted of the slow and halting political development of a reactive conservative movement and the rising intensity of conservative identities: Christian, morally traditional, patriotic, rooted in God, family, nation—and white usually by implication. "Identity politics," that insult often hurled against the post-1960s progressive project, has always had more than one form and more than one side. But the conservative side took decades to gather momentum.

The common practice of dating the rise of the modern right to Barry Goldwater's 1964 presidential campaign now looks out of date. The conservative movement from Goldwater to Reagan and the Bushes was only an intermediate step toward the truly right-wing reactionary movement that has emerged in recent years and taken over the Republican Party (and that has much in common, particularly on foreign policy, with the right wing of the 1930s). Republican conservatism from the 1960s through the 1980s had an obvious strategic logic. Liberal Democrats' support for Blacks' civil rights and later for feminist and LGBTQ+ demands created political opportunities for what had been America's minority party since 1932. Republicans saw a chance to turn themselves into the nation's majority party by appealing to racial and cultural backlash, though they had to use carefully modulated and coded language to avoid alienating more centrist voters. The early fruits of this strategy were the defection of Southern whites from the Democrats beginning in the 1960s and the surge of conservative evangelicals into the Republican Party toward the end of the 1970s—crucial factors in reversing the party's electoral fortunes from 1968 on.

The historical commitments of Republicans initially limited or at least slowed the party's shift to the right. The Republicans had long been the more liberal of the two major parties on racial and gender issues, a tradition that did not disappear overnight. In the early to mid-twentieth century, they had provided more support than Democrats did for civil rights and the Equal Rights Amendment. Higher percentages of congressional Republicans than of Democrats voted for the Civil Rights Act in 1964 and the Voting Rights Act in 1965. Liberal sympathies persisted among some congressional Republicans, officials in Republican administrations, and, perhaps most important, Republican appointees to the Supreme Court.

Consequently, the policies Republicans adopted in office and the decisions their appointees made on the bench did not always match the appeals Republicans used to win elections. Richard Nixon exemplified the pattern. Although he courted the forces of backlash to win the presidency in 1968, his domestic policies were not just moderate but surprisingly liberal (Democrats later had reason to regret that they rejected his proposals for national health insurance and a nationally guaranteed income). Nor did Reagan push the agenda of social conservatives. He prioritized a hardline foreign policy and conservative economics—cutting taxes and spending, undermining unions, rolling back economic regulation—but did not reverse the momentum of change in racial and gender relations. He even signed a 1986 bill that included an amnesty and path to citizenship for three million immigrants who had been living in the country without authorization.

Mainstream Republican leaders for a long time kept the radical right bottled up politically, doing enough to keep anti-liberal right-wing voters in the fold but usually denying respectability and power to conspiracy-minded fringe groups. The television networks and other dominant media also kept voices on both the radical right and the radical left from gaining access to a wider public than they could reach through their own newsletters, marginal radio shows, and other limited communication means. Until the 1990s, conservatives—and reactionaries to the right of conservatives—did not have media outlets with substantial national reach that reported the world the way they wanted to see it or gave far-right commentators and hosts a national platform.

The 1990s proved to be a turning point in American politics, though not entirely for the optimistic reasons many people had in mind at the time.

The collapse of Soviet communism at the start of the 1990s set off speculation that one world-historical era had ended and another had begun. What the British historian E. J. Hobsbawm called the "short twentieth century"—the years from 1914 to 1991, an "age of extremes" when the world had been wracked by total wars—was over.[1] The twenty-first century was beginning ahead of schedule, and it seemed pregnant with hopeful possibilities, not the least of which was that the "extremes" were finished. Just as the Soviet bloc was disintegrating, the rest of Europe was drawing together in a European Union committed to liberal democracy and the free movement of people, goods, and ideas across national borders. The prevailing trend in Southern Europe, Latin America, and elsewhere in the world, dating from the late 1970s, was from authoritarianism to democracy. Not only did dictators fall; so did political and economic barriers to global communication, travel, and trade. The future seemed to lie in an open and economically integrated liberal world. Locally too, a new era of connectivity was bringing both greater individual freedom and new forms of community. The internet, just then emerging as a medium for everyday communication, symbolized the excitement. By 1997, the joke went, the internet had already gone from a zero-million-dollar to a zero-billion-dollar industry. In the United States, you had to be an out-of-touch curmudgeon, or a manufacturing worker displaced by cheap imports, to refuse to join the celebrations.

The end of the Cold War might have lessened domestic political tensions by rendering moot long-running disagreements between liberals and conservatives about military and foreign policy. Instead, American politics in the 1990s turned more harshly partisan. Republicans in Congress, led by Newt Gingrich, rejected their predecessors' genteel ways and restrained rhetoric for a more accusatory, confrontational posture. Conservatives turned some of the energies they had put into the Cold War into a culture war at home, denouncing liberals as anti-American and a threat to morality (Bill and Hillary Clinton being the most conspicuous targets). It was during the 1990s that the engaged public—the people who paid politics and the news closest attention—became sharply polarized on a wide range of public issues. This was also the decade when right-wing talk radio took off and when Fox News was established. Political battles were especially fierce because the Democratic and Republican parties were so closely matched in electoral support. The future of the country often seemed to rest on small groups of swing voters, a few swing states, or even a single justice on the Supreme Court, as when the Court determined the outcome of the 2000 election in a 5–4 vote.

The idea of the United States as a "fifty-fifty country" appeared shortly after the 2000 election to describe the close balance in power between Democrats and Republicans. That was also when the media began dividing the country into "red" and "blue" states. Surveys showed that Republicans and Democrats now did not merely disagree, they detested one another with a passion. Partisanship had an emotional, negative character. Americans' trust in one another was also falling.

"Fifty-fifty" also came to describe the perceptions of the racial and cultural balance among the American people. Until the late twentieth century, America was a ninety-ten society—that is, Americans thought of the racial makeup of the United States as 90 percent white, 10 percent Black. Whites might dislike changes brought about by the civil rights movement, but they knew Blacks had no realistic chance of taking over. Other racial minorities were too small to figure in the dominant conception of the racial landscape. In fact, whites often forgot about Blacks too, equating the American people with the white supermajority. In much usage, the very word "American" implicitly meant someone who was white, straight, and Christian, and needed clarification when referring to anyone else. That was the national self-image, the image in movies and on television not just of the great and powerful but of the typical American.

As that national self-image has ceased to correspond to reality, it has set off a panic about what America is becoming. I do not mean here just to say that increasing racial and ethnic diversity triggers white anxieties. The overpowering anxiety is about being overpowered—specifically, about losing the power that comes from holding the majority position. In the early 1990s, based on new U.S. Census Bureau forecasts, the major media began proclaiming "the browning of America" and a future when whites would become a minority. These forecasts, as we will see, are deeply misleading. The idea that whites are headed for minority status is an artefact of federal statistical methods and the general practice of treating white-passing Hispanics as though they suffered from delusions about their ability to assimilate. While the American people are changing, whites are not close to losing the upper hand in either the economy or politics.

Nonetheless, at the turn of the twenty-first century, the belief in an imminent reversal in the position of whites became a political fact of the first importance. Immigration raised alarms among conservatives that America was near a social and political tipping point. Unnoticed at first, rising immigration proved to be a key trigger for turning the new phase of the American contradiction into an open conflict threatening to upend the entire society.

Marchers and Sleepwalkers

The leadership of the twentieth-century civil rights, feminist, and gay rights movements entered the struggle for equality and freedom with their eyes open. They knew that the legal and cultural changes they sought would stir up a backlash. But the story is different for changes in immigration law in the same era. The storm was slow to arrive, and supporters of new policies did not see it coming. Later market-oriented reformers, including centrists in the Democratic Party, also miscalculated the impact of deregulatory and free-trade policies not just on workers but on their own political fortunes.

In his book *A Nation of Immigrants*, President John F. Kennedy wrote that "centuries ago, migration was a leap into the unknown."[2] What Kennedy didn't realize was that the immigration reforms he proposed in 1963—one of his last actions as president—were also a leap into the unknown. When Congress passed the Immigration and Nationality Act in 1965, legislators said they did not expect any change in America's racial makeup, and the record provides no reason to believe they intended anything else. They eliminated the national-origins quotas from the 1920s mainly at the behest of Catholics and Jews who opposed the old limits on immigration as discriminatory against their European kin and co-ethnics. The 1965 law sought to keep America as it was by giving the highest preferences in immigration to relatives of families already in the United States and establishing the first cap ever on immigration from Latin America. Like other immigration reforms for the next twenty-five years, the legislation was adopted on a broad, bipartisan vote.

On the right, however, many now believe that immigration reform was part of a great plot to "replace" whites and change the nation's politics. "The worst attack on our democracy in 160 years?" Tucker Carlson said to Fox viewers in 2022. "How about the Immigration Act of 1965? That law completely changed the composition of America's voter rolls, purely to benefit the Democratic Party."[3]

While not seeing the 1965 law as a conspiracy, some liberals and progressives also believe the subsequent immigration set the nation on a radically different political course. They interpreted Barack Obama's election in 2008 as evidence that white America's dominance was over and the progressive project would ride to victory on a wave of demographic change. The collapse of Soviet communism had led to one kind of triumphalism; the demography-is-destiny narrative led to another. But triumphalism is a dangerous intoxicant. You may think you are destined to win when you're only sleepwalking into defeat—or into a new form of the American contradiction—you never thought possible.

If Democrats had been as farsighted as Tucker Carlson claimed and effectively used legislation to fortify their party's base, they would have strengthened the labor movement's ability to organize workers in the growing sectors of the economy during the unions' long slide in membership from 35 percent of the nation's labor force in 1955 to 11 percent in the 2020s. The labor movement had been vital in raising workers' standards of living as well as reinforcing their support for the Democratic Party. But in all the years after World War II when Democrats held congressional majorities, they failed to pass a single bill that aided private-sector union organizing. Anti-union Southern Democrats made it impossible to overcome Senate filibusters, and party leaders faced pressure from donors who might be liberal on other issues but not unions. Progressive Democrats devoted to causes like the environment did not necessarily prioritize organized labor's concerns, if they shared them at all.

That's not to say Democratic and Republican administrations had similar effects on working people. When Republicans were in office, their macroeconomic, tax, and spending policies redistributed income upward, which Democratic administrations did not do. But the Democrats' more progressive tax policies and public programs could not fully offset labor's loss of power in the marketplace. Democrats also supported economic deregulation under Jimmy Carter and free-trade measures under Bill Clinton that hurt unionized workers. The moderates who supported these immoderate measures also hurt themselves. In congressional districts most exposed to imports, moderate Democrats were the ones to lose their seats, primarily to far-right Republicans. Centrists went sleepwalking to their own political funerals.

The collapse of the center right in the Republican Party is the most important example of that phenomenon. In the early 2000s, when George W. Bush was president, conservative strategists like Karl Rove pronounced America a center-right country and envisioned a long future for center-right Republican rule. They never expected to be thrown into the political wilderness by forces within their own party. To right-wing Republicans, however, Bush's role in promoting immigration reform, free trade, the folly of the Iraq War, and the Wall Street bailout in the 2008 financial crisis epitomized the Republican establishment's betrayal of America's workers and middle class. Although two center-right politicians, John McCain and Mitt Romney, captured the Republican presidential nominations in 2008 and 2012, they both met defeat at the hands of Obama, further stoking anger in the Republican base about the ineffectuality of the party's leadership. As that anger was building up, an entrepreneur with an eye for an untapped market could see an opportunity. Donald Trump just happened to be the person who seized that opportunity, and when he captured the Republican nomination in 2016, he decapitated the party's old leadership. That year, however, he won the presidency only because of the Electoral College.

In seven out of eight presidential elections from 1992 to 2020, Democrats won the popular vote. They also won a majority of the votes cast nationally in Senate elections over every six-year cycle beginning in 1996 (it takes six years for every seat to come up for election). But in two of the presidential elections—in 2000 as well as 2016—the Electoral College gave Republicans the victory, and during twelve of the twenty-four years from 1996 to 2020, Republicans had Senate majorities.[4] In a normal democracy—the kind where majorities prevail—Democrats would have held the presidency in the 2000 and 2016 elections and likely the Senate as well and would therefore have appointed the majority of justices on the Supreme Court. Suffering those political losses, Republicans would have had strong incentives to change course and moderate their views, but instead they learned a different lesson: They could win power without conciliating the other side or moving toward the center. Both the Electoral College and the Senate reflect unchanged national institutions dating to the eighteenth century, which today advantage Republicans and have made it unnecessary for them to adapt to demographic and cultural change.[5] Trump did win the popular vote in 2024 (by the narrow margin of 1.47 percentage points). But over the whole period since the turn of the century, the skew of electoral institutions has allowed an older America to keep a new America in check and enabled the Republican Party to move right, and then further right.

As the battle for America has intensified, many political analysts have understandably focused on the two major parties, looking for signs as to which was gaining the edge. Their expectation has been that, as in the past, big changes would come when one party emerged as electorally dominant, which is likely to happen at some point. An entire theory of American politics has been built around the concept of "critical elections" that signal partisan realignments. But electoral realignment is the wrong way to think about recent change. Instead, the two major parties as of the mid-2020s have remained about evenly matched at the national level for three decades. The long duration of this close contest is significant in itself. The big change has come not from a shift in the balance of electoral support between the parties, but from an insurgency within one party, the Republicans, and from conservative Republican success in controlling the Supreme Court. The right has transformed American politics by taking over these two institutions, the Republican Party and the judiciary. While many analysts think of polarization as a phenomenon equally involving both parties, Republican radicalization has been the main change. With Trump's rise, not only has the center right of the party been liquidated (to use the proper revolutionary term); conservatism in the Goldwater–Reagan tradition, with its openness to immigration and free trade, has also been pushed to the margins.

Conservatives were right to recognize that gaining control of the Supreme Court would be crucial to their success. Just as the Court was central to the liberal rights revolution of the twentieth century, so it has been central to that revolution's undoing. Some critical steps in the legal counterrevolution, such as the Court's reversal of *Roe v. Wade*, have been at the center of national politics, but many others have attracted little public attention. In the quiet phases of the counterrevolution the Court has effectively nullified hard-won legal rights, as, for example, when it has approved the use of mandatory private arbitration and class-action bans in contracts imposed by businesses on workers and consumers.

The conservative legal movement has also turned the tables on liberals and progressives by pursuing its own rights revolution, focused on corporate rights, religious rights, gun rights, the rights of the unborn, and property rights. Most of this agenda is distinctly unpopular, but the Court has also not hesitated to put its finger on the scales of electoral politics, from *Bush v. Gore*, the case settling the 2000 election, to decisions about voting rights and presidential immunity. In the mid-twentieth century, law played an important role in legitimizing and catalyzing progressive changes in American culture. Can a Supreme Court in right-wing hands duplicate the catalytic role of the liberal Court? With Trump's return to the presidency in 2025, the chances have increased that the Court and executive branch will become fully aligned in favor of regime change, entrenching an anti-liberal, reactionary state. But both America's liberal constitutional heritage and the past half-century's progressive changes in American society and culture run deep.

The Progressive Project and American Identity

Although I use the term "progressive project," I do not mean to imply there has been a single progressive movement with unified beliefs. There has been an extended family of movements, each divided among different organizations and philosophies. Some of these tendencies fit within the broad compass of American liberalism and have sought to influence it, while others have rejected liberalism and sought to supersede it. The distinguishing element in the progressive project of the past three-quarters of a century has been the effort to achieve equal rights and respect for historically subordinated groups.[6]

In characterizing progressives and their ideas, some critics tendentiously focus on the most radical, often plainly illiberal forms the progressive project has taken—the more outrageous, the better. But the progressive struggles for freedom and equality would not have had a powerful effect on the American people if they did not have deep roots in American traditions and resonance in contemporary life. At bottom, those struggles are about making America great for more Americans than enjoyed its bounty in the past.

Still, even movements grounded in morally justified ideals unfold under unforeseen circumstances, take unexpected turns, and sometimes end up in a world of danger not their doing. The technological and economic transformation undermining the lives of working-class Americans has dealt a double blow to progressive hopes. After Black Americans made initial gains from civil rights reforms, their communities were devastated during the mid-1970s and 1980s by the loss of industrial jobs and the ensuing damage to family and community life. That same sequence unfolded again in the early 2000s in white working-class communities that came to feel they were no longer the priority of progressives and the Democratic Party. This was the tragic combination—the progressive focus on historically stigmatized and subordinated groups amid the collapse of working-class jobs with middle-class incomes—that laid the basis for a right-wing movement of rage and revenge in the twenty-first century against the revolutionary changes of the twentieth.

One consequence of these developments has been a three-way contest over the true basis of the American community. During the mid-twentieth century, most mainstream conservatives and liberals embraced the same theory of America. In the mainstream conception, what holds Americans together, what makes Americans one people and one nation, is not blood but belief—belief, that is, in the values of liberty and equality, often described as the American Creed. According to the mainstream understanding, the United States has differed from other countries because it has welcomed people of different faiths and races and enabled them to live and work together in harmony. Here is a vivid image of that America, not from a Democrat but from a Republican, Ronald Reagan, who explained in his Farewell Address in 1989 what he had in mind over the years by describing the country as a "city on a hill":

> In my mind it was a tall, proud city built on rocks stronger than oceans, wind-swept, God-blessed, and teeming with people of all kinds living in harmony and peace; a city with free ports that hummed with commerce and creativity. And if there had to be city walls, the walls had doors and the doors were open to anyone with the will and the heart to get here.[7]

This is a liberal version of American exceptionalism, the idea that the United States stands apart from other countries because of its unique values and institutions, which, in this interpretation, have ensured openness, tolerance, and pluralism and made the country dynamic and successful.

The mainstream conception gained sway at a time when the racial, cultural, and religious diversity of the United States was relatively contained. Conservative support for the mainstream view, however, eventually could not survive the rise of non-European immigration and changes in gender relations and religion: Did conservatives genuinely believe in a society as open to racial, cultural, and religious change as the mainstream theory of America implied? In Reagan's language, did they still want the doors to America to be "open to anyone with the will and the heart to get here"? Many didn't want the doors open even a crack. Fearful of losing control, they turned back to a more thoroughly right-wing national conservatism.

According to that older conception, the United States owes its greatness to its founding as a white, Christian nation. It is justified in limiting immigration to maintain the primacy of that pre-existing America and selecting whatever immigrants it chooses to admit with an eye to their ability to conform to the nation's moral and religious certainties. This reactionary nationalist vision is also a type of American exceptionalism: For America to be America, it must be the America that conservatives choose to remember and honor, a home principally to white Christians. Since Christianity, in this view, is the defining core of American nationhood, more secular and liberal ideas about America—like the mainstream view or, even worse, "woke" ideas about race and gender—are not merely mistaken but incompatible with, even traitorous to, America itself. One of the remarkable contemporary turnabouts is the endorsement of this view by conservative Catholics, who seem to forget that the Protestants who upheld it in the past regarded them as a threat to American morals and as heretics loyal to a foreign power, the Pope. Well into the twentieth century, Catholics were excluded from the tradition some of them want to bring back.

While this view of America as a Christian nation, with its strong evangelical support, has come to dominate the Republican Party, progressives have attacked the mainstream conception from the standpoint of a third theory of America. Progressives reject American exceptionalism in both its liberal mainstream and Christian nationalist forms; they fault both the mainstream and the conservative stories about the United States for failing to acknowledge its history of systemic racism and other denials of equality and dignity. In some progressive accounts, that is all America is. The story of slavery, not the story of freedom, becomes the prototypical American experience. American history collapses into the history of separate identity groups, and nothing is left of the idea of an American community, an American people, or an American nation. Although the progressive project does not necessarily lead to that conclusion, some of its exponents cannot resist taking it there. When they make that choice, however, they forfeit the opportunity to claim an American heritage and national identity for their own cause.

The mainstream and progressive theories of America often seem as unlike each other as day and night—the former, a sunny and uplifting story of a nation dedicated to universal ideals of freedom and justice; the latter, a dark and discouraging story of a nation that has always been racist, patriarchal, and exclusionary through and through. The view that underlies my account in the following pages takes the progressive project in a different direction, as a constructive criticism of the mainstream liberal conception and a contribution to a new American identity consistent with a new American people. Each of these two theories of America, the mainstream and the progressive, needs a dose of the other to tell a more complete national story, to avoid an idle daydream on the one hand or a nightmare of despair on the other, and to define a shared identity and national purpose to enable the country to bind its wounds and move forward. The mainstream story of America often mistakes the aspiration of universality for an accomplishment, but it is a worthy aspiration nonetheless. The aspiration itself has consequences: It matters what ideals and stories about their nation Americans hold dear. Understanding the United States requires taking seriously both sides of the country's inconsistent history and contradictory forces, both its sins and its virtues. Rather than resting comfortably on unified values, the United States has developed uncomfortably on the basis of opposed ideas, interests, and institutions that have repeatedly torn it apart.

This is the American situation again, a people pitted against one another in what appears to be a dire struggle over the nation's identity and future. But the past is not entirely discouraging. Out of their contradictory heritage, Americans have fashioned an imperfect, divided, but flourishing nation, home now to a wider range of people than ever. This is the history that the progressive project, best understood, has been trying to deepen and extend by taking on impossible challenges. If we want to understand how America can emerge from its present crisis and reach a new equilibrium in the twenty-first century, we need to begin with the old equilibrium of mid-twentieth-century America, which, before it broke down, provided a powerful though ultimately inadequate vision of what America should be.

PART I

American Revolutions of the Twentieth Century

CHAPTER ONE
Midcentury Normal

We Americans are reared with a feeling for the unity of our history and an unprecedented belief in the normality of our kind of life to our place on earth.

—DANIEL BOORSTIN, 1953[1]

People wanted change; they did not want to be changed.

—GODFREY HODGSON, 1976[2]

EVEN AS IT RECEDES into the past, mid-twentieth-century America continues to serve as a benchmark for measuring how far American society has come, or how far it has fallen. The United States emerged from the Great Depression and World War II as a global economic and political hegemon, and at the height of the Cold War the country enjoyed considerable prosperity and a sense of national unity. After the trauma and privations of the Depression and wartime, Americans welcomed the chance for a good life, and many who grew up during the postwar years—whites especially—later took that era as a standard of normality, from which all that happened afterward was a deviation. In later movies and novels as well as in political rhetoric, the 1950s represent the before-time: before Black insurgency, before the Vietnam War, before drugs, before women's and gay liberation, before the decline of blue-collar jobs for men that could support a family. Perhaps because of all the turbulence that followed, the America of the 1950s has lingered in early twenty-first-century memory as normal America, a period so exceptionally normal that it was unlike any time before or since.

Midcentury normal wasn't the normal of pre-Depression America, the "normalcy" that President Warren G. Harding promised in 1920 or that Sinclair Lewis described that same year in the novel *Main Street*, or that the sociologists Robert and Helen Lynd analyzed in their 1929 study of what was supposed to be a typical American community, *Middletown* (actually Muncie, Indiana). The pre-Depression image of normality was still small-town white America.

Midcentury normal, in contrast, was self-consciously modern and up to date. It had assimilated the growth of the big cities, mass media, the New Deal, labor unions, and earlier waves of immigration. It was a normal that was forward-looking, albeit in a particular way: It looked forward to continual improvements in the American standard of living but not to a change in the American way of life or how Americans thought about themselves.

The mid-twentieth century was the era of peak consensus, a historical parenthesis between the more overtly divided 1930s and 1960s. By peak consensus I don't mean that Americans were in general agreement; their disagreements mainly just became less conspicuous. The consensus was to a large extent engineered, the product of constraint and repression, but it was not entirely an illusion. Ethnic, class, and political differences among whites narrowed, and the idea of shared national values and an American national character became plausible under the constrained circumstances of the Cold War. In some ways the era was stifling and in other ways admirable, which is why American society subsequently could seem, even to the same people, both liberating and a disappointment, a story neither wholly of progress nor wholly of decline but an unexpected combination of both.

Much of what was admirable about midcentury America can now be appreciated more clearly than it could then. According to well-documented statistical trends, disparities in income and wealth between rich and poor were substantially lower than both earlier and later in the twentieth century. From 1947 to 1973, real income growth averaged about 2.6 percent annually for all families—except that families in the lower fifth did slightly better, with average income growth of 3 percent, while the top 5 percent of families did slightly worse, with average growth just above 2 percent.[3]

Americans had greater trust in their institutions and one another than they have had since.[4] American society was child oriented: the nation went on a school-building spree, unlike its later prison-building spree. Voter turnout and other forms of civic engagement were at high levels, while partisan antagonisms were low.[5] Churches, local sports leagues, civic associations, and other groups brought together people with different partisan affiliations. Religious participation was exceptionally high. People who voted Democratic or Republican sat next to each other in church and worked together in their communities—cross-cutting social affiliations that took the edge off partisan conflict.[6]

Yet the postwar consensus was far from all-embracing. Politics, the media, and intellectual life largely took for granted a white, patriarchal world. People on both the radical right and the radical left were left out. Labor unions, which continued to be large and powerful, had no consensus with American business about workers' rights and wages. Strikes were common. Blacks and whites surely had no consensus about desegregation and racial equality. The exclusions from public life of women, Black people, and other minorities followed long-established patterns, although those exclusions were beginning to be challenged. The society was so completely heteronormative that alternative forms of sexuality or gender expression were not even discussed, although new reports from sex researchers had begun to break through the reticence. Pressures toward conformity were overwhelming, yet everyone who wrote about conformity—a cultural preoccupation of the time—deplored it as inconsistent with ideals of freedom and individualism. But even those who sincerely condemned conformity had little idea what the coming decades' challenges to social norms would bring.

Consensus as a Contested Political Project

The post–World War II climate of belief in the United States is often described as a liberal consensus, but it could just as easily be described as a conservative consensus. Its liberalism was conservative, and its conservatism was liberal. Most liberals gave up the hopes for fundamental changes in capitalism that many had entertained during the Depression, while the dominant voices in Republican politics gave up trying to repeal Social Security and other major reforms that Franklin Roosevelt's New Deal had introduced. Liberal politicians and organizations distanced themselves from socialists, communists, and radicals of all kinds, while their conservative counterparts distanced themselves from anti-Semitic and anti-Catholic currents on the far right. The far right never disappeared; it remained influential in religious and business circles that were unreconciled to the New Deal, and it flared up in anticommunist crusades. But the gravitational forces in politics drew the two major parties toward the middle, marginalizing groups to either side that respectable opinion ruled out of bounds.

The pull toward the center was also visible in Western Europe, though the left was a more significant force in European politics. At a conference in Milan in 1954, European and American intellectuals identified a general trend that came to be summed up as "the end of ideology."[7] Mostly this referred to a loss of faith in Marxism, but it also applied to both fascism and laissez-faire. This wasn't, of course, the final end of ideology, but it represented an important, if temporary, political and intellectual shift away from ideological polarities in favor of support for a welfare state and mixed economy with considerable government involvement.

In the United States, the Democratic and Republican parties did not offer voters clear-cut choices framed around competing ideologies. Although the parties had long been loose coalitions, the ideological differences between them were especially blurred in an era when many foreign and domestic issues were matters of bipartisan consensus. The national broadcast networks, newsmagazines, and other leading news media studiously avoided being identified with an ideological position, adopting a nonpartisan, independent posture. According to an influential line of argument in political science based on studies of public opinion, only a small proportion of the electorate understood politics through a consistent worldview that could reasonably be characterized as ideological.[8]

Nonetheless, groups in the public arena did appeal to a common worldview, often citing such notions as "the American Way" and "Americanism." In the House of Representatives, investigations of communist influence in American society were carried out by a committee on "un-American activities." The historian Richard Hofstadter captured the moment in an often-repeated quip: "It has been our fate as a nation not to have ideologies but to be one."[9]

Yet even within these constraints, there were significant differences in how Americans understood what they supposedly agreed upon. Leaders in business, politics, and cultural life sought to define what the American Way meant. While these elites shared a commitment to a cohesive American society, they differed about the substantive content of the consensus they sought to consolidate. In this sense, consensus was a contested project. It did not just emerge on its own. Elite groups sought to develop and mold it to suit different purposes.

The elite efforts to build national unity went back to the 1930s, when the rise of radical movements on both the left and right aroused concerns about social cohesion. The outbreak of war in Europe in September 1939 heightened those concerns, and after France fell to the Nazis in June 1940, some Americans argued that the French had been fatally weakened by internal divisions. A new organization, the America First Committee, brought together pacifists, isolationists, and Nazi sympathizers in a campaign to keep the United States from entering the war. Sixty years later, the historian Arthur Schlesinger Jr. would recall that none of the "fierce national quarrels" in his lifetime—over communism in the late 1940s, McCarthyism in the 1950s, or the Vietnam War in the 1960s—so tore families and friends apart as the divisions among Americans that broke out between the European war's beginning in September 1939 and Japan's attack on Pearl Harbor in December 1941.[10] But the anxieties about national unity, which began during the Depression and intensified in the run-up to America's entry into World War II, led to an organized response. As the historian Wendy Wall shows in her account of the "invention" of the American Way, it was then that the elite project to strengthen national cohesion and morale had its roots.[11]

The consensus project had both a cultural and an economic aspect. Culturally, it sought to overcome religious, ethnic, and racial divisions and instill commitments to a broadened understanding of American national identity. But how inclusive was it, and did it call for equality or only for tolerance? In its economic aspect, the project sought to cultivate support for American capitalism. But did it imply a mixed economy that built on the New Deal, or did it mean, to use a term business groups introduced in the 1930s, "free enterprise" unfettered by government?

At the heart of the cultural project was the incorporation of religious and ethnic minorities from Europe into the American mainstream. The American Way, in this interpretation, meant the ability of diverse groups to live and work together in harmony according to shared values. An interfaith movement, led by such organizations as the National Conference of Christians and Jews, emphasized a shared religious heritage. Unlike those who identified America's religious tradition with Protestantism alone, the interfaith movement celebrated a "Judeo-Christian" heritage encompassing Protestants, Catholics, and Jews. Public occasions now often had not one man of the cloth but three, a minister, a priest, and a rabbi.

The consensus campaign sought to make white ethnics of diverse national origins at home in America, and it reconciled diversity with unity by elevating pluralism in the hierarchy of patriotic values. After the U.S. entry into the war, the government became directly involved in the effort to combat religious and ethnic prejudice, warning that anyone who sought to divide Americans was aiding the country's wartime enemies. But there was no consensus, during the war or after, about racial inclusion. Treating Black people as equals repeatedly led to resistance from white segregationists; during the war, Japanese Americans were denied the most basic of rights when they were sent to internment camps.

And there were still limits to white ethnic inclusion. After the war, when Congress revised the immigration laws, it left largely untouched the quotas that discriminated against Southern and Eastern Europeans, mainly Catholics and Jews. "It is incredible to me," President Truman wrote in a veto message, "that, in this year of 1952, we should again be enacting into law such a slur on the patriotism, the capacity, and the decency of a large part of our citizenry."[12] But Congress overrode his veto; the national-origins quotas would last until 1965.

In the struggle to define an economy that reflected American ideals, business leaders pursued one vision and New Dealers another. Business groups such as the National Association of Manufacturers and the U.S. Chamber of Commerce undertook a concerted campaign in the Depression years to promote a picture of free enterprise as the basis of prosperity and class harmony, the happy vision that their advertising and publicity labeled "the American Way." New Dealers countered with their own American narrative, emphasizing the nation's democratic ideals as the basis for an expansion of economic equality. In 1944, Roosevelt explicitly framed his principles for expanding opportunity and security as an "economic bill of rights," implying that these were a direct extension of the nation's original Bill of Rights. Socialists used the term "industrial democracy" to describe their goal of empowering labor to participate in running firms and planning the economy.

But the 1948 election, which sent both the Socialist and Progressive parties to defeat, devastated the left and crushed the radical aspirations remaining from the 1930s. By that point, liberals were in retreat, reconciled to the basic structure of capitalism. Rather than challenge the prerogatives of private capital, they focused instead on fiscal and monetary policies that, amid the postwar economic expansion, seemed sufficient for continued growth and stability. Unions became more narrowly focused on wages and benefits rather than economic planning or a role for labor in corporate management. But because they represented about one-third of workers and frequently used their most powerful weapon—the strike—the unions were a formidable countervailing force to employers and ensured that American workers shared in the benefits of rising productivity.[13]

The economic expansion, which was to last, with minor interruptions, for thirty years after World War II, was one of several background conditions that shaped which version of the postwar consensus predominated. Many people had feared that once the war was over, the United States would relapse into the Depression. Instead, the economy grew, the middle class expanded, and by the 1950s Americans were enjoying a sustained boom. During the early twentieth century, the United States had led the world in the proportion of people going to high school. After World War II, thanks to the GI Bill for veterans and federal and state spending on higher education, the United States again led the world in education, this time in the share of the population that went to college. The early 1940s had seen what later economists have called a "great compression" in earnings.[14] Not only did disparities in pretax incomes remain relatively low; high marginal income tax rates kept in check disparities in after-tax income, and those high tax rates continued into the Cold War. The top marginal rate during the Eisenhower administration in the 1950s was 91 percent, inconceivable today, especially under a Republican president. Marginal tax rates on inheritances were also high. Even though the wealthy had legal means to minimize taxes, they still paid effective rates that were higher than at any time since.[15]

A second background condition was the low level of immigration in the four decades between the restrictions of the early 1920s and the abolition of those restrictions in 1965. High levels of immigration replenish ethnic communities and help maintain strong ethnic identities.[16] A cut-off of new streams of immigration tends to weaken those identities, an especially likely result during an economic expansion that enabled many immigrants and their children to move up socioeconomically, move out of ethnic neighborhoods, and intermarry with other groups. Economic expansion and low levels of immigration both dampened nativist hostilities toward immigrants; in an expanding economy, the native-born have less reason to feel that the gains for the foreign-born come at their expense. Building interfaith and interethnic unity among white Americans was much easier under these conditions than if immigration had been high and economic growth low.

The postwar culture of consensus endorsed a strong commitment to religion while limiting religious expression in public life to certain common elements of the Judeo-Christian tradition. As a proportion of the American population, church membership in the 1950s was at an all-time high, reaching 59.5 percent, according to counts by churches, in 1953. Asked in surveys about their "religious preference," 95 percent of Americans described themselves as Protestant (68 percent), Catholic (23 percent), or Jewish (4 percent). In a well-known book of the period, *Protestant Catholic Jew*, Will Herberg wrote that the three major faiths had come to be understood as three interpretations of the same spiritual values, "equally and authentically American." They had become the primary way in which Americans expressed their identity within the broader society; indeed, Herberg wrote, one or another had become almost mandatory as a basis of "belonging," even though American society was overwhelmingly secular.[17] Patriotism demanded piety, though not of a particular kind. In an extemporaneous speech in New York shortly after being elected president, Eisenhower said, "Our government has no sense unless it is founded on a deeply felt religious faith—and I don't care what it is." He was, one commentator argued, "a very fervent believer in a very vague religion." The election in 1960 of John F. Kennedy as the nation's first Catholic president was greeted as a milestone in putting religious prejudices to rest, but Kennedy did not avoid references to God or faith in his Inaugural Address. Rather, he gave a powerful, activist expression to America's civil religion—the common religious elements of the national tradition—ending with the words, "With a good conscience our only sure reward, with history the final judge of our deeds, let us go forth to lead the land we love, asking His blessing and His help, but knowing that here on earth God's work must truly be our own."[18]

A fourth background condition shaping the postwar consensus was the change in international conflict, the shift in the United States from the antifascism of World War II to the anticommunism of the Cold War (or what we may soon need to call the "First Cold War"). Antifascism united liberals and the left, whereas anticommunism divided and weakened them. By the late 1940s, anticommunism was an overriding preoccupation in American politics and cultural life, reaching its zenith in the crusade led by Senator Joseph McCarthy and the House Un-American Activities Committee to root out communists in high places. The Red Scare affected virtually every major institution, from the federal government to Hollywood, the universities, schools, and labor unions. But while the Cold War led to repression of the left, it also led to self-restraint in corporate America in dealing with labor leaders who were partners in the anticommunist struggle. Concerned to maintain labor peace, corporate managers in large-scale industry preferred to compromise with America's mainstream unions rather than go on the warpath to eliminate them, as they would later.

These general patterns contributed to the blurring of lines between the Democratic and Republican parties. Both parties were ideologically mixed. The Democrats had their Southern conservatives, the Republicans had their Northern liberals, and both parties had moderates who were sometimes barely distinguishable from each other. "Checks and balances" in the American political system usually refer to offsetting, constitutionally assigned powers among the branches of government. But in the mid-twentieth century, the two major parties had internal checks and balances. The liberalism of the Democratic Party was checked by its dependence on Southern segregationists, and the conservatism of the Republican Party was checked by its Northern, urban liberal wing. In practice, however, this did not mean an even balance. It meant the status quo was safe, at least from national legislation.

It is misleading to identify this era as part of a "New Deal order," as if New Deal ideas and priorities governed. The persistence of strong unions was the greatest link between the New Deal and the 1950s. But from 1937 through the Kennedy administration in the early 1960s, a coalition of Southern Democrats and Republicans prevented any congressional action on national health insurance, education, civil rights, and many other liberal priorities. The passage of the Taft-Hartley Act in 1947 (over President Truman's veto) severely limited the growth of unions, particularly in the South, and had lasting effects on the entire political order. Unions were a central institution of American political economy at midcentury, but contrary to notions of a general labor–business accord, hostility to organized labor in the highest reaches of corporate America never went away and was ready to spring back once given the chance.

The lack of clear distinctions between the two parties troubled some analysts. In 1950, a committee of the American Political Science Association called for a system of "responsible" parties that would commit themselves to distinct programs and be cohesive enough to carry them out when they were in office. The political scientists were not worried about ideological polarization. The responsible parties, they confidently declared, would not erect "an ideological wall" between themselves because "there is no real ideological division in the American electorate."[19]

"The Area of American Agreement"

The years from 1945 to the early 1960s were a time of both economic growth and cultural constraint, and it was this culturally constrained prosperity that gave American society in that era its distinctive character.

Prosperity did not come psychologically unencumbered. In the wake of the Depression, many Americans were still haunted by memories of hardship. Cold War anticommunism intensified demands for sexual as well as political conformity, heightening concerns about anyone who might be a "subversive," a "deviant," or a "pervert." Later in the twentieth century, the culture would relax and the economy would tighten, but nearly every aspect of postwar life reflected the contrary influences of an expansive economy and restrictive culture. Nowhere was their impact more evident than in the institution that Americans generally agreed lay at the foundation of society, the family.

Before World War II, the birthrate had been falling in the United States for at least a century, and by 1940 it was down to 2.3 children per woman of childbearing age. It began rising during the war, and it remained above 3.0 until the early 1960s in the postwar baby boom—"the only period of sustained rising fertility in the nation's history," the demographer Andrew Cherlin observes—before falling back to, and then below, its level in 1940.[20] Before the 1940s, the long-term trends had also been toward later ages of marriage, smaller families, and greater educational equality between men and women, and by the end of the 1960s those trends would also resume. But from the mid-1940s to the early 1960s, the era of the baby boom, couples married earlier and the size of families increased. Women's educational attainment also fell relative to men's as women in their teens and twenties gave priority to getting married and having babies. In all these respects, the baby-boom era was unlike previous or subsequent years, a parenthesis in the history of the American family.[21]

The trends in marriage and birth rates corresponded to the rise of what the historian Elaine Tyler May calls a "reproductive consensus" in favor of early marriage and childbearing.[22] The birthrate rose among all social groups, across the usual divisions of race, ethnicity, education, and region. With the help of a strong economy and federal aid (notably subsidized home mortgages), many Americans who had grown up during the

Depression and war were able to establish their own homes and families and find the security and stability that had been missing from their lives. The change in relative income from the 1930s, not just its absolute level after the war, may have mattered for their family choices.[23]

But to see the turn toward marriage and family only in economic terms would be to miss the cultural strictures that ruled out other courses in life for both women and men. Popular culture, as well as religious and political leaders, unambiguously reinforced the message that a woman's ultimate fulfillment lay in marriage and motherhood. Young men faced strong pressures too. The novelist Philip Roth, who went to college in the early 1950s, later wrote in a quasi-autobiographical short story:

> A young college-educated bourgeois male of my generation who scoffed at the idea of marriage ... laid himself open to the charge of "immaturity," if not "latent" or blatant "homosexuality." Or he was just plain "selfish." Or he was "frightened of responsibility." Or he could not "commit himself" (nice institutional phrase that) to a "permanent relationship." Worst of all, most shameful of all, the chances were that this person who thought he was perfectly able to take care of himself on his own was in actuality "unable to love."[24]

Suspicion of the unmarried extended outside Roth's circles. A survey in 1955 found that only 9 percent of Americans believed a single person could be happy.[25] In a 1957 survey, one-third of the respondents checked off "mentally ill" when asked what they would think about someone if all they knew was that he was single.[26] The Red Scare of the 1950s was accompanied by a "lavender scare." The FBI and other federal agencies investigated the private lives of government employees, leading to 2,611 being fired as "security risks" and another 4,315 resigning under pressure.[27] A young man intent on rising the corporate ladder needed a presentable wife to get promoted. Staying single invited questions.

For a young unmarried couple to live together was also unacceptable. By this time, the rules of dating for teens revolved around "sexual brinksmanship," in Tyler May's charming Cold War phrase. A young man was expected to be sexually aggressive; that was natural and not to be held against him. It was up to the young woman to draw the line and limit "how far" he could go. The difference between "liberal" and "conservative" sexual morality lay in where that line was. Sexual liberalism did not condone premarital intercourse, but it accepted intimate physical relations, whereas conservative norms were less permissive. Whatever rules young couples were trying to follow, the rate of "shotgun weddings" (that is, weddings with a pregnant bride) increased during the postwar years.[28] Those weddings reaffirmed the social norm: If you wanted to have both sex and respectability, there was no alternative to marriage. As the 1955 hit song "Love and Marriage" ran, "Dad was told by Mother / You can't have one without the other."

But Americans did have sex without marriage, quite a bit of it according to Alfred C. Kinsey, who published a book on male sexuality in 1948 and one on female sexuality in 1953. Based on interviews with more than 11,000 people, the Kinsey reports found that more than four-fifths of men and two-thirds of women had sexual intercourse before marriage, and half of men and one-quarter of women had extramarital sex (though these numbers may have been inflated by the special circumstances of World War II).[29]

Like so much else about midcentury America, the idealized family combined old and new elements. The postwar reassertion of men's role as breadwinners was a return to the old ideal of female domesticity. But whereas the classic nineteenth-century bourgeois family had servants to do the housework, most wives in postwar America had to do it themselves. Despite new labor-saving devices like washing machines, they even spent more time on it than their counterparts in the 1920s. "Housewifery expands to fill the time available," Betty Friedan claimed in her 1963 book *The Feminine Mystique*.[30] Although husbands did not share equally in housework, they were expected to be more involved in family life, particularly in raising the children. "Togetherness," a term popularized by women's magazines in the 1950s, expressed the new ideal of a more fully shared marriage, centered on children while also providing sexual fulfillment to husband and wife. As Stephanie Coontz writes of family values in the 1950s, "The emphasis on producing a whole world of satisfaction, amusement, and inventiveness within the nuclear family had no precedents."[31] It was an ideal that imposed a tremendous burden on the family, especially on the women.

Among Black families, it was more common for the wife to work outside the home, and not only for material reasons: Black working-class men were not as inclined to think that a working wife compromised their masculinity. Although Black men and women both suffered from racial bias in the labor market, they made gains as they fled the rural South for cities in the North, West, and South. Previously confined largely to agricultural and private-household work, they were able to find jobs with better pay and benefits. Between 1940 and 1970, the share of employed Black women ages 18 to 49 working as domestics dropped from 58 percent to 13 percent, while those working in clerical occupations rose from 1 percent to 23 percent and in professional occupations from 5 percent to 11 percent. From 1940 to 1970, the average income of Black men rose from 43 percent to 64 percent of white men's average income; by 1970 the proportion of Black men with jobs in manufacturing approached that of white men, though they were still largely excluded from the most desirable positions. A Black steelworker later recalled that if one of their wives had a clerical job in a government agency, "we thought we had it made."[32]

The choices made by women of all races reflected their exclusion from the professions and better-paying jobs. A 1955 marriage study of a hundred white, middle-class couples in New England, originally interviewed in the 1930s, asked the wives what they had given up by marrying and raising a family. "Nothing," said a majority.[33] Analyzing the detailed responses of those women, however, Tyler May writes that many had given up professional careers, and they complained about "the burdens of their household tasks" and "their husbands' selfishness, demands on them, and need to be the boss." But the women nonetheless "put up with these problems" and said they were satisfied with their marriages. Their explanations were revealing: "life was 'economically comfortable and secure'; marriage provided 'complete peace,' a 'stable, comfortable life,' 'status,' and 'stability, children, a nice home,' which made them the 'envy' of many of their friends."[34] Economic security has always counted a great deal. For women in the generations haunted by the Depression, it was apparently enough to put up with a lot.

Two new worlds emerged in postwar America, one in suburbia, the other on television sitcoms. Although the first was real and the second fictional, they had one thing in common: both were populated almost entirely by white families. Suburbia and television illustrate how a consensus understanding of an idealized American way of life took shape under the social and political circumstances of the postwar era.

The spectacular increase in new single-family homes in the suburbs put the family ideals of the time into material form. The dream of living in "a home in a garden" beyond the dirt and danger of a city long predated the midcentury period. A spurt of suburban growth had followed World War I, but more Americans were able to fulfill the aspiration of moving from city to suburb after World War II. Public and private choices both played a role in opening the suburbs to more working- and middle-class families and shaping the communities that developed there.[35]

In 1945, after a decade and a half of limited construction, the pent-up demand for housing was enormous. Millions of house-hungry returning veterans and other Americans were doubling up with family and friends or even living in cars or temporary shelters. Several options for a government response were under debate. New Deal housing reformers favored affordable and walkable planned communities in the suburbs, like the one the Roosevelt administration had built in the late 1930s in Greenbelt, Maryland, just outside Washington, D.C. A bipartisan bill in Congress offered a variety of housing subsidies, including money for new multifamily rental housing to be built and run under public auspices. But neither of those proposals could overcome the opposition of the real estate industry and right-wingers like the junior senator from Wisconsin, Joseph McCarthy, who first made a name for himself in Congress by attacking public housing as a "breeding ground" for communists.[36]

The course that Congress primarily followed was to pump money into loan guarantees for private construction of single-family homes, about ten million of them between 1946 and 1953. Under legislation passed in 1944, veterans could get a low-interest mortgage for the entire appraised value of a home, little or no money down; others benefited from mortgages subsidized under the Federal Housing Administration. Of all housing starts in the postwar years, 85 percent were in the suburbs, overwhelmingly built on the premise that they would be for two-parent families in which the husband would commute to work and the wife would be a full-time homemaker. A massive program of highway construction provided the necessary complement to suburbanization.

Public reliance on private homebuilders raised a question: Could they build affordable suburban homes—affordable at least for middle- or lower-middle-class families if not the poor? Houses had traditionally been custom built, mostly for the affluent. Housing reformers and real-estate interests agreed that home construction for a wider market would require transforming the industry from its craft traditions to industrial methods of mass production. Emergency wartime projects at military bases and production facilities had already spurred development of those methods; applying the same techniques in peacetime would also require changes in financing to meet projected demand. A change in federal mortgage policies proved to be crucial for providing working capital to merchant builders: Under a new provision for federally insured loans, builders could borrow money in installments as construction advanced even without a prospective buyer in hand. Large-scale builders were far better able than small ones to master the financing as well as production requirements.

Federal policy thereby enabled the development of large suburban tracts with standardized houses, usually just a few models that were slight variations of a basic design. In 1947, a company that had built wartime housing, Abraham Levitt and Sons, offered homes in the first of several projects that would become a symbol of postwar suburbia. On what had mostly been potato fields in the Long Island suburbs of New York, the Levitts built thousands of nearly identical 800-square-foot, two-bedroom Cape Cod houses. They divided the construction process into twenty-six steps, with crews trained to do one step each, making maximum use of prefabricated parts. "The only difference between Levitt and Sons and General Motors," William Levitt declared, "is that we channel labor and materials to a stationary outdoor assembly line instead of bringing them together inside a factory on a mobile line." The original houses sold for $6,990; later, larger models were priced slightly higher. In a decade the Levittown on Long Island would have more than 17,040 houses and 82,000 residents, making it the largest community erected by a single builder. It was also the largest all-white community in the United States because the Levitts refused to sell to Black families.[37] This was no idiosyncrasy on their part. Federal housing programs not only accepted racial segregation; they actively promoted it. In some cases, the housing financed with federal money exclusively for whites displaced communities that had been integrated.[38]

Postwar policy also allowed tract developers to neglect public infrastructure and amenities. Unlike the New Deal planned communities, the new subdivisions were built without providing for diverse kinds of households, walkable greenways, parks, or public transportation. The original Levittown did have baseball diamonds, but it lacked a sewage system; each house had its own cesspool (the federal government would later provide funds to install sewers).

The physical form and social makeup of the first suburban subdivisions earned them a reputation for sameness and conformity. Not only did individual houses typically look alike; the subdivisions were also similar in design across the United States. Socially, suburban communities were more ethnically diverse than the immigrant neighborhoods from which many residents had come. In this respect, they were melting pots, for (white)

Americans with different religious traditions and European origins. In other respects, though, the young families that flocked to the suburbs were remarkably alike. "Our lives are held closely together," a writer in a Levittown community paper wrote, "because most of us are within the same age bracket, in similar income groups, live in almost identical houses and have common problems."[39] They didn't necessarily see that homogeneity as a problem. As one woman later recalled about moving into Levittown, "It was a whole new adventure for us. Everyone was taking courage from the sight of another orange moving van pulling in next door, a family just like us, unloading pole lamps and cribs and formica dining tables like our own, reflections of ourselves."[40]

Social critics and novelists were merciless in skewering suburban blandness and uniformity, but close students of suburban communities found a more lively and differentiated community life than the critics imagined. The sociologist Herbert Gans, who lived in a Levitt development that he studied in the late 1950s, argued that the residents were reasonably happy with life there.[41] Postwar suburbanization was in some respects an undeniable success. It raised material standards of living. In 1940, 45 percent of homes in the United States had lacked indoor plumbing, but the suburban tract homes offered not just plumbing but also central heating, washing machines, refrigerators, and other appliances.[42] For many of the second-generation immigrants who had grown up in crowded urban tenements, owning their own homes was the American dream come true. From 1940 to 1960, the proportion of Americans who were homeowners rose from 43 percent to 62 percent. Previously, as the historian of suburbia Kenneth Jackson writes, buying a home had "required savings and effort of a major order," as it does today. But government subsidies, the low cost of land and building materials, cheap energy, and new mass-production construction techniques made buying a home during the postwar decades more affordable to a wider group of Americans than ever before. It became cheaper to buy a new home in the suburbs than to rent housing at the market price.[43]

The advantages of suburban development accrued almost exclusively to white families. National housing policy had developed on two levels. Under the banner of "urban renewal," slum clearance became a priority for cities, often to make way for highways or commercial developments without any concern for the low-income communities being destroyed. While some money went toward public housing for the poor, most federal housing aid went to homeowners in the form of subsidized mortgages, tax deductions for mortgage interest and property taxes, and money for highway construction. The suburbs were built on that basis, and suburbanites enjoyed one further advantage. They benefited from public largesse without being conscious of it or feeling in any way indebted to government. While the white majority came to despise public housing and resent the money spent on it, they kept subsidizing suburbia without protest.

The suburbs changed with time. The residents landscaped, altered, and expanded their homes, reducing the architectural monotony. Communities added the infrastructure and amenities the developers didn't provide. Neighborhoods turned over, and some became more socially diverse. But suburban sprawl, dependence on the automobile, and the dominance of single-family houses were entrenched in American middle-class life in a way that made them highly resistant to change. And even after some of the realities did change, the early myths of suburbia persisted. Much the same happened with the second new midcentury world, the world that emerged on television.

Although television emerged as a technology before World War II, its diffusion as a medium of communication came after the war, to about 5 percent of households during the late 1940s and then rapidly toward saturation during the 1950s. In 1954, in an article in *Variety* entitled "Making TV the 'Shining Center of the Home' and Helping Create a New Society of Adults," the president of NBC wrote that television would make it impossible to raise children within the narrow horizons of separate groups. This power of television, he argued, "makes it most important in our stewardship of broadcasting to remain within the 'area of American agreement,' with all the implications of that statement, including however some acknowledgement in our programming of the American heritage of dissent."[44] Despite that nod, dissent didn't get much airtime. Television not only stayed within the "area of American agreement," it helped define and eventually change what that area was.

The cultural form of postwar television reflected early constraints on both broadcasting and viewing. Even many large cities had just three TV channels, while other areas had only one or two. At the same time, families with television normally had only one set, and watching TV together became an important part of family experience. The twin limits at both the sending and receiving ends of the TV signal shaped programming and led to the medium's early identification with family-oriented mass entertainment.

Like the suburban single-family home, television became an aspect of the family-centered 1950s. Surveys of early television use found that families with children were especially likely to buy a television, and when they did, more family members stayed home more of the time. This was part of the attraction: The kids stayed off the streets, Dad was more likely to come straight home to relax after work. Women's magazines worried over exactly where the TV should go—in the living room, the basement, the "family room" (a new concept), or perhaps "some strategic spot where you can see it from the living room, dining room and kitchen."[45] In homes where space was scarce, the old focal point of middle-class family life, the piano, sometimes had to go. Even in the early 1950s, the set was on in television households an average of five hours a day. Neighbors who didn't yet have one came over to watch—people even held "TV parties"—but by the end of the decade, nearly nine out of ten American homes had a TV set.[46]

The popular family sitcoms of the era—weekly shows like *The Adventures of Ozzie and Harriet* (1952–1966), *Father Knows Best* (1954–1960), and *Leave It to Beaver* (1957–1963)—portrayed, as David Halberstam writes, "idealized homes in an idealized, unflawed America" where there were no financial problems, no class distinctions, no divorces, no serious illness, no poverty, and no voices raised in anger. Living in single-family homes someplace in America, the families were comfortable but not rich. Moms were always home and dads worked at jobs that apparently paid enough so that they never worried about expenses. As Halberstam writes,

> Things could go wrong in a small way, but never in a way that threatened the families watching at home or cut too close to the nerve in dealing with the real issues of real American homes, where all kinds of problems lay just beneath the surface. Things in sitcoms never took a turn for the worse, into the dangerous realm of social pathology. Things went wrong because a package was delivered to the wrong house, because a child tried to help a parent but did so ineptly, because a dad ventured into a mom's terrain, or because a mom, out of the goodness of her heart, ventured into a dad's terrain. When people did things badly, they almost always did them badly with good intentions.

The sitcoms offered gentle lessons about social norms—the rules, for example, about a woman's terrain and a man's—not only for those who lived in leafy suburbs but for the millions of economically struggling viewers who might as well have been in a different country. Halberstam suggests that the shows later became objects of nostalgia because they left people with memories of an idyllic time, even if that was not the life they had lived: "Television reflected a world of warm-hearted, sensitive, tolerant Americans, a world devoid of anger and meanness of spirit and, of course, failure."[47] It was an America that Americans wanted to live in and believe in. It was an America that some remembered decades later when they said they wanted to "make America great again."

The combination of television's rapid adoption and limited viewing alternatives gave the most popular shows immense reach. On an evening in March 1955, one out of every two Americans watched the Broadway star Mary Martin in a live production of the musical *Peter Pan*. As an early sociologist of television pointed out, "Never before in history had a single person been seen and heard by so many others at the same time."[48] On ceremonial occasions like a presidential inauguration and in moments of crisis like a political assassination, television brought Americans together and conveyed the sense of being on the scene. Radio had already assembled national publics for national events; television increased these broadcasts' emotional power. Events came to be staged with media in mind, produced for television and experienced and remembered the way they were broadcast. At this early phase of television's development, it was possible to think of the medium as a basis of "national integration," a way of coordinating perceptions and beliefs, part of the larger project of building consensus.

This sharing of the experience of television, both in families and in the nation as a whole, was a cardinal fact of the midcentury era. The impact of communication does not depend only on the relation of individuals to the medium or to the message; it also depends crucially on the relation of readers, listeners, and viewers to one another.[49] The rise of mass-circulation daily newspapers had created a public whose members understood they were reading the same stories at the same time and could later talk about them. Newspapers set tongues in motion. One nineteenth-century editor defined news as "anything that will make people talk," a criterion that applies to successful entertainment of any kind (today it's called "buzz"). The sense of sharing a common experience, even if not in other people's physical presence, was all the greater for audiences listening to radio or watching television. They too turned mass media into conversation, recapping, rehashing, and reinterpreting stories, sometimes in ways the scriptwriters and broadcasters might not have intended or imagined. So it's a mistake to think of television viewers as merely passive. Nonetheless, televised experience was shared on a massive scale, and the economic incentives and political constraints shaping TV had wide-ranging implications for the culture that Americans had in common.

The mass audiences assembled by American television reflected the workings of a highly concentrated commercial market. Since broadcast reception was over-the-air and free, a TV station made money not by enrolling subscribers but by attracting eyeballs for advertisers. And since television programming was expensive to produce, local stations had overwhelming incentives to affiliate with a national network that would supply popular programs and give the stations a share of the revenue from the programs' sponsors. During the postwar decades, given the limited number of stations licensed in local areas, only three networks (CBS, NBC, and ABC) developed, and they supplied 90 percent of primetime shows.

With viewers having so few options, the rational strategy for each network was not to specialize in a niche and tailor programming to specific tastes or ideological viewpoints but to pursue the widest audience possible. While many viewers would not get the shows they might have wished, the networks and their affiliates would prosper with programs that were broadly acceptable. This incentive for conventional entertainment within "the area of American agreement" also fit with the demands of the family audience and the veto power of a network's local affiliates, which could refuse to clear more adventurous programs for local viewing. Sponsors and advertising agencies were also risk averse and closely involved in programming decisions, especially during television's early development, when many programs were sole-sponsored, like the *General Electric Theater* introduced every week by Ronald Reagan.

The bias toward standard family entertainment was reinforced, and to some extent created, by national policy. The three-network commercial oligopoly resulted from decisions by the federal government, which could have generated more competition in television from the start, including a role for public broadcasting, by allocating spectrum differently. The government involved itself in broadcasting far more than it had in earlier media. While constitutional protections of freedom of the press were long understood as barring any government licensure of printers, Congress and the courts justified the licensing and ongoing regulation of broadcasters for two reasons. The first was the scarcity of spectrum: If left unregulated, over-the-air signals would interfere with each other. So for broadcasting to work at all, the government had to allocate spectrum. That was the basis for assigning licenses and regulating their use consistent with "the public interest." The second rationale was that broadcasting was invasive: it intruded directly into the home. Hence the government could set standards for permissible speech on the air, including standards of "decency" that it could not set for print. Although the government rarely denied a station's application for a renewal of its license, the threat lay in the background, and broadcasters were acutely conscious of even a raised eyebrow by federal regulators.

What mainly kept television in line, however, was a wider set of sensitivities to advertisers and public opinion. Broadcasters knew that television was a "guest" in the family home, but they did not pay attention to every home's sensitivities. Stock characters and plots that portrayed Black and Native people in demeaning ways or as villains were taken for granted. The public that television's leaders worried about offending was white. That's not to say the networks were particularly concerned about pleasing the cultural elite. During the 1950s, they did run some programs with high-culture aspirations, such as original drama performed live to give the audience the sense of being in a theater.[50] But one-off dramas and "spectaculars" like *Peter Pan* didn't create a weekly viewing habit. By the end of the decade, the era of original TV drama and other live performances was over. American television mostly settled down to a few filmed genres such as sitcoms, westerns, and detective and mystery programs. The violence in westerns and crime shows didn't prevent them from attracting a family audience. "One of television's greatest contributions," the director Alfred Hitchcock said, "was that it brought murder back into the home, where it belongs."[51]

Although federal regulation could not turn commercial television into high art, it did affect the coverage of news and public affairs programs. Television stations carried news programs to fulfill their obligation under Federal Communications Commission (FCC) rules to serve the public interest.[52] Under a rule established in 1949 (the "fairness doctrine"), stations were subject to two requirements: to broadcast programs about controversial matters of public importance, and to present contrasting views. Exactly which contrasting views and how much time they should receive was left to the broadcasters' good-faith judgment. Like other content-related regulations, the fairness doctrine was not much enforced, and some historians and critics of later policies have retrospectively exaggerated its importance.[53]

Television networks, however, had another reason for telling news stories from a seemingly detached and balanced perspective. Doing so made business sense because the networks sought to build mass audiences that transcended regional and partisan lines. The economic logic dictated a particular kind of television journalism. To make potentially controversial stories more acceptable, news programs reported them in a point–counterpoint format, giving both sides and typically ending with an anodyne or wry comment by the correspondent.[54] Network news programs did have to find one kind of significance in news stories—national significance. The visual nature of the medium demanded pictures of particular people and places, but those individuals and places had to illustrate themes of national interest. A story about a local development, or several local stories stitched together, would show "in microcosm" a national trend.[55] In short, television nationalized the news. TV told stories about America.

In television's early days, news wasn't a priority for the networks or their local affiliates, but it developed into a source of profit as well as influence, particularly after CBS and NBC expanded their evening news programs from fifteen minutes to half an hour in 1963, allowing for more ads and more feature stories. As these programs gained viewership, the three networks became Americans' most important and trusted source of national and world news, with viewership of the evening news reaching one-fourth of the U.S. population.[56] This audience was extraordinary not only in its size but also in its composition. Surveys showed that unlike the readership of newspapers and newsmagazines, the TV news audience included disproportionate numbers of people with relatively little education. Much of this was an "inadvertent audience" made up of viewers who were already tuned to a channel and sat through the news.[57] Most local affiliates of the national networks ran their news broadcasts at the same hour, generally 6:00 P.M. After coming home from work, many people watched the evening news because there was nothing else on TV. The low-choice structure of TV probably made many Americans more informed about public affairs than they would have been if they had more options for TV entertainment.[58]

That low-choice structure of television also gave an enormous amount of power to the men—they were almost all men—who ran the networks and affiliates and decided what programs and news would go on the air. Many Americans today would view early television's offerings as limited and unappealing, but that was not what most viewers thought at the time. Just as Americans who moved to a suburban tract house were thrilled to own their own home, so they were thrilled to have their own home theater, no matter that the chairman of the FCC decried television as a "vast wasteland." The networks did not have an entirely free hand. They had to worry about ratings, sponsors, and federal regulation. But they had a degree of cultural and political influence that became fully apparent only in the mid- to late 1960s, when the "area of American agreement" turned into an area of conflict.

Consensus as Intellectual Framework

Midcentury America, I have been emphasizing, was not an era of universal consensus. The consensus did not extend to marginalized minorities or to political dissenters on either the left or the right, and even those who recognized an "area of American agreement" did not necessarily agree about what lay within it. Did the economic consensus rest on the ideas of the New Deal or the free enterprise system? Were Black and indigenous people included within the circle of equal respect? Nonetheless, people in positions of political power and cultural authority like television executives were confident enough of a consensus on social norms and political beliefs to be able to make decisions on that basis.

Intellectuals also discovered consensus where previously they had seen conflict. Historians, literary critics, and social scientists in the postwar era found a deep and lasting unity in American life that had escaped their predecessors' notice. They wrote about "the American mind" as though there were one such mind, and about "the American character" as though there were one such character. Many of them believed America had a meaning and a mission in the world and that its whole history had been a great experiment, a test of its principles and its people, which the nation had passed in World War II and which the Cold War was testing again. Like the TV news, intellectuals told stories about America. Although they did not all tell the same stories, the prevailing narrative viewed Americans as sharing a common political culture throughout its past, which presumably indicated that the consensus would prevail in the future too. But even here there were notable contrasts.

The work of two influential postwar historians, Daniel Boorstin and Richard Hofstadter, illustrates the range of views that came to be called "consensus history." Conflicting economic interests had been at the heart of the scholarship of such earlier figures as Frederick Turner, Charles A. Beard, and Vernon Parrington, historians deeply influenced by the politics of the Progressive Era who continued into the 1940s to dominate thinking about America's past. Boorstin and Hofstadter, in contrast, claimed that American history was characterized by a durable consensus and the absence of persistent class conflict. But whereas Boorstin wrote from within that consensus and celebrated it, Hofstadter wrote from outside the consensus and criticized it.[59]

Although Hofstadter later expressed misgivings about consensus history, he gave the perspective its defining formulation in 1948 in the introduction to *The American Political Tradition*, a book with unusual influence (it sold more than one million copies and became the text for countless courses in American history). Calling for "a reinterpretation of our political traditions which emphasizes the common climate of American opinion," Hofstadter claimed that the "fierceness" of political conflict was only superficial. "The major political traditions," he wrote, "have shared a belief in the rights of property, the philosophy of economic individualism, the value of competition; they have accepted the economic virtues of capitalist culture as necessary qualities of man." The "business of politics" in the United States had always been to protect and bolster this system. "American traditions," he granted, "also show a strong bias in favor of equalitarian democracy, but it has been a democracy in cupidity rather than a democracy of fraternity."[60]

Hofstadter's argument that no effort to break out of the framework of entrepreneurial capitalism had amounted to anything reflected the despair he shared with fellow radicals and socialists in the late 1940s. Franklin Roosevelt, Hofstadter acknowledged, stood out among American statesmen "for his sense of the failure of tradition," but while Roosevelt took bold measures, he was "neither systematic nor consistent" in his thinking and had failed to find an alternative to the ideology of self-help and free enterprise. Despite Hofstadter's view that America needed such an alternative, his irreverent portraits of central figures in American history and debunking of liberal myths could mostly be read as affirming that the United States was founded and had prospered on the basis of conservative ideas. "In material power and productivity," he wrote, "the United States has been a flourishing success. Societies that are in such good working order have a kind of mute organic consistency. They do not foster ideas that are hostile to their fundamental working arrangements. Such ideas may appear, but they are slowly and persistently insulated, as an oyster deposits nacre around an irritant."[61] Like a defeated political candidate's gracious acknowledgment that an opponent has more accurately read the electorate, *The American Political Tradition* amounts to a concession speech for Hofstadter's generation of radical intellectuals.

While Hofstadter questioned the merits of the American consensus, Boorstin sang its virtues. His 1953 book *The Genius of American Politics* claimed that in contrast to Europeans, Americans had never sought to realize any abstract ideal. In place of a general political theory, they had a "satisfactory equivalent" that he called "givenness," the belief that American values were "given" by the "facts" of history and geography, the "gifts" of the country's founding, its landscape, and the absence of any great changes from the founding to the present. These facts added up to "the idea that the 'American Way of Life' harbors an 'American Way of Thought.'" In Boorstin's telling, the American Revolution was not really a revolution, and even the Civil War was not a "discontinuity." Slavery receded into insignificance. American history had rolled out with no great hills or valleys.[62]

This placid view was consensus history in its purest form, relegating conflict to irrelevance, an unapologetic originalism more encompassing than the legal theory that later took that name. Even where consensus historians acknowledged conflict, they tended to see it as having such diverse and changing forms that there was no consistent or underlying pattern. Americans were one people, with one set of ideals. They had always been that way and presumably would never change. The idea of a deep contradiction in American society, of recurring lines of conflict, was completely foreign to the consensus school.

The same was true of the dominant school in American sociology, which conceived of societies as self-maintaining systems based on shared values. The sociologists outdid the historians by turning consensus into a basis for understanding all societies and as a framework for all of the social sciences. This argument was laid out by a group under the leadership of Talcott Parsons in the introduction to a work intended as a grand synthesis, *Toward a General Theory of Action* (1951). According to the synthesis, a functioning social system institutionalizes the roles that individuals are held to perform, creating "expectations of conformity." Integrating the "value-orientations" of individuals into a "common system," that is, a "moral consensus," is a "functional imperative." Social pathologies result from failures to align all individuals with the society's norms.[63] The theory, known in the field as "structural functionalism," did not envision the possibility that societies suffered from contradictions stemming from their core institutions and norms or from class or group conflict. There might be "dysfunctions," but they were secondary to the grand design.

The idea of a single ruling consensus also shaped these sociologists' understanding of ethnicity. In the early twentieth century, some writers on assimilation, such as Horace Kallen and Randolph Bourne, had disputed the idea that immigrant groups had to surrender entirely to Americanization. Kallen had called for "cultural pluralism," the idea that they could preserve distinct ethnic identities; Bourne envisioned a continual enlargement of American culture from new immigrants. But midcentury sociology took a dim view of any alternative to ethnic capitulation. "The future of American ethnic groups seems to be limited," W. Lloyd Warner and Leo Srole concluded in a 1945 book. The demands of assimilation required non-Anglo-Protestants to "unlearn" their cultural traits, which American culture viewed as inferior. Ethnic and racial groups formed a hierarchy, with white, English-speaking Protestants at the top and Blacks at the bottom. Among the in-between groups, Warner and Srole wrote, the "dark-skinned" Mediterranean Catholics like Italians would take a "moderate" period to assimilate, which they put at six generations. This was moderate only in comparison to Blacks, whose assimilation was so distant that Warner and Srole had no timetable for it. In *Assimilation in American Life* (1964), the canonical study of the subject, Milton Gordon offered a complex analysis of the forces affecting change in ethnic and racial groups along several dimensions of assimilation. He too saw no possibility of inclusion in American society except through conformity with the "core culture," the culture of white, Anglo-Saxon Protestants.[64]

The assumptions of American sociology in that era were not fundamentally different from those of American TV sitcoms. Both envisioned a society fundamentally in harmony with itself, based on a consensus culture. That Parsons and his colleagues believed they had a universal theory applicable to all societies is testimony to the peculiar but short-lived power of the midcentury moment. The consensus vision did not last long in either the broader culture or the intellectual world. If it was your framework for understanding the American future, you had surprises coming.

CHAPTER TWO

Black Americans, Model Minority

Through centuries of Black resistance and protest, we have helped the country live up to its founding ideals. And not only for ourselves—Black rights struggles paved the way for every other rights struggle.

—NIKOLE HANNAH-JONES[1]

TWO MODEL MINORITIES emerged in post–World War II America, though they were models in different ways.

By the mid-1950s, academic studies and popular magazines were celebrating the success of Japanese Americans in entering the middle class, a remarkable story since only a decade earlier they had been vilified as an "enemy race" and interned in concentration camps. In a 1966 article in the *New York Times Magazine,* William Petersen, a sociologist at the University of California, Berkeley, spelled out how "by any criterion of good citizenship that we choose, the Japanese Americans are better than any other group in our society, including native-born whites." They had a high "achievement orientation" and exceptionally low levels of crime, teenage delinquency, and other forms of "social pathology." Introducing a segment on Japanese Americans on *60 Minutes* in 1972, the CBS reporter Mike Wallace declared: "'The model minority,' they are called. . . .

They've become the very model of the way that white Americans like to think of themselves."[2]

The second group, Black Americans, served as a model of a different kind. Their collective struggle for freedom and dignity became the template for movements among other racial and ethnic minorities and among women, LGBTQ+ people, and people with disabilities. The role of Black Americans in that broader family of movements represented a stark break from the past. From the end of Reconstruction in 1876 to the 1940s, Black Americans had not been able to count on any reliable political allies, not in the federal government, not in the two major parties, not even among other ethnic or racial groups who shared their history of social and political subordination and exploitation. Other minorities who were not treated as white insisted that they were not Black, lest they be subjected to the same indignities as Black people. This long history of Black political isolation makes all the more remarkable the transformation set in motion by Black Americans in the following decades. From a caste apart, they became the driving force and moral center of the struggle for freedom and equality, expanding the range of possibility for other groups as well as themselves.

Black Americans became a true model minority in several ways. Their freedom struggle provided the prototype for the strategies and tactics that other movements adopted. Collective action always involves a "repertoire of contention," in Charles Tilly's phrase, and Black Americans were pattern-setters for other movements.[3] They were also the prototypical minority in the minority rights revolution—the judicial decisions and civil rights legislation of the mid-twentieth century that the courts and government agencies made primarily in response to Black protest but which they then applied to other historically subordinated groups as well. Other groups also followed the Black model in combining demands for both jobs and justice. And Black Americans set the cultural model for those groups in challenging the psychology of oppression by insisting on respect as well as rights and cultivating their own artistic and intellectual traditions. In short, despite the continuing racism they faced, Black Americans served as a model for collective action, legal redress, group economic advance, and cultural transformation, challenging hierarchies of power and worth that had long been simply taken for granted as facts of American life.

The publication in 1944 of Gunnar Myrdal's landmark study, *An American Dilemma: The Negro Problem and American Democracy*, was a signal event in highlighting the idea that bigotry and bias against Black Americans contradicted what Myrdal called "the American Creed." Myrdal, a

Swedish economist, had been brought to the United States by a New York philanthropy, the Carnegie Corporation, to direct a far-reaching study of the conditions of Black America. In 1940, while working on the project, he returned for a while to Sweden, which failed to take sides as the Nazis advanced across Europe. In Myrdal's mind, the United States offered a more inspiring example, though it had not yet entered the war. He took the American Creed to be the "cement" holding a disparate nation together: "These ideals of the essential dignity of the individual human being, of the fundamental equality of all men, and of certain inalienable rights to freedom, justice, and a fair opportunity . . . were written into the Declaration of Independence, the Preamble of the Constitution, the Bill of Rights and into the constitutions of the several states . . . [and] have thus become the highest law of the land." Americans recognized, he added, that they did not live up to the Creed, and they even acknowledged their collective sins: "The cultural unity of the nation is this common sharing in both the consciousness of sins and the devotion to high ideals."[4]

But Myrdal's reference in the title of his book to an "American dilemma" reflected what at the time was only a wishful premise. A "dilemma" describes a psychologically and often ethically difficult choice; genuine dilemmas force us to wrestle with alternatives. In 1944, however, most white Americans were not wrestling with their own or the nation's treatment of Black people.[5] Myrdal himself brilliantly analyzed the patterns of denial and escapism in the thinking of whites. At the time, the gap between the American Creed and the Black experience was only what I called in the introduction a "latent contradiction."

To be sure, some Americans, especially Black people themselves, were aware of the contradiction, and a few tried to make an issue of it. That same year, 1944, a group of Howard University students picketed a racially segregated Washington, D.C., restaurant with signs that read, "Are you for Hitler's Way or the American Way?"[6] Myrdal ultimately counted on the moral conscience and goodwill of white Americans to bring about change: "a great majority of white people in America would be prepared to give the Negro a substantially better deal if they knew the facts." Studies like his could be part of "an educational offensive against racial intolerance" that he said had never been seriously attempted. Using italics for emphasis, he wrote, "*To get publicity is of the highest strategic importance to the Negro people*"—and as the civil rights struggle eventually proved, that much was true.[7] But better information and goodwill would never be enough. It took a sustained movement led by Black people themselves to bring the American contradiction fully to the surface and force white Americans to confront a dilemma they had habitually avoided.

The Black freedom struggle of the twentieth century repeatedly confronted a dilemma of its own concerning its relation to sympathetic whites: whether to involve them directly in reform efforts, thereby potentially becoming dependent on them, or to organize separately and independently. For a long time, the issue of separatism bedeviled the movement for racial change, until it was transformed by the Black freedom struggle itself. By inspiring other movements for racial and gender equality, Black Americans found themselves from the late 1960s on in a different environment. The increasing Hispanic and Asian American populations also expanded the potential for alliances. Those relationships were often complicated and ambivalent, but they helped Blacks overcome their earlier political isolation.

The ensuing transformation of American life was both political and cultural. Black Americans for the first time became a major integral force in a national party coalition and in the process precipitated a regional partisan realignment as the white-dominated South began passing from Democratic into Republican hands. Black culture became more central in American life, and Black Americans became more fully represented in national media, school curricula and higher education, music, and the arts. The larger family of ethnoracial and gender minorities also gained greater media access and cultural representation in what had been a nearly homogeneous white culture. This upheaval had radical implications. It promised—or threatened, from the standpoint of conservative whites—to change the very idea of America.

Although this transformation would never have happened without the Black-led freedom struggle, it depended on responsive institutions that continued to be white dominated. However brilliant its leaders, however committed its grassroots members, the civil rights movement would never have succeeded without institutional support. That support is critical to understanding how the movement overcame the nation's status quo bias and why it did so in post–World War II America. The courts and cultural institutions, two spheres particularly influenced by liberal ideas, helped establish the legitimacy of new frameworks of rights and group identity. But they were not sufficient to change Blacks' economic situation. Despite significant material progress for Black Americans (particularly in the South), the epochal shifts in law and culture were not matched by an equivalent transformation in economic security, ownership of property, and institutional power. That gap between formal rights and culture, on the one hand, and economic resources, on the other, had explosive repercussions.

Black Prototypes

Prototypes are initial models or designs for building things, and the Black freedom struggle and its repertoires of contention served as a prototype in the building of other movements. But the term "prototype" also has a meaning in cognitive psychology that is relevant to the changing position of Black Americans in national consciousness. When we think of an abstract category, a particular instance often first comes to mind as the "best example," the one that most clearly stands for the category as a whole.[8] For example, a robin may come to mind as the prototypical bird. More than one group has suffered oppression, even genocide—Native peoples during colonization; Jews during the Holocaust. It does not diminish the suffering of either of those groups to recognize that in mid-twentieth-century America, the Black freedom struggle catapulted Black people from the margins to the center of American public consciousness. They became the prototypical, top-of-mind oppressed minority. Their struggle came to dominate the progressive imagination of social justice and social change. And because of the moral legitimacy that struggle enjoyed, other groups came to emulate it.

The decade-long "heroic" phase of the civil rights movement, which did more than anything else to bring about this change, is now the stuff of legend. From the bus boycott in Montgomery, Alabama, in 1955–1956 to the beatings of civil rights marchers on the Edmund Pettus Bridge in Selma, Alabama, in 1965, the movement led by Martin Luther King Jr. brought national attention to the Black struggle and precipitated the passage of the Civil Rights Act in 1964 and Voting Rights Act the following year. In the standard narrative, this heroic era came to a tragic end amid ghetto riots in the mid-1960s, assassinations, and rising racial tensions within the movement itself. Some blame often falls on the turn within the movement in 1966 from civil rights and integration to Black Power. But whatever the national political impact of Black Power, it too represented an important prototype for other emerging movements. To understand the broader influence of the Black freedom struggle, we need to consider what the historian Jacquelyn Dowd Hall calls the "long civil rights movement," beginning earlier in the twentieth century and extending after the national media's attention went elsewhere.[9]

Studies of the civil rights movement have sought to correct for all the attention given King and other national leaders by emphasizing the movement's base in local grassroots activities and institutions. That social base within Black communities was crucial—and as the authors of those studies recognize, so was the way those local activities connected with one another and reached the national public and national politics.[10] As Bayard Rustin, one of the movement's leaders, said of the Southern Christian Leadership Conference (SCLC), which played a coordinating role under King's leadership, "its most magnificent accomplishment" was "the creation of a disciplined mass movement of Southern blacks" that had no historical precedent.[11] Developments at both the base and the top of the movement enabled it to overcome barriers that previously seemed insuperable.

Analysts of the civil rights movement also point to the critical importance of its historical context. Black Americans had no political leverage in the first three decades of the twentieth century. In the South they were disenfranchised, and in the rest of the country they were too small a share of the electorate to influence either of the major parties. They also lacked the requisite economic and organizational resources to challenge white supremacy effectively. When Democrats became the majority party in the 1930s, white Southerners dominated the congressional leadership, and they saw to it that major legislation like the Social Security Act and National Labor Relations Act (also known as the Wagner Act), both passed in 1935, excluded both agricultural and domestic workers, the job categories where Blacks were most numerous. The Wagner Act also did not bar racial discrimination by unions. Civil rights organizations sought an amendment to impose a "duty of fair representation" to require unions to represent all workers, not just whites, but that effort failed. Nonetheless, the New Deal did begin to improve the situation of Black Americans, and by the 1940s demographic change and the onset of war dramatically increased their political opportunities and capacities.

The demographic change was the Great Migration that transformed Black Americans from a predominantly rural to a predominantly urban people. Nearly six million Black Americans left the South for the North and West between 1910 and 1960, with most of that shift coming after 1930. The causes were economic, chiefly the collapse of cotton farming and the growth of opportunities in Northern industry at a time when immigration from Europe was largely cut off. But the migration also had major effects in national politics. Black Americans moved to places where they had political rights they were denied in the South, settling overwhelmingly in seven major industrial states whose electoral votes were crucial in presidential elections. Even within the South, the migration into the cities had a political impact. The cities brought Black people into closer relations with one another and enabled them to free themselves from rural debt bondage, obtain more education, raise their incomes, and develop more substantial community institutions, particularly churches. By the 1940s, the Black vote in the North and the Black church in the South were emerging as new sources of leverage for civil rights. In the 1960s, Black college students would become another base for change.[12]

Wartime, the second major contextual influence, has a long history of strengthening interests in equality. Concessions of rights have often resulted from a state's need to recruit solders and motivate support during a war, and from pressure by veterans in its aftermath. In the United States, the ideological justifications of war have also legitimated and reinforced demands for equality. Before the twentieth century, the two greatest periods of Black advance both occurred in conjunction with war. The Revolutionary era led to the adoption of laws ending slavery in the North, the Civil War to a general emancipation and the passage of the Reconstruction Amendments to the Constitution.[13]

Both World War II and the Cold War also led to Black advances in civil rights. Emboldened leadership coincided with expanded political opportunity. The first indication of a shift came in 1941, when the Black labor leader A. Philip Randolph, head of the Brotherhood of Sleeping Car Porters, made an unprecedented call for tens of thousands of Black people to march on Washington. One of the demands of the March on Washington movement was an end to bias in defense jobs, and the mere threat drew a positive response. Before the march could take place, President Roosevelt issued an executive order banning racial discrimination in war production and establishing a Fair Employment Practices Commission to monitor compliance. Amid a tight labor market during the war, Black Americans' real incomes doubled, many obtained jobs in industry, and some joined interracial union organizing drives.

Despite the risk of being fired, denied credit, or subjected to violent reprisals, Black people signed on as plaintiffs in lawsuits demanding an end to discrimination in education, denial of voting rights, and exclusion from public facilities. The organization that provided the legal representation in many of these cases, the National Association for the Advancement of Colored People (NAACP), saw its membership climb from 50,000 in 355 local chapters in 1940 to almost 450,000 in 1,073 chapters in 1947. Some Black soldiers returned home fighting, in the sense that their military experience gave them both the impetus and the confidence to challenge white supremacy and segregation. Black World War II veterans later became mainstays of the civil rights movement.[14]

The ideological climate of both World War II and the Cold War and the new international position of the United States worked in favor of these Black efforts. The government's propaganda during World War II stood in glaring contradiction to practices at home: How could Americans who were fighting the Nazis with their ideology of Aryan supremacy accept the ideology of white supremacy behind Jim Crow? During the Cold War, as the United States competed with the Soviet Union for influence in the Third World, Jim Crow undermined America's legitimacy abroad. Southern racism became an embarrassment for American foreign policy. Earlier in the century, the Northern Protestant elite had been drawn toward eugenics and ideas of white racial superiority, but the Nazis helped discredit those views. By midcentury, the social sciences had also largely rejected the belief that racial differences were biologically based. "Hardly anywhere else or in any other issue is there ... such a wide gap between scientific thought and popular belief," Myrdal had already written in 1944.[15] Although the shifts in social science and elite opinion did not immediately reshape popular opinion, they affected judges, journalists, educators, and others in positions of influence.

These developments created a potential for challenges to white domination, but they did not determine the forms that those challenges would take or whether they would succeed. Some modes of contention would prove more successful and durable than others. Two different prototypes of struggle—civil rights unionism and civil rights litigation—made advances during World War II but fared very differently during the Cold War.

Civil rights unionism emerged from the left wing of the Congress of Industrial Organizations (CIO), the alliance of unions that organized workers in manufacturing. Originally founded in 1935 as a committee within the American Federation of Labor (AFL), the CIO broke away from the federation in 1938 (they would reunite in 1955 to form the AFL-CIO). Racial exclusion was the prevailing practice in unions in the United States, especially the AFL's craft unions. But the CIO's industrial unions faced an imperative to organize Black workers, especially when Black factory employment surged during World War II. The CIO's radical organizers, some of them communists, were also committed to racial equality. Unlike others in the labor movement, they challenged racism in the workplace, enabled Black workers to win union leadership positions, and favored broader reforms, including political enfranchisement and enhanced provision of social benefits such as national health insurance. They worked with the

NAACP to try to open union membership and jobs to Black workers. Legal cases in defense of exploited Black workers during the 1940s held the promise of developing a labor-based civil rights law.[16]

During World War II, Roosevelt's National Labor Relations Board enabled interracial organizing drives to succeed, but the political environment changed drastically after the war. The Taft-Hartley Act, passed by a Republican Congress in 1947, made union organizing more difficult, particularly in the South, by enabling states to pass "right-to-work" laws that allowed workers in a unionized workplace to hold jobs without paying dues for union representation. Cold War anticommunism broke up the broad coalition of progressive forces of the earlier Popular Front against fascism. In 1949, the CIO expelled unions with communist influence, and many progressive organizations, including the NAACP, "cleaned house" by conducting internal investigations and purging both Communists and "fellow travelers" who had taken part in what were deemed to be Communist-front organizations. Civil rights unionism didn't end entirely, but civil rights law took a different path in the 1950s and became disconnected from the labor movement. Rights consciousness and the pursuit of individual compensation for past discrimination would lead in a different direction from union organizing and working-class solidarity. These developments set back civil rights unionism and effectively ended the possibility that labor and civil rights groups might form a shared movement.

Progress on civil rights and racial integration, however, came via other means in Cold War America. During the late 1940s, Blacks gained entry to a variety of institutions that had previously excluded them, including professional sports. No event symbolized that change more than Jackie Robinson taking the field for the Brooklyn Dodgers on April 15, 1947. By the mid-1940s, the Black vote in the big, closely contested industrial states had become too large to ignore. In 1948 both major parties competed for that vote and adopted civil rights planks in their platforms; during the campaign, Truman desegregated the armed forces and the federal government and introduced civil rights legislation. Those civil rights efforts cost him the backing of Southern Dixiecrats, who bolted from the Democrats in favor of the third-party presidential candidacy of South Carolina's Strom Thurmond. But Black support proved decisive in the big industrial states that carried Truman to victory.

The Cold War also did not block progress in the civil rights litigation chiefly undertaken by the NAACP's Legal Defense Fund, led by Thurgood Marshall. Even before the Supreme Court declared segregated schools unconstitutional in *Brown v. Board of Education* in 1954, it was moving in a racially progressive direction. This was not a result of presidential nominations deliberately intended to shift the Court's rulings on racial issues. Although Roosevelt and Truman were concerned about how their appointees would rule on the government's economic powers, neither paid close attention to prospective justices' racial views. Both appointed Southerners whose earlier careers suggested they might be unsympathetic to Black legal claims. Nonetheless, the Court did become more receptive to those claims. During the 1940s, the NAACP won key rulings on voting rights (overturning exclusively white Democratic primaries in the South) and higher education (requiring Southern states first to spend more on Black colleges and professional programs and later to admit Black applicants to historically white, state-financed professional schools). By 1950, four years before *Brown*, the NAACP had a better than 90 percent winning record in the Supreme Court.[17]

The Court's new racial progressivism reflected a major shift in constitutional interpretation that was first signaled inconspicuously in a footnote in a 1938 case, *U.S. v. Carolene Products*, which involved the interstate commerce clause and had nothing to do with race. Just when the Court was deferring to Congress on regulation of the economy, the footnote singled out another area of law that might require judicial intervention. Ordinarily, the Court said, the democratic political process could be relied on to correct a bad law—but not if the law itself curtailed the political process. The Court might therefore need to step in to safeguard the constitutional rights of "discrete and insular" minorities when those minorities had no hope of winning elections. This was the origin of judicial activism on behalf of minority rights. It was no accident that the justices staked out this new role for the courts in the late 1930s. Soon after writing the opinion, Justice Harlan Fiske Stone told a friend, "I have been deeply concerned about the increasing racial and religious intolerance which seems to bedevil the world, and which I greatly fear may be augmented in this country."[18]

The Court's emerging racial progressivism did not, however, determine how it ruled in 1944 on the constitutionality of government internment of Japanese Americans. The internment policy had been adopted without due process and with no evidence of disloyalty, but rather solely based on racial ancestry. The majority opinion upholding the internment declared "that all legal restrictions which curtail the civil rights of a single racial group are immediately suspect" but added that a restriction might still be constitutional if it could survive the "most rigid scrutiny" by the courts.

"Pressing public necessity may sometimes justify the existence of such restrictions; racial antagonism never can." That is just what the majority found: Wartime necessity justified the internment of Japanese Americans, even though German and Italian Americans were not being similarly treated. But in the course of that shameful decision, the Court introduced into constitutional law a new interpretative rule: Any use of a criterion such as race that the Court deemed a "suspect classification" would require "rigid" or "strict" scrutiny and would have to be justified by a "compelling" public necessity.[19]

These "political process" and "strict scrutiny" rationales for judicial intervention on behalf of minority rights would become enormously important for Blacks and other groups. But whether—or under what conditions—U.S. courts on their own can produce significant social change is not a simple question.

One view emphasizes the constraints on judicial power. Judges have no control, in Alexander Hamilton's words, over "either sword or purse"; they cannot ensure their decisions are carried out by directly enforcing them or offering economic incentives for compliance. When the other branches of government resist or ignore their rulings, the courts may be at an impasse. They are also constrained in other ways. The executive and legislature can change the judiciary with new appointments, limit the courts' jurisdiction, or simply override them in matters of statutory interpretation by passing new laws. Because constitutional amendments are rare and difficult in the U.S. system, the courts do have more power in constitutional law. But even when the courts accept claims of a constitutional right, the other branches may do nothing to turn that formal right into a social reality.[20]

In contrast to this view of a constrained court, a more dynamic interpretation of the judiciary insists that it has a capacity to bring about social change that the other branches lack. The courts may be free to ignore electoral considerations and powerful interest groups, and even if the other branches do not immediately enforce their rulings, those rulings may have a catalytic effect, indirectly promoting social change through their impact on social norms and public opinion.[21]

The NAACP's litigation strategy was a bet on the dynamic interpretation of judicial powers. But as the Supreme Court moved to embrace racial progressivism in the 1940s and 1950s, it largely acted on its own, without support from either Congress or the presidency. Even as the NAACP won landmark cases, the practical effects on the lives of Black

Americans were limited. Although litigation might remove one obstacle to equality, others remained, and white-dominated institutions at the state and local level could create new ones. For example, the Supreme Court first struck down the whites-only primary in 1927, but Southern states preserved white primaries by revising their laws in ways the Court upheld in 1935. In 1944, the Court reversed its position and overturned white primaries a second time—which left one further Southern dodge that the Court struck down in 1953.[22] And even after the Court finally blocked racially exclusive Democratic primaries, the white South limited Blacks' voting rights through literacy tests, poll taxes, and other means of voter suppression, including outright violence. The NAACP's strategy of relying on the Supreme Court required supreme patience.

Nothing better illustrates both the triumph and limits of the NAACP's litigation strategy than the *Brown* decision and its aftermath. On May 17, 1954, the Court unanimously declared that "in the field of public education the doctrine of 'separate but equal' has no place. Separate educational facilities are inherently unequal." Soon the Court also barred segregation in both interstate and intrastate commerce and in public facilities from parks to courtrooms. At the time of the *Brown* ruling, which set no deadline for the end of segregated schools, seventeen Southern and border states, along with the District of Columbia, had laws segregating schools, while four other states allowed local segregation. A year after *Brown*, the Court issued a ruling about implementation that left compliance to lower courts and local officials, calling on them to proceed with "all deliberate speed." Rather than comply with the ruling, however, Southern legislatures enacted nearly 500 laws to impede it. "If one remedial law is ruled invalid," declared one Southern newspaper, "then let us try another; and if the second is ruled invalid, then let us enact a third." A decade after the Court's decision, school integration had made some progress in the border states (where it had been advancing even before *Brown*), but virtually none in the South. In the 1964–1965 school year, fewer than 3 percent of Black schoolchildren in Southern states attended formerly all-white schools.[23]

Civil rights unionism and civil rights litigation, the two main repertoires of contention that emerged from the New Deal era, had both opened paths toward racial equality. The first, coming out of the left wing of the labor movement, was a road not taken, or more accurately, a road whose full potential was blocked by Cold War anticommunism and anti-union legislation. Although the NAACP's court-oriented strategy made more headway, it seemed incapable of overturning segregation and guaranteeing Black Americans equal rights. There needed to be a different prototype for struggle, a new repertoire of contention.

The New Model Movement

A new repertoire of contention emerged during the mid-1950s that became the model for popular struggles for rights. While the NAACP relied mainly on sending lawyers to court, the new movement called for direct action by masses of Black people and allied whites: economic boycotts, marches, sit-ins, walk outs, freedom rides, and other forms of nonviolent protest.

The direct-action civil rights movement departed from the NAACP in how it mobilized power. In contrast to the NAACP's adherence to law, the new movement entailed civil disobedience, disruption of institutions, and a willingness to go to jail. The NAACP was a secular, professionalized organization based in New York that required its local branches to get clearance from headquarters for any actions they took, whereas the direct-action movement was based in the Black church in the South and relied, as the sociologist Aldon Morris writes, "on charisma, mass emotionalism, and mass enthusiasm."[24] Yet the movement's leaders kept that emotionalism in check by instilling discipline, self-restraint, and a commitment to nonviolence. Organizers were trained in the techniques of nonviolent action, and they admonished protesters not to retaliate against official or mob violence.

The civil rights movement also departed from the NAACP in making strategic use of the national media. It sought to expose Southern racism to public shame, and instead of avoiding the most rabid, violent white Southerners, it initiated public confrontations with them. The movement's most effective moments came when white sheriffs and mobs lived up to expectations and attacked peaceful Black demonstrators, and those attacks were witnessed by national reporters, caught on camera by national television, and shown around the world to the distress of the White House, State Department, and other officials who were concerned about America's image in the Cold War.

But while departing in its methods, the direct-action movement shared the NAACP's goals. Both aimed to end Jim Crow, enfranchise Black voters, and expand equal educational and economic opportunities for Black people. Although it began partly with spontaneous local acts, the direct-action movement also developed national leaders who planned and coordinated campaigns, and who often worked closely with the NAACP's lawyers to defend protesters and consolidate victories in court.

The civil rights movement consequently combined a new repertoire of direct action with the older courtroom repertoire. Repertoires of contention, in Tilly's analysis, are "learned cultural creations" that "emerge from struggle," not from any abstract theory. In an essay about contentious repertoires in Britain from 1758 to 1834, Tilly notes that "people learn to break windows in protest, attack pilloried prisoners, tear down dishonored houses, stage public marches, petition, hold formal meetings, organize special-interest associations." Contentious repertoires also encompass the responses of antagonists, including the authorities; they are "the established ways" in which protesters and their opponents confront each other over claims relevant to their interests.[25] In establishing those forms of struggle, the participants do not simply choose from a historically given set of routines. As the example of the civil rights movement shows, they also adapt or add to the repertoire, and success is so unpredictable that innovations often come from unexpected sources.

Mass action in the Black community was not entirely new. From 1929 to 1941, there had been "Don't buy where you can't work" campaigns, aimed at businesses that refused to employ Black workers despite the patronage of Black customers. In 1953 in Baton Rouge, Louisiana, a brief boycott of the local, segregated bus service secured some concessions. But it was a boycott of buses in Montgomery beginning in December 1955 that signaled a new political moment in America.

The Montgomery bus boycott showed a capacity for sustained collective action in an urban Black community that no one, not even its own leaders, could have counted on in advance. What began as a one-day boycott—famously triggered by the arrest of the 42-year-old Rosa Parks for refusing to vacate her seat for a white passenger—ended up lasting more than a year. Some 17,500 Black riders in Montgomery had been taking buses every working day and might have quickly returned to them because they needed to get to and from their jobs. But segregation on buses touched a nerve. A bus was a small theater where, in the words of an earlier Black protester, "the public humiliation of black people [was] carried out in the presence of privileged white spectators, who witnessed our shame in silence or indifference."[26] Perhaps because of that daily indignity, the boycott drew an immediate and sustained response. On the evening of its first day, an astonishing 5,000 Black people showed up at a meeting held at Montgomery's Holt Street Baptist Church to discuss what to do next. After some hesitation, the young pastor at a smaller church, the 26-year-old Martin Luther King Jr., had agreed to head a new community organization to lead the boycott. Though the original aims were only to institute more acceptable seating arrangements and stop abusive treatment by bus drivers, the city's intransigent leadership refused to make concessions, and the boycott's goal became eliminating segregation entirely.[27]

Both the organizational infrastructure of the Black church and the charismatic leadership of King and other Black ministers proved crucial. The new church-based group that King headed, the Montgomery Improvement Association, organized a carpool with dispatchers and drivers to enable Black workers to get to their jobs. The Black community in Montgomery at the time had no elected political representatives, no radio or TV station, and no daily newspaper, so the churches and their frequent mass meetings were essential in providing an alternative communications network. Shared practices of worship and song—the civil rights movement was a singing movement—also helped bind people together. And in King himself, the movement found a leader who was able to inspire trust, solidarity, and perseverance. "Blacks," Morris writes, "would come from near and far to get a glimpse of King and to hear him speak," drawing crowds from "the poolrooms, city streets, and backwoods long enough for trained organizers to acquaint them with the workshops, demands, and strategies of the movement."[28] Despite its original modest goals, the boycott ultimately won a bigger victory than it had initially sought when in December 1956 the Supreme Court declared bus segregation in the city unconstitutional.

Yet King and the other leaders who formed the SCLC in January 1957 had trouble following up the electrifying victory in Montgomery with further gains through direct action. The primary initiative for the sit-ins and freedom rides that represented the next phase of the struggle came from other quarters, primarily college students. On February 1, 1960, four young Black men, all students at the North Carolina Agricultural and Technical College, sat in at a whites-only lunch counter at an F. W. Woolworth store in Greensboro, North Carolina. The sit-in grew larger in the following days, and the protests soon spread to other lunch counters in Greensboro, to other cities in North Carolina, and then throughout the South. Although national civil rights organizations lent their support, college students initiated and drove the movement, a signal of the generational turn that would become a characteristic feature of protests in the 1960s. A new organization, the Student Nonviolent Coordinating Committee (SNCC), arose from the sit-ins. The repertoire of contention expanded further with similar protests, such as "wade-ins" at segregated pools and beaches and "pray-ins" at segregated churches.[29]

The freedom rides were initially a project of a relatively minor civil rights organization, the Congress of Racial Equality (CORE), founded in Chicago in 1942 by an interracial group of Christian pacifists. In 1947, after the Supreme Court ruled segregation in interstate transportation unconstitutional, CORE sent two small interracial groups on buses into Virginia and North Carolina. Several of the riders were arrested and sentenced to prison terms, but little came of the protest. In the spring of 1961, however, CORE gained more of a public profile when it organized what it now called a "Freedom Ride" to test desegregation in buses and bus stations. Leaving from Washington, D.C., two interracial groups planned to ride all the way to New Orleans but were beaten so savagely by a mob in Anniston, Alabama, that they stopped. Volunteers from the Nashville student movement, however, stepped in to continue the ride, only to be attacked again in Montgomery, where they took shelter for a night in a Black church surrounded by a white mob. With national attention now focused on the protest and new volunteers on board, the Freedom Riders continued on to Mississippi, where 400 of them were arrested. Like the 1956 bus boycott in Montgomery, the Freedom Rides led to a federally codified victory: Attorney General Robert F. Kennedy asked the Interstate Commerce Commission to issue regulations on the desegregation of interstate transportation.[30]

The culmination of the direct-action movement came in two historic confrontations in die-hard Alabama: campaigns for desegregation of downtown businesses in Birmingham in 1963 and for voting rights in Selma in 1965. Civil rights organizations planned and trained for these confrontations like a military campaign. They chose the two cities because they symbolized racist intransigence and had police authorities who were unrestrained in their brutality. The demonstrations in Birmingham started off slowly, but after King was arrested and jailed, his aides recruited high school students by the hundreds, and the police under Bull Connor met waves of teenagers and other marchers with snarling police dogs and high-powered firehoses, to the disgust of television audiences nationwide. The eventual settlement with Birmingham's businesses netted modest gains, but the protests had national impact. It was only after Birmingham that President Kennedy decided to propose comprehensive civil rights legislation; it passed after Kennedy's death and was signed into law by Lyndon Johnson in 1964. The scenario in Selma in 1965 was similar to Birmingham: marches and arrests of demonstrators (more than 2,600 were jailed) and overt police violence that produced national outrage and helped generate both a shift in public opinion and the passage of federal legislation, the Voting Rights Act.[31]

The success of the direct-action confrontations depended critically on the roles played by two national institutions, the mass media and the courts. The media not only enabled the movement to reach the national public; they also served a protective function. During the protests, Black churches were bombed, some civil rights workers were murdered, and many were beaten and severely injured—but the history of white terrorism suggests it could have been far worse. As King wrote in a letter in October 1961 after the Freedom Rides: "Without the presence of the press, there might have been untold massacre in the South."[32] Protest was dangerous, but the press made it less so.

And the press in turn was protected by the courts. In *New York Times v. Sullivan*, a 1964 case with wide ramifications, the Supreme Court struck down the decision of an Alabama court in which the jury had awarded $3 million to Alabama officials who claimed they were libeled in an advertisement in the *Times* by the Committee to Defend Martin Luther King and the Struggle for Freedom in the South. Without naming any individuals, the ad had accused "Southern violators of the Constitution" of responding to "Dr. King's peaceful protests with intimidation and violence," but the ad's drafters had made several minor misstatements of fact that the *Times* failed to correct. By the time the Supreme Court handed down its decision, other Southern officials had sued national media for a total of $300 million in damages, an amount large enough, if upheld, to have deterred the press from continuing to provide critical coverage of the South's racist practices and its efforts to suppress the movement. But the Court held unanimously for the *Times*, requiring public officials in libel cases to prove the press guilty of knowing falsity or reckless disregard of the truth. The national coverage continued.[33]

Surveys asking Americans about the most important issue facing the nation registered the change in the public agenda that the movement, the media, and the courts jointly brought about. In mid-1963, the share of Americans picking civil rights as the most important national issue reached 48 percent, up from 5 percent the previous year. During 1964–1965, civil rights was rated more important than the economy, foreign affairs, or any other issue.[34] That was the climate of opinion when Congress passed the

Civil Rights Act of 1964 and the Voting Rights Act of 1965, the two most important pieces of civil rights legislation since Reconstruction.

The federal attack on Jim Crow was fortified in 1965 by the passage of key elements of Johnson's Great Society, including Medicare and the Elementary and Secondary Education Act, both of which enabled federal agencies to impose substantial financial penalties on Southern institutions that failed to desegregate. Federal measures combating employment discrimination also combined legal and financial pressure. The Civil Rights Act's Title VII made it unlawful to discriminate in employment on the grounds of "race, color, religion, sex, or national origin" and created the Equal Employment Opportunity Commission (EEOC) to hear complaints. (Congress subsequently authorized it to initiate litigation but never gave it its own enforcement powers.) An executive order in 1965 created a second agency, the Office of Federal Contract Compliance, which had authority to impose fines on federal contractors if they failed to comply with civil rights laws. Title VII expressly prohibited the government from imposing racial quotas in employment, though the Nixon administration later finessed that provision when it required federal contractors to adopt affirmative action plans.[35]

As civil rights leaders always emphasized, their struggle had two aims that in practice were inseparable—jobs and justice. Title VII was crucial to breaking out of a world where white men had exclusive access to the work that commanded respect and made an independent life possible. As a Black woman who got her job at a North Carolina textile company thanks to the civil rights movement put it, "The best thing that has ever happened to black women in the South in my lifetime is a chance to be full-fledged citizens. And that comes from their work. You can't even pretend to be free without money."[36]

The gains in equal economic opportunity depended critically on privately initiated litigation. Even though the Civil Rights Act withheld enforcement powers from the EEOC, it created a private right to sue in federal court that, in combination with new procedural rules allowing class-action suits, led to an outpouring of claims of racial discrimination against both employers and unions. Private attorneys as well as civil rights organizations entered the field, often representing thousands of workers in class actions. By awarding back pay, punitive damages, and attorneys' fees, the courts imposed penalties that were large enough to force unions and companies to adopt strict timetables for hiring minorities and women. Contrary to the idea that the judiciary is constrained because it has neither sword nor purse, the courts assumed formidable powers of financial coercion under Title VII to achieve important breakthroughs.[37]

The Black movement's struggle for economic opportunity also benefited from Great Society policies that generally promoted full employment and higher living standards for low-wage workers. In a series of measures, Congress expanded both the coverage and the value of the minimum wage, raising it to $1.60 in 1968 (its highest level ever in purchasing power, equal to about $14.47 in 2024 dollars), which was enough for a full-time worker to support a family of three just above the poverty threshold. The establishment of Medicare and increases in Social Security helped reduce poverty among seniors and people with disabilities. Medicaid enabled many low-income pregnant women and children to obtain regular medical care for the first time and brought both immediate benefits in health and a long-term payoff in higher earnings, lower rates of disability, and greater longevity. Ronald Reagan would later say, "We had a war on poverty, and poverty won," but from 1960 to 1972, the poverty rate dropped from 23 percent to 11 percent. Infant mortality fell by 30 percent, and life expectancy at birth rose by two years. School attendance for both Black and low-income white children increased. Unemployment and poverty continued to run much higher in Black than in white America; some of the programs under the war on poverty failed, and others were too small and short-lived to have much impact. But unlike the Progressive Era and New Deal, when many reforms had effectively excluded Black people, the big policy changes in the 1960s improved life for low-income Americans of all races, Black Americans included.[38]

After the 1960s, the myth would develop that the civil rights movement had failed to produce any economic benefit for Blacks, but the evidence shows otherwise. The movement produced the most substantial improvements in the region where its efforts were targeted—the South. New legislation and backing from both the executive and judicial branches made possible the kind of coordinated attack on Jim Crow that the Supreme Court on its own had been unable to carry out. After being dead in the water for a decade, school integration in the South began to move forward. The proportion of Black children in schools with whites in the South increased from 2.3 percent in 1964–1965 to 91.3 percent in 1972–1973 (a major shift, though this statistic fails to distinguish between schools with many white children or only a few).[39] Other areas of Southern life also saw important changes. Previously, waiting rooms and treatment facilities in Southern hospitals had been segregated, and physicians typically saw white patients before seeing any Black patients. But with the new financial leverage over Southern hospitals that Medicare provided, federal officials succeeded in both desegregating health-care facilities and improving Black people's access to care.[40]

The impact on Black employment in the South was also substantial. Previously, Black Southerners had limited job options and faced a severe wage penalty relative to their white counterparts. Before the civil rights revolution, the economic gains made by Black Americans resulted from their leaving the South. The decade from 1964 to 1974 saw strong gains in both absolute and relative earnings for Black workers nationally; but unlike the earlier period, two-thirds of those gains came for Blacks *remaining* in the South. The most plausible explanation for this change lies in the Civil Rights Act and the Southern focus of federal enforcement of the law's provisions. Federal intervention in the Southern economy seems to have given some firms in the textile industry an excuse to do something that was in their own interest: abandon Jim Crow practices and tap into an underused pool of Black workers, which kept down their labor costs and for a time helped them remain competitive against mills overseas. Still, despite their economic self-interest, most Southern employers resisted integration and had to be forced through litigation and protests to comply with the law. But as they did, Southern Black workers' prospects for better jobs and higher incomes improved. One result was that Black migration out of the South slowed and, by the mid-1970s, even reversed.[41]

Political change probably also contributed to the new reverse migration. The Voting Rights Act accomplished what no previous law or court decision had done in breaking down barriers to Black voting in the South, chiefly by abolishing literacy tests and authorizing federal examiners to register voters in specially covered jurisdictions (six Southern states and forty counties of North Carolina). During the 1960s, the registration rate of Black voters rose from 29 percent to 60 percent of the voting-age Southern Black population. White resistance to Black voting had been fiercest in the areas where Blacks formed a majority of the population. In the covered jurisdictions before 1965, not one of the eighty-nine counties with a majority-Black population had a majority-Black electorate. By 1968, 40 percent of those counties did. Despite continuing white resistance, Blacks were able to elect local officials and representatives to state legislatures and Congress in numbers not seen in the South since Reconstruction. They were still underrepresented and needed federal enforcement to deal with the white establishment's schemes to limit their power, but they were no longer locked out.[42]

These and other changes gave the civil rights movement new political opportunities. Energies that formerly went into mass action now went directly into electoral politics and implementation of policy. Some activists ran for office and instead of asking supporters to march, asked them to turn out to vote. To say that the civil rights movement ended in 1965 is misleading; especially in the South, litigation and direct action aimed at enforcing the law at the local level continued into the 1970s. But far from being an unqualified triumph, the late 1960s and early 1970s revealed the movement's limits and saw much of the Black community turn to new prototypes of struggle, summed up in the term "Black Power."

Black Power as a Political and Cultural Prototype

The emergence of Black Power as a redefinition of the Black freedom struggle after 1965 had an underlying logic. During the 1960s Black people were arriving in a variety of social contexts where they confronted whites in authority. The number of Black students soared on university campuses, but except at historically Black institutions, the faculty and top administrators were nearly all white. Black workers arrived in growing numbers in many industries, but their bosses were also nearly all white. Black athletes had risen throughout professional sports—by 1968 they comprised a quarter of professional baseball players, a third of football players, and more than half of basketball players—but their managers and head coaches were white with only one exception, Bill Russell of the Boston Celtics.[43] Blacks were moving inside the American circle but rarely to the points of control.

Three historical developments—the Great Migration, the postwar baby boom, and white flight to the suburbs—created an especially combustible situation in American cities. As Blacks arrived in the cities of the North and West, much of the white middle and working class moved out to the suburbs, depleting the tax base. But whites still held most of the positions of power in city governments, businesses, housing, schools, social welfare agencies, and perhaps most important, the police. Conflicts especially increased between white-controlled instrumentalities of power and the Black baby-boom generation, now teenagers and young adults. In all these situations, the issue was no longer limited to civil rights. The fundamental source of conflict was unequal power.

What Black Power was and wasn't, however, is not easy to pin down. It had different expressions that varied in ideology and form. As a political idea, Black Power was framed in both pluralist and nationalist terms. In city politics, the pluralist demand was for a share of power along with other groups; in this respect, Blacks were only knocking on the doors of power the way the Irish, Italians, Jews, and others had done before. The nationalist versions of Black Power insisted on more: self-determination, separatism, armed self-defense, revolutionary transformation. Those demands reflected a deep pessimism about achieving equality within institutions that the nationalists considered unalterably racist. Both pluralists and nationalists shared a commitment to a thoroughgoing cultural change: deepening the Black community's understanding of its history and culture and promoting greater pride and a sense of self-worth. This cultural and social psychological dimension was integral to Black Power in all its incarnations.

These political and cultural expressions coincided, however, with another development that stemmed from increased friction with whites in positions of power: the outbreak of ghetto riots, often sparked by clashes with the police in big cities during the "long hot summers" of the mid-1960s, and in smaller cities and towns during the following years. The riots took the media spotlight away from nonviolent civil rights protest and lent themselves to a framing of the nation's most urgent problem as "law and order." By 1967, public opinion surveys found "social control" rising above "civil rights" as the public's choice for the nation's most important problem.[44]

If the rise of Black Power was a source of fear among the many whites who associated it with riots and revolutionaries, it was a source of inspiration to young Black people who saw in the militancy of leaders like Stokely Carmichael and Malcolm X a manly assertion of dignity in the face of continuing racism and oppression. Perhaps more surprisingly, Black Power also inspired other racial minorities, feminists, gay people, and people with disabilities, who were struggling with their own issues of identity and self-worth and in search not just of rights but of political empowerment and cultural change.

The advocates of Black Power often contrasted their outlook with that of the civil rights movement. The phrase "Black Power" entered the American political language in 1966, its arrival usually dated to June 16 that year, when Carmichael, then a leader of SNCC, told a meeting of civil rights workers in Mississippi: "The only way we gonna stop them white men from whoppin' us is to take over. We been saying freedom for six years and we ain't got nothin'. What we gonna start saying now is Black Power!"[45]

The slogan caught on in part because the strategies of the civil rights movement seemed ineffective when the movement moved north. What the movement had achieved economically, it had achieved primarily for Southern Blacks; it was not able to bring about immediate material improvement in the Northern Black ghettoes. An "End the Slums" campaign led by King in Chicago in 1966 was a notable failure. Using a language of constitutional rights and universal brotherhood, the civil rights movement had sought full citizenship and inclusion for Blacks in American society, but now the very goal of integration came into question. Critics equated integration with assimilation in the old sense of Anglo-conformity as if integration into American society required the abandonment of Black culture, when other groups had found space for their own traditions.[46] Defiantly rejecting any shared ground, Black Power emphasized the particularities of Black American experience and its connections to Africa and the developing world (in today's academic language, the "Global South"). The shift in usage from "Negro" to "Black" and rising interest in Black history and Black literature, including demands for Black Studies in universities, were all indicative of the turn in Black political culture that the term "Black Power" symbolized.

Every movement has a theory of change. Black Power proposed that political empowerment would come through changes in Black consciousness, especially racial solidarity and pride. For example, Carmichael's 1967 book *Black Power: The Politics of Liberation*, co-written with the political scientist Charles Hamilton, defined Black Power as "a call for black people in this country to unite, to recognize their heritage, to build a sense of community" in the interest of creating "power bases" and changing "patterns of oppression." Carmichael and Hamilton did not rule out coalitions, but Black solidarity came first.[47] Since the late 1950s, Malcolm X had emerged as a leader of the Nation of Islam (popularly known as the Black Muslims), though his ideas evolved, particularly during the last year of his life after he broke from the Nation in March 1964. But he consistently celebrated Blackness, rejected appeals to white benevolence, and called for a bold, unapologetic assertion of Black interests "by any means necessary." More than anyone else, Malcolm X became the symbol of Black Power even though the phrase came into use only after he was assassinated, in February 1965.[48]

The civil rights and Black Power movements captured media attention in different ways. King and other civil rights leaders aimed to reach a public that crossed racial lines, using a preacherly language steeped in the Bible and the American Creed that exposed the ugliness and violence of racism. In contrast, Black Power advocates seized attention with words that they hoped would awaken Black America even as—and partly because—they scandalized white America. Explaining his use of violent language, Carmichael in 1970 said: "The first stage is waking up our people. We have to wake them up to the impending danger. So we yell, Gun! Shoot! Burn! Kill! Destroy! They're committing genocide! until the masses of our people are awake."[49] Bobby Seale, one of the founders of the Black Panthers, once explained that hostile press coverage could help their recruitment: "The brothers on the block gon say, 'Who is these THUGS and HOODLUMS? . . . I'm going to check out what these brothers is doing.'"[50]

Hostile media attention sometimes does redound to the advantage of the target. Malcolm X became nationally known through a constant stream of hostile coverage, beginning with a 1959 TV documentary, *The Hate That Hate Produced*, which introduced him to the public as a "Black supremacist." Instead of being banished, he became a regular on TV talk shows and a top speaking attraction at universities and other venues. As the representative of the Nation of Islam, he called for the separation of the races, opposed racial intermarriage, and denounced civil rights leaders as Uncle Toms and their nonviolent methods as demeaning and unmanly. He stepped over boundaries no one else would dare transgress. After a plane crash killed 121 whites from Atlanta in 1962, he told a large audience the crash was "a very beautiful thing." The following year, he cheered John F. Kennedy's assassination as "the chickens coming home to roost." At a Harlem rally in July 1964, he said, "You have to walk in with a hand grenade and tell the man, 'Listen, you give us what we've got coming or nobody is going to get anything.' Then he might listen to you." (The first of the big-city riots began in Harlem later that month while he was out of town.) The media cast Malcolm X as a demon and a demagogue but didn't ignore him, perhaps because he confirmed whites' worst fears. Shortly before he was assassinated, he told an interviewer that his media image "was created by them and by me. . . . They were looking for sensationalism, for something that would sell papers, and I gave it to them."[51]

The ghetto riots reached a peak with 137 outbreaks between the summer of 1967 and the assassination of King in April 1968, but they weren't over. From May 1968 through 1972, according to the historian Elizabeth Hinton, the "rebellions," as she calls them, continued with some 1,949 uprisings in Black communities. Hinton estimates 40,000 people were arrested, 10,000 injured, and 220 killed in that time. As she explains, they typically began with teenagers throwing rocks in response to police surveillance, arrests, or other interventions by white authorities.[52] Throwing rocks at the police was direct action of a kind—a distinct repertoire of contention—but it differed from the methods of the civil rights movement, which had brought the Black struggle into the streets under charismatic leadership that simultaneously aroused and restrained mass emotionalism and made deliberate choices about where to confront white authority and what to seek from it. While the urban rebellions also brought Black youth into the streets, they did so without focus or discipline. According to later follow-up studies, the outbreaks brought long-term economic damage to the communities where they erupted.[53] While nonviolent protests gained Blacks public support, violent protests diminished it.[54] They also failed to sustain support within the Black community for the radical visions of Black Power in the face of suppression by the police, FBI, and other agencies. Within a few years, nationalist and revolutionary organizations like the Black Panthers were dead. Meanwhile, together with continuing litigation and pressure for compliance with the civil rights laws, the pluralist forms of Black Power survived and expanded as elected Black officials grew in number and formed new organizations like the Congressional Black Caucus and the National Conference of Black Mayors.

Black Power's most durable effect was on Black culture and consciousness. "The Black Power movement was not exclusively cultural, but it was essentially cultural," the historian William L. Van Deburg writes.[55] It fostered connections with Africa and the study of Black history; it celebrated Black food, dress, and hairstyles and contested white norms of beauty and speech, fighting old tendencies to downplay or escape Black identity. It resisted measuring Black literature, art, or music by the approval of white critics or producing it with white audiences in mind. That is not to say this wasn't also an era of Black crossovers. The work of Black musicians, writers, and artists infused all of American culture. But the struggle now was for crossovers that refused to conform to old stereotypes.

Just as demographic change and war had earlier given Blacks new political opportunities, so broader changes in American society gave Blacks increasing cultural opportunities. The extreme centralization in broadcast media of the 1950s and early 1960s began eroding with the advent of a new multichannel environment with the development of FM stations and later cable TV. In both cases, increased competition and new channels with specialized audiences created opportunities for Black performers and other artists. The only options for their work had once been more limited Black venues and institutions, rich in creative ferment but mostly cut off from the patronage and revenue streams that white institutions enjoyed. Now they had opportunities not only to be more fully represented in the mainstream culture but to do more work and earn a living on their own terms. Black cultural power grew faster than Black political or economic power. The success of Black musicians and other performers in the movies, television, and other spheres inspired creative talent in other historically marginalized groups, who now also had more opportunity to break into a diversifying culture.

The four major prototypes of the Black freedom struggle—civil rights unionism, civil rights litigation, civil rights nonviolent direct action, and Black Power—were often in tension with one another, but they formed a logical succession. The blockage of civil rights unionism had left the NAACP's litigation strategy as the primary model of struggle after World War II. The limits of litigation then gave rise to the direct-action civil rights movement, and the limits of direct action gave rise to Black Power. But they were not mutually exclusive: all four could, and in different contexts did, advance Black interests and serve as prototypes for other movements. Black Power might seem to be the least adaptable to other groups, since it turned away from universal ideals to an emphasis on Black identity and collective consciousness. But in doing so it served as a model of collective assertion for other groups. As a model minority, Black Americans created the prototypes of struggle for an entire family of minorities, as that term "minority" came to be understood.

The New Family of Minorities

As a political concept, the term "minorities" had its origins in an Atlantic crossing after World War I. When maps were redrawn in Europe as part of the postwar settlement, "minorities" referred primarily to the nationals of one country who ended up on the wrong side of a border, such as Germans in Czechoslovakia. Public discussion of the fate of national minorities in the peace settlement helped give the term currency among Americans. In the United States, "minorities" became understood as groups, whether religious or racial, who were considered less than 100 percent American.[56] White Protestants were the majority, and "minorities" included Catholics, Jews, and Blacks as well as Mexicans in the Southwest and Chinese and Japanese on the Pacific Coast. In the interwar years, they were subject to both informal bias and institutionalized forms of overt social exclusion, variously justified by theories of racial inferiority and accusations that their true loyalty was to foreign powers—the Pope in the case of Catholics;

secret conspiracies of international bankers and communists in the case of Jews; and during World War II, the Japanese Empire in the case of Japanese Americans.

The new family of minorities that emerged during the mid-twentieth century resulted from two different processes. The first was the consolidation of white identity. The promotion of interfaith tolerance and unity during World War II, postwar prosperity, and the long cut-off of new immigrants from the 1920s to 1965 all weakened felt distinctions among whites and eased the assimilation of white Catholics and Jews into the white majority. Anti-Semitism did not disappear, but it ceased to be respectable in the wake of the fight against the Nazis and increasing knowledge about the Holocaust.

But while the consolidation of whiteness tended to reduce the family of minorities, other political and demographic changes enlarged it. Non-European immigrants began coming to the United States, partly as an unintended result of the 1965 Immigration and Nationality Act. Discussions about minorities now also included women, who obviously were not an arithmetic minority. The gay rights and disability rights movements would later further enlarge the family of publicly recognized minorities.

The key criterion in determining who counted as minority became whether they were discriminated against and consequently underrepresented in higher education, employment, government, and other contexts. Were they in an analogous position to the group that was now the prototypical minority—Blacks? The Black freedom struggle had both an indirect and a direct influence on the public definition of minorities. The indirect effect came via the Civil Rights Act and other civil rights measures whose adoption the Black movement stimulated. The direct effect came from the example of the Black freedom struggle and, curiously, from people who left it, particularly women and gay people whose troubled experiences in the civil rights movement led them to organize new movements for their own liberation.

The role of civil rights law in the minority rights revolution was central. In standard accounts of the history of rights, mobilized social movements and shifts in public opinion bring about the expansion of legal rights, an explanation that applies well to the adoption of civil rights protections for Blacks. Equal rights for Black people were nearly the entire focus of the protests leading up to the passage of civil rights legislation. From 1940 to 1972, the *New York Times* reported on almost 3,800 civil rights demonstrations, more than 95 percent of which concerned bias against Blacks.[57]

But what the legislation achieved for Blacks, it did not achieve for them alone. The civil rights laws generally prohibited discrimination based on race, color, national origin, religion, and sex. In the case of Blacks, the movement preceded the law, but the sequence was different for other minorities. The law helped generate other equal rights movements or propelled them into a more active phase. Minority status had earlier implied being less than fully American, and some Americans continued to think of minorities that way. But now minority status became the basis for making legal claims about discrimination and the right to redress.[58] Recognized group disadvantage became, at least for some legal purposes, an advantage—or to put it differently, not to be recognized as being subject to discrimination when discrimination existed became a disadvantage.

The Black civil rights and Black Power movements during the 1960s directly inspired other movements, even among whites. Most studies of the era's social movements focus on one or another of those movements, almost as though they were independent occurrences. But as several sociologists have argued, social movements tend to come in "families" or "cycles of protest," and studies of individual movements often understate their interconnected development.[59] Without recognizing the role of the Black freedom struggle as an initiator, there is no accounting for the 1960s family of movements.[60] The daring of Black people encouraged others to be daring too and to formulate their grievances in analogous terms.

The Black freedom struggle's sit-ins, marches, and boycotts, even their songs, had echoes on college campuses. The student uprisings began in the fall of 1964 with the "free speech" movement at the University of California, Berkeley, where nearly 800 students were arrested in a sit-in protesting university restrictions on where political literature could be distributed and what outside speakers could come to campus. The core of the sit-in leadership had spent the previous summer in the South. "Last summer, I went to Mississippi to join the struggle there for civil rights," Mario Savio, the students' spokesman, told a crowd. "This fall I am engaged in another phase of the same struggle, this time in Berkeley." The two "battlefields," he insisted, were basically alike, a somewhat inflated idea of the dangers in Berkeley. "The same rights are at stake in both places—the right to participate as citizens in democratic society and the right to due process of law."[61]

The Berkeley leaders were representative of many white radicals of the 1960s whose political education came through the civil rights movement. Savio had joined a program called Freedom Summer, organized mainly by

SNCC, which brought nearly 1,000 college students to Mississippi along with lawyers, physicians, and clergy to conduct voter registration drives and "freedom schools." SNCC's organizing in Mississippi had previously met violent white resistance but received relatively little national attention or support. The organizers believed the national media might give their cause the attention it needed if white students were willing to put their lives on the line too. And just as Freedom Summer began, the nation's attention was riveted when three volunteers, two of them white, disappeared in Philadelphia, Mississippi, and were later found murdered. That was not the end of the toll: One other volunteer would be killed that summer, 4 critically wounded, 80 beaten, and 1,000 arrested, as well as 37 churches bombed or burned and 30 Black homes or businesses burned.[62]

Like the sit-ins and freedom rides, Freedom Summer helped shift the national agenda in 1964. Part of the long-run impact came from the program's returning white student veterans. As the sociologist Doug McAdam found in a follow-up study, they served as a "political and cultural bridge" between the Southern Black struggle and the campuses of the North and West, one of several ways in which the Black struggle diffused into the student, antiwar, and women's movements.[63] The diffusion increased during the mid-1960s when the leaders of SNCC and CORE adopted separatist policies and told white staffers and volunteers to go do their own thing.

Perhaps the most important transfer—and transformation—of ideas came through the Black freedom struggle's influence on the women's movement. Some of the first stirrings of women's liberation came from within SNCC. Two SNCC staff members, Mary King and Casey Hayden, circulated an unsigned position paper on "Women in the Movement" at a staff retreat in November 1964. The paper drew an analogy between white supremacy in the South and masculine domination in SNCC, arguing that women did most of the day-to-day work running the organization but had no "say-so" in it. Mary King later recalled her anxiety and fear of ridicule as she wrote it: "My heart was palpitating and I was shaking as I typed it." She had reason to worry. What attendees at the retreat later mostly remembered was Stokely Carmichael's rebuttal, which the men found hilarious: "The only position for women in SNCC is prone." Ignored within SNCC, King and Hayden distributed a paper on women as a subordinate "caste" to other women in the "peace and freedom" movement, one of the key spurs to the revival of feminism in the 1960s.[64]

The key figure linking racial and gender discrimination in the law was the Black attorney Pauli Murray. Ever since her years as a law student at

Howard in the early 1940s, she had written about using the Reconstruction amendments to overthrow both Jim Crow and what she called "Jane Crow." Race was her early focus. Thurgood Marshall called her 1951 book, *States' Laws on Race and Color*, the "bible" of civil rights litigators, and Murray's arguments influenced Marshall's decision to make a frontal assault on racial segregation in *Brown v. Board of Education*. The same legal theories, Murray believed, also applied to discrimination against women. During the congressional debate on the Civil Rights Act in 1964, she played a critical behind-the-scenes role ensuring that the act banned discrimination in employment on account of sex, and the following year in a law review article, "Jane Crow and the Law," co-authored with Mary Eastwood, she spelled out the legal arguments for treating race and sex as analogous. As a young law professor in 1969, Ruth Bader Ginsburg found that article "an enormous eye-opener" when she first taught a course on women and the law, and two years later she credited Murray as a co-author in her brief on behalf of the American Civil Liberties Union in *Reed v. Reed*, the case in which the Supreme Court for the first time ruled that gender-based discrimination violated the Equal Protection Clause of the Fourteenth Amendment—the argument Murray had been making for nearly three decades.[65]

The civil rights and Black Power movements also raised consciousness about rights, identity, and power among Hispanics, Native Americans, and Asian Americans. "Black Power," the Native American leader Vine Deloria Jr. wrote in 1970, "spoke not only to blacks but also to a longing with the other racial minorities to express the dignity and sovereignty of their own communities.... Soon every minority community in the nation formed its own power organization. Thus we have had Black Power, Chicano Power, Red Power, Flower Power, and Green Power."[66] The shift among people of Mexican descent was particularly noteworthy because, in the face of threats of being deported (as many were in the 1930s and 1950s) or segregated together with Blacks, their organized representatives had long insisted they were white. In a 1954 Supreme Court case, the League of United Latin American Citizens argued that by putting Mexicans in the same category as Blacks, a Texas county had violated their rights, not because racial discrimination was wrong but because the county had acted as though "the term 'white' excludes the Mexican." Many Mexicans preferred to call themselves "Mexican American," which suggested they were like other assimilating white immigrants, or "Spanish" to make themselves fully European.[67]

Not until the late 1960s did Mexicans begin embracing a nonwhite racial identity. A study by the legal scholar Ian Haney López of changes in racial identity and the law in East Los Angeles in 1968 suggests how the Black example led some Mexicans to see themselves differently. After thousands of students walked out of high schools to protest educational conditions, a grand jury indicted thirteen community leaders and college students for conspiring to disrupt the schools. But the lawyer representing them had trouble showing in court that Mexicans were a distinct group subject to discrimination because the community had repeatedly said Mexicans were white and the government had accepted that self-definition.

But racial consciousness was shifting. After the arrests on conspiracy charges and other clashes with authorities, the East Los Angeles activists began to proclaim themselves as members of a "brown" race, heralding, in Haney López's words, "the emergence of a new, quintessentially racial politics that sought to turn non-white status into a badge of pride." There is no doubt, he writes, that "the Black Power movement directly influenced this rhetoric" as it had influenced their protest tactics, but the movement's influence on what he calls "racial common sense" was even more profound: "Since the mid-1950s, the spectacle of black protesters encountering violent repression had transfixed the nation.... Chicano activists turned to race—and not to other potential bases of group solidarity such as class, nationality, or culture—because the social context made it 'obvious' to them that Mexicans were yet another racial minority protesting social injustice and in turn encountering legal violence."[68]

Turning a negative stereotype into a proud identity was what all the movements in the new family of minorities aimed to do. "Normative inversion," the sociologist Andreas Wimmer calls it.[69] The two model minorities of the post–World War II era had shown two ways of doing that—the individual striving and social mobility of Japanese Americans and the collective action the Black movement had undertaken.

Individual versus Group Striving

During the 1940s, liberals and progressives saw parallels between the racial obstacles that Japanese and Black Americans confronted. In two books published during the war, the writer Carey McWilliams—later the editor of *The Nation*—argued that bigotry against Japanese Americans was part of the same "race problem" afflicting Blacks and that overcoming white supremacy would require Congress and the federal courts to establish clear principles of racial equality and apply the Fourteenth Amendment.[70] During the war, antagonism toward Japanese Americans had intensified, but instead of deporting them afterward (as exclusionists had wanted), the federal government resettled them around the United States, scattered in the hope of avoiding "little Tokyos." Now that the postwar United States had an alliance with Japan, efforts to stoke hostility to Japanese Americans did not catch fire. Postwar anti-Japanese agitation was a "Hate That Failed," in the words of the *Saturday Evening Post*. To both independent observers and the representatives of Japanese Americans, their postwar success was a story of American redemption, evidence that Americans could overcome racism.[71]

That was the spirit of a memo President Johnson received in 1965 from an assistant secretary of labor who was previewing a report he had written about how to follow up civil rights legislation with a program to achieve full equality for Black Americans. "Many people think the color problem is insoluble," the assistant secretary told Johnson, but that was "nonsense." The experience of Japanese Americans showed discrimination against Blacks was a solvable problem:

> A quarter-century ago Japanese Americans were subject to the worst kind of racial discrimination and mistreatment. All of which has practically disappeared before our eyes. The reason is that Japanese (and the Chinese) have become a prosperous middle-class group. They now send twice as large a proportion of their children to college as do whites. Have twice as large a proportion of professional persons. Having solved the class problem, we solved the color problem.[72]

The memo arguing that solving the "class problem" of a racial minority could solve the "color problem" came from Daniel Patrick Moynihan— Harvard professor of government, later Democratic senator from New York—whose report, "The Negro Family: The Case for National Action," was about to provoke a storm of controversy. What Moynihan identified as a key source of Japanese Americans' success—their strong, intact families—was what he saw as missing among Black Americans. It seemed to many people that despite his protests to the contrary, Moynihan was blaming the victim by claiming that the "root" of Black poverty was the "crumbling" family in the ghettoes. He associated that pattern with the undermining of male authority, which he traced to slavery and, more immediately, to the high unemployment and low earnings of Black men.[73]

Although the Japanese American example had initially served as a reason for hope and support for the Black freedom struggle, it became the opposite in the hands of conservatives: Since Japanese Americans had made it through hard work, why couldn't Blacks? Some Japanese Americans worried that their story could be used in just this way, to divide racial minorities from one another. In 1969, when the Japanese American Citizens League announced that a new book it had sponsored would be called *Nisei: The Quiet Americans*, one Japanese American wrote that the title implicitly told "Black Americans and Mexican Americans to behave like 'good little Orientals' who know their place." As a new "Asian American" movement developed among college students, its leaders denounced the model minority narrative as an invidious attack on the Black movement. In a 1969 manifesto, "The Emergence of Yellow Power in America," Amy Uyematsu declared that by "allow[ing] white America to hold up the 'successful' Oriental image before other minority groups as the model to emulate," Asian Americans had been complicit in racial oppression.[74]

Some writers have depicted the "model minority" story about Asian Americans as a conservative white invention.[75] That is not accurate. Liberals and Japanese Americans themselves initially contributed to the narrative, often believing it would aid the cause of anti-racism. The conservative spin on Asians as a model minority—the "model minority myth" as scholars came to describe it—was only a new version of an old pattern, the tendency to identify success with individual virtues, particularly virtues associated with a traditional, family-oriented culture. Even poor Americans have generally identified economic success with individual striving, while attributing poverty to personal deficiencies. At least that has been the dominant historical picture of the white majority, with its relatively low levels of class consciousness.

Black Americans, however, have had access to a communal explanation of their situation, and the Black freedom struggle has exemplified the use of collective action to overcome institutionalized subordination. In the second half of the twentieth century, although Asian Americans became, at least in some minds, a model minority in the traditional, individualistic sense, Black Americans became a model minority in a collective sense. Their collective striving offered a model of struggle—actually a series of prototypes—for other groups. That is not to say collective action precludes individual effort, which would assume a false choice. But instead of emphasizing a single-minded devotion to individual advancement, the Black freedom struggle called for a commitment to solidarity and a concerted attack on both the structural obstacles and insidious cultural stereotypes that stood in the way of racial equality. That was the model that other minorities, including many Asians, sought to emulate.

Yet as a once-enslaved people who continued to be subjugated long after slavery, Black Americans did not immediately rise to economic parity with whites. Given the position from which they started—not just deprived of land and education in the aftermath of enslavement but excluded from access to jobs in industry and from the opportunity to acquire assets—that lag in economic mobility is hardly surprising, although many others used it against them. The civil rights and Black Power movements made considerable progress in overcoming the collective indignities visited on Blacks in American law and cultural life, but they had less success in changing the deeply entrenched hierarchies of power and wealth. The civil rights revolution, as we have seen, substantially improved employment opportunities and income for Southern Blacks. For Northern Blacks, however, economic advances were more limited, and nowhere did economic gains come close to eliminating the Black–white gaps in income and wealth.

Large-scale changes in the U.S. economy deprived Blacks of the opportunities to prosper from industrialization that European immigrants had enjoyed. The unskilled Europeans who came to the United States in the late nineteenth or early twentieth century had the benefit of as much as a century of industrial expansion before the country began to lose manufacturing jobs in the 1970s. The Southern Blacks who moved North in the Great Migration had a comparatively short time before deindustrialization and de-unionization knocked the lower rungs of social mobility out from under them. Anti-Black discrimination also did not disappear, perhaps most critically in the housing market. The primary basis for middle-class wealth accumulation is homeownership, and in the mid-twentieth century the European immigrants and their children benefited from rising suburban homeownership and preferences in public policy. But Blacks became renters when they moved to the North, faced red-lining and white resistance in moving out the ghettoes, and were unable to build housing wealth the way white immigrants and their children did. Asian Americans also did not face the level of housing discrimination that Blacks faced. In short, Black people ran into forces in the 1970s and later that did almost as much to undermine their economic position as the civil rights revolution and Lyndon Johnson's Great Society did to improve it. In later decades, the jump in income and wealth among the superrich increased Black–white inequality because the people in the top 1 percent, many of whom started out with inherited wealth, were nearly all white.

In both its successes and limitations, the Black freedom struggle confronted Americans with the contradiction that Gunnar Myrdal had written about in *An American Dilemma*. When Martin Luther King declared at the March on Washington in 1963 that he still had a dream that "one day this nation will rise up and live out the true meaning of its creed," he was evoking the creed Myrdal had written about two decades earlier. As Myrdal hoped, many white Americans did respond sympathetically, though Black people had to take great personal risks in places like Birmingham and Selma to elicit that response. What Myrdal did not anticipate was that Black Americans would establish a model for a whole series of revolutions in favor of a comprehensive vision of equal rights and dignity. It was through that process that Black Americans brought the American Creed closer to an American reality, though perhaps more for other groups than for themselves. The Black freedom struggle had spillover effects, none more important than in the struggle for gender equality.

CHAPTER THREE

How Sex Got Serious

Once the light began to dawn, I couldn't understand why I hadn't figured out any of this before.

—GLORIA STEINEM[1]

FROM THE FIRST STIRRINGS of change in sexuality and social relations in the 1960s, the idea of "gender equality," as we would call it today, did not just meet opposition—it met ridicule. In 1963, when John F. Kennedy's President's Commission on the Status of Women issued its report, much of the media response was "humorous, condescending or tinged with sexual undertones," one of the commission's members later recalled. The next year, "ripples of laughter" greeted Representative Howard Smith's introduction of an amendment to the Civil Rights Act adding "sex" to race, color, religion, and national origin as a prohibited ground of discrimination in employment. An arch-segregationist, Smith did not necessarily have what in those days would have been described as honorable intentions. To show "how some of the ladies feel about discrimination," the Virginia congressman read a letter purportedly complaining that the greater number of women than men in the population denied "the right of every female to have a husband of her own." The House erupted in laughter. In keeping with the mood, the chair of the Judiciary Committee, Emmanuel Celler, observed that at home he always had the last two words, "Yes, dear." A Louisiana attorney, later one of the regional directors of the National Organization for Women (NOW), recalled how a "wave of laughter" filled the courtroom when she tried to bring an early sex discrimination suit. "Of course," she said afterward, "it is better than being spat upon." Needless to say, relentless derision met the protests of the "women's libbers" and "gay libbers" at the end of the decade.[2]

Conservatives with old-fashioned ideas were not alone in regarding demands for gender equality as frivolous. Many men on the left thought the same thing. They did not want to be bothered with women's or gay rights, which amid the Vietnam War and Black struggle seemed like a distraction if not a downright embarrassment. The liberal men of that time, and even the radicals, could not have imagined how deeply the politics of gender and sexuality would change what liberalism and radicalism would mean.

Nor could anyone else have foreseen how consequential gender issues would soon become in American politics. In the 1960s there was no significant gender divide in voting for the Democratic and Republican parties. Only toward the end of the decade did gender-related issues begin receiving much attention from the media. Before the passage of the Civil Rights Act in 1964, few Americans saw a parallel between the issues of race and gender; there had been no public agitation to include "sex" in the law. When Americans first heard about claims of discrimination against women in employment, many thought the notion was preposterous. They took it as an established fact that men and women had different roles in life and different jobs in the economy because of their innate differences. Differences didn't imply discrimination. Homosexuals' claims to equality seemed even more ludicrous. At the time, the American Psychiatric Association classified homosexuality as a mental disorder. To most Americans, it could not be a basis of discrimination because it was a disqualification.

The women's and gay rights movements would not only overturn many of these assumptions; over the next half-century they would bring about a conceptual revolution in the understanding of gender and sexuality that has continued to unfold. Many of the harms suffered in silence by women and gay people to their health, physical security, and economic potential had never been seen as legitimate public concerns. But the new movements raised awareness of the problems, broke through the barriers to open discussion, and altered both social norms and law.

Yet there remains a tendency in the mainstream of historical and political thinking to treat the politics of gender as part of a secondary set of soft, social, and personal concerns, distinct from the hard material realities at stake in the primary fields of politics, especially political economy. Consider the term "identity politics," which in some circles carries the connotation of being subjective, artificial, and self-absorbed, unlike interest-group and class politics. But no politics, not even class politics, can do without concerns about identity. People who work do not automatically self-identify as workers, much less organize with others according to a shared worker identity. That identity has to be created. Moreover, if people are regularly humiliated based on who they are, that experience may be more important to them than being underpaid. And if movements need to focus on changing how others think about marginalized, often invisible people and how they think about themselves, that does not mean they are unconcerned about material realities. Like the Black freedom struggle, the women's and gay—or as it later became known, LGBTQ+—movements have always had economic opportunity and physical security as central concerns.

But while material interests and identity are intertwined, they often arise in political conflict in different ways and create different challenges and complications. The demand for equal rights under law, including full economic citizenship, leads to specific legal reforms that fit readily into a liberal framework, whether or not the law or liberals themselves have previously acknowledged those rights. Concerns about identity, sexuality, and interpersonal relations plunge into moral and psychological issues that have often been considered not just irrelevant to politics but indecent to bring up. The famous axiom of the women's movement, "The personal is political," correctly points to the connections between private life and larger patterns of power and domination. But the personal may not always be political in the same sense as problems like a right to equal pay, that is, with remedies that the law can provide.

Mid-twentieth-century American culture regarded a sharp contrast between men's and women's social roles as an unalterable fact. Maturity for both sexes required the acceptance of biologically given differences and the lives that arose from them. Men had agency denied to women. During the 1960s, however, an alternative conception began gaining ground that saw the relation of masculine and feminine not as a dichotomy but as a continuum that allowed for fluidity and change. In an influential 1964 article, the sociologist Alice Rossi, one of the founders of NOW, made a case for the acceptance of greater androgyny as a basis for greater equality: "An androgynous conception of sex role means that each sex will cultivate some of the characteristics usually associated with the other . . . tenderness and expressiveness should be cultivated in boys and socially approved in men . . .

achievement need, workmanship, and constructive aggression should be cultivated in girls and approved in women."[3]

Although Rossi could not yet see it, American culture was about to move in that direction. A revived feminist movement inspired more active models for young girls and claimed rights to independent agency for women, and critics attacked aggressive masculinity as responsible for heart disease, "emotional constipation," and a futile war overseas. Changing styles in popular culture suggested men could be both sensitive and straight.[4] These new cultural tendencies went along with ideals of equal partnership and greater freedom in sexual relations and marriage.

Like the Black freedom struggle, the women's and gay movements had two sides: one that chiefly had to do with equal rights achievable through legal reform, and another side that was concerned with liberation from traditional hierarchies and stereotypes through changes in consciousness, culture, and interpersonal relations. Both sides had implications for social and political power, but the rights revolution was more readily understood as an effort to bring American reality more closely into line with the American Creed. (In an appendix to *An American Dilemma*, Gunnar Myrdal had recognized a parallel to Blacks in the subjection of women, quoting a remark attributed to Dolley Madison that the Southern wife was "the chief slave of the harem."[5])

The "liberation" side of the women's and gay movements was more unsettling than legal equality. Did it mean, for example, overthrowing the basic understandings of what it means to be a man or a woman? Did it require people to reevaluate their lives, marriages, and moral understandings—the ways they had been brought up to think and act? One reason many people underestimated how consequential gender issues would become is that the challenges were so surprising and intimate and at first could be jokingly dismissed, until they became impossible to ignore. The demands for gender equality awakened a new consciousness among women and gay people that offended how many tradition-minded Americans thought about natural hierarchy and the nation's ideals and its heroes. This, too, was part of the new form that the American contradiction was taking.

Feminism as Equal Rights

The idea that women should have equal rights to men in education, the workplace, and all aspects of public life, as well as an equal partnership with men in interpersonal relations and domestic life, is now so widely accepted, at least in principle, that it is hard to recapture how radical it seemed to Americans when it became the basis of a revived feminist movement in the 1960s. Although that movement, like the Black freedom struggle, involved collective action, its objectives were in some respects highly individualistic: It aimed to have women treated in the economy as individuals apart from their marital status and from any stereotypical ideas about what women were capable of doing.

As of the mid-twentieth century, the ruling norms in the economy treated women not as individuals but as wives and mothers. For example, Americans generally accepted the practice of paying women less than men on the premise that their jobs were temporary before marriage, or their earnings only supplemented their husband's. Men, meanwhile, deserved a "family wage," sufficient to support a family that included a wife at home with the children. The idea of the family wage for men survived despite the patently obvious facts that some working men were single, while a working woman might be her family's breadwinner. But the norm did have a basis in the dominant patterns of family life on the eve of a massive transformation in women's economic role. In 1960, the male breadwinner model (that is, with a wife as a homemaker out of the labor force) described 66 percent of families with children up to age 17. Three decades later, that proportion was down to 27 percent.[6]

Americans' ideas about economic fairness followed from the priority they gave to employment for men and family responsibilities for women. Just as they favored the family wage, Americans had also overwhelmingly agreed at the end of World War II that women needed to relinquish the skilled, high-paying jobs they had filled during the war to make way for returning veterans, even though polls showed the great majority of working women wanted to keep their jobs. Similarly, it was a general practice for employers to discharge women when they got married or had children. Wasn't it improper for a wife to work when she should be at home supported by her husband, while a man might need that job to support his family? Americans' everyday theory of gender justice presupposed a society of male breadwinner families.

These gender stereotypes also had a flip side. Progressive social reformers in the early and mid-twentieth century, many of them labor feminists, used the stereotypes to win protective state legislation for women workers, including required lunch and rest breaks, prohibition of night work, and maximum hours of work or what labor organizers referred to as limits on "forced overtime." Many labor activists would have liked to win some of these protections for men as well, but the best they could do was to persuade state legislatures to enact them for women. As a result, not only was the labor force divided into largely sex-segregated occupations; labor law reflected the same underlying ideas. Gender stereotypes permeated other areas of law as well, including Social Security, welfare, and tax law. A benefit for some women, however, could be a hindrance to others. For example, while limits on overtime protected some working women who wanted to get home after their regular hours, they prevented others from earning extra pay, and many jobs requiring overtime were entirely off-limits to women.

Protective labor legislation was the source of a long-running split among women activists. After ratification of the Nineteenth Amendment in 1920 gave women the right to vote, some leaders of the suffrage movement proposed a further constitutional change, the Equal Rights Amendment (ERA). In 1943, the proposed amendment read, "Equality of rights under the law shall not be denied or abridged by the United States or by any state on account of sex." For decades the main organization promoting the ERA was the National Women's Party, a small, mostly Republican group of elite women who were unconcerned that the ERA might endanger protective labor laws. Some of its leaders opposed any government regulation of free enterprise. But feminists in the trade unions saw the ERA as a threat to the rights they had won for working-class women. Although some liberal Democrats supported the proposed amendment, Republicans and Southern Democrats provided the main support when it came before Congress in the 1940s and 1950s. In other words, the original political battle over the ERA was altogether different from what it later became. Among women, labor feminists made defeating the ERA a priority, whereas probusiness feminists sought to pass it. As the 1960s began, this fissure had not been healed.[7]

When a women's movement revived in the 1960s, some called it feminism's "second wave," lumping together all feminist thought and activity from the 1840s to 1920 in a "first wave" and setting aside everything since 1920 as irrelevant. The notion of a "second wave," popularized in a *New York Times Magazine* article in 1968, accurately reflected how little explicit activism on behalf of women there had been between 1920 and the early 1960s, when the word "feminism" had virtually disappeared from politics. But it was not true that advocacy on behalf of women had vanished in those years, or that the young women of the 1960s produced the new upsurge wholly on their own. Much of the impetus came from older women long involved in labor unions, some of them in labor's left wing. These included women of color and others with working-class backgrounds, contrary to the later image of second-wave feminism as a movement only of white, middle-class women.[8]

The first two major political initiatives in the 1960s, the Equal Pay Act of 1963 and the report of President Kennedy's Commission on the Status of Women later that year, reflected the changes, tensions, and compromises of the time. As originally drafted, the Equal Pay Act, a priority for reformers since the 1940s, would have required equal pay for "comparable work" and would have created a legal basis for equalizing pay across sex-segregated occupations. But the bill was amended to require equal pay only for "equal work"—that is, for the same jobs—a more limited though still significant reform.[9]

President Kennedy's commission was instigated and managed by the highest-ranking woman in the administration, Esther Peterson, assistant secretary of labor and director of the Labor Department's Women's Bureau. Peterson had previously worked as a labor organizer in the garment industry and a legislative lobbyist for the AFL-CIO. The commission sought to improve women's economic position without offending a public that still largely adhered to traditional conceptions of women's role. "Of the 68 million women and girls 14 years and over in the United States today," the commission noted, "44 million are married and keeping house."[10] One out of three married women worked for pay despite stark inequities that included low pay and limited benefits, barriers to promotion, and lack of organized childcare (as the government had arranged for working mothers during World War II). Studies of "national manpower" had already argued that to meet the challenges of the Cold War, the United States needed to draw more fully on the talents of America's women. Yet the overwhelming message in popular culture to women was that they belonged in the home.

Under pressure to avoid any policies that might undermine the family, the commission did not issue a clarion call for equal rights. "Equal opportunity for women in hiring, training, and promotion should be the governing principle in private employment," the commission declared, but rather than call for legislation it suggested an executive order in which the president would state the principle of equal opportunity but would require it only for federal contractors and the government itself. While proposing to extend protective labor laws for women, the commission also accepted the proposal of Pauli Murray, the Black civil rights lawyer, that women pursue their rights to equality in the courts under the Fifth and Fourteenth

Amendments, which the commission's members saw as a more reasonable and workable course than support for the ERA.[11]

That same year, 1963, Betty Friedan published *The Feminine Mystique*, the book often credited with setting second-wave feminism in motion. Eventually selling more than three million copies, it struck a popular nerve like no feminist book before (though it bore an intellectual debt to Simone de Beauvoir's more erudite 1949 work, *The Second Sex*). Friedan argued that despite being told by professional experts and popular media that life as a housewife raising children in the suburbs would bring happiness, many women suffered from what she called "the problem that has no name," a sense of incompleteness and despair from living vicariously through their husband and children, without being able to achieve their own potential. The feminine mystique was a trap, the suburbs a "comfortable concentration camp." In the book's final chapter, she wrote that "when society asks so little of women, every woman has to listen to her own inner voice to find her identity.... She must create, out of her own needs and abilities, a new life plan, fitting in the love and children and home that have defined femininity in the past with the work toward a greater purpose that shapes the future." Dabbling would not be enough; it would take a lifelong commitment to a fulfilling pursuit. "Even if a woman does not have to work to eat, she can find identity only in work that is of real value to society—work for which, usually, our society pays."[12]

Friedan preferred not to discuss her earlier career, claiming she had only discovered women's issues when, as a suburban mother, she began work on the book. In fact, she was one of those 1960s feminists with roots in the labor movement. From 1940 to 1953, she had worked as a radical labor journalist, employed for much of that time by one of the country's leading left-wing unions, the United Electrical, Radio and Machine Workers, where, among other things, she had written a pamphlet that was a guide for women fighting wage discrimination. But by the time *The Feminine Mystique* came out, she avoided mentioning that background, probably because she feared being smeared as a communist and no longer had the same left-wing political commitments. As a judgment of how best to reach her audience, Friedan's focus on the suburban wife made perfect sense, but the story she told about her political education helped conceal the connections between earlier radicalism and the women's movement of the 1960s.[13]

While it had links to the labor movement, equal rights feminism was even more indebted to the civil rights movement and civil rights law. Even though feminism reflected broader structural changes, such as women's growing role in the economy, and Congress had already passed the Equal Pay Act, the women's movement might not have developed *when* it did if not for the model and legal foundations created through the Black freedom struggle. The passage of the 1964 Civil Rights Act was the critical turning point in establishing the parallelism of race and gender in law and social thought. Once that parallel was established in law, no one could think about women's position in society the way they had before.

The inclusion of women in civil rights law, however, came about through the strangest of strange-bedfellows coalitions. During congressional hearings on the Civil Rights Act, the small National Women's Party lobbied for a provision against sex discrimination, but none came out of committee. When Virginia's Howard Smith proposed on the House floor to add "sex" to the act's Title VII concerning equal opportunity in employment, he was likely hoping that it would lead to the bill's being watered down, if not defeated. Like many other Southerners, however, Smith had supported the ERA, and in the ensuing debate on his amendment, other Southerners applauded it as a defense of white womanhood. "Unless this amendment is adopted," said one Alabama congressman, "the white women of this country would be drastically discriminated against in favor of a Negro woman." A South Carolina congressman declared, "It is incredible to me that the authors of this monstrosity . . . would deprive the white woman of mostly Anglo-Saxon or Christian heritage equal opportunity before the employer." Worried that the segregationists were trying to sink the bill, many liberals opposed Smith's amendment. At the behest of the administration, one of the leading Democratic women in the House, Edith Green of Oregon, argued against it on the grounds that Blacks had suffered far more than women. But other women representatives favored the amendment, and it passed—with the backing of Southern segregationists, even though they later voted against the Civil Rights Act as a whole.[14] And so it was that the representatives of the white South, the region with the most patriarchal laws in the country as well as the most racist, advanced the cause of women's equality. When the laughter in Congress had died down, the joke was on them.

The Civil Rights Act, the historian Alice Kessler-Harris argues, "helped to create a self-conscious women's movement" by linking race and sex.[15] It put sex discrimination on the same plane as racial discrimination, a conceptual as well as legal breakthrough (the contemporary meaning of "sexism" as an analog to racism originated around this time). The law opened the floodgates to suits about sex discrimination, the basis of 37 percent of employment discrimination complaints filed in the first year of the Equal Employment Opportunity Commission (EEOC), the administrative agency the law created. In 1966, as the commission dithered on moving against sex discrimination—initially approving separate "help wanted" ads for men and women—feminists under Friedan's leadership established NOW as a counterpart to the NAACP. For most women, Friedan later wrote, "nothing was going to happen... unless we organized a movement to change society, as the blacks had done."[16]

Over the next several years, the EEOC and the courts overturned much of the old employment regime, including the protective laws. The EEOC directed employers, for example, not to take marital status into account in decisions to hire or promote women unless they also did so for men. The law did allow employers to take sex into account if an employee's sex was a "bona fide occupational qualification," but that exception became hard to establish. In a 1969 case, an appellate court ruled that to exclude women as a class, an employer had to show that all or "substantially all" women—not just "many" or even "most" women—were unable to perform the work. Otherwise, an employer had to consider each woman for a job on her own individual merits.[17] That same year, the EEOC declared that state laws and regulations originally intended to protect women were discriminatory because they were no longer "relevant to our technology or to the expanding role of the female worker" and failed to consider "the capacities, preferences and abilities of individual females." As Kessler-Harris concludes, "Formally, at least, women of all races had become individuals under employment law."[18]

These changes in employment law promoted women's advance into better paid and more elite positions. During the first two decades after 1945, the percentage of women among college graduates had declined, and men began taking some of the professional positions in fields like school administration that previously had gone to women. But during the late 1960s and early 1970s, those trends reversed, and in rapid succession, women made a series of breakthroughs in higher education and the professions. One after another, the Ivy League colleges began admitting women. Women comprised sharply rising percentages of the entering classes in professional schools; they went from 10 percent to 25 percent of medical graduates in the 1970s. New legislation forced changes throughout higher education. For example, the relation of young women to athletics changed as a result of Title IX of the Education Amendments of 1972, which denied federal funds to colleges and universities if they discriminated against women in sports. The Women's Educational Equity Act, also passed in 1972, funded initiatives to promote changes in academic programs for women, such as reforming sexist curricula. Second-wave feminism was at such a high point that a Republican president, Richard Nixon, signed equal rights bills into law—with one crucial exception, the Comprehensive Child Development Act of 1971. The bill's chief sponsor, Senator Walter Mondale, said it was "in a class with Medicare" in its ambition to fund childcare nationally for all, not just for the poor. In a veto message written by the Nixon aide and future culture warrior Patrick Buchanan, the president declared that he was blocking the legislation because it would "commit the vast moral authority of the National Government to the side of communal approaches in child-rearing over against the family-centered approach" and lead to "the Sovietization of American children."[19]

By 1972, however, the old partisan division over putting equal rights for women into the Constitution had disappeared. This was the ERA's moment: Democrats had come around in support, while Republicans had not yet abandoned it. Congress passed the ERA overwhelmingly, with only twenty-four votes against it in the House and eight against it in the Senate, and sent the amendment to the states for what seemed like certain ratification. Meanwhile, in 1971, the Supreme Court had for the first time applied the Fourteenth Amendment's Equal Protection Clause to a sex discrimination claim. Whether through an amendment or a change in judicial doctrine, a constitutional foundation for gender equality seemed to be on its way.

The early 1970s also brought a revolution in family law, notably regarding divorce. Previously, states granted divorces only upon the showing of serious cause such as abusive treatment, adultery, desertion, or nonsupport. The apportionment of guilt then guided the division of property and post-marital obligations of the two parties. Divorce rates were already rising during the 1960s when, in just five years beginning with California in 1970, all but five states adopted "no-fault" divorce, making it possible to dissolve a marriage by mutual consent or according to such minimal criteria as "incompatibility." The women's movement originally supported no-fault divorce and other changes that treated such issues as child custody on what at the time seemed a more individualized and egalitarian basis.[20]

The Supreme Court had also begun to guarantee what would come to be called "reproductive rights," though it justified those decisions on the grounds of a constitutional right to privacy, not to equality. The liberalization of laws regarding contraception and abortion was part of a broader relaxation of strictures on sexual behavior, which had begun independently of the feminist movement and was more in the spirit of laissez-faire than of equality.

During the postwar era, the first mainstream cultural breaks with the public norm tying sex to marriage came from sources that were, in sexual terms, wholly conventional. From its founding in the early 1950s, Hugh Hefner's *Playboy* magazine had catered to male heterosexual fantasies about voluptuous women in a life free of marital obligations. According to the double standards of the time, sexual desire was perfectly understandable for men; public legitimation of sexual freedom for single women was a bigger step. Helen Gurley Brown's 1962 bestseller *Sex and the Single Girl* took that step, celebrating the new possibilities for young, urban working women who were as interested as men in sex and, rather shockingly, not necessarily interested in marriage. "Nice girls *do* have affairs," Brown wrote cheerily, "and they do not necessarily die of them!" Beginning a thirty-two-year run as editor of *Cosmopolitan* in 1965, she turned the magazine into a how-to guide for "Cosmo girls" who wanted to have both sex and a career. At the same time, a new "singles culture," with singles bars and clubs, began spreading in major cities.[21]

The acceptance of sex outside of marriage for women came at a time when medical technology was making pregnancy less of a risk. In 1960, the Food and Drug Administration approved the first oral contraceptive, which had an emancipatory potential for women by giving them more control over childbearing. The "pill," however, did not suddenly cause a radical shift in sexuality; diaphragms and condoms were already in use, and the initial take-up of the pill was predominantly among married women who wanted more reliable means to control the number of children or the timing of childbirth. In a few states, though, the law prohibited the dispensing of contraceptives—that is until 1965, when the Supreme Court in *Griswold v. Connecticut* ruled that the Bill of Rights gave Americans an implicit "right to privacy" that included a right of married couples to use birth control in their bedrooms. The Court extended that right to the unmarried in 1971. Readily available contraception, while not causing the change in norms, contributed to the normalization of sex before marriage among young women as well as men. From 1969 to 1973, the proportion of Americans believing premarital sex was "not wrong" doubled from 24 percent to 47 percent, the result of a sudden and dramatic shift among the young: Roughly four-fifths of baby boomers accepted sex before marriage, while four-fifths of their elders disapproved of it. A story from the period illustrates the shift. After a young woman had asked for a birth control prescription, a physician cautioned her that she "might someday want to marry a man who holds virginity in high regard" and was startled when she replied: "Yes, but I'm not at all sure I want to marry a man like that."[22]

During the 1960s, reformers began challenging state laws banning abortion. The laws, dating from the nineteenth century, criminalized abortion but allowed it under the control of physicians if they judged it necessary for "therapeutic" reasons, chiefly saving the life of the mother. Abortion had quietly been available in doctors' offices for years, but as the procedure migrated into hospitals and maternal mortality declined, the justification of therapeutic abortion became a matter of professional dispute. The movement for reform emerged not from feminists but from physicians, lawyers, and hospital officials who wanted to clarify the law and ensure that it reflected a "broad" rather than a "strict" construction of medical authority to perform abortions. In 1959, the American Law Institute—an organization of noted lawyers, law professors, and judges concerned with simplifying and modernizing the common law—proposed a model bill legalizing abortion not just when the pregnant woman's life was at stake but under broader circumstances: when the pregnancy resulted from rape or incest; when it threatened her physical or mental health; or when the child would be born with grave physical or mental defects.[23]

Between 1966 and 1972, eighteen states enacted laws that liberalized abortion to varying degrees. Like the politics of the ERA, the politics of abortion at this point was not ideologically polarized. Seven of the eighteen states liberalizing their abortion laws were in the South: Mississippi (the first), North Carolina, Georgia, Arkansas, South Carolina, Virginia, and Florida. In 1967, California adopted a reform that resulted in an increase of legal abortions from 5,018 in 1968 to 15,952 the next year and 116,749 in 1972. The law was signed by the hero of American conservatism, Ronald Reagan, who three years later also signed the country's first no-fault divorce law.[24]

As far as feminists were concerned, however, even liberalized abortion laws still left decisions about abortion to the discretion of physicians. When those laws were originally under debate, no significant political constituency had argued that abortion was a woman's right. But in the late 1960s, activists began to insist that abortion and contraception fell within a woman's right to control her own body. And in 1973, following the logic of its *Griswold* decision, the Supreme Court ruled in *Roe v. Wade* that the right to privacy also guaranteed a constitutional right to abortion. At that time, according to public opinion surveys, the support for abortion rights enjoyed more support in the electorate from Republicans than from Democrats.[25]

Like a woman's right to equal economic opportunity, rights to reproductive freedom upset traditional ways of thinking, including the thinking of many liberals, but the new claims to equal treatment and privacy were not incompatible with a liberal legal framework. They required a shift from one liberal regime to another, a shift that brought the law into closer alignment with an expanded economic role for women. But the women's movement had more to it than that.

Feminism as Women's Liberation

The dictum that "the personal is political" was at the heart of the young, radical branch of the women's movement that emerged in the late 1960s. Its pioneers saw their personal experience as revealing a pervasive system of male supremacy. At first there was some disagreement between two self-descriptions—"radical women" or "women's liberation"—but "women's liberation" won out and for a time was associated only with the new groups. While it gradually became synonymous with the entire women's movement, I will use the phrase here to refer to the younger branch that broke from liberal, equal rights feminism and introduced new ideas, tactics, and organization.[26]

The very name "women's liberation" suggested linkages to the Black and Third World liberation movements that at the time were regarded as models on the left. The new movement's founders, as the historian and movement veteran Sara Evans writes, "saw themselves as revolutionaries. Their model was black separatism, and their driving passion was fury at cultural definitions of women as secondary, inferior sexual objects." One of the original women's liberation groups, Redstockings, emphasized both the personal immediacy and the comprehensive reach of women's liberation in its founding manifesto: "We regard our personal experience, and our feelings about that experience, as the basis of an analysis of our common situation. We cannot rely on existing ideologies as they are all products of male supremacist culture.... Our chief task at present is to develop female class consciousness through sharing experience and publicly exposing the sexist foundation of all our institutions."[27]

Equal rights feminism and liberation feminism roughly paralleled the two main branches of the Black freedom struggle. Just as equal rights feminism built on the civil rights movement and civil rights law, so women's liberation adopted the more fiercely oppositional posture of Black Power. In equal rights feminism, the battle was against "discrimination"; in women's liberation, it was against "oppression." Liberal feminism used litigation, lobbying, and orderly forms of direct action, the same repertoire of contention as the civil rights movement. Women's liberation rejected the politics of respectability and, like Black Power, sought to gain media attention by saying and doing things that, to the conventional public, were shocking and scandalous. Unlike NOW, which included men as members and opened its founding Statement of Purpose with the words, "We, men and women," the women's liberation groups made the exclusion of men a standing policy.[28] Both Black Power and women's liberation called for a shift in perspective. Just as Black Power rejected the white gaze as a standard of judgment and called upon Blacks to look to other Blacks, so women's liberation rejected the male gaze and called upon women to look to other women. And while the equal rights goals of liberal feminism demanded that women be treated as individuals, the goals of women's liberation were more collectivist, a mutually supporting and powerful sisterhood.

At the ground level, women's liberation spread through independently organized "consciousness-raising" groups, composed of from five to thirty women. They tended to be relatively homogeneous in age (mostly in their twenties), race (nearly all white), and class (generally college educated). Many of the early members had been unhappily marginalized in male-dominated civil rights, student, and antiwar groups. Committed to equal and uninhibited democratic participation, they came together to share personal experiences that they had often never discussed even privately, much less in public. These experiences had to do with such intimate matters as their sexual relationships with men and other women and with such mundane but infuriating issues as the "politics of housework," the seemingly endless excuses boyfriends and husbands gave for not doing household chores. Membership was informal and often ephemeral; the groups formed and dissolved so fast that it was impossible to keep track of them or to get an accurate count.[29] Even if the membership could have been counted, it would not have been a good measure of the movement's significance. The challenges that women's liberation initiated to prevailing norms of sexuality and gender, and to relations between men and women, extended far beyond the movement itself.

"Consciousness-raising groups," Barbara Ehrenreich, Elizabeth Hess, and Gloria Jacobs later wrote, "encouraged women to trust their subjective experience, even when it contradicted male judgment or expert opinion." One of the themes was that the sexual revolution of the 1960s was more in men's interest than in women's, sexual pleasure for men without pleasure for women.

> Sex—the area of secrecy and self-doubt and of maximum competition between women—was opened up to informal analysis and sharing. Did you worry that you might be frigid? Fake orgasms to please a boyfriend? Secretly prefer masturbation, or wonder about lesbianism? So, it turned out, did almost everyone else.... It did not take long for women, buoyed with the confidence of the new movement, to trace the links connecting women's widespread sexual anxiety to their feelings of worthlessness and self-hate, and hence to the social oppression of women as a group.[30]

In 1968 and 1969, the new feminism began spilling into print in the form of newsletters and mimeographed articles, and beginning in the fall of 1969 it became the subject of feature stories in the weekly newsmagazines and on television. The early media treatments were often humorous and patronizing, and the young feminists were not unreasonably hostile and suspicious of the mass media, refusing to talk with male and sometimes even female reporters. But they did seek attention and get it, as when they staged a protest at the 1968 Miss America Pageant with a "freedom trash basket" for bras, girdles, and false eyelashes (leading to the fiction they were "bra burners," though no bras were burned).

The media coverage stimulated interest from some women and alienated others. For example, in the 1968 *New York Times* article that popularized the term "second-wave feminism," the journalist Martha Weinman Lear focused on the 29-year-old Ti-Grace Atkinson, at the time (though only briefly) the president of NOW's New York chapter. After comparing marriage to slavery, Atkinson said, "I think it's time for us to go on the offensive. I think we ought to say, 'Listen, you dumb broad, you look funny. You stay home, you're kind of empty, you're bored, you take your frustrations out on your husband, you dominate your kids, and when you get older, you disintegrate.'" (Atkinson soon left NOW, finding it insufficiently radical, and formed a group called The Feminists.) In February 1969, another radical feminist group distributed a leaflet that called marriage "a dehumanizing institution—legal whoredom for women." Or as another radical feminist publication explained, "Freedom for women cannot be without the abolition of marriage." Friedan, hoping to build coalitions and pass legislation, was appalled at the young radicals' attacks on men, marriage, and motherhood.[31]

Although magazine and newspaper editors tried to avoid assigning stories about women's liberation to women whom they knew to be feminists, many of the early articles turned into "personal conversion stories."[32] In 1969, Gloria Steinem, a well-established, 35-year-old political columnist for *New York* magazine, went to cover a Redstockings "speak-out" about abortion after the group had protested a state legislative hearing where fourteen of the fifteen experts called to testify were men. The Redstockings had twelve women talk about abortion from personal experience. For Steinem, "a great blinding lightbulb" went on about her own abortion and her suppressed anger about being passed over for important assignments. It led her to think about "the assumption that any work I did get was the result of my being a 'pretty girl,'" and "a lifetime of journalists' jokes about frigid wives, dumb blondes, and farmers' daughters that I had smiled at in order to be one of the boys":

> That was the worst of it, of course—my own capitulation to all the small humiliations, and my own refusal to trust an emotional understanding of what was going on, or even to trust my own experience. For instance, I had believed that women couldn't get along with one another, even while my own trusted friends were women. . . . It is truly amazing how long we can go on accepting myths that oppose our own lives.

In the wake of the Redstockings event, Steinem wrote an article called "After Black Power, Women's Liberation" that led some of her male friends and colleagues to take her aside to ask: "Why was I writing about these crazy women instead of something serious, political, and important?"[33] Within three years, she had founded *Ms. Magazine* and become the most widely recognized representative of women's liberation in America. That movement, journalists would have to recognize, was something serious, political, and important.

Even as women's liberation outgrew its origins on the radical left, the movement retained a deep aversion to structure, hierarchy, or leadership. No national organization coordinated, much less controlled, the consciousness-raising groups, and the groups themselves functioned without elected leaders or formal rules. This "structurelessness," the political scientist Jo Freeman points out, created a vacuum that the media filled: "the movement had not chosen women to speak for it, believing that no one could, [and so] the media had done the choosing instead." In August 1970, to coincide with Women's Strike Day commemorating the fiftieth anniversary of the Nineteenth Amendment, *Time* magazine put on its cover Kate Millett, author of the new book *Sexual Politics*, identifying her as a spokeswoman for women's liberation. But in December, after Millett publicly declared herself bisexual, *Time* said she had been discredited. "No movement group," Freeman points out, "had a role in either her ascendancy or dismissal."[34] Within the movement, women who appeared to be speaking for it frequently got "trashed," and the groups suffered from continual fractures on personal, ideological, and group lines.

Race was a particular point of tension. Although the early groups were almost all white, they had no hesitation about speaking in the name of all women, raising criticism from Black women who said the feminists didn't speak for them and were ignoring racism. Within a few years, women's caucuses and organizations had emerged in other racial groups, but the divisions and recriminations over race persisted. The movement also had a "gay–straight split" in its early years. Friedan saw lesbians as a danger to the movement—she called them the "lavender menace"—and fought to keep them out of NOW, but by 1973 even NOW had fully welcomed lesbians.

While the consciousness-raising groups mostly disappeared by the mid-1970s, they played an important role in bringing to light what the historian Ruth Rosen calls "hidden injuries of sex." Not only did the groups raise awareness about rape, domestic violence, and the failures of the healthcare system to address women's health problems; some groups also turned to service projects to create new institutions such as rape crisis centers and battered women's shelters.[35] A women's collective in Boston, dissatisfied with the medical knowledge available to women, produced the book *Our Bodies, Ourselves*, which helped launch a women's health movement and spread feminist ideas.

Our Bodies, Ourselves sought to demystify the female body and to transform the way women thought about themselves. The authors provided explanations in plain English of anatomy and physiology along with a narrative contesting dominant cultural beliefs and insisting on women's rights to equality, autonomy, and personal and sexual fulfillment. "From our beginning conversations with each other," they wrote, "we discovered four cultural notions of femininity which we had in some sense shared: woman as inferior, woman as passive, woman as beautiful object, woman as exclusively wife and mother." Those notions "constricted us" but after first angrily rejecting "our old selves," they looked to a new synthesis: "We are women and proud of being women. What we do want to do is reclaim the human qualities culturally labeled 'male' and integrate them with the human qualities that have been seen as 'female' so that we can all be fuller human people. This should also have the effect of freeing men from the pressure of being masculine at all times"—the more androgynous conception of gender roles that Rossi had proposed a decade earlier.[36]

In its discussion of sexuality, *Our Bodies, Ourselves* exemplifies the shift of perspective that women's liberation called for. "Our feelings about our anatomy," the authors wrote, "have often been very negative." They argued that the "ideal woman in America" was "the ideal of the men, the judges, whom we are supposed to please and win approval from" and that a preoccupation with men's esteem "carried over into our sexual life, where we felt that pleasing men was more important than pleasing ourselves." That preoccupation had led to a preoccupation with genital sex, whereas "we have come to see our sexuality in broader ways ... to listen to our own rhythms ... to express our own needs ... [and to be] more open to a variety of sexual expression."[37] That new openness was characteristic of the era's general tendency toward acceptance of greater individual choice and diversity in sexuality.

Gay Rights and the Turn toward Sexual Pluralism

The sexual revolution that took off in the 1960s originally challenged limits on heterosexual freedom, but it ultimately broke down other constraints on sex and gender as well. Seen in a half-century's perspective, it initiated a turn toward sexual pluralism, which at first meant a greater variety of erotic expression in heterosexual relations, then increased acceptance of homosexuality, and later came to include multiple forms of nonconforming gender expression and identity.

Like other marginalized, struggling groups in mid-twentieth-century America, gay men and lesbians came to see themselves, and to have many others see them, as a minority suffering from discrimination, but that understanding was far from self-evident. Most Americans viewed homosexuality as an individual problem for which medical treatment, legal penalties, and public ostracism were appropriate. Gay people generally concealed their sexuality from their employers, landlords, and families and avoided openly flouting or confronting established norms and institutions. They had no precedent of their own for organizing a militant political movement. The Black freedom struggle had a history before the 1960s; the civil rights era was a "Second Reconstruction" following the original Reconstruction of a century earlier. The feminism of the 1960s could be conceived as a "second wave" because an earlier wave had won women the vote. But sexual minorities had no earlier historical reconstruction or political wave. They had to be the first wave. The very idea of gay men and lesbians as a political force, acting publicly and collectively on their own behalf, required a greater imaginative and organizational leap than those made by the Black and women's movements.

In other respects, though, the gay movement—as it became known by 1970—followed patterns similar to others in the post–World War II family of movements. It started out in the 1950s with organizational leaders who adhered to a cautious politics of respectability before developing at the end of the 1960s into an activist, confrontational mass movement that defied conventional opinion and demanded equality and power. Like the movements among Black people and women, the gay insurgency had both a legal and a cultural side. In line with the civil rights tradition, it sought changes in law to guarantee personal security and rights to equal justice; and to make those claims successfully in the American legal system, it had to conceptualize gay people as a minority group analogous to racial minorities. In the same vein as Black Power and women's liberation, it also sought to shatter preconceptions, win respect, and become a presence in American culture that could no longer be ignored or ridiculed.

Behind the legal persecution and public vilification of homosexuality lay a complex history. The condemnation of sodomy has biblical origins, but before the twentieth century it did not refer strictly to same-sex acts. The sodomite committed abominable "crimes against nature" that involved non-procreative sex. Nineteenth-century American courts understood sodomy to refer to "the penetration of a man's penis inside the rectum of an animal, a woman or girl, or of another man or boy," and the law primarily served as a means of punishing sexual assault. No state classified oral sex as a crime against nature until 1879, when Pennsylvania included it in a definition of sodomy and, for the first time anywhere, made women potential defendants against a sodomy charge.[38] The legal and cultural preoccupation specifically with homosexuality emerged around the turn of the century; the word "homosexual" entered the language only in the 1890s. As physicians acquired greater cultural authority in the twentieth century, their disease model became the dominant framework for public understanding of the homosexual as a dangerously sick and depraved person, who might receive psychotherapy, drugs, psychiatric institutionalization, or even possibly "asexualization" (castration). In twentieth-century law, sodomy was increasingly equated with same-sex acts, although statutes often did not specify which acts were prohibited.[39]

The laws that most directly impinged on gay people were primarily at the state and local level. From the 1890s to the 1920s, a distinct gay world had developed in a few neighborhoods in New York and other cities where gays were tolerated or at least not hounded. Beginning in the mid-1930s, however, anti-homosexual policing increased, and the clamor against "perverts" intensified in the late 1940s and early 1950s. At midcentury, sodomy was a crime in every state, potentially punishable by heavier sentences than all other crimes except murder, kidnapping, and rape. Local police raided gay bars and surveilled parks and other public places, entrapping and arresting homosexuals on such charges as public lewdness, disorderly conduct, and solicitation. Even when they avoided a prison sentence, those who had been arrested often lost their jobs and were stamped for life as criminals.[40] As a crime, a sin, and a disease, homosexuality bore a triple weight of social opprobrium. It was so deeply reviled that it was not to be spoken of. That taboo, enforced by broad censorship laws, created additional barriers to change: the silence of the press and educational institutions, the reluctance of scientists to study the subject, and the reticence of people with same-sex desires to act on them or those with same-sex experiences to discuss them.

It was partly because of that wall of silence that the publication of Alfred Kinsey's findings about homosexuality had the impact of a thunderbolt. In his best-selling 1948 book *Sexual Behavior in the Human Male*, Kinsey reported that 37 percent of white American men had at least one homosexual encounter after adolescence that led to orgasm, while 4 percent were exclusively homosexual. Kinsey emphasized that it was a mistake to think, as most Americans did, that homosexuality was all or nothing; his study classified men along a seven-point heterosexual–homosexual scale. The numbers Kinsey reported five years later for homosexual contacts for white women were only about one-third to one-half the levels for men, except that some women had what was rare among men, a same-sex relationship that lasted for many years. (Kinsey's statistics did not include Blacks.) The data lent themselves to two opposite interpretations—Kinsey's own view that so common a practice should not be punished, and the more widely expressed view that homosexuality was an even greater threat than Americans had imagined.[41]

Still, the entry of scientists, including social scientists, into the study of homosexuality created an opportunity for research to expose the limitations of the disease model. Studies by psychologists and sociologists that followed in Kinsey's wake laid the foundation for viewing homosexuality as a benign variation in human sexuality. Researchers would put the onus of responsibility on religious institutions, medicine, and the state for labeling homosexuals as deviant and making them into a despised caste.[42]

The first stirrings of an oppositional gay consciousness originated in left-wing circles in the fraught McCarthy era. In Los Angeles in 1951, a member of the Communist Party, Harry Hay, convened a small meeting of homosexuals to found an organization with the "heroic objective of liberating one of the largest minorities from . . . social persecution." Called the Mattachine Society, it was to have a secretive, cell-like structure modeled after the Communist Party, which would help protect the members, known to each other only by pseudonyms, from having their identities disclosed. By 1953, however, as the group grew and began attracting attention from the press, Hay and the other founders stepped aside in recognition of the threat to the group's survival from exposure of their communist backgrounds. The leaders who took their place rejected the conception of homosexuals as a persecuted minority and sought to gain acceptance as conventional, patriotic citizens differing only in their private sexual orientation. They were so cautious that they refused to undertake any litigation or lobbying, in the belief that such actions would only stir up hostility. Instead, they worked with psychologists and other experts to promote research on "sex variant problems" in the hope that respected professionals could make homosexuality better understood. A separate lesbian organization, the Daughters of Bilitis, founded in San Francisco in 1955, also eschewed any effort to change public policy, primarily offering personal assistance to lesbians.[43]

Together, the Mattachine Society and the Daughters of Bilitis formed the "homophile" movement. Neither group attracted a large following; as of 1960, the Mattachine Society had 230 members; the Daughters of Bilitis, 110. But along with the magazine *ONE*, an independent Mattachine offshoot, their publications provided a platform for discussing issues of interest to homosexuals. They had one significant victory in the 1950s, when the Supreme Court, in 1958, unanimously overturned the Post Office's decision to classify *ONE* as obscene and ban it from the mails. The case established that homosexuals had a right at least to publicize their viewpoint.[44]

The Court's ruling in that case was part of a general shift in legal rules and social norms about sexuality in the public sphere. Although the courts had begun in the 1930s to chip away at the legal regime undergirding literary censorship, much of the Victorian legacy remained. In a 1957 case, the Supreme Court declared that obscenity—what most people called pornography—did not enjoy First Amendment protection, but it defined obscenity more narrowly than before, making it harder to prosecute. Following that decision, the Court overturned obscenity convictions in a series of cases, and by 1973 it resolved that the government could ban material as obscene only if that material met three criteria: It appealed to an average person's "prurient interest" defined according to "community standards"; depicted sex or excretory functions in a "patently offensive" way; and, taken as a whole, lacked "serious literary, artistic, political or scientific value."[45] Although that definition left room for prosecution, American cultural standards were becoming more permissive, and the old censorship regime effectively collapsed. The Court did allow federal broadcast regulators to limit, though not entirely ban, material that met the single criterion of being "patently offensive," a category it called "indecency." Under that rule, the FCC could limit "indecent" broadcasts to the late-night hours.[46] Local governments could also keep theaters with X-rated movies out of residential areas. The overall trend, though, was toward increased freedom in the depiction and discussion of sexuality, and that freedom protected the growth of a gay subculture, including a gay press.

The legal world also moved toward the decriminalization of homosexuality. In 1961 Illinois became the first state to repeal a sodomy law. In 1967, after the Supreme Court had determined, in its decision on contraception, that there was a constitutional right to privacy, the American Civil Liberties Union took the position that consensual sodomy should also be protected on privacy grounds, a position the Supreme Court did not reach until 2003. Courts in California and several eastern states ruled, however, that gay people had a constitutional right to assemble in establishments serving liquor, which provided grounds for contesting police raids on gay bars. In cities such as San Francisco, New York, Boston, and Seattle. the enforcement of sodomy laws and police harassment of homosexuals eased significantly even before the late 1960s.[47]

These legal changes began to protect, if imperfectly, the development of gay communities and gay culture. A distinction took root between being homosexual and being gay—the first, a sexual orientation; the second, a shared identity and way of life that included "unique codes of language use, dress, sexual mores and ideals of self-fulfillment."[48] (By the early 1970s, "gay" often referred only to gay men, though it was still used as a generic term.) In contrast to the view of the Mattachine Society in the 1950s that homosexuals differed only in their sexual orientation and wanted just to be let alone, the new gay leaders and publications in the 1960s defended gay identity as a positive, collective expression of a minority unjustly denied rights and respect.

These emerging changes within the gay community laid the groundwork for the explosive transformation of the gay movement at the end of the 1960s. In early 1969, secrecy was still a way of life for most gay men and lesbians. They were mostly invisible to the public, without any legal protection if their homosexuality was disclosed and they were fired or evicted. Their collective coming out to the public took place on a Friday night in June 1969, when the New York City police raided a gay bar in Greenwich Village, the Stonewall Inn, which was operating without a liquor license. While the police were making arrests, drag queens and others in a crowd on the streets outside fought back in a highly theatrical confrontation that got national and even international attention, making the riot the gay equivalent of the storming of the Bastille. In the months and years that followed, gay men and lesbians appeared openly and defiantly in public in large numbers for the first time as they commemorated Stonewall in gay pride marches and demonstrations.

Although the gay movement of the 1970s was far more assertive than the earlier homophile movement, it was similar in one respect. Just as communists initiated the Mattachine Society and then gave way to a more mainstream leadership, so radicals initially dominated the new phase before giving way to leaders with more mainstream ideas. The group that formed in New York right after Stonewall called itself the Gay Liberation Front, the first group in history to use "gay" in its name ("liberation front" came from the name of the insurgency that the United States was fighting in Vietnam). In the superheated style of the time, the group's manifesto announced, "We are a revolutionary group of men and women formed with the realization that complete sexual liberation for all people cannot come about unless existing social institutions are abolished." They would dedicate themselves to "all the oppressed, the Vietnamese struggle, the third world, the blacks, the workers." But since revolutionary groups like the Black Panthers were mostly just as homophobic as the establishment, some members of the Gay Liberation Front who did not share the leaders' politics split off to form a separate group, the Gay Activists Alliance, which devoted itself solely to gay rights. This new group still used in-your-face tactics and held long, wide-open participatory meetings—perhaps forgetting Oscar Wilde's admonition that the problem with socialism is that it takes too many evenings—until yet another split occurred and a more conventional group, the National Gay Task Force, broke off to influence politics and policy through professionally run litigation and lobbying.[49] This was, in a nutshell, the history of much of the radical movement on the downslope from the late 1960s and early 1970s.

Another split developed after Stonewall between gay men and lesbians. Gay liberation was just as dominated by men as other New Left groups had been; the lesbians saw the men as misogynist and felt they weren't paying attention to women's concerns. Lesbians had a dual presence in the women's liberation and gay liberation movements, but in both they had troubles with the leadership and found it necessary to organize separately as well. The split with gay men was partly cultural. While the women usually had one partner at a time, the men were more often promiscuous.[50]

The culture of gay men in the 1970s exemplified the sexual libertarianism that at the time suffused much popular sex advice. The 1972 bestseller *The Joy of Sex*, for example, defined its aim as "pleasure" and taught readers "to use sex as play" without necessarily linking it to a relationship. The sequel *More Joy* explained that sex "can be reproductive (producing babies), relational (expressing love and bonding adults together), or recreational (play and fun)" and declared that the "adult of today has all three options," including "sex for fun accompanied by no more than affection." Although the original *Joy of Sex* approved only of heterosexual sex, the sequel abandoned any restriction on the sexual partners' gender.[51] A widening vista of sexual pluralism went with sexual laissez-faire. Even many of those who remained committed to a more restrictive, romantic sexual ethic believed the government had no business regulating noncommercial sex taking place in private between consenting adults. Sexual freedom was now one of the freedoms that Americans most definitely enjoyed.

The combination of an activist gay movement, changing sexual norms, and a political culture receptive to minority rights led to major shifts during the 1970s in the three institutions that had long defined homosexuality as deviant—medicine, religion, and law. The chief target of gay protest in medicine was the American Psychiatric Association, which had included homosexuality in the official listing of mental disorders in its *Diagnostic and Statistical Manual*. After Stonewall, gay activists began disrupting the association's meetings, denouncing the idea that homosexuals were sick and in need of treatment. When a psychiatrist at the association's 1970 convention reported research on conversion therapy using electroshock and drugs, one protester yelled, "Where did you take your residency—Auschwitz?" At another convention the next year, the gay leader Franklin Kameny declared, "It has been well and truly said that there is no black problem in this country—there is a white problem—and I feel very strongly that there is no homosexual problem—there is a heterosexual problem—and many of you people here *are* the problem to a significant degree." After agreeing to reassess their position, the psychiatrists began taking into account research that confounded their disease model, and in 1973 the association dropped homosexuality from its list of disorders. The change was treated as the medical equivalent of a Supreme Court decision. "Doctors Rule Homosexuals Not Abnormal," the headline in the *Washington Post* declared.[52]

The women's and gay movements in the 1970s confronted America's churches with fundamental theological and organizational challenges. The responses of different faiths split along lines that proved critical for politics as well as religion. On the one hand, mainline Protestants and Reform Jews moved toward accommodating changes in gender roles and sexuality. Some congregations welcomed gay men and lesbians; some of their leaders revised their beliefs and language in the interests of greater inclusiveness. On the other hand, Southern Baptists, the Catholic Church, and Orthodox Jews turned in the other direction, particularly in relation to homosexuality. They not only rejected any accommodation but entered the political arena to oppose the gains that gay people were making. They insisted that gay rights and recognition implied an assault on religion itself, even though other religious groups saw it differently.

By January 1975, eleven states had decriminalized consensual sodomy, typically as part of a general updating of the criminal code. California made a major breakthrough that year when it decriminalized consensual sodomy through stand-alone legislation on sex crimes. A flurry of other states followed as the decriminalization movement reached a peak.[53] But people who supported decriminalization often did so because they believed the government shouldn't be snooping into citizens' bedrooms; they didn't necessarily support extending protection to gay people against discrimination in employment or housing. In 1974, a referendum in the college town of Boulder, Colorado, overturned a gay rights ordinance passed by the local government, but the repeal got little national attention. Three years later, when a county commission in Miami-Dade, Florida, adopted an ordinance prohibiting discrimination in employment based on "affectional or sexual preference," the national attention intensified. The battle in Miami signaled the start of the religious right's countermobilization against gay rights.

The "Save our Children" campaign against Miami's ordinance brought together conservative political operatives with a coalition of Baptists, Catholics, and Orthodox Jews, led by a Baptist singer and former beauty queen, Anita Bryant, known nationally as the TV pitchwoman for "pure" Florida orange juice. The gay rights ordinance would protect gay teachers, among others. Bryant opposed it as infringing on her rights "as a citizen and a mother" to teach her children according to "God's moral code as stated in the Holy Scriptures." The opponents of the ordinance conjured up a picture, as one campaign ad put it, of a "hair-raising pattern of recruitment and outright seduction and molestation" by homosexuals that would only grow "if society approves laws granting legitimacy to the sexually perverted." The state's Democratic governor ("I would not want a known homosexual teaching my children") backed the campaign, as did the *Miami Herald*, which ran several stories about homosexual child molesters. When the voters went to the polls, they repealed the ordinance by more than a two-to-one margin, an outcome repeated within a year in referenda on gay rights in three other cities across the country.

Conservatives then mounted an initiative campaign in 1978 in California to ban homosexuals from teaching. By this time, however, gay organizations had mobilized, and their political strategists had learned from polling that rather than ask the public to support civil rights for gay people, they were better off framing the election around individual privacy. Two of the advisers obtained a private meeting to explain their case to Ronald Reagan, who was preparing to run for president. To the shock of both supporters and opponents of the anti-gay initiative, Reagan released a statement that the initiative could do "real mischief" and infringe "basic rights of privacy and perhaps even constitutional rights." Although the early polls had shown the initiative passing by a wide margin, the voters defeated it in November by a margin of 58 percent to 42 percent.

But the story of gay rights in California that month had a tragic side. A year earlier, San Francisco had elected an openly gay candidate, Harvey Milk, to its board of supervisors along with a mayor, George Moscone, who supported gay rights. Milk was the first openly gay man elected to public office anywhere in the United States, and the San Francisco board passed a gay rights ordinance. Three weeks after the vote on the state ballot initiative, a conservative member of that board, Dan White, who had resigned in protest over the city's policies, returned to the municipal offices with a gun and killed both Milk and Moscone. A jury refused to find White guilty of murder. His lawyer said he had been eating too many sugary foods—a claim that became known as the "Twinkie defense"—and he was convicted of voluntary manslaughter, for which he served five years in prison.[54]

A decade after Stonewall, gay people were no longer an invisible minority, at least in the big cities. The urban communities they had established had a rich variety of institutions and services oriented to their needs, including businesses of every kind as well as clinics, churches, social centers, and sports leagues. Cultural pluralism in America had long been thought of as a basis for ethnic, national, racial, and religious groups to get along. In metropolitan areas, pluralism now began to include sexual minorities. Gay men and lesbians were treated in some cities almost like an ethnic group to be courted by ambitious politicians.

But they had not overcome disapproval and hostility. Asked in surveys from 1973 to 1980 whether "sexual relations between two adults of the same sex" are right or wrong, about 70 percent of Americans consistently responded "always wrong," while only 11–15 percent said "not wrong at all."[55] The public was closely split, however, on whether those relations should be legal—and so were the states. As the 1970s ended, twenty-two states had decriminalized consensual sodomy (two other states had repealed their sodomy statutes but then reinstituted them).[56] The gay movement and its supporters had not persuaded the federal courts that the right to privacy recognized for heterosexuals should apply to same-sex partners, and the movement had not convinced the electorate that gays deserved civil rights protections in jobs and housing. But gay men and lesbians were a factor in politics, particularly within the Democratic Party; even their adversaries no longer dismissed them with a joke. The political and business world had to take them seriously. With the AIDS epidemic in the coming decade, sex would get serious in a different way, through an ordeal of suffering that would deepen gay identity and a sense of shared fate, even as it showed how far gay people had to go in gaining their fellow citizens' sympathy and support.

The New Centrality of Gender Politics

Some social movements are important in their own time but leave few deep and durable effects, while others are important both in their time and long after. The student movement, the antiwar movement, and the New Left of the 1960s fall in the first category. They were important in their time, but their footprints have been mostly washed away. That is why I don't write about "the Sixties" in general; some things have mattered in the long run more than others. The Black freedom struggle, the women's movement, and the gay rights movement fall in that category. They led to changes in law, consciousness, and social relations and caused a realignment of political forces that continues to shape America in the twenty-first century.[57] Other movements, particularly the environmental and disability rights movements, have also had important long-run consequences. I have not tried to give an exhaustive account of all the transformations since the mid-twentieth century; I've focused only on what I see as the central through-line stemming from the contradiction that has roiled America from the beginning, the contradiction between freedom and social subordination.

The social movements' lasting effects and continuing significance have arisen from both their achievements and their incompleteness. No one should take the achievements lightly. They have allowed millions of Americans who are not straight white men to enjoy richer and freer lives than had ever been open to them before. In so doing, they have brought American realities closer to the aspirations of the American Creed. But for a variety of reasons—the limits of reforms, structural changes in the economy, and a conservative countermobilization that gained power in the 1980s—the movements have remained incomplete. In some ways they have also hurt their own political fortunes, as even worthy movements often do.

During the 1970s and following decades, the limits of reform affected how women fared economically. Many women, especially the college educated, benefited from breakthroughs in civil rights law, higher education, and the professions. But other women fared poorly in an economy where the best opportunities they could find were low-wage service jobs. While more women advanced in professional fields, the status of some sex-segregated occupations like secretarial work fell. Congress never remedied the failure of the 1963 Equal Pay Act to require equal pay for jobs of comparable worth. After Nixon's veto of a national childcare program in 1971, Congress never passed another general program to finance childcare. Unionization might have improved pay and benefits for service-sector jobs, and Democrats did for the first time give public employees the right to organize. In 1962 President Kennedy issued an executive order allowing federal employees to join unions, and many state and local governments did the same for their employees. But despite their large congressional majorities in the mid-1960s, Democrats did nothing to make organizing easier in the private economy; in 1965 the Senate blocked repeal of a key provision of Taft-Hartley that enabled states to pass right-to-work laws undermining unions. Unions had been weak in the private service economy and they stayed that way, to the disadvantage of working women.

These limits of American labor and social policy partly explain why one of the principal reforms of the 1970s proved economically disastrous for many women. No-fault divorce laws treated husbands and wives equally in some respects, such as the division of assets accumulated during marriage, but in practice the effects were anything but equal. The husband's earning capacity was typically greater than that of his wife, who often had been out of the labor force for years. After divorce, men became single, while women often became single mothers, and many men failed to make child support payments. Even before the no-fault laws, courts were already awarding women alimony less frequently and in smaller amounts. Under earlier divorce laws, though, if a couple with children owned a home, the court usually awarded the house to the wife along with custody of the children. But under no-fault laws, the home, which usually represented most of the couple's wealth, had to be sold to allow for an equal division of their assets, which forced the wife and children to move. Research showed that in the first year after divorce, the standard of living for divorced women with minor children plunged by an average of 73 percent, while it rose 42 percent for their former husbands.[58] No-fault divorce did benefit women by making it easier for them to escape unhappy marriages; indeed, in states that changed their divorce laws, female suicide dropped by 8–16 percent, and the murder rate of women by their partners declined by 10 percent. But rising divorce rates, together with continuing inequalities in the labor market, contributed to what sociologists began to call the "feminization of poverty," the rising proportion of women in the poor population.[59]

A growing class divide also separated married women who worked for pay from stay-at-home wives. From the early 1960s to the late 1970s, the increase in wives working outside the home took place almost entirely among women with a better-educated (and higher-earning) husband. In 1962, 34 percent of wives whose husbands had only a grade-school education worked for pay, compared to 38 percent of women whose husbands attended college. But by 1978, while no change had occurred among those with grade-school-educated husbands, the proportion with paying jobs among married women with a college-educated husband had jumped to 65 percent. That difference suggests the change was driven by choice—

the search for the more complete life championed by Friedan—rather than financial necessity. Surveys also indicated that better-educated wives no longer took the same pleasure in housework. In 1957, college-educated wives expressed only slightly less satisfaction than the grade-school educated in doing housework, but by 1976 the college-educated wives were far less likely to say they enjoyed it. If a woman had little education, she was likely to find homemaking more attractive than any job she could get. College-educated women had wider career opportunities and more readily abandoned the role of stay-at-home wife. That choice, however, meant that the remaining full-time homemakers lost social status.[60]

These changes in the economic situation and social standing of women in different family and class positions help explain the divided response of American women to the ERA. Two women's movements developed in the United States—a feminist movement and an antifeminist movement—and they responded to social change in opposite ways. While feminists welcomed women's growing opportunities outside the home and favored policies to protect their rights as equals in the economy, antifeminists held ever more tightly to the traditional role of women as wives and mothers and continued to count on men as breadwinners.[61]

The battle over the ERA reflected these divisions and took on a symbolic importance during the 1970s that was far out of proportion to its likely practical effects. Ratification of the ERA, the political scientist (and ERA supporter) Jane Mansbridge argues, probably would not have produced the results that activists on either side expected. This was partly because the Supreme Court began using the Fourteenth Amendment "to declare unconstitutional almost all the laws and practices that Congress had intended to make unconstitutional when it passed the ERA in 1972. The exceptions were laws and practices that most Americans approved. Thus, by the late 1970s it was hard to show that the ERA would have made any of the substantive changes that most Americans favored." The entire ERA debate was enveloped in a thick fog of misunderstanding. Arguing for the amendment, supporters cited the fact that women still earned only 59 percent as much as men. That was true but irrelevant. The amendment applied only to state action and was unlikely to be interpreted by the courts as a basis for intervening in private wages. Supporters also said the ERA would mean women would be subject to the draft and, like men, could be sent into combat. But Americans at that time did not approve of that possibility, and the Supreme Court probably would not have interpreted the amendment as limiting the war-powers provision of the Constitution.[62]

The opposition to the ERA, led by the conservative activist Phyllis Schlafly, who founded Stop ERA in 1972, also made dubious claims in its efforts to rally women. The most important of these claims was that the ERA would end husbands' common-law obligations to support their wives. As long as a married couple lived together, however, courts did not enforce standards for a husband's support of his wife, and if a couple broke up, state laws regarding separation and divorce applied. Rather than ending a husband's duty to support his former wife, courts were likely to interpret the ERA as requiring that the obligations of former spouses depend on their ability to pay. To satisfy the amendment, judges would probably have imposed the same obligation on a working wife who had supported a homemaking husband (not a common situation) as they imposed on a working husband who had supported a homemaking wife (a much more common situation). In other words, contrary to Schlafly, the ERA was unlikely to lead courts to reduce husbands' obligations beyond what had already happened through no-fault divorce and the decline of alimony.[63]

But that troubling experience had already increased many women's anxieties. What if the ERA encouraged courts and legislators to believe that women could support themselves and their children just as well as men, when in fact they could not? Moreover, wasn't the ERA being promoted by a radical feminist movement that was hostile to marriage and full-time homemaking? By attacking marriage as "slavery" and "legal whoredom," radical feminists had given Schlafly material to work with. For many women who could not have sustained their living standards on their own, marriage was an economic necessity. "What was at stake in the battle over the ERA," the critic Barbara Ehrenreich writes, "was the *legitimacy* of women's claim on men's incomes, and for this there was reason enough to fear—and to judge from the intensity of the opposition, fear enough to abandon reason."[64]

Republicans had once been the primary supporters of the ERA; they were also more likely than Democrats to welcome *Roe v. Wade*. Conservatives like Reagan had signed laws liberalizing abortion and divorce; Reagan even helped defeat an anti-gay California initiative. But as the 1970s went on, the sides were lining up in a new way. Together with the anti-gay movement led by Anita Bryant, the Stop ERA movement became the vanguard for the religious right in the battle for "traditional family values" that became a central theme for Republicans. In 1980, for first time since 1936, Republicans dropped support for the ERA from their party platform. That same year, Democrats for the first time included gay rights in their party platform. The two changes were representative of the shifting positions of the parties and the increased centrality of gender politics in national political alignments. The 1980 presidential election was also the first with a clear gender gap in voting; men favored Republicans, while women inclined toward Democrats despite the growing conservatism of full-time homemakers.

Historians have tended to emphasize racial politics as critical to the realignment of parties in the late twentieth century, but gender politics became equally important. Since Republicans could use homosexuality and abortion to appeal to evangelical Christians, those issues fit perfectly into the party's long-standing efforts to win the South. Family values would give conservatives a moral high ground that race did not. The defense of the traditional family and traditional ideas of masculinity and femininity would become central to the identity conservatives sought to project in national politics. Identity politics was just as much a phenomenon of the right as of the left.

CHAPTER FOUR
Half a Counterrevolution

Don't pay any attention to what those little shits on the campuses do. The great beast is the reactionary element in the country.

—LYNDON JOHNSON TO GEORGE BALL, 1965[1]

The whole secret of politics [is] knowing who hates who.

—KEVIN PHILLIPS TO GARRY WILLS, 1968[2]

IF LIBERALS HAD SET OUT to enrage the great beast that Lyndon Johnson was worried about, they couldn't have done better. Liberal decisions by the Supreme Court, Johnson's own Great Society programs, the civil rights and other progressive movements, greater openness to sexual alternatives—what was there about the direction of American politics and culture for conservatives not to hate? And it wasn't just the "reactionary element." The progressive changes of the 1960s and 1970s also alienated working- and middle-class whites who had been a vital part of the coalition that brought the Democratic Party to power. What ensued seems, in retrospect, all too predictable: a backlash-driven conservative ascendancy, leading first to the election of Richard Nixon in 1968, then to the "Reagan Revolution" of the 1980s, and in 1994 to yet another "Republican

Revolution" with the takeover of the House of Representatives led by Newt Gingrich.

The rise of conservatism, its journey to the peaks of national power, dominates narratives of the last third of the twentieth century. If that had been the whole story, conservatives should have completely reversed liberal and progressive change, but what they accomplished does not match what they set out to do. They were unable, and sometimes unwilling when they held office, to repeal liberal programs and policies they had long opposed. Before Medicare passed in 1965, Ronald Reagan recorded a speech warning that if Americans did not rise up against the pending bill, "you and I are going to spend our sunset years telling our children, and our children's children, what it once was like in America when men were free."[3] As president, though, Reagan did not try to abolish Medicare—he signed some modest reforms of its hospital payment rules—one of many accommodations that he and other conservative leaders made. Despite ten consecutive Supreme Court appointments by Republican presidents between 1969 and 1991, major elements of the liberal rights revolution and the progressive project remained in place, and some even advanced. However much conservatives deplored the direction of cultural change, they could not do much about it. They never came close to returning America to the social world of the 1950s. Liberalism retained more support and proved far more resilient than the narrative of backlash-driven conservative triumph suggests.

Yet conservatives did succeed in significant ways. They created a coherent political movement by fusing old but reinvigorated opponents of the modern liberal state together with new forces of racial, cultural, and corporate backlash. They summoned new intellectual and moral energies in law, economics, and religion. They elected legislators, governors, presidents. Still, they got just half a counterrevolution, which is not to say that all conservatives got half a loaf. Some who supported the half-turn right got a lot more, and many got nothing.

The surprise was where they had their biggest impact. The right-wing counterattack hindered but did not reverse the racial and cultural transformation of American society that began in the 1960s. It had its greatest success in attacking the power of what by the late 1970s was the least militant element in the liberal coalition—the unions. Over the next decade, capital achieved a degree of control over labor it had not enjoyed since the 1920s. The growing class divide was also reflected in a massive increase in incarceration, which had a devastating impact on the Black poor even as the Black middle class expanded. National policy in areas like taxation and antitrust fostered increasing concentrations of wealth and economic power. The backlash against the liberalism of the 1960s, intensified by an economic crisis in the 1970s, created political opportunity for the right, and it used that opportunity mainly for purposes it had been pursuing since the New Deal.

The Conservative Project and Political Realignment

During the 1950s, American conservatives faced two daunting obstacles to their political ambitions. The first was that they controlled neither of the two major parties at the national level. The Republican Party under President Eisenhower largely accepted the legacies of the New Deal and looked to compromise with liberals. While the great reserve of conservative votes lay in the white South, political power in the region had belonged to the Democrats since the end of Reconstruction. The conservative road to power, as some Republicans saw even in the 1950s, lay through Dixie, persuading white Southerners to join conservative Republicans outside the South.[4] But the hope of enlisting Southern whites in the election of a conservative Republican president came to nothing in 1960, when the Republican presidential nomination went to Eisenhower's vice president, Richard Nixon, who then lost to John F. Kennedy. Conservatives did not consider Nixon one of their own, unlike Arizona Senator Barry Goldwater, whom many conservatives already looked to in 1960 to lead them out of the wilderness.

The second obstacle to conservative power was the troublesome heritage of the right-wing past. Republicans had the reputation of being the party of the rich, and they continued to be haunted by the failure of their free-market policies to alleviate the Great Depression after the stock market crash in 1929. The right also had a long history of anti-Catholicism and anti-Semitism as well as overt anti-Black racism. Conservatives needed a fresh image, free of those past associations, to convince Americans they had broken from the untenable aspects of the Old Right. The challenge lay in fashioning that new identity while also winning over the white South, which meant—not to put too fine a point on it—they would have to appeal to racists without appearing to be racist, lest they lose too many Republican moderates and other votes outside the South.

Transforming the party of Lincoln into a party attractive to white Southerners would be no easy trick. It meant abandoning not only the party's historic identity but also the racial liberalism of many of its current leaders. The vast distance Republicans had to travel to become the party of the white South may be summed up in the career of Earl Warren, chief justice of the U.S. Supreme Court from 1953 to 1969. Warren led the Court through the most liberal period in its history, beginning with *Brown v. Board of Education*, which made him a target of conservative fury. Other pathbreaking decisions by the Warren Court also enraged conservatives: The justices declared that interracial couples had a constitutional right to marry; banned officially organized prayer from the public schools; recognized the constitutional rights of criminal defendants, including a right to counsel if they could not afford an attorney; and provided broad protections to political dissent. Billboards in the South and other conservative areas demanded Warren's impeachment. Before serving on the Court, however, he had been one of the Republican Party's most popular figures. Elected three times as governor of California by overwhelming margins, he was the party's candidate for vice president in 1948 in the election that Thomas E. Dewey narrowly lost to Harry Truman. Running for the presidential nomination in 1952, Warren had no chance once a candidate with a similar political profile and an even wider appeal entered the race. That was the former commander of Allied forces in Europe, General Dwight Eisenhower, who in his first year in office appointed Warren as Chief Justice, assuming him to be a like-minded, middle-of-the-road Republican, a mistake he later regretted.[5]

At that time, Republicans had hardly any presence in the South. The party had none of the region's major elected offices and virtually no organization; only one out of every eleven Southerners identified as a Republican. Under Eisenhower, Republicans began building a party in the region, originally aiming to attract racially moderate, middle-class whites in the peripheral Southern states. This was the beginning of what became the Republicans' "Southern Strategy" and, ironically, the undoing of the center-right Republicanism Eisenhower stood for.[6]

The Warren Court's school desegregation decision drove politics in the South farther right. During the decade after *Brown*, when Southern politics was fought out almost entirely within the Democratic Party, unreconstructed white segregationists dedicated to "massive resistance" to federal authority regularly defeated moderates. After George Wallace lost the Alabama gubernatorial primary to a hardline racist in 1958, he said, "Well, boys, no other son-of-a-bitch will ever outn____r me again."[7] Four years later he race-baited his way to victory, and at his inauguration, standing where Jefferson Davis took office as president of the Confederacy, he famously pledged, "Segregation now! Segregation tomorrow! Segregation forever!" As the historian Michael Klarman notes about Southern politics in this period, "Most officials, including those who were ordinarily inclined toward racial moderation, became more extremist to survive, and those few who resisted were generally destroyed."[8]

The white South's turn to defiance did not put off the nation's emerging intellectual and political leaders on the right. Far from it: They themselves were none too enamored of the federal government, and they took up the Southern cause of states' rights as their own. No publication played a greater role than *National Review* in shaping the postwar conservative movement, and no one played a greater role in shaping *National Review* than William F. Buckley, who was just 29 years old when he founded the magazine in 1955 and became its editor and sole owner. (Buckley's family had Texas oil money, although he grew up on a grand estate in Connecticut and went to Yale.) Thirty years later, President Reagan would say that when "pundits and analysts" understood "the enormous force and deep roots of the conservative movement," they would realize that Buckley was "perhaps the most influential journalist and intellectual in our era."[9]

Buckley exercised his influence in part by using *National Review* to define what belonged in a "responsible" conservative movement and what should be excluded from it. He would have nothing to do with the old anti-Catholicism and anti-Semitism; he was a devout Catholic and, from his undergraduate days at Yale, rejected anti-Semitism. But he welcomed into *National Review*'s pages the apologists of the white South, and the magazine defended Southern resistance to racial integration. While its editorials mostly made the Southern case on states' rights grounds, Buckley argued in an August 1957 editorial ("Why the South Must Prevail") that nothing less than the claims of the "advanced race" and "civilization" were at stake:

> The central question that emerges . . . is whether the white community in the South is entitled to take such measures as are necessary to prevail, politically and culturally, in areas in which it does not predominate numerically. The sobering answer is *Yes*—the white community is so entitled because, for the time being, it is the advanced race. . . . The question, as far as the white community is concerned, is whether the claims of civilization supersede those of universal suffrage. . . . *National Review* believes that the South's premises are correct.[10]

Some internal dissent in the magazine notwithstanding, the editorial fit Buckley's brand: a brash willingness to defy polite conventions. In a Publisher's Statement for the first issue, he wrote that the magazine "stands athwart history, yelling Stop, at a time when no one is inclined to do so, or to have much patience with those who do." Buckley called himself an "intellectual revolutionary" and believed that conservatives were America's true nonconformists, boldly standing up to the "liberal order."[11] This self-conception became central to the identity of generations of conservatives who have flattered themselves about how nonconformist and courageous they are in fighting for tradition and privilege.

After Nixon's 1960 defeat, the argument that Republicans should look South received more attention within the party. "We're not going to get the Negro vote as a bloc in 1964 and 1968, so we ought to go hunting where the ducks are," Goldwater told a 1961 meeting of the Republican National Committee. He had already begun hunting for those ducks in 1959, when he gave speeches in the South attacking the Supreme Court's decision in *Brown* and supporting state resistance to federal authority.[12]

As a national candidate, Goldwater had an appeal to conservatives that no race-baiting Southerner could have. He made the case against federal intrusion not on racial grounds—he insisted he was personally in favor of racial integration—but on principles of constitutional limitation. A tireless proselytizer for the conservative faith who seemed indifferent to popularity, he was believable as a conviction politician. His 1960 book *The Conscience of a Conservative*, ghostwritten by Buckley's close friend and brother-in-law L. Brent Bozell, called for an unyielding conservatism. *Conscience* criticized Eisenhower for saying he was "conservative when it comes to economic problems but liberal when it comes to human problems," and Nixon for saying Republican candidates "should be economic conservatives, but conservatives with a heart." Goldwater's conservatism came without qualifications, apologies, or exceptions. Black children, he said, did not have a civil right to attend integrated schools under federal law because the Constitution did not give the federal government any power in education.[13] In 1964, he voted against the Civil Rights Act, further endearing himself to the South in the year that he won the Republican presidential nomination.

Goldwater's version of the Southern Strategy was a fiasco in 1964. He lost to Johnson in a landslide, carrying only five Deep South states besides Arizona. But he set the pattern for Republican deniability on racism: signaling support for the white South without using overtly racist language or endorsing segregation. The 1964 election brought the first Great White Switch, the first time white Southerners voted more Republican than Democratic in a presidential election.[14] It also decisively shifted the American public's perception of the two parties. As late as 1962, surveys showed Americans did not see a clear difference on racial liberalism between the parties, but Johnson versus Goldwater cleared that up. From 1964 on, Americans identified Democrats as the party more favorable to Blacks. This was also the period when congressional voting patterns changed. According to a study of Senate voting, Republicans had been more liberal on race until the 1958 elections, the two parties were relatively close from 1959 to 1964, and then Democrats became the more racially liberal party, with a large gap opening up in the 1970s. The pattern in the House was similar.[15]

The implications of the partisan shift in racial liberalism for political realignment became clear after the dust settled on the 1968 presidential election. The election was a three-way race. Nixon made a Lazarus-like return from the political grave as the Republican nominee; the liberal Hubert Humphrey, Johnson's vice president, was the Democratic candidate; and George Wallace ran as a third-party populist, claiming there wasn't a "dime's worth of difference" between the two major parties and that the elites looked down their noses at white working people. Wallace made inroads in the North but, like Goldwater, won only five Deep South states. The outer South went to Nixon, who adopted a moderate position on racial issues. Unlike Goldwater and future presidents Reagan and George H. W. Bush, Nixon had supported the major civil rights legislation of the 1960s. While not reversing his previous positions, he said he would appoint conservative judges, called for "law and order," saw no need for any further civil rights legislation, and suggested that he would go easy on enforcement of desegregation. Nixon eked out a narrow victory over Humphrey, 43.4 percent to 42.7 percent of the popular vote.

But the combined Wallace and Nixon vote, adding up to 57 percent, was stunning. In an influential postmortem to 1968, *The Emerging Republican Majority*, Republican analyst and Nixon campaign aide Kevin Phillips saw a historic watershed: "This repudiation visited upon the Democratic Party for its ambitious social programming, and inability to handle the urban and Negro revolutions was comparable in scope to that given conservative Republicanism in 1932 for its failure to cope with the economic crisis of the Depression."[16]

The Emerging Republican Majority was right about the changing regional basis of the parties. The new Republican base, Phillips argued, lay in the

"Sunbelt," a term he coined for the region stretching from the South through the Southwest to California.[17] His analysis became the basis for public discussion of "Nixon's Southern Strategy" (as though Nixon had invented it) and the perception that the 1968 election represented the end of the postwar liberal era.

But 1968 was no 1932. It was not a turning point in national policy comparable to the coming of the New Deal. In fact, much of what people now believe happened under Kennedy and Johnson took place under Nixon, and much of what people associate with the 1960s did not happen until the 1970s. That was partly because Democrats continued to control Congress, liberal influence did not disappear from the courts, and the consumer and environmental movements were gaining momentum just as Nixon took office. But it was also because Nixon did not carry out a Southern Strategy in policymaking. Despite his rhetorical appeals to conservative backlash—and despite conservative appointments to the Supreme Court—he was responsible for major liberal initiatives on a wide range of issues, perhaps most surprisingly Southern school integration and affirmative action.

As president, Nixon did enough to show that he was a friend of the South to retain Southern support, but he didn't produce the radical reversal in national policy that white Southerners wanted. In his first year, he had two Supreme Court seats to fill. To replace the retiring Earl Warren as chief justice, Nixon appointed a conservative Minnesota judge, Warren Burger. To fill the second seat, he first nominated one conservative white Southerner whom the Senate rejected, and then a second conservative white Southerner, whom the Senate also rejected. His third choice, whom the Senate confirmed, was Harry Blackmun, a Minnesotan who would at first vote so closely with Burger that the two were called the Minnesota Twins. (Blackmun, however, gradually shifted to the Court's liberal wing, one of several Republican judicial miscalculations.) In July 1969 the Nixon administration sought to mollify a powerful Mississippi senator before an important vote on defense policy by delaying the timetable for integrating schools in Mississippi. But in October the Supreme Court rejected any delay. "The obligation of every school district," the Court declared, "is to terminate dual school systems at once and to operate now and hereafter only unitary schools." Burger wrote the Court's unanimous opinion.[18]

In response, Nixon not only agreed to abide by the Court's ruling but proceeded to oversee school desegregation in the South. *Brown v. Board of Education*, he declared, was decided correctly in "both constitutional and human terms," but he believed the law required only that the government end *de jure* segregation, that is, segregation resulting directly from action by the government. To replace dual school systems with unitary systems for fall 1970, he set up interracial committees in the Southern states, telling his aides, however, that "high profile, overly aggressive" action would only "make the problem worse." Bragging about this effort would "get us no votes in the North while gravely abrading the entire South." His subordinates were "not [to] make a big deal of all we're doing.... Low profile is the key." When the aide in charge of the effort told the president that he was trying to keep liberals "convinced we are doing what the Court requires, and our conservative Southern friends convinced that we are not doing any more than the Court requires," Nixon responded: "*Good! Keep it up.*"[19]

And that is how the South came to desegregate its public schools. When Nixon took office in 1969, only 186,000 out of three million Black children in the South attended integrated schools; by the fall of 1970, 2.6 million did so. As *New York Times* columnist Tom Wicker wrote two decades later, "Richard Nixon received little credit then, and probably gets less today, for having overseen—indeed, planned and carried out—more school desegregation than any other president, and for putting an end, at last, to dual school systems in the South."[20]

Moreover, Nixon personally made the decision in 1970 to accept rather than fight a court ruling denying tax exemptions to the whites-only, private Christian academies established in the South as an alternative to the public schools.[21] While that decision infuriated white Southerners, Nixon angered Black leaders and many liberals by denouncing the busing of school children across district lines, ordered by courts to achieve integration primarily in metropolitan areas in the North and West. Court-ordered school busing aroused intense opposition and had little support; surveys consistently showed that 85 percent or more of whites opposed it, while Blacks were evenly divided. The issue eventually faded after the Supreme Court struck down a lower court order for metropolitan busing in Detroit in 1974.[22]

In two other areas, Nixon adopted affirmative-action policies that conservatives and many unionized white workers opposed as illegitimate racial preferences. "Affirmative action" had come up as a policy during the Kennedy administration, but neither Kennedy nor Johnson did much to carry it out beyond the federal civil service. Under Nixon, the government began using its power to set rules for federal contractors to open up high-paid jobs in the construction industry that craft unions had long hoarded for whites by limiting access to apprenticeships. (Blacks did have jobs in construction, but in the low-paid "trowel" trades.) Led by Secretary George Shultz, the Labor Department put into effect a model for minority hiring called the "Philadelphia Plan," which had initially been devised under Johnson but dropped in a dispute over whether it was legal under the Civil Rights Act's express prohibition of racial quotas. Under a revised plan, unions would have to meet "goals and timetables" for Black and other minority hiring. (The plan made no mention of women.) For example, out of 2,335 plumbers and pipefitters in the five-county Philadelphia area, only twelve were minority. The Philadelphia Plan set a minority hiring goal of 5–8 percent in 1970, rising to 22–26 percent by 1973. Employers, unions, and conservatives denounced the plan as setting just the kind of quotas that the Civil Rights Act forbade, though the administration insisted a "goal" was only a target and therefore legally distinct from a "quota"; no penalties would be imposed as long as there had been a "good faith effort" to reach the target. Years later, challenged on his role in establishing racial quotas in employment, Shultz responded that in the construction industry, "We found a quota system. It was there. It was zero."[23]

Nixon was not unhappy about a policy that pitted the NAACP against the AFL-CIO, and some suggest his motives for instituting affirmative action were political, which would hardly be a shocker. But for a president who was courting hard-hat workers for his re-election, the Philadelphia Plan was counterproductive, and his administration did not implement it consistently across the country. Enforcement was limited even in Philadelphia itself. In 1972, however, Nixon signed the Equal Employment Opportunity Act, which enabled the EEOC to file dozens of suits against the nation's biggest companies to get them to increase minority hiring. The courts did what federal administrative agencies could not do directly. By the mid-1970s, affirmative action in the form of goals and timetables had been institutionalized.[24]

The second area in which Nixon introduced racial preference was through minority set-asides in federal contracting, as a way of spurring minority-owned business. "It's no longer enough that white-owned enterprises employ greater numbers of Negroes," he said during the 1968 campaign. "This is needed, yes—but it has to be accompanied by an expansion of black ownership, of black capitalism," which would lead to "black pride, black jobs, black opportunity and, yes, black power in the best, the constructive sense of that often misapplied term." Nixon created an Office of

Minority Business Enterprise in the Department of Commerce and increased federal contracting with minority-owned firms and deposits of federal funds in minority-owned banks.[25]

Nixon's interest in creating minority jobs and businesses reflected a commitment to capitalism as the Republican answer to progressive policies. In private, he was no racial egalitarian; he told his aides Blacks were racially inferior. Yet he also believed in creating opportunity for those who could take advantage of it. He said to one aide: "It's clear that not everybody is equal, but we must ensure that anyone might go to the top."[26] As a man who had climbed to the top himself, he had sympathy with strivers and supported policies that opened a path for the exceptionally talented. Without subscribing to a liberal belief in equality, he had a surprising willingness to adopt policies like affirmative action that his liberal predecessors had been unwilling or unable to carry out.

Perhaps Nixon's biggest break with conservative orthodoxy was his support for a national guaranteed income (what today might be called a universal basic income) to replace Aid to Families with Dependent Children (AFDC), the welfare program that had exploded in size in the late 1960s with growing numbers of poor single-mother families. Under AFDC, recipients lost all public benefits, often including health care, if they took a paying job, a clear disincentive for work. Some of Nixon's advisers, such as Daniel P. Moynihan, believed AFDC also undermined stable families by discouraging marriages, which would cost recipients their eligibility. Nixon's Family Assistance Plan would have changed those incentives by allowing recipients to continue receiving benefits on a downward sliding scale as their family earnings increased. Instead of cutting back welfare by curbing "abuses"—the kind of welfare policy conservatives usually favored—the plan would have extended aid to the working poor. A kind of negative income tax, it called for a national income floor, not counting food stamps, of $1,600 (equal to $13,337 in 2024 dollars), with benefits extended to the working poor with earnings up to $3,920 ($32,676 in 2024 dollars).[27] By creating a national minimum, it would have sharply increased incomes for poor Blacks in Southern states and likely slowed migration to the North and West.

Although liberal policy advisers had developed the proposal under Johnson, it was Nixon who took it up. He was attracted by its boldness. It wasn't a reversal of the war on poverty but a new version that would have his signature on it. The basic proposition was that what the poor needed was more money and the right incentives, not more social services (an "incomes strategy," as Moynihan and others called it, as opposed to a "services strategy"). Astonishingly for so radical a change, the Family Assistance Plan passed the House of Representatives with about equal levels of Democratic and Republican support, only to die in the Senate mainly at the hands of conservatives on the Finance Committee, who saw the proposed income supplements to the working poor as a huge expansion of the welfare rolls. Liberals in the Senate, some of whom planned to run for the Democratic nomination in 1972, were ambivalent. Some favored the plan, others denounced it, and many just distrusted anything proposed by Nixon.[28]

Although he failed to establish a national floor for income, Nixon signed major expansions of both Medicare and Social Security in 1972, including a 20 percent increase in Social Security benefits and the indexing of those benefits to inflation, which became hugely important when inflation took off a few years later. He also signed legislation establishing a new program, Supplemental Security Income, which provided income on a national basis to the aged, blind, and disabled poor, superseding uneven state income support for those highly vulnerable groups. While these policies enlarged the American welfare state, Nixon's Supreme Court appointments were bringing to an end a line of Warren Court decisions that had expanded the rights of the poor and provided procedural safeguards to welfare beneficiaries. In addition to Burger and Blackmun, Nixon also appointed two other justices, William Rehnquist and Lewis F. Powell Jr. By the time both were seated, in January 1972, antipoverty lawyers had lost any hope that the Burger Court would give welfare rights a stronger foundation by recognizing a constitutional right to a guaranteed minimum subsistence.[29]

Nixon's Family Assistance Plan was one of several efforts he made to get out in front of liberal pressures for reform with his own alternative. Environmental protection and health-care reform illustrate the pattern. Amid rising concern about pollution, Nixon and congressional Democrats agreed to a new Environmental Protection Agency, merging programs from various departments. He signed the landmark National Environmental Policy Act in 1969 and Clean Air Act of 1970 as well as the legislation that created the Occupational Safety and Health Administration, the Consumer Product Safety Commission, the National Traffic Safety Administration, and the Mine Safety and Health Administration. Together with affirmative action, these measures created "the new social regulation," a source of dismay to free-market conservatives. Under Kennedy and Johnson, Congress had passed some regulatory measures in areas like auto safety, air pollution, cigarette labeling, and truth in lending. But the new regulatory apparatus created under Nixon amounted to the greatest expansion of federal authority over the economy since the New Deal.

In 1971, to counter Democrats led by Senator Ted Kennedy, who were calling for national health insurance, Nixon offered his own national health insurance plan, which he expanded in a second proposal in 1974. Under his approach, employers would be required to insure their workers and dependents, while the federal government would run a public program for everyone not otherwise covered. The government program would be broad in scope and have no income limits on eligibility. On February 5, 1974, just before sending the program to Congress, Nixon declared that comprehensive health insurance was "an idea whose time has come." Its time might have come that year if he had survived the Watergate scandal, but his resignation on August 6, 1974, prevented any final negotiation with congressional Democrats.[30]

At a time when Nixon was enlarging the Vietnam War into Cambodia and denouncing protesters as "bums" and "thugs," liberals were not inclined to give him credit for his domestic policies. And when the facts came tumbling out in 1973 and 1974 that White House officials had directed the Watergate break-in at Democratic Party headquarters and Nixon had conspired in the cover-up, the news confirmed all the suspicions liberals had about Nixon ever since his first congressional campaign in 1946. He was a cunning and devious politician who had long played a double game. But what liberals didn't appreciate was that he was playing that double game with conservatives too, appealing to racial backlash while pursuing more liberal policies. As one of Nixon's liberal aides later put it, his civil rights policy "was for the most part operationally progressive but obscured by clouds of retrogressive rhetoric."[31] Like most liberals then and later, some historians have been so distracted by the political symbolism that they have ignored the policy substance.

Since Nixon's greatest passions were in foreign policy, he may have adopted liberal domestic positions because he believed their popularity would give him a free hand in conducting foreign relations.[32] If that calculation lay behind his choices, it could only have been because the political winds were still blowing in a liberal direction after Nixon's election, and his presidency did not end the liberalism of the 1960s.

But he did more than go with the flow. His proposals for a national guaranteed income and national health insurance were the domestic equivalents of his decision to go to China and pursue détente with the Soviet

Union. He liked the idea that he would be the American equivalent of Benjamin Disraeli, the nineteenth-century British prime minister who, by embracing reforms, stole some of the Liberal Party's thunder and won working-class support for his own Conservatives. If Nixon's Family Assistance Plan and national health insurance plan had been enacted, he would properly be recognized as the American Disraeli. Republicans had ridden the Southern Strategy to the White House, but without the conservative triumph in ideology and national policy that they expected from it.

The Conservative Take-Off (1): Religion

Two independent developments propelled the take-off of the conservative movement as a force for ideological change in the mid- to late 1970s. The first was the growing cultural as well as racial backlash against contemporary liberalism, which contributed to the rise of conservative evangelicalism and opposition to feminism and gay rights. The second was an economic crisis that ended three decades of stable growth and widely shared prosperity. Like the Democrats' embrace of racial liberalism in the 1960s, the economic tumult of the 1970s created new political opportunities for the right, particularly for business interests and conservative intellectuals who found newly receptive ears for their old case against the modern liberal state. Together, these religiously and economically based forces gave conservatism a double thrust, driving an ideological shift first within the Republican Party, and then in national politics when Reagan became the Republicans' winning presidential candidate in 1980.

The 1970s were a period of religious realignment on political lines. Instead of being organized primarily around the three major faith communities—Protestant, Catholic, and Jewish—religious divisions on public issues began to fall along a liberal-versus-conservative axis. Liberal Protestants, liberal Catholics, and liberal Jews often aligned in support of changes demanded by the era's protest movements, while conservative Protestants and Catholics (and on occasion right-leaning Jews) joined in a cross-denominational alliance, variously called the religious right, the Christian right, or the new Christian right.[33]

The rise of the religious right took place amid a sharp decline in religiosity that began in the mid-1960s. In 1952, the proportion of Americans telling pollsters that religion was personally "very important" to them stood at 75 percent. That figure was still 70 percent in 1965, but it dropped to 52 percent by 1978. Weekly churchgoing also declined, primarily among baby boomers, whose attendance at church throughout their lives has run 25–30 percent lower than their parents' at the same ages. Just as many baby boomers rejected their elders' views on such matters as premarital sex, many abandoned the previous generation's churchgoing practices. The drop in churchgoing affected both Catholics and mainline Protestants, but evangelicals defied the trend. The share of Americans identifying with an evangelical denomination increased from 23 percent in the early 1970s to 28 percent in the mid-1990s (before falling back to 24 percent by 2008). The strengthening of evangelicalism was especially significant in light of the weakening of mainline Protestantism. Of 100 Americans on an average Sunday, the number going to an evangelical church rose from 12 to 15 between the early 1970s and mid-1980s, while the number going to a mainline Protestant church dropped from 10 to 8 (and continued falling into the early 2000s).[34]

The growth in evangelical Christianity does not correspond to any shift in public opinion about evangelical theological doctrine. The fraction of Americans believing in the literal truth of scripture declined throughout the 1970s and 1980s (and continued to do so).[35] An alternative sociological explanation for the increased share of evangelicals in the population points to demography and evangelical culture. Evangelical women born before 1973 had more children, and had them at an earlier age, than women in other denominations; evangelical families were also more successful than others in keeping their children within the faith. As the sociologists who make this argument put it, "Conservative denominations have grown their own."[36]

Evangelicalism, moreover, became a broad cultural and political movement that breached denominational boundaries. As evangelicals from early in the twentieth century rejected secular and liberal trends in the larger culture, they built their own institutions, not just churches and seminaries but schools and colleges, Bible camps and institutes, missionary societies, publications and radio stations. In the 1970s, they continued investing in cultural institutions with the creation of Christian bookstores, cable television broadcasting, film and video production and distribution, and a Christian consumer marketplace. Instead of belonging to a particular denomination, a growing number of evangelicals identified themselves only as "Christian," attended nondenominational megachurches, listened to Christian contemporary music and other Christian media, and developed an identity as conservative Christians in opposition to the liberal mainstream culture, sometimes apart from any regular churchgoing. In short, evangelicals developed their own counterculture—or what might better be thought of as a counter-counterculture, since they were fighting the mainstream's absorption of countercultural ideas of the 1960s.[37] Surveys vary considerably in estimates of the evangelical population because of differences in definitions and the cultural reach of evangelicalism beyond evangelical denominations. But while the exact dimensions are unclear, there was unquestionably a surge beginning in the 1970s in both the numbers and mobilization of evangelicals. That surge peaked two decades later before falling off.[38]

In the mid-1970s, evangelicals were a politically diverse population, with substantial numbers of moderates and even some progressives. They included many people who were culturally conservative but politically inactive, seeking primarily to insulate their families from dominant cultural and social trends. During the early nineteenth century, in the period known as the Second Great Awakening, evangelicals in the North had supported not only slavery's abolition but the rights of women, help for the poor, and expanded public education. In the late nineteenth century, however, evangelicals had turned away from social reform toward an emphasis on personal piety and individual salvation. But developments in the 1960s and early 1970s, particularly the civil rights movement, revitalized progressive evangelicalism, even, to a degree, in the South. Campaigning for president in 1976, the racially moderate Democratic governor of Georgia, Jimmy Carter, made no secret of his identity as a "born again" Christian. Rather than downplay his faith, he played it up, and his election—a narrow victory over Nixon's successor, Gerald Ford—served to inject evangelicalism into national political discussion before the emergence of the religious right. His presidency may even have contributed to the rise of the religious right by awakening conservative evangelicals to their potential power.

Prominent evangelical pastors had long had connections with conservative politics. In the post–World War II years, some had ties with business interests who fought against the New Deal.[39] Many denounced "godless communism" and opposed the 1962 Supreme Court decision disallowing organized prayer in the public schools (although the Southern Baptist Convention, long committed to separation of church and state, supported the Court's ruling). No evangelical enjoyed wider renown in that era than Billy Graham, who despite being a registered Democrat was close to both Eisenhower and Nixon. Nonetheless, conservative activists in the 1960s and early 1970s were frustrated by their inability to mobilize evangelicals as a force in electoral politics.[40]

According to conventional wisdom, the trigger for the religious right's mobilization was the Supreme Court's decision in *Roe v. Wade*, but this "abortion myth," as the religious historian Randall Balmer calls it, does not stand up to scrutiny. Until the late 1970s, evangelicals generally saw abortion as a "Catholic issue." In 1971 the Southern Baptist Convention resolved that Baptists should "work for legislation that will allow the possibility of abortion under such conditions as rape, incest, clear evidence of severe fetal deformity, and carefully ascertained evidence of the likelihood of damage to the emotional, mental, and physical health of the mother." As I noted in chapter 3, the Southern states were among the first to liberalize their abortion laws before the Supreme Court decided *Roe v. Wade* in 1973. When the Court issued its decision, one of the leading fundamentalists, W. A. Criswell, author of *Why I Preach That the Bible Is Literally True*, approved the ruling: "I have always felt that it was only after a child was born and had a life separate from its mother that it became an individual person." Balmer notes that James Dobson, later a prominent opponent of abortion, acknowledged at the time that "the Bible was silent on the matter." Mostly, evangelicals didn't react at all to *Roe*; abortion was not an issue for them until the end of the decade.[41]

The policy that did trigger evangelical mobilization was the denial of tax-exempt status to segregated private educational institutions, including Bob Jones University in South Carolina and private whites-only academies throughout the South. Nixon had instructed the IRS in 1970 to deny tax exemptions to segregated schools after a federal court issued a preliminary injunction to that effect in a case brought by Black plaintiffs in a Mississippi county where whites withdrew all their children from the public schools. But the matter dragged on as Bob Jones University and the private academies made pro forma changes in their admissions rules and admitted token Black students. Finally, under Carter in 1978, the IRS said it would rescind tax exemptions from schools that had an "insignificant number of minority students." That action, according to conservative direct-mail fundraiser Richard Viguerie, "kicked a sleeping dog." As Paul Weyrich, another key figure in the movement, put it, "The federal government's moves against Christian schools ... absolutely shattered the Christian community's notions that Christians could isolate themselves inside their own institutions and teach what they pleased."[42] And discriminate as they pleased.

Internally, evangelicalism was also changing during the late 1970s as fundamentalist forces took over the most important evangelical institution, the Southern Baptist Convention. The moderate faction that had controlled the denomination had diverse views—not all were progressives—but they were willing to tolerate theological and political diversity, whereas the fundamentalists sought to reassert the old orthodoxy of the rural South. Through what amounted to a hostile takeover, they won control of the denomination and purged liberals and moderates from its leadership.[43]

As important as the tax issue was for evangelicals, the defense of segregated schools could never serve as the basis for a wider mobilization. The religious right needed a righteous moral cause, and they found it by assembling several independently emerging issues into a defense of "traditional family values." Phyllis Schlafly's campaign against the Equal Rights Amendment in the name of marriage and motherhood and Anita Bryant's "Save Our Children" campaign against gay rights both fit into the family values crusade. So did concerns about rising divorce rates and rising welfare rolls, both of which conservatives blamed on liberal values and government. Fighting abortion became the preeminent cause. Even though most evangelical leaders did not originally see a problem with abortion, they began to appreciate its political potential after the primarily Catholic right-to-life movement scored several surprise upsets of Democratic incumbents by raising abortion as an issue in the 1978 congressional elections. A concerted campaign by anti-abortion advocates began to solidify evangelical opposition to abortion in 1979.[44]

As Kristin Kobes Du Mez writes in her book *Jesus and John Wayne*, "The evangelical political resurgence of the 1970s coalesced around a potent mix of 'family values' politics, but family values were always intertwined with ideas about sex, power, race, and nation." The family that was valued was a family with "male headship" in which the husband was the "head of the wife," the same patriarchal understanding that shaped evangelical views of authority in both church and nation. Cowboys and soldiers were held up as the models of masculinity. Several evangelical bestsellers in that decade, such as Marabel Morgan's *The Total Woman* and Schlafly's *The Power of the Positive Woman*, instructed women how to remain sexually alluring and submissive to their husbands. In the mainstream culture, more androgynous ideals were in ascendancy, calling for greater agency for women and greater emotional awareness for men. But evangelical culture was emphatically anti-androgynous in reasserting sharply defined ideals of submissive femininity and dominating masculinity. The evangelical media and consumer marketplace, Du Mez argues, "functioned less as a traditional soul-saving enterprise and more as a means by which evangelicals created and maintained their own identity—an identity rooted in 'family values' and infused with a sense of cultural embattlement." They were able to become an effective partisan force in the 1980s because they had already created a shared identity and a communications infrastructure.[45]

Mobilizing as a partisan political force required a reversal among evangelicals. Between 1953 and 1974, social scientists conducted more than a dozen studies with data on political participation by members of different religious denominations, and every study found that evangelicals were less likely than members of other denominations to be politically active.[46] Evangelical leaders said that ministers should stay out of politics. In a 1965 sermon called "Ministers and Marchers," the 32-year-old pastor Jerry Falwell had declared, "We have a message of redeeming grace through a crucified and risen Lord. Nowhere are we told to reform the externals.... Preachers are not called to be politicians, but soul-winners." The marching ministers Falwell clearly had in mind were Martin Luther King Jr. and other religious leaders supporting the civil rights movement. But by the mid-1970s, Falwell was leading rallies at state capitols and allying himself with the campaigns against gay rights and the ERA. In 1979, he founded the Moral Majority, which became one of several organizations of the religious right mobilizing their supporters for political campaigns. Between 1976 and 1981, ten social science studies compared political activism in different religious groups, and every study now found evangelicals to be more active than others.[47]

For the Republican Party to capture the religious right's energy also required a reversal. Just as Republicans had to repudiate their earlier racial liberalism to win the white South, so they had to repudiate their earlier support of the ERA. Despite having signed liberalized abortion and divorce laws (and rarely attending church himself), Reagan received an adoring welcome in August 1980 at a meeting of the Roundtable, an organization of the religious right. Acknowledging that churches could not make political endorsements, he said to thunderous applause, "I know you can't endorse me, but I want you to know that I endorse you and what you are doing."[48]

The Conservative Take-Off (2): Business and the Counter-Establishment

The conservative counterattack against liberalism received another powerful boost from business. During the 1960s and early 1970s, business interests had accepted liberal policies, or at least not united against them, because the economy continued to grow smartly, and business did well. But starting in late 1973, the economy entered a prolonged crisis that helped trigger a political mobilization among America's corporate elite, who were already facing a steep loss of public confidence coinciding with the rise of the consumer and environmental movements and the onslaught of regulation enacted under Nixon. The proportion of Americans with a "great deal of confidence" in business leaders, according to the Harris Poll, fell from 55 percent in 1966 to 29 percent in 1973 and 15 percent in 1975.

Corporate America felt just as embattled as evangelicals did. At a private conference of business executives, the meeting's chairman observed that while others saw them as privileged, "We see ourselves as the persecuted few."[49] In a thirty-three-page memo to the U.S. Chamber of Commerce in August 1971—two months before Nixon nominated him to the Supreme Court—Lewis F. Powell Jr. had lamented that "the American business executive is truly the 'forgotten man,'" inverting the meaning FDR had given to that phrase during the Great Depression. Powell saw attacks on the free-enterprise system coming not just from the left but "from perfectly respectable elements of society: from the college campus, the pulpit, the media, the intellectual and literary journals, the arts and sciences, and from politicians." Business needed to mount a comprehensive response. "The judiciary," he noted, "may be the most important instrument for social, economic, and political change."[50] In line with arguments like Powell's, business sought not only to regain political influence in Washington but to restore public faith in free markets and build up conservative think tanks, research centers, legal advocacy groups, and other institutions that would spread the faith and litigate on behalf of business. Like the institution-building on the religious right, the surge of corporate-financed institution-building on the free-market right represented an effort to overturn what conservatives saw as a liberal cultural and intellectual establishment.

The economic crisis of the 1970s was more than a temporary downturn in the business cycle. It arose from several long-term changes undermining post–World War II economic policies and labor arrangements. The U.S. economy had been so dominant after the war that the nation's manufacturing firms were largely sheltered from international competition, enabling labor unions in the auto, steel, and other industries to win a steady share of the gains from rising productivity and economic growth. Productivity had risen at an exceptionally high rate in the postwar years, in part because of technological advances and capital investments in infrastructure made during the Depression and war that were not fully exploited commercially until afterward. But by the 1970s, the insulation from international competition and unsustainable postwar productivity increases were both over. Sooner or later, trouble was coming.

It came sooner because of electorally motivated political choices. Like Johnson, Nixon ran the economy hot, except for the beginning of his first term in 1969, when there was a brief recession. In August 1971, amid rising prices and international pressure on the dollar, he imposed controls on wages and prices and suspended the dollar's convertibility into gold, effectively ending the Bretton Woods international monetary system. The policy worked in the short term, helping Nixon win re-election. But inflationary pressures built up, and in October 1973 the Arab petroleum-exporting states imposed an oil embargo on the United States and other countries that had supported Israel that year in the Yom Kippur War, quadrupling crude oil prices and setting off a wage-price spiral. This was the beginning of two crises that dominated the decade: the energy crisis, understood as a shortage of cheap, domestically produced energy; and "stagflation," a stubborn combination of stagnant growth, high unemployment, and inflation. Corporate profits also declined sharply from their levels in the 1960s.

From the standpoint of business, the stagnant economy had a clear explanation: Labor unions and government were imposing excessive burdens, threatening the competitiveness of American business and suffocating capital formation and investment. The regulatory legislation passed under Nixon provided an immediate impetus for a general mobilization of corporate America to reshape national policy. Between 1970 and 1975, employment in federal regulatory agencies rose from 9,707 to 52,098, and federal spending on regulation also increased fivefold.[51] Earlier forms of economic regulation had been industry-specific and thus highly susceptible to capture by the regulated industries. New regulatory agencies like the Environmental Protection Agency and the Occupational Safety and Health Administration, in contrast, set rules that applied across the whole economy, with some exceptions for small business. In addition, the new regulatory laws, beginning with the employment protections of the Civil Rights Act, included provisions allowing individuals to sue to enforce the laws and to have their legal fees paid by the defendants, along with damages, if they won their cases. These rights of private action inspired the growth of nonprofit public-interest law firms and private attorneys specializing in such areas as civil rights, consumer protection, and the environment. Employment discrimination cases, for example, increased by a factor of ten, from 400 to 4,000 a year between 1970 and 1975. In liberal politics, the public interest movement emerged as a supplement to the unions as a countervailing force to business, particularly on issues where unions were no help.[52]

During the mid-1970s liberals also discussed the use of national economic planning as a remedy for America's woes. A committee of luminaries, including some prominent businessmen, proposed a federal Office of National Planning "to guide the economy in a direction consistent with our national values and goals," a conception of the government's role that most business leaders found abhorrent.[53] A younger generation of Democratic leaders called for an industrial policy to promote economic development, particularly in high technology. In the coming decades, planning and industrial policy would be the road not taken for the national economy.

Faced with a slowing economy and growing governmental role, corporate America adopted a harder line toward unions and in national politics. Although the rate of union membership had been declining since the mid-1950s, unions continued to be a major force in the early 1970s and, in total membership, they were larger than ever. "No program works without labor cooperation," President Nixon said. The decade began with stirrings of labor activism, but they failed to take hold. The historian Jefferson Cowie writes, "The ingredients for labor's renewal—new organizing, democratization movements, insurgencies among women and minorities, youth, and quality of work life issues—added up to less than the sum of the parts." The economic conditions and corporate mobilization of the mid-1970s were a turning point. Even companies that had earlier accepted unions began adopting aggressive tactics to fight them, including efforts to decertify unions they had previously recognized. To keep labor demands in line, firms shut down plants without notification or threatened to move plants elsewhere in the country or abroad.[54]

Business elites do not necessarily act in concert, but the conditions of the 1970s encouraged them to join together in support of broad class interests, as they understood them. Through mergers with two other business groups, the Business Roundtable developed into the preeminent organization representing the CEOs of Fortune 500 companies. The U.S. Chamber of Commerce grew dramatically in membership, budget, and staff. The National Federation of Independent Business spoke for small business and had influence at the local and state levels. Instead of depending solely on lobbyists based in Washington, corporations and trade associations built up "grassroots" networks of managers, employees, stockholders, suppliers, dealers, and customers in congressional districts across the country. Corporate political action committees (PACs) sharply increased both their contributions to political candidates and their spending on advocacy advertising, promoting their positions on public issues.[55]

Conservative intellectuals had long lamented that they had no institutions to match the liberal establishment's think tanks and university research centers. Now corporations and donors poured money into old organizations like the American Enterprise Institute and Hoover Institution and new ones like the Heritage Foundation. The money paid not only for the research and publications that gave credence to conservative positions but also for publicity to get conservative ideas and arguments into the media and onto the public agenda. The enlarged right-wing counter-establishment also provided a home for conservative policy intellectuals and technical experts who would be prepared to take over government departments when the political moment arrived.[56]

The ideological offensive had two overlapping but distinct branches. The older and more familiar branch called for free markets and lower taxes. Since the 1940s, the economists Friedrich von Hayek and Milton Friedman had been making the case for what some called "neoliberalism," though the term was still not widely used in the free-market sense in the 1970s or 1980s.[57] Free-market neoliberalism is not identical to pre–New Deal laissez-faire. It is one thing to oppose government programs and policies before they are introduced; it is another thing to undo them later. While the first requires only a blocking power, the second requires a constitutive power—the paradoxically active use of the state to shrink the state and create markets with new rules. Privatization, deregulation (which often meant re-regulation), fiscal austerity, and the relaxation of antitrust enforcement were some of the key instruments of neoliberal policy.[58]

The second branch of the ideological offensive, neoconservatism, had its origins in disquiet among liberals and others formerly on the left about 1960s radicalism and Great Society overreach. Neoconservatism emerged chiefly in the pages of two publications: *Commentary*, the magazine of the American Jewish Committee edited by Norman Podhoretz, and *The Public Interest*, founded in 1965 by Irving Kristol (the "father" of neoconservatism) and Daniel Bell (who left the journal as it moved right in the 1970s). The original neoconservatives did not have a principled objection to the welfare state; they approved of the New Deal and some Great Society policies like Medicare and still supported labor unions, whose leadership at that time shared their anticommunist passions. But they were highly critical of Johnson's war on poverty, affirmative action, and the counterculture. They differed from the "paleoconservatives," who objected on principle to the New Deal, unions, and Great Society. Neoconservatism also drew much of its support from unease about Black Power, rising crime rates, and urban disorder—an unease summed up in Kristol's capsule definition of a neoconservative as a "liberal who has been mugged by reality." But that definition, as Podhoretz pointed out, was misleading because prominent neoconservatives, including both Kristol and Podhoretz themselves, were former radicals who had started to the left of liberalism and moved to the right of it. Liberalism itself had never appealed to them. By the 1970s, neoconservatives also became identified with a hardline anti-Soviet foreign policy.[59]

One line of neoconservative criticism argued that the Western democracies suffered not only from inflated prices but also from inflated confidence in the possibilities of government. By attempting to satisfy popular demands, the democracies had contributed to a revolution of rising expectations and created an "overload" of public responsibilities that raised doubts about their societies' "governability." On this point, the neoliberal and neoconservative arguments coincided. What the United States and other democracies needed, they agreed, was government retrenchment, a backing away from promises of equality, and a return to greater self-discipline.[60]

The turn from the Warren Court to the Burger Court (1969–1986) brought about a shift in American law that both reflected and contributed to the conservative ideological offensive. Hoping to shift the Court at the beginning of his term, Nixon orchestrated Justice Department investigations of two Democratic appointees, Justices Abe Fortas and William O. Douglas. Although Douglas survived, Fortas resigned after Nixon's Attorney General John Mitchell made a private threat, likely a bluff, of indictments of both Fortas and his wife.[61] The Burger Court, however, did not reverse the Warren Court's historic precedents on such questions as racial integration, school prayer, and the rights of criminal defendants. It also advanced women's rights. One book on the Burger Court calls it "the counterrevolution that wasn't."[62]

But with Nixon's four appointees, the Court did expand the rights of corporations and make American politics less democratic. Previously, the Warren Court had strengthened individual rights in the interests of a more equal democracy; for example, it declared poll taxes an unconstitutional barrier to voting by the poor and required states with legislatures that vastly overrepresented rural areas to create districts equal in population (the one-person, one-vote principle). Many other Warren Court decisions, including its enforcement of civil rights legislation, also imposed national rules on the states in the interests of a more consistently democratic national politics.

This thrust of the Warren Court was in line with other changes at the time such as reforms in the presidential nominating process, which expanded popular participation on a national basis. In 1968, liberal Democrats opposed to the Vietnam War were outraged that the party nominated Humphrey for president even though he had not entered a single primary. The reforms they secured—which Republicans subsequently adopted—shifted control of presidential nominations from state party organizations to the voters in primaries and caucuses, reducing the power of party bosses.[63] Another move toward a more popular politics came through legislation to limit campaign contributions and spending, adopted by Congress in response to the Watergate scandal. Investigations of Nixon's re-election campaign had shown, for example, that milk producers had pledged $2 million after his administration approved higher milk price supports.

Altogether, the Warren Court decisions, new party nomination rules, and campaign finance reforms appeared to be moving the country toward a more democratic politics—until the Burger Court intervened. In a 1976 case, *Buckley v. Valeo*, the Court struck down many of the newly enacted limits on campaign finance. The District of Columbia Court of Appeals had upheld nearly all the 1974 campaign finance law, which it described as tending "to equalize both the relative ability of all voters to affect electoral outcomes, and the opportunity of all interested citizens to become candidates for elective federal office." The Supreme Court, however, ruled that the promotion of political equality was not a constitutionally permissible basis for regulating campaign finance. It interpreted the First Amendment as prohibiting the government from regulating not only the content of speech but the purchase of audiences. Just like speech itself, the Court decided, money spent on speech was constitutionally protected: "The concept that government may restrict the speech of some elements of our society"—it meant the money spent on that speech—"in order to enhance the relative voice of others is wholly foreign to the First Amendment." The Court consequently distinguished between campaign contributions and expenditures and struck down any limits on expenditures. It did recognize the potential for corruption as a constitutional basis for regulating campaign finance, but it saw actual or apparent corruption, defined narrowly to mean bribery, as arising only from *contributions* to individual candidate campaigns. It did not see a potential for corruption in a candidate's total spending, in contributions to independent campaigns on behalf of a candidate, or in spending by wealthy candidates on their own campaigns. All those limits the Court overturned as unconstitutional infringements on free speech. The effect of the ruling was to defeat Congress's efforts to respond to public concern about the undue political influence of wealth. To raise the growing amounts required for campaigns in coming years, candidates who could not self-fund would have to devote increasing amounts of time to soliciting donors, to the detriment of their attention to ordinary voters.[64]

The Supreme Court under Burger was also more partial to business than it had been under Warren. It took the side of business in key cases involving labor unions and employee rights; it extended First Amendment protections to commercial speech, prohibiting regulation of advertising except insofar as it was fraudulent or misleading; and it gave corporations new rights to use their funds to influence public referenda. The Burger Court extended the Warren Court's broad interpretation of free speech rights, but it took those rights in an entirely different direction, enlarging the power of money in American politics.[65]

The conservative mobilization of American business, the creation of a counter-establishment, and the abolition of limits on campaign spending influenced both major parties, but in different ways. Since Republicans tended to agree with business on legislation and policy, the surge in corporate political contributions in the mid-1970s mostly reinforced positions they would have taken anyway. But political contributions from business and wealthy donors often cross-pressured Democrats who otherwise relied on support from labor unions and consumer groups. The neoliberal and neoconservative arguments also resonated among some Democrats, dividing the party just when it had an enormous opportunity after Watergate to make progress on a liberal agenda.

The Democrats' Squandered Opportunity

In the wake of the Watergate scandal, Democrats made huge gains in Congress in 1974, margins that they enlarged two years later when Carter won the presidency. In January 1977, Democratic majorities in the House and Senate were nearly as big as in 1965, when Johnson passed his Great Society programs.

But Carter was no Johnson, and both his party and the political context had changed. Many of the post-Watergate Democrats in Congress came from affluent suburban districts and had little connection with unions or old party organizations. Rather than deliver material gains to the party's traditional working-class base, they focused on procedural reforms and clean government, reforms that sometimes prevented public agencies from acting expeditiously and effectively. The post-Watergate moment created a Democratic Party high in moral rectitude and inattentive to the practical realities of getting things done. Carter himself campaigned as the personal antithesis of Nixon, promising that he would never lie and would give America "a government as good as its people." Even after his election, he presented himself as an outsider to Washington, frugal, morally upright, a scourge to special interests and the congressional pork-barrel.

It did not go well. One by one, Democratic legislative priorities went down to defeat—a new consumer protection agency, hospital cost containment, a modest labor law reform that would have expedited union claims of illegal union-busting efforts by management. A mobilized business community was the immediate cause, but instead of overcoming Democrats' internal divisions, Carter exacerbated them. He was, as the historian Arthur Schlesinger Jr. said at the time, the most conservative Democratic president since Grover Cleveland. His chief of staff, Hamilton Jordan, later remarked that "we . . . had no unifying Democratic consensus, no program, no set of principles on which a majority of Democrats agreed."[66] Stymied on the economy, energy, and other domestic issues, Carter prioritized foreign policy—the ratification of a treaty turning the Panama Canal over to Panama, peace in the Middle East, the pursuit of human rights abroad.

During Carter's first two years, the economy expanded at a healthy rate, but 1979 brought a second spike in oil prices and surge in inflation. That year Carter appointed a new head of the Federal Reserve, Paul Volcker, who fought inflation by raising interest rates to double-digit levels. The Volcker shock sent the economy into a recession in advance of the 1980 election and thoroughly demoralized the Democratic base; the 1980 election had the lowest voter turnout in a presidential election in forty years.[67] Carter's inability to carry out a coherent economic program and the recession late in his term doomed his re-election and allowed Reagan and the Republicans to claim that liberalism was bankrupt.

Carter was Nixon's opposite in both symbolism and substance. Rhetorically, Nixon appealed to white backlash, whereas Carter was high-minded. Substantively, Nixon advanced liberal goals and made bold proposals, whereas Carter was timid and ineffectual. It would be wrong, however, to say that Carter's record on progressive policy was zero. It was less than that. He had campaigned on progressive reforms of the income tax but signed legislation that gave big tax breaks to the wealthy. In promoting the deregulation of the airline and trucking industries, he helped legitimize a general neoliberal attack on regulation. He could see no way forward on such issues as universal health insurance. Much of what we now associate with Reagan and the 1980s began under Carter. The Reagan era began when the Democrats squandered their post-Watergate opportunity.

Unity might have also been a problem for conservatives and the Republican Party, as it was for liberals and the Democratic Party. The religious right, neoliberals, neoconservatives, paleoconservatives, and libertarians had profound philosophical differences. American conservatism in the late twentieth century consisted of so many disparate ideological tendencies that the right required something outside itself to hold it together. That source of unity was the one thing conservatives all agreed on then and since: their opposition to liberal government and liberal culture. Political unity is often built on a negative, and conservative unity was built on the negative of liberalism. During the 1960s and 1970s, conservatism gained not only unity but its sense of identity and purpose in fighting the more progressive liberalism that emerged from the movements of Blacks and other racial minorities, feminists, and gays and lesbians, and from the consumer and environmental movements. This was liberalism's gift to conservatism: the revitalized conservative project that Reagan brought to national power in 1981. But under Reagan, the full force of the right came down on a different target.

The Half-Truth of the Reagan Revolution

From the moment Ronald Reagan became president in January 1981, conservatives hailed his administration as a revolutionary rupture with the past. But how much of a rupture was it? The historian Julian Zelizer argues that from the start the Reagan Revolution was a myth, "born out of an explicit political strategy" aimed at cementing "the impression that Reagan's victory had been a mandate for conservatism." Even some who admire Reagan's leadership, like the historian Gil Troy, are skeptical about how revolutionary he was. Reagan himself, Troy writes, "knew that his governing approach had been more nuanced, more consensus-driven, less transformative than the grandiose title of 'Reagan Revolution' implied. Reagan's administration was never as radical as he occasionally promised, conservatives desired, or liberals dreaded." It only shifted America "slightly toward a less liberal future."[68]

This skepticism is warranted up to a point. Reagan's presidency did not provide the decisive turning point and historic repudiation of liberalism his supporters wanted. The changes he brought about, however, were radical in one critical respect—their class impact. His policies sharply increased economic inequality through their effects on taxes and spending, capital, and labor. They were not entirely a rupture with the past because the forces increasing economic inequality were already at work in the late 1970s, and Carter had helped prepare the way. But to say that Reagan shifted America only "slightly toward a less liberal future" understates the imprint his presidency had on America's social structure. Reagan helped create a society in which inequalities between rich and poor rose, the cultural transformations dating from the 1960s continued, and the conflicts from that mixed pattern intensified.

The economic program that Reagan ran on in 1980 called for reductions in the size of both the federal government and the federal deficit, on the premise that those changes would bring down inflation and restore economic growth. In his first memorandum to Reagan during the campaign, Martin Anderson, Reagan's policy director, wrote that "the main cause of inflation is the massive, continuing budget deficit of the federal government," and the "most effective way" to reduce the deficit was to reduce expenditures. They could then pass a constitutional amendment requiring a balanced federal budget. Reagan's program also included a military buildup with dramatically higher defense spending.[69]

Along with a balanced budget and a military buildup, Reagan planned to slash federal income taxes, a cause to which he had long been passionately devoted. As his income had risen, he had personally resented paying the top rate, and as a publicist for General Electric in the 1950s, he had denounced the progressive income tax. A nationwide tax revolt in the late 1970s made clear how powerful an issue taxes could be. In June 1978, California voters overwhelmingly approved a radical cut in property taxes, and by 1980 anti-tax measures had passed in thirty-eight states. During Reagan's 1980 presidential campaign, several "supply-side" economists bolstered his intuition that even with higher defense spending, he could make large tax cuts and still balance the budget because the resulting impetus to growth would make up for revenue lost from lower tax rates. Reagan proposed across-the-board reductions in federal income tax rates over three years, cutting the top rate from 70 percent to 50 percent and the bottom rate from 14 percent to 11 percent. Not only did he get his way on those reductions; Congress, in what became a notorious "Christmas tree," pinned on to the legislation a variety of tax shelters that enabled investors to cut their taxes further.[70]

The promised spending reductions and balanced budget never arrived. Deficits quickly hit unprecedented levels. The national debt increased by half during Reagan's first thousand days, ultimately tripling during his presidency.[71] But inflation did go down, chiefly because of Volcker's tight monetary policies and Reagan's good fortune to be president in a time of declining international oil prices. For his first two years, however, the economy suffered its most severe downturn since World War II. It began recovering only when Volcker eased interest rates in response to a new package of tax increases and budget cuts agreed to by Reagan and Congress.

Average annual economic growth in Reagan's first term was no greater than it had been under Carter. But as actors know, timing is everything. Whereas Carter's term began with growth and ended in recession, Reagan's began with a recession and blossomed into an expansion, enabling him to win a landslide re-election. Martin Feldstein, chair of Reagan's Council of Economic Advisers from 1982 to 1984, noted soon after leaving office that the recovery had been in line with previous history and that the experience since 1981 had "not been kind to the claims" that the tax cuts "would spur unprecedented economic growth, reduce inflation painlessly, increase tax revenue and stimulate a spectacular rise in personal saving. Each of those predictions has proved to be wrong." Still, the economy was strong enough in 1984 for Reagan to campaign for re-election on the slogan "Morning again in America," a sunny contrast to the dark national mood that Carter had personified a few years earlier.[72]

Despite the happy image of that rosy-fingered dawn, the changes in both the public and private sectors did not work out as well for ordinary Americans under Reagan as they did for the wealthy. Wealthy people's incomes soared, while those of most other Americans grew modestly or stagnated. Between 1980 and 1992—that is, under Reagan and his Republican successor, George H. W. Bush—the lower 50 percent of Americans saw their incomes fall from 20.1 percent to 16.0 percent of national income, while the top 10 percent saw their share rise from 33.8 percent to 39.4 percent. A third of the gains for the top 10 percent went to the top

1 percent.[73] This was the new pattern the Reagan era initiated: the extreme concentration at the top of the gains from economic growth.

To be sure, not all of this increase directly resulted from Reagan's policy choices. Long-term processes of technological change and globalization also contributed to rising inequality. But partisan control of policy affects whether the government reinforces or counteracts those trends; Republican administrations have been much more favorable to high-income than to middle- or low-income people. This was true for income growth both before and after taxes. Under Reagan, the top 1 percent paid less in taxes in 1988 than they had in 1981, while the bottom one-fifth paid more.[74]

The shift in the federal tax burden that began with the 1981 tax cuts continued with two subsequent measures. In 1983, a compromise agreement to save Social Security called for raising payroll taxes, which fall more heavily on lower-income workers because their earnings are fully taxed, whereas the earnings of high-income people are taxed only in part. In 1986, a major restructuring of income taxes further reduced the top personal rate from 50 percent to 28 percent, while also cutting the corporate rate from 46 percent to 34 percent. On the spending side, defense outlays and debt service increased during the 1980s—debt service actually became the third largest item in the federal budget—while spending on social programs other than Social Security fell from 9.9 percent to 7.6 percent of GDP. Among other things, the Reagan administration sharply reduced funds for community and regional development and employment programs and eliminated federal revenue-sharing with the states (a program established under Nixon), pushing fiscal pressures down to the state and local level. Federal spending choices helped intensify a growing urban crisis and the destitution of the "underclass," as social scientists and journalists now called the poorest of the poor.[75]

Reagan's policies toward labor and business also drove greater economic inequality. In August 1981, federal air traffic controllers went out on strike after failing to reach an agreement on a new contract with the administration, which said their demands would jeopardize the battle against inflation. Rather than negotiate with the union, Reagan gave its members forty-eight hours to return to work and then fired the 11,000 who didn't, replacing them initially with military air controllers, later with permanent replacements, and destroying the union. His actions helped legitimize private companies' use of permanent replacement workers and other anti-union measures. At a time when the manufacturing sector was in decline and companies were offshoring jobs, the labor movement was in a weak position. The fraction of non-agricultural workers represented by unions, already in decline, fell under Reagan from 23.3 percent in 1980 to 16.6 percent in 1989.[76]

Much of the damage to labor's interests came from government inaction—the failure of the National Labor Relations Board, for example, to penalize illegal union-busting, and Congress's failure to update labor and employment laws. When Reagan took office, the minimum wage was $3.35, and when he left office, it was still $3.35, with the result that its real value had fallen by 27 percent. At the Justice Department, Reagan's appointees relaxed antitrust enforcement, enabling companies to accumulate market power through mergers and acquisitions.[77] When government fails to act on behalf of those with little economic power, things rarely just stay the same. Those with greater private power usually acquire more of it.

Compared to his efforts on behalf of business, Reagan did little to advance the agenda of the religious right. During the 1980 campaign, when polls showed his support lagging among women, he promised to nominate the first woman ever for the Supreme Court; and when a vacancy appeared, he chose the Arizona judge Sandra Day O'Connor, even though the religious right objected that she had supported abortion rights and the ERA. Their misgivings proved accurate. Although a hardline conservative on economic matters, O'Connor evolved into a swing vote on social issues and refused to support overturning *Roe v. Wade* or affirmative action in higher education. Reagan's later judicial appointments, including his two other nominees to the Supreme Court, Antonin Scalia and Anthony Kennedy, were more strictly vetted than Nixon's for their fidelity to movement conservatism, and on the bench they narrowed abortion rights, affirmative action, and other earlier liberal rulings (although Kennedy sided with liberals on gay rights). Reagan also appointed some cultural conservatives to administration posts, but except for his second-term Secretary of Education William Bennett, they typically occupied symbolic rather than decision-making roles. Reagan avoided committing political capital to the religious right's causes.

But even neglect of culturally stigmatized communities could have grievous consequences, as it did for gay men and many others when the AIDS epidemic arrived. During his first term, Reagan failed even to acknowledge AIDS; he first mentioned it only when one of his Hollywood friends, the actor Rock Hudson, died from HIV in 1985. The following year he had Surgeon General C. Everett Koop prepare a report on the epidemic, which included the first discussion of safe sex from the administration. Yet even then, Reagan held back from promoting public health measures to control AIDS.[78]

Although his presidency also had adverse effects on racial equality, Reagan did not actively drive a conservative racial agenda. On the campaign trail, he had a history of using coded racial appeals. Running for president in 1976, for example, he often told a story about a woman in Chicago who supposedly had "eighty names, thirty addresses, twelve Social Security cards and is collecting veterans' benefits on four non-existing deceased husbands.... Her tax-free cash income alone is over $150,000." He did not need to say the supposed "welfare queen" was Black, nor did he or his supporters ever substantiate her existence. (The closest case that journalists could find involved a Black woman in Chicago who had fraudulently collected $8,000, not $150,000.) Reagan launched his 1980 campaign at the Neshoba County Fair near Philadelphia, Mississippi, the site where three civil rights workers were murdered in 1964. But following in the Republican tradition of plausible deniability on racism, he was generally careful to present himself as unprejudiced and took umbrage at any suggestion to the contrary.[79]

Since Reagan had opposed major civil rights bills, Black voters still had ample reason to expect the worst from his election, and they overwhelmingly voted against him. In line with those expectations, both the Reagan Justice Department and the EEOC rejected critical tools for enforcing civil rights laws that previous administrations had employed. But racial moderates in the Republican Party, including some members of his cabinet and senior White House staff, limited how far Reagan went. He initially supported the legal case brought by Bob Jones University and segregated Christian academies against the IRS on the issue of their tax-exempt status. But he backed off, claiming to have been misinformed about the issue, and in 1983 the Supreme Court upheld the IRS ruling in an 8–1 decision. When the 1965 Voting Rights Act came up for renewal in 1982, Reagan signed an extension, which in some ways strengthened the law, over the objections of William Bradford Reynolds, the conservative he had put in charge of the civil rights division of the Justice Department. Reynolds also wanted Reagan to revoke the executive order requiring federal contractors to adopt affirmative action plans, but others in the administration prevailed on the president to leave it alone. Reagan initially opposed legislation making Martin Luther King Jr.'s birthday a national holiday, but he grudgingly signed it.[80] Reagan didn't reverse the civil rights revolution, which would have been politically impossible. Not only did Democrats hold power in Congress but congressional Republicans still included enough racial moderates to prevent a 180-degree turn on civil rights. The same was true of the Supreme Court, now almost entirely made up of Republican appointees.

Nonetheless, the situation of Black Americans deteriorated significantly in the 1980s, as it had already begun to do in the 1970s, and the Reagan and Bush presidencies contributed to that pattern. Two general processes stand out. The first produced a sharp decline in manufacturing and the market for unskilled labor in the cities that adversely affected Black workers; the second led to a sharp rise in incarceration.

I outlined in chapter 2 how long-lasting discriminatory practices and structural change in the U.S. economy undercut Black economic opportunity. Anti-Black discrimination in the housing market, carried out for decades by government agencies as well as private builders and lenders, prevented Blacks from purchasing homes, the main form of wealth accumulation for working- and middle-class white families. Unlike earlier unskilled European immigrants, who benefited from the long era of U.S. manufacturing growth, the Southern Blacks of the Great Migration arrived in the cities only toward the end of that expansion. By the 1970s, industrial jobs were disappearing from old manufacturing centers, primarily due to automation and the movement of plants to other countries with lower wages and to suburban and exurban locations in the United States. Black Americans arrived in manufacturing, furthermore, on the eve of the collapse of private-sector unions, the institution that had raised industrial wages. During the 1970s, after more Black workers obtained unionized jobs, they became unionized at a higher rate than whites, helping to narrow the Black–white gap in wages. But the decline of unions in that decade and after thwarted the aspirations of Black workers.[81]

The civil rights revolution did create new educational and career opportunities that fostered the growth of middle-class Black families, many of whom were able to move out of the ghettoes. But they left behind neighborhoods of concentrated poverty, depleted of many of the people who formerly helped maintain community institutions and norms. It was in this situation, as the sociologist William Julius Wilson emphasized, that drug addiction, crime, and disorder flourished, compounding the problems of Black America.[82] And those very problems then served as justification for conservative policies cutting federal antipoverty programs and aid to the cities.

The staggering rise in incarceration during these years was a major factor in the growing cumulative disadvantage of the Black poor. Although the United States previously had a somewhat higher rate of incarceration than other Western countries, it began to diverge radically from them around 1975. From the 1950s to the early 1970s, state and federal prisons had held about 200,000 inmates. But by 1980, the incarcerated population was 300,000, and between 1981 and 1994, it tripled to 1,000,000 and continued rising, until it reached a peak of about 1.55 million in 2009. These increases gave the United States a rate of incarceration five to ten times greater than Western European countries.[83] The United States had distinguished itself after World War II by building schools and universities and creating a mass system of higher education. In the late twentieth century it distinguished itself by creating a mass system of imprisonment.

Objective increases in crime rates cannot fully explain the immense increase in incarceration. At the behest of law-and-order politicians and a public that largely approved of tough-on-crime measures, both the federal and state governments enacted stiffer sentences and gave judges less discretion. Average prison time for violent crimes tripled between 1975 and 1989, though this appeared to have no effect on rates of violent crime. "If locking up those who violate the law contributed to safer societies," a report of the Canadian House of Commons commented, "then the United States should be the safest country in the world."[84]

The United States also began locking up more nonviolent offenders. Reagan and Bush played a direct role in this process through their war on drugs. Drug convictions became the single biggest immediate cause of the rise in imprisonment, even though by the early 1980s, surveys already indicated drug use was declining. By 1992, drug offenders represented 58 percent of federal prisoners, up from 25 percent in 1980. Bush signaled the priority he gave the drug war by creating a White House Office of National Drug Control Policy, which mandated that the rising federal budget for the drug war be split 70–30 in favor of enforcement over treatment and education. As of 1977, 42 percent of those admitted to prisons had committed violent crimes; that number dropped to 35 percent in 1985 and to 27 percent in 1990.[85]

In the minds and memory of conservatives, one of the central ideas of Reaganism was to reduce government interference in Americans' lives. Black Americans did not have that experience of enlarged freedom from the state. On the contrary, the drug war had the entirely foreseeable effect of locking up large numbers of young Black men. Blacks did commit a disproportionate number of crimes, but they were also subject to disproportionate sentences as well as discriminatory policing that led to more arrests. Between 1980 and 1992, the number of Blacks in prison tripled; a 1990 study estimated that 23 percent of Black men in their twenties were under the control of the criminal justice system. Not only did they bear that lifelong stigma but the surge of incarceration did immense damage to family and community life. Law-and-order politics and the drug war piled an additional disaster on Black urban communities already suffering from de-industrialization and the loss of jobs.[86]

As they had done in similar situations, Republicans denied any racial motivation behind the drug war and the rise in incarceration. In 2000, when the younger George W. Bush was running for president, he was asked whether he did drugs when he was young, and he got away with saying, "When I was young and reckless, I was young and reckless." Most white voters just nodded their heads forgivingly because, after all, that's what young men do. When young Black men did the same things, that was a different matter.

The conservative movement of the post–World War II era set itself against the changes that twentieth-century liberalism brought about. Conservatives fought civil rights legislation and Great Society programs, government regulation of the economy and the environment, and higher federal taxes, spending, and deficits. They continued to oppose the power of organized labor and the steeply progressive federal income tax. They resisted the legal and cultural changes associated with the feminist and gay rights movements and called for a return to "traditional family values," "law and order," and a more central place for religion in public life.

At the end of the Reagan–Bush years, how much of that agenda had conservatives accomplished? Not nearly as much as the notion of a Reagan Revolution suggested. The backlash against liberalism was powerful, but it failed to reverse the changes in the role of government that began under Franklin Roosevelt or the cultural transformation wrought by the movements that grew out of the Black freedom struggle. It is important here, as it is in thinking about liberalism, to distinguish between developments that were important only in their time and those that left a lasting impact. As long as government power continues to rotate between political parties, long-lasting effects depend on the enactment of changes in a form that successors cannot easily reverse.

The Reagan–Bush era brought about no general rollback of the federal government. Conservatives had big hopes for the privatization of government functions in the 1980s, but little came of those ideas. Deregulation had mixed results. In telecommunications, for instance, deregulation had begun under Carter, reflected a political consensus, and became well established. In the environment, Reagan's measures provoked controversy and resistance and were cut short. The loosening of oversight in the savings and loan industry led to an epic and costly scandal that discredited deregulation as a general movement. As a share of national income, neither federal spending nor federal taxes declined. The Reagan presidency did have a long-run effect on deficit spending, but it was the opposite of what conservatives had hoped for. "Reagan proved deficits don't matter," no less a conservative stalwart than Vice President Dick Cheney declared in 2002.[87] As Republicans came to see it, deficits didn't matter when they were in power and wanted to cut taxes, though they mattered very much when Democrats were in office. The conservative idea that reconciled these contradictions was "starving the beast," but the beast survived. Americans wanted and needed the government more than conservatives recognized.

There was, however, a unifying theme in the three major areas where conservatives did bring about major institutional change: taxes, the power of unions, and the system of mass incarceration. In all three, Republicans increased class inequality. The highly progressive tax rates and relatively high levels of unionization that characterized mid-twentieth-century America proved to be exceptional patterns—legacies of the New Deal and World War II that the Cold War originally helped Democrats to maintain. Republicans didn't entirely eliminate the progressive income tax or wipe out unions, but Democrats proved not only unable but generally unwilling even to try to get them back to their previous levels. The rise of mass incarceration also generated powerful political forces that, for years, Democrats were unwilling to challenge.

While exacerbating economic inequality, the Republicans of the Reagan and Bush years did not give priority to the cultural issues that had particularly concerned the religious right and the neoconservatives. But a new Republican political leadership in the 1990s would take up arms in the culture war and help initiate a more ferociously hostile era of national politics. That radicalized leadership sought to extend the half-counterrevolution of the Reagan era and make it a full counterrevolution against progressive changes. Every line of social conflict—race, immigration, gender, religion, class, partisanship—would become part of the hostilities splitting the country in the new century. As the American people continued to change culturally and demographically, Republicans fought to rally the old America in the name of the nation, and with the help of its entrenched institutions, to stop the changes and turn back the clock. This was the new phase of the American contradiction. Much of the Republican leadership would itself be consumed in the process as the radicalization of their own party went further than those leaders expected. Democrats also unwittingly contributed to an explosive reaction by championing free-trade and deregulatory policies. Americans on both sides of the great divide went sleepwalking into an upheaval they never imagined possible.

PART II

Sleepwalking into Revenge

CHAPTER FIVE

Americans as Enemies

The 1990s as Historical Pivot

Now that the other "Cold War" is over, the real cold war has begun.

—IRVING KRISTOL, 1993[1]

AFTER THE COLLAPSE of the Soviet Union in 1991, the United States enjoyed a position in the world similar to the one it had enjoyed after the defeat of Germany and Japan in 1945. In both instances, it stood for a brief period unchallenged as a global power, and Americans felt both relief and validation. The Soviet collapse ended not one but two threats—nuclear annihilation and communism. Once again, America's system had worked, and its enemy's had not. Triumph bred triumphalism.

The 1990s also brought, as the 1950s had, a tide of optimism about technology, another apparent confirmation of the vitality and superiority of American capitalism. In the 1950s, technological advances inspired dreams of space travel and brought down-to-earth improvements such as new home appliances and medical innovations like the polio vaccine. Now, in the 1990s, Americans looked to the ever-growing power of computers, new means of free and open communication, and the possibilities of a new information economy. After a brief recession in 1990–1991, the decade also saw steady economic growth. There were reasons for confidence and even excitement about the future.

Culturally and politically, however, the 1990s were a reverse 1950s. Even though America in the 1950s never had an all-encompassing consensus, it did have a consensus culture and a consensus politics. The dominant media and cultural institutions stayed within what the president of NBC referred to as "the area of American agreement," and national political leaders emphasized bipartisanship and civility. In the 1990s, the tenor of public life was altogether different. There was growing talk of a "culture war" as the right and left announced their irreconcilable moral differences, and Americans sorted themselves into different associations, churches, and political parties based on their varying ways of life and belief. The media afforded increased choice, and Americans used that freedom to find news and entertainment that more closely fit their opinions and tastes. More partisan outlets became fixtures of a changed media world. National politics became an unrelenting, partisan struggle. The end of the Cold War might have brought an era of good feeling, but it didn't work out that way.

In the first post–Cold War presidential election in 1992, the Republican incumbent George H. W. Bush was the early favorite, riding high in public opinion in the glow of the quick U.S. victory over Iraq in the Gulf War. After the Iraqi dictator Saddam Hussein had seized Kuwait in August 1990 and threatened to gain a stranglehold over Middle Eastern oil, Bush had responded decisively, assembling an international coalition and driving the Iraqis from Kuwait without, however, trying to take over Iraq itself and thereby involving the United States in a prolonged occupation (as his son would do a decade later). But in a surprising turn, like Winston Churchill's defeat in Britain's 1945 election after the nation's wartime triumph, Bush lost in 1992 to the young Democratic governor of Arkansas, Bill Clinton. The Democrats of the 1990s were not to be confused with Britain's Labor Party of 1945—the Democrats were a more centrist party. But amid a sluggish economy at the decade's start, the voters were ready for change and receptive to Clinton's youth, energy, and new ideas.

Some historians nonetheless treat Clinton as a reverse Eisenhower. Just as Eisenhower in the 1950s helped consolidate the liberal, New Deal political order, so Clinton, in this interpretation, helped consolidate a Reaganite, neoliberal political order in the 1990s.[2] A similar argument in the early 2000s posited that the United States had become a "center-right country," a supposed fact of national life that Democrats could not change.[3] Such arguments sometimes made use of an old metaphor suggesting American politics has always had a "sun" (a dominant majority party) and a "moon" (a minority party). From 1932 to 1980, the story went, the Democrats had been the sun and Republicans the moon, but the parties had changed places and Republicans were now the sun and Democrats the moon.[4] Similarly, a liberal political order had been followed by a neoliberal political order. These notions of neoliberal or center-right Republican dominance are consistent with important aspects of Clinton's presidency. But they are incomplete as a description of Clinton's policies and ultimately misleading about the broader historical significance of the 1990s.

The 1990s were more of a turning point than these interpretations suggest. They inaugurated an era of harsh partisan and ideological conflict that does not conform to the notion of a consistent political order or the sun/moon analogy. The idea that one party or the other, or a single ideologically driven order, must dominate politics and that Republicans or neoliberals had risen to that position ignores the possibility that the two parties may become locked in a conflict in which neither party can claim long-term dominance or impose a consistent ideology.[5]

In national voting, rather than extending a Republican era, 1992 initiated a period of rising Democratic support. Going into that year, Republicans had won five of the previous six presidential elections. Clinton's 1992 victory, however, proved to be the first of seven out of eight in which Democrats won the popular vote over the next twenty-eight years. Yet that edge in presidential voting did not translate into political dominance in either the 1990s or the early twenty-first century. After winning both the presidency and Congress in 1992, 2008, and 2020, Democrats immediately lost control of Congress in the first midterm elections in 1994, 2010, and 2022. Twice, in 2000 and 2016, Democrats won the popular vote but lost the presidency in the Electoral College. The 2000 election, decided by a 5–4 ruling by the Republican-dominated Supreme Court, was the ultimate expression of a "fifty-fifty country" in which the parties were almost equally matched and the Democrats found themselves stymied and unable to sustain progress on their agenda.

Partisan conflicts have two dimensions that were both relevant to the changed character of American politics in the 1990s. Conflicts between parties vary in how *deep* their divisions are—the separation of the parties from each other, ideologically and socially. Conflicts also vary in how *close* the divisions are—whether each party stands a reasonable chance of winning elections. The first dimension concerns the level of partisan polarization; the second, the level of electoral competitiveness. At various times, the major parties have been deeply but not closely divided; at other times, they have been closely but not deeply divided. But at the end of the twentieth century, they became *both deeply and closely divided*.[6] That combination, plus the end of the Cold War, which had restrained partisanship, led to a new era of intense conflict in which Americans on different sides increasingly looked at each other as enemies.

From Cold War to Culture War

Culture was not a new dimension of political conflict in the 1990s. Every phase of political development has a cultural aspect to it, and all the elements that went into the "culture war" in the 1990s had antecedents in previous decades, such as the attacks on "sexual perverts" in the 1950s, the divisions over drugs, sex, and the counterculture in the 1960s, and the family-values crusade of the late 1970s. In each decade, conservatives— usually Republicans, though sometimes Democrats—launched attacks on liberal politics for its association, real or presumed, with non-traditional forms of expression or modes of life that offended older, often religiously justified moral understandings. The idea that the end of the Cold War signaled a culture war at home came from the right. In the opening prime-time speech at the Republican National Convention in 1992, Patrick Buchanan defined that year's election as a struggle over American identity and portrayed the Democrats as a threat to the very core of American being:

> This election is about much more than who gets what. It is about who we are. It is about what we believe. It is about what we stand for as Americans. There is a religious war going on in our country for the soul of America. It is a cultural war, as critical to the kind of nation we will one day be as was the Cold War itself.[7]

In the Cold War, conservatives had accused liberals and progressives of being "un-American"—disloyal agents or unwitting "fellow travelers" of international communism. Now Buchanan and others sought to identify liberalism as another kind of enemy, an enemy entirely within. The issues that Buchanan highlighted were mostly the same ones the religious right had been agitating about—"abortion on demand," "homosexual rights," "discrimination against religious schools," "women in combat." Buchanan singled out Bill Clinton's wife Hillary as an exponent of "radical feminism," and he called attention to what he thought was a notably outrageous statement by Clinton's running mate, Tennessee Senator Al Gore:

> In New York, Mr. Gore made a startling declaration. Henceforth, he said, the "central organizing principle" of all governments must be: the environment.
>
> Wrong, Albert! The central organizing principle of this republic is freedom. And from the ancient forests of Oregon to the Inland Empire of California, America's great middle class has got to start standing up to the environmental extremists who put insects, rats and birds ahead of families, workers and jobs.

If the word "woke" had been in circulation, Buchanan would have used it.

An amped-up attack on liberal culture and values came from conservative intellectuals as well as politicians. Neoconservatives took the lead in criticizing liberals and the left (and confusing one with the other), as they had been doing since the 1970s. Now that communism had collapsed and American ideas were triumphant, wasn't it curious, the neocons asked, that so many Americans continued to complain about their society? The answer to this puzzlement was that "the left" had holed up in its last redoubt—America's cultural institutions—from which it spread pernicious, anti-American ideas. According to the critic Hilton Kramer, the left's agenda was rooted in the notion that "Amerika" is "intolerably repressive" and the "principal source of evil" in the world—a view, Kramer argued, that "prevails at almost every level of cultural life," from our universities down to our "wretched pop music." Or as a writer in *Commentary*, Charles Horner, put it, there was "one-party control of our major media and of our cultural, intellectual, and academic life." That one party, Horner claimed, was the "Anti-America Party," which was responsible for "the hateful anti-Americanism which suffuses public discourse."[8]

Sweeping right-wing accusations of disloyalty against liberals and leftists were nothing new, but there was an irony here. The neoconservatives, like other conservatives, believed in capitalism, and much of the culture they were attacking was wholly commercial and depended on the verdict of the market. If "pop music," for example, was "wretched," why was that? An older conservatism could be more openly derisive of popular taste and direct in its advocacy of censorship. But the picture conjured up by the neoconservatives was of a wholesome, chaste public seduced and degraded by anti-American liberal elites. The charges of anti-Americanism implied that the neoconservatives knew and stood for what was truly American. From their standpoint, as Hendrik Hertzberg pointed out at the time, "condemning American business or American military interventions is 'anti-American,' whereas wholesale vilification of American newspapers, American schools, American universities, American movies, American museums, and American book publishers is the least that can be expected of defenders of American values."[9]

Cultural conflicts may arise primarily from below, that is, from a deep divide within a society, or primarily from above, as a split among elites that may or may not diffuse to the public at large. In the 1991 book *Culture Wars: The Struggle to Define America*, the sociologist James Davison Hunter presented the conflict as a divide among ordinary Americans arising from two different kinds of moral commitments, orthodox and progressive. According to Hunter, whether the orthodox are Protestant, Catholic, or Jewish, they share a commitment to "an external, definable, and transcendent authority" that "tells us what is good, what is true, how we should live, and who we are. It is an authority that is sufficient for all time." The cultural progressives, in Hunter's contrast, define moral authority "by the spirit of the modern age, a spirit of rationalism and subjectivism," which changes with the zeitgeist.[10]

This conception was heavily loaded with conservative assumptions. Although liberals readily acknowledge that they are open to revising their views as circumstances and understandings change, that is not to say, as Hunter's conception implied, that they have no deep and abiding moral principles, having to do with freedom, dignity, and equality. And while conservatives may claim they are guided by a transcendent authority "sufficient for all time," they differ among themselves and have changed their minds historically about what that authority means. Only recently, in the early 1970s, leading evangelicals and fundamentalists had accepted the Supreme Court's legalization of abortion and acknowledged the Bible provided no guidance on the question; by the 1990s, they took the position that abortion was so inimical to their religious beliefs that compromise was impossible. The notion that conservatives are guided by a transcendent authority alone obscures the role of conservative religious and political leaders in changing that guidance.

As of the early 1990s, contrary to Hunter, surveys of public opinion failed to show an American public that had become sharply divided into opposing culture-war camps. Over the twenty-year period from 1972 to 1992, Americans had not become polarized on major moral and policy issues, with one exception—abortion.[11] What had happened with abortion, though, was instructive. Partisan polarization had begun at the top. Partisan differences had been minimal in the 1970s when Republicans were slightly more pro-choice than Democrats. By 1984, Republican Party leaders and activists had turned "pro-life," while Democratic leaders and activists had turned "pro-choice," but not until the 1990s did each party's rank and file reflect that split.[12] This pattern of "issue evolution," with divisions first emerging among party elites, was an early signal of what was coming across a wide range of issues. Some Americans would change their positions on the moral issues to align with their party, while others would change their party identification to align with their views. Party leaders who were out of line would give way to people with more consistent positions or change their own to keep in step.[13]

The idea of a popularly based culture war in the early 1990s was also hard to square with another widely discussed contemporary finding about the American public. The phrase "culture war" suggests a high intensity of feeling, but studies indicated that interest in the news and involvement in public life had fallen to a low point, particularly among the young. Going back to the 1940s, surveys had found relatively small differences in attention to news between young and older adults. But a 1990 study called "The Age of Indifference" found a younger generation (ages 18 to 29) that "knows less" and "cares less" and "is less critical of its leaders and institutions than young people in the past." Other studies later in the decade showed the same trend over the preceding two decades toward declining interest in the news, with the young paying the least attention and knowing the least about public and especially world affairs.[14]

Related research by the political scientist Robert Putnam, culminating in his best-selling book *Bowling Alone* (2000), found a generational basis for declining civic engagement in the United States. The proportion of Americans reporting one of a dozen civic activities—such as signing petitions, attending rallies and public meetings, working for a political party, or serving as an officer or committee member of a local organization—declined 10 percent from 1973–1974 to 1983–1984, and then fell another 24 percent in the next ten years. Over the entire twenty-year period, civic activity dropped 44 percent among those aged 18 to 29, compared to just 11 percent among those over age 60. "Generational math," Putnam argued, was "the single most important explanation for the collapse of civic engagement over the last several decades." Americans born between 1910 and 1940 had contributed disproportionately to civic life throughout their lives—voting, joining, reading, and trusting at a high rate. As that "long civic generation" died off, the overall level of civic participation in the United States was falling.[15]

These research findings were in line with a caricature that emerged in the early 1990s of the generation after the baby boomers, people born between 1966 and 1981, dubbed "Generation X" after a 1991 novel by that name. They were supposed to be ironic, cool, detached, uninterested in anything so earnest as enlisting in a culture war. It was a time when a rock group could sell ten million copies of an album whose signature lyric ran, "Oh well, whatever, never mind." In a recent book on the 1990s, the writer Chuck Klosterman remarks, "When informed that they were apathetic, the most common Xer response was disinterest in the accusation, inadvertently validating the original assertion."[16] Irony was having a moment. Later it drew a response, the "New Sincerity," though that seems to have been more of a hope than a trend.

Still, while the young may not have been especially interested in the culture war, the protagonists in the culture war were mightily interested in the young. Education was a primary site of conflict. Liberal and radical advocates of racial and gender equality sought to change curricula at all levels, from primary and secondary schools to the universities. In the schools, the battles were over such issues as multiculturalism in history and English classes and the introduction of sex education. Could textbooks and teachers recognize as legitimate other perspectives than the dominant tradition? Could the schools even venture into the sensitive terrain of sexuality and provide students the information to make better choices for themselves?

The very idea that the public schools should recognize a diversity of values and help students make choices for themselves—about sexuality, of all things—was anathema to conservatives. It implied that moral choices were open and, in the eyes of conservatives, it interfered with the rights of parents. When it suited conservatives, they were not above invoking pluralism, as they did in continuing efforts to introduce biblically based "creation science" alongside evolutionary biology into the science curriculum. But in fighting against multicultural and sexual diversity, they were carrying on the struggle that they had been consistently waging for years against "moral relativism" and "secular humanism." The televangelist Pat Robertson, who ran for the Republican presidential nomination in 1988, declared that the U.S. government was "attempting to do something that few states other than the Nazis and the Soviets have attempted to do, namely, to take the children away from the parents and to educate them in a philosophy that is amoral, anti-Christian and humanistic and to show them a collectivistic philosophy that will ultimately lead toward Marxism." Regarding sex education, for example, conservatives wanted either no role for the schools or "abstinence-only" instruction without the discussion of contraceptives that they regarded as how-to lessons for premarital sex.[17]

Rather than having a single outcome, these kinds of culture-war battles led to divergences in philosophy and policy in different organizations, communities, and regions. The diverging practices of the Boy Scouts and Girl Scouts illustrate the pattern. From their founding in the early twentieth century, both organizations reflected traditional gender roles and ideals. But after experiencing severe losses of membership in the 1970s—the Boy Scouts fell from 6.3 million to 4 million, the Girl Scouts from nearly 4 million to under 3 million—the organizations responded in opposite ways. From the 1970s on, the Girl Scouts adopted a more progressive program for girls. For example, it added skill-building in scientific and technical fields and accepted lesbians and nonbelievers as local leaders and members—and its membership grew. Meanwhile, the Boy Scouts held fast to its traditions, such as excluding members based on their sexual orientation and willingness to take a religious oath—and its membership continued to decline. Conservatives denounced the Girl Scouts; liberals spurned the Boy Scouts.[18] The clash reflected a widening pattern: the spread of cultural and ideological conflict into arenas of civil society where it had long been absent or at least subdued.

A division along liberal versus conservative lines had already appeared within the Protestant, Catholic, and Jewish communities, as discussed in chapter 4. By the 1990s, religiosity itself became an increasingly significant political demarcation. The correlation between religious attendance and Republican Party identification, which had been zero in the 1960s, rose slightly in the 1970s and 1980s and then sharply in the 1990s. Unlike their elders, young people were coming of age in an era when religion was politically charged, and some were turning away from it entirely. The emergence of "the nones," primarily young people who said they had no religious affiliation, was a growing development in the 1990s (and about to grow much larger in coming decades). American religion has always had a lot of ferment, with rising and falling waves of religious sentiment. Instead of sticking in adulthood with the religious tradition in which they had been raised, many people have moved from one church to another, discovered faith, or abandoned it. Due to this "churn," Robert Putnam and David Campbell pointed out in a 2010 study, "people gradually, but continually sort themselves into like-minded clusters—their commonality defined not only by religion, but also by the social and political beliefs that go along with their religion." In the 1990s and early 2000s, Putnam and Campbell argued, this sorting was producing a new pattern: Americans were becoming polarized over religion itself, "increasingly concentrated at opposite ends of the religious spectrum—the highly religious at one pole, and the avowedly secular at the other. The moderate religious middle is shrinking."[19] In this respect, the culture war was reaching down into the lives of ordinary Americans.

Americans were sorting themselves into different associations in other ways as well. According to measures of racial segregation, cities and suburbs were becoming more racially segregated in the late twentieth century. Gated communities became a symbol of the "secession of the affluent" from their surrounding neighbors. Americans were choosing neighborhoods based on lifestyle choices correlated with their partisan views.[20]

Perhaps the most important sorting process occurred in the teen years, when the young made critical choices about their future. Broadly speaking, two kinds of family patterns were associated with differing levels of education and career options. The older pattern involved marriage and childbearing at a relatively early age, which, especially for women, tended to limit the possibilities for higher education. The new pattern involved delays in both marriage and childbearing, which allowed for college and professional training.[21] In an emerging trend, Americans with a high school education or less were moving toward the Republicans, while the college-educated were beginning to move toward the Democrats. As a result, the choices that Americans were making in their teen years—insofar as they had any choice about continuing their education—were sorting them politically as well as by educational level.

As Americans sorted themselves into different associations, lifestyles, and family types, they also sorted themselves into different media. Since the 1970s, the once highly centralized media system had grown increasingly fragmented. The old midcentury system, for all its faults, led Americans to share more of a common culture by exposing them to much the same news, popular entertainment, and, not incidentally, the same advertising. As early as the 1920s, a leading advertising executive had said, "We're making a homogenous people out of a nation of immigrants."[22] A more fragmented media system tended to split up that wider public into market segments. The emergence of right-wing news media on radio and television in the 1990s was an outgrowth of this process.

Analysts often make two common mistakes in understanding the growth of partisan news media since the late twentieth century. The first is to attribute exaggerated importance to the repudiation of the "fairness doctrine" in 1987 by the Reagan administration's Federal Communications Commission. The doctrine had applied only to over-the-air broadcast stations, though it was inconsistently enforced even there; its repudiation probably did have a short-term impact on the rise of conservative talk radio. But the fairness doctrine had not previously blocked the syndication of right-wing radio broadcasters or the formation of 1,500 Christian radio stations. It never applied to cable television, which was where Fox News, the most important right-wing news outlet, developed in the 1990s, nor did it apply to the internet. One historian writes, "The repeal of the Fairness Doctrine was a major neoliberal victory" because it "freed radio and television stations from an obligation to present news that strove for objectivity and balance."[23] As I argued in chapter 1, however, it was not the fairness doctrine so much as economic incentives that led the three networks that originally dominated broadcast news to adopt a style of balanced, point–counterpoint reporting. When the number of TV channels was limited, the networks competed for a mass audience across regional and partisan lines and had no economic incentive to identify themselves with one party. When the number of channels increased, the incentives in news shifted toward market segmentation.

The second mistake analysts have sometimes made is to counterpose the mid-twentieth-century mass media to the internet and social media of the early twenty-first century, as though nothing had changed in the interim. In that oversimplified contrast, the online media seem to be the cause of fragmentation and polarization. But the fragmentation of the national public was already well advanced before the internet began to serve as a major means of communication, which happened only toward the end of the 1990s.

The breakup of the national public stemmed from complementary developments in consumer marketing and the media. The undifferentiated audience of midcentury mass media had its limitations from the advertisers' perspective. Companies were paying for "eyeballs" they didn't want. Especially as companies offered more differentiated brands, they sought out media that could efficiently reach finer segments of the market and encourage consumers to see the goods being advertised as reflections of their identity. The shift from mass to targeted advertising stimulated the multiplication of magazines and other media aimed at distinct groups. Conversely, the increasing number of channels in radio (with the advent of the FM band) and in television (with the spread of cable TV) also invited more targeted advertising. Both the marketers and the media companies were headed in the same direction, segmenting consumers to maximize profits.[24]

Targeted media were not a new phenomenon, but they grew rapidly in the last decades of the twentieth century. For example, as women's magazines proliferated, they sought to appeal to different groups of women based on their stage of life, ethnicity, education, and lifestyle. Radio too adapted to advertisers' interest in segmenting the public. During the late twentieth century, most stations adopted one or another type of talk or music that would attract a known demographic, no matter what time those listeners tuned in: Country, Urban Contemporary, Mainstream Rock, Classic Rock, Alternative, Oldies, Easy Listening, Gospel, Christian Contemporary, News/Talk, and numerous other formats. Television had taken away the old prime-time evening audience that radio had in its early decades. But as commuting time lengthened, many Americans spent hours listening during "drive time" in the morning and late afternoon. This was a disproportionately male audience, perfect for such formats as sports talk and conservative talk radio.

No medium was more wholly devoted to market segmentation than direct mail—"junk mail," as most people called it—which used data from credit cards and other sources to track purchases and classify households into different lifestyle clusters. Marketing by zip code became a high art. One system identified some forty lifestyle groups with such colorful names as "Blue-Blood Estates" and "Shotguns and Pickups" ("In *Shotguns & Pickups*, even the smallest home can come equipped with a giant-sized TV, wood stove, a ceramic bird collection and a dusty pickup in the driveway.")[25] Direct mail also became critically important for fundraising by nonprofit advocacy groups that used the money to support a staff of lawyers and other professionals lobbying Congress and litigating cases in the courts. Computerized direct mail was a major reason for declining civic engagement. Instead of organizing local chapters with regular meetings, advocacy groups were contacting supporters by mail and asking them just to write a check. Political candidates were doing the same thing, raising money to fight campaigns on the air rather than on the ground. It wasn't necessarily apathy that was responsible for diminished civic involvement; it was at least partly atrophy from lack of exercise of the civic muscles due to the changing forms of political struggle. Citizens don't show up to participate if no one asks.[26]

Television followed other media in moving from mass to specialized audiences. The more TV channels in an area and the more TV sets in a home, the more sense it made for programmers and advertisers to target market niches rather than the mass public. Liberals as well as conservatives generally thought the expansion of channels on radio and TV was a good thing because it provided for more competition and variety, including more programs for minorities that the old mass media had neglected.

But more choice had its downside. It diminished the culture Americans had in common, and it led to greater disparities in exposure to news. Compared to earlier years, when many viewers sat through the news because the networks all scheduled their half-hour evening news programs at the same time, the news audience split. News junkies could take in hours of cable news, while other viewers could avoid the news entirely and watch entertainment shows instead.[27] News dropouts, consisting disproportionately of people with low political interest, probably accounted for much of the decline in attention to news that researchers found in the 1990s. The cable news audience tended to include more people with high political interest, who also tended to be older and more partisan. In short, the same process produced falling audiences for news, the rise of partisan news media, and less consensus about what counted as important public problems and even what counted as fact.

The new right-wing electronic media of the 1990s—first on talk radio, then on cable TV—emerged because new means became available to satisfy long-standing grievances. Conservative anger at the mainstream media was not a new phenomenon. Conservatives had helped elect Republican administrations from Nixon to Reagan, but to their perennial disappointment, liberalism remained culturally dominant. According to data from the early to mid-1990s, Republicans were more than twice as likely as Democrats to report that the news media confronted them with a different perspective from their own.[28] The new structure of the media finally gave conservative Republicans opportunities they had not had before to watch news the way they wanted it framed and reported. To be sure, the right previously had its radio broadcasters, newspapers, magazines, and book publishers. But those voices had mostly been secondary to the mainstream media that came out of New York and Hollywood. Even when

Reagan became president, the conservative media barely survived financially. What emerged after Reagan—Rush Limbaugh's radio show went national in 1988; Fox News launched in 1996—was new: conservative media that were aggressively partisan, immensely profitable, and operating with resources and at a scale that dwarfed their predecessors.[29]

Partisan media were not necessarily incompatible with democracy. Partisan newspapers played a central role and, on the whole, a positive one in the United States in the nineteenth century. They were the primary means by which parties and elected officials communicated with the public, fought their adversaries, kept voters up to date, and got them to the polls. In the early 1800s the ties between local parties and newspapers were often so tight that their offices were in the same building and their leaders were the same people. Beginning with the "penny press" in the 1830s, however, some urban newspapers held themselves out as politically independent, a posture that enabled them to build a readership that stretched across party lines and had wider appeal to advertisers. With urban growth, more newspapers in the 1870s and later turned to this business strategy, which served as the organizational foundation for the rise of ideals of journalistic independence, professionalism, and objectivity.[30] Those ideals then influenced journalism as it developed on radio and television. The rise of partisan journalism in the electronic media in the late twentieth century reversed this historical sequence. As more segmented media developed, it made business sense to build news organizations around partisan identities.

Mainstream journalism itself had already adopted a more adversarial stance toward political leaders. Since the 1970s, leading news organizations had taken it as their highest duty to investigate wrongdoing in high places. Political corruption was not the only target; journalists became more aggressive in reporting sexual misconduct, as they had done earlier in American history. During the nineteenth century, the press subjected Thomas Jefferson, Andrew Jackson, Grover Cleveland, and others to accusations of sexual turpitude. In the early and mid-twentieth century, however, while journalists knew about the infidelities of Presidents Warren G. Harding, Franklin D. Roosevelt, and John F. Kennedy, they revealed nothing to the public. Even political opponents often held back from making charges of sexual misconduct when they knew about it. If Kennedy had been subjected to the same coverage as Clinton was three decades later, he would have been viewed differently at the time and he would be remembered differently now. The press corps and political leaders, however, formed a kind of club that saw the protection of the government's authority as their obligation. Clinton had the misfortune of serving as president too late to be protected in the simultaneous enjoyment of power and illicit sex in the White House. In the new political climate of the late twentieth century, the norms of journalism and politics changed, and the media feasted on sexual scandal. As the journalist Gay Talese observed in a different context, "Nothing pleased editors more than news that allowed them to express moral indignation while satisfying their prurient interest."[31]

Social and political divisions have always existed in the United States. A nation's institutions and its leaders can minimize or at least paper over those differences, or they can enlarge and aggravate them. As I emphasized in chapter 1, consensus in midcentury America was not a naturally occurring phenomenon. It was a political and cultural project. The same was true of public trust in that era. National leaders were determined to resist and suppress sources of division and distrust that could weaken the United States during the long international crisis that began during the late 1930s and extended through World War II and into the Cold War. Mass consumer markets and mass media provided a convenient foundation for carrying out that consensus project. Now, at the end of the century, instead of promoting mutual accommodation, marketers and the media reinforced and aggravated social and ideological differences, and political rivalries turned them into a general struggle for national power. When the sides in a conflict are closely matched, they do not necessarily tone down their differences and look for a middle ground. They may see a winning strategy in playing up those differences and annihilating their opposition.

The 1990s as the Beginning of a New Era

The early 1990s were one of those rare historical moments when the world seemed to be moving in a great rush toward democracy, peace, and economic growth all at once. The collapse of Soviet communism and end of the Cold War, the formation of the European Union and diminishing importance of national boundaries, the expansion of global trade and travel, the advent of the internet—all these developments appeared to signal a new era of progressive change. Perhaps naively, I shared in the enthusiasm. In spring 1990, Robert Kuttner, Robert Reich, and I launched a new political magazine that we called *The American Prospect*. The cover of the first issue showed an egg breaking open to reveal a new world inside, a world reborn. But the promise of that new world would not be fulfilled over the next three decades. Politics in the 1990s took a particularly ugly turn in the United States.

For nearly a half century after 1932, with only brief interludes, Democrats had enjoyed overwhelming control of both the Senate and House. It was a surprise in 1980 when Republicans won a Senate majority, which they held for six years. But from the 1980s on, control of Congress became much more hotly contested. As the political scientist Frances Lee argues in a study of the U.S. Congress, parties act differently depending on their prospects for control. If they see no chance of winning a majority, members of the minority are likely to try to achieve what they can through cooperation in writing legislation. But when control is up for grabs, both parties invest more in party-building and image-making and become more aggressive in drawing distinctions. The incentives for the minority change from legislating to messaging. Instead of taking part in writing laws that could redound to the majority's advantage, the minority party is likely to become more confrontational, assailing the majority as feeble and corrupt and accentuating issues where public opinion appears to be on its side.[32]

This was the strategy that Republicans in the House adopted during the late 1980s and early 1990s, when Newt Gingrich led the party's drive for power even before he became its formal leader and Speaker of the House in the wake of the 1994 election. Ferociously partisan, he brought down a Democratic Speaker in 1989 and broke from the old norms of civility, restraint, and partnership in government that previously shaped the workings of Congress. He had a grandiose vision of himself as a transformative leader. "People like me," he said in 1994, "are what stand between us and Auschwitz. I see evil all around me every day."[33] In a guide to other Republicans about language as a "mechanism of control," Gingrich set out a glossary of terms for describing their opponents, including "sick," "pathetic," "lie," "betray," "traitors," "corruption," "obsolete," "they/them," "cheat," "steal," and, of course, "liberal."[34] He advised, "The number one fact about the news media is they love fights," and so to draw attention and "educate" the public, combat was the best policy. While irony may have been having a moment among the young, vitriol was having a moment in politics. Like Buchanan at the 1992 convention and Limbaugh on the radio, Gingrich infused the culture war into partisan politics, accusing Democrats of every random outrage and of being "anti-child" and "anti-flag" (words he also recommended). If this style had been Gingrich's alone, it would have had limited significance. But other Republicans learned to "speak like Newt," and even some of the party's moderates in the House supported Gingrich for leadership, believing he could carry them to power.[35] The same pattern later led most of the dwindling number of moderate Republicans in Congress to support Donald Trump, ultimately reducing the center right in the United States to political impotence.

After losing three presidential elections in a row, Democrats in the early 1990s also faced an imperative for renewal. But the winner of the party's presidential nomination in 1992, Bill Clinton, adopted a strategy that combined progressive and neoliberal elements to achieve that renewal. No Democrat nominated that year could have succeeded by going as far to the left as Gingrich went to the right. Democrats did not have the luxury of writing off the South because they lacked sufficient support elsewhere to win a national election. (In defeating Bush, Clinton would take every state on either side of the Mississippi River, except Mississippi itself; in 1996 he would be the last Democrat, as of 2024, to win five of those states: Arkansas, Missouri, Louisiana, Kentucky, and Tennessee.) A Democrat could also not afford to write off either the so-called Reagan Democrats—Northern working- and middle-class whites who had defected to the Republicans—or the party's liberal base, or its support in minority communities. The Democrats needed support from all those heterogeneous groups to build a winning coalition.

Faced with that imperative, Clinton called for a mix of policies framed in terms that implicitly acknowledged the reservations of culturally conservative voters even while backing liberal priorities. For example, he called for universal health insurance, more support for education and training, and fairness in taxation as mere justice for "people who work hard and play by the rules." He defended reproductive rights but said he would seek to make abortion "safe, legal, and rare." In his first year, he had two major priorities, a plan for economic recovery and a plan for health-care reform, neither of which was especially left wing. But, in this new era of partisan warfare, he had no cooperation from Republicans in passing either one.

The economic program, presented in Clinton's first budget in 1993, gave a surprising priority to a presumably conservative goal—deficit reduction. Together, Reagan and Bush had generated in twelve years more than three times as much debt as the federal government had accumulated in its previous 192 years. Clinton reversed direction despite promises he had made during the campaign for an economic stimulus. Proposing long-term reductions in the deficit, he called for a combination of tax increases and spending cuts in the belief that interest rates would fall and the economy would get a stimulus by that means. This was the case that Clinton's Wall Street advisers, backed by Federal Reserve Chairman Alan Greenspan, were making, and during the 1990s their strategy seemed to work. As the economists Alan Blinder and Janet Yellen show, the 1993 budget proved to be a "fiscal turning point": Interest rates did fall afterward, and the economy grew faster than it otherwise would have, an average 4 percent annual growth rate.[36] Not only did Clinton's presidency cut the deficit; in his final three years, the government ran a surplus. After a dozen years of mammoth deficits, Clinton and the Democrats served as the party of fiscal repair and responsibility, while unemployment fell to its lowest point in more than two decades. The budget that set the government on that path, however, did not receive a single Republican vote in either the House or Senate and, because of its tax increases, probably contributed to the Democrats' loss of Congress in 1994.

Clinton and his advisers on health care—I was one of them—originally expected that his proposal for reform would lead to a negotiation with congressional Republicans as well as Democrats.[37] This hope did not seem far-fetched: Business groups at the time supported reform, Republican senators had sponsored a bill that included universal coverage, and Clinton's plan retained private insurers under a system of regulated competition, a model consistent in its rough outlines with what many conservatives were advocating. The plan, however, also called for a government cap on the rate of growth of total health spending, a provision aimed at long-term health-care cost containment that conservatives did not support. Unlike Clinton's federal budget plan, the health legislation could not pass without Republican votes because Democrats alone had fewer than the sixty needed to overcome a Senate filibuster. But congressional Republicans abandoned their own bills and turned against any deal. In a memo to party leaders three months after Clinton sent his plan to Congress, Republican strategist Bill Kristol (Irving Kristol's son) warned that the Clinton proposal was "a serious political threat to the Republican Party." It would "help Democratic prospects in 1996" and in the long term "revive the reputation of the party that spends and regulates, the Democrats, as the generous protector of middle-class interests." Republicans had to "adopt an aggressive and uncompromising counterstrategy" to "delegitimize" the Clinton proposal and bring about its "unqualified political defeat." They should reject any compromise proposal "sight unseen." When they killed the Clinton plan, one Republican senator remarked that they just had to make sure they left no fingerprints.[38]

Clinton's economic and health proposals did call for something highly distasteful to Republicans—economic redistribution. Besides increasing the gasoline tax (after a failed effort, at Gore's suggestion, to pass a broader carbon tax), the 1993 budget raised the top income tax rate back up to 39.6 percent. It also doubled the Earned Income Tax Credit (EITC), a benefit for people with earnings in 1993 under $23,050 (equivalent to about $50,000 in 2024 dollars). Higher taxes on the rich plus the EITC for the working poor probably made the budget the most economically progressive policy measure adopted by Congress in at least two decades. Like the EITC, the health plan had particular benefit for low-wage workers, a population likely to be uninsured for lack of coverage from either their employers or Medicaid. Furthermore, universal health coverage had appeal across class and racial lines at a time when many middle-class people with pre-existing medical conditions were unable to obtain insurance. Healthcare reform had risen to the top of the Democratic agenda partly because resolving the system's deep problems could help rebuild a broad coalition, which was precisely why, as Kristol clearly explained, Republicans decided to be "uncompromising" in their opposition.

At the beginning of a meeting in the Roosevelt Room of the White House in early 1993, Clinton mused aloud that he was making two gambles—one on the economy and the other on health-care reform—and that he might get re-elected if just one of them paid off. The gamble on the economy did get him re-elected in 1996, but it didn't pay off fast enough to avert the loss of Congress in 1994. From then on, much of his presidency was consumed in a defensive battle against congressional Republicans and the investigations of scandals that proved to be groundless but led to the disclosure of his sexual encounters with a White House aide in her early twenties. The report on those encounters by the special prosecutor Kenneth Starr provided enough lurid detail to have been banned under the old Comstock Act. Like the defeat of the Clinton health plan, the Starr Report and ensuing impeachment by House Republicans aimed to humiliate the president, but he survived the show trial in the Senate and emerged more popular. In a remarkable reversal of the midterm curse on the party in office, Democrats even picked up House seats in the 1998 elections.

The Republican attack on Clinton held him up as the chief exhibit in the conservatives' culture war against loose liberal morals. Instead of Clinton falling, however, it was Gingrich who was forced to resign after the 1998 midterm due to his rising unpopularity and the electoral reverses his party had suffered. But then the new Republican speaker-designate,

Robert Livingston, stepped down acknowledging extramarital affairs, and he gave way to another Republican, Dennis Hastert, who subsequently was convicted and served time in prison in connection with payoffs he made to conceal his sexual abuse of a teenage boy. Republicans' later willingness to excuse Trump for his high—and low—crimes and misdemeanors is also helpful in putting in perspective their attacks on Clinton's morals and how seriously they upheld their role as exemplars of traditional family values.

Clinton's policies, as I indicated, combined progressive and neoliberal elements. The progressive policies mainly concerned taxes, health care, and education and training and especially boosted the position of the working poor, which reduced inequality. The neoliberal policies related primarily to trade, telecommunications, and finance, areas where Clinton often sought support from corporate interests and relied on Republican votes to pass legislation. Those policies increased inequality in two ways, by boosting top incomes and by undermining economic security for working people.

During the 1970s and 1980s, the Democrats had been the more protectionist of the two major parties, but Clinton reversed that stance. He championed ratification of the North American Free Trade Agreement (NAFTA), which went into effect on January 1, 1994, and called for the periodic renewal of nondiscriminatory trade relations with China, culminating in the establishment of Permanent Normal Trade Relations in 2000. The resulting increase in trade with Mexico and China had major economic and political effects primarily because it accelerated the decline of U.S. manufacturing jobs. NAFTA's net impact on employment was relatively small nationally, but together with another trade agreement in 1994 phasing out import quotas on textiles and clothing, it did result in large losses of manufacturing jobs in one region, the South. Since the NAFTA-impacted communities had been low income to start with and suffered persistent employment losses in the following years, the agreement exacerbated regional as well as class inequalities. In post-NAFTA presidential and House elections, the white workers who lived in those communities in the South, as well as people elsewhere with protectionist views, abandoned the Democrats. The shift was particularly strong among white men without college degrees.[39]

Increased trade with China proved even more significant. Renewal of nondiscriminatory trade relations with China had depended on determinations that it was making improvements in human rights. In 1994, however, Clinton agreed to "de-link" trade from rights in response to lobbying by U.S. businesses heavily reliant on low-cost Chinese production. At the time, Clinton justified his decision by posing the question, "Will we do more to advance the cause of human rights if China is isolated or if our nations are engaged in a growing web of political and economic cooperation and contacts?" Clinton's premise reflected the post–Cold War confidence that increased trade would undermine authoritarianism in China. No one expected it might eventually undermine democracy in the United States. Trade with China took a much larger toll than NAFTA on U.S. manufacturing employment, much of it coming after Clinton left office. Again, however, the manufacturing jobs lost were not large in relation to the total U.S. economy, but because they were regionally concentrated, this time in the Midwest, they had a major political impact. Some of the financial policies adopted under Clinton, such as the failures to regulate derivatives and sub-prime mortgages, also did not blow up until after his presidency. During the 1990s, neoliberal economic policy seemed to be a bipartisan triumph. It was only afterward, especially with the 2008 financial crisis, that Americans began to see the damage.[40]

The decision of Clinton's that liberals objected to most strenuously at the time was his acceptance of a Republican-passed welfare reform bill in 1996. He had already vetoed two versions of the legislation that would have cut back Medicaid, food stamps, and the EITC. The version he signed dropped those cuts, but it still replaced the old cash assistance program, Aid to Families with Dependent Children (AFDC), with a restrictive program of block grants to the states called Temporary Assistance to Needy Families. The new policy eliminated the federal entitlement to benefits and introduced time limits and work requirements. Because AFDC had been colloquially known as "welfare," its elimination carried enormous symbolic weight even though it had represented only a small fraction of federal welfare spending. Moreover, AFDC had left eligibility and benefits largely to the states, which meant that public assistance was already minimal in some Southern states. Having promised to change "welfare as we know it," Clinton signed the Republican bill in the midst of the 1996 campaign despite the opposition of his liberal aides.

Clinton could, and did, rationalize his decision privately on the grounds that AFDC wasn't worth defending. The basic premise of AFDC seemed out of date; even liberals were finding it difficult to defend a program of cash assistance to poor mothers to stay at home with their children now that most mothers were in the labor force. In signing the bill, Clinton took a political burden off Democrats' backs at the cost of putting a heavier burden on the backs of the poorest of the poor. In retrospect, Clinton was responsible for two major changes in antipoverty policy: an enlarged, federally set EITC and diminished state-based cash assistance. The first lifted up poor people who worked, while the second left in deep poverty those who didn't have or couldn't keep a paying job. The combined effect was to "make work pay," as welfare reformers had intended, but it made life harder for the most destitute.[41]

Clinton achieved something that no Democrat had done since Franklin Roosevelt. He was re-elected (indeed, by a comfortable margin in 1996), but much of what Clinton did as president divided his own party, which suffered historic reverses in his own home region. Many observers attribute the Democrats' loss of the South to the party's embrace of civil rights in the 1960s. They often cite Lyndon Johnson's rueful comment to his aide Bill Moyers after signing the 1964 Civil Rights Act, "I think we just handed the South to the Republicans for a long time to come." But that is not exactly what happened. It wasn't until the 1990s that Democrats truly lost the South. During the intervening thirty years, Southern Democrats had continued to be competitive with Republicans. The enfranchisement of Black voters resulting from the Voting Rights Act helped make up for losses among whites. By building coalitions of Black and working-class white voters, a generation of moderate Democrats such as Carter and Clinton won elections in Southern states. According to an index of party competition, nine of eleven Southern states were still "two-party competitive" as late as 1994. But the interracial coalitions that supported relatively progressive policies broke down in the 1990s as working-class whites in the South abandoned the Democrats. Although certainly not the whole explanation, NAFTA and the resulting plant shutdowns in the South contributed to that shift. Working-class whites elsewhere in the country would later become alienated from the Democratic Party partly for the same reason, the Democrats' embrace of free trade.[42]

The Limits of Democratic Victories

The 1990s set a pattern for the Democratic Party that would be repeated over the thirty years from 1992 to 2022. The party won national elections but was unable to build on its victories. All three Democrats elected president in that period—Clinton, Barack Obama, and Joe Biden—came to office and immediately undertook repair work: Clinton addressed the looming overhang of debt; Obama the 2008 financial crisis; Biden the 2020

COVID pandemic. In each case, Democrats acted as a party of responsibility. Each time they carried out that work successfully and in ways that mitigated the impact on the poor far more than Republicans would have. For example, although recessions usually increase poverty rates, Obama's policies prevented a surge in poverty during the Great Recession in 2009.[43]

For their troubles, however, all three Democratic presidents immediately lost control of Congress and then had to defend themselves against Republican threats to shut down the government or default on the federal debt, as though Republicans had no responsibility for accumulating the debt in the first place. With a divided government, the three Democratic presidents not only lost the ability to move ahead legislatively with an agenda of their own but were forced to make concessions. After Republicans returned to undivided control of the presidency and Congress in 2001 and 2017 (both times with a president who had lost the popular vote), they did the one thing they prioritized—cutting taxes in ways that favored the rich, at the expense of government solvency. Although Democratic administrations shifted policy back in a more egalitarian direction, they were unable to shift it back entirely. In the thirty-two years from 1992 to 2024, Democrats held the White House for twenty years, but only for six of them with control of Congress. Even then they always lacked a sixty-vote, filibuster-proof Senate majority, except for the half-year from July 2009 to January 2010, which proved indispensable for passing the Affordable Care Act.[44] To have achieved progress on as deeply rooted a problem as inequality, Democrats would have needed large, sustained congressional majorities, the kind of majorities that in the 1930s and 1960s made possible historic breakthroughs. They have not had that power during Democratic administrations of the fifty-fifty era, when the parties have been close competitors.

The three decades after 1992 had other similarities that gave the whole period a consistent political character. Compared to the trends from the 1970s to the early 1990s, voter turnout and other forms of citizen engagement increased, but partisan polarization increased too, and it increased the most among Americans who were the most politically attentive and engaged. In the early 1990s, as I suggested earlier, Americans began polarizing on party lines, in the sense that Democrats and Republicans increasingly divided into opposed camps on public issues. According to one interpretation, partisan polarization even in the early 2000s continued to be limited to a narrow elite of leaders and activists who were disconnected from a predominantly moderate mass public.[45] But the evidence by then was unmistakable that polarization was rising among a wider "engaged public," people who reported even a minimal level of political involvement, such as trying to persuade someone else to vote for a candidate, displaying a political bumper sticker, or attending a rally. Polarization wasn't just elite zealotry. As the political scientist Alan Abramowitz showed, while the least attentive were bunched in the center, ideological and partisan polarization was "greatest among those individuals whose beliefs and behavior most closely reflect the ideals of responsible democratic citizenship, that is, the engaged public."[46]

Three additional aspects of polarization were also apparent.

First, partisanship became an important social identity. The late twentieth-century spread of polarization into civil society and the media anticipated and contributed to a widening pattern of "social polarization." Groups with different social characteristics and life experiences became arrayed against each other across America's culturally inflected partisan and ideological divide.[47]

Second, this conflict became highly emotional. Americans not only favored their own in-group but also developed an intense dislike of the other side. "Negative partisanship" became a key feature of American politics. Republicans and Democrats both came to rate each other more coldly and use terms like "immoral," "close-minded," and "unpatriotic" to describe members of the other party.[48]

Third, despite a tendency to treat the two sides of the conflict as equal and opposite, Republicans became more homogeneously conservative, while Democrats remained more ideologically and socially mixed. This asymmetric pattern appeared in congressional voting and surveys of party activists; Republicans moved further to the right than Democrats moved to the left.[49] Conservatives' social networks were more ideologically homogeneous; liberals were more likely to have exposure to people with other views.[50] But the most important difference lay between the experiences of the center right in the Republican Party and the center left in the Democratic Party.

The center right—consisting of people who are conservative and business-oriented on the economy but moderate to liberal on civil rights, immigration, and other social issues—traditionally had its home in the Republican Party. Center-right politics, however, have not been fixed in place. During the late twentieth century, the center right itself moved right, thanks in part to the shift of the white South into the Republican Party and the shift of the Northeast out of it. First, liberal Republicans in the tradition of Nelson Rockefeller disappeared from national politics; next, moderate Republicans with the positions of Richard Nixon became scarce. The group of Republican Senate moderates known as the Wednesday Club, which had nearly two dozen members in the 1970s, had shrunk to five by 2009 and all except one were gone eight years later.[51]

While hostility across partisan lines received the most attention, the rising hostility of conservatives toward moderates within the Republican Party was arguably just as politically significant. The right-wing media called out moderates as RINOs (a term that appears to have originated in 1992), denouncing them at times with as much fury as they denounced Democrats. One of the imperatives facing right-wing leaders and parties around the world is to clear the field of moderate to conservative rivals. This was what was happening in the Republican Party, beginning with Gingrich's attack on the old gentlemanly leadership that preceded him. In the early 2000s, while George W. Bush was president, the United States may have seemed to be a "center-right country," a phrase that Bush's strategist, Karl Rove, often repeated. But Bush's presidency was a fiasco for the center right. Not only did Bush's Iraq War become a symbol of official deceit and the futile expenditure of life, his administration's support for immigration reform and free trade coincided with rising disillusionment in the Republican base with both immigration and trade. In 2008, when Bush's presidency ended in financial crisis, recession, and the Wall Street bailout, the loss of the presidency may have seemed only to be a temporary setback to center-right Republicans. It turned out, however, to be much more serious.

In the coming decade, no political grouping in the United States would suffer a more complete wipeout than the center right. As a result of its collapse, the Republicans became a far different party than in the past. To be sure, the Democrats became more liberal since they lost their white Southern base, but the center left remained, and still remains, the party's core in Congress, state governments, and the electorate. Among Democrats there has been nothing comparable to the purge of RINOs among Republicans.

During the three decades after 1992, Americans moved across party lines in both directions, but the struggle for national power remained tight. Closely fought battles helped maintain deep divisions. Party leaders and activists had incentives to highlight their differences to raise money and drive voters to the polls.

Under these circumstances, anything that might change the balance in one direction or the other took on heightened importance. In the early

2000s, a change that had remained in the background began to stir hope on the left and fear on the right about the nation's future political direction. That change was demographic: the growing population of immigrants from Latin America, Asia, and Africa. As things turned out, it did lead to an upheaval. It just wasn't the one that liberals and progressives were expecting.

CHAPTER SIX

Sleepwalking (1)

Immigration

The ethnic mix of this country will not be upset.

—SENATOR TED KENNEDY, 1965, opening a hearing on immigration reform[1]

We are the boiling pot. We have open arms.

—REPUBLICAN PRESIDENT CANDIDATE BOB DOLE, 1996, presumably intending to say "melting pot"[2]

THE IDEA OF THE UNITED STATES as a refuge for freedom, taking in the persecuted and oppressed from other corners of the world, has been the theme of a long-cherished national story. Walt Whitman rhapsodized about America as a "nation of many nations." Emma Lazarus celebrated America's "world-wide welcome" to "your tired, your poor / Your huddled masses yearning to breathe free," words inscribed below the Statue of Liberty. This was a beloved truth, but it was not the whole truth. Under a law enacted by Congress in 1790, no one coming to America's shores could be naturalized except a "free white person," a racial prerequisite for the acquisition of citizenship by the foreign born that remained in effect, amazingly, until 1952.[3]

The new immigrants since the mid-twentieth century have not just added to the American mix; they have brought America closer to what the poets earlier imagined it to be. The single most important fact about the rise in immigration in the late twentieth and early twenty-first centuries is that it has taken place in the wake of the Black struggle for civil rights and respect and other progressive ethnic-consciousness movements. Those movements did not originally cause the rise in immigration, but they affected where the new immigrants have come from, how other Americans have seen them, and how they have seen themselves. The United States previously did not just have a white majority; it had a white supermajority, a nine-to-one, white-to-Black ratio, the racial cleavage that was uppermost in public consciousness. The new immigrants have changed that picture. Grouped together with Black people in census forecasts and popular discussion, they have brought the white-to-nonwhite ratio into a more even balance and raised the prospect of a flip in majority status and power.

This change would never have been easy for whites to accept, but it has been especially difficult because of the second most important fact about the rise in immigration. It accelerated during an economic and political transformation that has disrupted the lives of many native-born whites. Immigration did not cause their problems, but it has come to symbolize the sense many of them have had about being abandoned by their own country.

During the twentieth century's second half, Congress adopted major changes to immigration laws, including the Immigration and Nationality Act of 1965 and the Immigration Reform and Control Act (IRCA) of 1986, with little understanding of the immense effects they would have in racially and ethnically diversifying the American people. The effects of immigration policies may seem easy to foresee, but that is not always the case. In 1924, Congress passed the Johnson-Reed Immigration Act, which tightened and made permanent restrictions temporarily enacted three years earlier. That legislation did succeed in its primary objectives: drastically reducing the total yearly number of immigrants, nearly eliminating immigration visas for Southern and Eastern Europe, and barring all immigration from Asia. But by cutting off the supply of foreign labor, the 1924 law had unforeseen long-term consequences on migration within the United States. It created economic opportunities for Black people to move North, a result that the Northern elites who supported the 1924 law surely did not intend. Whether in closing the gates to foreigners (as in 1924) or in opening the gates more widely (as in 1965), immigration policy in the twentieth century irreversibly changed American society. But expectations and impact were two different things.

By the 2010s, the foreign born were nearly as large a proportion of the U.S. population as they had been a century earlier, when opposition to immigration was mounting. In 1910, 14.7 percent of the population was foreign-born, a share that dropped to a low of 4.7 percent in 1970 before climbing back up past 10 percent in the late 1990s, reaching 14.3 percent in 2023, and possibly setting a historical record in 2024.[4]

No law of political demography says that immigration at any particular level triggers a backlash. Still, nativist movements have been a recurrent phenomenon in the United States—against the Irish from the 1840s to the 1860s; against the Chinese and later the Japanese from the 1860s to the early 1900s; against Southern and Eastern Europeans, mainly Catholics and Jews, from the 1890s to the 1920s; and against Mexicans in the 1930s and 1950s. The pattern, to be sure, is not peculiar to the United States. Rising levels of immigration are associated internationally with support for anti-immigrant, right-wing parties.[5] In the late twentieth century, however, nativism was slow to re-emerge in the United States. Rising immigration did not provoke a sharp reaction until the 1990s, and at least at first, the impact of the "new nativism" was limited.

The growth of immigration, as already mentioned, coincided with the wrenching shift in jobs from manufacturing to services and information, a shift that would have taken place if only because of new technology and more rapid productivity increases in manufacturing than in other sectors. Rising global trade accelerated de-industrialization. When factories shut down, comparable, post-industrial jobs did not spring up for the same people. Conservative policies holding down the minimum wage, fighting unions, restricting the coverage of unemployment insurance, and cutting back other welfare provisions did not make things easy for displaced workers and the communities where they lived. Employers were also cutting back pension and health insurance plans, if they provided them at all. The costs of the changing structure of the economy fell where the costs of change usually do—on those with the least power to protect themselves.

According to the preponderant economic evidence, the gains experienced by immigrants in the United States have not come at the expense of the native born. A 2017 report of the National Academies of Sciences, Engineering, and Medicine concluded that immigration's impact on the wages of the native born "may be small and close to zero" particularly "when measured over a period of 10 years or more." But, the report acknowledged, some studies did find negative effects on native-born, low-skilled workers.[6] Whether or not immigration had such effects, many people saw job opportunities as limited and believed immigrants were a drag on their incomes. At the turn of the twenty-first century, insecurities among native-born whites were rising for multiple reasons. Many of them were poorly positioned to prosper in a globalizing economy. The September 11, 2001, terrorist attacks set off worries about foreigners as national security threats. Yet another source of insecurity came from the widely publicized reports that whites were on their way to becoming a minority, assuming current trends in immigration continued. Some conservative whites already felt like a minority, convinced that Blacks, immigrants, liberal Democrats, and untrustworthy Republicans were taking their country away from them.

In the 1990s and early 2000s, the national Democratic and Republican parties both supported internationalist policies, including support for free trade and NATO and other alliances. Presidents Bill Clinton and Barack Obama as well as the two George Bushes supported immigration, even as Republicans in Congress and state government were turning against it. Although both parties backed policies to fortify the southern border, these measures were largely symbolic and failed to stop unauthorized crossings. But politically exploitable fears and resentments of immigrants were building, and it should not have been a surprise when those fears and resentments eventually found a national leader willing to exploit them in full.

A Quiet Explosion

Two new streams of immigration flowed from changes in national policy in the mid-1960s. One stream was congressionally authorized, while the other was not, though it was long tolerated in practice. Both contributed to what was, for a long time, a quiet explosion in the numbers of immigrants.

The law principally responsible for the authorized stream, the Immigration and Nationality Act of 1965, was one of Lyndon Johnson's great legislative triumphs, yet its significance was little appreciated at the time by government officials, social scientists, or the public. The usual criticism of Johnson's Great Society is that it achieved less than it promised. That cannot be said of immigration reform. It did more than anyone promised.

The primary impetus behind reform was to undo the bias against Southern and Eastern Europeans in the national-origins quotas dating from the 1920s, but the legislation was far more sweeping. It provided that no person could be "discriminated against in the issuance of an immigrant visa because of his race, sex, nationality, place of birth or place of residence."[7] That provision for the first time extended principles of equal treatment to non-citizens beyond U.S. borders. In the age of civil rights and the Cold War, the flagrant racism of earlier immigration law had become unacceptable for both moral and foreign policy reasons. So instead of just ending the quotas favoring immigration from northwestern Europe, the law put prospective immigrants from Asia and Africa on the same footing as Europeans. Altogether, the law capped immigration from the Eastern Hemisphere—Europe, Africa, the Middle East, Asia, and the Pacific—at 170,000 annually, with no more than 20,000 visas to be issued annually to people from any one country.

Officials anticipated, however, that the breadth of the legislation would make little practical difference. Asked about likely immigration from Asia at a congressional hearing in 1964, Attorney General Robert F. Kennedy testified that "5,000 immigrants could come in the first year [because of a backlog in applications], but we do not expect that there would be any great influx after that." On the opening day of a hearing on the legislation the following year, Senator Ted Kennedy declared that the net increase in immigration would be small, only about 60,000, and would not disrupt America's existing "ethnic mix."[8] The expectations for minimal change reflected the bill's provisions: the priorities it gave to the skilled and to relatives of U.S. citizens, the continued cap on total "quota" immigration, and low estimates for "nonquota" immigrants (chiefly immediate family members). Legislators insisted on reversing the preference order in the original bill, putting family-based ahead of employment-based applicants, because they expected the family preferences would preserve the American "ethnic mix" as it was.[9] That was a reasonable assumption. Legislators were not dissembling when they said they didn't expect a major change in American society.

As the sociologist Nathan Glazer later wrote: "The United States was giving itself the moral satisfaction of passing a nondiscriminatory immigration act that it expected would in no substantial way change the sources or volume of American immigration. The people who were fighting for the bill were Jews, Italians, Greeks, and Poles, who hoped their relatives, their fellow countrymen, and their co-religionists would have an easier time getting in, and the bill itself favored strongly the principle of family unification."[10] What lawmakers failed to anticipate was that Europeans were no longer the primary ones interested in coming to America. Instead, new immigrants from other areas of the world would shortly make more use of the employment-based and then the family preferences. Social scientists had no role in the debate about the law and little to say when it passed. Hardly any population experts had been studying U.S. immigration because there had been hardly any immigration to study. "Demographers might consider reviving immigration as a field of inquiry," an article in the new journal *Demography* concluded in 1967.[11]

Many people believe the 1965 law also led to increased immigration from Latin America, but that is a misunderstanding. Latin America had previously been exempt from the overall immigration cap and national-origins quotas. The 1965 Immigration and Nationality Act for the first time set a numerical limit on immigration from Western Hemisphere countries, to go into effect in 1968.

The new hemispheric cap of 120,000 visas—introduced in Congress, initially over the administration's objections—was considerably lower than the number of Mexicans alone who had been entering the country legally on a temporary or permanent basis. Under the Bracero program first established by Congress in 1942, the U.S. government arranged for Mexicans to come to do seasonal work in the fields, ranches, and orchards of Texas, California, and other Western states. ("Bracero" translates roughly as "farmhand.") As of the late 1950s, the program brought in more than 400,000 Mexicans annually. But labor unions and other liberal groups saw the arrangement as exploitative, and Congress and the Johnson administration refused to extend it beyond 1964.[12] The agricultural growers who employed the braceros, however, continued to welcome Mexicans as a source of cheap labor, legal or not, and the border at that time was mostly unpoliced. In addition, from 1960 to 1968, while Mexican immigration was uncapped, about 368,000 Mexicans received permanent resident visas. But this level of legal immigration became impossible under the new restrictions.[13] In short, Congress put a stamp of illegality on an immigration stream that its earlier policies had encouraged.

Even after the end of the Bracero program, Mexicans coming to work in the United States were mainly circular migrants, that is, going back and forth across the border, earning money for their families back home. By the 1980s, as Mexico's own baby boom came of age and an economic crisis led more of its citizens to go north in search of work, Congress came under growing pressure to combat what was now defined as an "invasion" of "illegal aliens." The result was congressional passage of IRCA, the 1986 compromise legislation signed by President Reagan that became the model in the following years for a "grand bargain" over immigration reform. On the one hand, IRCA increased spending for border patrol and made it illegal for employers to knowingly hire the undocumented. On the other, it also granted temporary legal status to people who had been continuously in the country without permission for at least five years, enabling them, as well as a special category of agricultural workers, to obtain permanent residency and citizenship.[14]

About three million people eventually gained legal status under IRCA, and once citizens, they were legally able to bring family. But the measures intended to curb the undocumented population were ineffective. Employers found it easy to avoid the sanctions, and the increased policing of the border failed to keep out migrants. If apprehended and sent back, they could just try again. So while IRCA became a model of a successful grand bargain for reformers sympathetic to unauthorized immigrants, it became a model of failure for those who saw the unauthorized as a threat.

By the 1990s, more intensive border enforcement—forcing migrants to go through the desert and pay *coyotes* (guides) to get them across—did affect immigration, though in an unexpected way. By making it more dangerous and costly for the undocumented to return periodically to Mexico, it encouraged them to settle permanently in the United States. Just as policymakers didn't grasp the demographic implications of the Immigration and Nationality Act of 1965, so they didn't foresee that high-intensity policing of the Southern border would turn circular migrants into immigrants. Nor did they see that NAFTA would conflict with the aim of keeping out the unauthorized. From 1994 on, as more Mexicans did legitimate business across the border, they became more likely to learn English and acquire the contacts and information that made it easy for them to settle in the United States after entering legally and overstaying their visas.[15] As of mid-1989, the unauthorized population had fallen to 2.5 million from 4 million at the time IRCA was enacted in 1986. But by 2005, the estimated number of unauthorized migrants would reach 11.1 million, despite enormous investments in border enforcement during the intervening years.[16]

While failing to prevent the increase in unauthorized migrants, government policies had a political logic, at least in the short term. Intensified enforcement demonstrated the government was acting to secure the border, while at the same time it did not actually block the growers and other low-wage employers from access to a workforce that was not only cheap but also largely quiescent for fear of being deported. The rise of undocumented labor was in line with a long history. Repeatedly, foreigners have been welcomed as workers but not as citizens. This was the case with enslaved Black and indigenous people in the nation's early history. It was also the case for the Chinese and Japanese who were brought to work in the Western mines, railroads, and fields in the nineteenth and early twentieth centuries. In such situations, racial distinctions have helped justify labor without citizenship. Undocumented workers from Mexico and Central America were only the latest instance of this pattern.

The Return of Nativism

Immigration legislation from 1965 to 1990, except for its treatment of migration across the Southern border, tended to be both expansionary and broadly bipartisan. Family-based and employment-based preferences remained the major bases for legal immigration, but others were added. After making special provision for refugees from Cuba and several other countries, Congress passed the Refugee Act of 1980, creating regular procedures for refugee admissions. The Immigration Act of 1990 added a "diversity" lottery for countries otherwise underrepresented among recent immigrants. Initially these were mostly Europeans, though the main beneficiaries proved ultimately to be African immigrants, another example of unintended consequences. Although Congress set overall caps on immigration, the caps were regularly exceeded mainly because they did not apply to the foreign-born spouses, children, or parents of U.S. citizens. By the early 1990s, the United States was admitting about a million legal immigrants annually. All the major legislation throughout this period passed Congress by overwhelming bipartisan margins.

But the large unauthorized population, combined with increased legal immigration, was stirring opposition on the right and testing the limits of public tolerance. Before the 1990s, Republican leaders and major conservative outlets had kept their distance from right-wing anti-immigration groups like the Federation for American Immigration Reform, founded in 1979. In the early 1990s, however, conservative voices with more influence began to decry the racial change that the immigration laws since 1965 had brought about.

In 1992, the conservative magazine *National Review* published a cover story by an economics journalist, Peter Brimelow, warning that immigration was bringing the Third World to America. Patrick Buchanan had recently created a stir while campaigning for the 1992 Republican nomination when he asked whether a million Zulus or a million Englishmen "would be easier to assimilate and would cause less problems" in Virginia if that state had to take them in. While some conservatives were outraged, Brimelow rose to Buchanan's defense, citing a news story from South Africa about crimes Zulus had been committing. Responding to an article that called for embracing Haitian immigrants, Brimelow wrote: "Be careful about those embraces. A significant proportion of Haitians are reported to be HIV positive." Brimelow denied he was racist; he was just giving the facts (the facts about HIV transmission apparently eluded him). The real problem with conservative elites, he argued, was that they were too fearful of being called racists. They should say clearly that Third World immigrants were responsible for crime, welfare dependency, overpopulation, and other problems, and they should recognize that the immigrants would vote for Democrats and therefore spelled political trouble for Republicans.[17]

Rather than a slowly growing, continuous trend, the political reaction against the new immigrants came in a series of waves. The first came between 1993 and 1996. According to Gallup, the proportion of Americans who favored a decrease in immigration hit a peak of 65 percent in 1993 and 1995, though even then immigration did not rank as a top priority for voters nationally.[18] It was in this period, however, that the undocumented population became a hot political issue in California.

California in the early 1990s was in the grips of a severe recession and state budget crisis, its high unemployment rate stemming in part from post–Cold War cuts in defense spending. The incumbent Republican Governor Pete Wilson, trailing in his bid for re-election in 1994, first attacked welfare recipients but then focused his campaign on illegal immigrants and the fiscal burden they imposed. A television ad for Wilson showed shadowy figures slipping through a border crossing as an ominous voice declared, "They keep coming. Two million illegal immigrants in California. The federal government won't stop them at the border yet requires us to pay billions to take care of them."[19]

While Wilson was campaigning for re-election, an independent grassroots group, partly financed by the Republican Party, put an initiative on the ballot known as Proposition 187 that called for denying illegal immigrants public benefits and services, including K–12 education. Schools would have to expel children for whom their parents could not produce proof that they were legally resident in the United States. Proposition 187 directly challenged a U.S. Supreme Court decision. In the 1982 case *Plyler v. Doe*, the Court had ruled that to deny education to undocumented children required a "substantial" state interest because the denial would impose "a lifetime hardship on a discrete class of children ... [who] can neither affect their parents' conduct nor their own undocumented status." By preventing the children from attending school, the state would create "a subclass of illiterates within our boundaries, surely adding to the problems and costs of unemployment, welfare, and crime" and therefore render any savings to a state "insubstantial."[20] California's voters were unpersuaded by arguments of this kind. In November 1994 they not only re-elected Wilson but approved Proposition 187 by a margin of 59 percent to 41 percent. A federal court, however, immediately enjoined the state from carrying out the initiative and eventually struck down its major provisions as unconstitutional. If Proposition 187 had been upheld, many of the undocumented children later known as "Dreamers" would never have had an education.

But the California vote sent a message at a moment when a new congressional majority in Washington was highly receptive to it. The next January, Newt Gingrich and a more radically minded Republican Party came to power on Capitol Hill. Coincidentally, a bipartisan commission created by Congress in 1990 issued its report on illegal immigration. The commission was headed by an African American Democrat, former Texas Representative Barbara Jordan, and while it lauded the contributions of immigrants, it said plainly that the control of immigration was a "right and responsibility" of a democratic society and took a hard line on enforcement: "The credibility of immigration policy can be measured by a simple yardstick: people who should get in, do get in; people who should not get in are kept out; and people who are deportable are required to leave." The commission's report called for new enforcement measures, including more rigorous worksite enforcement with a national registry of Social Security numbers that employers would have to check to verify if a prospective hire was legally eligible to work.[21]

Congressional Republicans wanted to go further. Gingrich established a task force on immigration reform that, in the same vein as Proposition 187, called for excluding undocumented children from public schools, an idea also endorsed by Bob Dole, the Republican Majority Leader in the Senate and leading candidate for the party's presidential nomination in 1996. (It was during his presidential campaign, while trying to soften his immigration stance, that he referred to America as a "boiling pot," a perfect malapropism for the times.) Republican congressional leaders proposed sharp reductions in legal immigration as well. In the end, however, more moderate Republicans blocked the denial of schooling and the reductions in legal immigration. But Congress nonetheless passed and Clinton signed the 1996 Illegal Immigration Reform and Immigrant Responsibility Act, which increased border enforcement and penalties for the undocumented and declared them ineligible to receive Social Security and other federal benefits (for many of which they were already ineligible). In addition, as part of welfare reform, Congress denied a variety of social welfare benefits to *legal* immigrants during their first five years in the United States.[22]

Soon, though, the anti-immigrant wave petered out. Republicans began to worry, especially after Dole's defeat in 1996, that the anti-immigration push was hurting them among the rising Hispanic electorate. In 1997, Congress restored some benefits it had just taken away from legal residents, and by the 1998 election, the *New York Times* was reporting that immigration had "disappeared" as an issue. "A couple of years ago people were advocating to build a wall around the country. That's no longer the case," stated Spencer Abraham, Republican of Michigan, the new chair of the Senate immigration committee.[23]

Republicans lost the gubernatorial election in California in 1998 with a candidate who had backed Proposition 187, but in Texas another Republican governor, George W. Bush, courted Hispanic support and won 49 percent of their votes on his way to a comfortable re-election. As a presidential candidate in 2000, Bush made clear how sharply he departed from the direction taken by congressional Republicans four years earlier. He called for both a guest-worker program and a "path to citizenship" for the millions in the country without permission. After taking office, Bush made his first foreign trip to Mexico and set up high-level discussions with the Mexican government over immigration, trade, and other issues. On September 6, 2001, Mexican President Vicente Fox came to Washington, where he addressed a joint session of Congress, asking the legislators to "give trust a chance" and extend "legal rights to people who are already contributing to this great nation." Although Bush faced objections within his own party, the Democratic leader in the House, Richard Gephardt, said he thought Congress might pass legislation by the end of the year. Senator Joseph Lieberman, the Democrats' vice-presidential candidate in 2000, said, "The bottom line is the fences are going to go down between these two countries."[24]

Five days later, however, the fears about dangerous foreigners and lax border controls came back literally with a vengeance, and a second anti-immigrant wave began. The September 11 attacks on New York's World Trade Center towers and the Pentagon were a turning point in domestic as well as foreign policy. They reframed immigration as a security issue and put to rest, for the time being, any effort to regularize the status of the undocumented. The failure of government agencies to detect the attackers on entering the United States, or even when they obtained training as pilots for the hijackings, led to a massive increase in surveillance and the establishment of the Department of Homeland Security. The department included a new bureau, Immigration and Customs Enforcement (ICE), formed in 2003 from the merger of the enforcement functions of the old Immigration and Naturalization Service and the U.S. Customs Service. The government intensified not just border enforcement but interior enforcement, including undercover agents in immigrant associations and churches. Muslims were the primary target of public and official suspicion. In the days after 9/11, federal authorities conducted mass roundups of recent Muslim immigrants in the hope of uncovering terrorist networks. Other immigrant communities were affected as well. In the following years, ICE stepped up raids on worksites, sweeping up many who were in the country illegally and deporting them, regardless of whether they represented a public danger.[25]

The 9/11 attacks also reawakened and legitimized aspects of nativism that had long been dormant. In *Strangers in the Land*, the classic 1955 study of anti-immigrant movements in the nineteenth and early twentieth centuries, John Higham defined nativism as "intense opposition to an internal minority on the ground of its foreign (i.e., 'un-American') connections." In Higham's account, three strands—political, religious, and racial—ran through the nativist tradition in the United States.[26] All three strands now reappeared in new forms. Politically, earlier nativists had feared immigrants as radicals and linked them to international communism. Now Americans feared immigrants as terrorists and linked them to international networks loyal to previously little-known enemies like Osama bin Laden. In the nineteenth and early twentieth centuries, the religious impetus behind nativism had been primarily anti-Catholic and anti-Semitic. Now the religious impetus behind nativism was anti-Muslim. And because the new nativists conflated Muslims and Arabs, the religious hostilities had a racial subtext.

Bush himself was caught between contradictory impulses. Amid a spike in hate crimes against Muslims in the two weeks after September 11, the president went to a mosque at the Islamic Center of Washington and declared, "The face of terror is not the true faith of Islam. Islam is peace." But just two days earlier he had evoked a history of religious war when he had used the word "crusade" to describe the new "war on terror" he was proclaiming. Mindful of the need to cultivate allies in the Middle East, Bush was careful not to describe the hijackers as "Islamic" or "Muslim," but others on the right did not hesitate to identify the enemy as "radical Islam" or as Islam itself. The prophet Mohammed was a terrorist, Rev. Jerry Falwell declared on the CBS news program *60 Minutes*.[27]

It took more than two years after 9/11 for Bush to revive his call for immigration reform. In January 2004, as he began campaigning for re-election, the president again proposed "a temporary-worker program" to regularize the legal status of many of the undocumented, who would be able to apply for permanent legal residency and later citizenship, though only by going to the back of the line behind others who had applied earlier. Never introduced as formal legislation, the proposal served mainly as a talking point for Hispanic audiences, helping Bush to win four out of ten Hispanic votes in 2004.[28]

After Bush's re-election, however, the Republican majority in the House rejected both a temporary-worker program and a path to legalization and instead passed a draconian bill that imposed a penalty of up to a year's imprisonment for residing illegally in the United States and five years' imprisonment for assisting illegal immigrants knowingly in disregard of their immigration status. Carrying out such a law would have taken the carceral state to a new level. In contrast, the Senate in May 2006 passed a bill supported by Ted Kennedy and John McCain (as well as by Bush), another "grand bargain" for "comprehensive immigration reform," now with three parts: a guest worker program, "earned legalization" for the undocumented, and increased border enforcement. With House conservatives dead set against anything that could be described as "amnesty," no agreement was possible. And even after Democrats won back control of the House and Senate in the 2006 elections, Congress was unable to bridge the differences over immigration reform. In an outburst against conservatives in May 2007, Bush said that the opponents of the reform legislation "don't want to do what's right for America." The effort collapsed in Congress the next month.[29]

As happened in many other areas of policy in the early 2000s, the search for bipartisan agreement on immigration ended in failure. Like Bush, Obama would not be able to get immigration reform through Congress.

By 2010, 50 percent of the undocumented had been settled in the United States for more than ten years, but they had none of the rights of citizens, leaving them vulnerable to exploitation by employers and landlords. Many mixed-status families were also at risk of family breakup; nearly five million U.S.-born children lived with an undocumented parent who might be deported at any time.[30] This legal insecurity put roughly a quarter to a third of the foreign born in the early twenty-first century in a radically different position from their European predecessors. But in other ways the old and the new immigrants were surprisingly similar.

The New Immigrants versus the Old

No matter which side Americans have taken in the debate about immigration, they have usually assumed that the new immigrants since the 1960s have differed from earlier European immigrants in the experience they have had in the United States. Supporters of the new immigrants see them as being treated differently because they are not white, while immigration restrictionists tend to believe that because of their Latin American, Asian, and African origins, the new immigrants are less likely than earlier Europeans to assimilate and contribute economically to American society. Neither the immigrants' supporters nor the restrictionists have been inclined to see what social science research has found: The earlier immigrants from Europe and the new non-European immigrants have had similar rates of social mobility and assimilation. Even with new and different people, the United States has still functioned as much the same nation it was earlier in its history.

Part of the difficulty in seeing the historical parallels arises, at least among restrictionists, because of a tendency to idealize earlier immigrants, beginning with colonial settlers. In his 1992 polemic against the post-1965 immigration, Brimelow wrote: "American immigration has typically been quite selective.... English settlers included Royalist gentry who went to Virginia, like George Washington's ancestors, and Puritan gentry who went to New England."[31] But the early immigration was not selective, and gentry were a tiny percentage of colonial settlers.[32] In fact, the colonies suffered from an endemic shortage of free and willing immigrants: "almost nine out of every ten people on British ships before 1800 were there under some obligation to labor for others upon their arrival in the Americas." Those destined for Britain's mainland colonies included enslaved Africans; indentured white servants, who also could be bought and sold; and some 50,000 convicts (about as many as were sent to Australia before 1824), who served out their time in unpaid labor in the colonies.[33] As a colonial-era Donald Trump might have said, the British were "not sending their best."

Both historical and contemporary studies have examined the "selection" of immigrants, that is, whether they have been higher or lower in socioeconomic status and education than others in their countries of origin. In the age of mass European immigration (1850–1914), the estimated thirty million people who came to the United States were overwhelmingly working class. The young men who left Ireland for America more often had fathers who were illiterate and poor than the Irishmen who stayed behind. In Norway, the fathers of migrants were also poorer than the fathers of men who stayed. A study of Italian men examined at Ellis Island finds that the immigrants were shorter in average height than men in Italy, which suggests those who left for America were less well-nourished while growing up. The general conclusion from this research is that European migrants were "negatively" selected—they were poorer and less educated than others in their home countries.[34]

In contrast, the post-1965 immigrants have been "positively" selected. They have averaged more years of education than the general population in their countries of origin, though there is a great deal of variability. Immigrants from Asia, particularly from Iran, India, and China, have had much higher levels of education than an average adult in those countries. Indeed, the major Asian American immigrant groups have been "hyper-selected." They have been more highly educated than both the average adult back home and the average American adult. Mexicans, in contrast, have been among the least positively selected. Compared to the Mexican adult population, Mexican immigrants to the United States have averaged slightly more years of schooling, but they have included a smaller share with a college education. They have been disproportionately drawn from the middle of Mexico's income distribution. Other Hispanic immigrants such as Cubans, Dominicans, and Peruvians have had relatively higher educational levels than their home-country populations.[35]

In their analyses of earlier European and more recent immigrants, researchers cannot measure such qualities as ambition and drive, what some people refer to as "get-up-and-go." But since immigrants are precisely the people in their home countries who got up and went, it seems reasonable to infer from the act of immigration itself that they differed from those who stayed put in qualities that have affected how well they have fared in

America. Those unmeasured qualities of immigrants, along with persistent aspects of American society, may help explain the parallels in social mobility between earlier and more recent immigrants.

The most systematic comparison of economic mobility among the earlier European and recent non-European immigrants comes from the work of the economists Ran Abramitzky, Leah Boustan, and their colleagues, who have used millions of census and genealogical records and other data in comparing immigrants who arrived in 1880 and 1910 with immigrants who arrived in 1980. For each group, they have tracked how the immigrants and their children fared between fourteen and thirty years after arrival. By moving to the United States, immigrants in both eras have substantially increased their incomes relative to their home country. After an initial boost, however, the dominant pattern for the immigrant generation has been persistence at their initial economic level after arrival. But the immigrants' children, the second generation, have taken a major socioeconomic leap. In fact, they have moved further up the economic ladder than children of the U.S. born. With some exceptions, this is still the pattern for immigrants who arrived in 1980 as it was for those who arrived in 1880 and 1910.[36]

The European and more recent non-European immigrants have also assimilated at comparable rates. This is, if anything, more surprising than the historical parallels in economic mobility since some advocates for immigrants today reject the ideal of assimilation, which they interpret as requiring Anglo-conformity. But we need not think of assimilation as demanding a complete abandonment of ethnic culture. As sociologists Richard Alba and Victor Nee propose, assimilation may be defined as a "decline of an ethnic distinction," a narrowing of social and cultural differences from the native-born group.[37] Drawing on that conception, Abramitzky and Boustan compare rates of immigrant assimilation in the earlier and more recent period by using English proficiency, residential clustering, intermarriage, and—in an original twist—the choices that immigrants have made in naming their children (that is, whether they use names from their own ethnic group or "American-sounding" names). On all these criteria, patterns of assimilation in recent decades fall in the same range as in the age of mass European immigration.[38]

Both in the past and recently, the evidence has not supported claims that immigrants bring disease and crime. In fact, immigrants enjoy a health advantage. By 2017, life expectancy among the foreign born, at 81.4 years for men and 85.7 for women, was 7.0 years greater than for

U.S-born men and 6.2 years greater than for U.S.-born women. Trends in health and life expectancy in the United States would all be worse if not for immigrants.[39] Contrary to popular perceptions in both the early 1900s and early 2000s, rates of crime and violence have been lower among immigrants, including the undocumented. From the 1990s to the 2010s immigrants were important contributors to lower crime rates and economic revival in American cities.[40] Nonetheless, Republican leaders have relentlessly focused on instances of violent crime by immigrants as though they were representative.

The Republican turn against immigrants in the 1990s followed the party's move to the right on race in the late 1960s and on women's rights during the 1970s. Republicans and Democrats long shared in a bipartisan pro-immigration consensus. From the 1960s to the early 1990s, according to an analysis of congressional speeches, members of both parties spoke effusively about immigration. But the 1990s were a turning point on immigration, as they were in partisan politics generally. During the anti-immigrant wave from 1993 to 1996, Republicans became especially hostile, while Democrats were close to neutral. Since then, despite some fluctuations, Democrats in Congress have become exceptionally positive about immigrants, while Republicans have reverted to the harsh view of the 1920s.[41]

The parallel between the anti-immigrant views of the 1920s and recent Republican opposition to immigration is not limited to rhetoric. A similar political calculus has been at work. In the early 1900s, the predominantly small-town and rural native-born Protestants feared the highly urbanized Southern and Eastern European immigrants as a political force. Not only were the new immigrants gaining political power in the cities; the cities were growing large enough to dominate national politics. For Republicans, the national origins quotas were a pro-active means of voter suppression, an electoral prophylactic.

By the early 2000s, Republicans came to see themselves in an analogous position in relation to the new immigrants. During the debate over immigration under the younger Bush, Rush Limbaugh began calling immigration reform legislation the "Destroy the Republican Party Act."[42] A growing number of Republicans regarded any compromise that included legal status for the undocumented as unacceptably benefiting Democrats. Republicans were giving up on the idea promoted by Bush and others in the center right that immigrants were a winnable constituency and that it was a mistake to alienate people whose numbers were rising. In this stark vision of the future of American politics, immigrants now fell irreversibly on the other side of a racialized political divide.

This was the deeper, tragic turn that American politics was taking. Nothing could escape partisanship. Nothing could escape race. The old contradiction that had beset American society from its beginnings was intensifying again.

CHAPTER SEVEN

Sleepwalking (2)

Race

They said this day would never come.

—BARACK OBAMA, January 3, 2008 (on winning the Iowa caucuses)[1]

I probably showed up twenty years sooner than the demographics would have anticipated.

—BARACK OBAMA, November 18, 2016[2]

THE ELECTION IN 2008 of a Black man as president of the United States defied every sober expectation about American politics. Before it happened, it seemed unthinkable, but when it did happen, it seemed to make clear that a much larger transformation was under way: the emergence of a new racial and political majority. It was a change, some suggested, from a "white America" to a multicultural and multiracial America, or perhaps the advent of a "post-racial" America, an America in either case utterly different from the nation the United States had previously been.

"Each election year," Garry Wills writes, "is a revelation."[3] Some election years like 1968, the one that Wills was writing about, are bigger revelations than others, or at least they seem to be at the time. The 2008 election had to shake up the understanding of who Americans were and what they were going to become. Barack Hussein Obama was not only a Black man; he was also a young man, known to the national public for only a few years, with a name that sounded foreign, possibly Muslim and definitely more African than African American. To that point, Jesse Jackson was the only Black candidate who had made a serious run for president, and in his two campaigns in the 1980s he hadn't come close. Obama was different. Unlike Jackson, he hadn't marched side by side with Martin Luther King Jr., and he didn't fit the image of a Black political leader who spoke for minorities. From the moment Obama seized the spotlight with a keynote speech at the Democratic Convention in 2004, he located himself in a national tradition and sought to speak for Americans as "one people." But no matter what he said, no matter how eloquently he said it, and no matter what he accomplished as president, many Americans could never get past one fact about him: he was Black. And that one fact tragically racialized American politics more intensely than ever.

The response to Obama partly reflected the larger expectations about America; the coming reversal in racial predominance reported to be looming on the horizon. In August 2008, the same month Democrats nominated Obama at their national convention, the U.S. Census Bureau issued new population projections to 2050 that forecasted two things: first, that "minorities" would become a majority by 2042; and second, that the share of the population identifying as white would change only slightly by that date, declining from 80 percent to about 75 percent. The reason for this apparent anomaly was that "minorities" included all Hispanics, whereas the half of Hispanics who identified as white went to the other side of the ledger in the white total.[4] With equal justification the media could have accurately headlined their stories, "In a Generation, Minorities May Be the U.S. Majority" (as the *New York Times* did) or "Whites to Remain a Large Majority through 2050" (as none of them did). Instead, the headlines often declared "White Americans No Longer a Majority by 2042" (ABC News) and "Whites in the Minority by 2042, U.S. Census Predicts" (Fox News), despite the fact that the Census had not made that prediction.[5] To be fair, the practice of referring to all Hispanics as nonwhite had become routine and unquestioned, and the Census Bureau itself often treated Hispanics as the equivalent of a racial minority even though its own reports stated that Hispanics "may be of any race." The Census Bureau also did not clarify key assumptions underlying its forecast that, in highly improbable ways, magnified its projection of the minority share of America's future population and under-projected the share who would likely identify as white.

The United States was becoming more racially and culturally diverse: that much was clear. Liberals and progressives celebrated "diversity"—the central idea of a new social vision—and expected to benefit politically from the shift, oblivious to the alarm bells ringing on the right and the possibility that the reaction could threaten the foundations of a liberal society. What they didn't foresee was that a fifty-fifty society—a society that seemed to be approaching a tipping point in majority status—was entering politically treacherous territory. The Census Bureau forecast was one contributing factor both to overconfidence on the left and to panic on the right.

Despite the ambiguities and uncertainties of the Census forecast, the idea that whites would become a minority became a taken-for-granted fact. It was not a new idea in 2008. In 1990, *Time* magazine reported, "In the 21st century—and that's not far off—racial and ethnic groups in the U.S. will outnumber whites for the first time. The 'browning of America' will alter everything in society." President Clinton had referred to the change in a commencement speech in 1998 when he said there would be "no majority race" in the United States by the middle of the twenty-first century; in 2000 the Census forecasted that minorities would be a majority by 2059.[6] The new 2008 projections moved up that date by seventeen years to 2042, but more important, Obama's candidacy and election made it seem as though that future had already arrived. The emerging demographic majority was now widely understood as favoring an "emerging Democratic majority."[7] Even though Obama had won the presidency in the midst of a severe economic crisis—and might well have lost without that crisis—his victory was taken, particularly by liberals, as a decisive, positive sign of the world to come. In some circles, a kind of diversity triumphalism erupted. Shortly after Obama's election, the critic Hua Hsu wrote in *The Atlantic* that not only was "white America" demographically on its way out; culturally, "it's already all but finished."[8] Behind this thinking lay the idea that the groups thought of as minorities, including the white-identifying Hispanics, formed one larger collective group, increasingly referred to as "people of color."

A Majority of Minorities?

During the mid-twentieth century, "minorities" in the United States came to signify four specific groups: Blacks, Hispanics, Asian Americans and Pacific Islanders, and American Indians and Native Alaskans. (In 1997, thanks to congressional intervention, "Native Hawaiian and other Pacific Islanders" were split off from Asian Americans into a separate U.S. Census category of their own.) These were the official minorities, the minorities defined for legal and statistical purposes in federal regulations and added together in census reports of the coming "majority minority" society.

Official statistics have unusual power. They create a seemingly irrefutable picture of a society, but they are neither strictly scientific nor a mere reflection of social reality. Political and cultural influences shape the data at three levels—first, within the government in the choice of ways to classify people and methods for counting them and projecting their numbers into the future; second, in the gathering of the data, when people are asked to report potentially consequential information, including classifying themselves and their children; and third, in the interpretation of the numbers by government agencies and political leaders, private groups, and the media.

The first and fundamental choice is whether to collect data of a particular kind. For example, the U.S. Census Bureau and other agencies do not collect information about Americans' religious beliefs and identities. In 1957, the Census Bureau undertook a preliminary survey of religion with a view to adding the question, "What is your religion?" to the 1960 census. But the proposal stirred opposition from "nearly every religious group that had experience of violent persecution in the United States," and those groups—especially Jews and Mormons who worried about the use of the information by bigots—objected that the inquiry was improper, a violation of the separation of church and state. With support from sympathetic members of Congress, the opponents forced the Census Bureau to back down.[9] In contrast to this official statistical blackout on religion, the U.S. legal and statistical system has been race-obsessed. From the first census in 1790, the federal government has enumerated the population by race, a subject to which census forms and other government reporting systems have given prominent and detailed attention.

Political considerations have shaped not only the choice to count by race but also the decisions about what races to count. In 1930, after having always counted people of Mexican descent as white, the census introduced "Mexican" as a separate racial category. Soon afterward, President Herbert Hoover undertook a massive effort to deport Mexican migrants in the Southwest. But in 1940, the Census Bureau dropped "Mexican" and again counted people of Mexican and other Latin American descent as white. At that point, Mexican American groups preferred to be invisible in government data, merged into the white population.[10]

Another Census Bureau change of that era also sharpened the Black–white dichotomy as the overriding racial distinction in American life. In 1930 the Census dropped the category "mulatto," introduced originally in 1850, for people with Black and at least one other identifiable racial ancestry, usually white. Dropping "mulatto" ended the recognition of a mixed-race identity in official data. As the Census Bureau's instructions to census takers in 1930 showed—in those days, census takers visiting homes defined a person's race—racial classifications were to follow the "one-drop rule," the rule that any Black ancestry whatsoever made a person Black.[11]

Racial minorities long had a rational basis for concern about the government's intentions in classifying and counting them in official records. Racial classifications were used for a variety of invidious purposes, such as denying people the right to marry across racial lines, to buy a home in areas with restrictive covenants, or to rent an apartment in housing reserved for whites. Despite a statutory requirement that census responses be confidential, Congress revoked that guarantee after Pearl Harbor, and the federal government used census data when it interned Japanese Americans on the West Coast.[12]

With the civil rights revolution, however, the relation of minorities to the census and other government data-gathering changed drastically. It became advantageous to be classified and counted as a member of one of the minorities that the law recognized as subject to racial discrimination. Representatives of racial minorities could get laws thrown out and decisions changed if they could demonstrate race was a factor in denying them equal treatment. But to prove their case, groups needed data, and if they were not fully counted or even represented in official statistics, they might not have that proof.

The reversal in Mexican American attitudes toward the census illustrates the general turnaround in minority views. In the late 1960s, representatives of Mexican Americans began to demand that people in their communities be counted separately from the Anglo population and by methods that fully represented them. As long as their numbers were merged with Anglos, it was difficult to prove in employment discrimination cases that they were underrepresented in certain fields or firms, or to apply for federal grants that required a showing of community need.[13]

Not only did Mexican American groups want to be counted separately from whites; they also wanted to be counted together with others of Latin American descent. The greater the numbers of any racial or ethnic group, the more political clout it is likely to have. As of that time, however, there was no shared panethnic identity or organization among the three principal groups of Americans of Latin American heritage: Mexicans mainly in the Southwest, Cubans in Florida, and Puerto Ricans in the Northeast and Puerto Rico itself. But during the 1970s, new Spanish-language networks like Univision were assembling the different Spanish-speaking populations into a national audience. New lobbying organizations and coalitions in Washington were advocating on behalf of a constituency they were calling "Hispanic." And Nixon and subsequent presidents were looking to gain electoral support from that constituency. In the late 1960s, the Census Bureau had resisted adding a Spanish-origin question to the 1970 census, though it agreed to test a question on a form that went to 5 percent of households. But after the bureau faced intense criticism that the 1970 census had severely undercounted Hispanics, it negotiated with Hispanic groups the adoption of a new question that would ask about "Spanish/Hispanic origin or descent."[14]

But would "Spanish/Hispanic origin or descent" be a *racial* category? Americans who had "Spanish" or "Hispanic" origins had different racial understandings. The Cubans who had come to the United States soon after Castro's takeover mainly identified as white, as did many others from South America who thought of their origins as European, whereas Chicano activists in the Southwest were adopting a "brown" racial identity (as discussed in chapter 2). Even among Mexican Americans, leaders of the older and more traditional groups did not want to give up their self-conception and status as white. The Census Bureau also faced objections from other groups that the introduction of Hispanic as a racial category could reduce their numbers. Some Afro-Caribbeans might identify as Hispanic rather than Black; some Filipinos as Hispanic rather than Asian.

To avoid these conflicts, federal officials decided to define Hispanic origin as an ethnicity rather than a race, a formulation that was incorporated in a 1977 directive from the Office of Management and Budget (OMB) that consolidated the racial classifications to be used across federal agencies. Consequently, the 1980 census would ask, "Is this person of Spanish/Hispanic origin or descent?" (the "ethnicity" question) as well as a separate question about race (which did not include a Hispanic response option). The two-question format gave Hispanics the opportunity to have it both ways: to be counted as the equivalent of a racial minority while continuing to identify racially as white if they wanted to. Still, it was odd that "Hispanic" and "non-Hispanic" would be the only "ethnicities" counted by the Census.

Another historical reversal illustrating the new appeal of minority identity involves people with origins in the Indian subcontinent and the Middle East. During the years when U.S. law made whiteness a prerequisite for naturalization, immigrants from those regions petitioned the courts for recognition as white. Although the courts never deemed petitioners from China, Japan, and the Philippines to be white, they sometimes did treat applicants from India, Syria, and Arabia as white. The conflicting decisions arose from a discrepancy between two kinds of criteria the courts used for determining race: science and common knowledge. According to the science of the time, people from India and the Middle East were Caucasians, but this was not the everyday belief of most white Americans. In a case that reached the Supreme Court in 1923, a high-caste man from India, Bhagat Singh Thind, claimed that he was legally eligible to become a citizen because, according to science, he was Caucasian. But the justices rejected that claim, ruling that a "white person" was a person recognized as white "in the understanding of the common man." Since Thind was not white according to common knowledge—that is, the beliefs of whites—he was not eligible for citizenship.[15]

Half a century later, when OMB issued a preliminary version of its 1977 racial classification directive, it classified people with origins in both India and the Middle East as white. But, instead of being pleased, representatives of both groups lobbied for reclassification as minorities. OMB agreed to reclassify those from India as Asian Americans, but it continued to deem Middle Easterners to be white, a decision that created legal barriers to discrimination claims by Arab Americans and others with Middle Eastern origins.[16] Groups representing Middle Easterners and North Africans (the "MENA" category) fought on to be recognized as a racial minority (a reclassification that the Biden administration made in 2024).

American Indians are a third example of the rising appeal of a minority identity, though in this case the change has primarily involved a rise in individual self-identification. The census counts since the mid-twentieth century give the impression of a population explosion among the Native tribes. In 1950, when census workers made the racial classifications, the census put the number of American Indians at 343,400. At the time, census workers were to mark "American Indian" only if an individual was an enrolled member of a tribe or recognized as American Indian in the community, or at least "looked" Indian to the census taker. But with the shift to mail-in census forms and racial self-identification, which began in 1960, the count of American Indians surged from one decade to the next at a rate that cannot be explained by natural increase (births minus deaths). In 1960, the count of American Indians rose 60 percent from ten years earlier; in 1970, 50 percent over 1960; in 1980, 70 percent over 1970; and in 1990, 40 percent over 1980. Many of the additions were, at least in statistical terms, "former whites." In 2020, the census count would hit 3.7 million for those reporting they were American Indian alone, plus another 6 million reporting American Indian in combination with another race.[17]

The growing count of American Indians was partly cultural in origin and partly the product, after 2000, of broader census definitions and changes in methods. During the second half of the twentieth century, Native identity lost its earlier stigma and even acquired a new cachet among many Americans who had not previously self-identified as indigenous. A study of Americans reclaiming their Native heritage reports that "many spent time with tribal elders seeking instruction in tribal history and traditions, many learned more of their tribal languages, [and] many abandoned Christian religions and turned to native spiritual traditions." But Native organizations also denounced "ethnic fraud" by "pretendians" who misrepresented themselves to get scholarships or jobs, market their crafts, or obtain other benefits. The tribes jealously guarded tribal citizenship, enforcing tests such as a minimum level of "blood quanta" (direct biological lineage) or cultural upbringing. Rights such as a share in tribal revenues, the right to live on tribal land, and the right to vote in tribal elections were too valuable to give to any "self-identified Indian," a term used scornfully by Native groups.[18]

But self-identified American Indians were what the census counted, and the general thrust of policy was to make the count more inclusive. In 2000, for the first time, the census counted as American Indians those with indigenous origins throughout the Americas, not just in the United States. Also for the first time, Americans could check off more than one racial identity on the census. Under a new federal policy announced in 2000, people claiming to be both white and a minority were to be "allocated to the minority race" for legal purposes. In the case of American Indians, many of the people newly listing Native origins had limited ties with Native American life. In a 2015 survey, the Pew Research Center found that 61 percent of people identifying as both white and Native said they had a lot in common with whites, compared with only 22 percent saying they had a lot in common with American Indians. Three-quarters said all or most of their friends were white; and 88 percent said a passerby in the street would identify them as white.[19]

The cases I've described—involving Hispanics, Asian Indians and Middle Easterners, American Indians, and multiracial people—all testify to a historic reversal in identity preferences of people who were at the blurred boundaries of whiteness. Rather than projecting and pursuing a white identity, representatives of these groups sought to have them recognized as minorities and to have them counted in a way that maximized their numbers. Federal statistical policies generally obliged these demands. The result has been to enlarge the official minority share of the population, especially when projected into the future.

Two policies have been particularly important in raising the forecast of the minority population: the decision to treat white-identifying Hispanics as part of what has been generally understood to be a nonwhite minority; and the decision to treat all individuals with both white and minority parents, and all their future descendants, as minority.

Comparisons of racial groups typically separate out "non-Hispanic whites" as the real whites. The argument for this widely followed practice, which implicitly treats Hispanic white self-identification as a kind of false consciousness, is that racial classification in Latin American societies has different rules; consequently, when Hispanics in the United States check off "white," they do not mean what white Americans of European descent mean. A study of Mexican Americans, for example, finds that many indicate "white" on the census because they believe it signifies they are American. Historically, Mexican American communities were committed to upholding a white identity not because they were treated the same as Anglos but because it affirmed their legitimacy as U.S. citizens and protected them from the indignities of Blackness.[20]

But many Hispanics do have white European ancestry, come from the stratum of Latin American societies seen as white, and mix easily with whites whose ancestors came directly to the United States from Europe without a stopover in Havana, Buenos Aires, Caracas, or Mexico City. To treat all Hispanics as a distinct group from whites also obscures the felt racial differences among people of Latin American descent and the discrimination that Hispanics with darker complexions often face from those with more European features.[21]

The underlying question about white-identifying Hispanics is whether to think of them as more similar to (1) European immigrants of the past, the "white ethnics" who assimilated into the white majority, or (2) Black Americans, who have remained separate from whites. The Black analogy may apply to some groups of white-identifying Hispanics who do not pass as white, but the immigrant analogy appears to have wider application. As the research on immigrants discussed in chapter 6 indicates, the patterns of mobility and assimilation among Hispanic immigrants up to 1980—leaving aside Afro-Hispanics—resemble those of European immigrants a century earlier. Hispanic immigrants after 1980 include a larger proportion of undocumented people who were unable to take advantage of the naturalization provisions of IRCA enacted in 1986 and have not experienced the same mobility.[22] But this should not obscure the large-scale entry into the mainstream of white-identifying Hispanics, most of whom do not see themselves as a permanently excluded racial caste.[23]

The second major problem with census projections of a majority-minority society arises from the federal rule that assigns a minority identity to the children of mixed (Hispanic-Anglo or white-nonwhite) parents. As the sociologist Richard Alba argues, these projections rest on the dubious assumption that the descendants of mixed white and minority parents will all grow up to identify as minority. By the 2050s, one of three babies with white ancestry will also have Hispanic or racially nonwhite ancestry, amounting to almost one-fifth of infants of all backgrounds. Classifying them all as minority tilts the projections toward the minority side, but people of mixed white-minority backgrounds vary in their experience and self-identification. Black-white multiracial people are exceptional in identifying mostly with their minority heritage and feeling more accepted by others with the same minority background.[24] Although the United States no longer follows a "one-drop" rule in the classification of Black people, Black ancestry continues in practice to be the "heaviest drop."[25]

The United States, however, has never had and shows no signs of developing a one-drop or heaviest-drop rule for other mixed minority-white backgrounds. Asian whites identify more as whites, say they have more in common with whites than with Asians, feel more accepted by whites, and have more contact with the white than the Asian side of their families. Since Asian-white families tend to be affluent and highly educated and to live in predominantly white neighborhoods, it is not surprising that two-thirds of Asian-white children say their friends are "all or almost all" white. Hispanic-Anglos are in an intermediate position between Black-white and Asian-white biracial people.[26]

If this pattern continues, Americans with mixed backgrounds are unlikely all to be minority-identified no matter how diluted their minority ancestry becomes, as the census projections have assumed. In fact, studies of the descendants of both Hispanic and Asian immigrants find significant rates of "ethnic attrition," that is, a decline of identification with their minority ancestry as a result of intermarriage, especially intermarriage with whites. Ethnic attrition is selective: "non-Hispanics of Latin American descent" are especially common among the upwardly mobile. According to Pew Research, 11 percent of all Americans with Hispanic ancestors do not identify as Hispanic; nearly 60 percent of this group say that a passerby would see them as white. By the third generation of people with Hispanic ancestry, 23 percent do not identify as Hispanic; by the fourth generation or higher, half do not see themselves as Hispanic. These data suggest that the share of Americans who identify as Hispanic will not rise correspondingly with the share who have Hispanic ancestry, contrary to Census Bureau assumptions.[27]

In 2020, the Census Bureau adopted a new method for reclassifying people by race that raised its count of multiracial people and reduced its count of whites. For the first time, under both "white" and "Black" on the census form, the 2020 census asked people to list their "origins." People who checked off only one race but listed an origin that the bureau's algorithm did not recognize as consistent with that race were reclassified as multiracial. The algorithm recognized only European origins as white. Consequently, someone who checked off white but listed Argentina (or any other Latin American country) as an origin was reclassified as multiracial, that is, as white and "some other race." Similarly, someone marking only white but listing South Africa as an origin was reclassified as multiracial because the algorithm treated all African origins as Black. If Elon Musk, for example, listed South Africa (where he was born) as an origin, he would have been counted as multiracial on the census. The Census Bureau announcement of its 2020 findings led the news media to report two stories: a "multiracial boom" and an absolute decline in the white population, both of which were the artificial result of a change in census methods. Those stories tended to confirm the beliefs on both the left and the right that white America was facing a demographic implosion.[28]

Demographic inevitability—the idea that "demography is destiny"—has been vastly oversold, at least so far as the future racial makeup of American society is concerned. Whether the United States has a white majority will depend on the meaning that Americans associate with different racial and ethnic identities and the incentives it creates for identifying in different ways. Instead of just facing an inevitable plunge into minority status, white America is being replenished—that is, sustained, perhaps even enlarged—through intermarriage, the assimilation of immigrants, and ethnic attrition among the descendants of those immigrants. If, however, the government's statistical agencies, social scientists, and journalists continue to focus on the narrowest possible definition of "white"—non-Hispanic white alone with no other heritage—a white majority may seem to be disappearing. But that won't necessarily mean what people take it to mean. It won't mean that a majority of Americans think of themselves as people of color.

The Return of "People of Color"

The rising numbers of Hispanics and Asian Americans and the growing rates of interracial marriage raised questions that the Census Bureau forecasts could not answer. American society was leaving behind the old binary Black/white world, but it wasn't clear what was coming next. Hispanics, Asians, and multiracial people had become, in effect, the swing vote of the emerging ethnoracial order. Would they align themselves more with Blacks or whites, or with neither? If aligned with Blacks, would they adopt a shared identity as "people of color"? Or would racial lines become so blurred and individual lineages so complicated and overlapping that the old racial distinctions ceased to have the clarity and power they have traditionally had?

Historically, the "color line" in the United States referred to a bright-line boundary chiefly between Blacks and whites that regulated social contact, space, opportunity, and power. The line was psychologically salient, institutionally entrenched, and pervasive in its consequences. Conceivably, growing populations of Hispanics and Asians might not fundamentally alter that reality. This, at least, was what some people believed. In this view, white supremacy was just being reproduced, with whites on top and all oppressed people of color below; the old color line was evolving into a new people-of-color line. Or there would be some minimal change of the kind that the sociologist Eduardo Bonilla-Silva envisioned. The United States, he suggested, was moving toward a "tri-racial stratification system similar to that of many Latin American and Caribbean nations," composed of whites at the top, a small intermediate category of "honorary whites" (assimilated Asians and Hispanics), and a large nonwhite bloc at the bottom incorporating "most immigrants."[29]

But nowhere was it foreordained that the new immigrants were mainly to be grouped, or group themselves, with Black and Native people, or that the people-of-color line would be as salient, entrenched, and pervasive in its consequences as the Black-white color line. Hispanics and Asians did share with Black and indigenous people a long history of racial oppression in the United States, but for many recent Hispanic and Asian American immigrants, America was what it had been for earlier immigrants, a land of opportunity. Social tensions were frequent between Black and immigrant communities, and anti-Black racism was not limited to the white native-born. The immigrant groups were heterogeneous, and Hispanics—as already noted—were heterogeneous on racial lines, with a much larger proportion self-identifying as white than as Black and with long-standing cultural biases in favor of lighter skin color. Asian Americans not only had higher median incomes than other minorities; they also had higher median incomes than whites and were doing exceptionally well in higher education and the professions. In the wake of the civil rights revolution and ethnic-consciousness movements, minority identities had a new appeal, but whiteness had not lost its gravitational pull. On many criteria, Hispanics, Asians, and most multiracial people were "leaning" white.

Instead of a model that equated all people of color, America's recent history offered a second model for the new immigrant minorities, the model of assimilation based on the experience of Southern and Eastern Europeans who came to America in the nineteenth and early twentieth centuries but were not considered as fully white. The relevance of that history may seem easy to dismiss because, after all, weren't the other Europeans also white, just ethnically different? But "ethnicity" and "race" are not fixed ideas. What one generation regards as a race another generation regards as an ethnicity. A century ago, Americans commonly made racial distinctions among Europeans. They believed that Celts, "Hebrews," Italians, Slavs, and other groups were races with inherent traits that could be read in their bodily features. Rather than seeing only one white race, influential race thinkers argued there were several white races varying in vitality and intelligence as well as phenotypic features. The "Nordics" ranked highest on the criteria of fitness for civilization and democracy, while the "Mediterraneans" ranked at the bottom—a belief used to justify the national-origins quotas in immigration laws in the 1920s.[30]

Despite being institutionalized in immigration law, these racial distinctions faded into ethnic distinctions by the 1950s and became so blurred by the 1980s that they lost their invidious power. Immigrants didn't just blend into the white majority; they diversified it, breaking up the old WASP (white Anglo-Saxon Protestant) hegemony. But ethnicity for most of them became what Herbert Gans in 1979 called a mere "symbolic identification," the basis for family traditions and cuisine and celebrations like St. Patrick's Day. In a late 1980s study of suburban white Catholics, many of whom had diverse European roots, another sociologist, Mary Waters, found that among white Americans being ethnic, and which ethnicity to be, was a "personal choice." Ethnic heritage still mattered; in fact, Waters described many of her subjects as clinging "tenaciously" to ethnic identities as a source of meaning. "Being ethnic makes them feel unique and special and not just 'vanilla,' as one person put it." Ethnicity was the flavoring that the bland vanilla of whiteness alone could not provide, a source of both community and freedom for whites, who could slip in and out of their ethnicity as circumstances suited them, in contrast to Blacks, who did not have the freedom to slip in and out of their racial identity.[31]

As of the late twentieth century, this difference in compulsion seemed a critical aspect of the distinction between ethnicity and race: Ethnicity was optional, while race was inescapable. Or at least Blackness was inescapable. It was never clear that the inescapability of race applied equally to all Hispanics, Asians, or people with a mix of white and minority ancestry. Race is not necessarily a fixed identity, not for those who are racially ambiguous in appearance, as a growing number of Americans with multiple ancestries are. Indeed, the change in American ethnic and racial patterns involves not merely a shift in the proportions of different groups but an increase in racial ambiguity that allows for more individual agency and fluidity in self-definition. Just as many whites came to have a choice about which ethnicity to be, so the mixing of peoples had already given some Americans—and will likely give more in future generations—a choice about which race to be. The growth of racial ambiguity also opened possibilities for the decline of hard-and-fast racial distinctions and erosion of barriers that many have accepted as an irreducible fact of American life.

Still, at the turn of the twenty-first century, there were forces pushing Blacks, Native people, and the new immigrant communities together as allies. They continued to face white racism in its various forms and had a shared interest in enforcement of the civil rights laws. While those laws were enacted in response to Black protest, they treated other minorities made up mostly of recent immigrants as suffering analogous injuries and deserving the same legal guarantees as Black people. The government thereby helped establish the idea that all the official minorities belonged to one larger group. Officially, there was no name for this larger group, no recognition of its collective existence. That collective recognition came from the left, born of a hope of solidarity among all the racially oppressed.

The term "people of color" originated in the 1700s, then largely disappeared in the mid-nineteenth century, until it re-emerged in the 1970s, when the Black, feminist, and other progressive movements were trying to build interracial coalitions that included growing numbers of Hispanics and Asian Americans as well as the indigenous. The term had two characteristics that made it an appealing candidate for revival. In its early history, "people of color" had served as a bridging identity, a response to the mixing of peoples in the Americas. In addition, it had avoided the fate of many other terms for subordinate groups that became terms of abuse. Instead, it was a term of respect, a name that had historical resonance but was free of history's worst baggage and was so long out of use that it could be used for new purposes.[32]

The formation of new bridging identities has been a recurrent historical development. "American Indian" and "Black" combine people with different origins who nonetheless came to be classified, counted, and treated as a group and, partly for that reason, to see themselves as sharing a social identity. Immigrants from Italy in the late nineteenth century mostly identified with their villages and regions; it was in the United States that many of them first became "Italians." The consolidation of the dispersed Mexicans, Puerto Ricans, and Cubans into a new Hispanic panethnicity in the 1970s followed this pattern. So did the emergence of an Asian American panethnicity. Panethnicity, as Dina Okamoto defines it, is a "process through which multiple ethnic groups relax and widen their boundaries to forge a new, broader grouping and identity." They may do so because they share similar social spaces (occupations, neighborhoods) and because the majority lumps them together and subjects them to the same prejudices. If you are discriminated against indiscriminately, you have a good reason to fight discrimination together.[33]

The new bridging identities of the late twentieth century, like others before them, first met resistance from within. Cubans initially did not see themselves as belonging to the same group as Puerto Ricans and Mexicans. As late as the 1990s a popular bumper sticker in Miami read, "No Me Digas Hispano. Soy Cubano." ("Don't call me Hispanic; I'm Cuban.")[34] "Asian American" had to overcome long-standing tensions among the Chinese, Japanese, and Korean communities, stemming in part from hostilities among their countries of origin. Even after federal law and statistical agencies adopted the categories Hispanic and Asian American, individuals continued to identify primarily with their national-origin group—as Mexican rather than Hispanic, or as Chinese rather than Asian American. But the formation of higher-level identities and broader coalitions was crucial in defending collective interests in the public arena. It was also an opportunity for minorities to influence how American institutions defined who they were, including the choice of a collective name free of old derogatory associations—"Asian Americans," for example, instead of "Orientals."

"People of color" had a dignified pedigree, though not many were familiar with it. A translation of the French *gens de couleur*, it came from the French colonies in the Caribbean and entered the mainland of North America chiefly through New Orleans and Charleston, South Carolina. The original people of color were free, mostly mixed-race people of African, white, and sometimes indigenous descent. Recognized as a distinct group in the law of Louisiana and other Southern states, they formed a third social stratum between enslaved Blacks and free whites. This was not the same as "mulattoes," as most mulattoes were enslaved and some people of color were solely African-descended or indigenous. Since free people of color were often educated and owned property, the term had positive associations, and in the 1820s and 1830s Northern Black leaders and journalists adopted "people of color" as a collective name for their own community. For example, the African Baptist Church of Boston, established in 1806, became the "First Independent Church of the People of Color" in the 1830s. But the term faded away as the Civil War approached and, with the end of slavery, virtually disappeared, thereby avoiding becoming tainted, as did "colored," by later association with Jim Crow.[35]

When Black and other progressive intellectuals and activists reappropriated "people of color" in the late twentieth century, they were using it not in a neutral, apolitical sense but to mean people who suffer racial oppression. The terms "nonwhite" and "minorities" implicitly centered whites. To speak of "people of color" was to signal a re-imagining of their status and potential political power on a co-equal plane with whites. There was some confusion at first as to whether "people of color" meant Blacks alone or referred to other minorities as well, but activists were generally clear about its wider scope. Partly due to the lingering confusion, however, African Americans remained the prototypical people of color—the group that the category first brought to mind.

The phrase "women of color" first gained attention in November 1977 at the federally sponsored National Women's Conference in Houston, where a delegation originally calling for a "Black Women's Agenda" attracted support from other minority women for an expanded resolution on the "double discrimination" faced by "women of color." The resolution was read in five parts on the convention floor by a Black woman, a Native American, a Japanese American, a Puerto Rican, and finally Coretta Scott King, the widow of Martin Luther King Jr. According to the Black feminist Loretta Ross, the focus on "women of color" was an expression of solidarity, "a commitment to work in collaboration with other oppressed women of color." Radical minority women made the implicit bias of white-dominated feminism a major target. "We women of color," wrote the editors of a 1981 anthology, "are the veterans of a class and color war that is still escalating in the feminist movement.... Racism affects all our lives, but it is only white women who can 'afford' to remain oblivious to these effects. The rest of us have had it breathing or bleeding down our necks."[36]

Like the introduction of the terms "Hispanic" and "Asian American," the re-introduction of "people of color" was part of an ethnoracial reframing of American society. Unlike "Hispanic" and "Asian American," "people of color" did not become an official legal or statistical classification. But aggregating minorities first into panethnic groups and then into the super-panethnic category "people of color" had the same cultural and political logic. The social categories Black, Native American, Hispanic, and Asian American all assemble what might otherwise be smaller fractions into more powerful wholes. The efforts to promote "people of color" as a collective name and identity was one step further in the push toward enlargement necessary for greater cultural visibility and political power.

Diversity as an Ideal and Legal Standard

While radical activists and intellectuals were trying to create a collective consciousness among people of color, "diversity" was emerging as a new cultural and political ideal and a new framework for law and social relations. The recognition of diversity had an imperative logic. The American people were changing, and America's institutions had to prepare for that reality. Schools had to prepare for more diverse students, employers for a more diverse workforce, media organizations and advertisers for more diverse audiences. The original focus of affirmative action was breaking down barriers to opportunity for Black people, and the justification was primarily compensatory: Race-conscious policies aimed to rectify the past denial of equal rights and continuing disadvantage. But how did a compensatory rationale apply to minorities composed chiefly of immigrants who had only recently come to the United States? What would they be compensated for? "Diversity" reflected a new social reality and provided a more capacious rationale for race-conscious policies. It looked less to the past and more to the future.

The immediate source of the turn toward diversity, however, was the opinion of a single Supreme Court justice who had the swing vote in a critical affirmative action case in 1978. The justice was a Republican appointee, Lewis F. Powell, and the case was *Regents of the University of California v. Bakke*. Allan Bakke, a white student, had applied twice to the medical school at the University of California, Davis, and been rejected both times even though he had better grades and scores than some other applicants admitted under a policy that reserved a specific number of places for underrepresented minorities. When the case reached the Supreme Court, the justices were so split that six of the nine wrote separate opinions. While four voted to uphold the medical school's policy, four others voted to strike it down and require the medical school to admit Bakke. Agreeing partly with the conservatives, Powell found for Bakke. He rejected the compensatory rationale for affirmative action and opposed quotas. But he also provided the liberals a fifth vote to allow affirmative action to continue if it involved taking race into account only as a "plus factor" in admissions. Affirmative action was constitutionally permissible, Powell wrote, because "an ethnically diverse student body" provides "educational benefits": "diversity adds an essential ingredient to the educational process."[37]

Even though Powell's argument about diversity was his alone—none of the other justices joined that part of his opinion, and it had no standing as law—"diversity" policies spread throughout American society in the following years. Universities and other institutions adopted diversity programs and created diversity offices (eventually under the term "diversity, equity, and inclusion" or DEI). Although exactly what diversity meant was not spelled out, it clearly referred to racial diversity (with Hispanics qualifying as a race-equivalent) rather than class diversity, ideological diversity, or religious diversity. Organizations took it to imply an obligation to increase the representation of racial minorities, but there was no numerical standard they needed to satisfy because the law prohibited explicit quotas. With the seeming imprimatur of the high court, though, "diversity" validated much of what had earlier been described as "multiculturalism." In a 1997 book, Nathan Glazer, who had earlier been a leading critic of affirmative action, proclaimed, with some regret, "We are all multiculturalists now."[38]

Twenty-five years after *Bakke*, in a 2003 case, *Grutter v. Bollinger*, the Supreme Court affirmed diversity as a compelling reason for affirmative action in higher education, this time in a majority opinion, though again as a result of a single swing vote by a Republican appointee, Sandra Day O'Connor. In addition to citing the educational benefits of diversity, O'Connor argued that "the path to leadership [must] be visibly open to talented and qualified individuals of every race and ethnicity" if America's leaders were to have "legitimacy in the eyes of the citizenry." Now diversity had two compelling grounds in the law—educational benefits and institutional "legitimacy"—but only on a temporary basis. O'Connor wrote that affirmative action wouldn't be justifiable after another twenty-five years.[39]

Diversity also received support from a source not generally known for its support of progressive causes—American corporations. By the late 1980s, business leaders became convinced that they needed to prepare for a diverse workforce, diverse consumers, and diverse global markets. Corporate diversity training programs gained momentum in the late 1990s and early 2000s after several leading financial firms had to pay out tens of millions of dollars in sex and race discrimination claims. The total payout by Merrill Lynch would eventually run to nearly half a billion dollars. Evaluations showed that antibias training programs were ineffectual in changing employee behavior and, when mandatory, were possibly counterproductive. Nonetheless, corporations continued the training because it strengthened their defense against lawsuits.[40]

In electoral politics, both the realities and the ideals of diversity came increasingly to separate the parties. Republicans in office were nearly all white, while Democratic elected officials included more of the rising immigrant groups as well as Blacks. It was not clear, though, where the partisan loyalties of Hispanic and Asian voters would eventually land. In 1992 Asian Americans voted for George H. W. Bush over Clinton by 55 to 31 percent; Republicans also had a long-standing base among Cuban Americans. But in the 1990s and early 2000s, as Republicans turned toward draconian anti-immigrant policies and their campaigns at times took on a xenophobic air, they pushed immigrant communities, both Asian and Hispanic, toward the Democrats. Still, the issue was not entirely settled. As late as 2007, President George W. Bush tried to pass pro-immigration reforms.

Although Democrats were becoming the party of racial and ethnic minorities, diversity was a political problem for them. In local politics they were often riven by competition between Blacks and Hispanics. In addition, while Democrats generally defended affirmative action, they knew it was unpopular, as voters made clear first in California in 1996 and then in other states by passing initiatives banning racial preferences in public universities and other governmental institutions.

The bigger problem for Democrats, however, was that high levels of racial and ethnic heterogeneity do not typically favor left-of-center parties or the egalitarian programs they want to carry out. Welfare-state policies tend to be stronger in societies that are more ethnically homogeneous.[41] There is a lively debate among social scientists about why more heterogeneous societies and local communities tend to be lower in social trust.[42] The United States, however, wasn't just becoming more ethnically diverse. It is one thing to have a society with a large and secure racial majority alongside groups firmly in the minority even if they are growing. It is another thing to have a society where racial minorities are growing large enough to be in a credible position to surpass the long-standing majority in numbers and political power. The latter is far more threatening to the pre-existing majority. This was why the framing and assumptions of the census forecasts were important. As experimental studies in social psychology repeatedly confirmed, whites became more hostile to minorities and more supportive of conservative positions when they were shown forecasts that they would lose majority status.[43]

The relationship between ethnic diversity and politics does not conform to some absolute law. Political leadership can and does make a difference. In the United States, it was probably not coincidental that the New Deal's labor and social policies were enacted and then sustained while immigration was cut off. But it was also crucial that national leaders during World War II and the Cold War actively sought to tamp down ethnic and religious divisions and build consensus, whereas by the 1990s prominent figures in the Republican Party and conservative media were using culture-war issues to inflame divisions over immigration, race, and sexuality. The melting pot was overheating and beginning to boil, and the right believed it stood to benefit from turning up the heat.

At the turn of the twenty-first century, America's growing diversity posed a political challenge. It was not a wholly new challenge, only a new version of the one that the nation had faced before, the challenge summed up in the motto, *e pluribus unum*, out of many, one. As Americans became not just more diverse but more polarized into two nearly equal camps, what some of them longed for was a leader who understood the danger and could bring them together.

Obama and the Racial Loop

To racialize politics is to infuse it with racial meaning. That can happen both through efforts to create racial distinctions and through efforts to reduce and overcome those distinctions. When Lyndon Johnson and the Democrats passed civil rights legislation in the 1960s, voters began to identify their party as racially liberal and the Republicans as racially conservative. Party identification and voting thereby became racialized. Choices between the two parties carried racial meaning they had not had before. From the late 1960s on, Republicans saw the racialization of electoral politics as being in their interest. Their political campaigns accordingly emphasized "wedge issues" such as busing, affirmative action, and welfare, which could split the Democratic vote and win over racially conservative whites; or they played the "race card" in more explicit ways, such as running campaign ads with images of Black crime.[44] This cycle was an instance of what might be called the *racial loop:* the reactive impact on race consciousness of the political dynamic set in motion by efforts to overcome racial inequality.

Barack Obama's election as president was another case of that racial loop. It was both a triumph over racial prejudice and an instance of the reactive heightening of race consciousness from efforts to break out of it. As Obama gained ground in the 2008 Democratic primaries, many of his supporters took his victories as a sign that Americans were putting racism behind them. After he won the South Carolina primary, the crowd at his victory rally chanted, "Race Doesn't Matter. Race Doesn't Matter."[45] Of course, they were wrong—and not just because Obama faced opposition from conservative whites on account of his race. Race mattered in the reverse way as well: He enjoyed support from both white liberals and African Americans who were excited by the prospect of electing a Black president and winning what seemed like the ultimate civil rights battle.

The racialization of elections doesn't just divide voters according to their racial identities; it also divides them according to their racial sympathies. Some white voters are antagonistic, some sympathetic, to African Americans. In an election involving a Black candidate, therefore, racialization can have two kinds of effects (leaving aside, for the moment, the response to a Black candidate from minority voters other than Blacks). Compared to a white candidate with similar views, the Black candidate may receive fewer votes from white racial conservatives, but that candidate may also receive more support from both Black voters and white racial liberals. These are what the political scientists Michael Tesler and David O. Sears call the "two sides of racialization." In the 2008 Democratic primary race, the enthusiasm Obama created among white liberals as well as high Black turnout proved to be decisive for his victory. In contrast, Obama probably suffered a net loss of votes in the general election because of his race, though not enough to prevent him from winning.[46]

Obama's distinctive identity set him apart from other Black politicians. Not only was he the biracial son of a father from Kenya and a mother from Kansas; he had been raised partly in Indonesia. To some Americans he was disturbingly foreign, while others saw him as the enthralling embodiment of the new American diversity, a welcome symbol of the nation's future. Obama was not reticent about his background. He had already published a memoir, *Dreams from My Father*, when he was 34 in 1995. By the time he ran for the U.S. Senate in 2004, he had figured out how to use his only-in-America life story to talk about the true basis of the American community. In his national political debut at the Democratic Convention that year, he denied that there was "a liberal America and a conservative America," or that there was "a Black America and a White America and Latino America and Asian America—there's the United States of America." The thought was not original; the man who said it was. He was a new figure on the American stage, unless you count celebrities from the world of entertainment. In an early focus group, white women seeing a video of him for the first time discussed whether he was more like Denzel Washington or Sidney Poitier.[47] If one America was disposed to hate and fear Obama, it was partly because there was another America ready to fall in love with him.

Besides sheer star power, Obama's appeal rested critically on his ability to straddle racial boundaries and the hope he offered of racial reconciliation. While embodying diversity, he showed insight into all sides of the racial divide and stirred excitement about transcending it. His ability to mediate differences had been crucial to his first election as president—president of the *Harvard Law Review*—when he was a student. Though clearly a liberal, Obama won the support of conservative students on the law review who believed he listened to their arguments and treated them fairly. From an early point in his political career, his "preternatural calm" ("no-drama Obama") was legendary. In a society where anger was rising on both sides of the national divide, he was America's least angry man. As a candidate and legislator, he was respectful of conservatives, sought to reach across the aisle, and acknowledged the reasons why whites might resent affirmative action. Obama never played down his Black identity; he would say he was "rooted" in the African American community but "not limited" by it. In short, Obama himself was not a racially polarizing personality. That he nonetheless became racially polarizing as a candidate and as president testifies to how powerful the underlying social forces were in that direction.

The 2008 Democratic primary race, pitting Obama against Hillary Clinton after Joe Biden and other candidates dropped out, represented an almost too-perfect culmination, at the presidential level, of the twentieth-century movements for racial and gender equality. But just as Obama did not run as the Black candidate, Clinton that year did not run as the women's candidate. If anything, each of them ran against type. Clinton believed she had to show she was tough enough to be commander-in-chief, while Obama tried to avoid racially fraught issues. Nonetheless, race and gender were inescapable when the two candidates' positions on the issues were nearly indistinguishable. Initially, many Black voters held back from fully embracing Obama's campaign because of doubts that whites would vote for a Black president. Besides, the Clintons had long and deep connections in the Black community, and key Black leaders such as the civil rights icon John Lewis at first endorsed Hillary. Obama's breakthrough came in the first big test, on January 3, 2008, when he won the caucuses in nearly all-white Iowa, proof for Blacks and whites alike that his candidacy was for real.

Although Black voters strongly supported Obama from that point on, he did not win the nomination on the backs of a people-of-color coalition. Clinton won large majorities of both Hispanics and Asian Americans. Liberal whites were the key to Obama's victory. The more racially liberal white Democrats were, the more they were likely to prefer Obama to Clinton.[48] Endorsing Obama, Ted Kennedy drew a parallel with his brother Jack's candidacy in 1960, suggesting that what his brother had achieved in overcoming religious bigotry Obama could achieve in overcoming racial bigotry. Of course, Hillary Clinton's election as the first female president would have been equally "historic." But among liberal whites, even among women, her candidacy in 2008 did not ignite the same history-making thrill. Still, it would be an error to make too much of the outcome of the contest between the two. The total popular vote in the Democratic primaries was virtually a tie, with only a sliver of an edge for Obama over Clinton—enough, however, combined with his caucus victories, to give him a decisive edge in convention delegates.

But while a people-of-color coalition did not give Obama the nomination, it was critical for his victory in November over the Republican candidate, John McCain. The Democrats might have won in a landslide in view of the circumstances in November 2008: an unpopular incumbent Republican and unpopular war, plus the collapse of the housing market, financial crisis, and sharp rise in unemployment in the months leading up to the election. Yet even under these conditions, Obama received only 43 percent of the white vote. If not for his overwhelming majorities among Hispanics (67 percent), Asian Americans (62 percent), and Blacks (95 percent), he would not have won.[49]

As the economy nosedived between the election and inauguration, political expectations of Obama rose to dizzying heights. When journalists were not comparing him to Lincoln, they were comparing him to Franklin Roosevelt. Some talked about him as a "transformational" rather than a "transactional" president, the kind of leader who reshapes the nation in a crisis instead of just negotiating within old constraints. Obama himself had that model in mind.[50] At the time he took office in January 2009, nearly 750,000 jobs were being lost each month, real GDP was falling at an annual rate of 6 percent, and the United States appeared to be on the verge of another depression.[51]

During the fall, while Bush was still president, Democrats had supported bipartisan efforts to stem the financial crisis, including the passage of the Troubled Asset Relief Program, better known as the "Wall Street bailout," which authorized up to $700 billion to buy distressed assets or equity in financial institutions. (The eventual sale of those assets netted the government a profit, though that might as well have been classified information.) The bipartisanship ended when Obama became president. Obama's economic stimulus program, the American Recovery and Reinvestment Act, passed the House solely on Democratic votes and with only three Republican votes in the Senate in February 2009. Democrats had to pass the Affordable Care Act (ACA) the next year on their own. Obama's third major legislative achievement, the 2010 Wall Street Reform and Consumer Protection Act, was enacted almost entirely on party lines. Other initiatives, notably legislation on climate and immigration, went nowhere in the face of steadfast Republican opposition, which made it impossible to get those measures through the Senate. Republicans were not coy about their intentions to withhold cooperation. "The single most important thing we want to achieve is for President Obama to be a one-term president," Mitch McConnell, the Republican Senate leader, declared before the midterm elections.[52]

While Obama's achievements did not fulfill the hopes of a transformational presidency, neither were they insignificant. Although the recovery would probably have been faster if the stimulus had been larger, it succeeded in mitigating what could have been far more serious effects.[53] The United States made a stronger recovery from the Great Recession than the countries in the Euro area or Japan.[54] Americans' income from wages and capital declined sharply from 2008 to 2010, but disposable income—what people had available to spend—had "extraordinary stability" because of expanded government benefits.[55] The poverty rate would have risen by 4.5 percentage points without government aid, but it rose only by half a percentage point.[56]

Obama's program nonetheless met intense opposition, particularly from the right-wing Republican movement known as the Tea Party that took off the second month of Obama's presidency in response to expanded government assistance. Over the next two years, public opinion surveys also showed highly unfavorable views of the "stimulus," which many people appeared to confuse with the deeply unpopular Wall Street bailout passed under Bush. In fact, 70 percent or more of the respondents favored government spending to help unemployed workers, cut taxes, and build roads and bridges—just the things Obama's stimulus did.[57]

But Obama's economic program had not been designed to ensure the public knew where the money was going. People didn't even realize when the money was coming to them. In early 2008, the Bush administration had sent taxpayers lump-sum rebate checks with a letter signed by President Bush. In contrast, the Obama administration distributed its tax cuts through reduced withholding, averaging so small an amount, $16 a week, that most people would hardly notice it. Much of the other stimulus money was channeled through existing programs or the states, where governors could take the credit. Unlike Roosevelt's New Deal, which built new dams and bridges, Obama's recovery program devoted most of its infrastructure spending to repairs. It erected no great physical monuments. The low visibility of benefits and their low traceability to Obama's stimulus then limited what he was able to do. When his economic advisers agreed in mid-2010 that he needed to go back to Congress for an additional round of stimulus, the support wasn't there from moderate Democrats for anything that could be labeled "stimulus."[58]

Health-care reform followed a similar pattern of substantive achievement without much political credit. Rather than redounding to Obama's advantage during his presidency, it generated intense opposition. Obama chose to make health care his top priority for institutional reform in part for the same reason that Bill Clinton had in 1993. By coupling an expansion of coverage with control of costs, comprehensive health legislation could simultaneously address problems of the poor, the middle class, and government itself. Health-care reform had a distinctive potential for a cross-racial, cross-class alliance because it could extend coverage both to low-income people and to many in the middle class who were being denied affordable insurance due to pre-existing health conditions. By reducing the rate of cost growth in existing federal health programs, legislation could also offset the cost of expanded coverage for the uninsured and produce long-run savings in the federal budget. No other reform had the same combination of moral, political, and fiscal possibilities.[59]

Obama had an additional reason to put health-care reform at the top of his agenda. It had a strong chance of being enacted because key interest groups and members of Congress had forged a rough consensus on a reform plan in behind-the-scenes negotiations over the previous two years. The approach followed a model that Mitt Romney had successfully championed as governor of Massachusetts. It called for covering the uninsured by expanding Medicaid for the poor and adding a new insurance marketplace with sliding-scale subsidies for individuals with incomes above poverty. On the one hand, the law would require individuals to carry coverage (an "individual mandate"); on the other, it would bar insurers from excluding people because of pre-existing conditions. Since the roots of this approach lay not only in Romney's policy but in earlier Republican proposals, Democrats had grounds for believing they could win at least some bipartisan support. Ultimately, they did pass legislation structured along those lines. But it was a case of "bipartisanship in one party," a bipartisan compromise with a Republican Party that no longer existed.

Like new techniques for minimally invasive surgery, Obama's health plan represented a kind of minimally invasive reform. Business groups did not mobilize against it because it left employer-based coverage largely untouched. Democrats also worked out deals with two powerful lobbies, the pharmaceutical and hospital industries. Private insurers were divided. Yet while the reforms were mild and the usual interest group opposition was relatively quiet, the reaction from Republicans and the Tea Party movement was anything but mild and quiet. They denounced "Obamacare" as a "government takeover" that would lead to "death panels" in which bureaucrats decided which of the elderly would die.

"If we're able to stop Obama on this, it will be his Waterloo. It will break him," South Carolina Senator Jim DeMint said in a conference call with conservative activists in July as they prepared for protests at town hall meetings called by congressional Democrats during the August recess. Although the counterattack did set back the reform effort, it activated progressive groups to rally in favor of the plan. It also led Obama to deliver a televised speech to Congress that reversed a slide in public support. Obama had not formulated the general approach to reform, and he had left it to Congress to write the legislation. But it passed only because he decided to make it a priority and personally intervened on more than one occasion to save it when it appeared to be near collapse. It also passed for one other reason. Despite failing to win a single Republican vote for the bill, Senate Democrats had a brief window in late 2009 when they had the sixty votes needed to overcome a filibuster and pass the ACA (which they were later able to modify, on final passage in March, with a "budget" bill that required only fifty-one votes).

Even though Obama had succeeded where Bill Clinton, Ted Kennedy, and others had failed in the past, health-care reform did not boost Democrats' political fortunes, at least not in the short run. It probably cost them votes in the 2010 midterm elections. That was partly because the main provisions of the ACA took effect only in 2014, four years after passage. Even then, Republicans continued to demand the law's repeal, and public opinion remained closely divided.

The sheer vitriol of the opposition to the ACA is hard to account for on the basis of the policy itself without taking into account the bitter partisan, racialized divisions of the time. The Tea Party movement, although ostensibly about government spending, had a distinct racial and anti-immigrant subtext in its outrage about government aid to the undeserving. Democrats elevated health-care reform to a top priority in part because it was a race-neutral idea with the potential of drawing white as well as minority support. But as Michael Tesler has shown, once Obama became "the face of health care reform," the racial attitudes of whites became a stronger determinant of their views on health care. Racial attitudes toward a Black political leader spilled onto issues that are not inherently racial.[60] To be sure, the opposition to health-care reform might have been just as ferocious if Hillary Clinton had been elected in 2008, except with gendered rather than racialized undertones. When health-care reform became "Obamacare," it got caught in the racial loop. Even race-neutral policy benefiting both whites and minorities couldn't escape the racial meaning that infused nearly every aspect of politics.

America, the Boiling Pot

Obama was re-elected in 2012, but with only 39 percent of the (non-Hispanic) white vote, down 4 percentage points from 2008. The racial division in voting was now greater than ever as the Democratic Party became increasingly multiracial while Republicans remained nearly all white. From 1988 to 2004, non-Hispanic whites had accounted for 74 percent of the Democratic presidential vote; in 2012, that number dropped to 56 percent. In contrast, 90 percent of the Republican vote in 2012 came from non-Hispanic whites. The shares of the voting eligible population represented by Hispanics (8.4 percent) and Asians (2.9 percent) were rising, though they were still relatively small. But with Obama at the head of the Democratic ticket, minority turnout was high, and he won their votes by exceptionally high margins: 72 percent of the two-party vote among Hispanics, 74 percent among Asians, and 94 percent among Blacks.[61]

Obama's performance among Hispanic voters was not a foregone conclusion. He had promised comprehensive immigration reform but had been unable to deliver it. To make matters worse, in the effort to win over congressional Republicans by showing a commitment to secure the border, his administration had even stepped up what had already been a record number of deportations under Bush. The administration, however, focused its removals of undocumented immigrants on "felons, not families," suggesting that it deported only the undeserving (though there were grounds for skepticism about that claim). It also made some administrative changes favorable to immigrants.

But in Obama's first two years, while Democrats had congressional majorities, they had not even passed legislation protecting the "Dreamers," the young undocumented people who had arrived in the United States as children. After that legislation died in December 2010 when it fell short of sixty votes in the Senate, the Dreamers themselves began coming out of the shadows and organizing marches and sit-ins to publicize their cause.

Two developments in the spring of 2012 pushed the Obama administration to act. In April, Marco Rubio, senator from Florida and a potential Republican vice-presidential candidate, proposed a bill to give the Dreamers temporary legal status. The next month, as the Dreamers sought action from the White House, a group of law professors signed a letter arguing that under Supreme Court precedents, the president had sufficient discretionary authority to protect the Dreamers. Inaction now seemed inexcusable. In June the administration finally took action, announcing Deferred Action for Childhood Arrivals (DACA), which invited the undocumented aged 31 or younger to apply for a renewable, two-year reprieve and right to work if they had come to the United States before age 16, were in high school or had graduated from it, or served honorably in the military. The Dreamers did Obama a favor by forcing his hand. DACA boosted his approval among Hispanics and contributed to his victory over Romney in 2012 in what otherwise might have been a tighter race.[62]

The ensuing debate among Republicans about the lessons of the 2012 election became a critical test of two different strategies for the party that would have fateful consequences for the future of American politics. In a March 2013 report that became known as the "GOP autopsy," the Growth and Opportunity Project of the Republican National Committee (RNC) argued that the party had to "focus its efforts to earn new supporters and voters" on minorities, women, and youth. The report presumed a demographic imperative: "The minority groups that President Obama carried with 80 percent of the vote in 2012 are on track to become a majority of the nation's population by 2050." It acknowledged the younger generation's alienation from the party: "Our Party knows how to appeal to older voters, but we have lost our way with younger ones. We sound increasingly out of touch." It even pointed to "a generational difference within the conservative movement about issues involving the treatment and the rights of gays—and for many younger voters, these issues are a gateway into whether the Party is a place they want to be." While identifying Republicans as "the Party of private-sector economic growth," the report declared that "our policies and actions must take into account that the middle class has struggled mightily and that far too many of our citizens live in poverty." It went so far as to say, "We should speak out when a company liquidates itself and its executives receive bonuses but rank-and-file workers are left unemployed." Although the authors of the Growth and Opportunity report acknowledged they were not a policy committee, they nonetheless took a position on one issue: "we must embrace and champion comprehensive immigration reform."[63] At that time, a group of moderate Republican senators was working with Democrats on such legislation, which passed the Senate in June 2013 by a vote of 68 to 32. But the bill died in the House, where a majority of Republicans had no interest in seeking another "grand bargain" on immigration and prevented a bill from coming to the floor.[64]

The day after the RNC report came out, one critic of its approach tweeted, "New @RNC report calls for embracing 'comprehensive immigration reform.' . . . Does the @RNC have a death wish?"[65] No one paid that tweet much attention. It came from the rich, perennial would-be presidential candidate Donald J. Trump.

A strategically minded response to the RNC report, laying out the alternative Trump would eventually follow, came at the time of the Senate immigration vote from Sean Trende, a political analyst at the website RealClearPolitics. Trende acknowledged that immigration reform "is probably part of one way for Republicans to form a winning coalition at the presidential level, but it isn't the only way." Most observers, Trende claimed, had overlooked a crucial fact. From 2008 turnout and population data, he calculated that the 2012 electorate was "missing" some 6.5 million mostly downscale and heavily rural white voters, who were turned off by both Obama and Romney. Trende conceded that even if those white non-voters had shown up and 70 percent had voted for Romney, they would not have been enough to give him a victory. But he suggested that in 2016, when Democrats wouldn't have Obama on the ticket to boost Black turnout, the Republican Party could win a narrow victory with a presidential candidate who could motivate those downscale whites. "This GOP," Trende observed, "would have to be more 'America first' on trade, immigration and foreign policy; less pro-Wall Street and big business in its rhetoric; more Main Street/populist on economics."[66]

Trende was right that Republicans could plausibly have gone either way in search of a presidential majority. They could have tried to win over more minority, women, and young voters, or to drive up turnout from downscale whites. The first strategy did not require them to win a majority from voters of color. With their well-established majorities among whites, they just needed to improve over Romney's performance. The Hispanic vote fluctuated substantially from one election to another. Just as Bush had won 40 percent of Hispanics in 2004, so another Republican might do substantially better than a candidate like Romney whose share of the Hispanic vote was only 28 percent. Obama's performance among Blacks and Asians also did not necessarily portend a continuing pattern.

Black turnout in 2012 was higher than white turnout; that was unlikely to happen again in 2016 without Obama on the ballot. The partisan loyalties of Asian Americans, like Hispanics, had not yet "crystallized"; Republicans had won a majority of their votes in the early 1990s and might reasonably expect to do better than they had in 2012. But, just as plausibly, a Republican could also ignore minority voters and tap into the deep well of alienated, downscale, and rural whites. This was the strategy that both the liberal and Republican establishments had failed to consider. To be sure, it would take a different kind of politics from the kind envisioned by the Growth and Opportunity Project. It would have to be more "America first," perhaps even, if only by indirection, white people first.

The choice Republicans faced after 2012 was a choice about the grounds on which American politics would be fought in coming years. If the 2012 RNC report had prevailed and the two major parties had both supported more inclusive policies, that joint effort would have had widely ramifying consequences for a shared sense of belonging in the United States. Republicans would have joined Democrats in trying to tamp down racial hostilities instead of amping them up. In that event, the United States would have been much more likely to have become a melting pot for the new immigrants.

Going in the opposite direction was a choice to make the pot boil. And making the pot boil was exactly what one candidate for the 2016 Republican presidential nomination had in mind. Race and immigration weren't the only ingredients needed to bring the pot to a boil. Class dissatisfactions were also crucial.

CHAPTER EIGHT

How America Stopped Working for Working-Class Americans

There's class warfare, all right. But it's my class, the rich class, that's making war, and we're winning.

—WARREN BUFFETT, 2006[1]

The vote for social democratic and affiliated parties... has gradually become associated with higher-educated voters... [turning those parties into] a "Brahmin left"... in nearly all Western democracies.

—AMORY GETHIN, CLARA MARTINEZ-TOLEDANO, AND THOMAS PIKETTY, 2022[2]

CLASS TOOK A BACK SEAT to race and gender in American politics during the second half of the twentieth century. The realities of class did not become any less significant at a time when economic inequalities were rising. Liberals and progressives, however, infused racial and gender issues with greater moral urgency. Beginning in the 1960s, many young liberals and progressives were at odds with organized labor because of its leaders' support for the Vietnam War and their resistance to racial and cultural change. The young thought of the unions as part of the establishment they were fighting. It wasn't until the 1990s that the unions had new national leadership committed to renewal, and it took the financial crisis in 2008 and ensuing Great Recession to put issues of economic justice into the center of national politics. The financial crisis intensified anger at Wall Street, and the recession highlighted economic insecurities that had been building up for decades. In the wake of those developments, a progressive class politics gained support on the left. The 2016 and 2020 presidential campaigns of Vermont Senator Bernie Sanders and the more aggressive criticism of financial interests by Massachusetts Senator Elizabeth Warren exemplified those shifts.

On the right too, there has been a turn toward class politics, albeit of a different kind. The central theme has been the betrayal of the American worker by both the Republican and Democratic establishments through their support of immigration, free trade, and a "globalist" foreign policy. Donald Trump rose to power on the basis of that repudiation of past leadership. Like Obama, he seemed before his election to be an unthinkable choice for president, not because of his race, of course, but because of his tabloid notoriety, multiple bankruptcies, and propagation of the lie that Obama wasn't born in the United States. But once Trump won the 2016 Republican nomination, his rise seemed, like Obama's, to be a logical culmination of long-term developments. In Trump's case, those developments included the hollowing out of industrial America, the radicalization of Republican rhetoric and tactics since Gingrich's rise in the early 1990s, and the integration of conspiracy-minded right-wingers into major conservative media such as Fox News, talk radio, and new online sites at a time when newspapers and other mainstream sources of news were in decline. These shifts were reflected in changes at the Republican Party's base as whites without a college education began voting more heavily for Republicans in the early 2000s and helped put Trump in the White House in 2016. The turn to the right of working-class voters was not limited to the United States. Trump's election paralleled the rise in Europe of populist parties with strikingly similar messages and bases of support.

Although the progressive and reactionary forms of class politics are opposed on substantive issues, they both make anti-elitist appeals. They focus their attacks, however, on different elites. Progressive class politics challenges the corporate and financial elites who dominate the accumulation of wealth, while reactionary class politics primarily aims its fire at the cultural elites who dominate the nation's major mainstream media, entertainment, and educational institutions. The two forms of class politics also both look back to that mid-twentieth-century era I described in chapter 1 as the reference point for much later thinking about America. They are nostalgic, however, for differently remembered pasts. Trump's slogan "Make America Great Again" is a call to return America to the time before the tumult, when America was at the top of the world, and white men like Trump were at the top of America—a time when the economy worked reasonably well for a majority of the white majority, and the national culture hardly noticed anyone else. Progressive class politics looks back to the same period for different reasons: that era's strong unions, robust Democratic majorities, expanded New Deal social protections, and widely shared prosperity. Both the reactionary and progressive versions of class politics hold that America broke its promises to working people, though they understand that promise differently.

The common practice today is to use levels of education as a basis for distinguishing different classes in contemporary advanced societies. I distinguish classes on two dimensions, wealth and education, and highlight two critical divides, a wealth and an educational divide. Educational credentials have become a critical economic asset in contemporary societies, and abundant data show that people with and without a college degree differ sharply in their health, life expectancy, and family circumstances as well as income. Although the lack of a college degree would not have marked out the working class in earlier historical periods, it does serve that function in the early twenty-first century. The new post-industrial economy has devalued not just their skills but seemingly their whole way of life, and it is entirely understandable why they have recoiled from the tidal shifts in American society—racial and cultural as well as economic—and want their old life, the old normal, restored.

Post-Industrial Capitalism: Two Elites, One Loser

In 1958 the British sociologist Michael Young published a satirical fantasy, *The Rise of the Meritocracy, 1870–2033*, written in the voice of a sociologist in 2033 trying to explain the "risings" that year of lower-class rioters inspired by the "Populist movement." By that time, the narrator explains, Britain had done away with inherited wealth and status and adopted a "splendid" system for classifying people by ability, assigning them brainwork or handwork, and creating a new ruling elite. "Today [in 2033] the eminent know that success is just reward for their own capacity, for their own efforts, and for their own undeniable achievement," whereas the lower classes, having been tested and retested, "know they have had every chance" and cannot escape recognizing their own inferiority. Although the new "meritocracy" (a term Young coined) had the support of all but the fringe Populists, the depressed morale of the workers posed a challenge. As the elite mated with one another based on tested IQ, opportunities for mobility from below had virtually disappeared, and the Conservative Party had even proposed restoring a hereditary aristocracy, this time an aristocracy of the genetically endowed. That proposal helped trigger the Populist revolt, which, according to a footnote from the publisher on the book's final page, led to the sociologist's murder just after he finished the manuscript.[3]

The Rise of the Meritocracy was the third of the great dystopian works of mid-twentieth-century Britain, after Aldous Huxley's *Brave New World* and George Orwell's *1984*. While less widely read, Young's book eerily anticipated central features of the twenty-first century's post-industrial societies: the role of higher education as a basis of social status and economic advantage; the despair of the less educated; and the potential for populist fury. In Young's imagined future, the meritocracy replaces the old upper class of wealth and then rigidifies into a new exclusive elite, whereas today's advanced capitalist societies have never done away with the power and high standing of wealth. Instead, we now have two class divides and two elites—one based on concentrated wealth, the other on education and culture. The two elites intersect, but they are not the same, and politics has to some extent become a fight between them.

The two class divides stem from inescapable aspects of technologically advanced, capitalist societies. The first, the divide between capital and labor, is inherent in capitalism. The second is newly prominent in a post-industrial era: the divide that separates a much-expanded college-educated and professional class from people with less education. The inequalities across both these dividing lines have increased in the past half-century. Since the late 1970s, capital has aggressively reasserted its influence, while labor has lost collective leverage and workers' incomes have stagnated. The "diploma divide," the distance in economic and social circumstances and political views between education-based classes, has also increased.

Each divide is associated with a different elite. The first is dominated by top executives and the holders of great wealth; the second by educational and cultural elites (the "Brahmin left"). But as both divides have widened, the same people—ordinary workers, those without financial or cultural capital—have lost out. In short, workers find themselves doubly diminished under post-industrial capitalism, especially in the form it has thus far taken in the United States.

During the mid-twentieth century in both the United States and Western Europe, the collective organization of labor and the strength of labor-oriented, left-wing parties served as a countervailing force against the economically rooted power of corporations and the wealthy. Unions and labor-friendly left-wing parties were the core institutions that offset the inherent power advantages of concentrated wealth. The vote for the parties of the left came from people with both lower incomes and less education. Conversely, the parties of the right generally attracted support from people who were both wealthier and more highly educated.[4]

But the emergence of new ethnoracial and cultural issues and the expansion of higher education have scrambled this earlier picture. Without having surrendered their working-class heritage, the parties of the left have become the home of both the more highly educated and ethnic and cultural minorities. And without having surrendered their connections to business, the parties of the right have become the home of much of the native-born, culturally conservative working class. The result has been to introduce class tensions into both the right and the left without eliminating the old opposition between a business-oriented right and a labor-oriented left. A gender divide has also emerged as the parties of the left have attracted more women and the parties of the right more men. The fact that political coalitions have become more complex does not mean that class has lost its significance. On the whole, corporations and the rich have benefited. The parties of the right have continued to act in their favor, while the parties of the left no longer prioritize support for unions and working-class interests.

Mid-twentieth-century visions of post-industrial society and politics did not anticipate the subsequent rise in income and wealth inequality, emergence of racial and cultural divisions, and scrambling of political coalitions. As of the 1960s, overwhelming evidence seemed to show a trend toward greater economic equality in industrial societies and provide grounds for believing it would persist.[5] Unions appeared to have won a secure place in the United States just as their counterparts had in Europe. In retrospect, this was a misjudgment about labor's situation, particularly in the United States. By enabling states to pass right-to-work laws and limiting union organizing in other ways, the 1947 Taft-Hartley Act had already set up unions for a long-term decline. Postwar growth also led to a misplaced complacency about labor's long-term future. U.S. industry was bound to face stiffer foreign competition as Western Europe and Japan recovered and other countries began challenging Western economic dominance. By the mid-1970s pressures from international rivals were pushing American manufacturing companies to close plants and take a tougher line against unions.

A post-industrial economy, however, offered an appealing long-term prospect as an alternative to continued dependence on manufacturing. The expansion of education, health care, and other services, as well as innovation in communications and information technology, promised to open new frontiers for economic growth and prosperity without necessarily sacrificing labor's interests. That high road to the future was the focus of the most influential accounts of a post-industrial society. In his 1973 book *The Coming of Post-Industrial Society*, the sociologist Daniel Bell envisioned a future that depended on scientific and technologic advance and demanded more planning, regulation, and socially responsible corporations that would be more responsive to concerns about the quality of life than to their shareholders' interest in profits. Scientists would become the "chief resource of the post-industrial society," the professional and technical class would become preeminent, research-oriented universities would become the society's central institutions, and the nonprofit sector would grow.[6] Much of Bell's forecast, particularly about the rising importance of services and technology, higher education, and the professional class, proved correct. But because of political choices, post-industrial America in the late twentieth and early twenty-first centuries became a far more market-driven, corporate-dominated, and unequal society than he and others anticipated.

Under the best of circumstances, the transition to a post-industrial economy would have been difficult for organized labor. Manufacturing was highly unionized; the private service economy was not. In a legal system where every new firm and establishment is born non-union, industrial change itself tends to erode unions' share of the labor force. The cost of union organizing in the small establishments typical in retail, restaurants, and other services also inhibited unions' ability to maintain their membership.

The shift from manufacturing to services and information did not mean that people laid off from factories would get the new jobs in high-skilled services and high tech; on the contrary, it implied the destruction of the livelihood of tens of millions of workers. Most workers displaced from industry had no realistic chance of reproducing the same living standards with the low-wage, non-union jobs in the private economy. The shutdown of manufacturing plants also affected far more than the laid-off workers and far more than their earnings. It affected their pride and sense of self-worth.[7] The effects ramified through local economies and led to family breakdown and declining health and life expectancy. As other countries showed, governments were not powerless in the face of threats to industrial employment. Sweden expanded public services, invested in a high-skilled workforce, and maintained high levels of both growth and economic equality. Germany was able to stem losses in manufacturing, slow down the rate of post-industrial change, and enable workers and communities to adjust to new conditions. But instead of adopting policies that softened the blows from economic disruption, the United States did the opposite.[8]

The turn toward neoliberal policies from the late 1970s through the early 2000s resulted in a massive shift in economic power and the distribution of income and wealth. Labor's share of national income began a long decline, while capital's share increased, and businesses offloaded risks for retirement income and health costs to their workers by shifting to fixed-contribution pensions and high-deductible health plans or by outsourcing jobs and shedding the associated obligations altogether. Under Carter, Reagan, and the Bushes, federal policies lightened the tax burdens on the rich (through lower personal income tax rates, lower taxes on capital income, and lower corporate taxes), while raising them on working people (through higher payroll taxes). Hostile government policies toward unions and aggressive corporate union-busting weakened labor, while relaxed antitrust enforcement allowed increasing monopoly power. The drug war and growth of mass incarceration disproportionately affected the Black poor. The entire period saw increased commercialization of the nonprofit sphere (for example, in health care), the rising power of finance (which commanded an increased share of profits), and a general shrinkage of public responsibilities not only by government but by business as well. The development of a new market for corporate control transformed corporations in the opposite way from what Bell and others had earlier envisioned. Instead of being bound to uphold social responsibilities, corporations were under even more pressure than before to deliver the maximum return to their shareholders. This "shareholder value revolution," together with judicial expansion of the rights of corporations (including corporate free-speech rights, interpreted to include unlimited contributions to political campaigns), empowered capital just as the labor's collective power was enfeebled.

The post–Cold War 1990s, as I suggested in chapter 5, recapitulated the technological and economic optimism of the 1950s. The marvels of the high-tech economy and the internet encouraged the idea that technology had "changed everything" and made obsolete all the old concerns that led to government intervention. At a time when hundreds of millions of workers in China, the former Soviet bloc, and the Third World joined the world economy, free-trade agreements sped up the losses of U.S. manufacturing jobs and undermined the bargaining power of workers. Still, economic growth during the 1990s was strong. As the internet and online economy developed, the prevailing view was that government's proper role was to get out of the way, even though decades of federal investment had nurtured and guided the computer and software industries, and the internet itself was a creation of the Department of Defense. But now government was retreating from all its traditional forms of intervention—public finance, public regulation, and public ownership. It seemed at first that the open architecture of the internet would guarantee unprecedented freedom of expression and a cornucopia of information.

One unexpected effect of the internet's development, however, was the collapse of the nation's newspapers and their role in reporting public-affairs news, which had been subsidized by plentiful advertising and readers who bought a paper for its other coverage such as sports and business. Despite gradual, decades-long losses in total circulation, newspapers had remained highly profitable through consolidation and the pricing power for ads that newspapers often gained as the sole surviving daily in a metropolitan area. The economic crisis of newspapers hit them with full force at the time of the Great Recession, but it came about for one reason above all: The internet undermined their role as market intermediaries. Advertisers no longer needed to piggyback on the news to reach consumers, and consumers had other ways to find out about products and sales. Newspapers also could not duplicate in the online environment the local monopolies that they had enjoyed in print. The readers who had come to them for news about sports or business or to find a job could now go to specialized online sites that offered more in-depth coverage or services like easily searchable employment ads. In just three years, from 2006 to 2009, advertising revenue fell nearly in half, and newspaper stocks plummeted. Newspapers laid off staff, but their problems were not short term. Social media platforms were taking off at the time, and the platforms would be able to scoop up data from all over the Web to target advertising more efficiently and deny the content-creating commercial news media the income that had been the basis of their business.⁹

Although newspapers were only one of the many industries disrupted and disabled by the internet, their decline had singular political implications because of the role they played in reporting news at the state and local level and assembling a local public from across the political spectrum. In the new online economy, it became impossible to duplicate those functions. The visionaries of the online economy as a liberating and decentralizing technology had not been able to see how it could become the basis for new concentrations of power and wealth. Some historical knowledge, however, might have disabused them of their illusions. The internet just followed the same path from open competition to monopoly power that had characterized earlier innovations in communication technology: the telegraph in the 1840s, the telephone from the 1890s to the early 1900s, and radio and television after radio's debut in the early 1920s. Americans went sleepwalking again—into monopoly power, this time the power of online platforms.

Lopsided shifts in national income provide the clearest picture of the surging fortunes of the superrich in the late twentieth and early twenty-first centuries. In 1980, the top 1 percent took in 10.4 percent of pretax income, while the share going to the bottom 50 percent was 20.1 percent. By 1997, the top 1 percent were making more than all the bottom 50 percent of Americans combined, and by 2016 the top 1 percent share reached 18.7 percent of pretax income while the bottom 50 percent share was down to 13.0 percent.[10] Bigger pay packages for top executives contributed to the growth of top incomes. In the 1970s CEO pay had ranged from 20 to 30 times average employee pay, but by the early 2000s CEOs were making between 240 and 399 times their employees' average pay.[11] A variety of other measures of income and wealth find the same pattern: breakaway gains among the top 1 percent and even bigger percentage gains among the top 0.1 percent.[12] The typical justification for cutting taxes on the rich under Reagan and George W. Bush was that the cuts would lead to faster economic growth. Nonetheless, real per capita GDP grew at about the same rate in the United States as in other rich countries that did not make radical cuts in taxes on top incomes. Those countries also did not see the share of income going to the top 1 percent rise to the levels in the United States.[13]

The soaring gains of the top 1 percent were a sharp turnaround from the mid-twentieth century and the principal story that progressives told about the shift to a "winner-take-all" political economy.[14] But those gains were not the only reason for rising inequality. Economic inequality was also increasing among the "other 99 percent," most starkly between people with and without higher education.

The Growing Divide among the 99 Percent

The Rise of the Meritocracy was right about the increasing importance of a highly educated class, and it turned out to be especially right about that class in the United States. Just as the United States now stands out among the advanced societies for the outsized gains of the top 1 percent, so it also stands out for the disproportionate gains of the college educated, who represent a much larger group than the top 1 percent, about one-third of adults. In the late 1970s, Americans who received a BA went on to earn about 40 percent more than those whose education ended with a high school degree, but by 2000 college graduates earned 80 percent more, a higher differential than in other wealthy democracies.[15]

This rise in the "college earnings premium" departed from patterns in the early twentieth century. Previously, both high school and college graduates shared in the expanding U.S. economy. Although high school graduates had earned less than college graduates, their earnings had risen at about the same rate until the 1970s, when the economic trajectories of high school and college graduates diverged. The divergence among men was particularly striking: Real hourly earnings for all men without a college degree (high school dropouts, high school graduates, and those with some college) began falling in the mid-1970s and were still lower in 2015 than they had been in 1973. In contrast, real earnings rose during that period for college graduates and jumped sharply for those with professional degrees.[16]

In another reversal from previous experience, the life circumstances of Americans without a college education have gotten markedly worse. During the twentieth century, life expectancy had risen dramatically for Americans of all educational levels. But after 2010, life expectancy for Americans without a college degree began falling even as it continued rising for the college educated. This divergence is not only unprecedented in U.S. history but extremely rare internationally.[17] The disparate trends in "deaths of despair"—deaths from suicide, drug overdoses, and alcohol-related disease—have been especially disturbing. As the economists Anne Case and Angus Deaton have shown, the increase in deaths of despair in the 2000s began among whites, particularly among whites in midlife without a college degree (the increase later spread to Black people without a BA as well). Other health data show the same pattern: a decline in mental health, ability to perform everyday activities, and ratings of overall health among middle-aged Americans without a BA, as their lives have measurably deteriorated.[18]

The declining health and growing social pathology among less-educated, middle-aged whites in the early 2000s paralleled what happened two decades earlier among the Black poor. Like Blacks who faced a mortality crisis with the arrival of crack cocaine and HIV in the 1980s, whites without a BA faced an analogous crisis in the early 2000s from the opioid epidemic. For both groups, good jobs were becoming scarce at the time drug-related deaths surged. As Case and Deaton explain, "When the labor market turned against its least skilled workers, blacks were the first to lose out, in part because of their low skill levels, and in part because of long-standing patterns of discrimination. Decades later, less educated whites, long protected by white privilege, were next in line."[19]

Although the divergence between the college and non-college population has more than one cause, changing policies toward education have played a key role. From early in the twentieth century, the U.S. economy demanded a more educated workforce. Thanks to the publicly financed expansion of high schools between 1900 and 1940 and of colleges and universities after World War II, the United States enabled a growing proportion of Americans to obtain the skills needed for economic success. In the "race between education and technology," education kept up. The supply of the educated met the demand, and consequently the earnings premium of the better educated was stable. But after 1982, the rate of growth in the college-educated population sharply decelerated, and the earnings premium began to rise in response.[20]

This is not to say that technology and market forces were alone at work. Political choices mattered. In the 1980s, state governments began putting funds into the construction of new prisons instead of expanding public higher education, and tuition started rising at public as well as private colleges as the national commitment to low-cost access to college weakened. The United States, which had led the world in broadening access to education, began losing its edge. American businesses looked increasingly to high-skilled immigrants to make up for shortfalls in scientific and technical fields and in the supply of physicians and nurses.

The college earnings premium also rose because of political choices that undercut the earnings of the less educated. During the late twentieth and early twenty-first centuries, Congress failed to adjust the minimum wage to keep pace with rising prices, and its real value fell; by 2006, it was worth only 55 percent as much in purchasing power as it had in 1968. The failure to update employment law allowed companies to shift work from employees to temps, part-timers, and contractors. Rising monopoly power and the spread of "noncompete" clauses in employee contracts gave firms growing power to underpay. Free-trade agreements and tax laws encouraged the offshoring of what had been good-paying jobs. Historically, Americans had grounds for believing that broad access to education helped make upward mobility a reality for many people. But in the early twenty-first century, the United States has had the highest inequality and lowest intergenerational mobility among the wealthy democracies. Education, instead of being the "great leveler" it once was, has become another obstacle to advancement.[21]

The new class system has had implications for family life. As in Michael Young's imaginary meritocracy, couples with higher education tend to marry each other. College leads not just to one but to two good incomes, greater marital stability, and substantially better odds of reproducing economic advantage in the next generation. Conversely, people with less education are now less likely than were their parents or grandparents to achieve economic security, a stable marriage, and the ability to raise children under circumstances that equip them for economic success.

This divergence in family life on educational class lines has compounded the inequalities in the labor market. It is almost entirely among the less educated that the rise in single-parent homes has taken place. From 1980 to 2019, among mothers with college degrees, there was only a slight increase, from 10 percent to 12 percent, in the share of children growing up with an "unpartnered" mother (that is, neither married nor cohabiting with a second parent). But the share of children in that situation jumped from 17 percent to 29 percent among mothers with only a high school degree. A diploma divide in the growth of single-mother homes occurred among all racial and ethnic groups, though it was smallest among Asian Americans. As extensive research has shown, single parenthood results in diminished resources for children, not just reduced household income but also less parental time and attention, and it has long-term effects on the children, who are more likely to struggle as adults. Without a father at home, the boys have been especially likely to get in trouble and reproduce the cycle of disadvantage.[22]

Conservatives attribute family instability to liberal cultural values. If that explanation were correct, two-parent homes should have declined more among the more liberal, college educated than among those without a BA, but the reverse is true. The more plausible explanation for the decline of two-parent homes is that disadvantage in the labor market for men without a BA translates into trouble starting and maintaining a family. Less able to fulfill the traditional breadwinner role, men with only a high school degree have lower self-esteem and are less attractive as marriage partners, more ambivalent about starting a family, and less likely to stay married when they do.

Like the decline in life expectancy and rise in deaths of despair in the United States, the decline in stable, two-parent families has been a sign of the severe stress experienced by Americans in the economy's lower tiers, white as well as minority. Economic inequality increases when the rich get richer, and that has certainly happened as the top 1 percent have pulled away from the rest of society. Inequality also increases when gaps widen among the other 99 percent, and that has happened too. In the early twenty-first century, many Americans remember a time when their lives were better. As children, they may have seen their parents moving into the middle class, but as adults they see themselves falling out of it. And many of them no longer believe that the party that once represented them still does.

Labor's Decline and the Struggle for Labor's Revival

Rising inequality and the deteriorating life circumstances of American workers did not happen independently of partisan politics or the changing focal concerns of social movements. While some accounts hold Democrats and Republicans equally responsible, that is not what the record shows. Republican administrations produced much worse economic results for people both at the middle and in the lower half of the income distribution. From 1948 to 2016, middle-class pretax incomes rose only about half as fast under Republican as under Democratic presidents, while incomes of the working poor (at the 20th percentile) grew just one-tenth as fast under Republicans. Americans with top incomes (at the 95th percentile) did about equally well before taxes no matter which party was in office, but Democrats taxed higher incomes more heavily than Republicans did. Even after overall economic growth slowed in the mid-1970s, lower- and middle-income people continued to do better under Democratic administrations in both before- and after-tax income.[23]

The dominant forces in both major parties, however, became more hostile or indifferent to labor unions and working-class interests in the late twentieth century. During the postwar decades, Nixon and other Republicans had often competed for union support, but that became rare in the GOP after the mid-1970s as its leaders moved further right. Once Republicans turned decisively against the labor movement, Democrats did little on its behalf, perhaps because they were able to take the backing of unions for granted. Despite opportunities under Presidents Carter and Clinton, Democrats failed to update labor laws to counteract the decline of unions or the growth in workers' insecurity—indeed, they intensified labor's problems through economic deregulation. At times, anti-union Southern Democrats in Congress blocked pro-labor measures, but a deeper, long-run shift was also at work. Working-class concerns fell as a political priority as unions shrank and both the Democratic Party and the progressive movement became an alliance between the educated professional class and advocacy groups representing minorities and women.

The declining membership and political influence of unions reconfigured American liberalism. Before the Black movement became the prototype for struggles for freedom and equality, the labor movement had been the leading force on the left and its major hope for a general attack on social injustice. In the 1930s and 1940s, as we saw earlier, labor's left wing supported interracial union organizing, and labor feminists were advocates for women workers. Civil rights unionism, however, was undermined by the Red Scare after the war, and labor feminism was eclipsed by feminism's "second wave" in the 1960s. Even then, however, leaders in both the labor and civil rights movements—none more important than Martin Luther King Jr.—sought to bring the two movements together, albeit with little success at a time when unions often blocked women and people of color from obtaining better jobs. The defeated alliance-building efforts from the 1930s to the mid-1960s were the lost possibilities that might have limited, even if they could not have entirely averted, the deep breach that developed in progressive politics between unions, on the one hand, and the Black, feminist, gay and lesbian, antiwar, immigrant, and environmental movements on the other.

Although the AFL-CIO supported the Civil Rights Act in 1964, conflicts between the unions and the rights-oriented movements began growing immediately afterward. The rights movements confronted the unions with demands for change in their racist and sexist practices and denounced their complicity in the Vietnam War. That attack cost the unions moral legitimacy and allies on the left as they came under siege in the following years by employers and the Reagan administration. Lawsuits against unions for racial and gender discrimination also weakened them financially. The AFL-CIO's budget for litigation costs doubled from 1966 to 1973, doubled again by 1979, and then quadrupled from 1979 to 1983. Unions had to pay out millions of dollars in consent agreements to settle discrimination cases while they were losing members from de-industrialization and corporate union-busting.[24]

To many of the post-Watergate generation of Democratic political leaders, unions were "dinosaurs," backward-looking relics of another era. During the early 1980s, some self-described "neoliberal" Democrats repudiated the party's close alliance with the labor movement, blaming it for inflation, failings of the public schools, and America's eroding position in international trade. "Neoliberal" at the time referred to a progressive updating of liberalism, often in connection with new technology and the use of industrial policy to promote economic growth. But like later free-market neoliberalism, the neoliberalism of the 1980s was hostile to unions.[25] By that point, the unions were being hit from all political directions at once, and the aging, stolid leadership at the AFL-CIO was incapable of effectively communicating organized labor's mission and fighting back.

The civil rights litigation against unions, however, initiated a transformation in the labor movement by opening unionized jobs previously monopolized by white men. In fact, Black workers became the most highly unionized of any racial group during the 1970s; in private-sector jobs, 40 percent of Black men and nearly a quarter of Black women belonged to a union (just in time to have the rug pulled out from under them with labor's decline). Not only were Blacks overrepresented in the heavily unionized manufacturing and transportation industries; they were also more likely than whites with similar characteristics to belong to unions, in part because they were especially supportive of unions in organizing drives. The share of union membership represented by minorities and women also increased because of labor's one bright spot in the late twentieth century; the growth of public employee unions. Unionization rose to just over a third of public employees during the 1970s and stayed at that level in the following decades, while private-sector unionization tumbled. A labor movement that had once mainly represented white men in blue-collar jobs increasingly represented women and minorities in pink- and white-collar jobs.[26]

Even as these changes were taking place and unions were vanishing from the private sector, the AFL-CIO remained an inert bureaucracy out of touch with a changing society and unwilling to put resources into renewing its ranks. Since the 1950s, the federation had "gone from viewing organizing as unnecessary to viewing organizing as impossible," as the journalist Harold Meyerson put it. Unions had mainly become service providers to their existing members, with little presence in the wider society. They wrote checks to Democratic candidates but were ineffective in marshalling support in elections or in congressional lobbying. Finally, in 1994, the passage of NAFTA and the Republican takeover of Congress under Gingrich sparked an internal revolt. The following year, for the first time in the AFL-CIO's history, an insurgent group of union leaders replaced the federation's leadership and began moving resources into organizing campaigns and attempting to rekindle labor activism.[27] Although those campaigns brought some victories, they failed to reverse the decline of union membership as a share of the labor force. Neither did a second insurgency in 2005, which resulted in the defection from the AFL-CIO of a half-dozen unions. Public opinion polls showed high interest in union representation among non-union workers. But union decline had gone so far that no internal efforts could enable the labor movement to regain its former role as an effective defender of general working-class interests. Unions had achieved that position during the New Deal only because they enjoyed the support of the national government. It would take another such political boost, in the form of a radical rewrite of federal labor law, if they were ever to recover their old role.

The changes in the makeup and leadership of the unions, however, did end the progressive breach. Instead of being an obstacle to the aspirations of working women and people of color, unions increasingly became their instrument. The union organizing drives that succeeded typically did so where the workforce had more women and more minorities.[28] Changes in union policy positions necessarily followed. To organize the rising numbers of Hispanic workers, unions rethought their position on immigration. By 2000, the AFL-CIO was supporting "comprehensive immigration reform," including a path to citizenship for the undocumented. The unions' limited ability to achieve objectives on their own made it imperative for them to build broader alliances, starting at the state and local level. The "Fight for 15," which called for a $15 minimum wage at a time when the federal minimum was less than half that, began with fast food workers in New York City in 2012. After the campaign had its first success in a suburb of Seattle that was home to workers at Seattle's airport, it spread to Seattle itself, then to cities elsewhere in the country, and eventually into national Democratic politics.[29]

Obama's presidency illustrates two seemingly contrary points about the Democrats and the working class. On the one hand, Democrats performed far better economically than Republicans for working people; on the other, they did little to arrest the long-term erosion of labor's power in the market or to help unions institutionally. The contrast in tax policies between Obama and his predecessor, George W. Bush, makes the first point. The big-ticket items in Bush's tax cuts benefited the rich: lower tax rates on high-income people (the top marginal rate fell from 39.6 percent to 35 percent), lower taxes on capital gains and dividends, and the abolition of the estate tax. The general thrust of the Bush cuts was to reduce taxes on capital income and put the burden of taxation on wage and salary income. Since the top 1 percent received about half of capital income but only one-tenth of wage and salary income, the shift was inevitably to their immense advantage. In Bush's 2001 tax cuts, the top 1 percent received 36 percent of the total value, about the same percentage as the bottom 80 percent of Americans.[30]

After Obama's election in 2008 amid the financial crisis and Great Recession, Democrats reversed the thrust of fiscal policy. The 2009 Recovery Act created or enlarged three tax credits aimed at mitigating the recession's impact on low- and lower-middle-income people. The legislation also expanded unemployment benefits, aid for housing, and the Supplemental Nutrition Assistance Program ("food stamps"), which by 2010 covered one in four children and one in eight adults and functioned as a minimum basic income. The 2010 Affordable Care Act created new tax credits for private health insurance for low- and middle-income people as well as expanding Medicaid. At the same time, Democrats raised taxes on people with high incomes. They undid the Bush income tax cuts on the higher brackets, mostly by allowing the cuts to expire; increased Medicare taxes for individuals with taxable income over $200,000; reinstated the estate tax; and for the first time required taxpayers to report foreign bank accounts worth more than $50,000 to cut down on the offshoring of wealth and tax evasion by the rich.[31]

The Obama-era tax changes made the federal income tax highly progressive, wiping out obligations for most Americans with incomes below the median.[32] One person who took note of the change was Obama's Republican rival in the 2012 presidential campaign. "Forty-seven percent of Americans pay no income tax," Mitt Romney told a private meeting of high-dollar donors in a speech captured on video in which he deplored the government benefits that the 47 percent received. "So our message of low taxes doesn't connect. . . . And so my job is not to worry about those people. I'll never convince them that they should take personal responsibility and care for their lives." The 47 percent figure was accurate, though it did not mean that "those people" paid no federal taxes (they paid payroll as well as excise taxes).[33] Romney's gaffe—an example of a "Kinsley gaffe," the kind where a politician creates an uproar by telling the truth—did more to publicize the progressivism of Obama's income tax changes than anything that Democrats said.

But while Obama's policies favored people of low and moderate means, the position of labor unions and workers continued to erode. For decades employers had been taking aggressive measures to stop unionization, including illegally firing pro-union workers during organizing campaigns, in the knowledge that it was cheaper to pay the minimal penalties under the law than to accept collective bargaining. To boost labor's chances of winning those campaigns, its supporters in Congress in 2009 put forward a bill, the Employee Free Choice Act, that would have expedited union elections and, if the union won, mandated arbitration whenever firms did not agree to a first contract through negotiations. Although the legislation had Obama's endorsement and passed the House, it died in the Senate for lack of sixty votes, even though Democrats had a sixty-vote majority during the second half of 2009, which enabled them to pass health-care reform. On the labor bill, however, a half-dozen Democrats defected, and Obama did not invest political capital in getting it passed. This was not an unusual occurrence. Progressive labor legislation had repeatedly failed because of defections from within Democratic ranks.

The Senate's supermajority requirement stood in the way of other updates to labor law that might have responded to outsourcing and other strategies adopted by business to escape obligations, such as paying the minimum wage, under the standard employment relationship assumed in federal labor law. New online platform companies like Uber, founded in 2009, claimed not to be employing workers such as drivers, only to be organizing a market for them, which consequently put them outside of employment law. But Democrats were unable to amend the laws to maintain fair labor standards, in part because of the considerable influence within their own party of the finance and tech industries. Despite polls showing overwhelming popular support for a higher minimum wage, legislation to increase it died in the Senate in 2014 (as it would again in 2019 and 2021). By 2019 a family of three living off a minimum-wage job would fall far below the poverty line, unlike their counterparts fifty years earlier.[34]

The two patterns of Democratic policymaking I have been describing—progressive tax and spending policies, along with a failure to reverse the downward drift of workers' rights and power—resulted from three distinct causes: corporate influence over the party, the institutional structure and procedures of Congress, and the growing dependence of the party on the votes of the affluent college-educated. Under Senate rules, budget bills required only a bare majority to pass, while other legislation needed a sixty-vote majority. The economically progressive measures with a chance of passage took the form of tax credits or incremental modifications to existing programs that could pass with a bare Senate majority. Tax credits for low-income workers provide aid to the low-wage employees of corporations, which indirectly helps the companies too. Legislation to bolster unions and employees' claims on their employers, however, would have needed the support of sixty pro-labor senators, which Democrats never had.

Traditional class allegiances—that is, the tendency of higher-income Americans to vote Republican and lower-income Americans to vote Democratic—continued to be strong in the 1990s but weakened around the turn of the century. While Democrats were losing working-class votes, they were picking up votes among the more highly educated, particularly those who lived in metropolitan areas and their suburbs. These voters tended to be liberal on racial and cultural issues. They wanted an active government in such areas as health care and childcare, but they did not have the same interests as the Democrats' old base in the industrial working class.

This shift in the Democratic base was the context not only for the party's failure to strengthen labor's position but its support for free-trade legislation. Lower trade barriers reduced consumer prices as well as the price of inputs for some domestically produced goods. But increased imports from low-wage countries, especially China, devastated U.S. manufacturing, accounting for about one-quarter of the total decline in manufacturing employment from 1990 to 2007. The decline accelerated between 2002 and 2004—the infamous "China shock." Labor-intensive manufacturing industries such as footwear, toys, textiles, clothing, furniture, and electrical appliances felt the biggest impact. In the local regions most exposed to import competition, jobs and wages fell, while receipt of public benefits for unemployment, disability, and health care increased. The effects were particularly harmful to young men. The social pathologies were the familiar ones: higher premature mortality (including higher rates of deaths of despair), more poverty, more unwed mothers, and more children living in single-mother families.[35]

The effects also ricocheted back on politics. Exposure to trade heightened political polarization in congressional districts, particularly from 2010 to 2016. If the districts were majority white, moderate Democrats were succeeded by conservative Republicans; if they were majority-minority, moderate Democrats gave way to more liberal ones. But because many more districts were majority-white (and the others led only to internal Democratic shifts), the primary impact was to raise the number of seats held by Republicans.[36] As a political strategist later remarked in summarizing a study of factory towns that had suffered manufacturing losses, "Democrats saw the bottom drop out" of their support between 2012 and 2016.[37] Centrists in both parties had done it to themselves when they voted for free-trade agreements—sleepwalking, as I suggested in the introduction, to their own political funerals.

By the 2010s, rising economic inequality became a focus of national debate, spurred in part by the contrast between Wall Street bankers who escaped the 2008 financial crisis with impunity and ordinary people who lost their homes. Instead of prosecuting bankers for financial crimes and sending some of them to jail, the Obama administration offered the firms "deferred prosecution agreements" that allowed them to pay fines that amounted to slaps on the wrist. The lack of legal accountability for the financial crisis, at a time when millions of people were losing their life savings, symbolized a widely shared sense of injustice. Technological inevitabilities no longer seemed an adequate explanation for rising inequality. A new generation of scholars and journalists argued that political choices were the primary reason the superrich had captured a vastly disproportionate share of the gains of economic growth. Beginning in September 2011, the short-lived Occupy Wall Street movement attacked the "one percent," and in December that year, in a speech in Osawatomie, Kansas, President Obama called inequality "the defining issue of our time," making it a theme of his 2012 re-election drive. Romney's background in finance made him a perfect foil for that campaign and its populist-themed ads. But Obama's foray into economic populism was as brief as the Occupy movement, and in his second term he reverted to more conciliatory policies responsive to Wall Street and Silicon Valley.[38]

The political campaign that did more than any other to put class politics back in the national discussion was the challenge by Bernie Sanders to Hillary Clinton for the 2016 Democratic presidential nomination. Clinton came into the campaign with such overwhelming party support that others who might have entered the race, such as Senator Elizabeth

Warren, decided to forgo it. As a political independent, Sanders was willing to buck the party consensus in favor of Clinton, and as the only senator who called himself a "democratic socialist," he had an ideological mission in launching a campaign and a ready-made organizing force of progressive activists. Unlike Clinton and other Democrats, he was relentless in his attacks on Wall Street and insistence that the economic system was "rigged." The high-paid speeches that Clinton had given to Wall Street firms provided fodder for Sanders the way Romney's background in finance had provided fodder for Obama four years earlier.

The odd thing about Sanders's "socialism," though, was that he identified it with Roosevelt's New Deal and could just as easily have described his politics as a return to New Deal liberalism. In Roosevelt's own day, socialists emphatically denied that the New Deal amounted to socialism; it was Republicans who equated the two. Now Sanders was validating an old Republican line, which Democrats had long regarded as a smear.[39] But, with the Cold War over, most Democratic voters were not preoccupied with ideological distinctions. On the left of the party, many identified themselves as both socialists and liberals, though the favorite choice was "progressive," a label that both Clinton and Sanders accepted. One attraction of "progressive" was that it covered over differences between center-left liberalism and more radical views.

Sanders did far better in the 2016 Democratic primaries than anyone expected, winning 43 percent of the vote, though some of that was mainly anti-Clinton (running against Joe Biden four years later, Sanders was unable to reproduce his 2016 numbers). He benefited from the choice of Republicans and conservative media during the 2016 primaries to train their attacks on Clinton, confident that if by some miracle the Vermont senator became the Democratic nominee, they had all the ammunition they would need to beat him in the general election. Like the earlier Occupy protests and other sudden spurts of activism in the digital age, the 2016 Sanders campaign was a brief efflorescence, not the basis of a durable movement. What it lacked and was unable to build was a substantial, ongoing organizational infrastructure.

The missing element was the infrastructure that a well-developed labor movement might have provided. By 2016, the proportion of private-sector workers belonging to a union was down to 6.4 percent.[40] Despite the rebirth of a progressive labor leadership, the unions did not have the reach or resources to mobilize the mass of working-class voters. By failing to support them institutionally and enacting trade legislation that destroyed working-class confidence in their leadership, Democrats had inflicted damage on their own party.

Unions continue to have important political effects. Through their communication with their members, unions increase voting for Democratic candidates and nudge their white members toward more liberal views on racial issues.[41] Without unions—and without the newspapers that had once dominated local and state news—other sources of political communication fill the void. That was one of many reasons for the rise of a reactionary class politics. A nation that had nearly eliminated unions as a basis for working-class aspirations left its workers open to other appeals. Without an infrastructure for a progressive class politics, there was another road for working people who felt the ground was being cut out from beneath them. Strangely enough, a billionaire and reality TV star from New York intuitively grasped the potential for a reactionary class politics more clearly than did anyone else.

CHAPTER NINE

Trumpism as Total Revenge

I bring rage out. I do bring rage out. I always have. I don't know if that's an asset or a liability, but whatever it is, I do.

—DONALD TRUMP, March 31, 2016[1]

I am your warrior. I am your justice. And for those who have been wronged and betrayed, I am your retribution.

—DONALD TRUMP, March 7, 2023[2]

UP TO ELECTION DAY, November 8, 2016, nearly everyone in politics, even in Donald Trump's own circle, assumed that Hillary Clinton would be the election's winner. Trump's victory, though, was not just a stunning finish to a presidential race. It contradicted what most people at home and abroad thought they knew about the United States. It upset the standing idea of America. The United States had long been seemingly immune to the appeal of right-wing political figures from outside the mainstream who were openly contemptuous of immigrants and other minorities. Trump's election broke that pattern. Americans had also just twice chosen a Black man as their president, which led many people to think the country was headed in a progressive direction. But how did *that* America, the one that had elected Obama in 2008 and 2012, suddenly make a U-turn and elect Trump? No event of sufficient proportions—no economic collapse, no defeat in war, no earth-shattering scandal—could explain such an abrupt and extreme reversal.

Explaining the 2016 election will provoke endless debate, however, not because there is a shortage of explanations but because there are so many. In a close election, any number of factors may plausibly be said to have caused the outcome. The United States in the early twenty-first century was a fifty-fifty country. Since the 1990s it had been split into evenly matched and highly polarized parties and societal blocs. Under these conditions, slight differences from one election to the next, due to individual candidates or transitory circumstances, could swing politics in diametrically opposed directions.

Trump's Electoral College victory in 2016 did not reflect an overall shift in the nation's values or public opinion toward his party or his views. He lost the popular vote to Hillary Clinton by 2.9 million, giving her the largest winning margin of a losing candidate in American political history. If just 78,000 of those 2.9 million votes had come in the right proportions from Michigan, Wisconsin, and Pennsylvania instead of California or New York, they would have swung the Electoral College majority to her. A last-minute intervention by the FBI director, reopening (and then closing) a case concerning Clinton's use of a private server for some of her emails, may well have shifted the race's outcome.

Seen in that light, Trump's victory belongs among the critical events that have altered the course of history because of contingent circumstances that tipped the outcome, like the sinking of the Spanish armada in 1588 off the English coast due primarily to bad weather, helping England surpass Spain as a global power. As a whole genre of historical scholarship tells us, slight perturbations at "critical junctures" can produce large consequences. Trump's narrow margin in a few swing states makes it impossible to say for certain that online disinformation, Russian interference in the election, Clinton's personal image or history, or misogyny in general did not make just enough of a difference to tip the result.

Nonetheless, in one influential account of Trump's 2016 victory, race is the whole story, or nearly all of it. This is the view that I described in the introduction as racial reductionism. It explains Trump's rise to power primarily as the product of "racial resentment," the fears of threatened whites. Class divisions do not figure centrally in this interpretation; even gender issues are secondary if a factor at all.[3]

Heightened racial anxieties no doubt were a factor in Trump's support. Earlier presidential candidates like George Wallace and Patrick Buchanan had appealed unsuccessfully to racial grievance, but by 2016 Obama's presidency and immigration had created a more receptive context for those appeals. On both the right and left, Americans had come to believe that the country was approaching a time when minority groups would equal the white population and then exceed it. Obama's election seemingly confirmed that idea, though it was not the clear signal about the future that many people took it to be. The notion that whites were becoming a minority was a mistaken reading of demographic change and likely to be misleading about American society for a long time to come. It was especially misleading about politics since whites remained an overwhelming majority of the electorate and were overrepresented in the Senate and Electoral College because of their domination of predominantly rural states. But the fiction of an imminent collapse of a white majority lent credence to right-wing fears of racial "replacement" and served as a powerful stimulus to white identity.

After Romney's defeat in 2012, as I indicated at the end of chapter 7, one strategic vision for Republicans saw a potential path to the presidency in a right-wing candidate who could mobilize alienated, downscale, irregularly voting whites. But that candidate, whoever it turned out to be, "would have to be more 'America first' on trade, immigration and foreign policy; less pro-Wall Street and big business in its rhetoric; more Main Street/populist on economics."[4] As that strategy suggested, an awakening of white power required a new economic appeal, not just a racial one. Republicans had been gaining support from non-college whites since the late 1990s, and as Trump showed in 2016, more of those votes were ripe for the picking in states that tipped the Electoral College to him. The racial reductionist account of the 2016 election underrates the significance of Trump's overthrow of neoliberalism and direct appeal to working-class pride. Class figures as strongly as race in explaining why the 2016 election tipped in favor of Trump.

The shock of Trump's rise to the presidency, however, arises from something deeper than the outcome in the Electoral College. Donald Trump was far out of bounds of what previously had been the bounds of presidential politics. The true puzzle is how someone like him ever came close to the presidency. He flouted the rules in his political as well as private life and flourished all the same. In this respect, Trump's victory revealed momentous changes on the right, within the Republican Party, and ultimately in American politics. Long-standing social norms no longer served as a deterrent to openly racist and sexist language and behavior. A candidate could breach those norms, retain Republican support, and still get elected president.

In fact, Trump used breaches of norms strategically. He first built sustained political attention and support among Republicans with the lie that Obama did not have a U.S. birth certificate. When he announced his candidacy in June 2015, he characterized Mexican immigrants as "rapists" and said they were bringing crime and drugs. Shock value helped vault his campaign into public consciousness. Shockwaves were his medium. Like shock humor in comedy and shock jocks on the radio, shock politics was the Trump method for seizing attention, his way of reaching people who ordinarily tuned out politics. Precisely because he did not hold back from bluntly offensive language, he proved himself, in the eyes of many supporters, to be more truthful and trustworthy than other politicians. He not only spoke his own mind; he spoke thoughts of theirs that they never heard from other public figures, and they idolized him for being their unfiltered and unashamed voice.

In an account of his initial attraction to Trump, Stephen Miller illustrates how Trump's breaches of social norms won a devoted following. Miller is a hardline, ethno-nationalist opponent of immigration who became a key figure in the Trump campaigns and White House. While working as an aide to Alabama Senator Jeff Sessions, he was impressed that Trump in his announcement speech not only called Mexican immigrants "rapists" but refused to apologize when criticized for saying so. Miller had been upset by what he called the "apology-retreat cycle" among Republicans. They would talk about cracking down on immigration to get elected and then back off afterward, but Trump's refusal to apologize showed he could be counted on, if elected, to get tough on immigrants. "The fact that he . . . doubled down, breaking that apology-retreat cycle, gave enormous confidence to a lot of people," Miller later told journalists Julie Hirschfeld Davis and Michael Shear.[5]

With the devotion Trump earned, no shock was too shocking, and no low was too low, for him to recover. An outtake from the TV show *Access Hollywood* showed him saying that "when you're a star, [women] let you do it. . . . Grab 'em by the pussy. You can do anything." At his rallies, he encouraged violence against protesters ("Knock the crap out of them. I'll pay the legal fees.").[6] He openly admired Vladimir Putin and other authoritarian leaders. Liberals and the mainstream media expected Trump's demonstrable lies, advocacy of violence, admiration of dictators, and sheer vulgarity would sink his candidacy. In another day, they would have, but not in 2016. Liberal consternation was a source of conservative delight. Some Republicans disapproved (or at least said they did), but most soon forgave his lapses despite his dismissive attacks on leaders they had celebrated as heroes, like Senator McCain. Trump belittled and demeaned his Republican rivals in the primaries, yet they later pledged loyalty to him. These displays of masculine dominance earned him admiration and deference, too, the kind of deference shown an apex predator.

Trump's views on policy, especially his repudiation of the Republican establishment's support for immigration, free trade, and "globalism," need to be seen in this light. Racial retribution was only part of his appeal. He was the total backlash package, an icon of unabashed masculine defiance of liberal values and the progressive project. In what was simultaneously a cultural and class message, he promised revenge for all the ills that had befallen much-aggrieved, hard-working Americans. Trump himself had no guiding principles besides his appetite for power. But in satisfying that appetite, he raised to a feverish heat a form of racially and culturally inflected, reactionary class warfare that has reconfigured American politics. And because, amid all the xenophobia and racism, Trump's outlook had an element of economic rationality from the standpoint of people whose interests had been ignored, it brought about major shifts in national policy and threatened to change the relationship of the United States to the world.

The Interplay of Elite and Base in the Republican Party

Part I of this book argues that conservatives succeeded in getting only "half a counterrevolution" from the Republican administrations of the last third of the twentieth century, despite the twenty years in office of Presidents Nixon, Ford, Reagan, and George H. W. Bush and their ten consecutive Supreme Court appointments from 1969 to 1991. The main Republican success lay in squelching unions and thereby finally undoing part of the New Deal political transformation. But they did not reverse the major post–New Deal legal and policy precedents regarding racial and gender equality or the momentum of cultural and racial change. Part of the explanation for that pattern is that Republicans had historically been the more liberal party on racial and gender issues, and many of the party's supporters and leaders—including judges—still upheld liberal principles or at least moderate versions of them. They also joined in a bipartisan pro-immigration consensus. By the early twenty-first century, however, those older influences were waning, and a series of developments had changed the social base and emotional appeal of right-wing politics. The half-counterrevolution itself had increased economic inequality and insecurity but left in place liberal policies related to race and immigration and even expanded them in connection with gender. Discontent was boiling below, especially among white men and to some extent among men who weren't white. That discontent created new political opportunities for the party that had traditionally drawn its support from higher-income and better-educated Americans.

In the late twentieth century, whites with and without a college education did not differ significantly in presidential voting. During the Reagan-Bush years from 1980 to 1988, Republican candidates received about 60 percent of the white vote regardless of educational level. But in 1992 and 1996 Bill Clinton brought the white vote back down to an even split as he won back many of the Reagan Democrats. During the 1990s, however, Republicans began moving right with the rise of Gingrich, Limbaugh and conservative talk radio, and Fox News, all of them elevating the salience of culture-war issues. Polarization first showed up among highly engaged partisans, but the shift in the Republican Party and conservative media affected the composition of the party's electoral base. At the turn of the century, Republicans began doing about five points better among whites without a college degree than among college-educated whites. A similar divergence developed in party identification—more whites without college degrees began identifying as Republicans—and that split grew much larger during Obama's presidency. As of 2015, when college-educated whites were about evenly split between the two parties, whites with only a high school education favored Republicans over Democrats by twenty-four points, 57 percent to 33 percent.[7]

As the decline of the labor movement had reconfigured American liberalism and the Democratic Party, so increased white working-class support changed the Republican Party and American conservatism. Like the first Great White Switch in the South that began with Goldwater in 1964, the switch of the white working class outside the South, particularly in rural areas, changed who Republicans were. In the run-up to the 2016 primaries, however, neither the media nor the old Republican establishment had fully registered the implications for what and whom the party's voters would support. The change at the base did not just give the party new political opportunities; it also created an opportunity for an outsider to seize power from slow-to-respond party leaders.

Although Trump did not initiate the second Great White Switch, he exploited and intensified it through his attacks on immigrants and Muslims and his substantive positions on economic and foreign policy. The rhetorical bombshells got the most attention, but the substantive positions were important signals too. Trump did not have well-worked-out ideas about policy, but compared to the Republican establishment, he had impulses that were a better match for what the Republican Party had become. As both a salesman and an entertainer, he also had the skills to get his message across. The party establishment was committed to free trade and global alliances and inclined to compromise on immigration, and Trump was against all those positions. He used political speeches and rallies to test out different themes—his rallies became his research—and when he found a theme or a meme that worked, he kept coming back to it. One of his advisers suggested the idea of building a wall on the border with Mexico as a way of prompting Trump to talk about immigration. In speeches in Iowa and Texas in 2015 he discovered that his audiences loved the idea of the wall as much as he did.[8] Pretending that he had never supported the Iraq War, he now lambasted it as an example of how much losing America had been doing thanks to the Bushes, Romney, and others from the old leadership. He revived the old pre–World War II isolationist slogan, "America First," appealing to a widespread fatigue and disgust with forever wars and foreign commitments.

Trump also broke with the Republican establishment on central questions about the domestic role of government. He rejected cuts in Medicare, Medicaid, and Social Security, said he would provide "everybody" with health care "much better" than Obamacare, and suggested that as president he would change unfair tax laws and even raise taxes on the wealthy. Like his repudiation of the Iraq War, his rejection of the politics of austerity seemed to position him as more moderate than his 2016 rivals. Most of this was not to be taken seriously—he also promised he would pay off the national debt in eight years (in the four years from 2017 to 2021 he would add nearly $8 trillion to it). What some voters and political analysts took to be moderation is better understood as what Europeans call "welfare chauvinism," nationalism and nativism applied to social spending. Native-born working- and middle-class voters who oppose spending on outgroups often depend on public benefits themselves and want to protect those programs from retrenchment. Trump's opposition to cutting Social Security as well as Medicare and Medicaid responded to that concern, an especially important one for the party's older constituency.

Trump did need to distance himself from previous positions he had taken on abortion and other social issues—"I am very pro-choice," he had said on NBC's *Meet the Press* in 1999—but the religious right was willing to forgive and forget. Just as easily as Trump the tycoon became Trump the populist, so Trump the notorious libertine became Trump the social conservative. As of 2011, white evangelicals had been the *least* likely of all religious groups to say that someone "who commits an immoral act in their private life" could ethically fulfill public duties, but in 2016 they became the religious group *most* likely to say that personal immorality was compatible with public office.[9] On matters of morality, evangelicals were more flexible than some gave them credit for.

Accounts of the race for the Republican nomination emphasize the fragmentation of the rest of the Republican field, but it was the party's nomination rules that put Trump in a position to capitalize on the establishment's failure to unite behind a candidate before the primaries began. The Republicans' procedures, unlike the Democrats', called for an early use of winner-take-all primaries that were designed to avoid a prolonged battle and enable a candidate to lock up the nomination with only a plurality of the vote. The party had set a trap that ended up snaring its own establishment.[10] No doubt Trump also benefited from his prior celebrity and domination of news coverage (he received more mentions on the cable networks than all the other Republican candidates combined). At points in the primary campaign when other candidates threatened his lead, Trump arranged for stories smearing their reputations in the tabloid *National Enquirer*, which at the same time was also "catching and killing" stories that might hurt Trump.[11]

But Trump's nomination was not just a fluke. He fit the party's core followers both substantively and emotionally, like the angry voices they listened to on conservative talk radio. No political figure better embodied the spirit of negative partisanship, the buildup of hatred of the other side. It just so happened that the 2016 general election also pitted Trump against the first-ever female presidential nominee of a major party, a woman who in the minds of many Republicans epitomized the social changes they abhorred. Yet the surprising fact about the 2016 contest is that despite the emotional furors surrounding Trump and Hillary Clinton, the election was in line with prior patterns, a statistically normal election. Nearly 90 percent of both Democrats and Republicans voted for their party's candidate, just under what they had done in 2012. The final popular vote turned out close to what forecasting models based on economic and political conditions had predicted. The most comprehensive average of those models pointed to a nearly fifty-fifty split of the two-party popular vote. Although many would later say Clinton was a weak candidate and attribute her loss to her missteps in the campaign, she beat the forecasting models by two points.[12]

The expectations for Clinton, however, had been much higher than for Trump. Throughout the campaign, the polls showed her leading the popular vote both nationally and in the three key Midwestern states that she ultimately lost. On the day of the election, prediction models based on polling data put her chances of victory at about 85 percent.[13] Clinton had particularly strong support at elite levels. Of the top 100 U.S. newspapers based on circulation, only two endorsed Trump while 57 endorsed Clinton, the greatest imbalance ever.[14] The astonishment at the election's results may have been due to the social distance of elites from less-educated whites and mistaken perceptions that had been built into the polls. In a post-mortem, a committee of the American Association for Public Opinion Research concluded the most likely explanation for polling error in 2016 was "a pervasive failure to adjust for overrepresentation of college graduates (who favored Clinton)," along with "a late swing in vote preference toward Trump." The committee also cited evidence that Trump benefited from a change in voter turnout from 2012 to 2016.[15] The failures to adjust for overrepresentation of college graduates and to pick up in advance the change in turnout were both class-related mistakes. They underestimated Trump's support in the white working class.

As post-election analyses showed, changes in the social bases of support for the two parties were crucial to the outcome. Among non-Hispanic white voters without a college education, a twenty-five-point edge in 2012 for Romney over Obama had grown to a thirty-one-point edge in 2016 for Trump over Clinton. Among college-educated non-Hispanic whites, in contrast, a 0.7 percent edge for Obama in 2012 had grown to a 6.3 percent edge for Clinton. But non-college whites outnumbered the college educated in the eligible-voter population by about two to one. Furthermore, relative to 2012, turnout rose by 3.0 percent among the non-college white voters but only 1.9 percent among the college educated, and Black turnout fell by 4.5 percent. All these factors together led to a shift in the composition of the electorate in 2016 toward non-college whites and a higher Trump vote than polls predicted.[16]

These effects were magnified in Michigan, Wisconsin, and Pennsylvania, which gave Trump narrow majorities after going Democratic in the previous six presidential elections. Non-college whites represented a relatively large share of the population in Michigan and Pennsylvania, and the fall in Black turnout was exceptionally steep in Wisconsin. If non-college whites had represented the same share of the vote in 2016 as in 2012 in these and other states, Clinton would have come out ahead—one of many possible alternative scenarios that would have given her the election.

Even if the two candidates had not been Trump and Clinton, the 2016 electorate would likely have shifted in the same direction, though not necessarily to the same degree. Non-college whites were trending toward the Republicans, and without Obama on the ballot Black turnout was likely to fall. But Trump and Clinton affected who turned out and how they voted because each of them heightened the focus on social identities. Trump's incendiary rhetoric had the clear purpose of arousing feelings about race and immigration, and his slurs against women inevitably made that a more salient issue too. In one of many such incidents, the day after Fox reporter Megyn Kelly asked Trump at a primary debate about his insulting language about women, he confirmed her point when he said about Kelly herself, "You could see there was blood coming out of her eyes, blood coming out of her—wherever." Trump's mark on the campaign was, to say the least, distinctive. As research later demonstrated, people with high animosity toward Democratic-linked social groups (Blacks, Hispanics, Muslims, and gays and lesbians) responded with especially high levels of support for Trump that they did not show for other Republicans. The same research also showed the reverse not to be true: Clinton did not bring out greater support from those with high animosity toward Republican-linked groups (whites and Christians).[17]

But Clinton had reasons for emphasizing identity issues too. If she was to have any hope of maintaining the support from racial minorities that Obama had, she needed to stand up for them in the face of Trump's attacks, even though in the process she risked further alienating prejudiced whites. In addition, in 2016, unlike 2008, she highlighted her identity as a woman and her potential to break America's ultimate glass ceiling. That framing gave her candidacy, like Obama's, a historic purpose, a basis for mobilizing followers for a cause greater than herself. This was not an unreasonable hope on her part, and the gender gap did hit a new high in 2016—but not because Clinton had a bigger edge among women than Obama had. It hit a new high because Trump had a bigger edge among men than Romney had. He drew especially strong support from men with intensely sexist attitudes, the most devoted to traditional ideals of masculinity. Trump also had the support of a majority of white women, disproportionately those without a college education, who shared many of the beliefs about gender that working-class men had. Once again, the diploma divide was simultaneously a class and cultural divide.[18]

After the election, political analysts tended to pit economics against identity and status as explanations for the outcome. Did Trump's support arise from a change for the worse in a voter's individual economic well-being over the previous four years? Or did it arise from threats that "dominant groups" (whites, men, Christians) perceived to their status from racial and cultural changes such as the prospect of a majority–minority society? When the question was framed that way, identity emerged as the principal or even the exclusive reason Trump had won.[19]

But looked at in other ways, the shift in support that enabled Trump to win did not come chiefly from "dominant groups," at least not members of a dominant social class. Nor was economic change irrelevant to the political earthquake that Trump represented. Trump gained disproportionately in areas exposed to rising import competition, costing Clinton enough votes in Michigan, Wisconsin, and Pennsylvania to decide the 2016 election. A study examining how manufacturing job loss affected the three presidential elections from 2008 to 2016 found a similar pattern. Manufacturing layoffs were associated with higher Republican support among whites and more Democratic support among Blacks, but the former was the larger and more electorally significant effect. A third study identified how economic conditions affected voting and non-voting. In areas of economic distress, whites were more likely to vote for Trump, while Blacks were less likely to vote for Clinton not because they switched to Trump but because they were less likely to vote at all. Economics and social identity both mattered. The economic effects did not stem from simple, individual pocketbook voting but from the collective experience of groups—not from random individuals down on their luck so much as from downwardly mobile communities.[20]

Still, the effects were starkly visible in how individual voters had changed in partisanship over the previous quarter-century. Between 1992 and 2016, whites without a college education had shifted in party identification from +10 Democratic to about +25 Republican, while whites with college degrees went in the reverse direction, from +10 Republican to about an even split.[21] Over the same period, economic disparities had increased between non-college and college-educated Americans; the social lives and health of less-educated whites had also deteriorated, and the geographic areas where this disruption took place had moved to the Republicans. The rise of industrial unions during the New Deal era had lifted the fortunes of the Democratic Party in the industrial heartland. In 2016, however, Trump won 80 percent of the electoral votes of the twenty-five states with the largest share of manufacturing employment, while Clinton won 61 percent of the electoral votes of the twenty-five bottom manufacturing states.[22]

For the moment, Trump's rise consummated a reactionary Republican alliance that many on the right had long been dreaming about: the white South and white workers outside the South, both of whom felt dispossessed from the Democratic Party, united with the old right-wing elements of the Republican Party, including most of corporate America. Each party was a cross-class coalition—the moneyed elite in the Republican Party joined with less-educated whites; the educational and cultural elite in the Democratic Party, which had its wealthy donors too, joined with racial and cultural minorities that included high proportions of low-income people. Democrats had long made an issue of the Republicans' partiality toward corporations and the rich; Republicans replied in turn by portraying Democrats as elite snobs.

The Trump presidency would take the old right-wing suspicion of intellectuals to a new level in its efforts to delegitimate the mainstream media, scientists, and other professionals in universities and government agencies. These were not just culture-war conflicts, as they are usually described. They were attempts to discredit rival sources of power. Trump didn't just criticize journalists; he denounced them as "enemies of the people." In an off-camera conversation, Lesley Stahl of CBS asked Trump why he attacked journalists, and he replied, "You know why I do it? I do it to discredit you all and demean you so when you write negative stories about me, no one will believe you."[23] That honest answer also applied to right-wing attacks on climate scientists and other experts who came to conclusions supporting policies Republicans opposed. These attacks were part of struggles, class struggles of a kind, over who Americans would believe and what the governing principles of American society would be. There was even class conflict within the new Trump administration, which showed up, above all, in the issue of trade and relations with China.

A Truly Hostile Takeover

Open and undisguised hostility was at the core of Trump's political temper—hostility to immigrants and minorities; hostility to women who gave him any trouble; hostility to reporters and the media; hostility to political rivals and the elites in both the Republican and Democratic establishments who stood in his way; hostility to anyone among his own appointees who failed to show personal loyalty. Jared Kushner described his father-in-law's presidential campaign as a "hostile takeover" launched against the ruling class. This was the premise behind Trump's Inaugural Address, which told a story of national betrayal by previous administrations that had created a bleak landscape of "American carnage." One of the men credited with writing that speech, Steve Bannon—the former head of Breitbart News and final manager of Trump's campaign—was the leading advocate in Trump's circle of the theory that Trump was at war with the "globalist" elites. On entering the White House, where he had a brief cameo as a top adviser, Bannon said, "It's time to take on the elites in this country; Take the torch to them. Hit them with a blowtorch."[24]

Objectively, that was not what Trump did, not close. He used populist appeals to gain power but didn't use power that way. To call him a "populist" is to fall for that deception. In his first year, Trump sought legislation on health care and taxes, two areas where he had promised help for ordinary Americans. But, according to the Congressional Budget Office, twenty-four million people would have lost coverage under the bill to "repeal and replace" Obamacare passed by House Republicans (no legislation passed the Senate). The 2017 tax legislation, one of the few significant measures that his administration did obtain from the Republican-controlled Congress, reduced the corporate income tax rate from 35 percent to 21 percent and included other provisions benefiting the rich. "You all just got a lot richer," Trump told wealthy guests over dinner at his private Mar-a-Lago club just after he had signed the bill.[25] While performing the part of a warrior against the elites, he had stocked the senior ranks of his government with plutocrats, generals, and others from the nation's highest circles of power. The administration's original top economic policy figures, Secretary of the Treasury Steve Mnuchin and director of the National Economic Council Gary Cohn, both came from Goldman Sachs. Kushner had close Wall Street ties. Trump's first secretary of state, Rex Tillerson, had been the CEO of ExxonMobil. Trump's billionaire friends outside the administration had direct channels to him and were frequently in touch on matters of interest to them.

Nonetheless, the idea that Trump was mounting a hostile takeover had a kernel of truth because of his deviations from Republican orthodoxy and his authoritarian temper. He was at war not with the ruling class but with the ruling consensus of national elites on trade, immigration, and foreign policy, and he was intent on imposing a form of personal rule of his own.

Even before Trump took office, Breitbart News published an article, "The Deep State vs. Donald Trump," warning that entrenched forces would conspire against him, a narrative that framed how conservative media came to understand Trump's presidency.[26] But career bureaucrats did not prove to be his biggest problem in his first term. After appointing conservatives with elite credentials to the cabinet or White House staff, Trump often fell out with them or judged them insufficiently loyal to his personal interests. The most serious internal resistance he faced came from many of these appointees—his national security advisers, secretaries of defense and state, even his own chiefs of staff—who belatedly concluded, one after another, that he was incorrigible and unfit for the presidency. The "adults" atop his administration continually tried to restrain him or to divert his attention from hare-brained schemes he entertained, and they rationalized their decisions to stay in their jobs as long as they did on the grounds that at least they were stopping Trump from violating the Constitution, the national interest, and common sense.

Sooner or later, though, most of the adults lost the battle and were out. Repeatedly, Americans were treated to the spectacle of a president using a tweet to insult or fire his top officials or contradict policies they had already announced. Even his aides and Republican members of Congress were often at a loss to figure out what he wanted because of his dizzying reversals and inconsistencies. The sheer chaos and unpredictability of Trump's White House made his every mood the constant obsession of the political world. He was a strongman only in the limited sense of having a whim of iron.

With his TV background, Trump paid close attention to how he and other members of his administration looked, how events were staged, and how news was framed, lest anything make him seem weak. But he had never shown much interest in the specifics of policy, and reaching the White House did not suddenly concentrate his mind on legislating and governing. Even on the 2017 tax legislation, Trump issued only a vague one-page proposal; the bill was written on Capitol Hill, negotiated among Republican legislators. He did not have the slightest grasp of the complexities of the health-care system or how hard it would be even to get Republicans to agree on legislation. "Nobody knew that health care could be so complicated," he announced. When the health bill devised by Senate Republicans finally came up, John McCain in one of his last votes killed it with a thumbs-down. Promoting himself as a great builder, Trump said he would restore America's infrastructure, but the program never materialized. He said he would cut regulation "massively," but the volume of federal regulations increased.[27]

The policies that Trump pursued and his conduct of the presidency failed to raise his popularity, which started out at a historical low point. The average net approval rating (positive minus negative evaluations) for elected presidents from Eisenhower to Obama was +49 immediately after the inaugurations. Obama's net approval was only slightly below average at +41. Trump's was –7, and this was as high as it would get. Over four years, it varied between –7 and –21, averaging –13. What is striking about that range is not only how low but how narrow it was compared to other presidents. For the first time in polling history, a president never reached 50 percent approval, yet he also never fell as low as some of his predecessors had. That low-and-narrow range reflected not just the fixed partisan divisions among Americans but the choices Trump made in governing. Some of the proposals he had made in his campaign, such as infrastructure investment, did poll well with both Republicans and the public at large, while others polled well only among Republicans. Which proposals did his administration go ahead with? The ones that appealed to Republicans alone. Other presidents made popular proposals their top priority after being elected. Trump's priorities were historically unpopular. The net approval on the tax plan was –19. On the House Republicans' health bill, it was –30.[28]

Things could have been worse for Trump. If Congress had passed and he had signed the health legislation depriving twenty-four million people of their health insurance, Trump's popularity might have fallen even further. Although Republicans controlled both houses of Congress for Trump's first two years, they passed little legislation of consequence. As far as Trump's popularity and re-election chances were concerned, that may have been just as well.

The chaos of the Trump administration and paucity of its legislative accomplishments should not, however, obscure the historical significance of the policy changes Trump did make. He used his executive powers to change the direction of national policy in two areas, immigration and trade. Both were closely identified with his "Make America Great Again" (MAGA) and "America First" campaign themes. Both broke with the national leadership of the preceding decades and implied a radical shift in America's relation to the world. Together with Trump's disdain for NATO and other alliances, they represented a turn back toward an old, pre–World War II Republican ideal, not just America First but America Alone, not a "city on a hill" but a Fortress America with walls against immigrants, barriers against imports, and indifference to the fate of human rights and democracy around the world.

As a candidate, Trump made immigration his signature issue and, once in office, he believed that following through on his promises would be decisive for his political fortunes. In a campaign speech in August 2016, he had laid out a ten-point plan beginning with construction of his border wall and including a series of other items sought by anti-immigration groups: No more "catch and release" of border crossers. "Zero tolerance for criminal aliens," whom he estimated at two million, to be placed in "immediate removal proceedings." No more funding of "sanctuary cities" (cities that refused to cooperate fully with immigration authorities). Cancellation of Obama's "illegal executive amnesties" (a reference to the DACA program for Dreamers). Suspension of visas in countries where "adequate screening cannot occur"—his examples were all Muslim-majority nations—a problem that he identified as responsible for terrorism in the United States. Cutting off employment and public benefits for illegal immigrants. Legislative reforms to make merit and skill (rather than family ties) the basis for selecting immigrants and to "keep immigration levels, measured by population share, within historical norms" (which implied reducing annual levels). "Countless Americans," he said, had died because of the Obama administration's "open border policies." In a signal of priorities, Trump's first executive orders after his inauguration included a ban on travelers from seven Muslim-majority countries and a directive to build the border wall for which Congress had yet to authorize funds.[29]

Objectively, illegal immigration was not the growing crisis that Trump depicted in 2016. According to the best estimates available, the unauthorized population had peaked in 2007 at 12.2 million and fallen to 10.5 million a decade later in the year Trump became president.[30] That decline resulted in part from the volume of deportations under Obama, and it flatly contradicted Trump's denunciations of the Obama administration as having wreaked havoc on American society with its supposed commitment to "open borders." Trump continually highlighted violent crimes committed by illegal immigrants, even though crime rates among immigrants were lower than among the native born. He claimed falsely that the great majority of people convicted of terrorism were foreign born. He pointed to immigration as a primary reason for low wages among American workers, even though studies indicated the long-term effects of immigration were, at most, small.[31] The idea that a Mexican border wall and the other immigration policies Trump advocated would substantially raise Americans' standard of living was an illusion. Nonetheless, Trump's framing of the issue had much greater political potency in 2016—and greater long-run significance—than Democrats and center-right Republicans had expected. Trump lit a fire in the Republican base that the supporters of immigration in the party gave up trying to put out.

Critics of Trump's immigration policies denounced them as racist, an argument for which he supplied plenty of evidence himself. Dehumanizing references to immigrants as "snakes," "animals," and a burden on the American people were standard tropes in Trump's speeches. In June 2016 Trump said he would be treated unfairly in a lawsuit because the judge was Mexican American, an accusation that Paul Ryan, the Republican Speaker of the House, called "the textbook definition of a racist comment" (which did not, however, prevent Ryan from supporting Trump).[32] In a notorious 2018 Oval Office exchange with Senator Lindsey Graham and other members of Congress about immigrants from Haiti and Africa, Trump asked, "Why would we want all these people from shithole countries?" The United States, he added, should have more immigrants from European countries—Norway was his example.[33] An underlying current in Trump's immigration initiatives might be described as deterrence through cruelty. Interesting himself in the architectural design of his border wall, he asked that it have steel spikes on top and be painted black so that it would puncture and burn the flesh of anyone who tried to climb over it. On a trip to South Korea, he admired the North Korean side of the border, with its land mines and guards who shoot to kill. "That's what they call a border," he said. "Nobody goes through that border."[34]

Deterrence through cruelty had its clearest expression in Trump's short-lived policy of family separations. During 2018, Trump became increasingly agitated about his administration's failure to close the southern border as the number of migrants rose, many of them fleeing violence and destitution in Central America. Kirstjen Nielsen, the secretary of the Department of Homeland Security, caught the brunt of Trump's anger. In a crowded meeting in the Cabinet Room, he exploded at her: "I got elected on this issue, and now I'm going to get unelected." Finally caving in to the pressure to get tough in early May, she signed off on a "zero-tolerance" policy to separate migrant children from their parents so the parents could be jailed and prosecuted. (Previous rules had required the release of families into the United States, pending a hearing, because U.S. law barred jailing children with adults.) The migrant children, some under four years old, were now reclassified as "unaccompanied" minors and caged in shelters without proper food or personal care before being sent, sometimes thousands of miles away, to "foster care or whatever," as John Kelly, Trump's chief of staff at the time, put it. A public uproar forced Trump to reverse himself on June 20. "The crying babies doesn't look good politically," he admitted to Republican lawmakers just before issuing the decision. A judge also ordered the administration to end the separations and reunite the children with their parents, but immigration authorities had already taken away about 5,500 children, 628 of whom had still not been reunited with their parents by the time Trump left office mainly because information about the children's parents had not been preserved.[35]

Trump's fury over immigration grew as the midterm elections approached, and conservative media hyped the story of an invading "caravan" of Central Americans traveling toward the border. He continually insisted that Secretary Nielsen simply "close" the border and turn away the migrants, which, she explained, her department had no authority to do because many of them were claiming asylum and had a right to a hearing under U.S. law. Just close it, Trump told her. He threatened to send in the military with orders to shoot to kill or at least maim the migrants, which would have violated laws concerning deployment of the military and standing rules about the use of deadly force; Nielsen and others talked him down from what they foresaw as another disaster, getting him to agree to a limited use of the National Guard. Once the midterm election was over, Nielsen's department reached a deal with Mexico under which asylum seekers would wait for a U.S. hearing on the Mexican side of the border, and Mexico would receive $4.8 billion in aid. Trump grudgingly approved the deal, but conservatives were irate: He had promised Mexico would pay for the wall, and now the United States was paying Mexico! The COVID-19 pandemic would later provide a public health rationale and new legal authority for the "Remain in Mexico" policy.[36]

Behind the scenes, Miller worked with other hardliners in the administration to limit the number of immigrants of all kinds, legal and illegal. Obama's regulations had prevented federal agents from arresting people who had no other legal problem besides their immigration status. Trump ended these rules, "unshackling" the agents so they could round up the undocumented in raids on workplaces and other locations often in Hispanic communities. The administration's enthusiasm for deregulation did not extend to immigrants: It added pages to immigration rules and forms, creating an "invisible wall" to reduce the number of legal immigrants. It also sharply cut back the number of refugees legally admitted for resettlement, which fell from 85,000 in 2016 to under 23,000 in 2018 and 12,000 in 2020, the lowest levels since the 1980 Refugee Act. It also reversed earlier practices in granting asylum. In 2018, for example, Attorney General Sessions ruled that the immigration courts, which are under the Department of Justice, would no longer treat domestic, gender-based, or gang violence as grounds for asylum. These were all measures that the executive branch could carry out on its own.[37]

Trump's inability to strike deals with Congress and pass legislation was the most important source of his frustrations in making progress on his immigration agenda. His difficulties increased with the 2018 midterms, when Trump tried to make immigration and the invading Central American caravan the number one issue, only to see Democrats regain a majority in the House of Representatives by picking up forty-one seats. But even while Republicans had controlled both chambers, they refused to appropriate the funds that Trump needed to build the border wall. After shutting down the government in late 2017, he used a declaration of national emergency to siphon money from the Defense Department budget to construct the wall but was unable to build much additional wall by the time he left office.

Trump's volatility also contributed to his failure to do anything, one way or the other, about DACA and the Dreamers. He had committed himself to canceling DACA, and in late 2017 Sessions announced it would end in six months, but influential voices in the Republican Party, as well as Trump's own family, sought to protect the Dreamers. At the start of a meeting with lawmakers in January 2018, Trump announced that he wanted a "bill of love" on immigration and could sign one that gave legal status to the Dreamers and even provided for comprehensive immigration reform. Yet he also stood by Miller's demands, which ruled out such concessions and included draconian limits that Democrats would never agree to. The congressional negotiators at one point were willing to meet Trump's insistence on $25 billion for the wall. Polls showed a deal to save the Dreamers would have been popular; Trump could also have claimed vindication on the wall. But the hardliners still called the provisions for the Dreamers an "amnesty," and Trump withdrew his support, once again preferring to stick with his base rather than reach for compromise. Despite Trump's self-promoted image as a master of the "art of the deal," there never was the DACA-for-border-security deal that a more artful dealmaker might have negotiated. Trump preferred to govern by proclamation insofar as he was able to do so.[38]

The courts were instrumental in holding Trump back from measures he might have taken. Immigration law did give the president considerable discretionary authority. Under Section 212(f) of the Immigration and Nationality Act, the president can suspend "the entry of all aliens or of any class of aliens into the United States" if the president determines their entry would be "detrimental to the interests of the United States." The Supreme Court cited that provision in approving the third version of Trump's travel ban.[39] But it ruled that the administration's decision ending DACA had been made unconstitutionally, and it also rejected Trump's efforts to put a question about citizenship on the 2020 census. Miller wanted to eliminate the access of undocumented children to primary and secondary schools; Trump at times said he wanted to eliminate birthright citizenship. Judicial precedents stood squarely in the way of these measures.

After four years, the impact of Trump's immigration policies was far less than what his followers were expecting. When he left the White House in 2021, the unauthorized population was still 10.5 million, the same size it had been in 2017.[40] Since he failed to pass any immigration legislation and relied on executive orders, his policies could be, and were, mostly reversed by a new administration and new executive orders in 2021. But Trump had changed the politics of immigration. The issue had become even more intensely polarized as the nativist right consolidated its hold on the Republican Party, while Democrats became more supportive of immigration. The "crisis" at the border, which had been mostly a phony issue at the beginning of Trump's presidency, was also turning into a real one. Increasingly, people from Latin America and elsewhere were not surreptitiously stealing across the border in violation of U.S. law but presenting themselves at the border to immigration authorities and seeking asylum under U.S. law. Democrats had succeeded in staving off the harshest of Trump's initiatives, but the demand for asylum was soon going to become a political problem for them too.

Politically, trade had resemblances to immigration. Free trade and high levels of legal immigration had been the shared positions of both party establishments from Reagan to Obama. They were seemingly twin policies in line with an America integrated into a global society. Trump and his supporters also viewed immigration and trade as twin issues, though in the opposite way. From Trump's perspective, they were both examples of how foreigners took advantage of Americans and how the U.S. government failed to stand up for the American people. But the two issues were fundamentally different. Trump's policies on trade, specifically trade with China, had a more rational basis than did his policies on immigration.

Two motivations—one idealistic, the other commercial, but both short-sighted—had led the U.S. government to open Permanent Normal Trade Relations with China and support its admission to the World Trade Organization in 2001. The idealistic motivation reflected the high tide of confidence about capitalism and liberal democracy after the Soviet collapse. The prevailing view held that once capitalism developed in China, democracy would not be far behind. China would then become an upstanding international citizen, follow the historical pattern of largely peaceful relations among democracies, and avoid any aggressive use of military force. This happy vision assumed that the repressive dictatorship of the Chinese Communist Party could not survive capitalist-driven economic growth and the rise of a middle class and consumer society. While not unreasonable, the gamble failed and now looks naive. Instead of liberalizing and democratizing, China went in the opposite direction. After Xi Jinping came to power in 2012, the regime aggressively recentralized control, cracked down on dissent, suppressed democracy and human rights in Hong Kong, expanded militarily into the South China Sea, and threatened Taiwan.

The second, commercial logic for opening normal trade relations with China proved successful at least in the short term for American business. Outsourcing production and importing cheap goods kept profits up and consumer prices down. Those gains, however, came at the expense of American manufacturing workers, whose interests might have carried more political weight if not for the decline of the labor movement. American policymakers also failed to factor into their decisions the widely ramifying economic and social consequences of lost jobs in the old Rust Belt, the basis for Trump's claims of "American carnage."

The commercial logic of the opening to China was short-sighted for other reasons as well. China did not reciprocate by obeying the dictates of the free market. It adopted an aggressively mercantilist strategy to build up its domestic industry, subsidizing its leading firms and requiring U.S. and other Western companies to enter joint ventures and share technology with their Chinese partners. Americans underestimated the ability of the Chinese companies to master those technologies and build on them with innovations of their own. The United States also had such a loose and outdated system of export controls that it allowed the transfer of technologies of military as well as civilian value.

Moving up the "value chain," China undertook a massive, planned effort to dominate high-tech and seize global leadership in technologies of the future.[41]

By 2016, the original political and economic assumptions about the effects of free trade with China had been discredited, but the business interests remained and the U.S. and Chinese economies had become so interdependent that completely decoupling them would have had staggering costs to both sides. Still, if Hillary Clinton had won in 2016, she might have been forced to adopt a more confrontational posture toward China, though it would likely have differed from Trump's in both priorities and methods. Clinton might have given higher priority to human rights and national security, whereas Trump was overwhelmingly focused on trade and had no interest whatsoever in human rights. John Bolton, who served as Trump's national security adviser from 2018 to 2019, later wrote, "Trump once told me, I never want to hear from you about Taiwan, Hong Kong or the Uyghurs." Trump never raised those issues with the Chinese. When a Republican senator tried to persuade him to help the dissidents in Hong Kong because a successful crackdown there by China would encourage it to take over Taiwan, Trump reportedly said, "Taiwan is like two feet from China. We are eight thousand miles away. If they invade, there isn't a fucking thing we can do."[42]

Clinton also would have emphasized alliance-building in contrast to Trump's unilateralism. As secretary of state under Obama, she had been involved in negotiating a new trade pact, the Trans-Pacific Partnership, which involved twelve Pacific Rim countries, called for reductions in tariffs and other trade barriers, and created a new mechanism for resolution of disputes. Part of the U.S. interest in the agreement, which excluded China, lay in bringing the other participants closer to the United States. Under fire from Trump in 2016 for supporting yet another free trade deal, Clinton repudiated the pact but was still a committed multilateralist. In contrast, Trump made no effort to forge cooperation with allies to gain leverage against China; indeed, he imposed tariffs on them and repeatedly threatened to withdraw the United States from alliances. Just as Trump generally ruled by proclamation at home, he had a go-it-alone approach to foreign policy.

Trade, like immigration, was an issue on which Trump had staked his campaign. In a June 2016 speech on the issue written by Miller and an economist named Peter Navarro, Trump addressed American workers and said he would bring back factories and jobs "fast" by taking aggressive measures to renegotiate trade agreements.[43] Getting tough on China had long been part of the Trump creed, but once in the White House, he had other interests to satisfy. This was where the class divisions in Trumpism came out. The Wall Street financiers within his administration, Mnuchin and Cohn, and billionaire friends with substantial business interests in China, such as the casino owners Sheldon Adelson and Steve Wynn, were dead set against any decoupling of China and the United States.

During 2017 Trump first gave Mnuchin the chance to negotiate a trade deal with China, but when Mnuchin failed to make progress Trump turned to the hardliners, who believed that the United States had to threaten to impose serious costs on the Chinese to obtain concessions. Under U.S. trade laws, the president has unilateral authority to impose those costs once investigations formally establish the factual basis for punitive measures. In February 2018, the Commerce Department announced an investigation justifying tariffs on steel and aluminum imports from Canada, the European Union, Mexico, South Korea, and, only incidentally, China. The following month, a report by the U.S. trade representative, Robert Lighthizer, found that Chinese practices such as forced technology transfer and unfair subsidies were costing the U.S. economy at least $50 billion annually and called for tariffs on $50 billion of Chinese imports, tighter export controls, and limits on Chinese investment in the United States. China then announced U.S. goods it would tariff. Trump responded that he would expand the list of Chinese imports to tax, and in July the trade war started as tariffs began going into effect on both sides. Since the Chinese retaliatory tariffs heavily targeted agricultural products from Republican states, Trump provided subsidies to affected agribusinesses, eventually totaling $36 billion in 2018 and 2019. The conflict with China peaked in the second half of 2019 with new rounds of tariff increases until negotiators reached an agreement late in the year. Under the agreement, the United States cut back some of its tariffs, and China promised to make some structural reforms and to buy large amounts of American farm products. The American side called it a "phase one" deal, an implicit acknowledgment of its limitations, though there was no plan for a "phase two." The major effect was that a new tariff regime had been established without decoupling the two economies, and Trump was able to claim that he had kept his promise on trade.[44]

"Performance" in politics can be of two kinds. To perform may mean delivering results, but it may also mean performing in a theatrical sense to convey the sense that results have been delivered. Trump performed on trade primarily in this theatrical "performative" sense. The bottom-line impact of his policies on jobs and the U.S. economy was not impressive. He had renegotiated NAFTA with Canada and Mexico, but the result was an agreement with only marginal changes. He had also raised tariffs on steel and aluminum imports from European and other trading partners, but those countries had adopted retaliatory tariffs. During his tenure, the average tariff on Chinese imports rose from 3.1 percent to 21 percent, but China retaliated by raising average tariffs on U.S. imports from 8 percent to 21.8 percent. A study by economists of these policies—the U.S. tariffs, the retaliatory tariffs, and subsidies to U.S. agricultural interests—finds their aggregate economic impact was "at best a wash" and perhaps "mildly negative." Employment did not increase in the protected industries; trade data suggest that importers shifted from China to even lower-wage countries like Vietnam. But the policies did have a net positive impact on Republican voting in 2020. Voters in areas with industries presumed to benefit from tariffs became more likely to favor Republicans, while people in areas affected by retaliatory tariffs did not punish Republicans. The free-trade Republican Party of the Reagan era was dead because the new tariffs were politically a winner.[45]

Part of the reason that Trump's trade policies failed to reshore jobs was that he had not combined the tariffs with a domestic industrial policy to offset the subsidies to firms that China and other governments were providing, especially in leading-edge industries. The next Democratic administration would leave in place nearly all of Trump's tariffs; in that respect, both parties moved the United States away from free trade. The difference was that Democrats added to it an industrial policy that had more promise of rebuilding manufacturing and protecting supply chains for critical products.

To celebrate his trade deal, Trump brought together Chinese representatives and some of the billionaires with stakes in China for a signing ceremony in the White House. "We now have a big investment in each other and in getting along with each other," he declared.[46] The date was January 15, 2020. Trump did not mention reports of a new flu-like illness in the Chinese city of Wuhan. Just four days earlier, Chinese scientists had posted the genome for a novel coronavirus (later named "sars-CoV-2") believed to be responsible for the illness. The world was about to change, and so was Trump's tone about China. Something new was in the air.

The Pandemic Stress Test

In 2020, as Trump began his fourth year as president and the election season got under way, the United States was hit by a scourge of almost biblical proportions, a plague that over the next two years would take 850,000 American lives and millions of others around the world.[47] Like wars and natural disasters, pandemics often serve as stress tests that reveal and clarify a society's character under pressure. This was true of the COVID pandemic in the United States. It was an abnormal time but a revealing one about America under Trump.

The COVID pandemic entered a society divided on racial, regional, and class lines, and it magnified those divisions. It set off wild conspiracy stories. It led not just to a rise in anxiety, which was true everywhere, but to a spike in aggressive behavior that seems to have been peculiar to the United States: a sharp increase in homicide rates, fatal traffic accidents, unruly behavior on airplanes, and sales of firearms.[48] Anti-Asian violence increased. The pandemic also became embroiled in partisan conflict, a pattern that did not emerge in most other countries and had not been generally characteristic of public health crises in American history. The distinct misfortune of the United States in 2020 was to confront a new and deadly virus at a time when a plague was already consuming its political life. That double misfortune made the impact of COVID worse than it might have been. The United States proved unable to contain the virus partly because it proved unable to contain the forces of unreason within it.[49]

Politics always matters for health and disease. Political decisions shape social structures and the allocation of resources, which in turn influence who gets sick and dies. Ordinarily, the chains of causality from politics to disease are long and complex. Not so in 2020. The impact of politics on the COVID pandemic was immediate and direct.

If COVID had struck the United States in the decades before Donald Trump became president, it probably would not have mattered whether the administration in office was Republican or Democratic. The president would have turned to the nation's leading experts in public health and medicine, relied on their counsel, and rallied the nation to cooperate in stopping the spread of the disease. A rational president of either party would have seen the pandemic as an opportunity of the same kind that presidents have had in wartime to rise above partisanship and become the nation's defender. The U.S. response would not necessarily have been ideal. It would have had to overcome the long-standing inequities of the health-care system and underinvestment in public health. The novelty of the virus posed inherently difficult choices. Any administration would have made mistakes, especially at the beginning of the pandemic when critical scientific questions about the disease were clouded in uncertainty and public health leaders made a series of what turned out to be bad decisions. Even today there continues to be dispute about the efficacy of different measures.

But Trump did not simply make mistakes stemming from inadequate scientific knowledge or other factors beyond his control. He deliberately misled the public, downplaying the dangers of the virus. He failed to organize a coordinated national effort at the pandemic's inception. He promoted bogus cures. He modeled antisocial behavior. He turned the White House itself into a superspreader venue. As the journalist Lawrence Wright observed, "Trump, by his words and his example, became not a leader but a saboteur."[50] Above all, Trump so thoroughly politicized measures like the adoption of masks and social distancing that he made the denial of scientific evidence and the defiance of scientific judgment into emblems of Republican identity.

Everything about the COVID pandemic, including where it struck first, came to be seen through the prism of partisan politics. The virus arrived early in 2020 in New York, California, Washington, and other blue states and had its most severe impact on Democratic constituencies. A contagious disease originating abroad and spreading through contact was bound to develop first in metropolitan centers with international connections. The demographic profile of the victims was also predictable because those areas had large numbers of low-income racial minorities who suffered from high rates of diabetes, heart disease, and other conditions that made them especially vulnerable to serious illness from the coronavirus. In addition, critical resources such as testing capacity and personal protective equipment were scarce throughout the first months, and no drugs were available to treat the disease. Nonetheless, based on the early geography and incidence of COVID, the president and other Republicans framed it in partisan terms. At a rally in February, Trump declared that COVID was the Democrats' "new hoax." As late as September, he said, "If you take the blue states out . . . we're really at a very low level." By that time, the incidence had already risen in the red states, but the Republican narrative was set: COVID was an overblown, liberal, blue-state problem.[51]

In the spread of a dangerous new contagion, the early response is critical. Trump got elected on the promise to protect Americans from foreign threats, but the threats he imagined did not include microbes. In 2018

Trump shut down the Directorate for Global Health Security and Biodefense in the National Security Council. In 2019 several government agencies conducted a simulation that showed how unprepared the United States would be if tourists visiting China became infected with a dangerous new influenza (for example, N95 masks and other personal protective equipment would be in short supply and the United States lacked the capacity to produce them). But the findings were kept secret and the administration did nothing to remedy the deficiencies. In January 2020, despite internal warnings about the dangers of the new virus, Trump told Americans not to worry. He was still basking in the glow of the China trade deal on January 24, when he tweeted how greatly the United States appreciated China's "efforts and transparency" in containing the coronavirus and added, "It will all work out well."[52]

Meanwhile, travel from China continued uninterrupted. More than 40,000 travelers arrived on direct flights between the first official reports of the outbreak and the announcement of travel restrictions on January 31. Since the restrictions did not apply to U.S. citizens, however, thousands of travelers continued to arrive directly from China and were often subject to nothing more than cursory questioning before being sent on their way and told to quarantine voluntarily for two weeks. The virus arrived via travelers from other places as well. Countries that succeeded in using travel restrictions to delay the virus's arrival and spread, such as Australia and Taiwan, used the time to develop testing, contact tracing, and other measures.[53]

But the United States had no coordinated response of that kind. February proved to be a "lost" month because of Trump's playing down of the pandemic and failures at the Centers for Disease Control and Prevention (CDC) and the Food and Drug Administration (FDA). While several countries immediately deployed a diagnostic test for COVID using instructions published by the World Health Organization on January 13, the CDC was unable to produce a successful test until February 28 due to a contaminated lab and the agency's decision to pursue its own, complicated test design. The FDA failed to license private alternatives promptly. Although evidence began emerging in January that people with no overt signs of illness could transmit the virus, CDC officials were slow to acknowledge asymptomatic spread. Initially, they discouraged the use of masks by the public. The president kept insisting the public had no reason for concern.

Trump did know better. In a conversation with the journalist Bob Woodward on February 7 that was not published until the following September, the president said, "You just breathe the air and that's how it's passed.... It's also more deadly than ... even your strenuous flus ... this is deadly stuff." When confirmed cases began to climb, he continued to deny publicly there was anything to worry about and resisted mobilizing a national effort. On February 25 Trump said he thought the coronavirus was "a problem that's going to go away." He was enraged when on that same day the stock market tumbled after Nancy Messonnier, director of the National Center for Immunization and Respiratory Diseases at the CDC, issued a scientifically warranted warning that community spread of the virus was inevitable and Americans needed to consider drastic changes in their everyday lives. CDC officials were thereafter directed to clear all public statements about COVID with the White House. Two days later Trump suggested that "like a miracle" the virus might just disappear.[54]

In mid-March, however, Trump changed direction. On March 13 he formally proclaimed a national emergency concerning COVID and three days later he agreed to adopt federal guidelines for "15 Days to Slow the Spread," a package of stay-at-home measures that he renewed for another thirty days at the end of the month. During March, Congress passed on a bipartisan basis three measures in the response to the pandemic. The third and most substantial of these, the Coronavirus Aid, Relief, and Economic Security Act, provided $2.2 trillion in economic stimulus, the largest economic relief package in U.S. history and the most popular legislation that Trump signed. Federal aid went to individuals and businesses, health-care systems, and state and local governments; it enabled businesses and public agencies to keep people at work, paid for increases in unemployment benefits, suspended payments on student loans, protected tenants from eviction and homeowners from foreclosure, financed the development of vaccines, and intervened in myriad other ways to support people through the pandemic. Despite the nosedive in the economy, the federal stimulus prevented Americans from suffering a decline in personal income. The Treasury ordered Trump's name to be on the stimulus checks for $1,200 sent to individuals. This period in the early spring was the time when Trump enjoyed the highest public approval for dealing with the pandemic. As John Sides, Chris Tausanovitch, and Lynn Vavreck suggest in an analysis of public opinion during 2020, "Had Trump been able to maintain the short-lived bump in approval he received because of the pandemic, he likely could have won the election."[55]

But in April Trump became impatient with restrictions and lockdowns and, changing direction again, called for the economy to reopen. For a few days in mid-April, he insisted that he had total control over the pandemic response. "When somebody is the president of the United States," he said on April 13, "the authority is total and that's the way it's got to be." Three days later, however, he decided he did not want to be fully responsible and told the nation's governors, "You're going to call your own shots." But he didn't mean that either and instead began tweeting denunciations of Democratic governors who failed to "liberate" their states. He frequently undermined his own public health officials. When the CDC on April 3 finally recommended that Americans wear cloth masks in public places, Trump said, "I don't see it for myself." Shunting aside the experts, he took over the daily public briefings on the pandemic and used that platform to make boasts, give false reassurances, and pass along misinformation, most notoriously about an unproven and later discredited treatment (hydroxychloroquine) and the supposed value of injecting disinfectant to kill the coronavirus. In May, after officials including Anthony Fauci, director of the National Institute of Allergy and Infectious Diseases, recommended greatly increased testing, Trump said that testing was "overrated": "If we didn't do any testing, we would have very few cases." At a rally in Tulsa on June 20, Trump said that he had asked public health officials to "slow testing down." How the numbers looked was more important to him than saving people from the disease. The CDC's chief of staff later told the *New York Times*, "Every time that the science clashed with the messaging, messaging won."[56]

This was all characteristic Trump chaos, bluster, magical thinking, divisiveness, and duplicity. In this case, his actions had especially devastating consequences for human life and the sense of linked fate and bonds of solidarity that have held Americans together in other times of crisis. The nation's public health leaders did not cover themselves in glory—schools, in particular, could and should have been reopened earlier than they did in many states—but Trump sowed misinformation, discord, and distrust on an unmatched scale. According to a Cornell University study of the online "infodemic," the single most important driver of the "misinformation conversation" about COVID was the president himself.[57]

By any reasonable standard, the United States failed in meeting the pandemic stress test. Among the world's high-income countries, it had the highest COVID mortality rates. Changes in life expectancy offer a particularly telling measure of how great a loss Americans suffered and who suffered the most. During 2020, life expectancy in the United States fell by 1.87 years over what it had been two years earlier. That drop was more than eight times the average decline (0.22 years) in sixteen other high-income peer countries. None of those other countries came close to the loss of life in the United States. The shortening of U.S. life expectancy was greatest among Hispanics and Blacks. Life expectancy fell by 3.88 years among Hispanics, 3.25 years among non-Hispanic Blacks, and 1.36 years among non-Hispanic whites. Even the decline in white life expectancy was greater than the average decline in any other peer country. The gap between life expectancy in the United States and its peers had already been growing over the preceding decade, but in 2020 it reached a new high, especially for U.S. men, who could expect to die more than five years earlier than the average for men in peer countries.[58]

Among all groups, the poor were hit the hardest for four reasons: pre-existing health conditions that increased their vulnerability; less access to health care; overcrowded housing; and higher occupational exposure.[59] A toxic combination of racism, ageism, and indifference toward the poor lay behind the right-wing view that the pandemic was overblown, or that the disease should be allowed to spread until the country reached "herd immunity." The "herd" would be culled not at random but primarily at the expense of people with the least economic or political power.

From the beginning of the pandemic, Americans were divided along class and racial lines in their exposure to the virus. The government defined a class of "essential workers" who to keep society running had to stay on the job in person in such fields as food, transportation, energy, and health care. Except for health-care professionals, the division roughly followed class lines. People who could work online from home and had food and other goods delivered to their door were generally safe, healthy, and even prosperous, while those who had to do their work in person were exposed to higher odds of infection and unemployment. The disparities in who got sick and died, and who survived but became afflicted with long COVID, partly followed from that objective difference in life situation.

Objective data about risks, however, do not translate directly into perceptions and choices. Americans could disagree about the dangers of the virus because of differences in their personal experience, what happened to people they knew, and what they heard from sources they trusted. The coronavirus did not kill or make seriously ill most people under age 65 who caught it, whereas shutting down their workplace or business immediately threatened their economic livelihood. Decisions about when to impose lockdowns or more targeted restrictions and when to lift them were genuinely difficult. But, as the cross-national differences in mortality rates indicated, other high-income countries proved more successful at protecting life during the pandemic. The people of those countries also generally rated their government's response much more favorably. In a Pew Research international survey in the summer of 2020, majorities in nearly all fourteen high-income countries said they thought their government had done "a good job dealing with the coronavirus outbreak." The median approval rate was 73 percent, but the United States, at 47 percent, was one of two countries with exceptionally low public approval. The other, at 46 percent, was the United Kingdom, where Prime Minister Boris Johnson and the Conservative leadership cavalierly ignored restrictions they asked others to follow, creating a scandal that ultimately led to Johnson's downfall.[60]

A cultural interpretation of America's polarized response to the pandemic may seem intuitively appealing. In that view, Americans became divided about public health measures such as masks and social distancing because conservatives and liberals generally differ in the value they place on individual liberty versus social obligation. Some evidence lends support to that interpretation. For example, in another Pew Research international survey, this one in spring 2021, American conservatives stood out from conservatives in other high-income countries; 52 percent of the U.S. conservatives, compared to significantly lower shares elsewhere, said there should have been fewer restrictions during the pandemic.[61] But what such data cannot tell us is whether that opposition to restrictions stemmed from a committed libertarianism or the influence of Republican leaders. In March, after Trump declared a national emergency, polls showed a sharp rise in concern about the virus among Republicans, but when Trump changed his tone and began opposing restrictions on business, polls showed that concern among Republicans fell sharply. Americans were not quite the dedicated libertarians during the pandemic that some people believe them to be. After Trump turned against restrictions in April, his public approval on the pandemic fell and stayed low. Between January and October 2020, Republican governors saw their net approval ratings fall by an average of nine points, while approval for Democratic governors rose by fifteen points. Surveys during 2020 continued to show strong support for precautionary restrictions despite Trump.[62] If a more traditional Republican had been president, Republican views of pandemic restrictions might have been similar to those of conservatives in other high-income countries—not wholly enthusiastic, but more accepting of the need for restrictions.

As traumatic as the pandemic was, it became normalized in the United States in a short time, perhaps partly because of who was doing most of the dying. The vehemence of right-wing denial did not decrease late in the year even with the rising number of cases and deaths in red states. By the final weeks of 2020, the number of Americans dying of the virus every day was about what the country had lost on September 11, 2001. But the shock had worn off, and it had become unimaginable for the United States to make the necessary changes in social behavior to control the pandemic. The only solution became a technological fix—a vaccine.

Vaccines have historically taken years to develop and test, but recent discoveries had made it possible to design a vaccine for sars-CoV-2 on an unprecedented schedule. Within two days of the genome's publication in January 2020, scientists who had been working on related medical problems had worked out the design for a COVID vaccine. Six weeks later, vials were being shipped for clinical trials on animals and on March 16, the first trials on human beings started. With financing provided under the legislation Congress adopted in March, the Trump administration's Operation Warp Speed guaranteed government purchases. The COVID vaccine turned out to be highly effective against serious illness with relatively rare serious side effects, one of the greatest achievements of modern medicine. It might have been a time for renewed faith in science, but in Trump's America it wasn't.

Tragically, many of Trump's own followers refused to be vaccinated because of another virus, the virus of distrust on the right that Trump had helped propagate. Counties that voted more for Trump in 2020 had sharply lower vaccination rates in 2021. According to a study of registered Republicans and Democrats in Ohio and Florida, there were only small differences in their death rates in the first year of the pandemic, but after vaccine eligibility opened excess death rates were 43 percent higher among Republicans than among Democrats, and the deaths were concentrated in counties with low vaccination rates.[63] Trump would later be booed at his own political rallies when he talked positively about the vaccine, and he stopped mentioning it. The harm he did to the body politic overshadowed his one good deed in dealing with the pandemic.

Trump and the American Contradiction

After Trump was elected in 2016, his critics thought something far outside the normal range threatened the country. Trump's treatment of women, vilification of immigrants, encouragement of violence, and abusive belittling of other leaders, including fellow Republicans, violated the elementary norms of public civility. His constant lying and demand that others repeat what one of his aides, Kellyanne Conway, famously called "alternative facts" threatened elementary norms of respect for the truth. (Conway was defending Trump's insistence that his inauguration crowd was the largest ever, despite photographic evidence to the contrary.) A genuinely enormous Women's March the day after his inauguration and the protests against his Muslim travel ban shortly thereafter registered a widespread fear that Trump's election threatened the progress achieved in the struggles for equality. Organizing into groups that called themselves the "Resistance," Trump's opponents did not just oppose his policies. They resisted accepting Trump's behavior and ideas as a normal part of American politics and American life. They wanted him to be treated not with the respect due a president but with the contempt due someone who routinely violated America's public values.

Nothing that happened over the next four years changed the minds of many people about Trump on either side of the American divide. Amid the disasters of the pandemic in 2020, his opponents were surprised to find that most of his supporters still lined up behind him. When Trump tried to overturn the 2020 election and incited an assault on the Capitol to interfere with the peaceful transfer of power, his opponents were surprised again that he still held on to his followers. By that point the shock was less about Trump than about the willingness of his party to go along with flagrant violations of the nation's laws and traditions.

Democrats desperately wanted to believe that Trump's election had been an aberration from American history, but deep and stubborn forces were at work in sustaining his hold on his party in the face of all his scandals and failures. Trump would be an aberration if the United States from its founding had truly been rooted solely in ideals of freedom and equality—but that wasn't so. Trump would also be an aberration if the civil rights revolution had finally put America's high ideals on an irrevocable foundation—but American history has had too many reversals to treat equal rights as irrevocable. Along with its seasons of progress, the United States has had its seasons of retrogression, seasons that have lasted for decades. Trump was less of an anomaly if we understand American history in a different way, as having developed unsteadily from the country's beginnings, careening back and forth, on the basis of contradictory forces that by the early twenty-first century had entered a new phase.

As Obama symbolized the new people that Americans were becoming, so Trump came to represent the old nation and the old normal that Americans angry about unfolding social changes wanted to restore. The idea of making America great "again" appealed to the sense shared by Trump's supporters that things had been great in a lost America. That longing for a lost America is as resonant among twenty-first-century conservatives as the myth of the "lost cause" was to the South after the Civil War. Now, however, what has been lost is not just a clear racial hierarchy but an entire worldview that involves gender, religion, immigration, and other relations of power and worth. Once again, those who are heirs to a culture of domination have found that culture being denied, disrespected, and taken from them. Trump stood for the return of that lost America.

Between the 2016 and 2020 elections, no wave of public support developed for Trump, not for his policies, not for his values, not for him personally. He ended his term just as he had begun it, with a negative overall rating in public opinion. But "waves" in public opinion may not be the right place to look for the causes of contemporary gains by the far right. In a study of European politics, the political scientist Larry Bartels finds no evidence in public opinion data of a wave of support for right-wing populism from 2002 to 2019. The more apt metaphor, he suggests, is that public opinion long held a *reservoir* of right-wing sentiment that political entrepreneurs have drawn on with varying success. The changing strategies of elites have been crucial to the emergence of authoritarianism. As Bartels puts it, "Democracy erodes from the top."[64]

In the United States, the critical shift began at the elite level in the conservative media and among the Republican leadership and most engaged partisans in the 1990s, when a more fully reactionary radical right challenged the old RINO leadership that conservatives despised. That shift toward a more highly charged politics, with its populist appeals, did help win over working-class whites defecting from the Democrats, but it didn't amount to a national majority. The culmination of that process, the takeover of the national Republican Party by Trump and his MAGA movement, was something new. The two major parties in the United States have usually been separate from social movements. Movements typically try to influence one or both of the parties without any hope of taking over either. Trump, however, merged movement and party, a singular turn in American politics also because of its cult-like character. The political fate of Republican politicians came to depend on their willingness to pledge fealty to Trump. Other party leaders faced a simple choice: kneel or quit. Most knelt, a few quit or were pushed out. What is puzzling about Trump's personal dominance is that public attitudes toward him as a person were consistently negative. In 2018 and 2019, only 34 percent of Americans saw him as "honest and trustworthy," 35 percent said he was someone they admired, and 38 percent said he shared their values.[65] Yet Republicans chose to identify their movement-party entirely with him. In the 2020 election, they broke with tradition when the party decided not to adopt a platform at its convention. A platform would only have become an annoyance. The party would stand for whatever Trump said it stood for.

Going into the 2020 election, Democrats had grounds for optimism. In the midterms two years earlier, they had ridden a nine-point advantage in the voting to win a smashing victory in races for the House. While losing two seats in the Senate, they had also netted seven governorships, including those in the battleground states of Michigan and Wisconsin that Clinton had lost. In 2020, the challenge of beating Trump was a powerful stimulus to Democratic unity. Progressive activists mobilized for the primaries, but without producing acrimonious divisions as in 2016. Biden, as Obama's former vice president, started out as the favorite, stumbled at first but then won decisively in South Carolina, reached out to his rivals (including Sanders in particular), and successfully united the party. While the Democrats had elements of a movement, they were more of a coalition, more heterogeneous in both their social and ideological makeup than the Republicans were. In the 2020 vote, for example, Republicans were 85 percent non-Hispanic white and only 2 percent Black, whereas the Democrats were spread across racial groups in closer relation to their distribution in the population. Three-quarters of Republicans self-identified as conservative, but nearly half of Democrats did not self-identify as liberal.[66] Biden had to bring along the whole coalition, including its moderate elements, without alienating the movement on the party's left, and he proved adroit at doing both. He represented the hope that Trump would only be an aberration and that America could return to a more normal politics, recover from the pandemic, and address problems like inequality and climate change that Republicans denied or neglected. In some ways, he was a figure out of the past, having been elected to the Senate in 1972 at the age of 29; indeed, he seemed so attached to the Senate's old bipartisanship that some critics thought he was caught up in a hopeless centrist nostalgia. But Biden's self-presentation was also a shrewd means of reassuring Republican defectors that it was safe to vote for him.

According to the early forecasting models based on presidential popularity and economic conditions, 2020 was going to be another close election. In fact, it turned out to be a close but not exact replica of 2016. Ninety-five percent of those who had voted for Trump in 2016 voted for him again in 2020, and 95 percent of those who had voted for Clinton voted for Biden. At the county level, a prediction of the 2020 voting for president solely based on how the county had voted in 2016 would have been off only by an average of 1.9 percent. The 2020 state-level votes were also closely correlated with 2016—but not identical. Five states that narrowly went for Trump in 2020 narrowly went for Biden, enough to give him a victory.[67]

The 2020 voting differed from 2016 in several respects. Voter turnout rose 7 percentage points over 2016 to an unprecedented 66 percent of U.S. adult citizens.[68] A tide of new voters arrived for both parties, with the younger ones decisively favoring Biden. Conducted in the midst of a pandemic, the 2020 election was necessarily unprecedented in other ways, including the widespread adoption of voting by mail. Without that change in voting, the extraordinarily high turnout would have been unlikely. The pandemic itself and how Trump responded to it may have been the crucial factor in Biden's victory. Trump's primary argument for re-election had been the state of the economy, but the recession accompanying the pandemic undermined that case, and the pandemic changed how people evaluated the candidates. By the fall, Trump's rating on COVID had fallen from the brief peak it had reached the previous March. In an October poll, 52 percent of respondents said they trusted Biden more to handle the pandemic, whereas only 40 percent trusted Trump more.[69] Support for Biden, however, did not carry over to the congressional elections. Democrats lost thirteen seats in the House (though they retained control) and only barely achieved a tie in the Senate when they won two seats in run-off elections in Georgia.

In both the popular vote for the presidency and the Electoral College, the final results in 2020 were not close. Biden won the popular vote by seven million and the Electoral College by a vote of 306 to 232. His popular-vote margin of 4.45 percent was larger than that of any Republican since George H. W. Bush thirty-two years earlier. By another measure, however, the 2020 election was tight, even tighter than 2016, when 78,000 more votes for Clinton in Wisconsin, Michigan, and Pennsylvania could have swung the election to her. In 2020 just 43,000 additional votes for Trump in Wisconsin, Arizona, and Georgia would have created a tie in the Electoral College. In that case, under the nation's antique Constitution, the election would have been decided in the House with each state's delegation casting a single vote, and Trump would have won. In other words, four years after winning the presidency while losing the popular vote by nearly three million, Trump almost won re-election while losing the popular vote by seven million.

The Electoral College, the source of such distorted outcomes, also creates opportunities to overturn a presidential election that other defeated incumbents had not sought to exploit. During the two months between Election Day and the January 6, 2021, counting of electoral votes in the Senate, Trump tried a variety of schemes to stay in power: failed legal challenges to the vote counting, efforts to get state legislatures to override the popular vote, fake electors, pressure on Vice President Mike Pence to use the fake electors to gavel him into a second term, direct pleas to Republicans in the states. "Fellas, I need 11,000 votes," Trump told Georgia's secretary of state in a recorded call on January 2. In Arizona he needed fewer than 11,000, in Wisconsin a few more than 20,000. If enough uncertainty could be created about the results, Republican-controlled state legislatures might step in or Congress might not certify the Electoral College result. The United States came close to an election that was genuinely stolen. When Trump's followers stormed the Capitol on January 6 claiming the election had been stolen, they were just projecting on to Biden what Trump had tried to do.

But Trump was not done. His defeat had not been resounding enough to end his domination of conservatism or the Republican Party. Immediately after the storming of the Capitol, a majority of Republicans in the House, 139 of them, voted against certifying the 2020 election. Weeks later, after Trump was impeached for trying to overturn the election, a conviction in the Senate would have made it impossible for him ever to become president again, but forty-three of fifty Senate Republicans voted to acquit him. In the coming years, Trump would be back, back for what he promised would be his own and his followers' full revenge. "I am your warrior. I am your justice," he told an audience of conservatives in 2023. "And for those who have been wronged and betrayed, I am your retribution."

It was what he had been telling his supporters all along. His own and their grievances were joined. In fact, Trump had already achieved something for the right that would endure past 2020 and give him a better shot at a second term: a supermajority on the Supreme Court. Even with Trump out of office, the power of the Court and its centrality in American life meant that the foundation for a new, old regime in the United States was in place.

CHAPTER TEN

A New, Old America

Counterrevolution through the Courts

The most important thing for the public to understand is that we're not a political branch of government. They do not elect us. If they do not like what we are doing, it's more or less just too bad.

—CHIEF JUSTICE JOHN ROBERTS, 2009[1]

Tradition is the living faith of the dead, traditionalism is the dead faith of the living.

—JAROSLAV PELIKAN, 1984[2]

REPUBLICANS HAVE DOMINATED the Supreme Court for half a century. A majority of the sitting justices have been Republican appointees ever since January 1972, except for one interval of just over a year after Justice Antonin Scalia died in 2016, when the Court's eight remaining justices were tied. Since 1953, every chief justice has been a Republican, and Republican presidents have nominated twenty of the twenty-nine people who have joined the Court.

For a long time, though, Democrats were not unduly concerned. Republican jurists of the mid-twentieth century shared many of the beliefs of their Democratic counterparts, and some Republican Supreme Court appointees, beginning with Earl Warren, turned out to be more liberal than expected at the time they were nominated. The Court's decisions in its liberal heyday gained greater legitimacy from the support of justices chosen by presidents of both parties. That bipartisan imprimatur also tended to confirm the idea that the justices made their rulings independent of politics based on the law alone.

Decade by decade, however, that view of the Court became less tenable. Conservatives in the legal world became better organized, vetted judicial nominees more carefully, and swore "no more Souters" after David Souter, nominated by George H. W. Bush in 1990, turned out to be more liberal than Republicans anticipated. In 2005, when George W. Bush nominated his White House counsel Harriet Miers to replace Sandra Day O'Connor, conservatives rose up in opposition, forcing Miers to withdraw and leading Bush to choose a more ideologically reliable conservative, Samuel A. Alito. With a few exceptions, the more numerous Republican-appointed justices of the late twentieth century retired only when Republicans held the presidency to ensure perpetuation of a like-minded majority. When Scalia's death in February 2016 threatened to cost the party a seat, Republican Senate Majority Leader Mitch McConnell ignored previous norms and blocked Obama's nominee Merrick Garland on the flimsy grounds that it was an election year. That "constitutional hardball" paid off in 2017 when Trump was able to fill Scalia's seat with Neil Gorsuch. But in September 2020, when Ruth Bader Ginsburg died, McConnell saw no problem in expeditiously confirming Trump's nominee Amy Coney Barrett to fill Ginsburg's seat just days before the election. During his 2016 campaign, Trump had placated conservatives by pledging to limit his Supreme Court nominations to a list of stringently vetted conservative jurists. Altogether, thanks to McConnell, Trump made three appointments to the Court—Brett Kavanaugh was the third, replacing Anthony Kennedy. The result was a 6–3 supermajority of conservative Republicans, far to the right of public opinion and further to the right than any Supreme Court majority since the early 1930s.

For the right, the aim has been to carry out the other half of the counterrevolution that late twentieth-century Reaganite conservatism did not deliver, a lasting consolidation of Republican power and decisive reversal of liberal and progressive change going back at least to the New Deal and in some respects even earlier. The political basis for bringing about that reversal has emerged through the rise of Trumpism and the remaking of the Republican Party in Congress and the states. The judicial basis has come from the conservative ascendancy in the Supreme Court.

The relationship of these two developments in politics and the judiciary, however, was not foreordained. The institutional independence of the Court enabled it either to limit Trumpism or to protect and advance it. If the political and legal sides of right-wing ascendancy became fully aligned, they could produce a shift in the constitutional order, perhaps even a kind of regime change in which liberalism and progressivism are shut down for the long term. But even if that proved true, it would still not reproduce the old America of the 1950s or 1920s. It would result in a new version of America's "old regime" because changes in American society and culture are harder to reverse than policies and legal precedents and because it would be difficult to achieve a full reversal while preserving democracy and rule of law.

The centrality of law and the courts in American society is as old as the republic. On the bicentennial of the Constitution in 1987, Thurgood Marshall, the first Black justice, noted the law's role in determining the condition of Black Americans: "They were enslaved by law, emancipated by law, disenfranchised and segregated by law, and, finally, they have begun to win equality by law."[3] During the mid-twentieth century, the Supreme Court played a central role in facilitating, authorizing, and defining a far-ranging rights revolution that "finally," as Marshall said, "began to win equality by law" for Black people—and for many others. That equality-promoting role, however, has not been typical of the judiciary in American history.

Supreme Court justices have more often been defenders of property and privilege. Early twentieth-century progressives opposed judicial power and were skeptical about a fixation on rights because conservative judges invoked property rights, due process, and freedom of contract as grounds for invalidating protective labor legislation and entrenching laissez-faire economics. This was the *Lochner* era, the era when the Court struck down a ten-hour limit on the working day for bakers on the grounds that it interfered with freedom of contract. Instead of pursuing litigation in unfriendly courts, progressives sought to extend democracy and the power of the people's elected representatives to pass measures regulating corporations, defending the rights of workers, and curbing the power of concentrated wealth. It was only later, particularly during the Warren Court and the struggles over racial equality, that liberals and progressives became converts to judicial activism.

Liberals and progressives embraced litigation as a strategy for social change when the courts became a more receptive venue than the elected branches for claims of constitutional rights to racial and gender equality and personal autonomy. As I described in chapter 2, when the Supreme Court abandoned its role in severely restricting economic regulation in the late 1930s, it supplied a new, democratic rationale for judicial review: The courts were needed to ensure the rights of "discrete and insular minorities" when the ordinary political process failed to protect them. The justices on the High Court also later distilled rights to privacy and personal liberty from principles in the Bill of Rights that served as a basis for limiting the government's reach into Americans' private lives. Turning to the courts made possible historic advances. But by contributing to the re-enlarged power of the judiciary, liberals and progressives exposed themselves to the risk that the Supreme Court might revert to its older pattern and become once again the defender of property and privilege, which is, in fact, what happened.

Rights revolutions, it turns out, can be of more than one kind. Liberals and progressives who put their hopes in litigation tended to assume that the pursuit of rights would necessarily advance equality. That understanding ignored the possibility that conservative judges could invoke rights to create a more unequal democracy, as the Supreme Court did in 1976 when in the first of a series of rulings it invoked free-speech rights to strike down limits on the use of money in elections. The liberal reliance on the courts also ignored the possibility that even as conservatives called for judicial restraint, they could become practitioners of their own variety of judicial activism. Exalting the judiciary failed to anticipate how the courts might become the vehicle for conservative traditionalism and a conservative rights revolution aimed at undoing the egalitarianism of the liberal rights revolution.

The law is powerful, but it is not all-powerful. Even a Supreme Court that asserts claims of judicial supremacy is not all-powerful. Its ability to bring about social and cultural change is not automatic. It is an open question whether a new conservative legal regime can do as much for conservative purposes as a liberal legal regime did for liberal purposes. The liberal rights revolution responded to and reinforced trends in American culture. The conservative analog is running against contemporary cultural trends. In the early twenty-first century, the dominant thrust of the law has been to subtract rights associated with liberal causes and constituencies (workers' rights, consumer rights, voting rights, reproductive rights) and to expand rights associated with conservative causes and constituencies (corporate rights, gun rights, religious liberty rights, property rights). At crucial moments, the Court has also favored the interests of the Republican Party and helped consolidate its power.

Legally and culturally, however, the liberal rights revolution wasn't entirely over once the conservative movement in the law was well under way. The contemporary progressive project had one chapter left to be written into law. That one chapter was so morally significant and politically salient that many people were unaware how much of the earlier egalitarian change in American law the Supreme Court was simultaneously undoing.

Gay Rights and the Waning of the Liberal Rights Revolution

The growing acceptance of gay men and lesbians between the 1980s and early 2000s was one of the most dramatic changes in American culture ever tracked in public opinion polls. It came about along with a growing openness about gay identity. A surge of gay activism in response to the AIDS epidemic in the late 1980s and early 1990s led the news media to cover gay people more sympathetically and encouraged national Democratic political leaders to support antidiscrimination protections for gay people. Together, gay activism and the changes in the media and Democratic politics bolstered the confidence of gay people to come out of the closet, and their willingness to come out forced others, including friends, co-workers, and members of their own family, to rethink their prejudices.[4]

Public opinion data record the changes. The share of Americans who said they had no contact with gay people fell sharply. In national polls by the *Los Angeles Times*, the share of people who said they knew of no friend, family member, or co-worker who was gay dropped from 54 percent in 1985 to 27 percent in 2005, and the share who said they were "sometimes" or "always" uncomfortable being around gay people dropped from 38 percent in 1983 to 20 percent in 2004. Americans who said they knew someone who was gay were also more supportive of gay-friendly public policies. Of course, gay people were more likely to come out to others with sympathetic views, but careful studies showed that interpersonal contact had an independent effect on heterosexuals' support.[5]

Growing interpersonal openness about gay identity had its parallel in the entertainment media. At the beginning of the 1980s, gay characters rarely appeared in any of the regular shows on the CBS, NBC, and ABC television networks, but by the early 2000s a dozen or more gay characters were on network shows. The 1990s were the breakthrough decade. Straight A-list actors like Tom Hanks took gay roles in major Hollywood movies; TV celebrities like Ellen DeGeneres came out of the closet. Whatever the relative importance of personal and parasocial relationships in changing public opinion, the trend was unambiguous. In a national 1983 *Los Angeles Times* poll, only 30 percent had described themselves as "sympathetic" to the gay community; by 2004, that proportion had doubled to 60 percent.[6]

From the late 1980s to the turn of the century, the conception of alternative sexual and gender identities also expanded. The gay rights movement as late as the 1980s encompassed lesbians and gay men. References to bisexuals and the "LGB" population rose in the early 1990s; the "T" for transgender appeared in the mid- to late 1990s as a grassroots movement of transgender people developed. It was not until after the turn of the century, however, that the term "LGBT" became widely used—and then later became further extended with "Q" for queer or questioning, "I" for intersex, and "A" for asexual and aromantic, often then reduced to "LGBTQ+" (the term I will use for the more recent period) to signify an indefinite, fluid set of additional identities.[7]

In the simpler, repressed world of the 1950s, Americans had defined the sexual terrain according to two binary distinctions: male versus female and heterosexual versus homosexual. As I discussed in chapter 3, the 1960s initiated a movement toward sexual pluralism, which at first meant a wider range of erotic expression in heterosexual relations and then wider acceptance of homosexuality. Gender pluralism, social acceptance of a range of gender identity and expression, was slower to emerge (and still faces intense resistance). But as the twentieth century ended, Americans began to confront greater gender diversity and gender fluidity just as they confronted greater racial diversity, racial intermixing, and racial ambiguity. Both sets of developments destabilized settled understandings. Social conservatives, older generations, and people in rural areas condemned and resisted the new pluralism in sexuality and gender identity, in parallel to their reaction against racial change. Liberals, younger people, and urbanites were more accepting of diversity and change in both dimensions.

The increased tolerance of nonconforming sexuality evidenced in late twentieth-century public opinion trends did not mean that by the early

2000s LGBTQ+ people were free of social disapproval, discrimination, and violence. The share of Americans saying that "sexual relations between two adults of the same sex" were "always wrong" had first risen during the AIDS epidemic to a peak of about 75 percent in the mid-1980s and then fallen sharply—yet about half of Americans continued to hold that view in the early 2000s.[8] In most states, LGBTQ+ people could still legally be denied housing, jobs, and other opportunities and faced considerable risk of harassment and assault.

Throughout these years, the politics of gay rights followed a characteristic pattern: short-term backlash to proposals for equal rights amid long-term trends toward rising support. From 1977 to 1993, some cities adopted gay rights protections against discrimination, but local referenda reversing those ordinances had a 79 percent success rate. Bill Clinton was the first national Democratic presidential candidate to support gay rights protections, but soon after taking office, he suffered a stinging reverse when he proposed that gay people be able to serve openly in the military. Instead, Congress wrote their exclusion into law; the result was a "don't ask, don't tell" policy, under which the military annually discharged about 1,000 gay service members. In 1994, liberals in Congress first introduced the Employment Non-Discrimination Act to ban discrimination in employment based on sexual orientation. Clinton supported the legislation, but it made no headway.[9]

The political history of same-sex marriage in the mid-1990s followed the same pattern. After Hawaii's Supreme Court raised the possibility in 1993 that same-sex couples might have the right to marry under the state's Equal Rights Amendment, the state's voters approved a constitutional amendment enabling the legislature to prohibit same-sex marriage, which it proceeded to do. Other states also passed prohibitions of same-sex marriage, and in 1996 congressional Republicans sought to exploit the issue to split Democrats. By overwhelming margins, both houses of Congress passed the Defense of Marriage Act (DOMA), which defined marriage for federal purposes as exclusively between a man and a woman and provided that no state would have to honor same-sex marriages performed in another state. Facing a battle for re-election, Clinton signed the bill.[10]

The chances of progress for gay rights protections through litigation in the federal courts also seemed dim after the Supreme Court upheld a Georgia law criminalizing homosexual sodomy in a 1986 case, *Bowers v. Hardwick*. Georgia had the discretion to outlaw sodomy, the Court declared, as a reflection of "majority sentiments about the morality of homosexuality."

To bar the state from making sodomy a crime would require showing that sodomy was a freedom "deeply rooted in this Nation's history and tradition," which the Court said was impossible because it had long been a crime.[11]

Seventeen years later, in 2003, when the criminalization of homosexual intimacy came back to the Court in *Lawrence v. Texas*, it not only reversed *Bowers* but explicitly repudiated the thinking of the earlier majority. "Liberty," Anthony Kennedy's opinion began, "protects the person from unwarranted government intrusions into a dwelling or other private places" and "presumes an autonomy of self that includes freedom of thought, belief, expression, and certain intimate conduct." The *Bowers* decision, Kennedy wrote, had framed the question wrongly by failing to understand that the issue was freedom from the state in personal relationships, not just sex. Texas's Sexual Conduct Law also violated the Constitution's Equal Protection Clause: "When homosexual conduct is made criminal by the law of the state, that declaration in and of itself is an invitation to subject homosexual persons to discrimination both in the public and the private spheres." Instead of limiting freedom to the way it was understood in the past, Kennedy presented freedom as historically evolving: "Times can blind us to certain truths and later generations can see that laws once thought necessary and proper in fact serve only to oppress. As the Constitution endures, persons in every generation can invoke its principles in their own search for greater freedom."[12]

What had changed from *Bowers* to *Lawrence*? Between 1986 and 2003, public attitudes toward LGBTQ+ people had become more sympathetic, and states had repealed laws criminalizing sodomy. By 2003, the number of states with such laws on the books was down to thirteen, only four of which explicitly referred to homosexual sodomy, and in none of those states was the law being actively enforced. On this specific issue, the Court was consolidating a change in public sentiment, not leading it. At the time of *Bowers* in 1986, the median age of the justices had been the highest in the nation's history; five had been nearing 80. One of them, Lewis Powell, was on the verge of retirement and wavered on *Bowers*, though in the end he cast the deciding vote upholding the Georgia sodomy law. During the deliberations, he said to a law clerk, "I don't believe I've ever met a homosexual." The law clerk, who was gay himself, as were four other recent law clerks of Justice Powell, replied, "Certainly you have, but you just don't know that they are." Powell's replacement in 1988 was Kennedy, who had been nominated by Reagan and confirmed by the Senate despite the worries of some conservatives about reports that as a judge in California he had employed law clerks who in those days would have been referred to as "known homosexuals." By 2003, Sandra Day O'Connor, who had voted with the majority in *Bowers*, had changed her views, influenced partly by gay and lesbian law clerks who were out of the closet. The Court was not just reflecting public opinion; it was a microcosm of social change.[13]

After *Lawrence*, national discussion about gay rights turned to same-sex marriage, though the gay movement itself was sharply divided about the issue, as it had been since the late 1980s. Some radicals, echoing ideas from the 1960s, had long viewed marriage as an inherently repressive institution and seen it as inconsistent with gay liberation. A same-sex wedding at a gay rights march in 1987 had drawn protests from other marchers. During the 1990s and early 2000s, the leading gay rights organizations saw same-sex marriage as unattainable and emphasized other priorities. Polls showed support for equal rights for gay people in employment running above 80 percent, compared to only 33 percent or less for same-sex marriage. Many gay rights leaders believed they had to "get to A and B before we can get to E." By "A and B" they meant more achievable objectives such as antidiscrimination laws and more funding for AIDS research.[14]

The initially small cadre of activists and writers who wanted to prioritize same-sex marriage held the counterintuitive view that marriage had both a public appeal and a legal foundation that others in the movement had not appreciated. The marriage advocates were not interested only in the material benefits, like tax advantages, that civil unions could provide. Fighting for marriage conveyed a message about the desire of gay people for love, commitment, and stability that suggested they shared the same values as everyone else and were interested less in rebelling against mainstream institutions than in joining them. Framing the issue as the "freedom to marry" also connected their cause to the principle that Chief Justice Warren enunciated in *Loving v. Virginia*, the Court's 1967 decision about interracial marriage: "The freedom to marry has long been recognized as one of the vital personal rights essential to the orderly pursuit of happiness by free men."[15] The "orderly pursuit of happiness" was surely a principle deeply rooted in America's "history and tradition."

In November 2003, just six months after the Supreme Court's decision in *Lawrence*, the Massachusetts Supreme Judicial Court ruled that under the state's constitution the freedom to marry could not be denied to same-sex couples. The state began issuing marriage licenses to them in May 2004. That put same-sex marriage on the national agenda, where conservatives were only too glad to have it. Ballot initiatives amending state constitutions to prohibit same-sex marriage became a mobilizing cause for Republicans in the 2004 election, and in thirty-one state ballot fights from 2004 to 2011 the opponents of marriage equality won all thirty-one times.[16]

Nonetheless, the issue became an example of the overall pattern of short-term backlash and long-term growth in support for equal rights. After 2004, support for same-sex marriage in public opinion polls increased until by 2011 the supporters outnumbered the opponents. In 2012, facing his own difficult re-election race, Obama made the opposite choice from the one that Clinton had made in 1996. Obama endorsed same-sex marriage, believing it would help his candidacy, especially with young voters. The next year, the Supreme Court struck down DOMA as unconstitutional, and proponents of same-sex marriage began winning votes on ballot initiatives. The movement culminated in 2015, when the Supreme Court declared by a 5–4 vote in *Obergefell v. Hodges* that the freedom to marry of same-sex couples was a constitutional right. By that time, according to Gallup, 60 percent of the public favored same-sex marriage. As in *Lawrence*, the Court in *Obergefell* was responding to a rising tide of public sentiment, though the Court ruled the way it did only because Kennedy defected once again from the conservative wing.[17]

Strikingly, though, neither Congress nor the Supreme Court had yet acted on the reform that had long enjoyed more support in public opinion than same-sex marriage did—making discrimination against LGBTQ+ people illegal under the civil rights laws. After the failure of Congress to pass the Employment Non-Discrimination Act in 1994, its supporters had continued unsuccessfully to press for its adoption. In 2007, they expanded the bill to ban discrimination based on gender identity as well as sexual orientation, but when that change created more opposition, the chief sponsor, Representative Barney Frank, divided the legislation in two. The ban on sexual-orientation discrimination passed the House, while the ban on gender-identity discrimination did not—and the LGBTQ+ movement then split over whether to support the non-inclusive bill, which failed to get through the Senate. In 2015, LGBTQ+ supporters in Congress proposed a renamed Equality Act with comprehensive protections against discrimination based on both sexual orientation and gender identity and applying not just to employment but to housing, public accommodations, and other areas—but it went nowhere. The transgender protections were a particular problem in getting support from Republicans, who, once the

Supreme Court resolved the issue of same-sex marriage, moved on to stoking outrage about transgender people.

In a stunning decision, however, the Supreme Court again took a step in support of LGBTQ+ rights that the elected branches had been unable to agree on. In a 2020 case, *Bostock v. Clayton County*, the Court ruled that Title VII of the Civil Rights Act of 1964, which bans discrimination because of "sex," prohibits discrimination based on sexual orientation or gender identity. Not only did two Republican appointees, Gorsuch as well as Roberts, defect from the Court's right wing to support the ruling; Gorsuch wrote the majority opinion and based it on a textualist reading of the law: "An employer who fires an individual for being homosexual or transgender fires that person for traits or actions it would not have questioned in members of a different sex. Sex plays a necessary and undisguisable role in the decision, exactly what Title VII forbids." Just before the Court's ruling, a CBS News poll had shown that 82 percent of Americans favored civil rights protections for gays and lesbians.[18] Perhaps the most surprising aspect of Gorsuch's ruling was that it also prohibited discrimination based on gender identity.

In late 2022, supporters of the right to abortion failed to get Congress to pass a national law protecting that right after the Supreme Court overturned *Roe*. But, with the votes of twelve Republican as well as forty-nine Democratic senators, Congress passed the Respect for Marriage Act, which repealed DOMA and guaranteed that all states would have to respect a same-sex marriage performed in another state. Forty years earlier, abortion rights had wide support, and gay rights were a fringe issue. One possible explanation for the reversal in relative support for the two causes has to do with patterns of self-disclosure. When gay people came out of the closet in the late twentieth century, they disrupted old stereotypes and gained greater acceptance. But women who had an abortion generally kept it a secret. As a result, most Americans said they did not know a woman who had an abortion and underestimated the share of women who did, while they drastically overestimated the risk of medical complications associated with abortion. The "abortion closet" contributed to the spread of misinformation about abortion and limited the support the pro-choice movement might have otherwise enjoyed.[19]

The role of both state courts and the U.S. Supreme Court in sustaining claims of LGBTQ+ equality seemed to be a validation of liberal faith in the courts and litigation. As in the past, while the elected branches long failed to act on urgent moral questions, the courts proved more receptive to change. Activists and lawyers worked together. The role of AIDS activists in spurring change, including high levels of sympathetic media attention, followed the model of earlier civil rights protests. The role of gay rights attorneys recalled the historic victories of the NAACP Legal Defense Fund and the women's rights lawyers at the American Civil Liberties Union. When Justice Kennedy wrote in *Obergefell*, "The nature of injustice is that we may not always see it in our own times," he summed up an understanding that the entire movement for equal rights since the breakthroughs of the Black freedom struggle had been imploring Americans to grasp.

But the rulings on LGBTQ+ rights came at a time when the Supreme Court was undermining those earlier victories. Sometimes in obscure ways, sometimes conspicuously, the Court was compounding the economic injustices of a society where inequality was on the rise.

Rights Subtraction, the Quiet Counterrevolution

The conservative legal counterrevolution had moments when it was in the public eye, but much of it proceeded quietly in cases that did not receive public attention. That obscurity had consequences. In American constitutional history one line of thought holds that the Supreme Court follows public opinion and thereby expresses the "will of the people."[20] The Court's decisions on gay rights did fit that interpretation; public opinion had shifted toward support of gay rights by the time the Court made its landmark decisions beginning with *Lawrence*. But that pattern did not necessarily apply to other areas of law, especially to below-the-radar decisions in which the Court's conservative majority was able to carry out an ideological agenda without any concern about triggering protest and weakening the Court's legitimacy.

The road to a right-wing Supreme Court began in the mid-twentieth century with conservative anger over the liberal judiciary. Whites in the South and conservatives elsewhere were irate about the Court's decisions about racial integration. Corporate interests opposed its decisions upholding broad authority for government regulation of business. The religious right was furious about the Court's rulings on tax exemptions for segregated private academies, separation of church and state, and abortion. "While their particular grievances differed," Steven Teles writes, "the conservative coalition was drawn together by a shared opposition to liberal judges, professors, and public interest lawyers and by a unified call for 'strict constructionism' and 'judicial restraint.'" Financed by foundations and wealthy donors, the conservative legal movement sought to gain support at elite levels, create a network of lawyers committed to conservative doctrines and causes, build up supporting legal scholarship, and gain control of Republican judicial nominations and ultimately the Supreme Court.[21] The Federalist Society, the legal organization of movement conservatives, was the core of these efforts. Few movements can claim to have been more successful in changing America's laws and institutions.

Like conservative politics more generally, the conservative legal movement became increasingly radical over the half-century from the 1970s to the 2020s. Starting from calls for "judicial restraint," the movement embraced active judicial intervention aimed at undoing the egalitarian rights revolution, establishing new rights for corporations, and remaking the law into a means of reinforced economic and political domination. After a slow beginning in the Burger Court, the counterrevolution won important victories in the Rehnquist Court (1986–2005), accelerated after John Roberts became chief justice in 2005, and gained full control when Trump's three appointments gave the Court's right wing a 6–3 supermajority.

The counterrevolution in the law began quietly because it proceeded through Supreme Court decisions about seemingly technical matters that were little reported in the media or widely understood at the time. Two aspects of the counterrevolution's quiet phase were particularly important. The first consisted of court decisions chipping away at the rules that enabled private parties to sue to enforce rights under liberal reforms. The rights remained on the books, but enforcing them gradually became difficult, if not impossible. The second line of court decisions allowed corporations to impose contracts on workers and consumers that effectively nullified rights at the heart of the rights revolution. The contracts privatized and individualized the resolution of conflicts by requiring employees and consumers to settle any disputes through private arbitration and preventing them from joining together in class actions.

One of the key innovations of mid-twentieth-century civil rights, environmental, consumer protection, and other liberal legislation—as discussed in earlier chapters—was to give private parties the ability to sue to enforce their rights. Unable to convince congressional Republicans to give the EEOC strong enforcement powers, liberals had to settle for private rights of action—that is, allowing private parties to sue to vindicate claims of discrimination. The compromise included a provision enabling the prevailing party to have its legal fees paid by the other side. In the following years, Democrats became converts to private enforcement because it turned out to be highly effective. They also worried, especially under Nixon and later Republican presidents, that the Justice Department and other federal agencies would not enforce the laws aggressively even when they had that power. The Civil Rights Attorney's Fees Awards Act of 1976 and subsequent legislation authorized the courts to award attorney's fees to "prevailing parties." This was the era when public-interest law was on the rise. Both nonprofit law reform groups and private attorneys sued companies for discriminating against minorities and women, polluting the air and water, endangering their workers' health and safety, and putting dangerous or mislabeled consumer products on the market.[22]

The feasibility of this litigation, however, depended on a variety of issues in addition to the allocation of attorney's fees. For example, who would have standing to sue? If the plaintiffs won their cases, what damages would they receive? Without the ability to recover substantial damages, most people who suffered injuries would have been unable to get lawyers to take their case. Beginning in the 1970s, Congress enacted laws that provided not only for fee-shifting but also for damage enhancements, including double, triple, or punitive damages. These were deliberate incentives for litigation as a means of social reform; the aim was not just to compensate individual victims but to use cases to shape law and public opinion and deter malfeasance. Litigation grew accordingly, to the distress of corporate interests. Republican administrations tried to get Congress to weaken litigation as a means of enforcing rights against companies, but even after Republicans won control of Congress in 1994, they were able to enact only limited changes.

The counterrevolution against private enforcement of rights came through the Supreme Court, which in a series of rulings limited damages, particularly punitive damages, and adopted procedural rules favorable to business defendants. By 2014, according to one study of Supreme Court cases with at least one dissent, plaintiffs suing to enforce their rights, usually against corporations, were losing at a rate of about 90 percent, "an outcome driven by the conservative justices." Republicans had failed to get some of these changes through Congress. What they were not able to do politically on behalf of corporations their Supreme Court appointees were able to accomplish through rulings that few people were aware of.[23]

The closely related changes in contract law had even greater effects in nullifying the rights of workers and consumers. When Americans take a job or buy a product or service, they usually accept, often unknowingly, standardized, take-it-or-leave-it form contracts imposed by businesses. Over the past four decades, the Supreme Court has allowed clauses in the "fine print" of these contracts to subtract many of the rights Americans previously had under the common law, the Constitution, and statutes enacted by Congress and state governments.

The contracts typically prevent workers and consumers from going to court and instead require that they accept binding arbitration of disputes in a system of privatized justice. A 2018 employment contract for summer associates in a Los Angeles law firm was unusually explicit about the implications. The contract explained that besides "giving up your right to a jury trial," the associates would surrender, "without limitation," all "federal, state and local statutory, constitutional, and contractual and/or common law claims." As illustrations, the contract listed all claims under the Fair Labor Standards Act (which provides for, among other things, a minimum wage), Equal Pay Act (which requires equal pay for men and women), Title VII of the Civil Rights Act of 1964 (barring discrimination based on race, religion, national origin, or sex), Age Discrimination in Employment Act, and Americans with Disabilities Act.[24]

As of 2024, according to one study, such clauses prohibited 80 percent of non-union, private-sector employees from going to court in a dispute with an employer. Pre-dispute binding arbitration is also now standard in consumer contracts for banking, credit cards, cell phones, rentals, airline tickets, and countless other services. People accept binding arbitration for online purchases when they click "I agree" to legal terms they are unlikely ever to read, and for many other purchases when they merely walk into a store or unwrap a product.[25]

The removal of disputes from the courts to private arbitration affects the entire system of justice as well as the immediate parties. Litigation serves public purposes. It takes place in public, with publicly appointed judges and, in some cases, a jury, none of whom are paid by either the plaintiff or defendant. Arbitration proceedings take place in private with arbitrators who may have no legal training, much less the qualifications of a judge, and make judgments that are often confidential. Courts are required to observe rules of evidence, compile an official record, and allow for appeals, whereas arbitration proceedings do none of these things. Courts establish precedents, arbitration does not. Perhaps most important, judges and juries are expected to perform a public service, while arbitration is a business. Arbitrators are paid by the parties, and because companies are likely to use arbitration services repeatedly, the arbitrators depend for their livelihood on being invited back by the businesses they serve. Unsurprisingly, businesses prefer arbitration. They win more often in arbitration than in court and, when they have to pay out claims, the amounts are smaller.[26]

The ubiquity of binding arbitration in the consumer marketplace and employment today is a recent development. Although Congress adopted the Federal Arbitration Act in 1925, it was originally intended for the resolution of disputes between businesses that voluntarily agreed to it instead of going to court. Only in the 1980s and 1990s did the Supreme Court begin approving binding arbitration for consumer transactions and employment contracts, contexts in which one party (typically a business or other large entity) imposes on the other a standard, non-negotiable agreement that the other is unlikely to understand or be able to resist. Instead of making one landmark decision, the Court made twenty different rulings, gradually broadening the role of arbitration. Were standardized form contracts used by companies in consumer transactions to be treated as though they were voluntarily bargained? The Court said they were. Did the 1925 Federal Arbitration Act apply to disputes between employers and employees? Yes, the Court said, it did. Was arbitration a sufficient forum for adjudicating civil rights? The Court decided it was. Did the Federal Arbitration Act preempt state laws that protected access to state courts? Yes, the Court declared, the law did that too.[27]

Instead of the idealized world of freedom of contract, which never fully existed, the Court created what was, in practice, its opposite: a world of unfreedom of contract. One further step it took was of particular importance. Businesses were anxious to rid themselves of class-action suits, in which the claims of large numbers of workers or consumers are aggregated into a single case. In a classic 1974 article, "Why the Haves Come Out Ahead," the legal scholar Marc Galanter distinguished between "one-shotters" (who rarely become a party to a legal dispute) and "repeat players" (who frequently do). The one-shotters typically suffer from a wide range of disadvantages, including lack of experience and sophisticated legal counsel. They also have an interest in immediate, tangible results, unlike repeat players who can follow patient, long-term strategies aimed at shaping legal rules to their advantage.[28] Class-action suits put groups of one-shotters on a more equal playing field with repeat players and for just that reason are anathema to big businesses.

According to a *New York Times* investigation, "a Wall Street coalition of credit card companies and retailers" led a legal campaign over more than a decade to persuade the courts to approve contract provisions waiving a right to join in a class action. A key figure in that effort was a lawyer for a bank, John Roberts, who tried unsuccessfully to appeal a case involving a class-action ban to the Supreme Court. When the Court finally did address that issue in 2011, Roberts was chief justice, and he voted with the other conservative justices for a ruling that reflected his earlier brief and gave the green light to companies to impose class-action waivers. By 2018, most big corporations that used consumer arbitration agreements also used class-action bans, and more than 40 percent of the workers subject to binding arbitration also had to agree not to join in a class-action suit. Class-action bans preclude an entire category of cases against businesses, those that involve small amounts of money from each member of a large class of consumers, such as hidden charges by credit-card companies, which nonetheless add up to large profits.[29] The Supreme Court's approval of class-action bans is one reason for the subsequent proliferation of "junk fees" by financial services, hotels and airlines, and other businesses.

The spread of mandatory arbitration and class-action bans has also had a major impact on labor relations, particularly because of the proliferation of two other provisions in employment contracts: non-compete clauses and non-disclosure agreements (NDAs). After first including these prohibitions in contracts with managerial and technical employees, companies made them routine even for many low-level, low-paid workers. To take an egregious example, an employment package provided by Jimmy Johns to its franchisees included a non-compete clause prohibiting hourly employees from going to work for any other business that receives 10 percent or more of its revenue from selling sandwiches within three miles of a Jimmy Johns location. Non-compete clauses prevent workers from easily changing jobs and enable employers to keep down wages. Even when they are legally unenforceable, they lead many workers to tolerate working conditions that they would otherwise not accept.[30]

Beginning in the 1980s, NDAs became widely used in the tech industry in agreements with employees and suppliers before spreading into employment contracts in other industries as well as many arbitration judgments and other legal settlements. The use of NDAs in efforts to keep workers silent received considerable attention in several high-profile public scandals. For example, the blood-test firm Theranos used NDAs to try to prevent employees from disclosing the company's dangerously fraudulent technology. NDAs were also central in the efforts by the movie producer Harvey Weinstein to silence women he had sexually assaulted.[31] But the effects of NDAs are more pervasive than those scandals may suggest.

Together with binding arbitration and class-action bans, these "contracts for silence" keep workers isolated from one another, unable to act collectively. They are a free-speech problem that America's free-speech law does not address. Having spread with the decline of unions, they reinforce the same pattern, the subordination of labor to a new, old regime of domination.

The privatization of justice and restriction of free speech brought about by the Supreme Court and unfettered corporate power have had wide ramifications. They have reversed much of the egalitarian rights revolution, weakened important deterrents of corporate malfeasance, and contributed to rising economic inequality. The quiet counterrevolution has prevented people from tracing everyday problems to their origins in politics and law. When Americans are mistreated or suffer injuries today, they often find that they have no recourse, but they don't know how that happened or who is responsible. They may blame "elites" in general, perhaps even pinning the blame on liberals who fought against many of these changes. The genius of the quiet phase of the conservative counterrevolution is that most of it happened in such obscure ways that the business interests and conservative Supreme Court justices who were responsible escaped any blame.

The Right's Rights

The more openly contested phases of the legal counterrevolution have also been concerned, at least in part, with weakening the enforcement of rights, such as the right to vote, or entirely undoing rights, such as the right to abortion. But the counterrevolution has had its own rights-expanding agenda too. That agenda has involved corporate rights, religious liberty rights, free-speech rights (understood in ways that increase inequality), and Second Amendment rights.

The long-term pattern in the LGBTQ+ rights struggle, I have suggested, was short-term reversals (when proposals for equal rights were first made) amid long-term gains in public opinion and eventually law. In contrast, the conservative rights revolution has not exhibited a similar pattern of convergence between law and public opinion (with one important exception, affirmative action, where liberal policies never had strong support in public opinion). Key rulings by the Supreme Court's conservative majority have not reflected long-term public opinion trends, nor have those rulings (thus far) resulted in cultural change in a conservative direction. By moving sharply to the right of public opinion, the Court has changed American institutions without necessarily changing American culture.

Corporate rights illustrate how far the conservative rights revolution has diverged from public opinion. The Supreme Court decision that symbolized the ascendancy of corporate rights came in a 2010 case, *Citizens United*, where the Court ruled that corporations had a right protected by the First Amendment to spend money from their treasuries to influence elections. This was a right, the Court declared, that neither Congress nor the states had any power to limit in the interests of political equality.

Citizens United overturned a prohibition on corporate campaign contributions that had been in effect since Congress passed the Tillman Act in 1907. It also reversed decisions the Court had made as recently as 1990 and 2003, when it had upheld laws banning corporate contributions. In 1990, the Court had pointed out that the "unique legal and economic characteristics" of corporations give them "special advantages," including limited liability and perpetual life, that were designed to help them raise capital. These advantages, the Court said, enable corporations to use "resources amassed in the economic marketplace to obtain an unfair advantage in the political marketplace." Reaffirming that view in 2003, the Court noted "the corrosive and distorting effects of immense aggregations of wealth . . . accumulated with the help of the corporate form."[32] The 5–4 majority in *Citizens United* swept away all such considerations. In 1976, the Court had ruled in *Buckley v. Valeo* that limiting corruption or the appearance of corruption was the sole permissible basis for campaign finance restrictions. By 2010, the Court's view was that unlimited corporate spending on elections did not even create the appearance of corruption—at least, not to the justices.

The *Citizens United* decision met overwhelming disapproval from Democrats and Republicans alike in public opinion polls.[33] But it was only one in a long series of rulings that gave corporations most of the rights of individuals. As the constitutional scholar Adam Winkler writes in a history of corporate rights, while the civil rights movement struggled to win over the public, the corporate rights movement did not face that challenge. Corporations never made, or needed to make, any effort to convince the public that they should have the same rights as individuals: "Corporate rights were won in courts of law, by judicial rulings extending fundamental protections to business, even in the absence of any national consensus in favor of corporate rights."[34]

In its decisions on campaign finance, the Roberts Court was consistently hostile to concerns about political equality. Two rulings illustrate the pattern. A 2008 case concerned a provision of campaign finance reforms passed in 2002 that raised the individual-contribution limits for candidates facing wealthy opponents who used their own money to fund their campaigns above certain levels. This "millionaires' amendment" allowed a non-wealthy candidate to raise more money to keep up with a wealthy opponent. In other words, it added to speech rather than reducing or censoring it. Nonetheless, in a 5–4 decision, the conservative justices struck down this provision as a violation of the First Amendment because it burdened the ability of rich candidates to exercise their First Amendment rights "robustly." In a similar case three years later, the Supreme Court overturned a program for public financing of elections in Arizona that gave additional money to candidates being outspent by rich candidates who funded their own campaigns. Once again the Court's conservative majority rejected a policy that tried to equalize spending because it diminished the "effectiveness" of the rich candidate's speech, even though it did so by adding to speech, not restricting it.[35]

The Roberts Court also turned the First Amendment into a basis for undoing economic regulation. Vermont's Prescription Confidentiality Law prohibited the sale of information about physicians' pharmaceutical prescriptions to drug marketers and data mining companies unless physicians gave their permission, while the law allowed the information to be used for scientific and public health purposes. But the Court held it to be unconstitutional under the First Amendment because it "disfavored" particular speakers (pharmaceutical companies) and blocked the creation of information (data mining for marketing). The decision continued a pattern that had begun in the 1970s with the Court's extension of the First Amendment to protect commercial advertising.[36]

The Supreme Court's enlargement of the free-speech rights of corporations stands in contrast to the pattern I have described of the silencing of workers' voices through mandatory private arbitration, class-action bans, and NDAs. A fundamental asymmetry has long characterized the free-speech rights of employers and workers. Employers' speech in the workplace is a constitutionally protected right, while workers' speech is not. During unionization drives, for example, employers can hold "captive audience meetings" for workers where management attacks the union, but unions have no corresponding rights to conduct workplace meetings.[37] In 2021 the Roberts Court increased that asymmetry in rights in a case involving a state law, the California Agricultural Labor Relations Act, enacted in 1975 to protect the rights of farmworkers. The law included an access rule that enabled union organizers four times a year to approach farmworkers during lunch breaks and for an hour before and after work. The Roberts Court declared the rule an unconstitutional "taking" of private property because it violated the property owner's right to exclude third parties—in this case, union representatives.[38]

In 2014, the Supreme Court created another right for corporations when for the first time it held that a privately held, for-profit corporation had a right to religious liberty, entitling it to opt out of any law (except taxes) that its owners deemed incompatible with their religion. The case involved the obligations of Hobby Lobby Stores, a retail chain with 13,000 employees, under a provision of the Affordable Care Act requiring large employers to offer contraceptive coverage in employee health plans. In 2020, the Court upheld a broader Trump administration exemption for employers that sought to opt out of birth control coverage on religious grounds. The Court took a further step in extending the religion-based opt-out rights of enterprises in 2023, when it upheld the right of a Christian website design company not to produce websites for same-sex weddings.[39]

The Roberts Court has been a historically pro-business court. One study, based on voting by Supreme Court justices between 1946 and 2011, found that over that entire period Alito and Roberts were the two most pro-business justices and Thomas, Kennedy, and Scalia ranked among the top ten.[40] Their decisions favoring business did not come without a cost to other groups' rights. By recognizing the right of Hobby Lobby and other employers not to cover birth control, the Court was sacrificing the right to insurance coverage of contraceptives that the companies' women employees would have had. The 2023 ruling on the Christian website designer created a right to deny service to LGBTQ+ customers, the first time the Court recognized a right to discriminate against a class that antidiscrimination laws were intended to protect.

Conservatives originally framed their response to the civil rights, women's rights, and gay rights movements as a defense of traditional community and family values. In resisting each of those movements, they first spoke with the confident force of the dominant, majority culture. By the early twenty-first century, however, they were no longer in that position even with respect to LGBTQ+ rights and instead assumed the role of a minority seeking the right to opt out from a culture that was no longer entirely theirs. They used rights to fight against rights, but they still believed that history and tradition were on their side. That belief, the claim of fidelity to "history and tradition," also lay at the center of rulings by the

Supreme Court's conservative majority aimed at remaking fundamental aspects of American law and American life.

History and Traditionalism

The great hope of the conservative legal movement was to reverse foundational changes in constitutional law and American society that liberals had brought about through the courts. And since the premise of the conservative attack on legal liberalism was that liberal judges had imposed their preferences on the Constitution, conservative judges could not simply say they were substituting their own preferences in overturning what were now long-established liberal precedents such as *Roe v. Wade*. They needed to make an argument on higher ground, and the argument that many of them made concerned two related methods for identifying the true meaning of the Constitution.

In the first of these two methods, conservative jurists held that the Constitution's true meaning was its original meaning, and the way to identify it was an objective inquiry into the meaning of constitutional provisions at the time they were ratified—1791, for example, in the case of the Bill of Rights and 1868 in the case of the Fourteenth Amendment. The second method was a looser inquiry into "history and tradition," which could look back centuries in English law and forward into nineteenth-century American law in establishing tradition, though "history" stopped strangely in the twentieth century. Originalism and "history and tradition" were how a conservative Court would determine what the Constitution required in disputed areas of contemporary life.

Two of the most important examples of how this kind of judicial reasoning worked in practice were the changes wrought by the conservative justices in the interpretation of gun rights under the Second Amendment and abortion rights under the Fourteenth Amendment. In each case, these methods would just so happen to yield precisely the results that the contemporary right was looking for, though it required the justices to falsify the history to reach those conclusions.

The rulings on the Second Amendment, beginning with *District of Columbia v. Heller* in 2008, broke with precedent in two ways. The first had to do with the meaning of the Second Amendment, particularly its scope. The second had to do with the standard of judicial review for regulation of firearms.

The Second Amendment reads, "A well regulated Militia, being necessary to the security of a free State, the right of the people to keep and bear Arms, shall not be infringed." Before *Heller*, the Supreme Court had only rarely in more than 200 years taken up cases involving the Second Amendment because it was considered a matter of settled law that the amendment protected the right of the people in each of the states to maintain a well-regulated militia. (The amendment was a response to concerns raised during the Constitution's ratification that the federal government's military powers might allow it to disarm the militias and threaten the sovereign rights that the states retained.) As of 2008, the leading precedent regarding the Second Amendment was a 1939 decision in which the Supreme Court had upheld a federal firearms law and ruled that the amendment did not apply to a weapon that did not have "some reasonable relationship to the preservation or efficiency of a well regulated militia."[41]

In its 5–4 ruling in *Heller*, however, the Court held that the amendment established an individual right to possess and carry a weapon for self-defense unrelated to service in a well-regulated militia. In an opinion written by Scalia, the majority set aside the amendment's first part as merely "prefatory" and said that the operative part guaranteed "the individual right to possess and carry weapons in case of confrontation."[42]

The liberal dissenters in *Heller* did not disagree that the amendment implied an individual right; they disagreed about the scope of that right. They held it was a right to "keep and bear arms" for military purposes, that is, for service in a well-regulated militia. As Stevens wrote for the dissenters, "Neither the text of the Amendment nor the arguments advanced by its proponents [at the time of its adoption] evidenced the slightest interest in limiting any legislature's authority to regulate private civilian uses of firearms." The very phrase, "keep and bear arms," was an idiomatic phrase in the founding era that referred specifically to military service, as overwhelming evidence from historical linguistics showed.[43]

The division over the Second Amendment, therefore, did not fit the picture of conservatives as being faithfully devoted to the Constitution's original meaning, while liberals supposedly ignored it. The liberal justices adhered to the original meaning, as the courts had long understood it. The dispute illustrated how susceptible that original meaning was to different interpretations, even concerning an amendment that historically had not provoked much legal controversy, so settled had its meaning been until conservatives chose to break with precedent.

Still, the conservative majority's decision to read into the Second Amendment a version of the common-law right of individual self-defense need not have greatly altered the practical implications for federal or state regulation of firearms. In 2002, John Ashcroft, attorney general under

George W. Bush, had issued a memorandum endorsing an individual rights view of the Second Amendment but said the recognition of that right did not mean "reasonable restrictions" could not be imposed on firearms, nor would it prevent the Justice Department from "vigorously" defending "the constitutionality, under the Second Amendment, of all existing federal firearms laws." When *Heller* was decided, forty-two state constitutions provided an individual right to bear arms, but state courts had nearly always applied a "reasonable regulation" standard, deferring to legislative judgments about gun regulations.[44]

That kind of deference to contemporary legislative judgment about "reasonable" regulations, however, was not what the Supreme Court's conservatives had in mind. Although *Heller* indicated that the constitutionality of a gun law would depend on whether it was rooted in history and tradition, the decision did not set a clear standard. It overturned a law in Washington, D.C., that required a license for keeping a gun at home, which the majority said would fail to pass constitutional muster under any of the standards applied in judicial review. Those standards vary along a spectrum from "rational basis" (the least demanding) to "intermediate scrutiny" to "strict scrutiny," the latter requiring a "compelling" government interest to justify a burden on a constitutional right. After *Heller*, lower courts conducted a two-step review. They first determined whether a challenged regulation fell under the Second Amendment's newly enlarged scope and then, in a second step, subjected it to "heightened" scrutiny. The scrutiny would be "strict" if it severely burdened the Second Amendment right; "intermediate" if it did not. In 2022, however, in an opinion by Clarence Thomas, the conservative majority threw out the second step. Striking down a New York law regarding licenses for concealed-carry of a gun in public, the Court ruled in *New York State Rifle & Pistol Association, Inc. v. Bruen* that a modern firearm regulation was constitutional only if it had an early American historical analog. Only history mattered; contemporary judgments about public safety and gun violence were not constitutionally relevant.[45]

Bruen set off a torrent of challenges to gun regulations in the lower courts and widespread confusion about whether various regulations had a match in 1791 and were therefore constitutional. In one of those challenges, a man in Texas, Zackey Rahimi, challenged the federal law under which he was indicted for possessing firearms. Rahimi had been under a domestic violence restraining order because he had threatened his girlfriend. After police identified him as a suspect in several shootings, they entered his home on a search warrant and found guns, ammunition, and a copy of the restraining order that prohibited him from possessing firearms. Following *Bruen*, the Fifth Circuit Court of Appeals agreed with Rahimi that the government failed to prove that the federal law in question "fits within our nation's historical tradition of firearm regulation." Narrowly conceived, that much was true: In 1791 there were no domestic violence restraining orders. In this case, though, the members of the Supreme Court (except for Thomas) reversed the appellate court, ruling that other historical regulations restrained people who posed a danger to others and "when a challenged regulation does not precisely match its historical precursors, 'it still may be analogous enough to pass constitutional muster.'"[46]

But what does "analogous enough" mean? The regulation upheld by the Supreme Court in *Rahimi* was at issue in only eight of roughly 500 federal court cases at the time in which gun regulations were being challenged as unconstitutional.[47] The Court left unclear the criteria for judging whether a modern regulation on, say, assault weapons was "analogous enough" to an early American regulation concerning muskets and swords. Judges did not have the relevant historical expertise to undertake detailed inquiries into the gun regulations of the founding era: "We are not experts in what white, wealthy, and male property owners thought about firearms regulation in 1791," one federal district judge admitted.[48] Although originalism was supposed to constrain judges by tethering their decisions to historical facts, an analysis of Second Amendment cases in federal courts from 2000 to 2023 found a growing gap in rulings, especially after *Bruen*, between judges appointed by different presidents. Trump-appointed judges were more likely to rule in favor of gun rights than were judges appointed by other Republican presidents, who were in turn more likely than Democratic appointees to rule that way.[49] Legislatures had no clear guide as to what laws regarding guns they could pass. Presumably, they were to make policy based on analogies to laws in force more than two centuries earlier.

The reasoning in the Court's Second Amendment decisions was similar to its reasoning in *Dobbs v. Jackson's Women's Health Organization* in 2022, when it struck down the constitutional right to abortion. In *Heller*, Scalia wrote that "constitutional rights are enshrined with the scope they were understood to have when the people adopted them."[50] *Dobbs* involved a Mississippi law banning abortion after fifteen weeks. According to Alito's majority opinion, a key question was whether the Fourteenth Amendment's scope, as understood when it was ratified in 1868, included a right to abortion.

Alito argued that the Fourteenth Amendment could not have included such a right because three-quarters of the states in 1868 outlawed abortion. Arguing on the basis of "history and tradition," he claimed "an unbroken tradition of prohibiting abortion on pain of criminal punishment persisted from the earliest days of the common law until 1973," despite a brief from the American Historical Association and Organization of American Historians showing "plentiful evidence ... of the long legal tradition, extending from the common law to the mid-1800s (and far longer in some American states, including Mississippi), of tolerating termination of pregnancy before occurrence of 'quickening,' the time when a woman first felt fetal movement."[51] Nonetheless, based on the version of history favored by the religious right, the *Dobbs* majority overruled both the original 1973 abortion rights decision, *Roe v. Wade*, and its successor, *Planned Parenthood v. Casey*, the 1992 case in which the Court had upheld a woman's right to choose an abortion prior to viability free of any "undue burden" imposed by government. Unlike the conservatives' expansion of Second Amendment rights, which limited legislative powers, their ruling in *Dobbs* left abortion wide open to restriction by Congress and the states. *Dobbs*, the liberal dissenters in the case pointed out, was the first time in history that the Court had rescinded a previously established constitutional right.

In the nearly fifty years since *Roe v. Wade*, the constitutional argument for reproductive rights had evolved. The Court in *Roe* based its holding on the right to privacy, which it had earlier distilled from the First, Third, Fourth, Fifth, Ninth, and Fourteenth Amendments in its 1965 decision *Griswold v. Connecticut*, regarding the right of access to birth control. *Casey*, reflecting Anthony Kennedy's views, emphasized rights to liberty and substantive due process, as grounded in the Fourteenth Amendment. A third approach, long advocated by Ruth Bader Ginsburg before she joined the Court, focused on women's rights to equality under the Fourteenth Amendment's Equal Protection Clause.

By the 2020s, equal protection was central to the argument for abortion rights. As three feminist legal scholars put it in connection with *Dobbs*, "Abortion bans expressly target women and require them to continue pregnancy, imposing motherhood over their objections." Abortion laws, they argued, were sex-based by their very nature. At Brett Kavanaugh's confirmation hearing, Senator Kamala Harris had made the same point, flummoxing the future justice with one question: "Can you think of any laws that give the government the power to make decisions about the male body?" In his opinion in *Dobbs*, however, Alito brusquely dismissed the equal-protection argument. The Court's precedents, Alito wrote, "establish that a State's regulation of abortion is not a sex-based classification and is thus not subject to the heightened scrutiny that applies to such classifications."[52]

Dobbs therefore did not require the governmental interest in "fetal life" to be weighed against any other concerns. Congress or the states could ban abortion outright, even when the life of the mother was threatened. Previously, under *Casey*, in the months before a fetus was viable, the government could not impose a "substantial obstacle" to a woman's right to make choices about her body. But the majority decision in *Dobbs*, as the three dissenters wrote, implied that "from the very moment of fertilization, a woman has no rights to speak of. A State can force her to bring a pregnancy to term, even at the steepest personal and familial costs." Forced childbirth did not, in the majority's view, implicate a woman's rights to equality and freedom.[53]

The conservative majority said that nothing in the *Dobbs* ruling "cast doubt on precedents that do not concern abortion," but the same logic applied to the whole line of cases from *Griswold v. Connecticut* to *Lawrence v. Texas* and *Obergefell v. Hodges*, all of which protect personal life decisions from government control. All those protections would fall if the laws in force in 1868 were the decisive criteria about their constitutionality. If *Roe* was "egregiously wrong," as Alito repeated more than half a dozen times in *Dobbs*, Thomas was egregiously right when he wrote in his concurrence that the other related precedents also had to be reversed. The originalist and history-and-tradition arguments put in jeopardy all rights to personal freedom that, in the dissenters' words, "have no history stretching back to the mid-19th century."

In an article on originalism, the legal scholar Reva Siegel asks, "Why does the Roberts Court appeal to history and tradition in *exactly* those cases in which it is *changing* the law?"[54] The answer is clearly not that history and tradition are fixed anchors. The conservative justices cherry-picked the past in rewriting the history of the Second Amendment; they misrepresented the legal history of abortion in overturning *Roe*. Originalism and history and tradition in the hands of the justices are best thought of as strategies of constitutional change that masquerade as a constitutionally strict basis of legal stability (even as they have produced legal and political havoc in the two areas of gun regulations and abortion). The two doctrines rationalize change of a particular kind, a reverting of the law to a tendentiously remembered past.

The general language of the Constitution expresses an intention, the intention to allow new generations to infuse its provisions with new meaning consistent with the principles in the text. That too is part of American history and tradition, the living constitutional tradition, not the deadening hand of constitutional traditionalism. It's the part of the tradition that Justice Kennedy referred to when he wrote about the ability of new generations to invoke the Constitution's principles in their "search for greater freedom" as they discover "that laws once thought necessary and proper in fact serve only to oppress." By limiting the Constitution's principles to centuries-old statutes, the doctrines of originalism and history and tradition try to return the nation to a time before that enlargement of freedom, when women and minorities excluded from the political community did not have their interests in freedom and equality reflected in the making of laws.

Law versus Culture

Since the mid-twentieth century, the conservative movement has been fighting trends in American culture, but the movement finally in the 2020s had a Supreme Court majority taking its side on important culture-war battles. The rulings on the Second Amendment, abortion, and religion answered conservatives' hope of turning the tables on liberalism. Yet since judicial power has its limits, control of the Supreme Court does not necessarily translate into change on the ground—how people think, feel, and act toward one another. One result has been a staggering decline in public confidence in the judiciary. According to Gallup, confidence in the courts dropped twenty-four percentage points between 2020 and 2024, from 59 percent to 35 percent, putting the United States about twenty points below peer countries and in ninety-second place in a ranking of countries according to that measure.[55]

The Roberts Court's decisions on the Second Amendment did not reflect any deeper current in American culture favoring conservative positions on gun control. In the years leading up to the Court's decisions, the predominant pattern in public opinion on gun control was stability, but it was a stable pattern mostly inconsistent with conservative preferences. While Americans generally believed the Second Amendment conferred an individual right, they also favored by large majorities a variety of registration requirements for guns and licensing requirements for gun owners, as well as numerous other gun regulations, which the Court under its criteria in *Bruen* would likely judge unconstitutional. About six in ten Americans have thought it is too easy to obtain a gun legally and favored stricter gun laws.[56]

Still, there was a long-standing gap between majority opinion about guns and the gun laws because of the political power of the gun lobby. The Roberts Court immediately affected blue states with stronger firearms regulations; its first three major Second Amendment decisions overturned gun laws in Washington, D.C., Chicago, and New York. Besides creating general confusion about what laws were constitutional based on eighteenth-century analogs, the Court's decisions promote an armed society where more people make it a practice to carry weapons "in case of confrontation." That kind of society does have roots at least in a Wild West image of the past, and the Court has ensured it has more of a future even in the states and cities where people want no part of it.

The Court's abrogation of a constitutional right to abortion also did not reflect a shift toward conservative preferences in public opinion. In Gallup polls on abortion from 1987 to 2019, an average of 58 percent said they favored keeping *Roe* against 34 percent who said *Roe* should be overturned. *Dobbs* predictably produced a backlash. In nine separate national polls soon after *Dobbs*, between 56 and 63 percent of Americans disagreed with the Supreme Court's decision to overturn *Roe*. In fact, the share of Americans who supported legal abortion "for any reason" increased from 49 percent to 61 percent between 2021 and 2024.[57] As noted earlier, Americans substantially underestimated the share of women who had an abortion and overestimated the procedure's risks; support for abortion rights might have risen even further if Americans had more accurate information. But, as it was, not only did a majority of Americans oppose *Dobbs* at the time; the Court's decision drew growing opposition in the following two years.

By throwing abortion back into the political arena, the Court intensified political conflict over the issue and gave an impetus to reproductive rights organizing and Democratic mobilization. What had been a constitutional right became a crime in some states while remaining a right in others, exposing women and health providers to a patchwork of laws and medical risks. Not satisfied with abortion bans in individual states, the anti-abortion movement sought to escalate the fight: to limit the ability of women to travel to another state to have an abortion; to prevent the abortion drug mifepristone from being conveyed through the mail or by other means; and ultimately to ban abortion nationally, either through enactment of new federal legislation or through a court decision reviving the 1873 anti-abortion Comstock Act, long considered a dead letter. After *Dobbs*, six states voted on initiatives regarding abortion, and in every state—including Kansas, Kentucky, and Ohio—the side favoring access to abortion won. Abortion, long an animating issue for the Republican base, became an albatross for the party. In 2024 Democrats put the issue on the ballot, while Republicans tried to keep it off. Seven out of ten states that year passed abortion rights measures.

The right did have a majority of the public on its side in one major legal victory. In contrast to the backlash against the overturning of *Roe*, the Court's decision to strike down race-conscious affirmative action in university admissions in 2023 elicited only a muted political response from liberals. Affirmative action had long been on politically tenuous ground; eight states including California had banned it in public institutions. In 2020, when Biden trounced Trump in California by twenty-nine points, 57 percent of the state's voters rejected a ballot measure to bring back affirmative action to the state government and public higher education. The opposition did not just come from whites; a majority of Asian Americans were also opposed, and Hispanics were split evenly. In 2023, as the Supreme Court was deliberating race-conscious university admissions, a national poll found a similar pattern: Americans disapproved of selective colleges taking race into account in admissions by 50 to 33 percent, again with Asian Americans almost as opposed as whites, and Hispanics evenly divided. Exploiting the division among minorities, the conservative group that brought the legal challenge to race-conscious admissions did so on behalf of Asian American applicants. As I discussed in chapter 7, when affirmative action in universities survived a test in the Supreme Court in 2003, the pivotal justice was Sandra Day O'Connor, who wrote that it would not be justifiable in another twenty-five years. The Court brought down the hammer in just twenty. Although the Court's decision was likely to affect the numbers of Black and Hispanic students at highly selective colleges, it seemed less likely to affect total admissions of Black and Hispanic students at all four-year colleges. The bigger factor was likely to be the future of financial aid for low-income students and the ability and willingness of colleges to weigh personal adversity in admissions and financial aid decisions.[58] But the conservative drive to kill "diversity, equity, and inclusion" policies in all aspects of education and employment was far from finished.

Dobbs, like the decisions creating religious-liberty rights for corporations, was part of a shift in the Roberts Court in favor of claims brought by the religious right and its allies. In some of these cases, the Court was taking away with one hand what it gave with the other, establishing religiously based rights to discriminate after voting for antidiscrimination protections for LGBTQ+ people. The Court had long held that religious institutions were subject to generally applicable laws with only limited exceptions, but in 2020 it declared that church-run schools were not bound by laws that protect teachers and other employees against discrimination based not just on sex but on race, pregnancy, age, disability, and other characteristics. During the COVID-19 pandemic, the Court reversed earlier precedents by exempting churches from emergency public health regulations that restricted public gatherings.

The overall historical change was dramatic. The Roberts Court was a historically pro-religion court just as it was a historically pro-business court. In cases involving religion, the religious parties had prevailed about 50 percent of the time in the Warren and Burger Courts from 1953 to 1986. That proportion rose to 58 percent in the Rehnquist Court from 1986 to 2005 and then soared to 81 percent after Roberts became chief justice. The five most pro-religion justices since World War II (Kavanaugh, Thomas, Roberts, Alito, and Gorsuch) all sat on the Court in the early 2020s.[59]

Like the decisions on the Second Amendment and abortion, the Court's shift on religion-related cases does not correspond to a broad current in American culture. On the contrary, it goes in exactly the opposite direction as churchgoing has fallen and fewer Americans maintain religious affiliations. Between 2000 and 2020, the proportion of Americans affiliated with a church, synagogue, or mosque fell by more than twenty points to 47 percent, for the first time representing less than a majority of the population. The share of Americans self-identifying as Christian fell from 90 percent in 1972 to 64 percent in 2020. Over the same period, the proportion of "nones"—people who identify with no religion—rose from 5 percent to 30 percent, many of them alienated from organized religion as it has become more entangled with conservative politics. Among evangelicals, religious identity and partisanship have become conflated. People who describe themselves as "evangelical" have become more likely to say that they seldom or never attend church; 43 percent say they do not believe in the divinity of Christ. What holds them together is a politicized religious identity. The core religious right insists that the United States has always been and remains a Christian nation, but the proportion of Americans who hold those views has fallen. The decline in their numbers and cultural predominance, the sense that America has become a "negative world" for them, may be the critical stimulus to political mobilization.[60]

Although the trends in American culture tell a story of religious decline, the changes in the Supreme Court and American law tell the oppositive story of the religious right's growing political power. Anyone who just looked at the data on Americans and their religious affiliations and observance would say that churches in America, including the conservative churches, were failing at their mission. But while the religious right might not be working in matters of faith, its integration into a political party has enlarged its footprint in matters of power. The religious right has shown that cultural failure and political success can go together. Failing at persuasion, they seek to prevail through the power of the state.

The Partisan Court

The law's separation from politics is one of the cardinal principles of a rule-of-law nation, and it is a cornerstone of the judiciary's expansive authority in the United States. Before the 1990s, justices of the Supreme Court nominated by presidents of different parties substantially overlapped in their voting on cases, a pattern widely seen as evidence of their nonpartisanship. The Court helped preserve its authority by achieving unanimity in two decisions with explosive implications: *Brown v. Board of Education* in 1954 and *United States v. Nixon*, the 1974 case in which the Court ordered President Nixon to release the White House tape recordings that brought down his presidency.

During the 1990s and early 2000s, however, both the Supreme Court and appellate courts increasingly split along partisan and ideological lines on major decisions. To be sure, not all cases divided the judiciary on a partisan basis; many rulings in the Supreme Court and appellate courts continued to blur party lines or to be unanimous in areas of the law that were not ideologically contentious. Liberals could still win major cases on issues like the constitutionality of the Affordable Care Act with a single defection from the conservative wing.[61] But, from the 1990s on, partisanship spilled into a wider range of judicial issues as it did throughout American society. As statistical analyses of judicial decisions showed, judges increasingly voted like polarized legislators. When Chief Justice Roberts said in 2018, "We do not have Obama judges or Trump judges, Bush judges or Clinton judges," he was not citing empirical evidence. He was expressing an official faith that underwrote judicial authority and that many Americans desperately wanted to believe because the American political system does not work without at least the pretense that it is true.[62]

One reason for growing doubts about the neutrality of the courts was the behavior of the Supreme Court itself in cases with large and unambiguous electoral consequences. Two cases, *Bush v. Gore* in 2000 and *Trump v. United States* in 2024, stand out, as do important cases related to voting rights. These decisions do not reflect any coherent conservative doctrine such as originalism. The rulings were typically ad hoc, ignored precedent, and, in *Bush v. Gore*, violated basic precepts of rule of law. The consistent element was that the Court's conservative majority came down on the Republican side. The whole pattern was one of circularity: Republican presidents had appointed a majority of the sitting justices, and they returned the favor, protecting Republican power at moments when that power was at stake.

By entrenching Republican electoral power, the Republican justices also entrenched their own control of the law. Few people would dispute that incumbents in the elected branches try to keep power and that their interest in political entrenchment explains much of what they do.[63] The idea that judges do so as well may seem too crude a way of explaining their decisions, but it is the most straightforward explanation for the behavior of the Republican justices on cases of high electoral consequence. The decisions from *Bush v. Gore* to *Trump v. United States* exemplified not just the politicization of the judiciary but also the "judicialization of politics": the active, critical intervention of the judiciary in electoral politics to the clear partisan advantage of the justices in the majority.[64]

In the 2000 presidential election, the Democratic candidate Al Gore won the national popular vote over George W. Bush, but the Electoral College hung on a near tie in Florida. Controversy in Florida swirled around the methods for manually recounting "undervotes," ballots that when tabulated by machine did not register a vote for president. Errors in machine counting were known to be a serious problem in areas using punch-card ballots when voters did not fully punch through the ballot, possibly leaving a "hanging chad." Immediately after Election Day, the two sides were in court fighting over recounts. On December 8, after an initial statewide machine recount and manual recounts in several counties, the Florida Supreme Court ordered a statewide manual recount of previously uninspected undervotes. At the time, Bush led Gore by 154 votes (out of nearly six million), though there were ongoing disputes about absentee ballots and other issues. Having already been cautioned by the U.S. Supreme Court in a previous case not to create any new law, the Florida court ordered local canvassing boards to follow the existing rule for evaluating ballots set in state law, which was to determine "the intent of the voter." On December 9, however, by a 5–4 vote, the U.S. Supreme Court issued a stay suspending the recount, and three days later the same five justices ordered the recount stopped. The total vote at that point stood at 2,912,790 for Bush compared to Gore's 2,912,253, making Bush the winner by 537 votes. The majority consisted of five conservative Republican appointees (Rehnquist, Scalia, Thomas, O'Connor, and Kennedy), while the four dissenters included two moderate Republican appointees (Souter and Stevens) as well as two Democrats (Breyer and Ginsburg).[65]

The conservative majority ruled that the manual recount ordered by Florida's Supreme Court violated the Equal Protection Clause because the "intent of the voter" standard was insufficiently specific, allowed for variation from one canvassing board to another, and therefore did not satisfy the "minimum requirement for nonarbitrary treatment of voters." According to the majority, time to resolve this issue had run out. Although the Electoral College did not cast its votes until December 18, the date for submitting a list of electors who could not be challenged, December 12, was "upon us." With allegedly no time left to conduct a constitutional recount, the conservative justices overturned the Florida court's order. Bush's strategy had been to run out the clock, and the Court announced that the clock had, in fact, run out.[66]

The four dissenting justices took issue not just with the rationale for the majority's decision but with the Court's decision to intervene in the recount. The standard for issuing a stay was "irreparable harm," but "counting every legally cast vote cannot constitute irreparable harm" and the stay therefore violated principles of judicial restraint. The dissenters also held that December 12 was not a deadline under state or federal law; the majority had no legitimate basis for treating it as an enforceable cut-off date. In fact, other states that year would submit their lists of electors between December 12 and December 18 and suffer no adverse effect. Stevens and Ginsburg saw no violation of the Equal Protection Clause in the use of an "intent of the voter" standard for the recount; American elections are rife with local variations in ballot design, voting technology, and counting rules, which had never been treated as constitutional deficiencies. Souter and Breyer did see an equal-protection issue, but one that should have been resolved by remanding the case back to the Florida court with instructions for making the standard more specific. Breyer wrote in his dissent that "in a system that allows counties to use different types of voting machines, voters already arrive at the polls with an unequal chance that their votes will be counted." He said he did not understand "why the Florida Supreme Court's recount order, which helps to redress this inequity, must be entirely prohibited based on a deficiency that could easily be remedied."[67]

Critics of the Court's ruling were particularly outraged that the conservative justices had overturned the Florida recount on equal-protection grounds but held that the decision was "limited to the present circumstances." Not only did the Court have no precedent for treating local variations in the counting of votes as unconstitutional; by applying only in the "present circumstances," the decision could not serve as a precedent in the future. But as Scalia himself had said in an opinion five years earlier, the Supreme Court "does not sit to announce 'unique' dispositions. Its principal function is to establish *precedent*—that is, to set forth principles of law that every court in America must follow."[68] Its ruling in *Bush v. Gore*, however, was like a train ticket "good for this day and train only" and, in this respect, violated rule-of-law principles.

Moreover, the justices who cited the Equal Protection Clause to overturn the Florida recount were the members of the Court most resistant to granting equal-protection claims by racial minorities in other cases. The majority did not appear to hold a principled, general conviction that local differences in voting with unequal effects (such as fewer polling stations or reliance on poorly functioning, outdated voting machinery in low-income, minority areas) warranted judicial intervention. As Georgetown law professor David Cole said at the time, the majority "created a new right out of whole cloth and made sure it ultimately protected only one person—George Bush."[69]

The Court's subsequent response to equal-protection claims in election cases bears out a point by the election-law scholar Richard Hasen that people should not take the Court's holding in *Bush v. Gore* seriously "because the Court itself did not take its holding seriously." In a series of decisions on ideological and partisan lines, the Court went on to dismiss equal-protection claims on such questions as voter ID laws requiring a government-issued photo ID (which disparately affect low-income and minority voters); purges of the voting rolls eliminating people who have not voted in the most recent elections (again disparately affecting low-income and minority voters); and partisan gerrymandering (which the Court ruled was a "non-justiciable" political question at a time when Republicans were the principal beneficiaries of partisan gerrymandering).[70]

Perhaps the most stunning and consequential of these decisions was the 2013 case *Shelby County v. Holder*, in which the Court overturned a critical part of the Voting Rights Act. Under the act, states and local jurisdictions with a history of discrimination needed to obtain federal approval ("preclearance") to make changes in voting procedures. The original 1965 legislation required Congress to reauthorize the act periodically. When Congress did so in 2006, it created an extensive documentary record of continued discrimination to show why preclearance was still needed. The vote for reauthorization was overwhelming (98 to 0 in the Senate, 390 to 33 in the House), and Bush signed the bill. Nonetheless, seven years later, the Supreme Court ruled by a 5–4 vote that the coverage formula (determining which jurisdictions were subject to preclearance) violated "the fundamental principle of equal sovereignty" of the states. Dismissing the congressionally assembled evidence from 2006, Roberts wrote that the legislation relied on "40-year-old data" and that the country had changed: Racial progress made the preclearance provisions unnecessary. Writing for the dissenters, Ginsburg referred to the majority's decision as "hubris" and added: "Throwing out preclearance when it has worked and is continuing to work to stop discriminatory changes is like throwing away your umbrella in a rainstorm because you are not getting wet." And what was the principle of "equal sovereignty of the states" invoked by Roberts? In a commentary, the federal appellate judge Richard Posner, a Republican appointee, said, "This is a principle of constitutional law of which I had never heard—for the excellent reason that . . . there is no such principle." What the Court was expressing, Posner said, was its "tenderness for 'states' rights,'" which it ignored in some cases (like gun control) but upheld in others. Posner had defended *Bush v. Gore* as necessary to avert a constitutional crisis on the grounds that the Court supplied what an overtly partisan Congress could not—a "tincture of justice." *Shelby County*, in his mind, did not even have a tincture: the decision "rests on air."[71]

While the *Shelby County* decision rested "on air," it produced a material impact on elections by opening the gates to restrictive voting laws. State governments can make voting more costly in both money and time by passing strict voter ID requirements (affecting the many people who don't have a driver's license or passport) or by allowing fewer options for voting and creating longer waiting lines. Research on the "cost" of voting, measured in both time and money, shows that between 2012 and 2020 those costs rose sharply in states that had been covered by preclearance requirements and in states controlled by Republicans. States with larger proportions of Republicans in their legislatures had already begun increasing voting costs after Obama was elected in 2008; that relationship between Republican control and voting restrictions became even stronger after *Shelby*. The evidence also shows an increase after *Shelby* in the gap between white and nonwhite voter turnout that was greatest in states formerly covered by preclearance. The effects were particularly evident among younger Blacks and Hispanics (older voters have more stably established voting habits). Using largely fictitious voter fraud as a pretext, Republicans carried out a successful campaign of voter suppression, blessed by the Supreme Court.[72]

In 2020, voter suppression and Trump's efforts to overturn the election failed to prevent Joe Biden from winning and taking office, a result that many took to be a vindication of confidence in both the electoral system and the judiciary. Trump's claims of a fraudulent and stolen election met no success with election administrators or in the courts, whether the judges were Republicans or Democrats. The situation, however, was different from 2000, when there was a legal dispute in a single state, and the Supreme Court had only to run out the clock (or rather make it appear the clock had run out) because Bush had a narrow lead in Florida at the time the Court shut down the recount. Blocking Biden in 2020 would have required far more blatant intervention involving several states and coordinated on an improbable scale.

The 2020 election consequently was not definitive on the partisan disposition of the Supreme Court's conservative justices, as became evident in their response to the federal indictment of Trump relating to his efforts to overturn the 2020 election. Like his indictment on charges of illegally retaining classified documents, the election case lent itself to the same strategy of judicial delay and running out the clock as in 2000. In 2024 judicial delay meant slow-walking the two federal criminal cases against Trump to avoid putting him in front of a jury in time for the November election. (The only criminal prosecution of Trump that did go to trial was his indictment in New York on falsification of business records concerning his hush-money payments to a porn star during the 2016 election, for which a jury unanimously convicted him.) The Supreme Court first declined to intervene in the election case in December 2023, when the special prosecutor Jack Smith asked for an immediate ruling on Trump's appeal of a district court decision that he had no immunity from the charges. In

February, the appellate court issued a lengthy opinion denying Trump immunity, but the Supreme Court again declined to expedite its deliberations on a Trump appeal. That response contrasted with another case in which the Court quickly rejected Colorado's disqualification of Trump from the ballot on the Fourteenth Amendment grounds that he had engaged in insurrection. By not issuing its decision on presidential immunity until the last day of its term, July 1, the Court effectively shielded Trump from a trial before the next presidential election for trying to overturn the previous one.

There is no mention anywhere in the Constitution of presidential immunity. Indeed, the Constitution's Impeachment Clause plainly assumes that former presidents are subject to the criminal law for the same actions that may lead to impeachment when it provides that an official impeached and convicted by the Senate "shall nevertheless be liable and subject to Indictment, Trial, Judgment and Punishment, according to Law." During Trump's second impeachment trial in the Senate, even the Republican majority leader McConnell, who favored acquittal because Trump was no longer in office, took for granted that Trump could be subsequently prosecuted. Trump's own lawyers said that if the Senate did not convict, it would not leave Trump "in any way above the law." Nonetheless, in its delayed decision in *Trump v. United States*, the Supreme Court's six conservatives ruled that a president's official acts are entitled to immunity that is "at least . . . presumptive" and potentially "absolute." The ruling, as Justice Sotomayor wrote in a powerful dissent, "makes a mockery of the principle, foundational to our Constitution and system of Government, that no man is above the law." The decision also made a mockery of the conservatives' profession of devotion to history and tradition. In a scathing aside citing *Dobbs* and *Bruen*, Sotomayor wrote, "It seems history matters to this Court only when it is convenient."[73]

Not only did the conservative justices say presidents enjoyed at least presumptive and potentially absolute immunity for their official acts; the majority defined "official acts" in an unusually expansive way.[74] As Sotomayor pointed out, the majority narrowed "the conduct considered 'unofficial' almost to a nullity" by saying "that whenever the President acts in a way that is 'not manifestly or palpably beyond [his] authority,' he is taking official action." The majority noted, for example, that the allegations regarding Trump's conduct on January 6, 2021, "largely" consisted of "Trump's communications in the form of Tweets and a public address." But, the Court continued, "most of a President's public communications are likely to fall comfortably within the outer perimeter of his official responsibilities" and would therefore enjoy presumptive immunity.[75]

Perhaps most disturbingly, the majority found that no president can be held criminally liable for any use of the government's prosecutorial powers: "The President cannot be prosecuted for conduct within his exclusive constitutional authority. Trump is therefore absolutely immune from prosecution for the alleged conduct involving his discussions with Justice Department officials." No matter that Trump told Justice Department officials to make groundless statements that the 2020 election was rigged. Information about those discussions could not even be entered as evidence as part of a prosecution for unofficial acts he undertook to overturn the election. In one of the most extraordinary aspects of the decision, the majority said no consideration could be given to motive or intent in regard to official acts.[76] If what Trump said to Justice Department officials can never be a basis for prosecuting him, all presidents are free to demand that those officials undertake investigations of an administration's enemies and instigate sham prosecutions. The Court's decision provided a license for presidential vengeance and intimidation, and it did so at a moment when a man standing on the threshold of the presidency openly called for "retribution" against his enemies and showed every intention of using the license that the Court invented.

This was not a reversion to an America of the 1950s or the 1920s. It recalled a much older, old regime. "In every use of official power," Sotomayor wrote in her dissent, "the President is now a king above the law."[77]

In the years from *Bush v. Gore* to *Trump v. United States,* Democrats had many occasions to be disappointed with the Supreme Court, but no major figure in the party called for defiance. In his concession speech after the Court decided the 2000 election, Gore called the rule of law "the source of our democratic liberties" and declared, "Let there be no doubt, while I strongly disagree with the court's decision, I accept it."[78]

After Trump lost the 2020 election and failed to overturn it, he set a different model for his party. He raged against the legal system, insisting at times that he be returned to power even before another election. "A Massive Fraud of this type and magnitude," he tweeted in 2022, "allows for the termination of all rules, regulations, and articles, even those found in the Constitution."[79] Trump's disregard for legality was not a surprise. It was more of a surprise, although by this point it was not a shock, that other

Republican leaders offered so little criticism even when Trump talked about terminating the Constitution.

What was most surprising, however, was that despite all the victories Republicans were winning in the Supreme Court, Trump-like talk of defying the courts and the Constitution spread among other Republican leaders. In 2022, a U.S. Senate candidate in Ohio said in a podcast interview that he would advise Trump if he won in 2024 to fire "every civil servant in the administrative state, replace them with our people," and when the courts intervened, tell the country (like Andrew Jackson in 1834) that "the chief justice has made his ruling. Now let him enforce it." The Senate candidate who gave that advice was Trump's future vice presidential running mate, J. D. Vance. His interviewer in 2022 responded, "Among some of my circle, the phrase 'extra-constitutional' has come up quite a bit." The more common phrase was "post-constitutional moment" as in the idea, popularized on the right by Russell Vought, that Trump would be justified in taking extreme measures because "the Left" had so distorted the Constitution. Trump named Vought, a self-described Christian nationalist, to be policy director for the Republican platform in the 2024 election (and later director of the Office of Management and Budget).[80]

With a conservative supermajority on the Supreme Court, Republicans already had the law moving decisively in their direction, as had been happening quietly for decades. They had scored historic victories on the Second Amendment, abortion, affirmative action, religion, and other issues. The Supreme Court's decision on presidential immunity offered Trump himself considerable legal protection for what he had done in the past and might do in the future. But it wasn't enough for Trump personally or for his movement and the party it had captured.

To Trump and the right, the United States is in a desperate situation, mired in decadence and facing moral and political collapse. What is required is a purge not just of the federal bureaucracy but of institutions outside the government: a program of "de-wokeification," some call it, to be imposed on schools and universities, the media, and other institutions, including business. In July 2024, the president of the Heritage Foundation, which prepared the detailed plans for a second Trump administration called Project 2025, said the country was "in the process of the second American Revolution, which will remain bloodless if the left allows it to be."[81] Conservatives discussed sending the military into Democratic cities under the Insurrection Act at the first demonstrations against Trump or on the pretext of controlling crime. They talked not just about a border wall but about mass deportations, in the millions, of long-settled illegal immigrants. Banning abortion was only part of a broader program to get native-born women to have more babies to make up for the missing labor that immigrants would otherwise provide. Christianity would be restored to what Christian nationalists believe to be its rightful place in American life.

These plans were so far-reaching that the MAGA Republicans knew they could not count on the courts, not even perhaps their own Supreme Court with its conservative supermajority, to rubber-stamp all they wanted to do. They needed a ruler with a strong hand who would not hesitate to use all possible means to bring about a second American revolution that would overturn the liberal and progressive side of the American tradition. The first step, the necessary step in this great crusade to bring back the old America even at the cost of making it a more authoritarian America, was to put Donald Trump back in power.

CHAPTER ELEVEN

The American Contradiction, 2024

He who desires or proposes to change the form of government in a state ... must needs retain at least the shadow of its ancient customs, so that the institutions may not appear to its people to have been changed.

—NICCOLÒ MACHIAVELLI, 1531[1]

RUNNING FOR PRESIDENT for the third time in 2024, Donald Trump campaigned for a double restoration: his own restoration to the office that he claimed had been stolen from him in 2020 and a restoration of the old America, the way of life that he said the elites had stolen from the people. Kamala Harris summed up the Democrats' response in a single sentence when she accepted her party's presidential nomination: "America, we are not going back."

The prospect of a national restoration, or at least what Trump could claim would return America to its past greatness, divided Americans primarily according to their historical experience. It had little appeal to Black Americans, LGBTQ+ people, or women concerned about equality and reproductive rights, groups who tended to see a MAGA restoration as a threat to their freedom. Neither was a restoration generally attractive to people with college and professional degrees, who have done well in the contemporary economy.

But the idea of a MAGA restoration did appeal to the many Americans who saw themselves on the losing end of changes that the country had undergone since the mid-twentieth century. Two opposite developments have been central to those changes: advances toward greater equality on racial and gender lines and a shift in political economy that has created a less equal society by undercutting the earning power of working people. Much of the support to "make America great again" has come from people who believe that they have lost out from both the inclusion of others and their own dispossession. They have been the most eager to embrace a narrative of national decline, the story of contemporary America that Trump was telling.

The outlook of the right has reflected a deep anger about the direction of American society. Asked in surveys about changes in America's "culture and way of life since the 1950s," two-thirds of Republicans have said that the changes have been for the worse, while two-thirds of Democrats have said the changes have been for the better.[2] American politics in the early twenty-first century hasn't just been a response to how presidents and parties have performed in the previous few years. It has been a fight over whether the tides of history have been lifting Americans up or sweeping them away.

In post–World War II America, the push to lift up the historically excluded to a position of equality began with the Black freedom struggle, which served as the model and the spark for an entire family of movements for egalitarian change, including women's and LGBTQ+ rights. The demand for racial equality also indirectly contributed to new immigration laws that had unexpected effects on America's racial and ethnic balance, and the Black example inspired ethnic-consciousness movements among the new immigrants. The sheer scale of the socially inclusive movements and their effects was unprecedented.

Yet, as I have been arguing throughout this book, while the American people changed, the nation and its institutions did not adjust for two interrelated reasons: entrenched institutional obstacles and the pushback among elites and in the electorate from people who wanted the old America back. The entrenched obstacles primarily lay in the structural bias of the Senate and Electoral College and now a Supreme Court back firmly in right-wing hands. After the mid-twentieth-century era when the Court had facilitated progressive change, conservative Republicans had succeeded in gaining control and opportunistically invoked "history and tradition" to justify reverting to a past when Black people, other racial minorities, and women had no say in the law. By the twenty-first century, the Court's majority was fully committed to a far-reaching legal counterrevolution long sought on the right. Together with other entrenched obstacles, the Court empowered the pushback against progressive change.

The pushback also came from traditional conservative political constituencies, now enlarged by economic reversals and racial, nativist, and gender backlash. The progressive movements upset traditional social hierarchies at both the interpersonal and societal levels and set off countermobilization by traditionalists across the entire social terrain. Interpersonally, the progressive project challenged the dominance of whites over racial minorities and of men over women. It encouraged people with nonconforming sexual orientations and gender identities to come out and insist on equal rights and respect. These changes offended conservatives' moral and religiously grounded beliefs about right and wrong and the proper order of social life. At the societal level, the demographic and cultural changes associated with the progressive project raised fears not just that whites would become a minority but that Americans with traditional moral and religious beliefs would be outnumbered and overpowered.

The conflict between a new and an old America did not appear suddenly with Trump. It was recognizably a continuation of the deep fissure that has run through American history, the fissure that I refer to as the American contradiction. Its principal historical origin was racial slavery—America's founding contradiction. Slavery, as I suggested in the introduction, was not just a paradox or an example of hypocrisy; it was also a social contradiction in that it generated conflict over first principles and could be resolved only through change. In its early history, the United States became divided into two economies: one based on the enslaved labor of Black people in the South, the other on free labor in the North. Two fundamentally different societies emerged as a result, and the conflict between them turned into a struggle for control of the West and ultimately the nation that produced the Civil War, the defeat of the South, and slavery's abolition.[3]

But the racial legacies of slavery persisted, and those legacies were the starting point for the Black freedom struggle in the twentieth century that ignited the new phase in the history of the American contradiction. The old and the new fissures have some clear continuities; the former Confederacy has continued to be the core of reactionary politics. But this time a crisis over control of the national government developed through a different route. The struggle for racial equality ramified into a general assault on social inequality in multiple dimensions, while an economic transformation arising for independent reasons destroyed working-class livelihoods and gave the right an expanded base of support. The crossing of those two currents, the broadening of social equality and the exacerbation of economic inequality, produced a crisis threatening the nation's constitutional foundations.

It is a mistake, though, to think that the opposition to progressive change has come entirely from whites or that white men were the whole force behind it. The multiple fronts of the progressive attack on traditional social relations alienated others who saw themselves as threatened or disrespected. As we saw in chapter 3, for example, the mid-twentieth-century battles over gender equality gave rise not to one women's movement but to two—both a feminist and an antifeminist movement. The latter drew support from women who identified with their traditional roles as wives and mothers.

Similarly, a Black or Hispanic man might identify more with traditional ideals of masculinity or with conservative moral ideals than as a member of a discriminated-against racial minority. Most discussions of identity politics focus on one aspect of identity—who people identify *as*—but neglect the equally important question of who people identify *with* and the aspirations linked to those identities. An immigrant may identify as Hispanic or Asian but still identify with white Americans and America's idealized traditions. Some of the greatest admirers of the old America have been new Americans. It seemed to make sense under Obama that the new immigrants would join Blacks in forming a unified progressive bloc of people of color, but the unity was fragile and it soon began to fray.

Still, the old fault lines did not disappear in the 2024 election. On the contrary, race, immigration, and gender were inescapably at the center of the political battle, and Trump sought to accentuate all of them. Trump was an instinctual believer in the American contradiction. He constantly sought to exploit it. Like the old radicals on the left who believed in "heightening the contradictions" of capitalism, he tried to heighten the American contradiction—to intensify the old nation's fear of America's changing people and changing culture. He waged the most relentlessly xenophobic presidential campaign by a major-party candidate in American history. He represented himself as the alpha male alternative to a feminized Democratic Party and a society with powerful women. He seized on both the racial and the gender identity of his Democratic opponent, Kamala Harris, in his characteristically denigrating ways.

When Trump had left office in January 2021 after scheming to prevent the peaceful transfer of power, many people doubted that he could possibly regain control of the Republican Party and become its nominee again in 2024. But after Republicans in the Senate refused to convict him in his second impeachment trial, the Supreme Court effectively blocked his prosecutions. The troubles of the Biden years provided him a new opening, and Trump emerged in more complete control of the Republican Party than he had before without softening his appeals in the least. He summoned all the anxieties, resentments, and fears that the progressive project had aroused. The 2024 election underlined once again the supremely high stakes that American politics had taken on, the sense that the country's foundations, its future, and its very existence as a liberal democracy could radically change depending on who won power in Washington.

The Third Trump Election

By standard criteria, the Democrats' prospects did not look good in the run-up to the 2024 presidential election. In a late September analysis, Gallup used ten conventional measures of the election environment and found a Republican edge on nearly every criterion, including party identification (48 percent Republican to 45 percent Democratic); the job approval of the Democratic incumbent (39 percent); economic confidence (low); party better able to keep America prosperous (50 percent Republican to 44 percent Democratic); and party better able to keep America safe from international threats (54 percent Republican to 40 percent Democratic). The picture also looked grim for Democrats on another oft-cited criterion, the share of voters saying the country was headed on the "right track." As of a late September NBC poll, only 28 percent of registered voters said America was on the right track, whereas no party holding the White House in the previous half-century had been returned to office when that number was below 39 percent. Some forecasting models suggested that the Democrats could win the national popular vote, though the election might again be decided by swing states critical to an Electoral College victory.[4]

But partly because of what happened in Trump's previous races and during his presidency, the 2024 election was far from normal. The shadows of 2020 and the assault on the Capitol on January 6, 2021, fell over 2024. No major-party candidate had ever run for president while facing trial for attempting to overturn the previous election's results. Trump and other Republican leaders refused to acknowledge the legitimacy of the 2020 outcome, sowed doubts about the integrity of the 2024 election, and prepared to fight the counting of ballots and certification of the vote.

The 2024 election was also unusual in the personal unpopularity of both parties' original presumptive nominees. Biden and Trump coasted to victory in the primaries, even though each of them had unfavorable ratings of about 60 percent in public opinion polls; the same share of the public also thought they were too old to serve a second term.[5] Biden was now 81 years old, Trump 78, both of them visibly past their prime; the prospect of a rematch between them filled many people with dread. Democrats could no longer deny they were in trouble after Biden appeared physically frail as well as foggy and unfocused in a debate with Trump in late June. Pressed by party leaders, he finally stepped aside as the Democratic nominee on July 21 and endorsed Vice President Harris, who quickly consolidated support. In a September debate, she thoroughly dominated Trump, though he insisted, against the overwhelming judgment of observers, that he had won. A week later, he claimed that the audience had been on his side and "went crazy" in supporting him even though the debate had taken place without any audience in an empty hall.

Now it was Trump whose age and mental acuity became an issue as he rambled on in long, disjointed speeches and seemed more forgetful than he had been in earlier races. At one event in October, he talked about the size of the golfer Arnold Palmer's penis. Observers debated whether Trump's disinhibited behavior was early-stage dementia or just his characteristic willingness to break norms, the sexual disinhibition that enabled him to abuse women and the political disinhibition that enabled him to assault a major party and upend the political system.[6]

In other respects, the 2024 race resembled the previous Trump elections but was still historically abnormal. With his customary venom and insulting racist subtext, Trump said that while Biden had become "mentally impaired," Harris was "born that way." Appealing to sexist stereotypes, he said that foreign leaders would treat Harris as a "play toy." He also variously described her as a "lunatic," "a Marxist, communist, fascist person," and a "shit vice president." His opponents were "vermin." Democrats were "the enemy within"; he could use the military against them (singling out former House Speaker Nancy Pelosi and Representative Adam Schiff, the California Democrat running for Senate in 2024). He said that if he lost, Jews would have "a lot" to do with it.[7]

While the polls indicated a large majority of Americans thought the country was on the "wrong track," the significance of that opinion in 2024 was unclear. Trump, after all, was a former president campaigning for a restoration. Harris framed her entire candidacy about "not going back," pursuing "a new way forward," and "turning the page" on the kind of politics that Trump represented. If 2024 was a "change election," which side represented change? By the fall, some polls showed more people thought of Harris, not Trump, as the change candidate. But she undercut her own efforts to distinguish herself when she said in a television interview that nothing "comes to mind" when asked what she would have done differently from Biden over the previous four years. Trump turned that sound bite into an ad.[8]

Democrats could take encouragement from the 2022 midterm elections. That year the polls had also indicated a majority of voters thought the country was on the wrong track. Most analysts expected a "red wave," conforming to the usual midterm pattern favoring the party out of the White House. But the usual expectations did not account for another incumbent power: the Republican Supreme Court majority, who had just overturned *Roe v. Wade.* Many people who thought the country was on the wrong track may have had abortion rights in mind and feared other policies supported by Republicans.

Instead of a red wave, the 2022 midterms brought surprising results. Democrats defended all the party's senators up for re-election and even took one additional seat. They also won most of the hotly contested gubernatorial races, while only narrowing losing the U.S. House of Representatives. In fifteen states with closely contested races for governor or senator, Democrats outperformed their vote in Biden's 2020 victory by 1.5 percentage points and won thirteen of eighteen races. High voter turnout was critical to the Democrats' success. In the other thirty-five states, however, Democrats suffered the kind of fall-off in support, 6.8 percentage points, typical in midterm elections for the incumbent party. In two Democratic states where turnout declined, New York and California, the party lost twelve seats in the House, enough to give Republicans a nine-seat, 222–213 majority.[9]

The high turnout in contested states in 2022 was potentially relevant to the presidential election because the United States would not conduct a national election for president in 2024. Instead, it would conduct an election for president in a small number of contested swing states. There weren't even fifteen projected battlegrounds, only seven, where the parties and groups aligned with them invested their resources: Pennsylvania, Michigan, and Wisconsin in the North and Georgia, North Carolina, Arizona, and Nevada in the Sunbelt. Political observers expected that, as in 2016 and 2020, the election would depend on a small fraction of the national electorate, the voters who could make the difference in the few closely divided states of a closely divided country. If, as in 2022, Democrats again did better in contested races than elsewhere, they might win the swing states even if they lagged elsewhere.

The Democrats' success in the 2022 midterms and in special elections proved to be significant in another way: it led to complacency among Democratic leaders as they approached the 2024 primaries. With party leaders lined up behind Biden, no prominent Democrat challenged him for the nomination despite his age and public disapproval of his administration. Unlike Clinton in 1994 and Obama in 2010, Biden didn't reorient his administration to win back voters who disapproved of his performance. To win in 2024, Democratic leaders thought they just needed to mobilize anti-MAGA voters against Trump. But the midterms and special elections that gave Democrats this false confidence had much lower turnout than a presidential election. In 2016 and 2020, Trump had already demonstrated an ability to draw infrequent voters to the polls, and in 2024 he would have new developments working in his favor.[10]

The 2024 Fault Lines

Changed circumstances on the Southwestern border, in the tech and media environment, and in the economy put Trump in a stronger position in 2024 than he had been four years earlier.

Ever since 2016, Trump had portrayed an America under siege by migrants. Although those appeals to fear had failed in the 2018, 2020, and 2022 elections, a surge in migrants had created a political crisis for Democrats by 2023 and enabled Trump to find broader support for his anti-immigrant campaign.

The media environment had also become more favorable to Trump as a result of an emerging tech-MAGA alliance. Biden's appointees at the Federal Trade Commission were aggressively pursuing antitrust cases to break up the major tech monopolies; his administration was also considering regulations of cryptocurrencies and artificial intelligence that tech interests opposed. In 2020, the major social media companies had tried to limit electoral as well as public-health misinformation, but by 2024 they had dropped those efforts. After buying Twitter in 2022, Elon Musk turned it into a right-wing propaganda platform and allied himself with Trump.

Trump also benefited politically from a spike in prices under Biden, chiefly an effect of the COVID-19 pandemic and related supply-chain problems. After hitting a peak annualized rate of 9 percent in early 2022, inflation gradually receded, but Trump could point to his own term as president as a time when the cost of living and interest rates were lower. Voters rated the economy and immigration as the two top issues facing the country, and on both of those the polls indicated Trump had the advantage.

When Biden took office in 2021, the United States was in an unusually pro-immigration mood, probably due to the sympathy for immigrants generated by Trump's family separations and other harsh policies. Since 1965, Gallup has asked whether immigration should be "kept at its present level, increased or decreased." The only years Gallup has ever found more Americans favoring an increase rather than a reduction were 2020 and 2021. Gallup also asked whether immigration was a "good" thing or a "bad" thing. At the start of the 2020s, about three-quarters of Americans said it was a good thing.[11]

Biden's initial policies reflected that singular moment and his own determination to adopt a humane approach to migrants, in stark contrast with his predecessor's cruelty. But by the beginning of 2024, the public mood and the politics of immigration had taken a radical turn. Americans favored a reduction over an increase in immigration by a more than 3-to-1 margin, and only 32 percent of Americans expressed any confidence in Biden's immigration policies.[12] Confronted with mass disapproval in an election year, the president reversed course and sought to shut down the border. It was too late, however, to change the public's verdict on his immigration policies. Biden's reversal, and the little that Harris had to say about immigration in her campaign, also seemingly validated Trump's view that a humane, welcoming immigration policy is a mistake.

One of the tragic aspects of Biden's presidency was the setback he dealt to public support for immigration by failing to act promptly to avert a border crisis. After taking office, Biden reversed many of the policies that Trump had used to deter migrants and provided new ways for migrants to get temporary authorization to stay in the United States. With the end of the COVID pandemic and the eventual lifting of emergency restrictions that had imposed a blanket ban on asylum seekers, the number of migrants on the Southwestern border increased dramatically. No doubt desperate conditions in many countries such as Venezuela and Ukraine pushed migrants to flee. The prospect of jobs in the United States, where an economy recovering faster than others had millions of job openings, also pulled migrants in America's direction.

But Biden's immigration policies also pulled them to the United States in such large numbers that border regions seemed in chaos and the asylum system was overwhelmed. Migrant apprehensions on the border rose to record levels, exceeding two million in both 2022 and 2023. Furthermore, a majority of those apprehensions, far more than in previous years, resulted in migrants staying in the United States rather than being expelled. As the number of migrants seeking asylum overwhelmed detention centers, they were released into the interior with instructions to show up at an uncertain date, perhaps years later, in immigration court. Many people in distant countries learned about these conditions through online and personal networks and made a rational decision to risk a dangerous journey to reach and cross the U.S. border, knowing that they would likely be able to stay. In 2022, two Republican governors, Greg Abbott in Texas and Ron DeSantis in Florida, made sure that the migrants didn't all just stay in their states, and began shipping them to Democratic cities. Eventually tens of thousands of them arrived in New York, Chicago, Boston, Denver, and elsewhere, raising pressures on housing and other services as well as local budgets. The governors' strategy worked. It broadened concerns about the migrant surge and succeeded in splitting the Democratic Party.[13]

Biden was slow to recognize that his initial policies would contribute to a crisis. It wasn't until the end of 2023 that the administration secured Mexico's agreement to limit the number of migrants arriving at the U.S. border. In January 2024, Biden said that if Congress gave him the authority to shut down the border, "I would use it the day I sign the bill into law." He endorsed a bill being negotiated by congressional Democrats and Republicans that would have been a major enforcement-oriented shift in immigration law—until Trump, preferring to keep the issue boiling, shot the legislation down. In June, after long insisting that he needed authority from Congress, Biden discovered, lo and behold, that he could do on his own what was needed to stop the flood of migrants. He issued an executive order denying migrants asylum if they arrived illegally and established new border procedures making it less likely migrants would qualify for asylum. By September, border apprehensions fell to the lowest levels in years, but the election was now only weeks away.[14]

Biden had put the public's tolerance for immigrants to a stress test it should never have had to face. In 2022 and 2023, the administration began extending immigration parole on a nationality basis to migrants from Cuba, Venezuela, Haiti, and Nicaragua. If they passed background checks and had a financial sponsor, they could take flights to the United States and receive legal permission to stay for up to two years. In addition, border authorities began granting short-term parole to migrants encountered illegally crossing the border. Parole was only one of several forms of temporary protection. According to an estimate in the *New York Times* in November 2024, 2.3 million migrants had received temporary protections of one kind or another, while the number of migrants released into America's cities awaiting resolution of their asylum claims more than doubled to 7.6 million. The administration also raised the number of immigrants receiving permanent legal residency back up past one million a year.[15]

Even before Biden, the supporters of immigration needed to recognize that they have been asking a great deal of their fellow citizens. The United States has by far the most international migrants of any country in the world, more than the next four countries combined.[16] Nearly everywhere in the world, people fear outsiders, especially racial and religious outsiders; it is not unusual for them to see no benefit to themselves from immigration, even if that is incorrect. They may conceive of their nation's economy in static terms as producing a fixed number of jobs, which immigrants will only steal away. They may worry, not unreasonably, that their taxes will go up and housing will be in short supply when large numbers of immigrants arrive in their area from poverty-stricken countries.

Public officials who believe immigration is a good thing must take into consideration the many people who have reasonable worries that it is a bad thing for them. Political leaders have to give them as little basis for their fears as possible and make the case that all citizens can benefit from the infusion of energy that immigrants bring. Most of all, they must ensure that immigration is orderly and under control. Biden failed to do these things and as a result he squandered the support for immigration that existed at the start of his presidency. He also may have brought to an end a sixty-year period of immigration that enriched America culturally and economically, albeit at the cost of rising internal conflict.

The public, though, hadn't been entirely wrong in 2020 to think that immigration was a good thing, and not only for humanitarian reasons. The influx of immigrants did have positive effects on the national economy. A report of the Federal Reserve Bank of Dallas, based on estimates by the

Congressional Budget Office, projected that "as a result of the immigration surge," GDP over the 2024–2034 period would rise by $8.9 trillion, federal tax revenues would increase by $1.2 trillion, and the federal deficit would fall by $900 billion. Despite the influx of immigrants, unemployment didn't just stay low under Biden; it stayed lower for longer than during any other administration since the 1960s.[17]

For Trump, of course, immigrants never benefited Americans, only hurt them, taking their jobs, committing crimes, overrunning their communities. His tirades against immigration became even more strident than in the past. Channeling the Nazis, he said immigrants were "poisoning the blood of our country." Channeling eugenicists, he said they had "bad genes." Seizing on a debunked rumor from Springfield, Ohio, he told the millions watching his debate with Harris that Haitian immigrants were eating their neighbors' cats and dogs. Seizing on another debunked story from Aurora, Colorado, he said that gangs of Venezuelan immigrants had taken over whole areas of the town, which later became "sections of the state." He added, "Getting them out will be a bloody story." In an October speech in Aurora—an example of what Richard Hofstadter called the "paranoid style in American politics"—Trump declared, "Kamala has imported an army of illegal alien gang members and migrant criminals from the dungeons of the third world." Instead of just proposing a wall to keep migrants out, he promised "the largest deportation operation in history" to expel them en masse.[18]

Trump's turn to draconian policies brought a great many Americans along with him. Polls during the 2024 campaign were widely reported as showing that about half of Americans, including surprising proportions of Hispanics, supported "mass deportations"—but the same polls often had conflicting findings. For example, a Pew survey in August found 56 percent of voters in favor of mass deportations—but also 61 percent in favor of a pathway to citizenship for illegal immigrants. An October *New York Times/Siena* poll found 45 percent of Hispanics in favor of mass deportations—but also 67 percent in favor of "a pathway to citizenship for *all undocumented immigrants* currently living in the United States" (emphasis added). People who supported such a broad pathway to citizenship could not have understood Trump to be intending to deport long-settled unauthorized Hispanic immigrants. This failure to absorb Trump's announced intentions reflected a broader problem. Many people did not take seriously the enormity of what Trump was proposing, whether about immigration, tariffs, the federal civil service, America's alliances, or other matters.[19]

According to the polls, Trump's vilification of immigrants and plans for deportations weren't driving Hispanic voters to the Democrats. One of the unexpected changes between the 2016 and 2020 elections had been Trump's improved showing among Hispanics, up from 28 percent to 36 percent of the two-party Hispanic vote, within shouting distance of Bush's 40 percent level in 2004. But whereas Bush had been pro-immigration, Trump's hostility to immigrants had been clear from the start. As one Republican strategist, Patrick Ruffini, noted in a 2023 book, Trump had demonstrated the viability of "a hard turn toward populism" that not only "ran up margins in the white working class beyond the party's wildest hopes" but also surprisingly didn't cost the GOP votes among minorities. The Republicans, Ruffini argued, were now the party that could build a "multiracial populist coalition." That was still a long shot at the time; in 2022, 85 percent of the Republican vote came from non-Hispanic whites. But Trump's ability to use nativist appeals to win support from whites, while making gains among Hispanics and Blacks, offered Republicans hope for 2024 and beyond.[20]

The receptiveness of many Hispanic voters to Trump should not have been a surprise. The racially reductionist view of American politics assumed that Hispanics would vote as part of a bloc of people of color. One problem with that assumption was that not even a majority of Hispanics thought they were people of color. In a 2021 survey that asked Americans whether they considered themselves persons of color, only 45 percent of Hispanics said yes, compared with 62 percent of Asian Americans and 95 percent of Blacks. Hispanics who said they weren't people of color were identifying more with whites than with Blacks. Four of ten Hispanics born in the United States have been marrying outside their own ethnic group, chiefly with non-Hispanic whites. Most second- and third-generation Hispanics primarily or exclusively speak English, work in the mainstream economy rather than an ethnic enclave, and do not regard themselves as a permanently racialized outsider group in American society. When asked in surveys in 2024, two-thirds of Hispanics did not think Trump was talking about people like them when he attacked immigrants. They might be offended by some of Trump's rhetoric, but they did not necessarily rule out voting for him.[21]

Trump also continually sought ways to set minority groups against each other. Immigrants, he said, were taking "Black jobs." Speaking to a group of Black journalists, he said that Kamala Harris was not authentically Black: "She was Indian all the way, and then all of a sudden she made a turn and she became a Black person." Biden's program of humanitarian parole had benefited Cubans as well as Haitians, but Trump directed his attacks at the Haitians, the ones whom he had earlier referred to as coming from a "shithole" country. His efforts to drive wedges into the minority vote focused particularly on winning over Hispanic and Black men. Polls during the campaign showed that while Black and Hispanic women supported Harris, Trump ran better among the men.[22] Gender proved to be as important a fault line in 2024 as race and immigration.

Even before Harris became the Democratic nominee, the politics of gender had taken on high significance in the 2024 presidential race. In response to the Supreme Court decision on abortion, the supporters of reproductive rights mobilized to oppose Trump and block Republicans from passing a national abortion ban. Trump and his running mate, J. D. Vance, campaigned as the unreconstructed defenders of gender traditionalism and sought to capitalize on masculine backlash, especially among young men.[23]

The political gender gap, with men moving to the right of women, has been roughly a half-century in the making throughout the world's high-income countries. The geographic breadth of this political realignment suggests that the underlying causes are changes in the advanced economies that have reduced the advantages that men once enjoyed. Not only have men without higher education lost out economically from the decline of industrial jobs; women have made gains in education and the post-industrial labor market, and their increased earning power has given them more options and leverage in relations with men. This shift in relative economic fortunes has coincided with the rise of feminism and support from left-of-center parties for gender equality and LGBTQ+ inclusion. As a result of that support, Democrats and other parties of the left have taken the blame from men for an economic and social transformation that has not had strictly partisan origins. The decline of industrial unions has also eliminated a basis of left-wing fraternity.

Although American men overall have moved toward the Republicans in national politics since 1980, the youth vote has given Democrats grounds for hope that the losses among men have been transitional, a reflection of older men's difficulties in adjusting to more equal gender relations and a changed economy. Young men's support for Democrats reached a high point in Barack Obama's victories. According to exit polls in 2008, Obama won 62 percent of 18- to 29-year-old men, as well as 69 percent of women that age. As recently as the 2022 midterms, Democrats had won 54 percent of young men as well as 72 percent of young women. Their 65 percent of the 2020 vote among all 18- to 29-year-olds (male and female), 3 percentage points higher than Biden's support in 2020, was stunning. In each of the four elections from 2016 to 2022, the Democrats won at least 60 percent of the total youth vote, an auspicious sign for the party's future.[24]

Polling during the 2024 campaign, however, suggested that while Democrats were running up strong margins among young women, they were losing support from young men. The Democrats' deficit with young men was not specific to Harris; it had already emerged in polling while Biden was the presumptive Democratic nominee. Democrats faced the risk that rather than being a fluke in 2024, the drift of young men to the right might signal a long-term political development. Young men were diverging from women their age in their life chances as well as their political views. A narrative of national decline may have made sense to them because it fit the experience of many men in their generation. They were falling behind women in education, employment, and earnings and showing signs of rising distress in measures of mental health and suicide. The acceleration of these problems had occurred in an era when liberals and progressives had continually paired the words "toxic" and "masculinity." Young men had a basis for feeling that Democratic sympathies were entirely with women. Democrats weren't addressing themselves to young men at all.[25]

The alienation of young men from progressive politics represented a political opportunity for Trump and the Republicans. In the hope of reaping a harvest of new votes, Republicans mounted a voter registration drive targeted at young men, and Trump and Vance made masculinity a focus of their campaign. They appeared on YouTube shows and podcasts with large audiences of young men and cultivated influencers in the manosphere. But while both Trump and Vance upheld traditional masculine ideals, they represented two different sides of masculine backlash and reactionary gender politics.[26]

Trump offered young men a fantasy of manhood as an unapologetic assertion of dominance. He personified the enjoyment of fame, power, and sex without obligations—the fantasy behind his taped *Access Hollywood* line, "When you're a star, they let you do it. You can do anything." Perhaps as compensation for his lack of military experience, he identified himself with fighting sports, like Dana White's mixed martial arts Ultimate Fighting Championship, part of his carefully cultivated image of dominance and toughness. White introduced Trump for his acceptance speech at the Republican National Convention, and the former wrestler Hulk

Hogan stirred up the crowd for him, calling Trump a "gladiator." Trump entered the convention with "It's a Man's, Man's, Man's World" playing in the background.

Vance's appeal to male backlash was more closely tied to social conservatism, an exaltation of the old male-breadwinner family and sharply distinguished, biologically given roles for men and women. He gained notoriety for his mockery of "childless cat ladies," his view that women should de-emphasize careers and have more babies, and his suggestion that people with children should have more votes than those without. In a 2021 podcast interview, he said that when women prioritize careers over children, it "causes them to chase things that will make them miserable and unhappy." Presumably, men should chase those things because that is what they are meant to do according to their inherent, God-given nature. But, in Vance's view, the elites were trying to "suppress" masculinity, an insidious plot to thwart male vitality and turn boys into girls, all evidence of a liberal culture gone awry. At one point, though, Vance suggested that he and Trump had an appeal to gay men. In an interview with the podcaster Joe Rogan, he said he wouldn't be surprised if he and Trump won "the normal gay guy vote." Apparently, in Vance's mind, some gay men were normal—perhaps like his Silicon Valley mentor Peter Thiel or Trump's old mentor Roy Cohn—and consequently, unlike the abnormal ones and unlike lesbians, would vote Republican.[27]

Neither Trump's nor Vance's vision of masculinity was new. Trump's had its origins in Hugh Hefner's 1950s *Playboy* and its best-known contemporary expression in the online manosphere. The vision of manhood in that world has been primarily about men's freedom to say and do what they like, not about family obligations. In contrast, Vance's celebration of the family and distinct gender roles was an update of the campaign for "traditional family values" of the 1970s and 1980s, rooted in the Christian right. With his Silicon Valley connections, Vance (along with Elon Musk) personified a coming together of tech bros and religious conservatives, which lent gender traditionalism a veneer of novelty. The tech right was another testosterone-fueled expansion of the Trump coalition. In the fall, Musk, who had a trans daughter lost to what he called the "woke-mind virus," declared himself "dark MAGA." As the world's wealthiest man, with control of a major social media platform and 200 million followers, he became a formidable investor and partner in the Trump campaign.

No doubt substantial numbers of young men did and do respond to these traditionalist gender appeals. In different ways, Trump and Vance raised the possibility for young men of being the boss at home in the way their grandfathers could have been.

But neither Trump's model of unrestrained male dominance nor Vance's call to revive the old male-breadwinner ideal bears any relation to contemporary realities. Neither represents a successful way to be a man today, much less a practical way to help young men falling behind their female peers. In contemporary America, where women are doing better at school and are overrepresented in the most rapidly growing occupations, Vance's prescription for women to return to the home is as much a fantasy as Trump's unapologetic model of male domination. Relations between men and women are more equal today because, in the economy, men and women have become more equal. Women used to need men more than men needed women. Under those conditions, as the nineteenth-century feminist writer Charlotte Perkins Gilman put it, "The female of the genus homo is economically dependent on the male. He is her food supply."[28] That world was the source of Trump and Vance's ideas, but it is remote from the lives most men and women lead. The tradwife is a luxury most young men will not be able to afford. But the appeal of that old America to young men was another reason, like Trump's appeal to Hispanic and Black men, that Republicans had grounds for hope of not only beating Harris but changing the political calculus about the American future.

The Democrats Try to Occupy a New Center

The Democrats faced a democracy dilemma in 2024. After Harris replaced Biden on the Democratic ticket, the presidential race was virtually tied in both national and swing-state polls, a reflection of the obdurate fact that at least half the voters did not see Trump's overt violation of democratic norms as disqualifying. The party needed new ways of making its case against Trump and of overcoming the reservations that persuadable voters might have about Harris.

Four years earlier, Joe Biden had chosen Kamala Harris as his running mate amid a national "reckoning" with racism and injustice that had followed the murder of a Black man, George Floyd, by the Minneapolis police on May 25, 2020. Harris would probably not have been the party's presidential nominee in 2024 if not for that fleeting moment in 2020 when the Movement for Black Lives was at its height. Her speech to the Democratic convention as the party's vice-presidential candidate that year emphasized her identity as a woman and gave prominent attention to "structural racism."

That political frame nearly disappeared from the Democratic campaign in 2024. Harris and other party leaders wanted to occupy the center ground in American politics and culture that Republicans had vacated. In late July, two weeks before Harris asked Minnesota Governor Tim Walz to join her on the Democratic ticket, Walz introduced a new word into the national conversation about Trump and Vance: "These guys are just weird. They're running for He-Man Women Haters Club or something, that's what they go at. That's not what people are interested in."[29] The idea that Trump and Vance were "weird" epitomized an effort by Democrats to reset the debate about American culture and public norms. The opposite of weird is normal, and Democrats were intent on representing themselves as "team normal." But it was a different normal from what I described in chapter 1 as "midcentury normal," the old normal of the 1950s that social conservatives revered.

"The introduction of *weird*," Gal Beckerman pointed out in *The Atlantic*, "took one of the central subtexts of modern American politics and made it text." Since the 1960s, Republicans had represented themselves as speaking for the majority—the "silent majority" or the "moral majority"—and attacked Democrats as effete snobs, unpatriotic weaklings, and dangerous deviants from conventional morals. In 2024 Democrats sought to flip the script. They drew pointed contrasts to Trump's affinity for Putin and other dictators and the aspersions he cast on fallen or wounded American soldiers as "suckers" and "losers." The Democratic National Convention rocked with chants of "USA! USA!"; its theme was freedom, and much of the appeal was libertarian. On abortion, Walz said that in Minnesota "even if we wouldn't make those same choices for ourselves, we've got a golden rule: Mind your own damn business." Harris talked about "the freedom to live safe from gun violence in our schools, communities and places of worship," but in her debate with Trump, she noted that she owned a gun and, in an interview with Oprah Winfrey, she said, "If somebody breaks into my house, they're getting shot." She campaigned in a joyful key, but she emphasized her no-nonsense background as a prosecutor and pledged to maintain America's armed forces as the "most lethal fighting force in the world." She sought to dispel the stereotypes of a progressive Black woman that she had good reason to believe would make it impossible for her to win.[30]

In 2024, however, the Democrats weren't just making a play for centrists and conservatives. They were promoting a synthesis of American traditions and hard-won cultural changes. They were trying to overcome the American contradiction. They wanted Americans to understand freedom and normality in a new way appropriate to a changed America.

During the national convention the most moving description of a new normal came in Transportation Secretary Pete Buttigieg's description of an everyday meal with his husband and children, "when the dog is barking and the air fryer is beeping and the mac and cheese is boiling over and it feels like all the political negotiating experience in the world is not enough to get our 3-year-old son and our 3-year-old daughter to just wash their hands and sit at the table." It was an example, Buttigieg said, of what had been impossible "as recently as 25 years ago when an anxious teenager growing up in Indiana wondered if he would ever find belonging in the world.... This kind of life went from impossible, to possible; from possible to real; from real to almost ordinary, in less than half a lifetime." The ordinariness of a same-sex couple's family life, that new normal, was a revolutionary achievement.

"But that didn't just happen," Buttigieg declared. "It was brought about through idealism and courage, through organizing and persuasion, and storytelling and, yes, through politics. The right kind of politics."[31] This too was what Democrats meant when, in response to Harris, they chanted over and over, "We are not going back."

Republicans were having none of this, and in the fall the Trump campaign answered the Democrats' efforts at cultural repositioning by investing heavily in an ad about Harris's support for the use of public funds for surgery for transgender prisoners. In a 2019 clip used in the ad, Harris said, "Every transgender inmate in the prison system would have access." The ad ended with the devastating tag line, "Kamala is for they/them; Trump is for you." After a popular Black radio host, Charlamagne Tha God, saw the ad on football games, he said, "Hell no, I don't want my taxpayer dollars going to that." The Trump campaign then produced a second version with that clip (over Charlamagne's protests). Testing of the ad by a Democratic group found that it moved the race 2.7 percentage points toward Trump among voters who saw it. The ad worked because it conveyed the message that Harris was too liberal, her priorities were wrong, and her efforts to suggest otherwise were deceptive.[32]

In October, top generals who had served under Trump introduced another term for him into the national conversation—fascist. They weren't the first to call Trump a fascist, but they carried more weight, or at least it seemed they would. General Mark Milley, former chairman of the Joint Chiefs of Staff, called Trump "the most dangerous person to this country ... a fascist to the core." General Jim Mattis, Trump's original secretary of defense, later said he agreed with that assessment. Former Marine General John Kelly told the *New York Times* that Trump "certainly prefers the dictator approach to government," confirmed reports that Trump had made admiring comments about Adolf Hitler, and asked why American generals couldn't be like Hitler's generals. Reviewing a definition of fascism, Kelly said, "It's a far-right authoritarian, ultranationalist political ideology and movement characterized by a dictatorial leader, centralized autocracy, militarism, forcible suppression of opposition, belief in a natural social hierarchy.... [Trump] certainly falls into the general definition of fascist, for sure."[33] As Trump's longest-serving White House chief of staff, Kelly did know the man.

Since 2016 scholars had been debating whether Trumpism was a form of fascism, but Democrats had shied away from using that term. One noted historian of fascism, Robert O. Paxton, had initially resisted applying "this most toxic of labels." After January 6, 2021, however, he changed his mind because in assaulting the Capitol, Trump's supporters were virtually reenacting similar attacks on democratic governments by fascists in the 1920s and 1930s. Yet even Paxton did not think that using the word was politically useful. "Fascist" had long been thrown about so loosely that it had lost clarity and bite. Trump would (and did) just throw it back at Democrats. But Milley and Kelly broke a political and journalistic taboo by pointing out the obvious commonalities between fascism and Trumpism. Their blunt description of Trump gave Harris and the Democrats a new way of ringing the alarm about how dangerous Trump was. When asked whether Trump was a fascist, Harris said he was.[34]

The trouble with ringing the alarm was that Americans had apparently lost their capacity for alarm. Even Trump's new threats had somehow become old news. A group campaigning on Harris's behalf tested an ad using Kelly's charge that Trump was a fascist but found it wasn't effective.[35] In her closing argument, Harris did not ignore the threat to democracy, but she focused on the everyday economic problems that preoccupied the voters she needed to win.

In 2024, Democrats confronted an economic dilemma along with a democracy dilemma. The economic dilemma stemmed from the disconnect between the U.S. economy's strong performance and the public's consistently downbeat opinion about it. Economic commentators called the phenomenon a "vibecession." In surveys, many Americans rated their own personal economic situation as good while they said the national economy was bad.

Indeed, they said the economy was getting worse when it was getting better. Seventy-four percent of respondents in an April 2024 *Wall Street Journal* poll of swing states said inflation had gone in the wrong direction in the past year, when, in fact, inflation had fallen from 6 percent a year earlier to 3.2 percent. In a survey for the *Guardian* around the same time, 49 percent of Americans said they believed unemployment to be at a fifty-year high, even though it was under 4 percent and near a fifty-year low![36]

When inflation jumped early in Biden's term, some economists argued that bringing it down would take years of high unemployment. Instead, the economy had a "soft landing," and the United States avoided a recession. But that early spurt in prices left many people struggling to keep up with the cost of living and higher interest rates, and it exacerbated long-term problems of housing affordability. These realities were not just vibes, and they accounted for much of the dissatisfaction behind the low opinion that many Americans held about the national economy. By 2023, however, the U.S. economic recovery was the envy of many other countries and the United States had the lowest inflation rate of the leading economies in the Group of Seven, though Biden got little credit for it.[37]

Biden also got little credit for his efforts to deal with long-term economic needs, including a bipartisan infrastructure program, which Trump had promised but never delivered; the CHIPS and Science Act, which provided aid for rebuilding the U.S. semiconductor industry; the climate reforms in the 2022 Inflation Reduction Act, which were projected to cut U.S. net greenhouse emissions substantially by 2030; and the revived antitrust efforts under the Federal Trade Commission to break up monopolies.[38] The tepid response to these measures in public opinion partly reflected Biden's inability to communicate his own achievements, but it also illustrated a deeper problem. American politics was not rewarding political leaders who made compromise efforts to promote the long-term common good.

As the 2024 election campaign got underway, some analysts suggested that public opinion on the economy was just lagging the objective economic measures. By 2024 a variety of social indicators had improved after the pandemic-driven spike not only in inflation but in rates of violent crime, fatal accidents, and other problems.[39] The Misery Index—the sum of the unemployment rate and inflation rate—was at one time thought to be a good measure of the overall state of the economy. The index hit 20.13 in 1980, when Reagan defeated Carter, and it stood at 10.58 in 1992, when Clinton defeated Bush. On the eve of the 2024 election, the Misery Index was just 6.5—the most recently measured unemployment rate, 4.1 percent, plus the inflation rate, which was down to 2.4 percent. These were exceptionally good numbers, but the economic "vibes" were still bad. In October, according to Gallup, 46 percent rated the economy "poor," while only 25 percent said it was "good" or "excellent." Those numbers resulted from drastically different partisan views. Republicans overwhelmingly rated the economy "poor," but only a slight majority of Democrats called it "excellent" or "good."[40]

Surveys showed that Americans rated both their local economy and their own personal economic situation better than the national economy.[41] Those differences suggest that opinions about the national economy were based less on direct experience than on feelings of despair about America's direction, the emotions that the conservative media and Trump's story of a "dying" America reflected and amplified.

Trump's story of a dying nation also served as justification for the drastic measures that he was proposing. In a second term, he proposed doing what he had done in his first—raising tariffs, curbing immigration, and cutting taxes—only now on a much larger scale. These proposals were the source of a second disconnect. If what troubled you was inflation, Trump's economic policies did not make a lot of sense. "Groceries, cars, everything—we're going to get the prices down," he said in September. But the taxes on imports he was proposing, 10 to 20 percent tariffs on all imported goods and 60 percent tariffs on imports from China, would raise prices while triggering retaliatory tariffs against U.S. exports. Mass deportations on an unprecedented scale would also raise prices for groceries and other goods. The United States did not have a large pool of idle, able-bodied workers to replace the undocumented immigrants who accounted for about three-eighths of agricultural workers and one-fifth of construction workers. Trump was also proposing nearly $8 trillion of deficit spending. Many voters did not recognize the likely inflationary effects of Trump's policies, though the financial markets did—analysts called his policies a "reflationary cocktail."[42] Trump's policies were less a rational answer to Americans' economic problems than culture war by other means.

Commentators often referred to Trump as a "populist" and Harris and the Democrats as "elitist," but the objective facts about who would benefit from their policies were the reverse. Although Trump did pledge to make tips, overtime, and Social Security payments exempt from income taxes, his biggest giveaways would go to corporations and people with top incomes, and his tariffs would hit lower- and middle-income people hardest because of their effects on consumer prices. Harris, in contrast, proposed to eliminate Trump's earlier tax cuts for people making over $400,000 a year and to expand child tax credits with broader eligibility for low-income families. Trump's various proposals for exempting income from Social Security taxes would also accelerate a funding crisis in the Social Security system. He promised to lift regulations from financial institutions and cryptocurrencies, which would increase the risk of a financial crisis.[43]

After the election, analysts would point to Harris's edge among voters with incomes over $100,000 and Trump's edge among those with incomes under that amount as evidence that Trump's Republicans had turned the relation of class to politics upside down. But this misses the more complex reality. While Democrats had become the party of the more highly educated, they continued to favor policies benefiting working-class interests and for that reason had the backing of labor unions. While Republicans won working-class votes through xenophobic and culturally conservative appeals, they were still the party of business and favored policies benefiting those with capital and top incomes. American politics now pitted one party dominated by the educated against another party dominated by concentrated wealth, but the former still sought to build a bottom-up majority based on progressive taxes, redistributive programs, and other interests in a broadly shared prosperity.

But the inflation spike of 2021–2022 had hit many low-income people hard, and Harris struggled to make the Democrats' economic case to much of the party's own base. Personal experience with the rising cost of living probably mattered more to voters than anything she could say about the consequences of Trump's and her own policies. Harris was passionate about abortion and the rights of women, but she didn't have a message about the economy to match Trump's simple story that foreign countries and immigrants were taking unfair advantage of Americans and he would stand up to them. The gender and educational-class divides were now central to American politics. The outcome of the election would depend on whether Harris had a large enough margin among women and the highly educated to overcome Trump's margin among men and the less educated. As it turned out, she didn't, though the vote was close.

Trump's Restoration

The 2024 election restored Trump to the presidency, but whether his working-class supporters will also get their restoration, the restoration of the old America of their imagining, is another matter. They may get a new era of authoritarianism and crony capitalism instead, more unequal and corrupt than anything they have known.

Trump's victory was clear-cut. He swept all seven of the swing states and, for the first time in his three races, won the national popular vote. The United States, however, was still a 50–50 country, closely and deeply divided. Trump's popular-vote edge, 49.80 percent to 48.33 percent for Harris, was not exactly a landslide, though it may have seemed like one to Republicans since it was only the second time in nine presidential elections that they had won the popular vote.[44] Republicans picked up four seats in the Senate, while losing one in the House. If Democrats had won three more House seats, they would have had a majority.

From such a slim margin of victory for Trump and his party it would be a mistake to conclude that the final popular verdict had arrived in 2024 on who Americans are and what kind of nation the United States will be in the twenty-first century. The historical context of the election was crucial. Over the previous year, incumbent governments running for re-election all around the world had lost vote share, and many had lost power. These defeats did not depend on the ideology of the party in office; the losers included parties of every stripe. The simplest explanation for this global pattern is global inflation. The best formula for winning an election at the time was to have lost the previous election. Critics of Biden's American Rescue Plan, passed in March 2021 in response to the pandemic, argue that it caused higher prices, but internationally, inflation was unrelated to the size of fiscal relief packages. As an analyst in Britain's *Financial Times* put it, "Ultimately voters don't distinguish between unpleasant things that their leaders and governments have direct control over, and those that are international phenomena resulting from supply-side disruptions caused by a global pandemic or the warmongering of an ageing autocrat halfway across the world. Voters don't like high prices, so they punished the Democrats for being in charge when inflation hit."[45]

This tendency of voters to throw out incumbents when bad things happen regardless of their responsibility for misfortune has a name: "blind retrospection."[46] It's part of the normal seesaw in democracies. What made the voters' blind retrospection different in the United States in 2024 is that they brought back to power a man who was not committed to the rules of a democracy and who four years earlier did have substantial responsibility for what went wrong in a national crisis, the COVID pandemic. Although the United States had a stronger economic recovery than other major countries, that was not the comparison voters were likely to make. They compared what they were paying for groceries and rent under Biden to what they had paid under Trump, and they did not like what Biden appeared to have cost them. Trump also made significant gains within demographic groups, notably Hispanics and young men, that potentially carried long-run implications.[47]

Democrats had a well-financed campaign, with more ads and more volunteers knocking on doors in the swing states. That campaign made a difference, just not enough of a difference. From 2020 to 2024, the swing from Biden to Trump was less than half as much in the seven battlegrounds as in the other forty-three states.[48] Harris herself ran not only behind Biden's 2020 numbers but behind other Democrats running for Congress in 2024. In five of the swing states, Democratic senators were running for re-election, and four of them won their races even though Harris lost their states.

From the inception of the campaign, the public was dissatisfied with the economy and disapproved of the incumbent administration chiefly for that reason. That dissatisfaction put Harris at a disadvantage from the point when she became the candidate, late in the election cycle. Harris carried several other burdens, any one of which might explain the outcome in such a close election. As a Black woman, she undoubtedly lost votes because of racism and misogyny. As Biden's vice president, she could not escape the blame on the administration for the border crisis as well as the increased cost of living. A doddering Biden became the symbol of Democrats' lack of energy and forcefulness, and his failure to step aside earlier added to the party's difficulties. Harris's image and past positions, such as her support for the use of public funds for transgender surgery for prison inmates, undercut her effort to reposition herself and other Democrats in the cultural and political center. She was the wrong messenger for the campaign she tried to wage.

Much of the post-election commentary focused on the shifts to Trump among Hispanics and young men. The growing Hispanic population and the youth vote have been central to the Democrats' long-term expectations, but the party was on weak ground with the men in both groups. Many who had voted Democrat in the past were never on board with the progressive cultural views on gender the party's leaders had embraced. By highlighting those issues and making a concerted effort to win over young men, Trump peeled away support that Democrats were counting on. He also expanded his base by adding Musk and the tech right and winning over Robert F. Kennedy Jr. and his antivax and wellness followers.

Mostly, though, the causes of the election's outcome were less weighty than the consequences. The causes were of the moment, but the effects were likely to outlast the moment. The two sides of the American divide had been engaged in a decades-long tug-of-war. The question now was whether one side had won that struggle.

In the immediate aftermath of the election, some commentators called it a "turning point," but that conclusion neglected the possibility that a more important turning point had already come before 2024 with the far-right takeover of the Republican Party and the Supreme Court. After the collapse of the center right and Trump's consolidation of party control, it was only a matter of time before transitory circumstances like a recession or a spike in inflation under a Democratic administration led to a Republican victory, which would now mean a far-right victory. The occasion just happened to be the 2024 election. In America's two-party system, power had historically alternated between center-left and center-right administrations. The MAGA takeover of the GOP meant that if and when power shifted right, it wouldn't necessarily shift back again as it had in the past because of what Trump and those around him had already shown themselves willing to do to stay in power. In a two-party system, both parties need to be committed to democratic norms. Trump's repudiation of those norms and his indifference to legality put the future of American democracy in doubt.

The turning point may have also come before 2024 because of the counterrevolution through the courts discussed in chapter 10. The Supreme Court had already disposed of much of the twentieth-century rights revolution and weighted the scales of justice so far in favor of corporations, the rich, and the Republican Party that it had substantially disabled progressivism. One reason Trump had been able to win in 2024 is that the Court protected him from prosecution. The change in judicial power changed electoral politics. The Democrats might still win an election, but when they did, the Court provided the right with a veto over policy, which they were likely to keep for a long time.

Trump's restoration gave his movement-party an opportunity to entrench its power and policies in a more thoroughgoing way in the executive branch as well as the judiciary. A purge of the federal civil service might disable the government's capacities to regulate business and to protect civil rights, consumers, the environment, and labor's already diminished right to organize. A purge of the FBI, military, and Department of Justice might give it the power not just to exact retribution on Trump's enemies but to suppress opposition for the long term. Republicans were also intent on extending their power into spheres such as education, medicine and public health, and the media. They had an extensive list of policies for subjecting higher education to control; DeSantis's Florida, a laboratory of illiberalism, provided them with a model. The larger aim was to imprint their beliefs on all the independent institutions of a liberal democracy to prevent them from weakening the right-wing hold on power. They sought to turn back the currents of cultural change that they saw as a threat, and to do that they wanted to put Blue America under the supervision of Red America. With unrestrained use of presidential powers, Trump could try to do to other people and institutions what he had done to Republicans and the Republican Party—make them all pliable instruments of his will. This was what passed as conservatism in the 2020s.

Trump's determination to impose his personal rule was clear, and Project 2025 had explained in detail how he might institutionalize and entrench a right-wing state. In his first term, however, he had been mercurial, undisciplined, and ineffective—he had, as I suggested, a whim of iron. His performance during the COVID pandemic was not encouraging about how he would act in a future national crisis. His policy positions have always been highly transactional. During the 2024 campaign, he repeatedly reversed his stance on issues in response to donors and special interests. For example, after warning that cryptocurrency seemed "like a scam," he said he would make America "the crypto capital of the planet," received a windfall of financial support from the industry, and issued his own crypto coins.[49] He modeled the constant pursuit of self-interest; many of the people who came begging to Mar-a-Lago were looking for personal enrichment too. Crony capitalism seems a more likely outcome than a government that serves working-class interests or the common good. Short-term interests in making money may dominate long-term interests in economic stability, sustainable growth, and national unity.

The danger that Trump and his movement represent to the nation arises not only from personal interests in self-aggrandizement but from political interests in keeping America's social divisions at a high boil. The kind of politics Trump practices requires a continual need for outrage, enemies, and campaigns of retribution, even at the cost of undermining social solidarity and institutions of critical importance for national security, public health, and a stable and growing economy. Culture war drives choices that are unlikely to work out in the long run. Mass deportations and a trade war will make the economy smaller and the nation poorer. An assault on universities, medicine, and science may be deeply satisfying as the ultimate in "owning the libs," but if it damages those institutions, pushes researchers abroad, and compromises U.S. scientific leadership, it will hurt the country. Shutting down research on climate change won't make climate change go away.

The likely disastrous effects of right-wing power and the entrenchment of right-wing power will not sit well together. If Trumpism had solutions to the problems that America faces, it would have a better chance of achieving stable right-wing rule. In the days after the 2024 election, Biden was handing off an economy that was, ironically, in excellent shape: inflation was down, unemployment was low, the Federal Reserve was cutting short-term interest rates. But a large disturbance was on the way. That disturbance was Trump himself and the people he was putting in charge of the government.

In the preface, I suggested that instead of "a city on a hill," the United States might be thought of as a city on a geological fault, shaken often by tremors and periodically by earthquakes. What the current earthquake will leave standing of America's institutions, including the liberal and progressive achievements of the past, is not yet clear. During the twentieth century, the shocks of world war and depression caused staggering damage, but they also led to unexpected advances. The United States emerged in the aftermath as both a more powerful and a more just society than it had been. The twenty-first century will have its shocks too, including new ones from climate change, artificial intelligence, and an aging society. If Americans are to do in the twenty-first century what they did in the twentieth; if they are to live in a democracy with any hope of liberty and justice for all; if they are to establish a more perfect union—they will have to create new popular movements and new institutions capable of repairing the damage from Trumpism and from the shocks that lie ahead. It is not too early to start thinking about what form those movements and institutions should take.

Notes

Preface

1. Walt Whitman, *Democratic Vistas* (New York: J. S. Redfield, 1871), 4.
2. Daniel T. Rodgers, *As a City on a Hill: The Story of America's Most Famous Lay Sermon* (Princeton, NJ: Princeton University Press, 2018).

Introduction

1. E. J. Hobsbawm, *Age of Extremes: The Short Twentieth Century* (London: Michael Joseph, 1994).
2. John F. Kennedy, *A Nation of Immigrants*, rev. and enl. ed. (New York: Harper Perennial, 2008 [1958, 1964]), 4.
3. Media Matters Staff, "Tucker Carlson: 'The Worst Attack on Our Democracy in 160 Years? How about the Immigration Act of 1965?,'" Media Matters, April 29, 2021, https://www.mediamatters.org/tucker-carlson/tucker-carlson-worst-attack-our-democracy-160-years-how-about-immigration-act-1965.
4. America's first-past-the-post, single-member-district electoral system also tends to underrepresent Democrats in the U.S. House and state legislatures, even apart from partisan gerrymandering. The same bias affects all urban-based parties of the left in countries using single-member-district elections as opposed to proportional representation. See Jonathan A. Rodden, *Why Cities Lose: The Deep Roots of the Urban-Rural Political Divide* (New York: Basic Books, 2019). The current urban-rural divide is also the source of Democrats' disadvantage in the Senate and Electoral College. These institutions do not inherently disadvantage Democrats; they disadvantage them because of the high geographic clustering of Democratic votes.
5. Steven Levitsky and Daniel Ziblatt, *Tyranny of the Minority: Why American Democracy Reached the Breaking Point* (New York: Crown, 2023).

6. I have previously written about the "liberal project" as the centuries-long effort to establish rights to freedom and equality under a government of constitutionally restrained powers (*Freedom's Power: The History and Promise of Liberalism* [New York: Basic Books, 2008]; "Center-Left Liberalism," in David Coates, ed., *Oxford Companion to American Politics* [New York: Oxford University Press, 2012], 68–76). Here I am using the term "progressive project" to refer to the more recent efforts of both liberals and radicals on the left to achieve equality for historically subordinated groups. The term "progressive" has had other meanings, from the early twentieth-century Progressive Era (when it referred to a wide range of reformers, including Theodore Roosevelt and Woodrow Wilson) to the mid-twentieth century (when it became associated with Henry Wallace's left-wing Progressive Party) to the late twentieth century (when it supplanted "liberal" as the favorite term for political groups from the centrist Democratic Leadership Council to radicals to the left of the Democratic Party). In my use in this book, "progressive" is a bridging term that extends across left-of-center political and intellectual tendencies. There used to be many liberals who were not progressives in my sense; they were not much concerned about the historically subordinated. Today, most liberals are progressives, which is one result of the progressive project. But there are also progressives who are not liberal. Liberal progressives have serious differences with illiberal progressives, and in a better world they could devote their energies to that argument. Personally, I look forward to that day. For the moment, though, liberal progressives have a bigger fight on their hands with a right that has abandoned its own classically liberal tradition.

7. Ronald Reagan, "Farewell Address to the Nation," Ronald Reagan Presidential Library and Museum, January 11, 1989, https://www.reaganlibrary.gov/archives/speech/farewell-address-nation. For the view that American institutions rest on a single, consistent set of values, see the work of Seymour Martin Lipset, particularly *Continental Divide: The Values and Institutions of the United States and Canada* (New York: Routledge, 1990) and *American Exceptionalism: A Double-Edged Sword* (New York: W. W. Norton, 1996). See also chapter 1 in this book for a discussion of the "consensus" school of American history versus the conflict school that emphasized the battle between "the people" and "the interests." Rogers M. Smith, *Civic Ideals: Conflicting Visions of Citizenship in U.S. History* (New Haven, CT: Yale University Press, 1999) offers another narrative about conflict over "multiple traditions" of citizenship and identity. All of these are different from the idea of a central contradiction in American history, stemming from the founding contradiction between slavery and freedom and taking different forms at different times, including the contemporary contradiction between a changing people and an older, resistant nation.

Chapter One. Midcentury Normal

1. Daniel J. Boorstin, *The Genius of American Politics* (Chicago: University of Chicago Press, 1953), 33.
2. Godfrey Hodgson, *America in Our Time* (Garden City, NY: Doubleday, 1976), 7.
3. The data come from Claudia Goldin and Lawrence F. Katz, *The Race between Education and Technology* (Cambridge, MA: Harvard University Press, 2008), 46, 48. Their measure of income is the official U.S. Census Bureau measure of pre-tax, post-transfer money income (consequently including Social Security but not "in-kind benefits" such as health care). See also Claudia Goldin and Robert A. Margo, "The Great Compression: The Wage Structure in the United States at Mid-Century," *Quarterly Journal of Economics* 107(1) (1992): 1–34; Thomas Piketty and Emmanuel Saez, "Income Inequality in the United States, 1913–1998," *Quarterly Journal of Economics* 118(1) (2003): 1–39.
4. Seymour Martin Lipset and William Schneider, *The Confidence Gap: Business, Labor, and Government in the Public Mind* (New York: Free Press, 1983), 15; Robert Putnam, *Our Kids: The American Dream in Crisis* (New York: Simon & Schuster, 2015), 220.
5. On trends in civic engagement, see Robert Putnam, *Bowling Alone: The Collapse and Revival of American Community* (New York: Simon & Schuster, 2000), chs. 2–3; on relatively low partisan antagonisms, see Gabriel Almond and Sidney Verba, *The Civic Culture: Political Attitudes and Democracy in Five Nations* (Princeton, NJ: Princeton University Press, 1963), 125, 132–43; Robert E. Lane, "The Politics of Consensus in the Age of Affluence," *American Political Science Review* 59 (December 1965): 874–75, esp. table 2. For the subsequent rise of negative partisanship, see, e.g., Alan I. Abramowitz and Steven Webster, "The Rise of Negative Partisanship and the Nationalization of U.S. Elections in the 21st Century," *Electoral Studies* 41 (2016): 12–22.
6. Robert A. Dahl, *Democracy in the United States: Promise and Performance* (Boston: Houghton Mifflin, 1981), 284.
7. Edward Shils, "The End of Ideology?," *Encounter* 5 (November 1955): 52–58; Daniel Bell, *The End of Ideology: On the Exhaustion of Political Ideas in the Fifties* (Cambridge, MA: Harvard University Press, 1988 [1960]); for a review of the debate, see Howard Brick, "The End of Ideology Thesis," in Michael Freeden and Marc Stears, eds., *The Oxford Handbook of Political Ideologies* (Oxford: Oxford University Press, 2013).
8. Philip E. Converse, "The Nature of Belief Systems in Mass Publics," in David E. Apter, ed., *Ideology and Discontent* (New York: Free Press, 1964), 206–61.
9. Quoted in Hans Kohn, *American Nationalism: An Interpretive Essay* (New York: Macmillan, 1957), 13.

10. Arthur Schlesinger Jr., *A Life in the Twentieth Century: Innocent Beginnings, 1917–1950* (Boston: Houghton Mifflin, 2000), 241.
11. Wendy L. Wall, *Inventing the "American Way": The Politics of Consensus from the New Deal to the Civil Rights Movement* (New York: Oxford University Press, 2008). My discussion of consensus as a political project is generally indebted to Wall's book.
12. "President Harry S. Truman's Veto Message of the Immigration and Nationality Bill, June 25, 1952," in Michael Lemay and Elliott Robert Barkan, eds., *U.S. Immigration and Naturalization Laws and Issues* (Westport, CT: Greenwood Press, 1999), 225–31 (quotation, 227).
13. Alan Brinkley, *The End of Reform: New Deal Liberalism in Recession and War* (New York: Alfred A. Knopf, 1995).
14. Goldin and Katz, *The Race between Education and Technology*; Goldin and Margo, "The Great Compression"; Thomas Piketty, *Capital in the Twenty-First Century* (Cambridge, MA: Belknap Press of Harvard University Press, 2014), 272, 275, 291–94.
15. Thomas Piketty and Emmanuel Saez, "How Progressive Is the U.S. Federal Tax System? A Historical and International Perspective," *Journal of Economic Perspectives* 21 (2007): 3–24.
16. Tomás R. Jiménez, *Replenished Ethnicity: Mexican Americans, Immigration, and Identity* (Berkeley: University of California Press, 2010).
17. Will Herberg, *Protestant Catholic Jew: An Essay in American Religious Sociology* (Garden City, NY: Doubleday, 1955), 52–53, 59, 60. For the historical trends in church membership, see Roger Finke and Rodney Stark, *The Churching of America, 1776–1990* (New Brunswick, NJ: Rutgers University Press, 1992).
18. For Eisenhower's original words (slightly altered in Herberg and other books), see "Text of Eisenhower Speech," *New York Times*, December 23, 1952; and for subsequent commentary and disputes about what Eisenhower meant, see Patrick Henry, "'And I Don't Care What It Is': The Tradition-History of a Civil Religion Proof-Text," *Journal of the American Academy of Religion* 49(1) (1981): 35–49. The commentator who described Eisenhower as "a very fervent believer in a very vague religion" was William Lee Miller, *Piety along the Potomac: Notes on Politics and Morals in the Fifties* (Boston: Houghton Mifflin, 1964), 34. On the concept of "civil religion" and Kennedy's Inaugural, see Robert N. Bellah, "Civil Religion in America," *Daedalus*, Winter 1967, 1–21.
19. American Political Science Association Committee on Political Parties, *Toward a More Responsible Two-Party System* (New York: Rinehart, 1950), 20.
20. Andrew J. Cherlin, *Labor's Love Lost: The Rise and Fall of the Working-Class Family in America* (New York: Russell Sage Foundation, 2014), 95.
21. Stephen Mintz and Susan Kellogg, *Domestic Revolutions: A Social History of American Family Life* (New York: Free Press, 1988), 178–79.
22. Elaine Tyler May, *Homeward Bound: American Families in the Cold War Era* (New York: Basic Books, 1988), ch. 6.

23. Relative income is central, albeit at an aggregate level, to the "Easterlin hypothesis," that is, "a rise in the relative economic status of young persons... induces earlier marriage and childbearing, and a corresponding rise in fertility." Richard A. Easterlin, "Relative Economic Status and the American Fertility Swing," in E. B. Sheldon, ed., *Family Economic Behavior: Problems and Prospects* (Philadelphia: Lippincott, 1973), 215. For one of the many reviews, see Diane J. Macunovich, "Fertility and the Easterlin Hypothesis: An Assessment of the Literature," *Journal of Population Economics* 11 (1998): 53–111.
24. Philip Roth, *My Life as a Man* (New York: Penguin Books, 1985), 169–70.
25. Stephanie Coontz, *The Way We Never Were: American Families and the Nostalgia Trap* (New York: Basic Books, 1992), 25.
26. Cherlin, *Labor's Love Lost*, 97.
27. Coontz, *The Way We Never Were*, 33.
28. Tyler May, *Homeward Bound*, ch. 5; Cherlin, *Labor's Love Lost*, 96.
29. Regina Markell Morantz, "The Scientist as Sex Crusader: Alfred C. Kinsey and American Culture," *American Quarterly* 29 (1977): 563–89.
30. Betty Friedan, *The Feminine Mystique* (New York: W. W. Norton, 1963), ch. 10.
31. Coontz, *The Way We Never Were*, 27.
32. Cherlin, *Labor's Love Lost*, 94, 104; Black–white male income ratios computed from James P. Smith and Finis Welch, "Black Economic Progress after Myrdal," *Journal of Economic Literature* 27(2) (1989): 519–64, table 1.
33. Coontz, *The Way We Never Were*, 25.
34. Tyler May, *Homeward Bound*, 201–2.
35. The following discussion of suburbanization draws on Kenneth T. Jackson, *Crabgrass Frontier: The Suburbanization of the United States* (New York: Oxford University Press, 1985); Rosalyn Baxandall and Elizabeth Ewen, *Picture Windows: How the Suburbs Happened* (New York: Basic Books, 2000); and Dolores Hayden, *Building Suburbia: Green Fields and Urban Growth, 1820–2000* (New York: Pantheon Books, 2003).
36. On McCarthy's role, see Baxandall and Ewen, *Picture Windows*, 89–105.
37. Baxandall and Ewen, *Picture Windows*, ch. 10 (Levitt quoted, 125); Hayden, *Building Suburbia*, 133–37.
38. Richard Rothstein, *The Color of Law: A Forgotten Story of How Our Government Segregated America* (New York: Liveright, 2017).
39. Jackson, *Crabgrass Frontier*, 235.
40. Baxandall and Ewen, *Picture Windows*, 167.
41. Herbert J. Gans, *The Levittowners: Ways of Life and Politics in a New Suburban Community* (New York: Columbia University Press, 1982 [1967]).
42. For statistics on indoor plumbing, see U.S. Census Bureau, "Historical Census of Housing Tables: Plumbing," https://www.census.gov/data/tables/time-series/dec/coh-plumbing.html.
43. Jackson, *Crabgrass Frontier*, 240–41.

44. Sylvester L. "Pat" Weaver, "The Task Ahead: Making TV the 'Shining Center of the Home' and Helping Create a New Society of Adults," *Variety*, January 6, 1954, 91.
45. Lynn Spigel, *Make Room for TV: Television and the Family Ideal in Postwar America* (Chicago: University of Chicago Press, 1992), 37, 45; Leo Bogart, *The Age of Television* (New York: Ungar, 1956), 15, table 5.
46. Bogart, *The Age of Television*, 67, table 19; U.S. Bureau of the Census, Current Housing Reports, Series H-121, Table 743, "Percent of Households with Television Sets, 1955, 1960, and 1965," 521.
47. David Halberstam, *The Fifties* (New York: Villard Books, 1993), 508–11.
48. Bogart, *The Age of Television*, 1.
49. I develop this framework for understanding media in "The Relational Public," *Sociological Theory* 39(2) (2021): 57–80.
50. James L. Baughman, *Same Time, Same Station: Creating American Television, 1948–1961* (Baltimore: Johns Hopkins University Press, 2007), 82–120.
51. Baughman, *Same Time, Same Station*, 153–91 (Hitchcock quoted, 188).
52. Baughman, *Same Time, Same Station*, 220; Edward J. Epstein, *News from Nowhere: Television and the News* (New York: Vintage Books, 1973), 54, 60.
53. Steven J. Simmons, *The Fairness Doctrine and the Media* (Berkeley: University of California Press, 1978).
54. Epstein, *News from Nowhere*, 242.
55. Epstein, *News from Nowhere*, 5–6, 58, 103, 105–12, 243.
56. Epstein, *News from Nowhere*, 3–4, 54.
57. Michael J. Robinson, "Public Affairs Television and the Growth of Video Malaise," *American Political Science Review* 70 (1976): 409–32.
58. Markus Prior, *Post-Broadcast Democracy: How Media Choice Increases Inequality in Political Involvement and Polarizes Elections* (New York: Cambridge University Press, 2007).
59. For contemporary discussion of the consensus framework, see John Higham, "The Cult of the 'American Consensus': Homogenizing Our Past," *Commentary* 27 (February 1959): 93–100; John Higham, "Beyond Consensus: The Historian as Moral Critic," *American Historical Review* 67(3) (1962): 609–25; Irving Howe, "This Age of Conformity," *Dissent*, January 1, 1954.
60. Richard Hofstadter, *The American Political Tradition: And the Men Who Made It* (New York: Alfred A. Knopf, 1973 [1948]), xxix, xxx.
61. Hofstadter, *The American Political Tradition*, xxix, xxxi.
62. Boorstin, *The Genius of American Politics*, 8–9.
63. Talcott Parsons and Edward Shils, eds., *Toward a General Theory of Action* (Cambridge, MA: Harvard University Press, 1951).
64. Horace M. Kallen, *Culture and Democracy in the United States* (New York: Boni and Liveright, 1924); Randolph S. Bourne, "Trans-National America," *Atlantic Monthly*, July 1916, 86–97; W. Lloyd Warner and Leo Srole, *The Social Systems of American Ethnic Groups* (New Haven, CT: Yale University Press,

1945); Milton Gordon, *Assimilation in American Life* (New York: Oxford University Press, 1964). For a critical review of sociological thinking about assimilation, see Richard Alba and Victor Nee, *Remaking the American Mainstream: Assimilation and Contemporary Immigration* (Cambridge, MA: Harvard University Press, 2003).

Chapter Two. Black Americans, Model Minority

1. Nikole Hannah-Jones, "Democracy," in Nikole Hannah-Jones, Caitlin Roper, Ilena Silverman, and Jake Silverstein, eds., *The 1619 Project: A New Origin Story* (New York: One World, 2021), 11.
2. Ellen D. Wu, *The Color of Success: Asian Americans and the Origins of the Model Minority* (Princeton, NJ: Princeton University Press, 2013), 150–80, 249; William Petersen, "Success Story, Japanese-American Style," *New York Times Magazine*, January 9, 1966, 20–21, 33, 36, 38, 40–41, 43 (quotation, 21).
3. Charles Tilly, "Contentious Repertoires in Great Britain, 1758–1834," in Mark Traugott, ed., *Repertoires and Cycles of Collective Action* (Durham, NC: Duke University Press, 1995), 15–42; Charles Tilly, *Contentious Performances* (New York: Cambridge University Press, 2008), 14–19, 59–61. For Tilly, a "repertoire of contention" also includes the responses of opponents, including the authorities.
4. Gunnar Myrdal, *An American Dilemma: The Negro Problem and Modern Democracy* (New York: Harper & Brothers, 1944), 3, 4, 22. On the impact of Myrdal's interlude in Sweden in 1940, see William J. Barber, *Gunnar Myrdal: An Intellectual Biography* (New York: Palgrave Macmillan, 2008), 69–71.
5. On the book's twentieth anniversary, this was the criticism of Myrdal. Charles Silberman declared, "Myrdal was wrong. The tragedy of race relations in the United States is that there is no American Dilemma. White Americans are not torn and tortured." See Mitchel Duneier, *Ghetto: The Invention of a Place, the History of an Idea* (New York: Farrar Straus & Giroux, 2016), 111–12.
6. Wendy L. Wall, *Inventing the American Way: The Politics of Consensus from the New Deal to the Civil Rights Movement* (New York: Oxford University Press, 2008), 132.
7. Myrdal, *An American Dilemma*, 48, 49.
8. Susan Fiske and Shelley E. Taylor, *Social Cognition: From Brains to Culture*, 4th ed. (Thousand Oaks, CA: Sage, 2021), 120–22.
9. Jacquelyn Dowd Hall, "The Long Civil Rights Movement and the Political Uses of the Past," *Journal of American History* 91(4) (2005): 1233–63.
10. Aldon D. Morris, *The Origins of the Civil Rights Movement* (New York: Free Press, 1984); Charles Payne, *I've Got the Light of Freedom: The Organizing Tradition and the Mississippi Freedom Struggle*, 2nd ed. (Berkeley: University of California Press, 2007).
11. Quoted in Morris, *The Origins of the Civil Rights Movement*, 77.

12. Doug McAdam, *Political Process and the Development of Black Insurgency, 1930–1970* (Chicago: University of Chicago Press, 1982), 65–116.
13. Paul Starr, "Dodging a Bullet: Democracy's Gains in Modern War," in Elizabeth Kier and Ronald R. Krebs, eds., *In War's Wake: International Conflict and the Fate of Liberal Democracy* (New York: Cambridge University Press, 2010), 50–66; Philip A. Klinkner and Rogers M. Smith, *The Unsteady March: The Rise and Decline of Racial Equality in America* (Chicago: University of Chicago Press, 1999).
14. Robert Korstad and Nelson Lichtenstein, "Opportunities Found and Lost: Labor, Radicals, and the Early Civil Rights Movement," *Journal of American History* 75 (1988): 786–811; Patricia Sullivan, *Lift Every Voice: The NAACP and the Making of the Civil Rights Movement* (New York: New Press, 2009), 287–332; Michael J. Klarman, *From Jim Crow to Civil Rights: The Supreme Court and the Struggle for Equality* (New York: Oxford University Press, 2004).
15. Myrdal, *An American Dilemma*, 93.
16. Korstad and Lichtenstein, "Opportunities Found and Lost"; Hall, "The Long Civil Rights Movement"; Risa L. Goluboff, *The Lost Promise of Civil Rights* (Cambridge, MA: Harvard University Press, 2007); Paul Frymer, *Black and Blue: African Americans, the Labor Movement, and the Decline of the Democratic Party* (Princeton, NJ: Princeton University Press, 2008).
17. Klarman, *From Jim Crow to Civil Rights*, 173, 193–95.
18. Robert Cover, "The Origins of Judicial Activism in the Protection of Minorities," *Yale Law Journal* 91(7) (1982): 1287–316; Klarman, *From Jim Crow to Civil Rights*, 196.
19. Korematsu v. United States, 323 U.S. 214 (1944).
20. Gerald N. Rosenberg, *The Hollow Hope: Can Courts Bring About Social Change?*, 2nd ed. (Chicago: University of Chicago Press, 2008), 14–28; Alexander Hamilton, "The Federalist No. 78," May 28, 1788, The Founders Online, National Archives, https://founders.archives.gov/documents/Hamilton/01-04-02-0241.
21. Rosenberg, *The Hollow Hope*, 28–34.
22. Mark V. Tushnet, *Making Civil Rights Law: Thurgood Marshall and the Supreme Court, 1936–1961* (New York: Oxford University Press, 1994), 99–115; Rosenberg, *The Hollow Hope*, 57–58.
23. Clive Webb, ed., *Massive Resistance: Southern Opposition to the Second Reconstruction* (New York: Oxford University Press, 2005), 6; Klarman, *From Jim Crow to Civil Rights*; Rosenberg, *The Hollow Hope*.
24. Morris, *The Origins of the Civil Rights Movement*, 46.
25. Tilly, "Contentious Repertoires in Great Britain," 26, 27.
26. The words are those of the young Pauli Murray, who was arrested in 1940, when she and a companion refused to give up their seats on an interstate bus in Virginia. Kathryn Schulz, "The Many Lives of Pauli Murray," *New Yorker*, April 17, 2017, http://www.newyorker.com/magazine/2017/04/17/the-many-lives-of-pauli-murray.

27. David Garrow, *Bearing the Cross: Martin Luther King, Jr., and the Southern Christian Leadership Conference* (New York: Morrow, 1986), 11–82; Morris, *The Origins of the Civil Rights Movement*, 40–63; Thomas E. Ricks, *Waging a Good War: A Military History of the Civil Rights Movement, 1954–1968* (New York: Farrar, Straus and Giroux, 2022), 11–36.
28. Morris, *The Origins of the Civil Rights Movement*, 61.
29. Garrow, *Bearing the Cross*, 127–34; Clayborne Carson, *In Struggle: SNCC and the Black Awakening of the 1960s* (Cambridge, MA: Harvard University Press, 1981), 9–30.
30. August Meier and Elliott Rudwick, *CORE: A Study in the Civil Rights Movement, 1942–1968* (New York: Oxford University Press, 1973); Carson, *In Struggle*, 31–44; Garrow, *Bearing the Cross*, 154–61.
31. Morris, *The Origins of the Civil Rights Movement*, 250–74; Garrow, *Bearing the Cross*, 231–69, 357–430. For a general analysis of the movement as a series of quasi-military campaigns, see Ricks, *Waging a Good War*.
32. Garrow, *Bearing the Cross*, 172.
33. Anthony Lewis, *Make No Law: The Sullivan Case and the First Amendment* (New York: Random House, 1991).
34. Omar Wasow, "Agenda Seeding: How 1960s Black Protests Moved Elites, Public Opinion and Voting," *American Political Science Review* 114(3) (2020): 638–59.
35. Hugh Davis Graham, *The Civil Rights Era: Origins and Development of National Policy 1960–1972* (New York: Oxford University Press, 1990), 329–40.
36. Nancy MacLean, *Freedom Is Not Enough: The Opening of the American Workplace* (Cambridge, MA: Harvard University Press/Russell Sage Foundation, 2006), 6.
37. Frymer, *Black and Blue*, ch. 4.
38. Martha J. Bailey, John DiNardo, and Bryan A. Stuart, "The Economic Impact of a High National Minimum Wage: Evidence from the 1966 Fair Labor Standards Act," *Journal of Labor Economics* 39(S2) (2021): S339–67; Ralph E. Smith and Bruce Vavrichek, "The Minimum Wage: Its Relation to Incomes and Poverty," *Monthly Labor Review* 110(6) (1987): 24–30. The January 2024 figure comes from the Bureau of Labor Statistics Consumer Price Index Inflation Calculator; Andrew Goodman-Bacon, "The Long-Run Effects of Childhood Insurance Coverage: Medicaid Implementation, Adult Health, and Labor Market Outcomes," *American Economic Review* 111(8) (2021): 2550–93; "Share of the Population Living in Poverty by Race and Hispanic Origin in the United States from 1959 to 2022," Statista, September 2024, https://www.statista.com/statistics/1225017/poverty-share-by-race-race-us/.
39. For a careful analysis of the change in school integration in the South before and after *Brown*, see Klarman, *From Jim Crow to Civil Rights*, 344–63.
40. David Barton Smith, *The Power to Heal: Civil Rights, Medicare, and the Struggle to Transform America's Health System* (Nashville, TN: Vanderbilt University Press, 2016).

41. Gavin Wright, *Sharing the Prize: The Economics of the Civil Rights Revolution in the American South* (Cambridge, MA: Harvard University Press, 2013), esp. ch. 4; John J. Donohue and James Heckman, "Continuous versus Episodic Change: The Impact of Civil Rights Policy on the Economic Status of Blacks," *Journal of Economic Literature* 29(4) (1991): 1603–43; Leah Platt Boustan, *Competition in the Promised Land: Black Migrants in Northern Cities and Labor Markets* (Princeton, NJ: Princeton University Press, 2016).
42. James E. Alt, "The Impact of the Voting Rights Act on Black and White Voter Registration in the South," in Chandler Davidson and Bernard Grofman, eds., *Quiet Revolution in the South: The Impact of the Voting Rights Act, 1965–1990* (Princeton, NJ: Princeton University Press, 1994), 351–77; Lisa Handley and Bernard Grofman, "The Impact of the Voting Rights Act on Minority Representation: Black Officeholding in Southern State Legislatures and Congressional Delegations," in Davidson and Grofman, *Quiet Revolution in the South*, 335–50.
43. William L. Van Deburg, *New Day in Babylon: The Black Power Movement and American Culture, 1965–1975* (Chicago: University of Chicago Press, 1992), 83.
44. Wasow, "Agenda Seeding."
45. Van Deburg, *New Day in Babylon*, 31.
46. Stokely Carmichael and Charles V. Hamilton, *Black Power: The Politics of Liberation in America* (New York: Random House, 1967), 62; Harold Cruse, *The Crisis of the Negro Intellectual* (New York: New York Review Books, 2005 [1967]), 3–10. The idea of "cultural pluralism" as distinct from "Anglo-conformity" comes from Horace Kallen; see, e.g., Horace M. Kallen, *Culture and Democracy in the United States* (New York: Boni and Liveright, 1924).
47. Carmichael and Hamilton, *Black Power*, 4, 46.
48. Manning Marable, *Malcolm X: A Life of Reinvention* (East Rutherford, NJ: Penguin, 2011).
49. Van Deburg, *New Day in Babylon*, 19.
50. Van Deburg, *New Day in Babylon*, 12–13.
51. Marable, *Malcolm X*; Peter Goldman, "Malcolm X: Witness for the Prosecution," in John Hope Franklin and August Meier, eds., *Black Leaders of the Twentieth Century* (Urbana: University of Illinois Press, 1982), 305–29 (quotation, 317).
52. Elizabeth Hinton, *America on Fire: The Untold History of Police Violence and Black Rebellion since the 1960s* (New York: Liveright, 2021).
53. William J. Collins and Robert A. Margo, "The Economic Aftermath of the 1960s Riots in American Cities: Evidence from Property Values," *Journal of Economic History* 67(4) (2007): 849–83.
54. Wasow, "Agenda Seeding."
55. Van Deburg, *New Day in Babylon*, 9.
56. Oscar Handlin, *Race and Nationality in American Life* (Garden City, NY: Doubleday Anchor, 1957 [1950]), 135–39.

57. Paul Burstein, *Discrimination, Jobs and Politics* (Chicago: University of Chicago Press, 1998 [1985]), 73–74.
58. John D. Skrentny, *The Minority Rights Revolution* (Cambridge, MA: Harvard University Press, 2002).
59. Sidney Tarrow, *Democracy and Disorder: Protest and Politics in Italy, 1965–1975* (New York: Oxford University Press, 1989); Doug McAdam, "'Initiator' and 'Spin-Off' Movements: Diffusion Processes in Protest Cycles," in Traugott, *Repertoires and Cycles of Collective Action*, 217–39; Craig Calhoun, "'New Social Movements' of the Early Nineteenth Century," in Traugott, *Repertoires and Cycles of Collective Action*, 173–215.
60. Aldon D. Morris, "A Retrospective on the Civil Rights Movement: Political and Intellectual Landmarks," *Annual Review of Sociology* 25 (1999): 517–39.
61. McAdam, "'Initiator' and 'Spin-Off' Movements," 234.
62. Doug McAdam, *Freedom Summer* (New York: Oxford University Press, 1988), 96.
63. McAdam, *Freedom Summer*, 6.
64. Sara Evans, *Personal Politics* (New York: Vintage Books, 1979), 83–89; Carson, *In Struggle*, 147–48; Mary King, *Freedom Song: A Personal Story of the 1960s Civil Rights Movement* (New York: William Morrow, 1987), 442–55 (quotation, 445), 467–68. For the two papers by King and Hayden, see King, *Freedom Song*, appendices 2 and 3, 567–74.
65. For Murray's role in applying the civil rights framework to women's subordination, see Pauli Murray, *Song in a Weary Throat: Memoir of an American Pilgrimage* (New York: Liveright, 2018 [1987]), 462–66, 470–80; Rosalind Rosenberg, *Jane Crow: The Life of Pauli Murray* (New York: Oxford University Press, 2017), 130–33, 145–50, 187, 297–300, 340–45; Pauli Murray and Mary Eastwood, "Jane Crow and the Law: Sex Discrimination and Title VII," *George Washington Law Review* 34(2) (1965): 232–56. And for a general analysis, see Serena Mayeri, *Reasoning from Race: Feminism, Law, and the Civil Rights Revolution* (Cambridge, MA: Harvard University Press, 2011).
66. Vine Deloria Jr., *We Talk, You Listen* (New York: Macmillan, 1970), 100.
67. Ian Haney López, *Racism on Trial: The Chicano Fight for Justice* (Cambridge, MA: Harvard University Press, 2003), 71, 76–80.
68. Haney López, *Racism on Trial*, 2, 9, 10.
69. Andreas Wimmer, "The Making and Unmaking of Ethnic Boundaries: A Multilevel Process Theory," *American Journal of Sociology* 113(4) (2008): 970–1022.
70. Carey McWilliams, *Brothers Under the Skin* (Boston: Little, Brown, 1943), 295–325; Carey McWilliams, *Prejudice—Japanese-Americans: Symbol of Racial Intolerance* (Boston: Little, Brown, 1944), 289–94.
71. Wu, *The Color of Success*, 156–68; W. L. Worden, "Hate That Failed," *Saturday Evening Post*, May 4, 1946, 22–23.
72. Wu, *The Color of Success*, 171.

73. For the report and the controversy around it, see Lee Rainwater and William L. Yancey, *The Moynihan Report and the Politics of Controversy* (Cambridge, MA: MIT Press, 1967).
74. Wu, *The Color of Success*, 174–76, 246, 247; Bill Hosogawa, *Nisei: The Quiet Americans* (New York: William Morrow, 1969).
75. Ronald Takaki, *Strangers from a Different Shore: A History of Asian Americans* (New York: Penguin, 1989), 474–75.

Chapter Three. How Sex Got Serious

1. Gloria Steinem, *Outrageous Acts and Everyday Rebellions*, 2nd ed. (New York: Henry Holt, 1995 [1983]), 23.
2. Dorothy Sue Cobble, *The Other Women's Movement: Workplace Justice and Social Rights in Modern America* (Princeton, NJ: Princeton University Press, 2003), 170 (quoting Katherine Ellickson, commissioner), 175 ("how some of the ladies feel"); Alice Kessler-Harris, *In Pursuit of Equity: Women, Men, and the Quest for Economic Citizenship in Twentieth-Century America* (New York: Oxford University Press, 2001), 241 ("ripples of laughter"), 283 ("better than being spat upon"); Ruth Rosen, *The World Split Open: How the Modern Women's Movement Changed America* (New York: Penguin, 2000), 71–72 (quoting Celler).
3. Alice S. Rossi, "Equality between the Sexes: An Immodest Proposal," *Daedalus* 93(2) (Spring 1964): 607–52.
4. Barbara Ehrenreich, *The Hearts of Men: American Dreams and the Flight from Commitment* (Garden Press, NY: Anchor Press/Doubleday, 1983), 126–27. I wrote about this at the time: Paul Starr, "Hollywood's New Ideal of Masculinity," *New York Times*, Sunday Arts & Leisure, July 16, 1978.
5. Gunnar Myrdal, *An American Dilemma: The Negro Problem and Modern Democracy* (New York: Harper & Brothers, 1944), 1073–78 (quotation, 1075).
6. Donald J. Hernandez, *America's Children: Resources from Family, Government, and the Economy* (New York: Russell Sage Foundation, 1993), 104 (figure 4.2, combining farm and non-farm families).
7. Cynthia Harrison, *On Account of Sex: The Politics of Women's Issues, 1945–1968* (Berkeley: University of California Press, 1988), 9–10, 14–23, 26–39; Cobble, *The Other Women's Movement*.
8. Martha Weinman Lear, "The Second Feminist Wave," *New York Times Magazine*, March 10, 1968; Nancy A. Hewitt, "From Seneca Falls to Suffrage? Reimagining a 'Master' Narrative in U.S. Women's History," in Nancy A. Hewitt, ed., *No Permanent Waves: Recasting Histories of U.S. Feminism* (New Brunswick, NJ: Rutgers University Press, 2010), 15–38; and Becky Thompson, "Multiracial Feminism: Recasting the Chronology of Second Wave Feminism," in Hewitt, *No Permanent Waves*, 39–60.
9. Harrison, *On Account of Sex*, 89–105.

10. President's Commission on the Status of Women, *American Women* (Washington, DC: Government Printing Office, 1963), 18.
11. President's Commission, *American Women*, 30–31, 45; Harrison, *On Account of Sex*, 109–67; Kessler-Harris, *In Pursuit of Equity*, 213–25.
12. Betty Friedan, *The Feminine Mystique* (New York: W. W. Norton, 1963), 281, 344, 346.
13. Daniel Horowitz, *Betty Friedan and the Making of The Feminine Mystique: The American Left, the Cold War, and Modern Feminism* (Amherst: University of Massachusetts Press, 1998), 1–2, 121–52.
14. Kessler-Harris, *In Pursuit of Equity*, 241–44 (quoting Southern congressmen); Jo Freeman, "How 'Sex' Got into Title VII: Persistent Opportunism as a Maker of Public Policy," in *We Will Be Heard: Women's Struggles for Political Power in the United States* (Lanham, MD: Rowman and Littlefield, 2008), ch. 12.
15. Kessler-Harris, *In Pursuit of Equity*, 246.
16. Betty Friedan, *"It Changed My Life": Writings on the Women's Movement* (New York: Dell, 1991 [1985]), xxxii.
17. Weeks v. Southern Bell Telephone & Telegraph Company, 408 F. 2d 228 (1969).
18. Kessler-Harris, *In Pursuit of Equity*, 267.
19. Jerome Karabel, *The Chosen: The Hidden History of Admission and Exclusion at Harvard, Yale, and Princeton* (Boston: Houghton Mifflin, 2005), 410–48; Janet Bickel, "Women in Medical Education," *New England Journal of Medicine* 319 (December 15, 1988): 1579–84; Frederika Randall, "The Hand That Rocks the Cradle: A Study of the Comprehensive Child Development Act of 1971" (MA thesis, Massachusetts Institute of Technology, 1973), https://dspace.mit.edu/bitstream/handle/1721.1/77366/25977492-MIT.pdf?sequence=2.
20. Lenore J. Weitzman, *The Divorce Revolution: The Unexpected Social and Economic Consequences for Women and Children in America* (New York: Free Press, 1985); Steven Mintz and Susan Kellogg, *Domestic Revolutions: A Social History of American Family Life* (New York: Free Press, 1988), 225–33.
21. Helen Gurley Brown, *Sex and the Single Girl* (New York: B. Geis, 1962), 246; Barbara Ehrenreich, Elizabeth Hess, and Gloria Jacobs, *Re-Making Love: The Feminization of Sex* (Garden City, NY: Anchor Press/Doubleday, 1986), 54–59.
22. David J. Harding and Christopher Jencks, "Changing Attitudes toward Premarital Sex: Cohort, Period, and Aging Effects," *Public Opinion Quarterly* 67(2) (2003): 211–26; Elaine Tyler May, *America and the Pill: A History of Promise, Peril, and Liberation* (New York: Basic Books, 2010), 71–91 ("Yes, but I'm not at all sure," 88); Griswold v. Connecticut, 381 U.S. 479 (1965).
23. Kristin Luker, *Abortion and the Politics of Motherhood* (Berkeley: University of California Press, 2008), 66–91.
24. Christopher Z. Mooney and Mei-Hsien Lee, "Legislative Morality in the American States: The Case of Pre-Roe Abortion Regulation Reform," *American*

Journal of Political Science 39(3) (1995): 599–627; Luker, *Abortion and the Politics of Motherhood*, 94.

25. See figure 5 in Greg D. Adams, "Evidence of an Issue Evolution," *American Journal of Political Science* 41(3) (1997): 718–37. Elite opinion, as measured by congressional voting, was slightly more favorable to abortion rights in the Democratic Party in the early 1970s and became more favorable over time.
26. Jo Freeman, *The Politics of Women's Liberation* (New York: Longman, 1975), 108–10.
27. Sara M. Evans, *Tidal Wave: How Women Changed America at Century's End* (New York: Free Press, 2003), 27; "Redstockings Manifesto," in Robin Morgan, ed., *Sisterhood Is Powerful* (New York: Vintage Books, 1970), 598–601.
28. "NOW: Statement of Purpose," in Friedan, *It Changed My Life*, 109–15; Freeman, *The Politics of Women's Liberation*, 115–16.
29. Freeman, *The Politics of Women's Liberation*, 103–4.
30. Ehrenreich et al., *Re-Making Love*, 68–69.
31. Lear, "The Second Feminist Wave"; WITCH, "Confront the Whoremakers at the Bridal Fair" (February 1969), in Morgan, *Sisterhood Is Powerful*, 610–13; Sheila Cronan, "Marriage," in Anne Koedt, Ellen Levine, and Anita Rapone, eds., *Radical Feminism* (New York: Quadrangle, 1973), 213–21 (quotation, 219); Friedan, *It Changed My Life*, 201–7; Rosen, *The World Split Open*, 87.
32. Freeman, *The Politics of Women's Liberation*, 114.
33. Steinem, *Outrageous Acts and Everyday Rebellions*, 21–23; Carolyn G. Heilbrun, *The Education of a Woman: The Life of Gloria Steinem* (New York: Dial Press, 1995), 168–74, 187–88.
34. Freeman, *The Politics of Women's Liberation*, 120n.
35. Rosen, *The World Split Open*, 143–95.
36. Boston Women's Health Book Collective, *Our Bodies, Ourselves: A Book By and For Women* (New York: Simon & Schuster, 1973), 6.
37. Boston Women's Health Book Collective, *Our Bodies, Ourselves*, 12, 23.
38. William N. Eskridge Jr., *Dishonorable Passions: Sodomy Laws in America, 1861–2003* (New York: Viking, 2008), 20, 50.
39. John D'Emilio, *Sexual Politics, Sexual Communities: The Making of a Homosexual Minority in the United States, 1940–1970* (Chicago: University of Chicago Press, 1983), 15–19; Eskridge, *Dishonorable Passions*, 75–76.
40. George Chauncey, *Gay New York: Gender, Urban Culture, and the Making of the Gay Male World, 1890–1940* (New York: Basic Books, 2019); Eskridge, *Dishonorable Passions*, 76–108.
41. Alfred C. Kinsey, *Sexual Behavior in the Human Male* (Philadelphia: W. B. Saunders, 1948), 650–51; Alfred C. Kinsey, *Sexual Behavior in the Human Female* (Philadelphia: W. B. Saunders, 1953), 450, 475, 487; D'Emilio, *Sexual Politics, Sexual Communities*, 37.
42. D'Emilio, *Sexual Politics, Sexual Communities*, 140–44.
43. D'Emilio, *Sexual Politics, Sexual Communities*, 57–107.

44. D'Emilo, *Sexual Politics, Sexual Communities*, 115.
45. Miller v. California, 413 U.S. 15 (1973). The earlier case was Roth v. United States, 354 U.S. 476 (1957). For the story behind these cases, see Gay Talese, *Thy Neighbor's Wife* (New York: Harper Collins, 2009 [1980]), 93–111, 408–14.
46. Federal Communications Commission v. Pacifica Foundation et al., 438 U.S. 726 (1978).
47. Eskridge, *Dishonorable Passions*, 121–27, 152–54, 170–73; D'Emilio, *Sexual Politics, Sexual Communities*, 211–12.
48. Steven Seidman, *Romantic Longings: Love in America, 1830–1980* (New York: Routledge, 1991), 164.
49. Dudley Clendinen and Adam Nagourney, *Out for Good: The Struggle to Build a Gay Rights Movement in America* (New York: Simon & Schuster, 1999), 42–51.
50. Clendenin and Nagourney, *Out for Good*, 92–93.
51. Seidman, *Romantic Longings*, 127–32.
52. Clendenin and Nagourney, *Out for Good*, 199–216.
53. Eskridge, *Dishonorable Passions*, 176–86, 197–201.
54. Clendenin and Nagourney, *Out for Good*, 383–84, 387, 391–404.
55. Alan S. Yang, "Trends: Attitudes toward Homosexuality," *Public Opinion Quarterly* 61(3) (1997): 484.
56. Eskridge, *Dishonorable Passions*, 201.
57. For a general history of the 1960s, see Maurice Isserman and Michael Kazin, *America Divided: The Civil War of the 1960s*, 6th ed. (New York: Oxford University Press, 2021). Isserman and Kazin give far more attention to the New Left than to the women's and gay rights movements, whereas in this book I do the reverse—a reflection of the different line of argument here. For a more extreme contrast, see Todd Gitlin, *The Sixties: Years of Hope, Days of Rage* (New York: Bantam Books, 1987). But in his preface, responding to the question of "what *did* all the uprisings accomplish for the good?," Gitlin puts first "the irreversible entry of blacks, women, and their concerns into American politics and professional life."
58. Weitzman, *The Divorce Revolution*, xii.
59. Betsey Stevenson and Justin Wolfers, "Bargaining in the Shadow of the Law: Divorce Laws and Family Distress," *Quarterly Journal of Economics* 121 (2006): 267–88; Sara S. McLanahan and Erin L. Kelly, "The Feminization of Poverty: Past and Future," in Janet Saltzman Chafetz, ed., *Handbook of the Sociology of Gender* (New York: Kluwer, 1999), 127–45. The article originally identifying the pattern was Diane Pearce, "The Feminization of Poverty: Women, Work and Welfare," *Urban and Social Change Review* 11 (1978): 28–36.
60. Jane J. Mansbridge, *Why We Lost the ERA* (Chicago: University of Chicago Press, 1986), 105–7.

61. Ehrenreich, *The Hearts of Men*, 152–53.
62. Mansbridge, *Why We Lost the ERA*, 2, 36–44, 60–66. Mansbridge nonetheless supported the ERA on the grounds that it would affirm the principle of equality and might have positive future effects. (It also would have entrenched the principle of gender equality in the Constitution, making it less likely that the Court would reverse the decisions it made based on the justices' reading of the Fourteenth Amendment.)
63. Mansbridge, *Why We Lost the ERA*, 91–112.
64. Ehrenreich, *The Hearts of Men*, 146 (italics in original).

Chapter Four. Half a Counterrevolution

1. Julian E. Zelizer, *Arsenal of Democracy: The Politics of National Security from World War II to the War on Terrorism* (New York: Basic Books, 2010), 194.
2. Garry Wills, *Nixon Agonistes* (Boston: Houghton Mifflin, 1970), 265.
3. The audio for Reagan's speech is available from the Ronald Reagan Presidential Library at http://www.youtube.com/watch?v=AYrlDlrLDSQ.
4. Rick Perlstein, *Before the Storm: Barry Goldwater and the Unmaking of the American Consensus* (New York: Hill and Wang, 2001), 6–16; Kevin M. Kruse, "The Southern Strategy," in Kevin M. Kruse and Julian E. Zelizer, eds., *Myth America: Historians Take on the Biggest Legends and Lies about Our Past* (New York: Basic Books, 2023), 169–96.
5. G. Edward White, *Earl Warren: A Public Life* (New York: Oxford University Press, 1982), 138–53, 185. On the Warren Court, see Morton J. Horwitz, *The Warren Court and the Pursuit of Justice* (New York: Hill and Wang, 1998).
6. Earl Black and Merle Black, *The Rise of Southern Republicans* (Cambridge, MA: Harvard University Press, 2002), 2, 24–25, 40.
7. Clive Webb, ed., *Massive Resistance: Southern Opposition to the Second Reconstruction* (New York: Oxford University Press, 2005), 5, 20.
8. Michael J. Klarman, "Why Massive Resistance?," in Webb, *Massive Resistance*, 38.
9. John B. Judis, *William F. Buckley, Jr.: Patron Saint of the Conservatives* (New York: Simon & Schuster, 1988), 13.
10. Judis, *William F. Buckley, Jr.*, 138–39. See also Joseph E. Lowndes, *From the New Deal to the New Right: Race and the Southern Origins of Modern Conservatism* (New Haven, CT: Yale University Press, 2008), 45–76.
11. Judis, *William F. Buckley, Jr.*, 135, 162.
12. Kruse, "The Southern Strategy," 178, 179.
13. Barry Goldwater, *The Conscience of a Conservative* (Shepherdsville, KY: Victor, 1960), 9–10, 33–34.
14. Black and Black, *The Rise of Southern Republicans*, 4.
15. Thomas Byrne Edsall and Mary D. Edsall, *Chain Reaction: The Impact of Race, Rights, and Taxes on American Politics* (New York: W. W. Norton, 1991), 36; Edward G. Carmines and James A. Stimson, *Issue Evolution: Race and the*

Transformation of American Politics (Princeton, NJ: Princeton University Press, 1989), 163 (figure 7.2).
16. Kevin P. Phillips, *The Emerging Republican Majority* (Princeton, NJ: Princeton University Press, 2015 [1969]), 1.
17. For a recent historical analysis that emphasizes deeper social and political connections between the South and the Southwest, see Heather Cox Richardson, *How the South Won the Civil War: Oligarchy, Democracy, and the Continuing Fight for the Soul of America* (New York: Oxford University Press, 2020).
18. Tom Wicker, *One of Us: Richard Nixon and the American Dream* (New York: Random House, 1991), 485, 493; Alexander v. Holmes County, 396 U.S. 19 (1969); Dean J. Kotlowski, *Nixon's Civil Rights: Politics, Principle, and Policy* (Cambridge, MA: Harvard University Press, 2001), 30–31.
19. Kotlowski, *Nixon's Civil Rights*, 34–35, 40.
20. Kotlowski, *Nixon's Civil Rights*, 37; Wicker, *One of Us*, 504.
21. Randall Balmer, *Bad Faith: Race and the Rise of the Religious Right* (Grand Rapids, MI: William B. Eerdmans, 2021), 39.
22. Howard Schuman, Charlotte Steeh, Lawrence Bobo, and Maria Krysan, *Racial Attitudes in America: Trends and Interpretations*, rev. ed. (Cambridge, MA: Harvard University Press, 1997), 123–25 (table 3.2); Edsall and Edsall, *Chain Reaction*, 89; Kotlowski, *Nixon's Civil Rights*, 42–43.
23. Hugh Davis Graham, *The Civil Rights Era: Origins and Development of National Policy, 1960–1972* (New York: Oxford University Press, 1990), 278–97, 322–45; John David Skrentny, *The Ironies of Affirmative Action: Politics, Culture, and Justice in America* (Chicago: University of Chicago Press, 1996), 193–204; Kotlowski, *Nixon's Civil Rights*, 105.
24. Kotlowski, *Nixon's Civil Rights*, 107–8; Kevin Yuill, *Richard Nixon and the Rise of Affirmative Action: The Pursuit of Racial Equality in an Era of Limits* (Lanham, MD: Rowman & Littlefield, 2006).
25. Richard Nixon, "Bridges to Human Dignity, The Concept," remarks on the CBS Radio Network, April 25, 1968, The American Presidency Project, https://www.presidency.ucsb.edu/node/326763; Kotlowski, *Nixon's Civil Rights*, 125–56.
26. Kotlowski, *Nixon's Civil Rights*, 2.
27. Daniel P. Moynihan, *The Politics of a Guaranteed Income: The Nixon Administration and the Family Assistance Plan* (New York: Vintage, 1973), 493. The 2024 calculations come from the CPI inflation calculator of the Bureau of Labor Statistics, https://data.bls.gov/cgi-bin/cpicalc.pl.
28. Moynihan, *The Politics of a Guaranteed Income*, 439–542; Brian Steensland, *The Failed Welfare Revolution: America's Struggle over Guaranteed Income Policy* (Princeton, NJ: Princeton University Press, 2008).
29. The key turning point was Dandridge v. Williams, 397 U.S. 471 (1970). See Adam Cohen, *Supreme Inequality: The Supreme Court's Fifty-Year Battle for a More Unjust America* (New York: Penguin, 2020), ch. 2.

30. I draw here on my account in *Remedy and Reaction: The Peculiar American Struggle over Health Care Reform*, rev. ed. (New Haven, CT: Yale University Press, 2013), 55–58.
31. Kotlowski, *Nixon's Civil Rights*, 1.
32. Wicker, *One of Us*, 413.
33. Will Herberg, *Protestant Catholic Jew: An Essay in American Religious Sociology* (Garden City, NY: Doubleday, 1955); Robert Wuthnow, *The Restructuring of American Religion: Society and Faith since World War II* (Princeton, NJ: Princeton University Press, 1988).
34. Robert D. Putnam and David E. Campbell, *American Grace: How Religion Divides and Unites Us* (New York: Simon & Schuster, 2010), 97–99, 103–4, 106–7.
35. Putnam and Campbell, *American Grace*, 111–12.
36. Michael Hout, Andrew Greeley, and Melissa J. Wilde, "The Demographic Imperative in Religious Change in the United States," *American Journal of Sociology* 107(2) (2001): 468–500.
37. Kristin Kobes Du Mez, *Jesus and John Wayne: How White Evangelicals Corrupted a Faith and Fractured a Nation* (New York: Liveright, 2020), 9–12; Balmer, *Bad Faith*, 15–19.
38. Surveys count evangelicals in three ways: by their self-definition (asking, for example, whether they are "evangelical or born again"), by their agreement with a list of theological doctrines deemed to be central to evangelicalism, and by membership in denominations deemed to be evangelical. Each method has its problems. For a succinct discussion, see Frank Newport, "Jimmy Carter and the Challenge of Identifying Evangelicals," Gallup, March 24, 2023, https://news.gallup.com/opinion/polling-matters/472772/jimmy-carter-challenge-identifying-evangelicals.aspx.
39. Kevin M. Kruse, *One Nation under God: How Corporate America Invented Christian America* (New York: Basic Books, 2015).
40. Balmer, *Bad Faith*, xii, 69–70.
41. Balmer, *Bad Faith*, xiv, 31–37.
42. Balmer, *Bad Faith*, 38–49.
43. Nancy Tatom Ammerman, *Baptist Battles: Social Change and Religious Conflict in the Southern Baptist Convention* (New Brunswick, NJ: Rutgers University Press, 1990).
44. Balmer, *Bad Faith*, 50–57. See also Frank Schaeffer, *Crazy for God* (New York: Carroll & Graf, 2007).
45. Du Mez, *Jesus and John Wayne*, 12.
46. Robert Wuthnow, "The Political Rebirth of American Evangelicals," in Robert Wuthnow and Robert Liebman, eds., *The New Christian Right: Mobilization and Legitimation* (New York: Aldine, 1983), 167–85.
47. Jerome L. Himmelstein, *To the Right: The Transformation of American Conservatism* (Berkeley: University of California Press, 1989), 117–18 (Falwell quoted, 118); Wuthnow, "The Political Rebirth of American Evangelicals," 168.

48. Donald T. Critchlow, *The Conservative Ascendancy: How the GOP Right Made Political History* (Cambridge, MA: Harvard University Press, 2007), 176.
49. Leonard Silk and David Vogel, *Ethics and Profits: The Crisis of Confidence in American Business* (New York: Touchstone, 1976), 21, 181.
50. Lewis F. Powell Jr., "Attack of American Free Enterprise System," Memorandum to Mr. Eugene B. Sydnor, Jr., Chairman, Education Committee, U.S. Chamber of Commerce, August 23, 1971, https://www.thirteen.org/wnet/supremecourt/personality/sources_document13.html.
51. David Vogel, "The Power of Business in America: A Reappraisal," *British Journal of Political Science* 13 (1983): 19–43.
52. Stephen B. Burbank and Sean Farhang, *Rights and Retrenchment: The Counterrevolution against Federal Litigation* (Cambridge: Cambridge University Press, 2017), 4–16; David Vogel, *Fluctuating Fortunes: The Political Power of Business in America* (New York: Basic Books, 1989), 68, 159, 293.
53. Silk and Vogel, *Ethics and Profits*, 82–101; Otis L. Graham Jr., *Toward a Planned Society: From Roosevelt to Nixon* (New York: Oxford University Press, 1979), 277–86.
54. Jefferson Cowie, *Stayin' Alive: The 1970s and the Last Days of the Working Class* (New York: New Press, 2010), 70–74, 288–91 (quotation, 70); Jake Rosenfeld, *What Unions No Longer Do* (Cambridge, MA: Harvard University Press, 2014), 2 (Nixon quoted). For more on labor's troubles in this period, see chapter 8 in this book.
55. Thomas Byrne Edsall, *The New Politics of Inequality* (New York: W. W. Norton, 1984), 107–40.
56. Sidney Blumenthal, *The Rise of the Counter-Establishment: From Conservative Ideology to Political Power* (New York: Times Books, 1986).
57. On the use of "neoliberal" in the 1980s, see Randall Rothenberg, *The Neoliberals: Creating the New American Politics* (New York: Simon & Schuster, 1984).
58. See my discussion of the meaning of neoliberalism in *Entrenchment: Wealth, Power, and the Constitution of Democratic Societies* (New Haven, CT: Yale University Press, 2019), 169–70.
59. Irving Kristol, *Neoconservatism: The Autobiography of an Idea* (New York: Free Press, 1995); Norman Podhoretz, "Neoconservatism: A Eulogy," *Commentary* 101(3) (March 1996): 19–27; Peter Steinfels, *The Neoconservatives: The Men Who Are Changing America's Politics* (New York: Simon & Schuster, 1979); Murray Friedman, *The Neoconservative Revolution: Jewish Intellectuals and the Shaping of Public Policy* (New York: Cambridge University Press, 2005); Justin Vaisse, *Neoconservatism: The Biography of a Movement* (Cambridge, MA: Harvard University Press, 2010). On Bell, who came to revile the neoconservatives, see my "Daniel Bell's Three-Dimensional Puzzle," in Paul Starr and Julian Zelizer, eds., *Defining the Age: Daniel Bell, His Time and Ours* (New York: Columbia University Press, 2021), 59–87.
60. Michel Crozier, Samuel P. Huntington, and Joji Watanuki, *The Crisis of Democracy: Report on the Governability of the Democracies by the Trilateral Commission*

(New York: New York University Press, 1975), 157–71. On the market as a form of political deflection, see Stefan Eich, "The Double Bind: Daniel Bell, the Public Household, and Financialization," in Starr and Zelizer, *Defining the Age*, 291–311.

61. Laura Kalman, *Abe Fortas: A Biography* (New Haven, CT: Yale University Press, 1990); Laura Kalman, *The Long Reach of the Sixties: LBJ, Nixon, and the Making of the Contemporary Supreme Court* (New York: Oxford University Press, 2017).
62. Vincent Blasi, ed., *The Burger Court: The Counter-Revolution That Wasn't* (New Haven, CT: Yale University Press, 1983).
63. Byron Shafer, *Quiet Revolution: The Struggle for the Democratic Party and the Shaping of Post-Reform Politics* (New York: Russell Sage Foundation, 1983); Elaine C. Kamarck, *Primary Politics: How Presidential Candidates Have Shaped the Modern Nominating System* (Washington, DC: Brookings Institution Press, 2009).
64. Buckley v. Valeo, 424 U.S. 1 (1976); Robert E. Mutch, *Buying the Vote: A History of Campaign Finance Reform* (New York: Oxford University Press, 2014), 139–50; Robert C. Post, *Citizens Divided: Campaign Finance Reform and the Constitution* (Cambridge, MA: Harvard University Press, 2014); Michael Graetz and Linda Greenhouse, *The Burger Court and the Rise of the Judicial Right* (New York: Simon & Schuster, 2016), 255–60.
65. Graetz and Greenhouse, *The Burger Court and the Rise of the Judicial Right*, 240–65, 269–78.
66. Quoted in Julian E. Zelizer, *Jimmy Carter* (New York: Times Books, 2010), 58.
67. U.S. Elections Project, "National Turnout Rates, 1789–Present," https://www.electproject.org/national-1789-present.
68. Julian E. Zelizer, "Reagan Revolution," in Kruse and Zelizer, *Myth America*, 283–98; Gil Troy, *The Reagan Revolution: A Very Short Introduction* (New York: Oxford University Press, 2009), 54.
69. Martin Anderson, *Revolution: The Reagan Legacy*, updated ed. (Stanford, CA: Hoover Institution Press, 1990), 116–21, 133.
70. Lou Cannon, *Reagan* (New York: Putnam, 1982), 91, 235–36; Thomas W. Evans, *The Education of Ronald Reagan: The General Electric Years and the Untold Story of His Conversion to Conservatism* (New York: Columbia University Press, 2006); Robert Kuttner, *The Revolt of the Haves: Tax Rebellions and Hard Times* (New York: Simon & Schuster, 1980); David O. Sears and Jack Citrin, *Tax Revolt: Something for Nothing in California* (Cambridge, MA: Harvard University Press, 1985); David Lowery and Lee Sigelman, "Understanding the Tax Revolt: Eight Explanations," *American Political Science Review* 75 (1981): 963–74; W. Elliot Brownlee, "'Reaganomics': The Fiscal and Monetary Policies," in Andrew L. Johns, ed., *A Companion to Ronald Reagan* (Malden, MA: Wiley Blackwell, 2018), 131–48.

71. Daniel P. Moynihan, "Reagan's Bankrupt Budget," *New Republic*, December 31, 1983, reprinted in Moynihan, *Came the Revolution: Argument in the Reagan Era* (New York: Harcourt Brace Jovanovic, 1988), 151–68.
72. Martin Feldstein, "Supply-Side Economics: Old Truths and New Claims," National Bureau of Economic Research, Working Paper 1792, January 1976; Brownlee, "'Reaganomics.'"
73. "Income Inequality, USA, 1820–2021," World Inequality Database, https://wid.world/country/usa/.
74. Larry M. Bartels, *Unequal Democracy: The Political Economy of the New Gilded Age*, 2nd ed. (New York: Russell Sage Foundation, 2016), 7–73.
75. Brownlee, "'Reaganomics'"; "Budget Policy: 3. Charles Schultze," in Martin Feldstein, ed., *American Economic Policy in the 1980s* (Chicago: University of Chicago Press, 1994), 279–84 (esp. table 4.16).
76. Michael R. Adamson, "Reagan and the Economy: Business and Labor, Deregulation and Regulation," in Johns, *A Companion to Ronald Reagan*, 149–66; Barry T. Hirsch, David A. Macpherson, and Wayne G. Vroman, "Estimates of Union Density by State," *Monthly Labor Review* 124(7) (2001): 51–55.
77. Adamson, "Reagan and the Economy."
78. Randy Shilts, *And the Band Played On: Politics, People, and the AIDS Epidemic* (New York: Penguin, 1988).
79. Lou Cannon, *President Reagan: The Role of a Lifetime* (New York: Public Affairs, 1991), 456–58; Jeremy D. Mayer, "Reagan and Race: Prophet of Color Blindness, Baiter of the Backlash," in Kyle Longley, Jeremy D. Mayer, Michael Schaller, and John W. Sloan, eds., *Deconstructing Reagan: Conservative Mythology and America's Fortieth President* (Armonk, NY: M. E. Sharpe, 2007), 70–89.
80. Sean Wilentz, *The Age of Reagan: A History, 1974–2008* (New York: HarperCollins, 2008), 180–85.
81. Jake Rosenfeld, *What Unions No Longer Do* (Cambridge, MA: Harvard University Press, 2014), ch. 5.
82. William Julius Wilson, *The Truly Disadvantaged: The Inner City, the Underclass, and Public Policy* (Chicago: University of Chicago Press, 1987), 22–23.
83. Marie Gottschalk, "Hiding in Plain Sight: American Politics and the Carceral State," *Annual Review of Political Science* 11 (2008): 235–60; The Sentencing Project, "Mass Incarceration Trends," https://www.sentencingproject.org/reports/mass-incarceration-trends/.
84. Michael Tonry, *Malign Neglect: Race, Crime, and Punishment in America* (New York: Oxford University Press, 1995), 17–18; John F. Pfaff, *Locked In: The True Causes of Mass Incarceration—and How to Achieve Real Reform* (New York: Basic Books, 2017).
85. Tonry, *Malign Neglect*, 25–26, 81–83.
86. Tonry, *Malign Neglect*, 29; Bruce Western, *Punishment and Inequality in America* (New York: Russell Sage Foundation, 2006).

87. Ron Suskind, *The Price of Loyalty: George W. Bush, the White House and the Education of Paul O'Neill* (Simon & Schuster, 2004), 291.

Chapter Five. Americans as Enemies

1. Irving Kristol, "My Cold War," *The National Interest*, Spring 1993, 141–44.
2. Gary Gerstle, *The Rise and Fall of the Neoliberal Order* (New York: Oxford University Press, 2022), 152–64.
3. John Micklethwait and Adrian Wooldridge, *The Right Nation: Conservative Power in America* (New York: Penguin, 2004); Jon Meacham, "We're a Conservative Country," *Newsweek*, October 17, 2008, https://www.newsweek.com/meacham-were-conservative-country-92333. In 2015, the eve of Brexit and Trump's election, David Brooks was still holding on to the idea of center-right preeminence: "The Center-Right Moment," *New York Times*, May 12, 2015.
4. The sun/moon analogy comes from Samuel Lubell, *The Future of American Politics* (New York: Harper & Row, 1965 [1951]), 191–92. For an application of the analogy to the 1990s written in the confidence that Republicans were and would continue to be the "sun" party, see Michael Lind, "Solar Eclipse: Behind Clinton's Moon the Republican Sun Still Shines," *New Yorker*, October 27, 1996, 7–8.
5. To put the point in more theoretical terms, these conceptions reflect assumptions of totality—that is, an underlying unity of a social and political order—and a failure to recognize how dissimilar, even antithetical policies and institutions can become entrenched in the same society, as I argue in *Entrenchment: Wealth, Power, and the Constitutions of Democratic Societies* (New Haven, CT: Yale University Press, 2019).
6. On the distinction between "closely and deeply divided" and "closely but not deeply divided," see Morris P. Fiorina, with Samuel J. Abrams and Jeremy C. Pope, *Culture War? The Myth of a Polarized America* (New York: Pearson Longman, 2005), 8 (figure 2.1). Fiorina tried to show Americans were closely but not deeply divided without recognizing how the first might lead to the second. For the argument that Americans had become both closely and deeply divided and that this was an "explosive combination," see Ronald Brownstein, *The Second Civil War: How Extreme Partisanship Has Paralyzed Washington and Polarized America* (New York: Penguin, 2007), 19.
7. Patrick J. Buchanan, "1992 Republican National Convention Speech," August 17, 1992, https://buchanan.org/blog/1992-republican-national-convention-speech-148. The wording of the speech as delivered was slightly different: "Pat Buchanan 1992 Republican Convention Address," C-SPAN, August 17, 1992, https://www.c-span.org/video/?31255-1/pat-buchanan-1992-republican-convention-address.
8. Hilton Kramer, "The Prospect before Us," *The New Criterion* 9(1) (1990): 6–9; Charles Horner, "The American 80s: Disaster or Triumph?," *Commen-*

tary, September 1990, 30–31. I am drawing here on my response to the neocons: "The Cultural Enemy Within," *The American Prospect*, Winter 1991, 9–11.
9. Hendrik Hertzberg, "Neoconfab" (Washington Diarist), *The New Republic*, May 21, 1990, 42.
10. James Davison Hunter, *Culture Wars: The Struggle to Define America* (New York: Basic Books, 1991), 43–46, 49.
11. Paul DiMaggio, John H. Evans, and Bethany Bryson, "Have Americans' Social Attitudes Become More Polarized?," *American Journal of Sociology* 102 (1996): 690–755.
12. The literature is extensive: Greg D. Adams, "Abortion: Evidence of an Issue Evolution," *American Journal of Political Science* 41(3) (1997): 718–37; Edward G. Carmines and James Woods, "The Role of Party Activists in the Evolution of the Abortion Issue," *Political Behavior* 24(4) (2002): 361–77; Geoffrey C. Layman and Thomas M. Carsey, "Why Do Party Activists Convert? An Analysis of Individual-Level Change in the Abortion Issue," *Political Research Quarterly* 51 (1998): 723–50.
13. John H. Evans, "Have Americans' Attitudes Become More Polarized? An Update," *Social Science Quarterly* 84 (2003): 71–90; David Karol, *Party Position Change in American Politics: Coalition Management* (New York: Cambridge University Press, 2009).
14. Times Mirror Center for People and the Press, "The Age of Indifference," June 28, 1990, https://www.pewresearch.org/politics/1990/06/28/the-age-of-indifference/#report-summary; Thomas E. Patterson, "Young People and News," Shorenstein Center on the Press, Politics, and Public Policy, July 2007; Martin Wattenberg, *Is Voting for Young People?* (New York: Pearson Longman, 2008), 63–68.
15. Robert Putnam, *Bowling Alone: The Collapse and Revival of American Community* (New York: Simon & Schuster, 2000), 44, 252, 255. Behind the generational differences, Putnam saw differences in social capital. For my criticism of that analysis, see my review, "The Public Vanishes," *The New Republic*, August 14, 2000, 35–37. See also, below in this chapter, the discussion of changing forms of political struggle.
16. Chuck Klosterman, *The Nineties* (New York: Penguin, 2022), 19. The album was Nirvana's *Nevermind*.
17. Pat Robertson, quoted in Hunter, *Culture Wars*, 202–3; Kristin Luker, *When Sex Goes to School: Warring Views on Sex—and Sex Education—Since the Sixties* (New York: W. W. Norton, 2006).
18. Barbara Arneil, "Gender, Diversity, and Organizational Change: The Boy Scouts vs. Girl Scouts of America," *Perspectives on Politics* 8 (March 2010): 53–68. The Boy Scouts won a Supreme Court case in 2000 affirming their right to exclude members based on sexual orientation, but in 2014 the organization abandoned that exclusion and five years later changed its name to Scouts USA (later Scouting America) and began admitting girls.

19. Robert D. Putnam and David E. Campbell, *American Grace: How Religion Divides and Unites Us* (New York: Simon & Schuster, 2010), 3–5, 127–31.
20. Douglas S. Massey and Nancy A. Denton, *American Apartheid: Segregation and the Making of the Underclass* (Cambridge, MA: Harvard University Press, 1994); Bill Bishop, with Robert G. Cushing, *The Big Sort: Why the Clustering of Like-Minded America Is Tearing Us Apart* (Boston: Houghton Mifflin, 2008). For a more recent study of partisan geographic sorting, see Ronda Kaysen and Ethan Singer, "Millions of Movers Reveal American Polarization in Action," *New York Times*, October 30, 2024. The concept of the "secession of the affluent," if not the exact phrase, comes from Robert B. Reich, *The Work of Nations* (New York: Knopf, 1991).
21. Ron J. Lesthaeghe and Lisa Neidert, "The Second Demographic Transition in the United States: Exception or Textbook Example?," *Population and Development Review* 32(4) (2006): 669–98; Naomi Cahn and June Carbone, *Red Families v. Blue Families: Legal Polarization and the Creation of Culture* (New York: Oxford University Press, 2010).
22. Albert Lasker, quoted in Joseph Turow, *Breaking Up America: Advertisers and the New Media World* (Chicago: University of Chicago Press, 1997), 23.
23. Gerstle, *The Rise and Fall of the Neoliberal Order*, 127.
24. Turow, *Breaking Up America*, 4–7, 31–36.
25. Turow, *Breaking Up America*, 44–46.
26. Theda Skocpol, *Diminished Democracy: From Membership to Management in American Civic Life* (Norman: University of Oklahoma Press, 2003); David Karpf, *The MoveOn Effect: The Unexpected Transformation of American Political Advocacy* (New York: Oxford University Press, 2012).
27. Markus Prior, *Post-Broadcast Democracy: How Media Choice Increases Inequality in Political Involvement and Polarizes Elections* (New York: Cambridge University Press, 2007).
28. Diana C. Mutz and Paul S. Martin, "Facilitating Communication across Lines of Political Difference: The Role of Mass Media," *American Political Science Review* 95 (2001): 97–114 (using data from surveys in 1992 and 1996).
29. Nicole Hemmer, *Messengers of the Right: Conservative Media and the Transformation of American Politics* (Philadelphia: University of Pennsylvania Press, 2016), 266–69; see also Paul Matzko, *The Radio Right: How a Band of Broadcasters Took on the Federal Government and Built the Modern Conservative Movement* (New York: Oxford University Press, 2020); and Brian Rosenwald, *Talk Radio's America: How an Industry Took Over a Political Party That Took Over the United States* (Cambridge, MA: Harvard University Press, 2019).
30. Paul Starr, *The Creation of the Media: Political Origins of Modern Communications* (New York: Basic Books, 2004), 130–39, 141–42; Michael Schudson, *Discovering the News: A Social History of American Newspapers* (New York: Basic Books, 1978); James T. Hamilton, *All the News That's Fit to Sell* (Princeton, NJ: Princeton University Press, 2004), 37–70.

31. John H. Summers, "What Happened to Sex Scandals? Politics and Peccadilloes, Jefferson to Kennedy," *Journal of American History* 87 (2000): 825–54; Gay Talese, *Thy Neighbor's Wife* (New York: Harper Collins, 2009 [1980]), 75.
32. Frances E. Lee, *Insecure Majorities: Congress and the Perpetual Campaign* (Chicago: University of Chicago Press, 2016).
33. In the *Atlanta Constitution*, January 17, 1994, as quoted in Amy D. Bernstein and Peter W. Bernstein, eds., *Quotations from Speaker Newt: The Little Red, White and Blue Book of the Republican Revolution* (New York: Workman, 1995), 33.
34. Excerpt from GOPAC guide reprinted as "Accentuate the Negative," *Harper's Magazine*, November 1990, 17–18.
35. Julian Zelizer, *Burning Down the House: Newt Gingrich and the Rise of the New Republican Party* (New York: Penguin, 2020); McKay Coppins, "The Man Who Broke Politics," *The Atlantic*, November 2018, https://www.theatlantic.com/magazine/archive/2018/11/newt-gingrich-says-youre-welcome/570832/.
36. Alan S. Blinder and Janet L. Yellen, *The Fabulous Decade: Macroeconomic Lessons from the 1990s* (New York: Century Foundation Press, 2001), 15–24.
37. I became involved as an adviser on health-care reform first to a Democratic Senate candidate (Harris Wofford in Pennsylvania), then to the Clinton presidential campaign, and finally in the White House from a week after the inauguration to the fall of 1993. Wofford's campaign director, James Carville, first contacted me because of an argument I had been making, first in *The American Prospect* and then in *Harper's*, on the potential middle-class support for health-care reform. During the Clinton campaign, while my friend Bob Reich was working with Ira Magaziner on the campaign's manifesto, *Putting People First*, Reich asked me to send Magaziner a copy of a new book of mine about to appear, *The Logic of Health-Care Reform* (n.p.: Grand Rounds Press, 1992), which laid out the case for combining universal coverage with a highly regulated system of competing private insurers under a cap on total spending. This was the hybrid I thought potentially attractive to Republicans as well as Democrats. Magaziner later brought me into the White House as a senior adviser on the design of the health plan. For better or worse, the plan Clinton submitted to Congress in September 1993 conforms closely to the design I favored. As they say, watch what you wish for. For an account of the Clinton health plan's origins, see Jacob S. Hacker, *The Road to Nowhere: The Genesis of President Clinton's Plan for Health Security* (Princeton, NJ: Princeton University Press, 1997). I console myself with the thought that it was a road to somewhere since many of the same elements were later passed in the more modest Affordable Care Act in 2010.
38. For my full account of the Clinton plan's defeat, including these details, see Paul Starr, *Remedy and Reaction: The Peculiar American Struggle over Health Care Reform* (New Haven, CT: Yale University Press, 2011), 103–28.

39. Jiwon Choi, Ilyana Kuziemko, Ebonya Washington, and Gavin Wright, "Local Economic and Political Effects of Trade Deals: Evidence from NAFTA," *American Economic Review* 114(6) (2024): 1540–75. For the best overall account, see Nelson Lichtenstein, *A Fabulous Failure: The Clinton Presidency and the Transformation of American Capitalism* (Princeton, NJ: Princeton University Press, 2023), ch. 8.
40. Lichtenstein, *A Fabulous Failure*, ch. 11 (Clinton quoted, 339).
41. I base part of this paragraph on a conversation with Clinton on New Year's Eve, 1996, Hilton Head, South Carolina. For more on the story of welfare reform, see David T. Ellwood, "Welfare Reform as I Knew It: When Bad Things Happen to Good Policies," *The American Prospect*, May–June 1996, 22–29; Jason DeParle, *American Dream: Three Women, Ten Kids, and a Nation's Drive to End Welfare* (New York: Penguin, 2005); Kathryn J. Edin and H. Luke Shaefer, *$2.00 a Day: Living on Almost Nothing in America* (Boston: Houghton Mifflin Harcourt, 2015); Christopher Jencks, "Why the Very Poor Have Become Poorer," *New York Review of Books*, June 9, 2016.
42. Gavin Wright, "Voting Rights, Deindustrialization, and Republican Ascendancy in the South," Institute for New Economic Thinking, Working Paper No. 135, September 2020.
43. Paul Starr, "Achievement without Credit: The Obama Presidency and Inequality," in Julian Zelizer, ed., *The Presidency of Barack Obama: A First Historical Assessment* (Princeton, NJ: Princeton University Press, 2018), 45–61.
44. Democrats had sixty votes in the Senate from July 2009, when Al Franken was finally seated after a long recount in Minnesota, to January 2010, when a Republican, Scott Brown, won a special election after the death of Ted Kennedy. Without that brief filibuster-proof majority, it is doubtful the Affordable Care Act could have been enacted.
45. Morris P. Fiorina, with Samuel J. Abrams, *The Disconnect: The Breakdown of Representation in American Politics* (Norman: University of Oklahoma Press, 2009).
46. Alan I. Abramowitz, *The Disappearing Center: Engaged Citizens, Polarization, and American Democracy* (New Haven, CT: Yale University Press, 2010), 4–5.
47. Lilliana Mason, *Uncivil Agreement: How Politics Became Our Identity* (Chicago: University of Chicago Press, 2018).
48. Shanto Iyengar and Sean J. Westwood, "Fear and Loathing across Party Lines: New Evidence on Group Polarization," *American Journal of Political Science* 59(3) (2015): 690–707; Pew Research Center, "Partisan Antipathy: More Intense, More Personal," October 10, 2019, https://www.pewresearch.org/politics/2019/10/10/partisan-antipathy-more-intense-more-personal/.
49. Jacob S. Hacker and Paul Pierson, *Off Center: The Republican Revolution and the Erosion of American Democracy* (New Haven, CT: Yale University Press, 2005); Pew Research Center for People and the Press, "Trends in American Values, 1987–2012," June 4, 2012, https://www.pewresearch.org/politics

/2012/06/04/partisan-polarization-surges-in-bush-obama-years/; Abramowitz, *The Disappearing Center*, 43–44; Fiorina, *The Disconnect*, 8.
50. Diana C. Mutz, *Hearing the Other Side: Deliberative versus Participatory Democracy* (New York: Cambridge University Press, 2006), 33.
51. Geoffrey Kabaservice, *Rule and Ruin: The Downfall of Moderation and the Destruction of the Republican Party, from Eisenhower to the Tea Party* (New York: Oxford University Press, 2012), 382.

Chapter Six. Sleepwalking (1)

1. U.S. Senate, *Hearings Before the Subcommittee on Immigration and Naturalization of the Committee on the Judiciary*, 89th Congress, 1st Session (1965), on S500, vol. 1, 1–2.
2. Maria L. La Ganga, "Dole's Ideas Often Stumble on Own Trips of the Tongue," *Los Angeles Times*, June 26, 1996.
3. "Act of March 26, 1790: An Act to Establish a Uniform Rule of Naturalization," reprinted in Michael LeMay and Elliott Robert Barkan, eds., *U.S. Immigration and Naturalization Laws and Issues* (Westport, CT: Greenwood Press, 1999), 11; Ian Haney Lopez, *White by Law: The Legal Construction of Race* (New York: New York University Press, 1996), ch. 1.
4. "U.S. Immigrant Population and Share over Time, 1850–Present," Migration Policy Institute, https://www.migrationpolicy.org/programs/data-hub/charts/immigrant-population-over-time.
5. Alberto Alesina and Marco Tabellini, "The Political Effects of Immigration: Culture or Economics?," National Bureau of Economic Research, Working Paper No. 30079, May 2022.
6. National Academies of Science, Engineering and Medicine, *The Economic and Fiscal Consequences of Immigration* (Washington, DC: National Academies Press, 2017), 247–48. For another review of recent evidence, see Ran Abramitzky and Leah Boustan, *Streets of Gold: America's Untold Story of Immigrant Success* (New York: Public Affairs, 2022), 139–62.
7. "Act of October 3, 1965: Immigration and Nationality Act of October 2, 1965 . . . ," in LeMay and Barkan, *U.S. Immigration and Naturalization Laws and Issues*, 258.
8. U.S. House, Subcommittee No. 1 of the Committee on the Judiciary, Immigration Hearings, 88th Congress, 2nd session (1964), 418; U.S. Senate, *Hearings Before the Subcommittee on Immigration and Naturalization of the Committee on the Judiciary*, 89th Congress, 1st Session (1965), on S500, vol. 1, 1–2.
9. Rep. Michael Feighan, chair of the key House committee, played the crucial role in elevating family preferences on the assumption it would protect the ethnic status quo. See Jia Lynn Yang, *One Mighty and Irresistible Tide: The Epic Struggle over American Immigration, 1924–1965* (New York: W. W. Norton, 2020), 235–40, 248–50.

10. Nathan Glazer, "Introduction," in Glazer, ed., *Clamor at the Gates: The New American Immigration* (San Francisco: ICS Press, 1985), 3–13 (quotation, 7–8).
11. Donald S. Akers, "Immigration Data and National Population Estimates for the United States," *Demography* 4 (1967): 272.
12. Kitty Calavita, *Inside the State: The Bracero Program, Immigration, and the I.N.S.* (New York: Routledge, 1992).
13. Douglas S. Massey, Jorge Durand, and Nolan J. Malone, *Beyond Smoke and Mirrors: Mexican Immigration in an Era of Economic Integration* (New York: Russell Sage Foundation, 2002), 40–47.
14. Massey et al., *Beyond Smoke and Mirrors*, 89–91. IRCA provided only an eighteen-month grace period for undocumented immigrants to apply for citizenship; it did not confer a permanent right.
15. Massey et al., *Beyond Smoke and Mirrors*, 5, 48–50, 105–41.
16. Jeffrey S. Passel, "The Size and Characteristics of the Unauthorized Migrant Population in the U.S.: Estimates Based on the March 2005 Current Population Survey," Pew Research Center, March 7, 2006, 3 (figure 2).
17. Peter Brimelow, "Time to Rethink Immigration," *National Review*, June 22, 1992, 30–46.
18. Gallup Poll, "Immigration," https://news.gallup.com/poll/1660/immigration.aspx#:~:text=Trend%20on%20Americans%27%20views%20of,believe%20they%20should%20be%20decreased; Andrew Wroe, *The Republican Party and Immigration Politics: From Proposition 187 to George W. Bush* (New York: Palgrave Macmillan, 2008), 31–34.
19. Wroe, *The Republican Party and Immigration Politics*, 38–52 (TV ad, 46).
20. Plyler v. Doe, 457 U.S. 202 (1982).
21. U.S. Commission on Immigration Reform, *U.S. Immigration Policy: Restoring Credibility*, vol. 1 (1994), iii, xii–xiii.
22. Wroe, *The Republican Party and Immigration Politics*, 121–50.
23. Mirta Ojito, "The 1998 Campaign: Immigrants; Once Divisive, Immigration Now a Muted Issue," *New York Times*, November 1, 1998.
24. Jim Yardley, "The 2000 Campaign: The Texas Governor; Hispanics Give Attentive Bush Mixed Reviews," *New York Times*, August 27, 2000; Ginger Thompson, "Fox Urges Congress to Grant Rights to Mexican Immigrants in U.S.," *New York Times*, September 7, 2001.
25. Tanya Golash-Boza, *Immigration Nation: Raids, Detentions, and Deportations in Post-9/11 America* (Boulder, CO: Paradigm, 2012); Spencer Ackerman, *Reign of Terror: How the 9/11 Era Destabilized America and Produced Trump* (New York: Viking, 2021).
26. John Higham, *Strangers in the Land: Patterns of American Nativism, 1860–1925*, 2nd ed. (New Brunswick, NJ: Rutgers University Press, 2002 [1955]), quotation, 4.
27. Dana Milbank and Emily Wax, "Bush Visits Mosque to Forestall Hate Crimes," *Washington Post*, September 18, 2001; George W. Bush, "Remarks by the President upon Arrival," White House, September 16, 2001, https://

georgewbush-whitehouse.archives.gov/news/releases/2001/09/20010916-2.html; "Threats and Responses; Muhammad a Terrorist to Falwell," *New York Times*, October 2, 2002.

28. A post-election analysis, with the benefit of additional data, found that the Hispanic vote for Bush was "probably closer to 40 percent than to the 44 percent widely reported last year by news organizations that had relied on national exit poll data." See Robert Suro, Richard Fry, and Jeffrey S. Passel, "Hispanics and the 2004 Election: Population, Electorate and Voters," Pew Research Center, June 27, 2005, https://www.pewresearch.org/race-and-ethnicity/2005/06/27/hispanics-and-the-2004-election/.

29. Border Protection, Antiterrorism, and Illegal Immigration Control Act of 2005, H.R.4437, Section 203, https://www.congress.gov/bill/109th-congress/house-bill/4437/text; Wroe, *The Republican Party and Immigration Politics*, 192–217.

30. Jeffrey S. Passel and D'Vera Cohn, "U.S. Unauthorized Immigrant Total Dips to Lowest Level in a Decade," Pew Research Center, November 27, 2018, 22, 25.

31. Brimelow, "Time to Rethink Immigration," 37.

32. Bernard Bailyn, *The Peopling of British North America: An Introduction* (New York: Vintage Books, 1988 [1986]), 60–63; Bernard Bailyn, *Voyagers to the West: A Passage in the Peopling of America on the Eve of the Revolution* (New York: Alfred A. Knopf, 1986), 147.

33. David Eltis, "Slavery and Freedom in the Early Modern World," in Stanley Engerman, ed., *Terms of Labor: Slavery, Serfdom, and Free Labor* (Stanford, CA: Stanford University Press, 1999), 25–49 (quotation, 31); Bailyn, *The Peopling of British North America*, 120–21.

34. Dylan Shane Connor, "The Cream of the Crop? Geography, Networks, and Irish Migrant Selection in the Age of Mass Migration," *Journal of Economic History* 79(1) (2019): 139–75; Ran Abramitzky, Leah Platt Boustan, and Katherine Ericksson, "Europe's Tired, Poor, Huddled Masses: Self-Selection and Economic Outcomes in the Age of Mass Migration," *American Economic Review* 102(5) (2012): 1832–56; Yannay Spitzer and Ariell Zimran, "Migrant Self-Selection: Anthropometric Evidence from the Mass Migration of Italians to the United States, 1907–1925," *Journal of Development Economics* 134 (2018): 226–47.

35. Cynthia Feliciano, "Educational Selectivity in U.S. Immigration: How Do Immigrants Compare to Those Left Behind?," *Demography* 42(1) (2005): 131–52; Daniel Chiquiar and Gordon H. Hanson, "International Migration, Self-Selection, and the Distribution of Wages: Evidence from Mexico and the United States," *Journal of Political Economy* 113(2) (2005): 239–81; Jennifer Lee and Min Zhou, *The Asian American Achievement Paradox* (New York: Russell Sage Foundation, 2015), 29–33.

36. Abramitzky and Boustan, *Streets of Gold*, 53–101. Among sons, the exceptions are Caribbeans; among daughters, some Europeans (see 83–84, figures 7A and 7B). Abramitzky and Boustan also acknowledge that the 1980 immigrants

include many who came without authorization but were able to regularize their legal status after IRCA's passage in 1986, whereas the undocumented who came later have not had that ability and have likely fallen behind as a result.

37. Richard Alba and Victor Nee, *Remaking the American Mainstream: Assimilation and Contemporary Immigration* (Cambridge, MA: Harvard University Press, 2003), 11. This allows for the possibility of "segmented assimilation," including assimilation "downward" into a stigmatized minority. Alejandro Portes and Min Zhou, "The New Second Generation: Segmented Assimilation and Its Variants," *Annals of the American Academy of Political and Social Science* 530 (1993): 74–96.
38. Abramitzky and Boustan, *Streets of Gold*, 103–37.
39. Arun S. Hendi and Jessica Y. Ho, "Immigration and Improvements in American Life Expectancy," *SSM: Population Health* 15 (2021): 1–9.
40. Michael T. Light and Ty Miller, "Does Undocumented Immigration Increase Violent Crime?," *Criminology* 56(2) (2018): 370–401; Robert J. Sampson, "Immigration and America's Urban Revival," *The American Prospect* 26(3) (Summer 2015): 20–24.
41. Dallas Card, Serina Chang, Chris Becker, Julia Mendelsohn, Rob Voigt, Leah Boustan, Ran Abramitzky, and Dan Jurafsky, "Computational Analysis of 140 Years of US Political Speeches Reveals More Positive but Increasingly Polarized Framing of Immigration," *Proceedings of the National Academy of Sciences* 119(31) (July 29, 2022): 1–9.
42. Wroe, *The Republican Party and Immigration Politics*, 209.

Chapter Seven. Sleepwalking (2)

1. "Barack Obama's Caucus Speech," *New York Times*, January 3, 2008.
2. David Remnick, "Obama Reckons with a Trump Presidency," *New Yorker*, November 18, 2016.
3. Garry Wills, *Nixon Agonistes* (Boston: Houghton Mifflin, 1970), 37. I owe the reference in this context to Donald R. Kinder and Allison Dale-Riddle, *The End of Race? Obama, 2008, and Racial Politics in America* (New Haven, CT: Yale University Press, 2012), 1.
4. The share of Hispanics self-identifying as white on the decennial census was 48 percent in 2000, 53 percent in 2010. See U.S. Bureau of the Census, "Census 2000 Shows America's Diversity," March 12, 2001, https://www.census.gov/newsroom/releases/archives/census_2000/cb01cn61.html; and Jeffrey S. Passel, D'Vera Cohn, and Mark Hugo Lopez, "Hispanics Account for More than Half of Nation's Growth in Past Decade," Pew Research Center, March 24, 2011, https://www.pewresearch.org/race-and-ethnicity/2011/03/24/hispanics-account-for-more-than-half-of-nations-growth-in-past-decade/.
5. Sam Roberts, "In a Generation, Minorities May Be the U.S. Majority," *New York Times*, August 13, 2008; Deenesh Sohoni, "The Coming Majority-

Minority State? Media Coverage of U.S. Census Projections, Demographic Threat, and the Construction of Racial Boundaries," *The Sociological Quarterly* 63(1) (2020): 94–113.
6. William A. Henry III, "Beyond the Melting Pot," *Time*, April 9, 1990, 28–30; Bill Clinton, "Commencement Address at Portland State University in Portland, Oregon," YouTube, June 13, 1998, https://www.youtube.com/watch?v=2VOi1RoylDs; U.S. Census Bureau, "2000 National Population Projections Tables," https://www.census.gov/data/tables/2000/demo/popproj/2000-national-summary-tables.html.
7. I was early in making that claim: Paul Starr, "An Emerging Democratic Majority," in Stanley Greenberg and Theda Skocpol, eds., *The New Majority: Toward a Popular Progressive Politics* (New Haven, CT: Yale University Press, 1997), 221–37. Five years later, John B. Judis and Ruy Teixeira published a book that gave that thesis its better-known formulation: *The Emerging Democratic Majority* (New York: Scribner, 2002).
8. Hua Hsu, "The End of White America?," *The Atlantic*, January–February 2009, https://www.theatlantic.com/magazine/archive/2009/01/the-end-of-white-america/307208/.
9. Kevin M. Schultz, "Religion as Identity in Postwar America: The Last Serious Attempt to Put a Question on Religion in the United States Census," *Journal of American History* 93(2) (2006): 359–84 (quotation, 374). See also my earlier discussion of statistical blackouts: "The Sociology of Official Statistics," in William Alonso and Paul Starr, eds., *The Politics of Numbers* (New York: Russell Sage Foundation, 1987), 7–57.
10. G. Cristina Mora, *Making Hispanics: How Activists, Bureaucrats, and Media Constructed a New American* (Chicago: University of Chicago Press, 2014), 85, 110.
11. Melissa Nobles, *Shades of Citizenship: Race and the Census in Modern Politics* (Stanford, CA: Stanford University Press, 2000), 65–72.
12. Margo J. Anderson, *The American Census: A Social History*, 2nd ed. (New Haven, CT: Yale University Press, 2015), 193–96.
13. Mora, *Making Hispanics*, 83–85.
14. Mora, *Making Hispanics*, ch. 3.
15. Ian Haney López, *White by Law: The Legal Construction of Race* (New York: New York University Press, 1996), 3–7; U.S. v. Bhagat Singh Thind, 261 U.S. 204 (1923), 211.
16. Nobles, *Shades of Citizenship*, 80; Amaney Jamal and Nadine Naber, eds., *Race and Arab Americans before and after 9/11* (Syracuse, NY: Syracuse University Press, 2008).
17. Jeffrey Passel, "The Growing American Indian Population, 1960–1990: Beyond Demography," in Gary D. Sandefur, Ronald R. Rindfuss, and Barney Cohen, eds., *Changing Numbers, Changing Needs: American Indian Demography and Public Health* (Washington, DC: National Academy Press, 1996), 79–102; U.S. Census Bureau, "Race: Decennial Census, Table P1, 2020"; Andrew

Van Dam, "The Native American Population Exploded, the Census Shows. Here's Why," *Washington Post*, October 27, 2023.
18. Joane Nagel, "American Indian Ethnic Renewal: Politics and the Resurgence of Identity," *American Sociological Review* 60, no. 6 (1995): 961; Eva Marie Garroutte, *Real Indians: Identity and the Survival of Native America* (Berkeley: University of California Press, 2003), 21, 42–51, 86, 96–98.
19. Kim Parker, Juliana Menasce Horowitz, Rich Morin, and Mark Hugo Lopez, *Multiracial in America: Proud, Diverse, and Growing in Numbers* (Washington, DC: Pew Research Center, June 11, 2015), 44, 66.
20. Julie A. Dowling, *Mexican Americans and the Question of Race* (Austin: University of Texas Press, 2014).
21. Tanya Katerí Hernández, *Racial Innocence: Unmasking Latino Anti-Black Bias and the Struggle for Equality* (Boston: Beacon Press, 2022).
22. Ran Abramitzky and Leah Boustan, *Streets of Gold: America's Untold Story of Immigrant Success* (New York: Public Affairs, 2022), 97–100.
23. Project Juntos, "Project Juntos: Latinx Race-Class," July 2020, https://static1.squarespace.com/static/5ef377b623eaf41dd9dfi311/t/5fc55c8d4e98326c02c48eb6/1606769814244/Project+Juntos.summary+briefing.092620.pdf.
24. Richard Alba, *The Great Demographic Illusion: Majority, Minority, and the Expanding American Mainstream* (Princeton, NJ: Princeton University Press, 2020), 4–5, 83–87.
25. Gregory John Leslie and David O. Sears, "The Heaviest Drop of Blood: Black Exceptionalism among Multiracials," *Political Psychology* 43(6) (2022): 1123–45.
26. Parker et al., *Multiracial in America*, 69, 73, 75, 77.
27. Brian Duncan and Stephen J. Trejo, "Tracking Intergenerational Progress for Immigrant Groups: The Problem of Ethnic Attrition," *American Economic Review* 101(3) (2011): 603–8; Mark Hugo Lopez, Ana Gonzalez-Barrera, and Gustavo López, *Hispanic Identity Fades across Generations as Immigrant Connections Fall Away* (Washington, DC: Pew Research Center, 2017), https://www.pewresearch.org/race-and-ethnicity/2017/12/20/hispanic-identity-fades-across-generations-as-immigrant-connections-fall-away/.
28. Paul Starr and Christina Pao, "The Multiracial Complication: The 2020 Census and the Fictitious Multiracial Boom," *Sociological Science* 11(40) (December 3, 2024): 1107–23, https://doi.org/10.15195/v11.a40.
29. Eduardo Bonilla-Silva, "From Bi-Racial to Tri-Racial: Towards a New System of Racial Stratification in the USA," *Ethnic and Racial Studies* 27(6) (2004): 931–50.
30. Matthew Frye Jacobson, *Whiteness of a Different Color: European Immigrants and the Alchemy of Race* (Cambridge, MA: Harvard University Press, 1999).
31. Herbert J. Gans, "Symbolic Ethnicity: The Future of Ethnic Groups and Culture in America," *Ethnic and Racial Studies* 2 (1979): 1–20; Mary C. Waters, *Ethnic Options: Choosing Identities in America* (Berkeley: University of California Press, 1990).

32. This section draws on Paul Starr, "The Re-Emergence of 'People of Color,'" *Du Bois Review: Social Science Research on Race* 20 (2023): 1–20.
33. Dina G. Okamoto, *Redefining Race: Asian American Panethnicity and Shifting Ethnic Boundaries* (New York: Russell Sage Foundation, 2014), 2.
34. Sheila L. Croucher, *Imagining Miami: Ethnic Politics in a Postmodern World* (Charlottesville: University of Virginia Press, 1997), 56.
35. Starr, "The Re-Emergence of 'People of Color.'"
36. Rick Perlstein, *Reaganland: America's Right Turn, 1976–1980* (New York: Simon & Schuster, 2020), 183; Loretta Ross, "Loretta Ross Recounts the Origin of the Phrase 'Women of Color,'" May 22, 2011, https://www.thesociologicalcinema.com/videos/loretta-ross-recounts-the-origin-of-the-phrase-women-of-color; Cherríe Moraga and Gloria Anzaldúa, eds., *This Bridge Called My Back: Radical Writings by Women of Color* (New York: Kitchen Table Press, 1983), 57, 58.
37. Regents of the University of California v. Bakke, 438 U.S. 265 (1978), 306, 322; Peter W. Wood, *Diversity: The Invention of a Concept* (San Francisco: Encounter Books, 2003), 137–200.
38. Nathan Glazer, *We Are All Multiculturalists Now* (Cambridge, MA: Harvard University Press, 1997).
39. Grutter v. Bollinger, 539 U.S. 306 (2003), 332.
40. Frank Dobbin and Alexandra Kalev, "Why Diversity Programs Fail: And What Works Better," *Harvard Business Review*, July–August 2016, https://hbr.org/2016/07/why-diversity-programs-fail.
41. Alberto Alesina and Edward L. Glaeser, *Fighting Poverty in the US and Europe: A World of Difference* (New York: Oxford University Press, 2004), ch. 6.
42. For two important contributions to the debate on ethnic diversity and truth, see Robert D. Putnam, "*E Pluribus Unum:* Diversity and Community in the Twenty-First Century; The 2006 Johan Skytte Prize Lecture," *Scandinavian Political Studies* 30(2) (2007): 137–74; and Maria Abascal and Delia Baldassarri, "Love Thy Neighbor? Ethnoracial Diversity and Trust Reexamined," *American Journal of Sociology* 121(3) (2015): 722–82.
43. Maureen A. Craig and Jennifer A. Richeson, "On the Precipice of a 'Majority-Minority' America: Perceived Status Threat from the Racial Demographic Shift Affects White Americans' Political Ideology," *Psychological Science* 25(6) (2014): 1189–97; Rachel Wetts and Robb Willer, "Privilege on the Precipice: Perceived Racial Status Threats Lead White Americans to Oppose Welfare Programs," *Social Forces* 97(2) (2018): 793–822.
44. Tali Mendelberg, *The Race Card: Campaign Strategy, Implicit Messages, and the Norm of Equality* (Princeton, NJ: Princeton University Press, 2001).
45. David Remnick, *The Bridge: The Life and Rise of Barack Obama* (New York: Random House, 2010), 555; Marc Ambinder, "Race Over?," *The Atlantic*, January–February 2009, https://www.theatlantic.com/magazine/archive/2009/01/race-over/307215/.

46. Michael Tesler and David O. Sears, *Obama's Race: The 2008 Election and the Dream of a Post-Racial America* (Chicago: University of Chicago Press, 2010), chs. 2–3.
47. Remnick, *The Bridge*, 409, 414, 440. The full text of Obama's 2004 DNC speech may be found at https://www.americanrhetoric.com/speeches/convention2004/barackobama2004dnc.htm.
48. Tesler and Sears, *Obama's Race*, 37–40; S. Karthick Ramakrishnan, Janelle Wong, Taeku Lee, and Jane Junn, "Race-Based Considerations and the Obama Vote: Evidence from the 2008 National Asian American Survey," *Du Bois Review: Social Science Research on Race* 6 (2009): 219–38.
49. Tesler and Sears, *Obama's Race*, ch. 5.
50. The distinction between "transformational" and "transactional" leaders comes from James MacGregor Burns, *Transforming Leadership* (New York: Grove Press, 2003); on Obama's interest, see Remnick, *The Bridge*.
51. Alan S. Blinder and Mark Zandi, "How the Great Recession Was Brought to an End," July 27, 2010, https://www.economy.com/mark-zandi/documents/End-of-Great-Recession.pdf.
52. Andy Barr, "The GOP's No-Compromise Pledge," *Politico*, October 28, 2010, https://www.politico.com/story/2010/10/the-gops-no-compromise-pledge-044311.
53. Justin Wolfers, "What Debate? Economists Agree the Stimulus Lifted the Economy," *New York Times*, July 29, 2014; Blinder and Zandi, "How the Great Recession Was Brought to an End"; Congressional Budget Office, "Estimated Impact of the American Recovery and Reinvestment Act on Employment and Economic Output in 2014," February 2015.
54. By 2016, U.S. GDP was up 10 percent from the precrisis peak, whereas it was nearly flat in both the Euro area and Japan. See Organization for Economic Cooperation and Development, "OECD Economic Surveys: The United States, 2016," June 16, 2016, 17, https://www.oecd-ilibrary.org/economics/oecd-economic-surveys-united-states-2016_eco_surveys-usa-2016-en.
55. Gary Burtless and Tracy Gordon, "The Federal Stimulus Programs and Their Effects," in David B. Grusky, Bruce Western, and Christopher Wimer, eds., *The Great Recession* (New York: Russell Sage Foundation, 2011), 249–93.
56. Executive Office of the President of the United States [Council of Economic Advisers], "The Economic Record of the Obama Administration: Progress Reducing Inequality," September 2016, https://obamawhitehouse.archives.gov/sites/default/files/page/files/20160923_record_inequality_cea.pdf.
57. CNN Opinion Research, Poll, press release, January 25, 2010, http://i2.cdn.turner.com/cnn/2010/images/01/25/rel1g.pdf; "Polls: Stimulus Unpopular, but Its Uses Have Broad Support," Wayback Machine, January 29, 2010, https://web.archive.org/web/20120330162508/http://articles.cnn.com/2010-01-29/politics/stimulus.poll_1_stimulus-bill-stimulus-plan-cnn-survey?_s=PM:POLITICS.

58. Lydia Saad, "Americans Back More Stimulus Spending to Create Jobs," Gallup, June 17, 2010, http://www.gallup.com/poll/140786/americans-back-stimulus-spending-create-jobs.aspx; Michael Grunwald, *The New New Deal: The Hidden Story of Change in the Obama Era* (New York: Simon & Schuster, 2012), 338.
59. This section draws on Paul Starr, *Remedy and Reaction: The Peculiar American Struggle over Health-Care Reform*, rev. ed. (New Haven, CT: Yale University Press, 2013).
60. Michael Tesler, *Post-Racial or Most-Racial? Race and Politics in the Obama Era* (Chicago: University of Chicago Press, 2016), ch. 5.
61. Tesler, *Post-Racial or Most-Racial?*, 165–67.
62. John D. Skretny and Jane Lilly López, "Obama's Immigration Reform: The Triumph of Executive Action," *Indiana Journal of Law and Social Equality* 2(1) (2013): [iii]–79.
63. Henry Barbour, Sally Bradshaw, Ari Fleischer, Zori Fonalledas, and Glenn McCall, "Growth & Opportunity Project," March 18, 2013, https://www.wsj.com/public/resources/documents/RNCreport03182013.pdf, 5, 6, 8, 12.
64. Ashley Parker and Jonathan Martin, "Senate, 68 to 32, Passes Overhaul for Immigration," *New York Times*, June 27, 2013.
65. Donald J. Trump (@realDonaldTrump), Twitter (now X), March 18, 2013, https://x.com/realdonaldtrump/status/313744229774008322.
66. Sean Trende, "The Case of the Missing White Voters, Revisited," RealClearPolitics, June 21, 2013, http://www.realclearpolitics.com/articles/2013/06/21/the_case_of_the_missing_white_voters_revisited_118893.html.

Chapter Eight. How America Stopped Working for Working-Class Americans

1. Ben Stein, "In Class Warfare, Guess Which Class Is Winning," *New York Times*, November 26, 2006.
2. Amory Gethin, Clara Martinez-Toledano, and Thomas Piketty, "Brahmin Left versus Merchant Right: Changing Political Cleavages in 21 Western Democracies, 1948–2020," *Quarterly Journal of Economics* 137(1) (2022): 1–48.
3. Michael Young, *The Rise of the Meritocracy 1870–2033: An Essay on Education and Equality* (Baltimore, MD: Penguin Books, 1961 [1958]), quotations 103, 106, 107.
4. Thomas Piketty, *Capital and Ideology* (Cambridge, MA: Harvard University Press, 2020), 807–61; Gethin, Martinez-Toledano, and Piketty, "Brahmin Left versus Merchant Right."
5. For the classic analysis of that period, see Simon Kuznets, "Economic Growth and Income Inequality," *American Economic Review* 45(1) (1955): 1–28.
6. Daniel Bell, *The Coming of Post-Industrial Society: A Venture in Social Forecasting* (New York: Basic Books, 1973), 221, 15, 269, 245–46.

7. Arlie Russell Hochschild, *Stolen Pride: Loss, Shame, and the Rise of the Right* (New York: New Press, 2024).
8. For more on this subject, see Paul Starr, "'Post-Industrial' versus 'Neoliberal': Rival Definitions of Our Age," in Paul Starr and Julian Zelizer, eds., *Defining the Age: Daniel Bell, His Time and Ours* (New York: Columbia University Press, 2021), 161–94.
9. Paul Starr, "Goodbye to the Age of Newspapers (Hello to a New Era of Corruption)," *New Republic*, March 4, 2009, 28–35.
10. "Income Inequality, USA, 1820–2021," World Inequality Database, https://wid.world/country/usa/.
11. Josh Bivens and Jori Kandra, "CEO Pay Has Skyrocketed 1,460% since 1978," Economic Policy Institute, October 4, 2022, 10 (figure A), https://www.epi.org/publication/ceo-pay-in-2021/. The data are for CEOs of the top 350 U.S. corporations.
12. Lawrence Mishel and Jori Kandra, "Wages for the Top 1% Skyrocketed 160% since 1979 while the Share of Wages for the Bottom 90% Shrunk," Economic Policy Institute, December 1, 2020, https://www.epi.org/blog/wages-for-the-top-1-skyrocketed-160-since-1979-while-the-share-of-wages-for-the-bottom-90-shrunk-time-to-remake-wage-pattern-with-economic-policies-that-generate-robust-wage-growth-for-vast-majority/.
13. Facundo Alvaredo, Anthony B. Atkinson, Thomas Piketty, and Emmanuel Saez, "The Top 1 Percent in International and Historical Perspective," *Journal of Economic Perspectives* 27 (Summer 2013): 3–20.
14. For two different versions of the winner-take-all story, see Robert H. Frank and Philip J. Cook, *The Winner-Take-All Society: How More and More Americans Compete for Ever Fewer and Bigger Prizes, Encouraging Economic Waste, Income Inequality, and an Impoverished Cultural Life* (New York: Free Press, 1995); and Jacob S. Hacker and Paul Pierson, *Winner-Take-All Politics: How Washington Made the Rich Richer—and Turned Its Back on the Middle Class* (New York: Simon & Schuster, 2010).
15. Anne Case and Angus Deaton, *Deaths of Despair and the Future of Capitalism* (Princeton, NJ: Princeton University Press, 2017), 50–51.
16. Ariel J. Binder and John Bound, "The Declining Labor Market Prospects of Less-Educated Men," *Journal of Economic Perspectives* 33(2) (2019): 163–90.
17. Anne Case and Angus Deaton, "Accounting for the Widening Mortality Gap between American Adults with and without a BA," BPEA Conference Draft, September 28–29, 2023, https://www.brookings.edu/wp-content/uploads/2023/09/1Case-Deatonunembargoed.pdf.
18. Case and Deaton, *Deaths of Despair and the Future of Capitalism*, esp. chs. 4–6.
19. Case and Deaton, *Deaths of Despair and the Future of Capitalism*, 62.
20. Claudia Goldin and Lawrence F. Katz, *The Race between Education and Technology* (Cambridge, MA: Harvard University Press, 2008).
21. David Autor, "Skills, Education, and the Rise of Earnings Inequality among the 'Other 99 Percent,'" *Science* 344(6186) (May 23, 2014): 843–51.

22. Sara McLanahan and Gary Sandefur, *Growing Up with a Single Parent* (Cambridge, MA: Harvard University Press, 1994); Melissa S. Kearney, *The Two-Parent Privilege: How Americans Stopped Getting Married and Started Falling Behind* (Chicago: University of Chicago Press, 2023), 30–32, 130.
23. Larry M. Bartels, *Unequal Democracy: The Political Economy of the New Gilded Age*, 2nd ed. (New York: Russell Sage Foundation, 2016), ch. 2.
24. Paul Frymer, *Black and Blue: African Americans, the Labor Movement, and the Decline of the Democratic Party* (Princeton, NJ: Princeton University Press, 2008), 90–91.
25. Charles Peters, "A Neo-Liberal's Manifesto," *Washington Post*, September 5, 1982; Randall Rothenberg, *The Neoliberals: Creating the New American Politics* (New York: Simon & Schuster, 1984).
26. Jake Rosenfeld, *What Unions No Longer Do* (Cambridge, MA: Harvard University Press, 2014), ch. 5.
27. Harold Meyerson, "A Second Chance: The New AFL-CIO and the Prospective Revival of American Labor," in Jo-Ann Mort, ed., *Not Your Father's Union Movement: Inside the AFL-CIO* (New York: Verso, 1998), 1–26.
28. Kate Bronfenbrenner and Dorian T. Warren, "Race, Gender, and the Rebirth of Trade Unionism," *New Labor Forum* 16(3/4) (2007): 142–48.
29. AFL-CIO, "Executive Council Statement: Immigration," February 17, 2000, https://aflcio.org/about/leadership/statements/immigration-0; AFL-CIO, "Convention Resolution, Resolution 5: A Nation of Immigrants," December 3, 2001, https://aflcio.org/resolution/nation-immigrants; Harold Meyerson, "The Fight for 15's Long, Winding, and Brandeisian Road," *The American Prospect*, July 18, 2019, https://prospect.org/labor/fight-15-s-long-winding-brandeisian-road/.
30. Peter R. Orszag and William G. Gale, "The Great Tax Shift," Brookings Institution, May 4, 2005, https://www.brookings.edu/articles/the-great-tax-shift/; Jacob S. Hacker and Paul Pierson, "Abandoning the Middle: The Bush Tax Cuts and the Limits of Democratic Control," *Perspectives on Politics* 3(1) (2005): 33–53.
31. U.S. Department of the Treasury, "Reducing Income Inequality through Progressive Tax Policy: The Effects of Recent Tax Changes on Inequality," September 26, 2016, https://home.treasury.gov/system/files/131/Report-Obama-Distribution-Changes.pdf.
32. Chuck Marr and Nathaniel Frentz, "Federal Income Taxes on Middle-Income Families Remain Near Historic Lows," Center on Policy and Budget Priorities, April 15, 2014, http://www.cbpp.org/research/federal-income-taxes-on-middle-income-families-remain-near-historic-lows; Urban-Brookings Tax Policy Center, "Average and Marginal Federal Income Tax Rates for Four-Person Families at the Same Relative Position in Income Distribution, 1955–2014," July 1, 2015, http://www.taxpolicycenter.org/sites/default/files/legacy/taxfacts/content/PDF/family_inc_rates_hist.pdf.

33. See the evaluation at Politifact, https://www.politifact.com/factchecks/2012/sep/18/mitt-romney/romney-says-47-percent-americans-pay-no-income-tax/.
34. Ralph E. Smith and Bruce Vavrichek, "The Minimum Wage: Its Relation to Incomes and Poverty," *Monthly Labor Review* 110(6) (1987): 24–30; David Cooper, Elise Gould, and Ben Zipperer, "Low-Wage Workers Are Suffering from a Decline in the Real Value of the Federal Minimum Wage," Economic Policy Institute, August 27, 2019.
35. David H. Autor, David Dorn, and Gordon H. Hanson, "The China Syndrome: Local Labor Market Effects of Import Competition in the United States," *American Economic Review* 103(6) (2013): 2121–68; David Autor, David Dorn, and Gordon H. Hanson, "When Work Disappears: Manufacturing Decline and the Falling Marriage Market Value of Young Men," *AER Insights* 1(2) (2019): 161–78.
36. David Autor, David Dorn, Gordon Hanson, and Kaveh Majlesi, "Importing Political Polarization? The Electoral Consequences of Rising Trade Exposure," *American Economic Review* 110(10) (2020): 3139–83.
37. Mike Lux, "A Strategy for Factory Towns," American Family Voices, February 22, 2023, https://www.americanfamilyvoices.org/post/a-strategy-for-factory-towns.
38. "Remarks by the President on the Economy in Osawatomie, Kansas," https://obamawhitehouse.archives.gov/the-press-office/2011/12/06/remarks-president-economy-osawatomie-kansas.
39. Harold Meyerson, "Bernie, Son of FDR," *The American Prospect*, June 12, 2019, https://prospect.org/economy/bernie-son-fdr/.
40. U.S. Bureau of Labor Statistics, "Union Members: 2016," Department of Commerce, January 26, 2017.
41. Rosenfeld, *What Unions No Longer Do*, ch. 7; James Feigenbaum, Alexander Hertel-Fernandez, and Vanessa Williamson, "From the Bargaining Table to the Ballot Box: Political Effects of Right to Work Laws," National Bureau of Economic Research Working Paper No. 24259 (2018); Paul Frymer and Jacob M. Grumbach, "Labor Unions and White Racial Politics," *American Journal of Political Science* 65(1) (2021): 225–40.

Chapter Nine. Trumpism as Total Revenge

1. Trump to Bob Woodward and Robert Costa, in Bob Woodward, *Rage* (New York: Simon & Schuster, 2020), ix.
2. Maggie Haberman and Shane Goldmacher, "Trump, Vowing 'Retribution,' Foretells a Second Term of Spite," *New York Times*, March 7, 2023.
3. For two influential versions of this interpretation, see Diana C. Mutz, "Status Threat, Not Economic Hardship, Explains the 2016 Presidential Vote," *Proceedings of the National Academy of Sciences* 115(19) (2018): E4330–E4339; and John Sides, Michael Tesler, and Lynn Vavreck, *Identity Crisis: The 2016*

Presidential Campaign and the Battle for the Meaning of America (Princeton, NJ: Princeton University Press, 2019). Sides et al. recognize a kind of "racialized economic anxiety" as a factor in the election but conclude from their analysis of public opinion data that "racial attitudes—more than economic anxiety—were the key" to explaining the educational divide among whites (93). Mutz is more emphatic about the primacy of racial identity.

4. Sean Trende, "The Case of the Missing White Voters Revisited," RealClearPolitics, June 21, 2013, http://www.realclearpolitics.com/articles/2013/06/21/the_case_of_the_missing_white_voters_revisited_118893.html.
5. Julie Hirschfeld Davis and Michael Shear, *Border Wars: Inside Trump's Assault on Immigration* (New York: Simon & Schuster, 2019), 32–33.
6. "Trump: 'Knock the Crap Out' of Protesters, I'll Pay Legal Fees," *Daily Beast*, February 1, 2016, https://www.thedailybeast.com/cheats/2016/02/01/trump-i-ll-pay-for-protester-beatings.
7. For the data on presidential voting by educational level, see Brian F. Schaffner, Matthew MacWilliams, and Tatishe Nteta, "Understanding White Polarization in the 2016 Vote for President: The Sobering Role of Racism and Sexism," *Political Science Quarterly* 133(1) (2018): 11 (figure 1, based on national exit polls). For the data on partisan identification, see Sides et al., *Identity Crisis*, 26 (figure 2.6, based on Pew Research surveys).
8. Davis and Shear, *Border Wars*, 24–25.
9. Interview on *Meet the Press*, October 24, 1999, https://www.nbcnews.com/meet-the-press/video/trump-in-1999-i-am-very-pro-choice-480297539914; "Backing Trump, White Evangelicals Flip Flop on Importance of Candidate Character | PRRI/Brookings Survey," PRRI, October 19, 2016, https://www.prri.org/research/prri-brookings-oct-19-poll-politics-election-clinton-double-digit-lead-trump/. For Republicans as a whole, the proportion agreeing that a public official who commits an "immoral act" in private life could behave ethically in public office nearly doubled from 2011 to 2020, rising from 36 percent to 71 percent. See Suzanna Krivulskaya, "The Diminishing Importance of Personal Morality in Politics, 2011–2020," PRRI, November 21, 2022, https://www.prri.org/spotlight/the-diminishing-importance-of-personal-morality-in-politics-2011-2020/.
10. On the origin of Republican winner-take-all rules for primaries, see Elaine C. Kamarck, *Primary Politics: How Presidential Candidates Have Shaped the Modern Nominating System* (Washington, DC: Brookings Institution Press, 2009), 84–85; on the consequences of those rules in 2016, see Sam Wang, "GOP Nomination Rules Tilt the Playing Field toward Donald Trump," *The American Prospect*, January 14, 2016, https://prospect.org/power/gop-nomination-rules-tilt-playing-field-toward-donald-trump/.
11. Sides et al., *Identity Crisis*, ch. 4; Matthew Haag, "David Pecker, Ex-National Enquirer Publisher, Details How He Aided Trump," *New York Times*, April 23, 2024.
12. Sides et al., *Identity Crisis*, 157–58.

13. Josh Katz, "Who Will Be President?," *New York Times*, November 8, 2016.
14. Gerhard Peters and John T. Woolley, "2016 General Election Editorial Endorsements by Major Newspapers," The American Presidency Project, ed. John T. Woolley and Gerhard Peters, University of California, Santa Barbara, CA, 1999–2021, https://www.presidency.ucsb.edu/statistics/data/2016-general-election-editorial-endorsements-major-newspapers.
15. Courtney Kennedy et al., "An Evaluation of the 2016 Election Polls in the United States," *Public Opinion Quarterly* 82(1) (2018): 1–33.
16. Exit polls show an even larger gap between college and non-college whites in 2016 than the data cited in this paragraph, which are drawn from Rob Griffin, Ruy Teixeira, and John Halpin, "Voter Trends in 2016: A Final Examination," Center for American Progress, November 2017, https://www.americanprogress.org/article/voter-trends-in-2016/. The CAP report uses Census and other data to correct for likely errors in the exit polls.
17. Lilliana Mason, Julie Wronski, and John V. Kane, "Activating Animus: The Uniquely Social Roots of Trump Support," *American Political Science Review* 115(4) (2021): 1508–16.
18. Sides et al., *Identity Crisis*, 185–89; Erin C. Cassese and Tiffany D. Barnes, "Reconciling Sexism and Women's Support for Republican Candidates: A Look at Gender, Class, and Whiteness in the 2012 and 2016 Presidential Races," *Political Behavior* 41 (2019): 677–700.
19. Mutz, "Status Threat, Not Economic Hardship, Explains the 2016 Presidential Vote." In a similar vein, see Schaffner et al., "Understanding White Polarization in the 2016 Vote for President," 9–34.
20. David Autor, David Dorn, Gordon Hanson, and Kaveh Majlesi, "A Note on the Effect of Rising Trade Exposure on the 2016 Presidential Election" (Appendix to "Importing Political Polarization"), MPRA Paper No. 112889, January 6, 2017, https://mpra.ub.uni-muenchen.de/112889/; Andrea Cerrato, Francesco Ruggieri, and Federico Maria Ferrara, "Trump Won in Counties That Lost Jobs to China and Mexico," *Washington Post* (Monkey Cage), December 2, 2016; Leonardo Baccini and Stephen Weymouth, "Gone for Good: Deindustrialization, White Voter Backlash, and US Presidential Voting," *American Political Science Review* 115(2) (2021): 550–67; Jon Green and Sean McElwee, "The Differential Effects of Economic Conditions and Racial Attitudes in the Election of Donald Trump," *Perspectives on Politics* 17(2) (2019): 358–79.
21. Griffin et al., "Voter Trends in 2016," 32. Data originated in Pew Research surveys.
22. Robert E. Scott, "We Can Reshore Manufacturing Jobs, but Trump Hasn't Done It," Economic Policy Institute, August 10, 2020, https://www.epi.org/publication/reshoring-manufacturing-jobs/#:~:text=Overall%2C%20the%20U.S.%20has%20suffered,Census%20Bureau%202020a%2C%202020b.

23. Peter Baker and Susan Glasser, *The Divider: Trump in the White House, 2017–2021* (New York: Doubleday, 2022), 47.
24. Baker and Glasser, *The Divider*, 15, 17.
25. Justin Fox, "Tax Bill Will Deliver a Corporate Gusher," *Bloomberg*, December 17, 2017; Baker and Glasser, *The Divider*, 141. For an evaluation of its long-term effects, see Chuck Marr, Samantha Jacoby, and George Fenton, "The 2017 Trump Tax Law Was Skewed to the Rich, Expensive, and Failed to Deliver on Its Promises," Center on Budget and Policy Priorities, June 13, 2024, https://www.cbpp.org/research/federal-tax/the-2017-trump-tax-law-was-skewed-to-the-rich-expensive-and-failed-to-deliver.
26. Virgil, "The Deep State vs. Donald Trump," Breitbart News, December 16, 2016, https://www.breitbart.com/politics/2016/12/12/virgil-the-deep-state-vs-donald-trump/; Beverly Gage, "'Nut Job,' 'Scumbag,' and 'Fool': How Trump Tried to Deconstruct the FBI and the Administrative State—And Almost Succeeded," in Julian E. Zelizer, ed., *The Presidency of Donald J. Trump: A First Historical Assessment* (Princeton, NJ: Princeton University Press, 2023), 298–314.
27. Baker and Glasser, *The Divider*, 138–41; Madeline Conway, "Trump: 'Nobody Knew That Health Care Could Be So Complicated,'" *Politico*, February 27, 2017, https://www.politico.com/story/2017/02/trump-nobody-knew-that-health-care-could-be-so-complicated-235436; Jonathan Cohn, *The Ten Years War: Obamacare and the Unfinished Crusade for Universal Coverage* (New York: St. Martin's Press, 2021); Cary Coglianese, Natasha Sarin, and Stuart Shapiro, "The Deregulation Deception," University of Pennsylvania Law School, Public Law Research Paper No. 20-44, June 21, 2021, SSRN, https://ssrn.com/abstract=3723915 or http://dx.doi.org/10.2139/ssrn.3723915.
28. John Sides, Chris Tausanovitch, and Lynn Vavreck, *The Bitter End: The 2020 Presidential Campaign and the Challenge to American Democracy* (Princeton, NJ: Princeton University Press, 2023), 37, 45, 59, 61.
29. "Full Text: Donald Trump Speech on Immigration in Arizona," *Politico*, August 31, 2016, https://www.politico.com/story/2016/08/donald-trump-immigration-address-transcript-227614.
30. Jeffrey S. Passel and Jens Manuel Krogstad, "What We Know about Unauthorized Immigrants Living in the U.S.," Pew Research Center, November 16, 2023, https://www.pewresearch.org/short-reads/2023/11/16/what-we-know-about-unauthorized-immigrants-living-in-the-us/.
31. Michael T. Light and Ty Miller, "Does Undocumented Immigration Increase Violent Crime?," *Criminology* 56(2) (2018): 370–401; Davis and Shear, *Border Wars*, 98; National Academies of Science, Engineering and Medicine, *The Economic and Fiscal Consequences of Immigration* (Washington, DC: National Academies Press, 2017), 247–48.
32. Jennifer Steinhauer, Jonathan Martin, and David M. Herszenhorn, "Paul Ryan Calls Donald Trump's Attack on Judge 'Racist,' but Still Backs Him," *New York Times*, June 7, 2016.

33. For the full context of the exchange, which concerned a DACA-for-immigration-restriction deal, see Davis and Shear, *Border Wars*, 219–25 (Trump quoted, 223).
34. Davis and Shear, *Border Wars*, 2–4.
35. John Bolton, *The Room Where It Happened: A White House Memoir* (New York: Simon & Schuster, 2020), 228; Jason Zengerle, "How America Got to 'Zero Tolerance' on Immigration," *New York Times*, July 16, 2019; Davis and Shear, *Border Wars*, chs. 22–23; Mae Ngai, "Immigration Politics and Policy under Trump," in Zelizer, *The Presidency of Donald J. Trump*, 144–61.
36. Davis and Shear, *Border Wars*, 329–48.
37. Davis and Shear, *Border Wars*, 309–23; "U.S. Annual Refugee Resettlement Ceilings and Number of Refugees Admitted, 1980–Present," Migration Policy Institute, https://www.migrationpolicy.org/programs/data-hub/charts/us-refugee-resettlement; Katie Benner and Caitlin Dickerson, "Sessions Says Domestic and Gang Violence Are Not Grounds for Asylum," *New York Times*, June 11, 2018.
38. Davis and Shear, *Border Wars*, 217–25, 237–51; Sides et al., *The Bitter End*, 40.
39. Zengerle, "How America Got to 'Zero Tolerance' on Immigration."
40. Passel and Krogstad, "What We Know about Unauthorized Immigrants Living in the U.S."
41. Josh Rogin, *Chaos under Heaven: Trump, Xi and the Battle for the 21st Century* (Boston: Houghton Mifflin, 2021); Ya-Wen Lei, *The Gilded Cage: Technology, Development, and State Capitalism in China* (Princeton, NJ: Princeton University Press, 2023). On the problems with U.S. trade policies with China and rationale for a tougher posture, see Robert Kuttner, "Trump and China: The Art of the Desperate Deal," *The American Prospect* 30(2) (Spring 2019): 16–23.
42. Rogin, *Chaos under Heaven*, 44.
43. "Donald Trump: Read Donald Trump's Speech on Trade," *Time*, June 28, 2016, https://time.com/4386335/donald-trump-trade-speech-transcript/; Rogin, *Chaos under Heaven*, 6.
44. Rogin, *Chaos under Heaven*, chs. 8, 13; Robert Lighthizer, *No Trade Is Free: Changing Course, Taking on China, and Helping America's Workers* (New York: Broadside Books, 2023).
45. David Autor, Anne Beck, David Dorn, and Gordon H. Hanson, "Help for the Heartland: The Employment and Electoral Effects of the Trump Tariffs in the United States," NBER Working Paper 32082, January 2024, https://www.nber.org/papers/w32082.
46. Rogin, *Chaos under Heaven*, 253.
47. For the U.S. numbers, see Centers for Disease Control, "Deaths by Selected Demographic and Geographic Characteristics: Provisional Death Counts for COVID-19," https://www.cdc.gov/nchs/nvss/vsrr/covid_weekly/index.htm.
48. Eric Klinenberg, *2020: One City, Seven People, and the Year Everything Changed* (New York: Knopf, 2024), 19–20, 338–42.

49. This section draws on an article I wrote during the pandemic: "Reckoning with National Failure: The Case of COVID," *Liberties* 1(3) (Spring 2021): 72–95.
50. Lawrence Wright, "The Plague Year," *New Yorker*, December 28, 2020.
51. Peter Baker and Annie Karni, "Trump Accuses Media and Democrats of Exaggerating Coronavirus Threat," *New York Times*, February 28, 2020; Philip Bump, "Trump Blames Blue States for the Coronavirus Death Toll: But Most Recent Deaths Have Been in Red States," *Washington Post*, September 16, 2020.
52. Wright, "The Plague Year"; Shana Kushner Gadarian, Sara Wallace Goodman, and Thomas B. Pepinsky, *Pandemic Politics: The Deadly Toll of Partisanship in the Age of COVID* (Princeton, NJ: Princeton University Press, 2022), 48.
53. Thomas J. Bollyky and Jennifer B. Nuzzo, "Trump's 'Early' Travel 'Bans' Weren't Early, Weren't Bans and Didn't Work," *Washington Post*, October 1, 2020.
54. Bob Woodward, *The Trump Tapes* (New York: Simon & Schuster, 2023), 205; Pam Belluck and Noah Weiland, "C.D.C. Officials Warn of Coronavirus Outbreaks in the U.S.," *New York Times*, February 25, 2020; David Leonhardt, "A Complete List of Trump's Attempts to Play Down Coronavirus," *New York Times*, March 15, 2020; Dan Diamond, "Trump Officials Interfered with CDC Reports on Covid-19," *Politico*, September 11, 2020, https://www.politico.com/news/2020/09/11/exclusive-trump-officials-interfered-with-cdc-reports-on-covid-19-412809.
55. Sides et al., *The Bitter End*, 137–38, 143, 215; Lisa Rein, "In Unprecedented Move, Treasury Orders Trump's Name Printed on Stimulus Checks," *Washington Post*, April 14, 2020.
56. Michael D. Shear, Noah Weiland, Eric Lipton, Maggie Haberman, and David E. Sanger, "Inside Trump's Failure: The Rush to Abandon Leadership Role on the Virus," *New York Times*, July 18, 2020; Aaron Blake, "Trump's Continually Strange Comments on Possibly 'Overrated' Coronavirus Testing," *Washington Post*, May 15, 2020; Noah Weiland, "'Like a Hand Grasping': Trump Appointees Describe the Crushing of the C.D.C.," *New York Times*, December 16, 2020.
57. Sarah Evanega, Mark Lynas, Jordan Adams, and Karinne Smolenyak, "Coronavirus Misinformation: Quantifying Sources and Themes in the COVID-19 'Infodemic,'" https://allianceforscience.org/wp-content/uploads/2020/10/Evanega-et-al-Coronavirus-misinformation-submitted_07_23_20.pdf.
58. Steven H. Woolf, Ryan K. Masters, and Laudan Y. Aron, "Effect of the Covid-19 Pandemic in 2020 on Life Expectancy across Populations in the USA and Other High Income Countries: Simulations of Provisional Mortality Data," *British Medical Journal* 373(1343) (2021). On the racial disparities, see also Theresa Andrasfay and Noreen Goldman, "Reductions in 2020 US Life Expectancy due to COVID-19 and the Disproportionate Impact on

the Black and Latino Populations," *Proceedings of the National Academy of Sciences* 118(5): e2014746118 (2021).

59. For a review of the evidence, see Zachary Parolin and Emma K. Lee, "The Role of Poverty and Racial Discrimination in Exacerbating the Health Consequences of COVID-19," *The Lancet*, March 2022, 7.
60. Kat Devlin and Aidan Connaughton, "Most Approve of National Response to COVID-19 in 14 Advanced Economies," Pew Research Center, August 27, 2020, https://www.pewresearch.org/global/2020/08/27/most-approve-of-national-response-to-covid-19-in-14-advanced-economies/.
61. Aidan Connaughton, "Those on Ideological Right Favor Fewer COVID-19 Restrictions in Most Advanced Economies," Pew Research Center, July 30, 2021, https://www.pewresearch.org/fact-tank/2021/07/30/those-on-ideological-right-favor-fewer-covid-19-restrictions-in-most-advanced-economies/.
62. Sides et al., *The Bitter End*, 150. For the shift in Republican views of the seriousness of the pandemic just after Trump's April 2020 turn, see Amy Mitchell, Mark Jurkowitz, J. Baxter Oliphant, and Elisa Shearer, "Three Months In, Many Americans See Exaggeration, Conspiracy Theories and Partisanship in COVID-19 News," Pew Research Center, June 29, 2020, https://www.pewresearch.org/journalism/2020/06/29/three-months-in-many-americans-see-exaggeration-conspiracy-theories-and-partisanship-in-covid-19-news/.
63. Ritu Agarwal et al., "Socioeconomic Privilege and Political Ideology Are Associated with Racial Disparity in COVID-19 Vaccination," *Proceedings of the National Academy of Sciences* 118(33) (2021): e2107873118; Jacob Wallace, Paul Goldsmith-Pinkham, and Jason L. Schwartz, "Excess Death Rates for Republican and Democratic Registered Voters in Florida and Ohio during the COVID-19 Pandemic," *JAMA Internal Medicine* 183(9) (2023): 916–23.
64. Larry Bartels, *Democracy Erodes from the Top: Leaders, Citizens, and the Challenge of Populism in Europe* (Princeton, NJ: Princeton University Press, 2023), 14.
65. Sides et al., *The Bitter End*, 64–66.
66. Ruth Igielnik, Scott Keeter, and Hannah Hartig, "Behind Biden's 2020 Victory," Pew Research Center, June 2021, 15.
67. Sides et al., *The Bitter End*, 222–24.
68. Igielnik et al., "Behind Biden's 2020 Victory," 3.
69. Sides et al., *The Bitter End*, 198.

Chapter Ten. A New, Old America

1. "Supreme Court Chief Justice Roberts and Justice Stevens," C-SPAN, October 9, 2009, https://www.c-span.org/video/?7654-1/supreme-court-chief-justice-roberts-justice-stevens.
2. Jaroslav Pelikan, *The Vindication of Tradition* (New Haven, CT: Yale University Press, 1984), 65.

3. Thurgood Marshall, "The Constitution's Bicentennial: Commemorating the Wrong Document?," *Vanderbilt Law Review* 40(6) (1987): 1341.
4. For the general causal argument about AIDS activism, the news media, and the Democrats and their relationship to openness about gay identity and support for gay rights, see Jeremiah J. Garretson, *The Path to Gay Rights: How Coming Out and Activism Changed Public Opinion* (New York: New York University Press, 2018).
5. For the *Los Angeles Times* polls, see Patrick J. Egan, Nathaniel Persily, and Kevin Wallsten, "Gay Rights," in Jack Citrin, Nathaniel Persily, and Patrick J. Egan, eds., *Public Opinion and Constitutional Controversy* (New York: Oxford University Press, 2008), 234–66. Besides Garretson's evidence on the liberalizing effect of coming out, see Gregory Lewis, "The Friends and Family Plan: Contact with Gays and Support for Gay Rights," *Policy Studies Journal* 39(2) (2011): 217–38.
6. Garretson, *The Path to Gay Rights*, 150 (figure 6.1); Elizabeth Mehren, "Acceptance of Gays Rises among New Generation," *Los Angeles Times*, April 11, 2004, https://www.latimes.com/archives/la-xpm-2004-apr-11-na-gaypoll11-story.html.
7. On the factors involved in the shifting terminology, see Kristopher Velasco and Pamela Paxton, "Deconstructed and Constructive Logics: Explaining Inclusive Language Change in Queer Nonprofits, 1998–2016," *American Journal of Sociology* 127(4) (2022): 1267–310. For the earlier history of transgender people, see Joanne Meyerowitz, *How Sex Changed: A History of Transsexuality in the United States* (Cambridge, MA: Harvard University Press, 2002).
8. Clyde Wilcox and Barbara Norrander, "Of Moods and Morals: The Dynamics of Opinion on Abortion and Gay Rights," in Barbara Norrander and Clyde Wilcox, eds., *Understanding Public Opinion*, 2nd ed. (Washington, DC: Congressional Quarterly Press, 2002), 121–48 (figure 6-5, data from General Social Survey).
9. William N. Eskridge Jr., *Dishonorable Passions: Sodomy Laws in America, 1861–2003* (New York: Viking, 2008), 279; Egan et al., "Gay Rights," 239.
10. Michael Klarman, *From the Closet to the Altar: Courts, Backlash, and the Struggle for Same-Sex Marriage* (New York: Oxford University Press, 2013), 56–57, 61–63; Nathaniel Frank, *Awakening: How Gays and Lesbians Brought Marriage Equality to America* (Cambridge, MA: Harvard University Press, 2017), ch. 5.
11. Eskridge, *Dishonorable Passions*, 248; Bowers v. Hardwick 476 U.S. 186 (1986).
12. Eskridge, *Dishonorable Passions*, 325–26; Lawrence v. Texas 539 U.S. 558 (2003).
13. Klarman, *From the Closet to the Altar*, ix; John C. Jeffries Jr., *Justice Lewis F. Powell, Jr.* (New York: Charles Scribner's Sons, 1994), 521, 531; Eskridge, *Dishonorable Passions*, 243–47, 286–87.
14. Frank, *Awakening*, 82–87; Klarman, *From the Closet to the Altar*, 176–78.

15. William N. Eskridge Jr., "Marriage Equality's Lessons for Social Movements and Constitutional Change," *William & Mary Law Review* 62(5) (2021): 1449–76; Jo Becker, *Forcing the Spring: Inside the Fight for Marriage Equality* (New York: Penguin, 2014); Frank, *Awakening*, 274–85; Loving v. Virginia, 388 U.S. 1 (1987).
16. Eskridge, "Marriage Equality's Lessons for Social Movements and Constitutional Change"; Frank, *Awakening*, 273.
17. Nate Silver, "How Opinion on Same-Sex Marriage Is Changing, and What It Means," *New York Times*, March 26, 2013; Eskridge, "Marriage Equality's Lessons for Social Movements and Constitutional Change"; Justin McCarthy, "Record-High 60% of Americans Support Same-Sex Marriage," Gallup, May 19, 2015, https://news.gallup.com/poll/183272/record-high-americans-support-sex-marriage.aspx.
18. Bostock v. Clayton County 590 U.S. 644; Jennifer De Pinto and Anthony Salvato, "Americans Weigh in on Issues before the Supreme Court: CBS News Poll," June 8, 2020, https://www.cbsnews.com/news/supreme-court-opinion-poll-cbs-news/.
19. Sarah K. Cowan, "Secrets and Misperceptions: The Creation of Self-Fulfilling Illusions," *Sociological Science* 1 (2014): 466–92; David E. Pozen, "The Abortion Closet (with a Note on Rules and Standards)," *Columbia Journal of Gender and Law* 161 (2017): 163–64; Sarah Kliff, "We Polled 1,060 Americans about Abortion: This Is What They Got Wrong," Vox, February 29, 2016, https://www.vox.com/a/abortion-statistics-opinions-2016/poll.
20. Barry Friedman, *The Will of the People: How Public Opinion Has Influenced the Supreme Court and Shaped the Meaning of the Constitution* (New York: Farrar, Straus & Giroux, 2009).
21. Steven M. Teles, *The Conservative Legal Movement: The Battle for Control of the Law* (Princeton, NJ: Princeton University Press, 2008), 2; Jefferson Decker, *The Other Rights Revolution: Conservative Lawyers and the Remaking of American Government* (New York: Oxford University Press, 2016).
22. Stephen B. Burbank and Sean Farhang, *Rights and Retrenchment: The Counterrevolution against Federal Litigation* (Cambridge: Cambridge University Press, 2017), 8–10, 35; Andrew M. Siegel, "The Court against the Courts: Hostility to Litigation as an Organizing Theme in the Rehnquist Court's Jurisprudence," *Texas Law Review* 84 (2006): 1097–202.
23. Burbank and Farhang, *Rights and Retrenchment*, 22, 31–32.
24. Sarah Staszak, *Privatizing Justice: Arbitration and the Decline of Public Governance in the U.S.* (New York: Oxford University Press, 2024), 1.
25. Staszak, *Privatizing Justice*, 2; Margaret Jane Radin, *Boilerplate: The Fine Print, Vanishing Rights, and the Rule of Law* (Princeton, NJ: Princeton University Press, 2013), 88, 130–35.
26. Staszak, *Privatizing Justice*, 10–11.
27. Siegel, "The Court against the Courts," 1140; Staszak, *Privatizing Justice*, 44.

28. Marc Galanter, "Why the Haves Come Out Ahead: Speculations on the Limits of Legal Change," *Law and Society Review* 9 (1974): 95–160.
29. Jessica Silver-Greenberg and Robert Gebeloff, "Beware the Fine Print, Part I: Arbitration Everywhere, Stacking the Deck of Justice," *New York Times*, October 31, 2015; Jessica Silver-Greenberg and Michael Corkery, "The Fine Print, Part II: In Arbitration, a 'Privatization of the Justice System,'" *New York Times*, November 1, 2015; Staszak, *Privatizing Justice*, 12.
30. Sandeep Vaheesan and Matthew Jinoo Buck, "Non-Competes and Other Contracts of Dispossession," *Michigan State Law Review* 1 (2022): 113–86; Joseph P. Beckman, "The New Wave of Non-Competes: Are They Enforceable?," *Litigation News* 43(1) (2017): 10–15; Evan Starr, J. J. Prescott, and Norman D. Bishara, "Noncompete Agreements in the US Labor Force," *Journal of Law and Economics* 64 (2021): 53–84.
31. Alan E. Garfield, "Promises of Silence: Contract Law and Freedom of Speech," *Cornell Law Review* 83 (1998): 261–362; Jeff John Roberts, "Why You Should Be Worried about Tech's Love Affair with NDAs," *Fortune*, April 29, 2019; John Carreyrou, *Bad Blood: Secrets and Lies in a Silicon Valley Startup* (New York: Alfred A. Knopf, 2018); Jodi Kantor and Megan Twohey, *She Said: Breaking the Sexual Harassment Story That Helped Ignite a Movement* (New York: Penguin, 2019); Ronan Farrow, *Catch and Kill: Lies, Spies, and a Conspiracy to Protect Predators* (New York: Little, Brown, 2019).
32. Citizens United v. FEC, 558 U.S. 310 (2010); Austin v. Michigan Chamber of Commerce, 494 U.S. 652 (1990); McConnell v. Federal Election Commission, 540 U.S. 93 (2003); Adam Winkler, *We, the Corporations: How American Businesses Won Their Civil Rights* (New York: Liveright, 2018), 335, 336.
33. Dan Eggen, "Poll: Large Majority Opposes Supreme Court's Decision on Campaign Financing," *Washington Post*, February 17, 2010; Greg Stohr, "Bloomberg Poll: Americans Want Supreme Court to Turn Off Political Spending Spigot," Bloomberg News, September 28, 2015, https://www.bloomberg.com/politics/articles/2015-09-28/bloomberg-poll-americans-want-supreme-court-to-turn-off-political-spending-spigot.
34. Winkler, *We, the Corporations*, xviii.
35. Davis v. FEC, 554 U.S. 724 (2008); Arizona Free Enterprise Club's Freedom Club PAC, et al. v. Bennett, et al., 564 U.S. 721 (2011), 736.
36. Sorrell v. IMS Health, 564 U.S. 552 (2011). Since data is central to the entire information economy, the Court's decision raised the specter of a new free-market doctrine akin to *Lochner*, updated for the information age. Jedediah Purdy, "The Roberts Court v. America," *Democracy*, Winter 2012; Jeremy K. Kessler and David E. Pozen, "The Search for an Egalitarian First Amendment," *Columbia Law Review* 118 (2018): 1953–2010.
37. Kate E. Andrias, "A Robust Public Debate: Realizing Free Speech in Workplace Representation Elections," *Yale Law Journal* 112 (2003): 2415–63.
38. Cedar Point Nursery v. Hassid, 594 U.S. __ (2021).

39. Burwell v. Hobby Lobby Stores, 573 U.S. 682 (2014); Adam Liptak, "Supreme Court Upholds Trump Administration Regulation Letting Employers Opt Out of Birth Control Coverage," *New York Times*, July 8, 2020; 303 Creative LLC v. Elenis (2023).
40. Lee Epstein, William M. Landes, and Richard A. Posner, "How Business Fares in the Supreme Court," *Minnesota Law Review* 97 (2013): 1431–73.
41. United States v. Miller, 307 U.S. 174 (1939), 178.
42. District of Columbia v. Heller, 554 U.S. 570 (2008).
43. District of Columbia v. Heller, 570 (Stevens dissenting, 592, 637); "Brief for Corpus Linguistics Professors and Experts as Amici Curiae Supporting Respondents," in *Bruen*, https://www.supremecourt.gov/DocketPDF/20/20-843/193271/20210921155937883_Amicus%20Brief.pdf.
44. Adam Winkler, "Scrutinizing the Second Amendment," *Michigan Law Review* 105(4) (2007): 683–734.
45. New York State Rifle & Pistol Association, Inc. v. Bruen, 597 U.S. 1 (2022).
46. New York State Rifle & Pistol Association, Inc. v. Bruen, 1; United States v. Rahimi, 602 U.S. ___ (2024), 2.
47. Rachel Weiner, "The Supreme Court Upended Gun Laws Nationwide: Mass Confusion Has Followed," *Washington Post*, July 7, 2024.
48. Judge Carlton W. Reeves, U.S. v. Bullock, No. 3:18-CR-165-CWR-FKB, U.S. District Court, Southern District of Mississippi, https://s3.documentcloud.org/documents/23255743/us-v-bullock-historian-order.pdf.
49. Rebecca L. Brown, Lee Epstein, and Mitu Gulati, "Guns, Judges, and Trump," Virginia Public Law and Legal Theory Research Paper No. 2024-51, Virginia Law and Economics Research Paper No. 2024-24, and USC Law Legal Studies Paper No. 24-31, June 22, 2024, SSRN, https://ssrn.com/abstract=4873330.
50. District of Columbia v. Heller.
51. "History, the Supreme Court, and *Dobbs v. Jackson:* Joint Statement from the AHA and the OAH," American Historical Association, July 6, 2022, https://www.historians.org/news/history-the-supreme-court-and-dobbs-v-jackson-joint-statement-from-the-aha-and-the-oah/.
52. Reva B. Siegel, Serena Mayeri, and Melissa Murray, "Equal Protection in *Dobbs* and Beyond: How States Protect Life Inside and Outside of the Abortion Context," *Columbia Journal of Gender and Law* 43(1) (2022): 67–97; for the Kamala Harris video, see "2018: Harris Questions Kavanaugh on Sex-Based Law," *Washington Post*, July 23, 2024; Dobbs v. Jackson Women's Health Organization, 597 U.S. ___ (2022).
53. Dobbs v. Jackson Women's Health Organization (Breyer, Sotomayor, and Kagan dissenting), 2.
54. Reva B. Siegel, "The 'Levels of Generality' Game, or 'History and Tradition' as the Right's Living Constitution," *Harvard Journal of Law and Public Policy* 47 (2024), Yale Law School, Public Law Research Paper (italics in original),

https://ssrn.com/abstract=4808688; Emily Bazelon, "How 'History and Tradition' Rulings Are Changing American Law," *New York Times*, April 29, 2024.

55. Adam Liptak, "Confidence in U.S. Courts Plummets to Rate Far Below Peer Nations," *New York Times*, December 17, 2024.

56. Tom W. Smith, "Public Opinion about Gun Policies," *The Future of Children* 12(2) (2002): 154–63; Colleen L. Barry et al., "Trends in Public Opinion on US Gun Laws: Majorities of Gun Owners and Non-Gun Owners Support a Range of Measures," *Health Affairs* 38(10) (2019): 1727–34; Jeffrey M. Jones, "Public Believes Americans Have Right to Own Guns," Gallup, March 27, 2008, https://news.gallup.com/poll/105721/public-believes-americans-right-own-guns.aspx; Katherine Schaeffer, "Key Facts about Americans and Guns," Pew Research Center, July 24, 2024, https://www.pewresearch.org/short-reads/2024/07/24/key-facts-about-americans-and-guns/.

57. Barbara Norrander and Clyde Wilcox, "Trends in Abortion Attitudes: From Roe to Dobbs," *Public Opinion Quarterly* 87(2) (2023): 427–58; AP-NORC, "Support for Legal Abortion Increased since Roe v. Wade Was Overturned," July 9, 2024, https://apnorc.org/projects/support-for-legal-abortion-increased-since-roe-v-wade-was-overturned/.

58. Michael Powell and Ilana Marcus, "The Failed Affirmative Action Campaign That Shook Democrats," *New York Times*, June 11, 2023; "More Americans Disapprove than Approve of Colleges Considering Race, Ethnicity in Admissions Decisions," Pew Research Center, June 8, 2023, https://www.pewresearch.org/politics/2023/06/08/more-americans-disapprove-than-approve-of-colleges-considering-race-ethnicity-in-admissions-decisions/; Thomas B. Edsall, "The Liberal Agenda of the 1960s Has Reached a Fork in the Road," *New York Times*, November 15, 2023.

59. Adam Liptak, "An Extraordinary Winning Streak for Religion at the Supreme Court," *New York Times*, April 5, 2021; Lee Epstein and Eric Posner, "The Roberts Court and the Transformation of Constitutional Protections for Religion: A Statistical Portrait," *Supreme Court Review* 2021 (2022): 315–47.

60. Jeffrey M. Jones, "U.S. Church Membership Falls Below Majority for First Time," Gallup, March 29, 2021, https://news.gallup.com/poll/341963/church-membership-falls-below-majority-first-time.aspx. The data on the decline of Christian self-identification and rise of the "nones" come from the General Social Survey, as cited in "Modeling the Future of Religion in America," Pew Research Center, September 13, 2022, https://www.pewresearch.org/wp-content/uploads/sites/20/2022/09/US-Religious-Projections_FOR-PRODUCTION-9.13.22.pdf. See also Shadi Hamid, "Trump Has Changed What It Means to Be Evangelical," *Washington Post*, June 13, 2024. On the growing proportion of evangelicals who reject the divinity of Christ, see "The State of Theology," 2022, https://thestateoftheology.com. On the falling

support for Christian nationalism, see Andrew L. Whitehead and Samuel L. Perry, *Taking America Back for God: Christian Nationalism in the United States*, updated ed. (New York: Oxford University Press, 2022), 44–53.
61. National Federation of Independent Business v. Sebelius, 567 U.S. 519 (2012). Roberts defected from the conservative wing by upholding the individual mandate (the requirement that individuals buy coverage or pay a fine) under the government's taxing power. If the conservative wing had prevailed, the decision would have called into question the constitutionality of Republican proposals to privatize Social Security. The individual mandate for health insurance had originally been the Republican alternative to an employer mandate. Roberts seemed to be the only conservative justice who remembered the larger scheme for transforming social policy that Republicans were promoting.
62. Adam Bonica and Maya Sen, "Estimating Judicial Ideology," *Journal of Economic Perspectives* 35(1) (2021): 97–118; Cass R. Sunstein et al., *Are Judges Political? An Empirical Analysis of the Federal Judiciary* (Washington, DC: Brookings Institution Press, 2006); Alma Cohen, "The Pervasive Influence of Political Composition on Circuit Court Decisions," Harvard John M. Olin Discussion Paper Series, Discussion Paper No. 1109, February 2024. For the quotation from Roberts, see Adam Liptak, "Chief Justice Defends Judicial Independence after Trump Attacks 'Obama Judge,'" *New York Times*, November 21, 2018.
63. I review and develop arguments about entrenchment in my book *Entrenchment: Wealth, Power, and the Constitution of Democratic Societies* (New Haven, CT: Yale University Press, 2019).
64. John Ferejohn, "Judicializing Politics, Politicizing Law," *Law and Contemporary Problems* 65(3) (2022): 41–68.
65. On the history of *Bush v. Gore*, see Howard Gillman, *The Votes That Counted: How the Court Decided the 2000 Presidential Election* (Chicago: University of Chicago Press, 2001), and Cass R. Sunstein and Richard A. Epstein, eds., *The Vote: Bush, Gore, and the Supreme Court* (Chicago: University of Chicago Press, 2001).
66. Bush v. Gore, 531 U.S. 98 (2000), 105, 110.
67. Bush v. Gore, 129 (Souter dissenting, 129; Ginsburg dissenting, 143; Breyer dissenting, 147); Bush v. Gore, 531 U.S. __ (2000) (Stevens dissenting, 1); Gillman, *The Votes That Counted*, 160.
68. United States v. Virginia, 518 U.S. 515 (1996) (Scalia dissenting, 596).
69. Gillman, *The Votes That Counted*, 162, 163.
70. Richard L. Hasen, "*Bush v. Gore* and the Future of Equal Protection Law in Elections," *Florida State University Law Review* 29 (2002): 377–406 (quotation, 387); Adam Cohen, *Supreme Inequality: The Supreme Court's Fifty-Year Battle for a More Unjust America* (New York: Penguin, 2020), ch. 6; Adam B. Cox and Thomas J. Miles, "Judging the Voting Rights Act," *Columbia Law Review* 108(1) (2008): 1–54.

71. Shelby County v. Holder, 570 U.S. 529 (2013), 2 (Ginsburg dissenting, 30, 33); Cohen, *Supreme Inequality*, 182–86; Richard A. Posner, "The Supreme Court and the Voting Rights Act: Striking Down the Law Is All about Conservatives' Imagination," Slate, June 26, 2013, https://slate.com/news-and-politics/2013/06/the-supreme-court-and-the-voting-rights-act-striking-down-the-law-is-all-about-conservatives-imagination.html; Richard A. Posner, *Breaking the Deadlock: The 2000 Election, the Constitution, and the Courts* (Princeton, NJ: Princeton University Press, 2001), 143.
72. Michael J. Pomante II, Scot Schraufnagel, and Quan Li, *The Cost of Voting in the American States* (Lawrence: University Press of Kansas, 2023); Kevin Morris and Coryn Grange, "Growing Racial Disparities in Voter Turnout, 2008–2022," Brennan Center for Justice, March 2, 2024, https://www.brennancenter.org/our-work/research-reports/growing-racial-disparities-voter-turnout-2008-2022; Michael Podhorzer, "Shelby County Opened the Door to Modern-Day Poll Taxes," Weekend Reading, March 21, 2024, https://www.weekendreading.net/p/voter-suppression-since-shelby.
73. Trump v. United States, 603 U.S.___, 1 (2024) (Sotomayor dissenting, 1, 8).
74. In *McDonnell v. United States* (2016), the Court narrowly defined an official act as a decision or action on a "question, matter, cause, suit, proceeding or controversy" involving a "formal exercise of governmental power." This was a case of public corruption, in which the accused could be convicted only for official acts. By defining official acts narrowly in that context, the Court made it more difficult to convict public officials of corruption—one of a series of such decisions, all consistently shielding officials from accountability to the criminal law. The Court's ruling in *Trump v. United States* also limited official accountability to the criminal law, but it achieved that result in the *opposite* way, by defining official acts broadly and finding that presidents are "absolutely" immune in core areas of presidential authority and presumptively immune in the "outer perimeter" of their functions.
75. Trump v. United States (Sotomayor dissenting, 12), 6, 7.
76. Trump v. United States, 4, 21.
77. Trump v. United States (Sotomayor dissenting, 30).
78. Gillman, *The Votes That Counted*, 151–52.
79. Maggie Astor, "Trump's Call for 'Termination' of Constitution Draws Rebukes," *New York Times*, December 4, 2022.
80. Jonathan V. Last, "The New Right Has Told Us Who They Are: Why Don't Americans Believe Them?," The Bulwark, April 21, 2022, https://www.thebulwark.com/p/the-new-right-has-told-us-who-they; Beth Reinhard, "Trump Loyalist Pushes 'Post-Constitutional' Vision for Second Term," *Washington Post*, June 8, 2024; Russell Vought, "Renewing American Purpose: Statesmanship in a Post-Constitutional Moment," The American Mind, September 29, 2022, https://americanmind.org/salvo/renewing-american-purpose/.

81. Maggie Astor, "Heritage Foundation Head Refers to 'Second American Revolution,'" *New York Times*, July 3, 2024.

Chapter Eleven. The American Contradiction, 2024

1. Niccolò Machiavelli, *Discourses on Livy*, ed. Bernard Crick (Baltimore: Penguin Books, 1970 [1531]), 175.
2. "Challenges to Democracy: The 2024 Election in Focus: Findings from the 2024 American Values Survey," PRRI, October 11, 2024, https://www.prri.org/research/challenges-to-democracy-the-2024-election-in-focus-findings-from-the-2024-american-values-survey/.
3. For the argument in full, see "Racial Slavery as an Entrenched Contradiction," in my book *Entrenchment: Wealth, Power, and the Constitution of Democratic Societies* (New Haven, CT: Yale University Press, 2019), 56–104.
4. Jeffrey M. Jones, "2024 Election Environment Favorable to GOP," Gallup, September 24, 2024, https://news.gallup.com/poll/651092/2024-election-environment-favorable-gop.aspx?utm_source=alert&utm_medium=email&utm_content=morelink&utm_campaign=syndication; Harry Enten, "Kamala Harris Needs to Beat the Fundamentals to Win," CNN, October 5, 2024, https://www.cnn.com/2024/10/05/politics/kamala-harris-trump-election-fundamentals/index.html; Rich Miller, "What Economic Models Say about the 2024 Presidential Election," Bloomberg News, February 5, 2024, https://www.bloomberg.com/news/newsletters/2024-02-05/what-economic-models-say-about-the-2024-presidential-election; Alan I. Abramowitz, "Time for Change Model Predicts Close Election with Slight Edge for Kamala Harris," The Center for Politics, August 22, 2024, https://centerforpolitics.org/crystalball/time-for-change-model-predicts-close-election-with-slight-edge-for-kamala-harris/.
5. According to a Pew Research survey, six in ten Americans had a negative opinion about Biden; six in ten had a negative opinion about Trump; and one in four had a negative opinion of both. Shanay Gracia and Hannah Hartig, "About 1 in 4 Americans Have Unfavorable Views of Both Biden and Trump," Pew Research Center, March 19, 2024, https://www.pewresearch.org/short-reads/2024/03/19/about-1-in-4-americans-have-unfavorable-views-of-both-biden-and-trump/. The data on age come from an ABC News/Ipsos survey: "Majority of Americans Think Both Biden and Trump Are Too Old to Serve Second Terms," Ipsos, February 11, 2024, https://www.ipsos.com/en-us/majority-americans-think-both-biden-and-trump-are-too-old-serve-second-terms.
6. Peter Baker and Dylan Freedman, "Trump's Speeches, Increasingly Angry and Rambling, Reignite the Question of Age," *New York Times*, October 6, 2024; Marianne LeVine and Isaac Arnsdorf, "Trump Fixates on Arnold Palmer as 'All Man' in Showers during Profane Rally," *Washington Post*, Oc-

tober 19, 2024; Ezra Klein, "What's Wrong with Donald Trump?," *New York Times*, October 22, 2024.

7. Ian Prasad Philbrick and Ashley Wu, "The 9 Elements of a Trump Rally," *New York Times*, October 8, 2024; Maegan Vazquez and Sabrina Rodriguez, "Trump Falsely Attacks Harris as 'Mentally Impaired' and 'Mentally Disabled,' Prompting Criticism," *Washington Post*, September 28, 2024; Summer Concepcion, "Trump Says Harris Would Be 'Like a Play Toy' to World Leaders if Elected," NBC News, July 31, 2024, https://www.nbcnews.com/politics/2024-election/trump-says-harris-play-toy-world-leaders-elected-rcna164483; Michael Gold, "At a Pennsylvania Rally, Trump Descends to New Levels of Vulgarity," *New York Times*, October 19, 2024; Marianne LeVine, "Trump Calls Political Enemies 'Vermin,' Echoing Dictators Hitler, Mussolini," *Washington Post*, November 13, 2023; Nnamdi Egwuonwu and Raquel Coronell Uribe, "'So Evil' and 'Dangerous': Trump Doubles Down on Calling Democrats 'Enemies from Within,'" NBC News, October 15, 2024, https://www.nbcnews.com/politics/2024-election/trump-democrats-enemies-within-rcna175628; Isaac Arnsdorf and Marianne LeVine, "Trump Says if He Loses Election, Jewish Voters Would Have 'a Lot' to Do with It," *Washington Post*, September 19, 2024.

8. Adam Nagourney, Ruth Igielnik, and Camille Baker, "Poll Finds Harris Rising as She Challenges Trump on Change," *New York Times*, October 8, 2024; Hanna Panreck, "Kamala Harris Tells 'The View' She Can't Think of Anything She Would Have Done Differently from Biden," Fox News, October 8, 2024, https://www.foxnews.com/media/kamala-harris-tells-the-view-she-cant-think-anything-she-would-have-done-differently-from-biden.

9. Catalist, "What Happened in 2022: An Analysis of the 2022 Midterms," https://catalist.us/whathappened2022/; Michael Podhorzer, "All Politics Is Local; All Political Data Is National," Weekend Reading (Substack), July 31, 2023, https://www.weekendreading.net/p/all-politics-are-local-all-political?r=103bk&utm_campaign=post&utm_medium=web&triedRedirect=true; Michael Podhorzer, "Turns Out, Turnout Matters: But Only if You Care about Winning Elections," Weekend Reading (Substack), August 5, 2023, https://www.weekendreading.net/p/turns-out-turnout-matters.

10. Ezra Klein, "The Democratic Blind Spot That Wrecked 2024," *New York Times*, November 10, 2024.

11. Gallup, "Immigration," https://news.gallup.com/poll/1660/immigration.aspx. This section draws on Paul Starr, "The Social Triumph and Political Tragedy of Immigration," *The American Prospect* 35(7) (December 2024): 20–25.

12. Muzaffar Chishti and Sarah Pierce, "Biden Sets the Stage for a Remarkably Active First 100 Days on Immigration," Migration Policy Institute, January 27, 2021, https://www.migrationpolicy.org/article/biden-immigration-reform-agenda; Gallup, "Immigration"; "Assessments of Joe Biden," Pew

Research Center, December 14, 2023, https://www.pewresearch.org/politics/2023/12/14/assessments-of-joe-biden/.

13. Muzaffar Chishti, Kathleen Bush-Joseph, and Colleen Putzel-Kavanaugh, "Biden at the Three-Year Mark: The Most Active Immigration Presidency Yet Is Mired in Border Crisis Narrative," Migration Policy Institute, January 19, 2024, https://www.migrationpolicy.org/article/biden-three-immigration-record; Michael D. Shear, Hamid Aleaziz, and Zolan Kanno-Youngs, "How the Border Crisis Shattered Biden's Immigration Hopes," *New York Times*, January 31, 2024. For the rising numbers of border encounters and increased proportions resulting in release into the United States, see Pia M. Orrenius et al., "Unprecedented U.S. Immigration Surge Boosts Job Growth, Output," Federal Reserve Bank of Dallas, July 2, 2024, chart 3, https://www.dallasfed.org/research/economics/2024/0702#:~:text=Estimates%20from%20the%20Hamilton%20Project,absent%20the%20surge%20of%20immigration.

14. Hamed Aleaziz, "A Quick Plunge," *New York Times*, October 4, 2024; Gallup, "Immigration"; John Gramlich, "Migrant Encounters at U.S.-Mexico Border Have Fallen Sharply in 2024," Pew Research Center, October 1, 2024, https://www.pewresearch.org/short-reads/2024/10/01/migrant-encounters-at-u-s-mexico-border-have-fallen-sharply-in-2024/.

15. Department of Homeland Security, "Fact Sheet: Data from First Six Months of Parole Processes for Cubans, Haitians, Nicaraguans, and Venezuelans Shows That Lawful Pathways Work," July 25, 2023, https://www.dhs.gov/news/2023/07/25/fact-sheet-data-first-six-months-parole-processes-cubans-haitians-nicaraguans-and; Michael D. Shear and Hamed Aleaziz, "Biden Wanted to Fix Immigration, but Leaves Behind a System That Is Still Broken," *New York Times*, November 3, 2024.

16. "Frequently Requested Statistics on Immigrants and Immigration in the United States," Migration Policy Institute, March 13, 2024, https://www.migrationpolicy.org/article/frequently-requested-statistics-immigrants-and-immigration-united-states-2024.

17. Orrenius et al., "Unprecedented U.S. Immigration Surge Boosts Job Growth, Output."

18. Russell Contreras, "Axios Explains: The Racist History of Trump's 'Poisoning the Blood,'" Axios, December 30, 2023, https://www.axios.com/2023/12/30/trump-poisoning-the-blood-racism; Philip Bump, "Saying Immigrants Bring 'Bad Genes' Echoes Trump's History: And the World's," *Washington Post*, October 7, 2024; Kris Maher, Valerie Bauerlein, and Tawnell D. Hobbs, "How the Trump Campaign Ran with Rumors about Pet-Eating Migrants—After Being Told They Weren't True," *Wall Street Journal*, September 18, 2024; Bente Birkeland, "Trump Rallies in Aurora: A City He Has Demonized as Overrun by Migrant Crime," National Public Radio, October 11, 2024, https://www.npr.org/2024/10/11/nx-s1-5147400/donald-trump-aurora

-colorado-rally'; Isabel Fattal and Stephanie Bai, "A Brief History of Trump's Violent Remarks," *The Atlantic*, October 31, 2024, https://www.theatlantic.com/politics/archive/2024/10/trump-violent-rhetoric-timeline/680403/; Richard Hofstadter, *The Paranoid Style in American Politics* (New York: Knopf, 1965); Brooke Singman, "Trump Says He Will Carry Out the 'Largest Domestic Deportation Operation in American History' if Elected," Fox News, September 20, 2023, https://www.foxnews.com/politics/trump-says-he-will-carry-out-the-largest-domestic-deportation-operation-in-american-history-if-elected.

19. Michael Podhorzer, "Poll-Washing Trump's Fascist Plans," Weekend Reading (Substack), October 25, 2024, https://www.weekendreading.net/p/poll-washing-our-way-to-fascism?utm_source=post-email-title&publication_id=808381&post_id=150582929&utm_campaign=email-post-title&isFreemail=true&r=a61qk&triedRedirect=true&utm_medium=email; Shawn McCreesh, "The Trump Voters Who Don't Believe Trump," *New York Times*, October 14, 2024.

20. Jennifer Medina, Ruth Igielnik, and Jazmine Ulloa, "Harris Struggles to Win Over Latinos, While Trump Holds His Grip, Poll Shows," *New York Times*, October 13, 2024; Patrick Ruffini, *Party of the People: Inside the Multiracial Populist Coalition Remaking the GOP* (New York: Simon & Schuster, 2023), 14. Not all polls found a shift from 2020: Mark Hugo Lopez and Luis Noe-Bustamante, "In Tight U.S. Presidential Race, Latino Voters' Preferences Mirror 2020," Pew Research Center, September 24, 2024, https://www.pewresearch.org/race-and-ethnicity/2024/09/24/in-tight-u-s-presidential-race-latino-voters-preferences-mirror-2020/.

21. Paul Starr and Edward Freeland, "'People of Color' as a Category and Identity in the United States," *Journal of Ethnic and Migration Studies* 50(1) (2024): 47–67; Medina et al., "Harris Struggles to Win Over Latinos."

22. Matt Dixon, Yamiche Alcindor, and Michelle Garcia, "Trump Falsely Accuses Harris of Deciding to 'Turn Black' during a Combative Panel with Black Journalists," NBC News, July 31, 2024, https://www.nbcnews.com/politics/donald-trump/trump-focuses-harris-race-black-jobs-combative-panel-black-journalists-rcna164271; Maya King, "Behind the Republican Effort to Win Over Black Men," *New York Times*, June 10, 2024.

23. This section draws on Paul Starr, "What Should Democrats Say to Young Men?," *The American Prospect*, October 2024, 50–54.

24. Tom Rosenstiel, "Young Voters in the 2008 Election," Pew Research Center, November 13, 2008, https://www.pewresearch.org/2008/11/13/young-voters-in-the-2008-election/; "2022 Exit Polls," CNN Politics, https://www.cnn.com/election/2022/exit-polls/national-results/general/us-house/20; Catalist, "What Happened in 2022."

25. Claire Cain Miller, "Many Gen Z Men Feel Left Behind: Some See Trump as an Answer," *New York Times*, August 24, 2024; Richard V. Reeves, *Of Boys*

and Men: Why the Modern Male Is Struggling, Why It Matters, and What to Do about It (Washington, DC: Brookings Institution Press, 2022).

26. John Branch, "Donald Trump Courts the Manoverse," *New York Times*, August 30, 2024; Alex Leary, "Trump Allies Launch $20 Million Effort to Reach Young Men," *Wall Street Journal*, August 1, 2024; Ezra Klein, "Manliness, Cat Ladies, Fertility Panic and the 2024 Election" [podcast], *New York Times*, August 16, 2024.

27. Jason Wilson, "'Dangerous and Un-American': New Recording of JD Vance's Dark Vision of Women and Immigration," *Guardian*, August 31, 2024; "J.D. Vance Reveals Why Trump Chose Him as VP and Exposes Kamala Harris and the Democrats!," YouTube [Nelk Boys], August 2, 2024, https://www.youtube.com/watch?v=-re1pBdMD8I.

28. Quoted in Barbara Ehrenreich, *The Hearts of Men: American Dreams and the Flight from Commitment* (Garden Press, NY: Anchor Press/Doubleday, 1983), 5.

29. "Gov. Walz: 'People Like JD Vance Know Nothing about Small Town America,'" *Morning Joe*, July 23, 2024, https://www.msnbc.com/morning-joe/watch/gov-watz-people-like-jd-vance-know-nothing-about-small-town-america-215470661588.

30. Gal Beckerman, "Who's Normal Now?," *The Atlantic*, August 22, 2024, https://www.theatlantic.com/books/archive/2024/08/democrats-are-redefining-normal-dnc/679558/; "Full Transcript of Tim Walz's Speech at the Democratic Convention," *New York Times*, August 22, 2024; "Full Transcript of Kamala Harris's Democratic Convention Speech," *New York Times*, August 23, 2024; Jess Bidgood, "Kamala Harris Tells Oprah if Somebody Breaks into Her Home, 'They're Getting Shot,'" *New York Times*, September 20, 2024.

31. CNN Transcripts, Democratic National Convention, August 21, 2024, https://transcripts.cnn.com/show/se/date/2024-08-21/segment/04.

32. Leigh Ann Caldwell, Liz Goodwin, and Justine McDaniel, "Republicans Lean into Anti-Transgender Message in Closing Weeks," *Washington Post*, October 22, 2024; Shane Goldmacher, Maggie Haberman, and Jonathan Swan, "How Trump Won, and How Harris Lost," *New York Times*, November 11, 2007; Glenn Thrush, "Under Trump, U.S. Prisons Offered Gender-Affirming Care," *New York Times*, October 16, 2024.

33. Peter Bergen, "Military Leaders Who Served under Trump Sound the Alarm about Him Winning a Second Presidency," CNN, October 19, 2024; Michael S. Schmidt, "As Election Nears, Kelly Warns Trump Would Rule Like a Dictator," *New York Times*, October 22, 2024.

34. Robert O. Paxton, "American Duce: Is Donald Trump a Fascist or a Plutocrat?," *Harper's*, May 2017; Elisabeth Zerofsky, "Is It Fascism? A Leading Historian Changes His Mind," *New York Times*, October 23, 2024; Tyler Pager, Patrick Svitek, and Jonathan Edwards, "Harris Says She Concurs with Assessment That Trump Is a Fascist," *Washington Post*, October 23, 2024.

35. Michael Podhorzer, "Sleepwalking Our Way to Fascism," Weekend Reading (Substack), October 18, 2024, https://www.weekendreading.net/p/sleepwalking-our-way-to-fascism; Shane Goldmacher and Maggie Haberman, "Pro-Harris Super PAC Raises Concerns about Focusing on Trump and Fascism," *New York Times*, October 27, 2024.
36. Greg Ip, "What's Wrong with the Economy? It's You, Not the Data," *Wall Street Journal*, April 4, 2024; Lauren Aratani, "Majority of Americans Wrongly Believe US Is in Recession: And Most Blame Biden," *Guardian*, May 22, 2024, https://www.theguardian.com/us-news/article/2024/may/22/poll-economy-recession-biden; Paul Krugman, "America Is Still Having a 'Vibecession,'" *New York Times*, May 23, 2024; John Cassidy, "Will Historic Job Growth Bring an End to the 'Vibecession'?," *New Yorker*, April 9, 2024.
37. Louis Jacobson, "Joe Biden Is Mostly Right That the US Inflation Rate Is the Lowest among Other Leading Economies," PolitiFact, September 1, 2023, https://www.politifact.com/factchecks/2023/sep/01/joe-biden/does-the-us-have-less-inflation-than-other-leading/.
38. For an estimate at the time, see Jesse D. Jenkins et al., "Preliminary Report: The Climate and Energy Impacts of the Inflation Reduction Act of 2022," REPEAT Project, August 2022, https://repeatproject.org/docs/REPEAT_IRA_Prelminary_Report_2022-08-04.pdf.
39. Steven Pinker, "Trump Says the Country Is 'Dying': The Data Say Otherwise," *New York Times*, October 29, 2024.
40. Alex Harring, "Economic 'Misery Index' That's Predicted Every Election Winner since 1980 Looking Good for Harris, but It's Close," CNBC, September 10, 2024, https://www.cnbc.com/2024/09/10/misery-index-looks-good-for-kamala-harris-in-presidential-race.html; Lydia Saad, "Final Election Indicators Give Mixed Signals," Gallup, October 30, 2024, https://news.gallup.com/poll/652850/final-election-indicators-give-mixed-signals.aspx?utm_source=alert&utm_medium=email&utm_content=morelink&utm_campaign=syndication.
41. Aaron Zitner, "Trump Leads Biden in Six of Seven Swing States, WSJ Poll Finds," *Wall Street Journal*, April 2, 2024.
42. Ian Smith, "Inflation Worries Seep Back into U.S. Bond Market," *Financial Times*, November 7, 2024; Paul Krugman, "Why Trump's Deportations Will Drive Up Your Grocery Bill," *New York Times*, November 11, 2024; Committee for a Responsible Federal Budget, "The Fiscal Impact of the Harris and Trump Campaign Plans," October 28, 2024, https://www.crfb.org/papers/fiscal-impact-harris-and-trump-campaign-plans.
43. Chuck Marr and Samantha Jacoby, "Principles for the 2025 Tax Debate: End High-Income Tax Cuts, Raise Revenues to Finance Any Extensions or New Investments," Center on Budget and Policy Priorities, September 25, 2024, https://www.cbpp.org/research/federal-tax/principles-for-the-2025-tax-debate-end-high-income-tax-cuts-raise-revenues-to#_ftnref9; Committee

for a Responsible Federal Budget, "What Would the Trump Campaign Plans Mean for Social Security?," October 24, 2024, https://www.crfb.org/blogs/what-would-trump-campaign-plans-mean-social-security.
44. The popular vote percentages come from the Cook Political Report, "2024 National Popular Vote Tracker," November 29, 2024, https://www.cookpolitical.com/vote-tracker/2024/electoral-college.
45. Peter R. Orszag, "The Real Story of Inflation: Pandemic-Era Stimulus Isn't the Culprit," *Washington Post*, November 14, 2024; David Dayen, "A Globally Predictable Result," *The American Prospect*, November 6, 2024, https://prospect.org/economy/2024-11-06-globally-predictable-result-election-inflation-trump/; John Burn-Murdoch, "Democrats Join 2024's Graveyard of Incumbents," *Financial Times*, November 7, 2024.
46. Christopher H. Achen and Larry M. Bartels, *Democracy for Realists: Why Elections Do Not Produce Responsive Government* (Princeton, NJ: Princeton University Press, 2016), 116–18.
47. Michael Podhorzer, "Is This What Democracy Looks Like?," Weekend Reading (Substack), November 11, 2024, https://www.weekendreading.net/p/is-this-what-democracy-looks-like. According to an analysis of the AP VoteCast Survey, Trump won young men by fourteen points but lost young women by eighteen points; consequently, Harris had a narrow four-point edge among young voters overall, the only age group she won. News Staff, "Young Voters Shifted toward Trump but Still Favored Harris Overall," TUFTS Now, November 12, 2024, https://now.tufts.edu/2024/11/12/young-voters-shifted-toward-trump-still-favored-harris-overall.
48. Podhorzer, "Is This What Democracy Looks Like?"
49. Shane Goldmacher, Maggie Haberman, and Jonathan Swan, "How Donald Trump Is Making Big Promises to Big Business," *New York Times*, October 26, 2024.

Acknowledgments

Since I straddle two worlds, the academy and political journalism, I've incurred debts to two distinct sets of colleagues over the many years of thinking and writing about the historical developments discussed in this book. The first debts are to my colleagues in sociology, history, and political science; the second are to my colleagues at the *American Prospect*. At Princeton, I am especially grateful to those who in the fall of 2024 read and responded to the manuscript, many of whom participated in a workshop on the book: David Bell, Dorothy Sue Cobble (from Rutgers), Dalton Conley, Matt Desmond, Mitch Duneier, Patricia Fernandez Kelly, Shamus Khan, John Robinson, Sam Wang, and Julian Zelizer. Frances Lee and Tali Mendelberg gave me critical comments but were unable to attend. Leah Boustan and Deborah Pearlstein responded to specific chapters, as did current and former graduate students, Shay O'Brien and Christina Pao. I thank participants in a small conference organized by Kim Scheppele where I presented an early version of chapter 10. Over the years, both undergraduate and graduate students have given me feedback on my ideas about the American contradiction, a theme in my teaching about American society and politics. I am grateful to a former undergraduate, River Reynolds, who did fact-checking on the book.

I owe a large debt as well to the members of the *American Prospect* community, particularly my fellow editors Bob Kuttner, Harold Meyerson, and David Dayen. Although none of the chapters in this book is reprinted from the *Prospect*, some make use of work I originally published there, going back decades. The final chapter includes material that I wrote simultaneously for this book and for the *Prospect:* "What Should Democrats

Say to Young Men?" (October 2024) and "The Social Triumph and Political Tragedy of Immigration" (December 2024).

Some of my discussion of race in chapter 7 draws on my article "The Re-Emergence of 'People of Color,'" *The Du Bois Review: Social Science Research on Race* 20(1) (2023): 1–20. Some of what I write about Obama's presidency in chapters 7 and 8 appeared originally in my article "Achievement without Credit: The Obama Presidency and Inequality," in Julian Zelizer, ed., *The Presidency of Barack Obama: A First Historical Assessment* (Princeton, NJ: Princeton University Press, 2018), 45–61. The discussion of the COVID pandemic in chapter 9 draws on my article "Reckoning with National Failure: The Case of Covid," originally published in *Liberties*, a journal of culture and politics, in spring 2021.

Needless to say, I am alone responsible for the book's errors and other limitations.

I first gave a public talk about the "American Contradiction" at Oxford in January 2009, just after Obama's election, when, like many others, I thought we might finally overcome the racial legacies of the nation's founding contradiction. I wish I could retain the optimism of that moment. But it is better to face up to the realities and renew the fight for a good society than to pretend that the arc of the universe will carry us there on its own.

In these years when not all was well in the world, I have fortunately had sustenance at home. I thank my wife Ann and our children and grandchildren for that love, joy, and support without which this book would have been impossible.

Index

Abbott, Greg, 341
abortion, 94–95, 96–97, 133, 134, 261; abortion rights, 148, 162–63; laws, 315–17, 319–20; misinformation concerning, 301. *See also* reproductive rights; *Roe v. Wade* (1973)
Abraham, Spencer, 193
Abraham Levitt and Sons, 37
Abramitzky, Ran, 197
Abramowitz, Alan, 180
Access Hollywood (television series), 257
activism: Black Americans as model for, 50; on college campuses, 76–77; gay rights, 103, 108–9, 295; judicial, 58, 294; labor, 138, 247; and racial identity, 79, 216; women's rights, 89
Adelson, Sheldon, 276
Adventures of Ozzie and Harriet, The (television series), 40
advertising, 42–43, 166–68, 169, 239–40. *See also* consumer culture
affirmative action, 125–26, 127, 140, 217–19, 320
Affordable Care Act (ACA) (2010), 179, 224, 226–28, 248, 266, 311, 322, 385n37
AFL-CIO, 126, 245–46, 247
African Baptist Church, Boston, 216

Age Discrimination in Employment Act, 305
Agricultural Labor Relations Act, California, 310
AIDS epidemic, 148–49, 242, 295, 297, 302
Aid to Families with Dependent Children (AFDC), 127, 177
Alba, Richard, 198, 210
Alito, Samuel A., 292, 311, 315, 317, 321
"alternative facts," 286
America, theories of, xi–xii, 16–18
America First Committee, 27
America First slogan, 260, 268
American Association for Public Opinion Research, 262
American Civil Liberties Union (ACLU), 78, 106
"American Creed," 17, 50–51, 71, 112
American Dilemma, An (Myrdal), 50–51, 83, 87
American Enterprise Institute, 139
American exceptionalism, 17–18
American Federation of Labor (AFL), 56. *See also* AFL-CIO
American Indians. *See* Native Americans
American Jewish Committee, 139
American Law Institute, 96

American Political Science Association, 31

American Political Tradition, The (Hofstadter), 46–47

American Prospect, The (magazine), 171–72

American Psychiatric Association, 108–9

American Recovery and Reinvestment Act, 224

American Rescue Plan, 355

Americans with Disabilities Act, 305

American Way: "invention" of, 26–28; "givenness" of, 47

Anderson, Martin, 145

anticommunism, 25–26, 30–31; and labor unions, 57

anti-elitist elites, 233–34

antifascism, 30–31

antifeminist movement, 114; opposition to ERA, 115. *See also* women's movements

antipoverty policies, 178

anti-Semitism, 75, 121

arbitration, mandatory, 305–6

Ashcroft, John, 313–14

Asian Americans, 8, 78; anti-Asian violence, 278; Asian American movement, 78; Asian whites, 210; as a "model minority," 49–50, 81–82; as an official racial category, 203–4, 207; as a panethnicity, 215–16; as "people of color," 215, 344; success as immigrants, 196–99; as a swing group in racial order, 212, 213; view of affirmative action, 320; as voters, 224, 228, 231

assimilation: defined, 198; models of, 48, 213, 390n37; of post-1965 immigrants, 198; "segmented assimilation," 390n37; of white ethnics, 17–18, 28, 29–30, 37–38, 48, 197–98, 209–10, 214

Assimilation in American Life (Gordon), 48

Atkinson, Ti-Grace, 99

Atlantic, The (periodical), 203

baby boom, 32, 69

backlash: antifeminist, 114–15; conservative movement as, 117–19, 124, 152; masculine, 345, 346–47; racial, 3, 8–11, 129; timing of, 8–11; Trump as, 258, 346–47. *See also* counterrevolution

Bakke, Allan, 218

Ball, George, 117

Balmer, Randall, 133

Bannon, Steve, 266

Barrett, Amy Coney, 292

Bartels, Larry, 287

Baton Rouge, Louisiana, boycotts, 62

Beard, Charles A., 46

Beauvoir, Simone de, 91

Beckerman, Gal, 349

Bell, Daniel, 139, 237

Bennett, William, 148

Biden, Joe, 223; choice of Harris as vice presidential nominee, 348; and economy, 340, 343, 352, 359; election as president, 288–90, 327; immigration policy, 340–42; presidency, 178–79, 340–42, 352; as symbol of Democrats' lack of energy, 356; 2024 campaign withdrawal, 337, 339

Birmingham, Alabama, 64, 83

"birtherism" attacks, Trump and, 257

birthrates, in United States, 32

Black Americans: and changing U.S. racial order, 52, 184–85, 212; economic advances, 34–35, 67–68, 82, 118–19, 150; families, 34–35, 80; Great Migration, 7, 54–55, 69, 82; incarceration, 151–52; and labor unions, 246; model of collective action, 49–50, 79–83; one-drop rule, 205, 210; performers and artists, 73–74; professional sports, 57, 69; as

prototypical minority, 75; urban riots, 72–73
Black freedom struggle: and "American Creed," 50–51; integration vs. separatism, 52–53, 71, 97–98; model for a family of movements, 2, 74–79, 81–83. *See also* Black Power; civil rights movement; civil rights unionism
Blackmun, Harry, 124, 128
Black Panthers, 72, 82
Black Power, 53, 69–74; contrasted with civil rights movement, 70–71; impact on Black consciousness, 73; model for other ethnic-consciousness movements, 78–79; model for women's liberation, 97–98; pluralism vs. nationalism, 69–70; theory of change, 71
Black Power (Carmichael and Hamilton), 71
Black Studies, 71
Blinder, Alan, 174
Bob Jones University, 133, 149
Bolton, John, 275
Bonilla-Silva, Eduardo, 212
Boorstin, Daniel, 23, 45–46, 47
border enforcement, 189–90, 193, 340–41
Bostock v. Clayton County, 301
Bourne, Randolph, 48
Boustan, Leah, 197
Bowers v. Hardwick, 297–99
Bowling Alone (Putnam), 163
boycotts, 62–63
Boy Scouts, 165, 383n18
Bozell, L. Brent, 122
Bracero program, 188–89
Brave New World (Huxley), 235
Breitbart News, 266, 267
Bretton Woods international monetary system, 137
Breyer, Stephen, 324–25
Brimelow, Peter, 190–91, 196

Brotherhood of Sleeping Car Porters, 55
Brown, Helen Gurley, 95
"brown" racial identities, 79, 206
Brown v. Board of Education (1954), 58, 60, 78, 120, 124–25, 322
Bryant, Anita, 110, 115, 134
Buchanan, Patrick, 94, 160–61, 191, 255
Buckley, William F., 121–22
Buckley v. Valeo, 141, 309
Buffett, Warren, 232
Burger, Warren, 124, 128
Burger Court, 140–42, 303, 321
Bush, George H. W., 123, 146, 158, 219, 289, 292
Bush, George W., 13, 152, 181, 193, 292; immigration policy, 186, 195, 199, 219; 9/11 terror attacks, 194–95; tax policy, 248
Bush v. Gore (2000), 323–25, 327, 329
business/corporate interests: corporate diversity policies, 219; corporate mobilization of 1970s, 135–40; corporate rights, 140–42, 309–11; declining confidence in, 136; and the law, 142, 304–11; mandatory arbitration and class-action bans, use of, 13, 304–7; minority-owned business, 126–27; in national politics, 26, 27, 28, 135–40, 236; response to labor, 25, 31–48, 147, 238, 249; "shareholder value revolution," 238; support for trade, 176–77, 274–75; as target of civil rights protest, 62, 64; in Trump administration, 266, 276
Business Roundtable, 138
Buttigieg, Pete, 350

California: affirmative action as issue, 320; gay rights as issue, 110–11; immigration as issue, 191–92; 1978 tax revolt, 145
campaign finance law, 141–42, 309–10

Campbell, David, 166
capitalism: American visions of, 25–28, 46; Black capitalism, 126–27; development of in China, 274; expansion, post–World War II, 28–29; post-industrial, 235–39; "shareholder value revolution," 238. *See also* business/corporate interests
Capitol insurrection (January 6, 2021), 290
Carlson, Tucker, 12
Carmichael, Stokely, 70, 71–72, 77
Carnegie Corporation, 51
Carter, Jimmy: as "born again" Christian, 132; as president, 142–44
Case, Anne, 241–42
Catholics: acceptance vs. exclusion, 27–28, 30, 48, 74–75, 119, 185; conservative Catholics, 18, 109–10; cross-denominational alliances, 130–31; Kennedy's election (1960), 30; right-to-life movement, 133, 134; William F. Buckley, 121
Celler, Emmanuel, 84–85
center right (liberal-moderate Republicans), collapse of, 13–14, 15, 173, 180–81, 199, 357, 382n3
Centers for Disease Control and Prevention (CDC), 280, 281, 282
Chamber of Commerce, 138
Cheney, Dick, 153
Cherlin, Andrew, 32
childcare, federal funding for, 94, 112
Child Development Act (1971), 94
China, trade with, 176–77, 250, 274–77
CHIPS and Science Act, 352
Christian nationalism, 18, 330
Christian radio stations, 167
Christian right. *See* religious right
church attendance, statistics, 30, 130–31. *See also* religion
citizenship: birthright, 275; Census question, 273; full and equal citizenship as recurrent conflict, 6, 71; labor without citizenship, 190; white identity as a prerequisite for naturalization, 183–84, 207
Citizens United (2010), 309
"city on a hill," xii, 17, 359
civic engagement, 25, 163–64
civil religion, in United States, 30
Civil Rights Act (1964), 53, 64–65, 75–76, 78, 178, 245, 301, 305; employment protections, 137–38; impact of, 92–93; Title VII, 66–67, 92
Civil Rights Attorney's Fees Awards Act, 304
civil rights movement, 3; Black Americans, economic benefit, 67–68; and Black Power, 70–71; Black prototypes, 50–61; civil rights unionism, 56–57; direct action phase, 61–69; grassroots base, 53–54; historical context, 54; male domination of, 77; mass action, turn to, 62; non-violent vs. violent activism, 72–73; progress in North vs. South, 71. *See also* Black freedom struggle
civil rights unionism, 56–57, 60, 74, 245
class action suits, 306–7; bans on, 310
class divisions: "diploma divide," 241–43, 264; education and wealth as bases of class division, 234–36; and family structure, 243–44; and political party allegiances, 250–53; Reagan's impact, 146–48, 153; top 1 percent, 240–41; working class, 232–34. *See also* economic inequality
Clean Air Act (1970), 128
Cleveland, Grover, 143, 170
Clinton, Bill: combination of progressive and neoliberal policies, 173–75; elections as president, 158–59, 161, 173, 178, 259; and gay rights, 297; immigration policy, 193; sex scandal, 170–71, 175–76; as target of conser-

vative attacks, 10; trade policy, 176–77; welfare policies, 177–78
Clinton, Hillary: as target of conservative attacks, 10, 161; on trade policies, 275; 2008 presidential campaign, 223–24; 2016 presidential campaign, 251–52, 254–5, 261–65
Cohn, Gary, 266, 276
Cohn, Roy, 347
Cold War, 30
Cole, David, 325
college education. *See* higher education
Coming of Post-Industrial Society, The (Bell), 237
Commentary (periodical), 139, 161
Commission on the Status of Women, 90
Committee to Defend Martin Luther King, 65
communications. *See* media
communism: during Cold War, 160; collapse of Soviet, 10, 12–13, 157, 171. *See also* anticommunism
Comstock Act, 175, 320
Congressional Black Caucus, 73
Congressional Budget Office, 266
Congress of Industrial Organizations (CIO), 56
Congress of Racial Equality (CORE), 64; and Black separatism, 77
Connor, Bull, 64
Conscience of a Conservative, The (Buckley), 122
consensus, sense of: contested, post–World War II, 25–32; contrast with in 1990s, 157; elite efforts to define, 26–27; as intellectual framework, 45–48; role of media in promoting or reducing, 39–40, 41–42, 171
consensus history, 45–46, 47
consensus project, 27, 171
conservatism: conservative ascendancy, 117–18, 144, 173–74, 258–59, 292–93; conservative movement, 8–9, 15, 121–22, 130–40; conservative vs.

reactionary/radical right, 8, 9, 15, 16–18, 330–31, 357, 358; conservatism vs. liberal establishment, 31, 122; corporate, 135–39, 306–8; cultural/religious, 130–35, 148, 160–62, 164–66, 173, 243–44, 261, 318–22, 335, 347; free market/libertarian, 136, 139, 184; and immigration, 190–96, 199, 220, 257, 271; longing for a lost America, 287, 333; and media, 169–70, 233; neoconservatism, 139–40, 142, 144, 161–62; in post–World War II consensus, 25–26; and race, 121, 123, 133, 221–22, 227, 258, 335, 344; and Republican Party, 15, 119, 142, 181, 287, 288; and Supreme Court, 15, 120, 140, 292–95, 302–22, 323, 333–34, 357
conservative legal movement, 15, 292–95, 302–3, 312
Constitution, U.S., 1–2, 5, 293; and American Creed, 51. *See also individual clauses and amendments*
constitutionalism/constitutional law: constitutional interpretation, major shifts in, 58–59, 106, 120, 308–18; constitutional limitation, 122, 141–42. *See also* Supreme Court
consumer culture, 167–68. *See also* advertising
Consumer Product Safety Commission, 128
contraception, 94–96, 165, 311
contradiction, concept of, xi, 6–7, 112, 334, 335
Conway, Kellyanne, 286
Coontz, Stephanie, 34
Coronavirus Aid, Relief, and Economic Security Act, 281
corporations, rights of, 142, 309–11. *See also* business/corporate interests
Cosmopolitan magazine, 95
counterrevolution, 117–18, 135–42, 153–54, 258–59, 330–31; legal, 15, 302–22, 357. *See also* backlash

courts: as agents of social change, 52, 58–60, 66–67, 106, 114–15, 124, 293–95, 318–2; judicial activism vs. restraint, 58, 294, 303. *See also* Supreme Court
COVID pandemic, 277–85; anti-Asian violence, 278; coordinated response, lack of, 280–81; and life expectancy, 282–83; misinformation, 282
Cowie, Jefferson, 138
crime: crime rates, 140, 150–52, 352; hate crime, 194–95; and homosexuality, 103–4; and immigration, 191, 192, 198–99, 257, 269, 343
Criswell, W. A., 133
"cultural pluralism," 48, 111, 370n46
"culture war," 10, 148, 153–54, 157–58, 160–71, 220, 243–44, 318–22, 335, 345–48; and partisan polarization, 172–73
Culture Wars (Hunter), 162

Daughters of Bilitis, 105
Davis, Jefferson, 121
Davis, Julie Hirschfeld, 257
"deaths of despair," 241–42, 244
Deaton, Angus, 241–42
Defense of Marriage Act (DOMA), 297
Deferred Action for Childhood Arrivals (DACA), 229, 269, 272
DeGeneres, Ellen, 296
Deloria, Vine, Jr., 78
DeMint, Jim, 227
democracy: American, 14, 46, 170; China, possibilities of, 274; Democrats' democracy dilemma (2024), 148; Trump's threat to, 286, 331, 351–52, 357
Democratic Party: blurring of divide with Republican Party (1950s), 26, 31–32; class composition of support, 117, 250–51, 264–65, 353–54; economic policies, 12, 13, 29, 46, 138, 143, 153, 154, 171–72, 175, 177, 178–79, 224–26, 244–45, 247–49, 249–50, 352–54; and gay rights, 111, 115–16, 295, 297; and gender gap in voting, 85, 116, 345–46; growing divide from Republicans, 159–60, 180; immigration policy, 12, 28, 186, 199, 340–43; internal tensions, 31, 158–59, 180, 181, 251–52; and labor unions, 13, 112–13, 245, 249–51, 252–53; limits of Democratic victories (1974–1980), 142–44; limits of Democratic victories (1992–2020), 178–82; 1968 election, 123–24; and race, 54, 123, 203, 221–24, 227–28, 348; reform of presidential nomination process, 141; Southern Democrats, 31, 52, 54, 57, 58, 60, 89, 120, 123, 178, 245; and Supreme Court, 58, 292, 329; and trade, 176–77, 178; 2020 election cycle, 288–89; 2022 midterm elections, 338–39; 2024 election cycle, 336–37, 348–54, 356; youth vote, 345–46
Democratic Vistas (Whitman), xi
demographic change, 7; Census forecast of majority-minority society, 202–4, 209–11; changes in birthrates, 32; changes in immigration, 12, 29, 75, 184–85, 189; "demography is destiny" narrative, 12, 211; and Obama's election, 203, 256. *See also* Great Migration
Demography (journal), 188
Department of Commerce, 127
Department of Homeland Security, 194
Depression. *See* Great Depression
deregulation, 139, 144, 153, 245, 267–68, 271, 354
DeSantis, Ron, 341
desegregation, schools, 60, 124–25. *See also* segregation
Dewey, Thomas E., 120

Diagnostic and Statistical Manual of Mental Disorders (American Psychological Association), 109
disability rights, 75, 112
Disraeli, Benjamin: as model for Nixon, 130
District of Columbia v. Heller, 312–13
diversity: celebration vs. fear of, 11, 203; diversity, equity, and inclusion (DEI), 218; as ideal and legal standard, 217–21
divorce, 94; gender-based impacts, 113, 115
Dixiecrats, 57
Dobbs v. Jackson's Women's Health Organization, 315–17, 319–21
Dobson, James, 133
Dole, Bob, 183, 192
Douglas, William O., 140
"Dreamers," 228–229, 269, 272
Dreams from My Father (Obama), 222
drugs, war on, 151–52
Du Mez, Kristin Kobes, 134–35

Earned Income Tax Credit (EITC), 175
Easterlin hypothesis, 365n23
Eastwood, Mary, 78
economic inequality: increasing, xii, 2, 3, 145, 153, 240–44, 251, 308, 335; as a political issue, 232–33, 251; reduced in midcentury America, 24, 29, 145. *See also* class divisions
economic policies: free market vs. New Deal, 28–29; industrial policy, 138, 246, 277; mercantilist, 274; mixed economy, 26; "supply-side" economics, 145–46. *See also under individual presidents, policy areas, and political parties*
Edmund Pettus Bridge, Selma, Alabama, 53
education: as basis of class position, 234–36, 241–44; and culture wars, 164–65, 265; diploma divide (in voting), 262, 264, 354; educational attainment of immigrants, 197; educational attainment of women, 32, 93–94, 112–14, 166, 345; Elementary and Secondary Education Act, 66; immigrants' right to K–12 education, 191–92; organized prayer in public schools, 120, 132; U.S. leadership vs. lag, 29, 242–43; whites-only schools, tax-exempt status, 125, 133, 149. *See also* higher education; segregation
Education Amendments, Title IX, 93–94
Ehrenreich, Barbara, 98–99, 115
Eisenhower, Dwight, 29, 119, 120; on religious values, 30
Electoral College, 1, 159, 255, 289–90, 323–24; vs. popular vote, 14–15; urban-rural divide, 361n4
Elementary and Secondary Education Act, 66
elites: anti-elitism of both left and right, 233–34; corporate elites, 136, 138–39; meritocracy, 234–35, 243; Northern Protestant elites, 56, 184–85; post-industrial, 235–37; and public opinion, 26–27, 136, 162, 163, 179–80, 262; Republican, 258–60; top 1 percent, 240–41; Trump's relation with, 233–34, 260–61, 265–67. *See also* business/corporate interests; higher education; intellectuals
Emerging Republican Majority, The (Phillips), 123–24
Employee Free Choice Act, 249
employment: apprenticeships, 126; fair labor standards for, 249; law and sex discrimination, 92–94, 297, 300–301; minimum wage, 67, 127–28, 148, 243, 247; minority hiring goals, 126. *See also* unions
Employment Non-Discrimination Act, 297, 300

"End the Slums" campaign, 71
environmental movement, 112, 124, 128–29, 136, 144, 153, 161, 245
Environmental Protection Agency (EPA), 128–29, 137
Equal Employment Opportunity Act, 126
Equal Employment Opportunity Commission (EEOC), 66, 93, 126, 303
Equality Act, 300
Equal Pay Act (1963), 90, 92, 112, 305
Equal Protection Clause, 78, 94, 298, 316, 324, 325
Equal Rights Amendment (ERA), 9, 89, 94, 376n62; battle over in 1970s, 114; campaign against, 115, 134
equal rights and feminism, 87–97
ethnicity: assimilation, 17–18, 28, 29–30, 37–38, 48, 197–98, 209–10, 214; bridging identities and panethnicity, 205–6, 215–16; definitions and frameworks, 48, 198, 213–14; ethnic attrition, 211–12; ethnic-consciousness movements, 184, 213, 333; ethnic heterogeneity and politics, 220; gay men and lesbians as quasi-ethnic group, 111; immigration and "ethnic mix" in United States, 183, 187–88; vs. race, 214. *See also* immigration
European politics, 26, 27, 287; European Union, 10
evangelical Christianity, 131, 261; evangelicalism as cultural movement, 131–32, 378n38
Evans, Sara, 97

Fair Employment Practices Commission, 55
Fair Labor Standards Act, 305
"fairness doctrine" (FCC), 43–44, 167
Falwell, Jerry, 135, 195

families: Black families, 34–35, 80; divorce law, 94, 113, 115; family entertainment, 40–41, 42; family types and politics, 166; "family wage," 88; and gender roles, 34–35; single-parent homes, 243–44. *See also* marriage
"family values," 94, 134–35, 347, 350
"family wage," 88
farm workers, migrant, 188–89
fascism: antifascism, 30; Trump and, 350–51
Father Knows Best (television series), 40
Fauci, Anthony, 282
Federal Arbitration Act (1925), 306
Federal Communications Commission (FCC), 43, 167
Federal Housing Administration, 36
Federalist Society, 303
Federal Reserve, 174
Federal Trade Commission, 339, 352
Federation for American Immigration Reform, 190
Feldstein, Martin, 146
Feminine Mystique, The (Friedan), 34, 91
feminism. *See* women's movements
financial crisis (2008), 181, 233, 251
firearms, 312–15, 318–19
First Amendment, 141–42, 310
Floyd, George, 348
Food and Drug Administration (FDA), 280
food stamps, 248
Ford, Gerald, 132
Fortas, Abe, 140
Fourteenth Amendment, 78, 80, 90–91, 114, 315–16, 328; Equal Protection Clause, 94
Fox, Vicente, 193
Fox News, 10, 167, 170, 233, 259
Frank, Barney, 300
freedom: American ideal, xii, 2, 3–5, 16, 183, 318; collective struggle for,

50–52; and conformity, 25; men's vs. women's, 95, 99; and public health restrictions, 284; religious, 311; reproductive, 317–18; sexual, 95, 106, 108, 298. *See also* Black freedom struggle; free speech; slavery
Freedom Rides, 64
Freedom Summer, 76–77
Freeman, Jo, 101
free speech, 76, 142, 308
"free speech" movement, 76–77
free trade. *See* trade policy
Friedan, Betty, 34, 91, 93, 100
Friedman, Milton, 139

Galanter, Marc, 306
Gans, Herbert, 38, 213–14
Garland, Merrick, 292
Gay Activists Alliance, 108
Gay Liberation Front, 107–8
gay rights movement, 85, 87, 102–11, 295–302; and Democratic Party, 111, 115–16, 295, 297; gay men/lesbian split, 108; gay representation in the mass media, 296, 302; "homophile" movement, 105–6; LGBTQ+ community, 296–97; same-sex marriage, 297–300; sodomy, laws criminalizing, 297–99. *See also* homosexuality
gender-based discrimination, 78
gender equality, 345–46; feminism as equal rights, 87–97; feminism as women's liberation, 97–102; identity formation, 85–87; opposition to and belittling of, 84–85; and race equality, parallels with, 85; reproductive rights, 94–97; women's movement, lasting impact of, 111–16
gender gap, political, 85, 116, 236, 345–46
gender identity: discrimination based on, 300–301; gender stereotypes in media, 40–41; growth of androgenous norms, 86–87, 134; growth of gender identity pluralism, 102, 296; stereotype of wife and mother in midcentury law and economy, 88–89
gender traditionalism: and religious right, 134; and Trump-Vance campaign, 345–48
General Electric Theater (television series), 42
generational differences: baby boomers, 32, 69, 95–96, 131; in churchgoing, 131; in civic engagement, 163–64; Generation X, 164; among immigrants, 198, 211, 213, 344
Genius of American Politics, The (Boorstin), 47
Gephardt, Richard, 193
Gethin, Amory, 232
Gilman, Charlotte Perkins, 348
Gingrich, Newt, 10, 118, 172, 175, 247; task force on immigration, 192–93
Ginsburg, Ruth Bader, 78, 292, 316, 324; *Shelby County v. Holder,* 326
Girl Scouts, 165
Glazer, Nathan, 187–88, 218–19
Goldwater, Barry, 119, 122–23, 259
Gordon, Milton, 48
Gore, Al, 161, 323–24, 329
Gorsuch, Neil, 292, 301, 321
Graham, Billy, 132
Graham, Lindsey, 270
Great Depression, 32, 33, 119, 136, 359
Great Migration, 7, 54–55, 69, 82, 150, 184–85
Great Society programs, 66–67, 82, 139–40
Great White Switch, 123, 259–60
Green, Edith, 92
Greenbelt, Maryland, 36
Greensboro, North Carolina, 63
Greenspan, Alan, 174
Griswold v. Connecticut (1965), 95, 316, 317

Growth and Opportunity Project (RNC report), 229–30, 231
Grutter v. Bollinger, 219
Gulf War, 158
gun laws, 312–15, 318–19

Halberstam, David, 40–41
Hall, Jacquelyn Dowd, 53
Hamilton, Alexander, 59
Hamilton, Charles, 71
Haney López, Ian, 79
Hanks, Tom, 296
Hannah-Jones, Nikole, 49
Harding, Warren G., 24, 170
Harris, Kamala, 316, 332, 337, 344–45, 348; 2024 election cycle, 338, 348–54, 356
Hasen, Richard, 325
Hastert, Dennis, 176
hate crimes, 194–95
Hate That Hate Produced, The (television documentary), 72
Hay, Harry, 105
Hayden, Casey, 77
Hayek, Friedrich von, 139
health and life expectancy, 241–42, 244; COVID impact, 278, 282–83; immigrants, 198–99
health care reform, 31, 56; Clinton administration, 173–75, 385n37; Nixon administration, 9, 129; Obama administration, 226–28
Hefner, Hugh, 95, 347
Herberg, Will, 30
Heritage Foundation, 139, 330
Hertzberg, Hendrik, 162
Hess, Elizabeth, 98–99
Higham, John, 194
higher education: as basis of class position, 234–36, 241–44; changing accessibility of, 4, 19, 242–43; college students and protest, 63–64, 76–77, 117; conservative efforts to control, 358–59; racial equality and affirmative action in, 58, 148, 219, 320; women's participation, 32, 93–94, 113–14, 166
Hinton, Elizabeth, 72–73
Hispanics: ambiguity and change in racial definition, 11, 78, 202–3, 209–11; ethnic pride and rights consciousness, 78–79; as an official statistical category, 206, 209–10; as a panethnicity, 205–6, 215–16; as "people of color," 215, 344; success as immigrants, 196–99; as a swing group in racial order, 212, 213; view of affirmative action, 320; as voters, 193, 195, 228, 230–31, 343–44, 356, 389n28. *See also* Mexican Americans
Hitchcock, Alfred, 43
Hitler, Adolf, 351
HIV/AIDS, 148–49, 242, 302
Hobby Lobby (retail chain), 311
Hobsbawm, E. J., 10
Hodgson, Godfrey, 23
Hofstadter, Richard, 26, 45–47, 343
homosexuality, 33, 85; conversion therapy, 109; criminalization of, 103–4; decriminalization of, 106–7; disease model, limitations of, 105; orientation vs. identity, 106–7; same-sex marriage, 297, 299–300; secrecy vs. coming out, 107, 295–96; statistics on prevalence, 104–5; use of word "homosexual," 103–4. *See also* gay rights movement
Hong Kong, 274, 275
Hoover, Herbert, 204
Hoover Institution, 139
Horner, Charles, 161
House Un-American Activities Committee (HUAC), 26, 30–31
housework, politics of, 98
housing: Black vs. white homeownership and wealth accumulation, 82; collapse of housing market (2008), 224, 251; housing policy after World War II,

36–37; public housing, 36, 38–39; racial discrimination, 37, 82, 150, 205; suburban development, 37–39
Howard University, 51
Hsu, Hua, 203
Hudson, Rock, 148
Humphrey, Hubert, 123, 141
Hunter, James Davison, 162–63
Huxley, Aldous, 235

identity formation: ethnicity and bridging identities, 215–16; gay identity, 107; "identification as" vs. "identification with," 335; and politics, 86–87, 180, 221. *See also* gender identity; racial identity and classification; white identity
identity politics, 8, 86, 116, 335
ideology. *See* conservatism; liberalism; neoconservatism; neoliberalism; progressivism/"progressive project"; socialism
Illegal Immigration Reform and Immigrant Responsibility Act (1996), 193
immigration: anti-immigrant sentiment, 29, 185, 190–96; from Asia, 187, 207; border enforcement, 189–90, 340–41; Bracero program and farm workers, 188–89; changing patterns post-1965, 186–90, 196–200; Commission on Immigration Reform (Jordan Commission), 192; and concept of "minorities," 74–75; declining levels, midcentury, 29–30; "diversity lottery," 190; "Dreamers," 228–29, 269, 272; economic benefits of, 342–43; and "ethnic mix" in United States, 187–88; immigrants and racial stratification systems, 212–13; and industrialization, 82; from Middle East, 207; new vs. old immigrants, 196–200; public opinion, 191, 340–41, 342–43; quotas in immigration law, 213–14; racial prerequisite for naturalization, 183–84; social selectivity of immigrants, 196–97; and Trump, 230, 269–73, 339, 343–44. *See also* assimilation; *individual immigration laws*
Immigration Act (1990), 190
Immigration and Customs Enforcement (ICE), 194
Immigration and Nationality Act (1965), 12, 75, 184, 186–87, 188, 273
Immigration Reform and Control Act (IRCA), 184, 189, 210, 389–90n36
incarceration, increased rates of, 118–19, 151–52
industrial policy, 138, 246; Biden vs. Trump administration, 277
inequality. *See* class divisions; economic inequality; education; gender equality; racial discrimination and racism; racial inequalities
Inflation Reduction Act (2022), 352
Insurrection Act, 330–31
intellectuals: conservative vs. liberal, 121, 136, 139–40, 161–62; post–World War II, 16, 45–48; right-wing suspicion of, 265
internet, 10, 239–40; online economy, 240
interracial coalitions, 214–15
interracial marriage, 212
Iraq War, 181
IRS (Internal Revenue Service): tax-exempt status for schools, 133
isolationism, 260, 268–69
Israel, support for, 137

Jackson, Andrew, 170, 330
Jackson, Jesse, 202
Jackson, Kenneth, 38
Jacobs, Gloria, 98–99
"Jane Crow," 78
January 6 Capitol insurrection, 290
Japanese American Citizens League, 81

Japanese Americans: government internment of, 58–59; as model minority, 49–50, 79–82; during World War II, 28; post–World War II success of, 80
Jefferson, Thomas, 170
Jesus and John Wayne (Du Mez), 134–35
Jewish Americans, 7–8, 27–28, 30, 74–75, 109, 130, 165, 204
Johnson, Boris, 284
Johnson, Lyndon, 117; and civil rights, 64–65, 80, 178; Immigration and Nationality Act (1965), 186–87, 188; war on poverty, 140
Johnson-Reed Immigration Act (1924), 184
Jordan, Barbara, 192
Jordan, Hamilton, 143
journalism: mainstream, 170–71; newspaper, 41, 170–71, 239–40; television, 43–44. See also media; news media
Joy of Sex, The (Comfort), 108
"Judeo-Christian" heritage, 27–28

Kallen, Horace, 48
Kameny, Franklin, 109
Kavanaugh, Brett, 292, 316, 321
Kelly, John, 271, 351
Kelly, Megyn, 263
Kennedy, Anthony, 148, 292, 298, 302, 311, 316, 318, 324
Kennedy, John F., 119; and civil rights, 64; Commission on the Status of Women, 84, 90; and immigration, 12; and media, 170; and public employee unions, 112; and religion, 30
Kennedy, Robert F., 64, 187
Kennedy, Robert F., Jr., 356
Kennedy, Ted, 129, 183, 187, 195, 223
Kessler-Harris, Alice, 92, 93
King, Coretta Scott, 217
King, Martin Luther, Jr., 53, 63, 65, 71–72, 83, 149, 245; birthday as federal holiday, 149
King, Mary, 77
Kinsey, Alfred C., 34, 104
Klarman, Michael, 121
Klosterman, Chuck, 164
Koop, C. Everett, 148–49
Kramer, Hilton, 161
Kristol, Bill, 174
Kristol, Irving, 139–40, 157, 174
Kushner, Jared, 266
Kuttner, Robert, 171

labor law, 89, 90, 143, 245, 247, 249. See also unions
labor movement. See unions
labor relations, 307–8
Latinos. See Hispanics
Lawrence v. Texas, 298–99, 317
Lazarus, Emma, 183
League of United Latin American Citizens, 78
Lear, Martha Weinman, 99
Leave It to Beaver (television series), 40
Lee, Frances, 172
lesbians, 101, 104, 105, 108, 111, 165, 295, 296, 301. See also gay rights movement
Levitt, William, 37
Levittown, Long Island, 37, 38
Lewis, John, 223
Lewis, Sinclair, 24
LGBTQ+, origin of term, 296–97. See also gay rights movement; gender identity
liberalism: backlash against, 130, 135–40, 144, 160–61; contested consensus, post–World War II, 25–32; cultural liberalism, 33–34, 52, 85, 134, 160–61, 164, 244–45; in Democratic Party, 181, 250, 288; liberal courts, 52, 120, 292, 294–95; liberal New Deal order, idea of, 31; "liberal

project," 362n6; racial liberalism, 120, 123, 135, 222, 223; and religious realignment, 130; in Republican Party, 31, 119–20, 124, 127, 129, 180–81, 258; and theories of America, 16–19. *See also* rights revolution
Lieberman, Joseph, 193
Lighthizer, Robert, 276
Limbaugh, Rush, 170, 199, 259
Livingston, Robert, 176
Loving v. Virginia, 299
Lynd, Helen, 24
Lynd, Robert, 24

Machiavelli, Niccolò, 332
Madison, Dolley, 87
Main Street (Lewis), 24
"Make America Great Again" (MAGA), 268, 286–87; impact on Republican Party, 357–58; restoration (2024), 333
Malcolm X, 70, 71–72
Mansbridge, Jane, 114, 376n62
March on Washington movement, 55
marriage: and childbearing, 32–34; divorce, 94, 113; radical feminist view of, 99–100, 115; same-sex marriage, 297–300. *See also* families
Marshall, Thurgood, 57–58, 78, 293
Martin, Mary, 41
Martinez-Toledano, Clara, 232
masculinity: binary vs. androgenous conceptions of masculine-feminine distinction, 86, 102, 134; male backlash, 5, 335, 345–48; male breadwinner ideal, 34, 88, 114, 244, 347–48; "toxic," 346; Trump's and Vance's use of, 258, 346–48. *See also* gender gap, political
Mattachine Society, 105, 107
Mattis, Jim, 350–351
McAdam, Doug, 77
McCain, John, 14, 195, 224, 258, 267
McCarthy, Joseph, 30, 36

McConnell, Mitch, 225, 292, 328
McDonnell v. United States (2016), 411n74
McWilliams, Carey, 79–80
Media, 4, 9, 26; Black freedom struggle and media, 61, 65, 71–72, 77; Black representation in mass media, 53, 73–74; Christian media, 131–32, 134; conservatives and the media, 169–70, 172, 220; decline of newspapers, 239–40; gay representation in mass media, 296, 302; midcentury television, 39–45; rise of multichannel system and breakup of mass public, 158, 166–71; Trump's relationship with, 265, 339–40, 358; and women's movements, 84, 98, 99, 101. *See also* journalism; news media
Medicaid, 67, 248, 260
medical profession: medical school admissions, 93, 218; women's health movement, 101
Medicare, 66, 67, 118, 248, 260; expansion of, 128
Meet the Press (television series), 261
meritocracy, 234–35, 243
Messonnier, Nancy, 281
Mexican Americans, 78–79, 185, 188, 197, 204, 205, 206, 209, 216, 257, 270. *See also* Hispanics
Mexico: and border enforcement, 189–90, 341; G. W. Bush, negotiations with, 193; immigration to United States, 188–89, 197; Mexican immigrants denounced by Trump, 257; Trump negotiations concerning immigration, 271; trade with, 176–77
Meyerson, Harold, 247
Miami, Florida: gay rights, 110
Michigan as swing state, 262–63, 264, 288
Middletown (Lynd and Lynd), 24

Miers, Harriet, 292
military buildup, Reagan administration, 145
Milk, Harvey, 110–11
Miller, Stephen, 257, 271, 272, 273, 275–76
Millett, Kate, 101
Milley, Mark, 350, 351
Mine Safety and Health Administration, 128
minimum wage, 67, 127–28, 148, 243, 247
minorities: as concept, 74–75, 204; incorporation into America, 27–28; Japanese and Black Americans as two model minorities, 49–50, 81–82; majority-minority society, Census forecast of, 202–4, 209–11; as "people of color," 212–17; stigma vs. legal advantages of minority status, 102, 125–27, 205–8; whites as a minority, 11, 186, 203, 211–12, 220, 256
minority rights revolution, 50, 58–59, 75–76, 125–27
Misery Index, 352–353
Miss America Pageant protest (1968), 99
Mitchell, John, 140
Mnuchin, Steve, 266, 276
Mondale, Walter, 94
Montgomery, Alabama, bus boycott, 53, 62–63
Montgomery Improvement Association, 63
Moral Majority movement, 135
More Joy of Sex (Comfort), 108
Morgan, Marabel, 134
Morris, Aldon, 61, 63
Moscone, George, 110–11
Movement for Black Lives, 348
Moyers, Bill, 178
Moynihan, Daniel Patrick, 80, 127–28
Ms. Magazine, 100
Murray, Pauli, 77–78, 90–91, 368n26
Musk, Elon, 211, 340, 347

Muslims, 194–95, 202, 207, 260, 263, 269, 286; Black Muslims, 71
Myrdal, Gunnar, 50–51, 83, 87

NAFTA (North American Free Trade Agreement), 247, 277
National Academies of Sciences, Engineering, and Medicine (NASEM), 185–86
National Association for the Advancement of Colored People (NAACP), 55; on affirmative action, 126; Legal Defense Fund, 57–58, 302; litigation strategies, 59–60; Supreme Court record, 58
National Association of Manufacturers, 28
National Conference of Black Mayors, 73
National Conference of Christians and Jews, 27–28
national debt, 145–46, 260
National Enquirer (tabloid newspaper), 261
National Environmental Policy Act (1969), 128
National Federation of Independent Business, 138
National Gay Task Force, 108
National Institute of Allergy and Infectious Diseases, 282
National Labor Relations Act (1935), 54
National Labor Relations Board (NLRB), 57, 148
National Organization for Women (NOW), 85, 93, 101. *See also* women's movements
National Review (magazine), 121–22, 190–91
National Traffic Safety Administration, 128
National Women's Conference (1977), 216–17
National Women's Party, 89, 92

Nation of Immigrants, A (Kennedy), 12
Nation of Islam, 71
Native Americans: colonization, 53; increased Census count, 207–8; as a minority, 204; as a panethnicity, 215, 217; rights movements, 78
nativism, 29, 185, 190–96; and social spending, 260
Navarro, Peter, 275–76
Nee, Victor, 198
"Negro Family, The" (Moynihan), 80
neoconservatism, 139–40, 142, 144, 161–62
neoliberalism: Clinton and, 173, 176–77; Democratic industrial-policy neoliberals of 1980s, 246; free-market, 139, 238; neoliberal order, idea of, 158, 159; Trump's overthrow of, 256
Neshoba County, Mississippi, 149
New Deal: efforts to repeal, 25–26; housing reform, 36; New Deal Order, 31; programs, 54, 252
news media: Black Power coverage, 72; and civil rights movement, 61, 65; feminist movement coverage, 99–100; nonpartisan vs. partisan, 26, 170. *See also* journalism; media
newspapers: decline of, 239–40; newspapers and the mass public, 41; as partisan media, 170
New York State Rifle & Pistol Association, Inc. v. Bruen, 314–15, 318–19
New York Times v. Sullivan, 65
Nielsen, Kirstjen, 270, 271
9/11 terror attacks, 194–95
1984 (Orwell), 235
Nineteenth Amendment, 89; fiftieth anniversary, 101
Nisei: The Quiet Americans (Hosokawa), 81
Nixon, Richard: contrasted with Carter, 143–44; defeat in 1960 presidential election, 119; economic policies, 128–29, 137; election as president (1968), 117, 123–24; guaranteed income policy (Family Assistance Plan), 127–28; health policy, 129; on labor unions, 138; liberal initiatives, 124, 129–30; and race, 124–27; re-election campaign, 141; regulatory expansion, 128–29; and school desegregation, 124–25; Southern Strategy, 124; Supreme Court appointments, 124, 128, 140–141; *United States v. Nixon*, 322; veto of Comprehensive Child Development Act, 94; Watergate, 129
"no-fault" divorce, 94, 113
"noncompete" clauses, 243, 307
non-disclosure agreements (NDAs), 307–8, 310
"normality": conflicting claims of in 2024, 349–50; Democrats' labeling of Trump-Vance as "weird," 349; homosexual orientation as normal vs. pathological, 25, 104–5; midcentury, 23–24; "normal gay guy vote" (Vance), 347; Trump as normal vs. aberration, 286; Trump's breaches of norms as strategic, 257
normative inversion, 79
North American Free Trade Agreement (NAFTA), 176
North Carolina Agricultural and Technical College, 63

Obama, Barack: "birtherism" attacks on, 257; economic policies, 178–79, 224–26, 247–49; elections as president, 201–3, 221–24, 228–29, 251, 345–46; health-care reform, 226–28, 248, 311, 322; immigration policy, 195, 228–29, 269; labor law reform, 247–48; and race, 203, 221–24, 227–28; on rising inequality, 251

Obamacare. *See* Affordable Care Act
Obergefell v. Hodges, 300, 302, 317
Occupational Safety and Health Administration (OSHA), 128, 137
Occupy Wall Street movement, 251
O'Connor, Sandra Day, 148, 219, 292, 299, 320, 324
Office of Federal Contract Compliance, 66
Office of Management and Budget (OMB), 206–7
Office of Minority Business Enterprise, 126–27
Office of National Planning, calls for, 138
Okamoto, Dina, 215
ONE (magazine), 105–6
"one-drop" rule, 205, 210
online media, 167
online platform companies, employment at, 249
Operation Warp Speed, 285
opioid epidemic, 242
originalism, constitutional, 312–13, 317–18
Orwell, George, 235
Our Bodies, Ourselves, 101–2

paleoconservatives, 140
Palmer, Arnold, 337
panethnicity, 215–16
Parks, Rosa, 62
Parrington, Vernon, 46
Parsons, Talcott, 47–48
partisanship: courts, 291–92, 322–31; media, 26, 170; as social identity, 180. *See also* polarization; political parties
patriotism, 161–62
Paxton, Robert O., 351
Pelikan, Jaroslav, 291
Pelosi, Nancy, 337
Pence, Mike, 290
Pennsylvania as swing state, 262–63, 264
"people of color," 212–17, 343

Permanent Normal Trade Relations with China, 274
Peter Pan (musical), 41
Petersen, William, 49
Peterson, Esther, 90
Philadelphia, Mississippi, 77, 149
Philadelphia Plan, 126
Phillips, Kevin, 117, 123–24
Piketty, Thomas, 232
"pill, the," 95. *See also* contraception
Planned Parenthood v. Casey (1992), 316, 317
Playboy magazine, 95
pluralism: American ideal of, 17, 28, 48; cultural, 48, 111, 370n46; sexual, 102, 108, 296
Plyler v. Doe, 192
Podhoretz, Norman, 139–40
Poitier, Sidney, 222
polarization: ideological, 31–32; partisan, 10, 159–60, 163, 179–80, 251, 259; and public health, 284; vs. Republican radicalization, 15. *See also* partisanship
political action committees (PACs), 139
political parties: and class allegiances, 236, 250; ideological homogeneity vs. heterogeneity, 180–81; partisan realignments, 14–15, 119–30; presidential nomination process, 141; racial realignment, 52, 116, 123. *See also* Democratic Party; gender gap, political; partisanship; polarization; Republican Party
populist movements, 234–35
pornography and obscenity, 106
Posner, Richard, 326
post-industrial economies, 235, 236–37
poverty: and COVID pandemic, 283; homeownership and wealth accumulation, 82; income and wealth disparities, 24; national guaranteed income, 127–28; progress in war on, 67; working poor, 127

Powell, Lewis F., Jr., 128, 136, 218, 298
Power of the Positive Woman, The (Schlafly), 134
Prescription Confidentiality Law, 310
presidency: Electoral College vs. popular vote, 14–15; presidential elections, 14, 54, 116, 123, 143, 158, 173, 264, 323; presidential immunity, 327, 328–29, 330; presidential nominating process, 141. *See also* Electoral College; *individual presidents*
President's Commission on the Status of Women, 84
privatization, 139, 153
Progressive Era, 67, 362n6; impact on historians' paradigms, 46
Progressive Party, 28, 362n6
progressivism/"progressive project," 3–4, 5, 8, 16–19, 118; acceptance of label "progressive," 252; defined as against "liberal project," 16, 362n6; impact of Black struggle on progressive vision of social justice, 53; progressive breach with unions, 232–33, 245, 247; progressive vs. reactionary class politics, 233–34; relation of mainstream liberal and progressive theories of America, 18–19
Project 2025, 330–31, 358
Proposition 187 (California), 191–92
Protestant Catholic Jew (Herberg), 30
Protestants, 18, 48; and Judeo-Christian heritage, 27, 30; liberal-conservative axis, 130–31, 165; Northern Protestant elites, 56. *See also* evangelical Christianity
"prototype," concept of, 53
public health, 149, 271, 278–79, 282, 284, 321, 358
public housing, 36. *See also* housing
Public Interest, The (periodical), 139
public-interest law, 137, 302, 304

Puerto Rican immigrants, 206
Putin, Vladimir, 257
Putnam, Robert, 163–64, 166

racial discrimination and racism: anti-Asian violence, 278; anti-Black discrimination, 150; demeaning stereotypes on television, 43; double discrimination toward women of color, 217; exposure of in South, 61; in housing, 37, 82, 150, 205; racial prerequisite for naturalization, 183–84, 207; "structural racism," 348; systemic racism, 18; white denial of, 51; within women's movement, 101.
racial identity and classification: bridging identities, 205–6, 215–16; fixed vs. fluid, 214; Hispanics, ambiguity and change in racial definition, 11, 78, 202–3, 209–11; one-drop rule, 205, 210; racial statistics, 11, 186, 202–11. *See also* "brown" racial identities; white identity
racial inequalities: in health and life expectancy, 242, 279, 282–83; in income and wealth, 34–35, 82, 150
racial politics: interracial coalitions, 214–15; race and conservatism, 121, 123, 133, 221–22, 227, 258, 335, 344; race and Democratic Party, 54, 123, 203, 221–24, 227–28, 348; race and foreign policy, 56, 61; race and liberalism, 120, 123, 135, 222, 223; race and Republican Party, 122–27, 129, 149–50, 229–31, 344–45; racialization ("racial loop"), 221–28; "racial reductionism," 4–5, 255–56; "racial replacement," 256
radio, 41–42; Christian radio stations, 167; talk radio, 167, 233, 259, 261
Rahimi, Zackey, 314–15
Randolph, A. Philip, 55

Reagan, Ronald, 42; and abortion, 96; on civil rights, 123, 149–50; and conservative movement, 121, 130, 135, 148; economic policies, 145–48; elections as president, 143, 259; "fairness doctrine," 167; Farewell Address, 17; on gay issues, 110, 115, 148–49; immigration reform, 189; opposition to Medicare, 118; presidency, 144–52; and race, 149–50; Supreme Court appointments, 298–99; on war on poverty, 67

"Reagan Revolution," 117; myth and reality of, 144–45, 152–54

RealClearPolitics (website), 230

Recovery Act (2009), 248

Red Scare, 33

Redstockings (feminist nonprofit organization), 97–98, 100

Reed v. Reed, 78

Refugee Act (1980), 190, 272

Regents of the University of California v. Bakke, 218

regulatory frameworks: federal agencies, 137; Kennedy and Johnson administrations, 128–29; Nixon administration, 129

Rehnquist, William, 128, 324

Rehnquist Court, 303, 321

Reich, Robert, 171

religion: civil religion in United States, 30; interfaith movements, 27–28; and law, 311, 320–22; liberal-versus-conservative axis/polarization, 130, 165–66; "nones," 165, 321; religious affiliation and participation, 25, 30, 131, 321–22; religious realignment, 3, 130; response to women's and gay rights movements, 109. *See also* Catholics; Jewish Americans; Muslims; Protestants

religious right, 109, 130–31, 148; as part of conservative movement, 130–35; 311, 320–22

reproductive rights, 94–97, 345. *See also* abortion

Republican Party: blurring of divide with Democratic Party (1950s), 26, 31–32; collapse of center right (liberal-moderate Republicans), 13–14, 15, 173, 180–81, 199, 357; conservative attacks on "Republicans in name only" (RINOs), 181, 287; counterrevolution, incomplete, late twentieth century, 258–59; culture war issues, 160–61, 220; economic policies, 119, 146, 181, 244–45, 340; elite vs. base, twenty-first century, 258–65; ERA and gay rights, 115–16; Great White Switch, 123, 259–60; immigrants, turn against, 199–200; MAGA takeover, 357–58; mobilization of alienated voters, 256; as "multiracial populist coalition," 344; Obama, opposition to, 224–25; and partisan polarization, 159–60, 163; racial composition, 219, 228, 344; "Republican autopsy" (2013), 229–30, 231; Southern strategy, 119–24; South's shift to, 52; strategies in 1990s, 172–73; "sun/moon" model, 159; Supreme Court domination/supermajority, 291–93, 323, 329–31; tax cuts for the wealthy, 179, 353–54; Trump, and shifts in base, 233, 261–63, 264–65, 287–88; Trump's control of, 287–88, 335–36; winner-take-all primaries, 261

Respect for Marriage Act, 301

Reynolds, William Bradford, 149

rights revolution: conservative, 294–95, 303, 308–9; liberal, 15, 118, 294–95

right-to-life movement, 134. *See also* abortion

"right-to-work" laws, 57

Rise of the Meritocracy, 1870–2033, The (Young), 234–35, 241

Roberts, John, 291, 301, 303, 307, 311, 322–23; *Shelby County v. Holder*, 326
Roberts Court, 310–11, 318, 320–21, 410n61
Robertson, Pat, 164–65
Robinson, Jackie, 57
Rockefeller, Nelson, 181
Roe v. Wade (1973), 96–97, 115, 133, 148, 162–63, 316, 319. *See also* abortion
Romney, Mitt, 14, 226, 230, 248–49
Roosevelt, Franklin D., 170; economic bill of rights, 28; Hofstadter critique, 46; wartime response to Black job demands, 55, 57. *See also* New Deal
Rosen, Ruth, 101
Rossi, Alice, 86–87, 102
Roth, Philip, 33
Rove, Karl, 13, 181
Rubio, Marco, 229
Ruffini, Patrick, 344
Rustin, Bayard, 54
Ryan, Paul, 270

Saddam Hussein, 158
same-sex marriage, 297–300. *See also* gay rights movement
Sanders, Bernie, 233, 251–52
"Save our Children" campaign, 110
Savio, Mario, 76–77
Scalia, Antonin, 148, 291, 311, 313, 315, 324, 325
Schiff, Adam, 337
Schlafly, Phyllis, 115, 134
Schlesinger, Arthur, Jr., 27, 143
schools: school construction, 25; segregated, 57–58, 60, 124–25; tax exemptions for private schools, 125. *See also* education
Seale, Bobby, 72
Sears, David O., 222
Second Amendment, 312–15
Second Great Awakening, 132
Second Sex, The (Beauvoir), 91
Seeger, Pete, 2

segregation: armed forces, 57; on buses, 62–63, 64; downtown Birmingham, 64; educational institutions, 133; and George Wallace, 120–21; housing and red-lining, 82; lunch counters, 63–64; in medical settings, 67–68; occupational, 88–89; restaurants, 51; schools, 57–58, 60, 124–25
Selma, Alabama, Edmund Pettus Bridge, 53
September 11 terror attacks, 194–95
Sessions, Jeff, 257, 272
Sex and the Single Girl (Brown), 95
sex education, 165
Sexual Behavior in the Human Male (Kinsey), 104
"sexual brinksmanship," 33
sexuality: and feminist movement, 101–2; sexual freedom, 95–96; sexual morality, 33–34; sexual pluralism, 102–3, 108, 296
Sexual Politics (Millett), 101
sexual revolution, 99
"shareholder value revolution," 238
Shear, Michael, 257
Shelby County v. Holder, 326–27
Shultz, George, 126
Sides, John, 281
Siegel, Reva, 317
single-family homes/suburbanization, 35–37
single-parent homes, 243–44
"singles culture," 95
60 Minutes (television news program), 195
slavery, 6–7, 18, 47, 55, 334–35
slum clearance, 38–39
Smith, Howard, 84, 92
Smith, Jack, 327–28
socialism: "industrial democracy," 28; Oscar Wilde on, 108; Sanders and democratic socialism, 252; Socialist Party in 1948 election, 28
social media, 167, 239–40, 339–40

social movements: important in their time vs. continuing impact, 111–12; interconnected families of movements, 50, 76; "repertoires of contention" (Tilly), 50, 62, 64, 73, 98, 367n3
Social Security, 67, 147, 260; efforts to repeal, 25–26; expansion of, 128; Social Security Act (1935), 54
socioeconomic stratification. *See* class divisions
sodomy: decriminalization of, 109–10, 111; definitions and legal frameworks, 103–4
Sotomayor, Sonia, 328
Souter, David, 292, 324
South: Black employment in, 68; Democratic to Republican shift, 52; Great White Switch, 123; racism, exposure of, 61; Southern strategy, Republican Party, 119–24; whites-only primaries, 60
Southern Baptist Convention, 109–10, 132, 134; on abortion, 133
Southern border, 189–90, 193, 340–41
Southern Christian Leadership Conference (SCLC), 54, 63
Southern Democrats, 31, 52, 54, 57, 58, 60, 89, 120, 123, 178, 245
Southern Dixiecrats, 57
Soviet Union, collapse of, 157
Srole, Leo, 48
Stahl, Lesley, 265
Starr, Kenneth, 175
States' Laws on Race and Color (Murray), 78
Steinem, Gloria, 84, 100
Stevens, John Paul, 313, 324
Stone, Harlan Fiske, 58
Stonewall Inn raid (1969), 107
Stop ERA, 115
Strangers in the Land (Higham), 194
structural functionalism, 47–48
Student Nonviolent Coordinating Committee (SNCC), 63–64; segregation among volunteers, 77

suburbanization, 35–37; and conformity, 37–38; and material success, 38; and segregation, 37; and slum clearance, 38–39; and white flight, 69
"Sunbelt," 124
Supplemental Nutrition Assistance Program (food stamps), 248
Supplemental Security Income, 128
"supply-side" economics, 145–46
Supreme Court: abortion/reproductive rights, 94–95, 96–97, 133, 311, 315–17; affirmative action, 218–19, 320; *Buckley v. Valeo* (1976), 141–42; *Bush v. Gore* (2000), 323–25, 327, 329; *Citizens United* (2010), 309; conservative counterrevolution (quiet phase), 302–8; conservative historical role, 293–95; conservative rights revolution, 308–12; constitutional interpretation, 58–59, 312–18; on gay rights, 105–6, 297–302; immigrant rights, 192; internment of Japanese Americans, 58–59; judicial intervention for minority rights, 58–59; legal change vs. cultural change, 318–22; liberal rights revolution, 15, 120, 294; NAACP cases, 58, 59–60; *New York Times v. Sullivan*, 65; Nixon's impact, 124, 128, 136, 140; on obscenity, 106; partisanship, 322–29; *Plyler v. Doe*, 192; on prayer in public school, 132; on racial perquisites for citizenship, 207; Reagan nominees, 148; Republican domination, 291–93, 330–31; *Shelby County v. Holder*, 326; Trump appointees, 292; *Trump v. United States* (2024), 328–29. *See also* Burger Court; Rehnquist Court; Roberts Court; Warren Court

Taft-Hartley Act (1947), 31, 57, 113, 236–37
Taiwan, 274, 275
Talese, Gay, 171

talk radio, 167, 233, 259, 261
tariffs: between China and United States, 276, 353; on steel and aluminum imports, 276, 277; by Trump in a second term, 353
Tausanovitch, Chris, 281
tax policy: Clinton administration, 175; George W. Bush tax cuts, 248; labor vs. capital, 238; Obama administration, 248–49; Reagan administration, 145–47; Republican tax cuts, 179, 240; tax rates during 1950s, 29
Tea Party movement, 225, 227
tech industry, 239, 249; MAGA/tech alliance, 339–40, 347, 356; NDAs, 307; tech monopolies, 339
technology: confidence in, 157–58; high-tech economy, 239; technological change, 4
Teles, Steven, 302–3
television: and advertising, 42; cable television and minorities, 73–74; Christian broadcasting, 131; federal regulation of, 42–43; gay characters, rise of on network shows, 296; low-choice structure in early years of, 44–45; midcentury era, 39–45; news and public affairs, 43–44; rise of multichannel system, 169–70; and shared experience, 41–42
Temporary Assistance to Needy Families, 177
Tesler, Michael, 222, 227
Theranos (blood-test firm), 307
Thiel, Peter, 347
Thind, Bhagat Singh, 207
Thomas, Clarence, 311, 321, 324
Thurmond, Strom, 57
Tillerson, Rex, 266
Tilly, Charles, 50, 62
Time magazine, 203
Title IX, Education Amendments, 93–94
Title VII, Civil Rights Act, 301, 305
tolerance vs. equality, 27

Total Woman, The (Morgan), 134
Toward a General Theory of Action (Parsons), 47–48
trade policy: Clinton administration, 176–77, 178; impact of free trade policy, 243, 250–51, 274; Trump administration, 273–77, Trump 2024 campaign, 353
transgender people, 296, 300–301, 350
Trans-Pacific Partnership, 275
Trende, Sean, 230
Troubled Asset Relief Program (Wall Street bailout), 224, 225
Troy, Gil, 144–45
Truman, Harry, 120; desegregation of armed forces, 57; on immigration laws, 28; veto of Taft-Hartley Act, 31
Trump, Donald J.: abortion position, 261; approval ratings, 268; "birtherism" attacks, 257; breaches of social norms, 256–68, 285–86, 337; chaos and unpredictability, 267; COVID pandemic, 277–85; criminal cases against, 327–28; defeat in 2020, 288–90; efforts to overturn 2020 election, 290, 328–29; elections as president, 254–58, 261–65, 332–59; emergence in politics, 233; fascism, accusations of, 350–51; and Hispanic voters, 343–44; health policy, 267, 268; hostility of, 265–68; immigration policy, 230, 269–73, 343–44; Inaugural Address (2017), 266; misogyny, 263; policy changes as president, 268–78; rallies, use of, 260; Republican establishment, differences with, 260; Resistance against, 285–86; second Great White Switch, 260; trade policies, 273–77, 353; travel ban, 273, 286
Trump v. United States (2024), 323, 328, 411n74
Turner, Frederick, 46

Twitter, 340
Tyler May, Elaine, 32, 33, 35

Uber, 249
unions, 25; breach with rights-oriented movements, 245–46; civil rights unionism, 56–57, 245–46; as countervailing force to business, 29, 138, 236; Democratic Party and, 13, 245, 249–51, 252–53; labor law reform, 249–50; loss of membership and influence, 13, 138, 244–53; in post-industrial economies, 237–38; race and, 54, 56–57, 126, 245–47; Republican Party and, 147–48, 245; Taft-Hartley Act (1947), 31, 57, 113, 236
United States v. Nixon, 322
universal basic income, 127
University of California, Berkeley, 76–77
Univision (television network), 206
"urban renewal," 38–39
U.S. Census Bureau: data collected by, 204–5
U.S. Chamber of Commerce, 28
U.S. Labor Department Women's Bureau, 90
U.S. v. Carolene Products, 58
Uyematsu, Amy, 81

vaccines, 285
Vance, J. D.: anticipating "normal gay guy vote," 347; calling for defiance of Supreme Court, 330; as defender of gender traditionalism, 345, 347–48
Van Deburg, William L., 73
Vavreck, Lynn, 281
Vietnam War, 129, 141, 233, 245
Viguerie, Richard, 133
Volcker, Paul, 143, 146
voting rights, 58, 64, 68, 141; *Shelby County v. Holder*, 326–27; voter ID laws, 325–26; voter registration drives, 76–77; women and Nineteenth Amendment, 89
Voting Rights Act (1965), 53, 65, 66, 149, 326
Vought, Russell, 330

wages: immigrant impact on native born, 185–86; minimum wage, 67, 127–28, 148, 243, 247
Wagner Act (1935), 54
Wall, Wendy, 27
Wallace, George, 120–21, 123, 255
Wallace, Mike, 49–50
Wall Street bailout, 181, 224, 225
Wall Street Reform and Consumer Protection Act, 224
Walz, Tim, 349
Warner, W. Lloyd, 48
War on Drugs, 151–52
war on poverty, 67, 127, 140
Warren, Earl, 120–21, 124, 292, 299
Warren, Elizabeth, 233, 251–52
Warren Court, 120, 140–42, 321
Washington, Denzel, 222
Watergate scandal, 129, 141; Democratic Party reaction, 142–44
Waters, Mary, 214
wealth: as dimension of class divide, 234. *See also* class divisions; economic inequality
Wednesday Club, 181
Weinstein, Harvey, 307
"welfare chauvinism," 260
welfare policy: Clinton administration, 177–78; and ethnic composition of society, 220; "incomes strategy" vs. "services strategy," 128; and legal immigrants, 193; Nixon administration, 127–28. *See also* war on poverty
Weyrich, Paul, 133
White, Dana, 346
white flight, 69
white identity: blurring of boundaries of

whiteness, 209–10; consolidation of, 75; and demographic change, 11, 201–12; and Mexican Americans, 78–79, 204, 205–6, 209; and mid-century culture, 35, 37, 38, 43; as prerequisite for naturalization, 183–84, 207; shift from racial to ethnic distinctions among whites, 213; white Anglo-Saxon Protestants, 48, 213; white ethnics, 28, 214; white "replacement," 12; white replenishment, 211–212; whites as a future minority, 11, 184, 186, 203, 210–11, 256; whites-only primaries, 58, 60; whites-only private Christian academies, 125, 133. *See also* racial identity and classification

white supremacy, 6, 56, 212

Whitman, Walt, xi, 183

Why I Preach That the Bible Is Literally True (Criswell), 133

Wicker, Tom, 125

Wilde, Oscar, 108

Wills, Garry, 117, 201

Wilson, Pete, 191–92

Wilson, William Julius, 150

Wimmer, Andreas, 79

Winfrey, Oprah, 349

Winkler, Adam, 309

Winthrop, John, xii

Wisconsin as swing state, 262–63, 264, 288

"women of color," 216–17

Women's Educational Equity Act (1972), 94

women's health, 101–2

women's movements: antifeminist movement vs. women's liberation, 114; civil rights law and race-sex analogy, 91–93; civil rights movement, roots of second wave in, 77–78; feminism as equal rights, 87–97; feminism as women's liberation, 97–102; first wave, 89; gay-straight split, 101; labor movement, roots of second wave in, 91–92; race and, 101, 216–17; second wave, 89–90, 91, 99–100, 245; structure, lack of, 100–101. *See also* gender equality; National Organization for Women (NOW)

women's roles, 32–34, 88, 91, 93–94. *See also* gender identity

Women's Strike Day (1970), 101

Woodward, Bob, 280–81

working class, 232–34

working poor, 127

World Health Organization (WHO), 280

World Trade Organization, 274

World War II: and American patriotism, 28; employment of women, 88; and equality, 55–56; GI Bill for veterans, 29; government propaganda during, 56; opposition to U.S. involvement, 27

Wright, Lawrence, 279

Wynn, Steve, 276

Xi Jinping, 274

Yellen, Janet, 174

Yom Kippur War, 137

Young, Michael, 234–35, 243

Zelizer, Julian, 144